# WildFly Cookbook

Over 90 hands-on recipes to configure, deploy, and manage Java-based applications using WildFly

**Luigi Fugaro**

BIRMINGHAM - MUMBAI

# WildFly Cookbook



First published: July 2015

Production reference: 1170715

Published by Packt Publishing Ltd.
Livery Place
35 Livery Street
Birmingham B3 2PB, UK.

ISBN 978-1-78439-241-3

www.packtpub.com

# Credits

**Author**
Luigi Fugaro

**Reviewers**
Brian Dwyer
Juraci Paixão Kröhling
Fabio Marinelli
Kylin Soong

**Commissioning Editor**
Amarabha Banerjee

**Acquisition Editor**
Indrajit Das
James Jones

**Content Development Editor**
Ritika Singh

**Technical Editor**
Vijin Boricha

**Copy Editors**
Sarang Chari
Sonia Mathur

**Project Coordinator**
Judie Jose

**Proofreader**
Safis Editing

**Indexer**
Monica Ajmera Mehta

**Production Coordinator**
Arvindkumar Gupta

**Cover Work**
Arvindkumar Gupta

# About the Author

**Luigi Fugaro** had his first encounter with computers back in the early 1980s, when he was still a kid. He started with a Commodore VIC-20, passing through a Sinclair, a Commodore 64, and an Atari ST 1040; here, he spent days and nights giving breath mints to Otis. Then, he took a big jump with a 486DX2 66 MHz, and he started programming in Pascal and BASIC.

GOTO 1998.

He started his career as a webmaster doing HTML, JavaScript, Applets, and some graphics with PaintShop Pro. He then switched to Delphi and Visual Basic, and finally, he could start working on Java projects.

While working on Java, Luigi met his mentor, Gianluca Magalotti, who helped him a lot in acquiring more hard and soft skills. Luigi has been developing all kinds of web applications in Java—dealing with both backend and frontend frameworks for various system integrators.

In the last system integrator he worked for, Luigi met another special person, Pierluigi Lucci, who trusted and helped Luigi in his career, which earned Luigi the SCJP 6 and SCEA 5 Java certifications. Then, he took the big jump toward Red Hat.

Luigi is now working with Red Hat as a senior middleware consultant, where he can count on a group of highly talented people to help him daily. He would like to mention all of them, but two of them need a special mention: uL, the pragmatist, and aL, the grandpa, for helping Luigi during his hard days at work.

# Acknowledgments

I'd like to thank James Jones for giving me this big opportunity and the experience of a lifetime—of authoring a book.

A special thanks goes to the content editor, Ritika Singh, who helped me a lot with her talent and patience. Thanks to the technical editor, Vijin Boricha, for his precious work of testing all the technical aspects of the book.

A big thank you goes to my friend and colleague, Fabio Marinelli, who reviewed the entire book without missing a chapter!

More and more thanks go to all the other reviewers: Kylin Soong, Juraci Paixão Kröhling, and Brian Dwyer.

I would also like to thank Stefano Linguerri and Matteo Bernacchi, who helped me a lot in writing the messaging and the Docker and OpenShift recipes, respectively.

Last but not least, I really need to mention and thank my daughter, Giada, who is definitely my life. Without even knowing, she helped me in different ways, giving me the right distractions at the right moments.

I'd like to dedicate this book to Giada.

# About the Reviewers

**Brian Dwyer** is an IT infrastructure architect in the Greater New York City area. His current focus is DevOps and the IaaS cloud architecture, but his expertise spans multiple IT realms, including network engineering, security, and virtualization. He authored the popular book *Chef WildFly Cookbook* to automate the deployment and provisioning of the WildFly Java Application Server. He also holds multiple certifications, including Cisco Certified Network Professional (CCNP) and Microsoft Certified IT Professional (MCITP).

**Juraci Paixão Kröhling** is a developer working for Red Hat in open source projects within the middleware division. In the past decade, he has worked in several development positions and has lead quality engineering teams.

> I'd like to thank all the individual contributors to JBoss projects who make Wildfly possible; each single commit in any of the several components is a piece that keeps this engine working.

**Fabio Marinelli** has been a developer since he was a little child—doing experiments and trying out any new technology, no matter how hard he has to try. Growing up in the Java environment taught him how great and valuable the open source world is, but only working at Red Hat gave him the time and tools to really participate in this big family—the open source community. He had the time to dive deep into Wildfly, Camel, JGroups, and Vertx. He contributed the JGroups clustering plugin to Vertx.

**Kylin Soong** is a software engineer and JBoss product committer with over 6 years of JBoss/WildFly experience and was a reviewer of *WildFly Performance Tuning, Packt Publishing*. He works and lives in Beijing. He loves open source, is good at open source development and maintaining, has proficiency in Java and Java EE programming, has knowledge of middleware architecture, knows performance tuning, and so on.

# www.PacktPub.com

## Support files, eBooks, discount offers, and more

For support files and downloads related to your book, please visit `www.PacktPub.com`.

Did you know that Packt offers eBook versions of every book published, with PDF and ePub files available? You can upgrade to the eBook version at `www.PacktPub.com` and as a print book customer, you are entitled to a discount on the eBook copy. Get in touch with us at `service@packtpub.com` for more details.

At `www.PacktPub.com`, you can also read a collection of free technical articles, sign up for a range of free newsletters and receive exclusive discounts and offers on Packt books and eBooks.

`https://www2.packtpub.com/books/subscription/packtlib`

Do you need instant solutions to your IT questions? PacktLib is Packt's online digital book library. Here, you can search, access, and read Packt's entire library of books.

## Why Subscribe?

- Fully searchable across every book published by Packt
- Copy and paste, print, and bookmark content
- On demand and accessible via a web browser

## Free Access for Packt account holders

If you have an account with Packt at `www.PacktPub.com`, you can use this to access PacktLib today and view 9 entirely free books. Simply use your login credentials for immediate access.

# Table of Contents

# Preface

Java has been around for years, and if you count them all, you should get the number—20-plus years. This does not mean that Java is obsolete or dead; rather, Java is more than lively, and the new Java 8 language specification is the proof.

Because Java is not dead, WildFly wants to give you more power than ever. Thanks to its small memory footprint, WildFly can run in your pocket using the Raspberry Pi, it can be spread on Linux containers using Docker (the basis of microservice architectures), or it can hit the cloud using the OpenShift Online platform.

Furthermore, WildFly's new, modular nature lets you customize its system as needed. You can extend WildFly by providing your own extensions and subsystems.

WildFly's modular class loading gives you fine-grained control over the libraries and Java classes an application requires to load, which allows you to have the proper traction to use WildFly in your continuous integration and continuous delivery practices.

Moreover, WildFly provides a set of management APIs that can be used to manage the overall platform. You can interact with WildFly through the command-line interface (CLI), which is a powerful tool to manage the whole system. If you feel more comfortable with a UI, you can rely on the well-designed Web Console.

One more reason to choose WildFly is its vibrant community and the whole Java EE environment. Don't forget that WildFly is the only open source Java EE 7 application server supported by its community!

## What this book covers

*Chapter 1, Welcome to WildFly!*, introduces the WildFly Java application server and its main features in relation to the Java EE 7 platform.

*Chapter 2, Running WildFly in Standalone Mode*, explains the standalone operational mode and how you can manage your instances in this way.

*Chapter 3, Running WildFly in Domain Mode*, explains the domain operational mode and all that it comes with, such as the domain controller and the host controller.

*Chapter 4, Managing the Logging Subsystem with the CLI*, describes how you can configure and manage the logging subsystem to trace the operation of both WildFly and applications.

*Chapter 5, Managing the Datasource Subsystems with the CLI*, describes how you can configure and manage the datasource subsystem.

*Chapter 6, Clustering WildFly*, introduces and explains how you can run WildFly in a cluster for both operational modes; TCP and UDP network configurations are shown.

*Chapter 7, Load Balancing WildFly*, covers how you can balance WildFly instances with mod_cluster using Apache HTTP Server—with the HTTP and AJP protocols.

*Chapter 8, Commanding the CLI*, explains how to retrieve configuration and runtime information using the CLI; both operational modes are used.

*Chapter 9, Conquering the CLI*, talks about how, using the CLI in both operational modes, you can alter WildFly's state, such as deploy, undeploy, stop server, stop server-group, and so on.

*Chapter 10, Hardening the WildFly Communication*, explains how you can harden WildFly communication, such as Web Console communicating on secure channels via HTTPS, domain controller, and host controller.

*Chapter 11, Hardening the WildFly Configuration*, describes techniques to harden WildFly configuration, such as hashing passwords and using vaults.

*Chapter 12, Role-based Access Control with WildFly*, introduces the RBAC provider to access WildFly Web Console and shows how you can customize it.

*Chapter 13, Messaging with WildFly*, describes how you can configure and manage the messaging subsystem (embedded HornetQ) and its components, such as Queue and Topic.

*Chapter 14, WildFly into the Cloud with OpenShift*, introduces the OpenShift Online platform and how you can deploy your application on WildFly directly on the cloud.

*Chapter 15, Using WildFly with Docker*, introduces the Linux containers using Docker, and how you can run WildFly on it.

*Appendix, WildFly Domain and Standalone Modes*, is a bonus chapter that takes you through understanding WildFly's domain and standalone modes. You can download it from `https://www.packtpub.com/sites/default/files/downloads/24130S_Appendix.pdf`.

# What you need for this book

To fully benefit from this book, you first need a PC with 4 GB of RAM and pretty much 50 GB of free disk space. Also, an Internet connection is a must.

From a software point of view, if you want to follow the book, you need a Fedora 21 OS, along with JDK 8 and WildFly 9.

We will also use other tools, such as Maven, Git, Apache JMeter, and MySQL.

# Who this book is for

This book is intended for middleware system administrators and Java developers, actually good Java developers, who care about architecture design and implementation. Whether you are new to WildFly, come from a previous version, such as JBoss AS 5, 6, and 7, or are an expert in it, you will be able to master both the basic and advanced features of WildFly.

By the way, most of the core components of WildFly are totally new, such as its administration tool, that is, the CLI; its operational modes, which are, the standalone and domain modes; and its web server provided by Undertow, you can benefit from this book even if you have no experience in JBoss and WildFly at all.

# Sections

In this book, you will find several headings that appear frequently (Getting ready, How to do it, How it works, There's more, and See also).

To give clear instructions on how to complete a recipe, we use these sections as follows:

## Getting ready

This section tells you what to expect in the recipe, and describes how to set up any software or any preliminary settings required for the recipe.

## How to do it...

This section contains the steps required to follow the recipe.

## How it works...

This section usually consists of a detailed explanation of what happened in the previous section.

### There's more...

This section consists of additional information about the recipe in order to make the reader more knowledgeable about the recipe.

### See also

This section provides helpful links to other useful information for the recipe.

## Conventions

In this book, you will find a number of text styles that distinguish between different kinds of information. Here are some examples of these styles and an explanation of their meaning.

Code words in text, database table names, folder names, filenames, file extensions, pathnames, dummy URLs, user input, and Twitter handles are shown as follows: "The `WFC` folder is used just to not interfere with your current environment."

A block of code is set as follows:

```
<VirtualHost 10.0.0.1:6666>
    <Directory />
      Order deny,allow
      Deny from all
      Allow from 10.0.0.1
    </Directory>
      ServerAdvertise off
      EnableMCPMReceive
</VirtualHost>
```

When we wish to draw your attention to a particular part of a command line block, the relevant lines or items are set in bold:

```
$ cd $WILDFLY_HOME
$ ./bin/standalone.sh -Djboss.bind.address=10.0.0.1
...
22:56:05,531 INFO  [org.wildfly.extension.undertow] (MSC service
thread 1-3) WFLYUT0006: Undertow HTTP listener default listening on
/10.0.0.1:8080
```

Any command-line input or output is written as follows:

```
[disconnected /] connect
[standalone@localhost:9990 /] /socket-binding-group=standard-sockets/
socket-binding=http:read-attribute(name=port)
{
    "outcome" => "success",
    "result" => expression "${jboss.http.port:8080}"
}
```

**New terms** and **important words** are shown in bold. Words that you see on the screen, for example, in menus or dialog boxes, appear in the text like this: "Where you first need to mark the option of **Accept License Agreement** to enable the links."

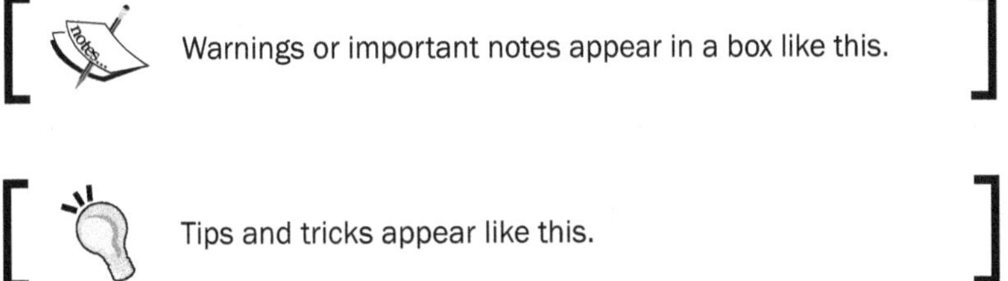

Warnings or important notes appear in a box like this.
Tips and tricks appear like this.


# Reader feedback

Feedback from our readers is always welcome. Let us know what you think about this book—what you liked or disliked. Reader feedback is important for us as it helps us develop titles that you will really get the most out of.

To send us general feedback, simply e-mail `feedback@packtpub.com`, and mention the book's title in the subject of your message.

If there is a topic that you have expertise in and you are interested in either writing or contributing to a book, see our author guide at `www.packtpub.com/authors`.

# Customer support

Now that you are the proud owner of a Packt book, we have a number of things to help you to get the most from your purchase.

## Errata

Although we have taken every care to ensure the accuracy of our content, mistakes do happen. If you find a mistake in one of our books—maybe a mistake in the text or the code—we would be grateful if you could report this to us. By doing so, you can save other readers from frustration and help us improve subsequent versions of this book. If you find any errata, please report them by visiting `http://www.packtpub.com/submit-errata`, selecting your book, clicking on the **Errata Submission Form** link, and entering the details of your errata. Once your errata are verified, your submission will be accepted and the errata will be uploaded to our website or added to any list of existing errata under the Errata section of that title.

To view the previously submitted errata, go to `https://www.packtpub.com/books/content/support` and enter the name of the book in the search field. The required information will appear under the **Errata** section.

## Piracy

Piracy of copyrighted material on the Internet is an ongoing problem across all media. At Packt, we take the protection of our copyright and licenses very seriously. If you come across any illegal copies of our works in any form on the Internet, please provide us with the location address or website name immediately so that we can pursue a remedy.

Please contact us at `copyright@packtpub.com` with a link to the suspected pirated material.

We appreciate your help in protecting our authors and our ability to bring you valuable content.

## Questions

If you have a problem with any aspect of this book, you can contact us at `questions@packtpub.com`, and we will do our best to address the problem.

# 1
# Welcome to WildFly!

In this chapter, you will learn the following recipes:

- Software prerequisites
- Downloading and installing WildFly
- Understanding WildFly's directory overview
- Running WildFly in standalone mode
- Running WildFly in domain mode
- Running WildFly as a service

## Introduction

In this first chapter, we will describe WildFly's history, its prerequisites, where to get it, and how to install it. We will also explain the standalone and domain running modes, that is, how to run them up.

JBoss.org community is a huge community, where people all over the world develop, test, and document pieces of code. There are a lot of projects in there other than JBoss AS or the recent WildFly such as Infinispan, Undertow, PicketLink, Arquillian, HornetQ, RESTeasy, AeroGear, and Vert.x. For a complete list of all projects, visit the following site: `http://www.jboss.org/projects/`.

Despite marketing reasons, as there is no preferred project, the community wanted to change the name of the JBoss AS project to something different that would not collide with the community name. The other reason was the Red Hat JBoss supported version named JBoss **Enterprise Application Platform** (**EAP**). This was another point towards replacing the JBoss AS name.

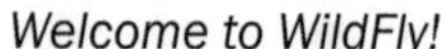



How did the community change the name? How would they have decided? Easy—ask us, the community, for new names. The election process started, people from the JBoss Community, **JBoss User Group** (**JBUGs**), **Java User Group** (**JUGs**), and related communities all over the world, expressed their preferences.

The new name for JBoss AS should have suggested Java application server capabilities and affinities such as integration, cloud, mobile, messaging, nimbleness, strength, open source, free spirit, and so on. You guessed the winner!

> *"A wild fly is extremely agile, lightweight, untamed and truly free."*

The brand new name was announced during the JUDCon 2013 in Brazil. Zzzzhhh... Welcome to WildFly!

Let's talk about the WildFly features and characteristics:

- WildFly replaces JBoss AS. The first version of WildFly was 8.0, which was based on JBoss AS 7.1. To keep things simple the community decided to keep the same numbering.
- WildFly has gained the Java EE 7 Full platform compatible implementations badge, which means it has the newest Java technologies. Easy development, better security, better integration, better management!
- WildFly boots in seconds. All its services start up together, but just the ones that it needs. This is because there is a centralized metadata cache and a modular classloading system, which prevents the famous classpath hell.
- Another big change is the default web server; WildFly now utilizes Undertow.

  > *"Undertow is a flexible performant web server written in java, providing both blocking and non-blocking API's based on NIO."*

- It is lightweight, less then 1 MB for its core jar, and less then 4 MB at runtime. Undertow is embeddable, flexible; it supports WebSocket (HTTP upgrade protocols) and Servlet 3.1. Later in the book, we will see how to configure and tune Undertow embedded in WildFly.
- With this new release of WildFly has been introduced a **Role Based Access Control** (**RBAC**) system. This new feature actually gives functionalities to define users, groups and roles. This way you will have not simply a Superuser, but a user to do its proper task without compromising on security. It's highly customizable and it can be integrated with most identity stores such as LDAPs and ADs.
- WildFly has just one configuration file, so that all your settings are centralized in one place.
- You can manage your configurations through the Admin Console (also known as Web Console), the **Command Line Interface** (**CLI**), the REST API and the Java API. All these tools give great powers to customize your management settings. Within this book we will concentrate mainly on the CLI and the Admin Console.

WildFly has been built using Java SE 1.7; thus, it requires you to have at least a JRE version 1.7.

Having said that, let's start for real!

In the following recipes we will see what we need to start JBoss AS, ops, and WildFly, where to get it, what does its folder structure look like, and where to find its configuration files.

# Software prerequisites

WildFly runs on top of the Java platform. It needs at least a **Java Runtime Environment** (**JRE**) version 1.7 to run (further references to versions 1.7 and 7 should be considered equal—the same applies for versions 1.8 and 8 as well), but it also works perfectly with the latest JRE version 8.

As we will also need to compile and build Java web applications, we will need the **Java Development Kit** (**JDK**), which provides the necessary tools to work with the Java source code. In the JDK panorama we can find the Oracle JDK, developed and maintained by Oracle, and OpenJDK, which relies on community contribution.

Nevertheless, after April 2015, Oracle will no longer post updates of Java SE 7 to its public download sites, as mentioned at `http://www.oracle.com/technetwork/java/javase/downloads/eol-135779.html`. Also, keep in mind that the Java Critical Patch Updates are released on a quarterly basis; thus, for reasons of stability and feature support, we will use the Oracle JDK 8, which is freely available for download at `http://www.oracle.com/technetwork/java/javase/downloads/index.html`.

While writing this book, the latest stable Oracle JDK is version 1.8.0_31 (as well as 8u31). Hereby, every reference to **Java Virtual Machine** (**JVM**), Java, JRE, and JDK will be intended Oracle JDK 1.8.0_31. To keep things simple, if you don't mind, use that same version.

In addition to the JDK, we will need Apache Maven 3, which is a build tool for Java projects. It is freely available for download at `http://maven.apache.org/download.cgi`. A generic download link can be found at `http://www.us.apache.org/dist/maven/maven-3/3.2.5/binaries/apache-maven-3.2.5-bin.tar.gz`.

## Getting ready

To fully follow the recipes in the book, using the same environment is a fundamental requirement. As I cannot replicate the same recipe to suit different settings (such as Windows, Mac, and Linux), I'll use Linux (actually, Fedora 21) as the base operating system.

If you are running a different system and you want to carefully follow what's in the book, you can easily install and run Fedora 21 inside a virtual machine using the VirtualBox software, available at `https://www.virtualbox.org/wiki/Downloads`.

1. Choose the version that is compatible with your actual system. You can install Fedora 21 by downloading its image at `https://getfedora.org/en/workstation/`.

The installation of the above software is out of the scope of this book.

2. To install the Oracle JDK, you need to open your browser and point it to `http://www.oracle.com/technetwork/java/javase/downloads/index.html`.
3. Once there, click on the JDK download link, as depicted in the following image:

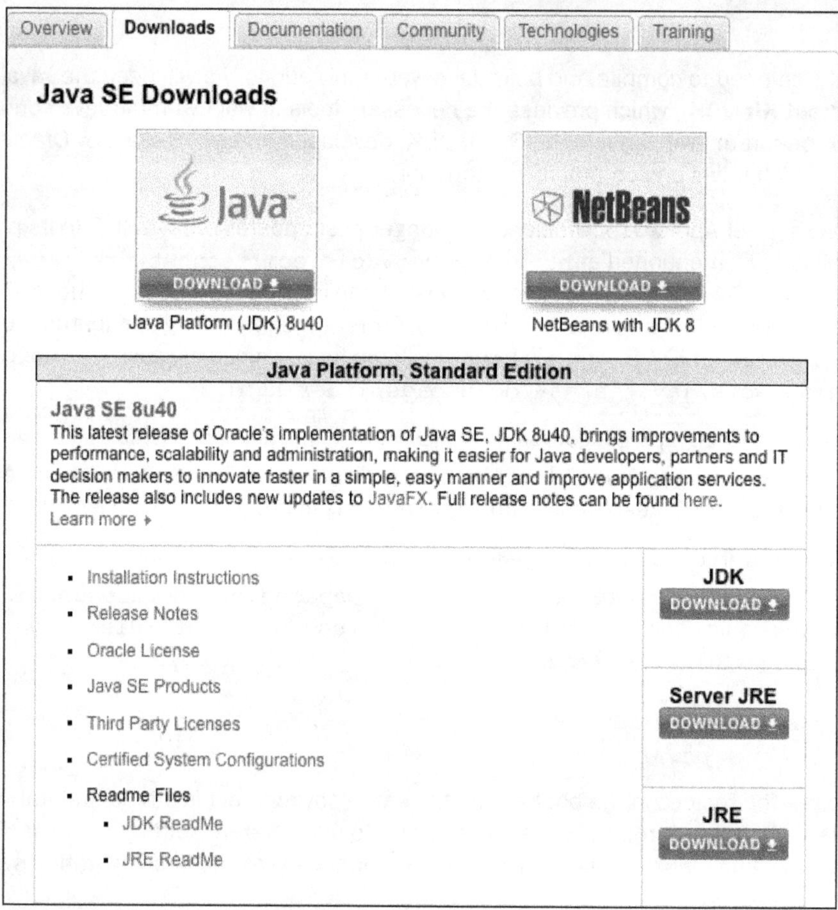

4. The link will take you to the download page, where you first need to mark the option of **Accept License Agreement** to enable the links, as depicted in the following screenshot:

Overview | Downloads | Documentation | Community | Technologies | Training

**Java SE Development Kit 8 Downloads**

Thank you for downloading this release of the Java™ Platform, Standard Edition Development Kit (JDK™). The JDK is a development environment for building applications, applets, and components using the Java programming language.

The JDK includes tools useful for developing and testing programs written in the Java programming language and running on the Java platform.

See also:

- Java Developer Newsletter (tick the checkbox under Subscription Center > Oracle Technology News)
- Java Developer Day hands-on workshops (free) and other events
- Java Magazine

JDK MD5 Checksum

Looking for JDK 8 on ARM?
JDK 8 for ARM downloads have moved to the JDK 8 for ARM download page.

**Java SE Development Kit 8u40**

**You must accept the Oracle Binary Code License Agreement for Java SE to download this software.**

Accept License Agreement    Decline License Agreement

| Product / File Description | File Size | Download |
|---|---|---|
| Linux x86 | 146.84 MB | jdk-8u40-linux-i586.rpm |
| Linux x86 | 166.85 MB | jdk-8u40-linux-i586.tar.gz |
| Linux x64 | 145.14 MB | jdk-8u40-linux-x64.rpm |
| Linux x64 | 165.17 MB | jdk-8u40-linux-x64.tar.gz |
| Mac OS X x64 | 221.91 MB | jdk-8u40-macosx-x64.dmg |
| Solaris SPARC 64-bit (SVR4 package) | 139.09 MB | jdk-8u40-solaris-sparcv9.tar.Z |
| Solaris SPARC 64-bit | 98.68 MB | jdk-8u40-solaris-sparcv9.tar.gz |
| Solaris x64 (SVR4 package) | 130.57 MB | jdk-8u40-solaris-x64.tar.Z |
| Solaris x64 | 89.91 MB | jdk-8u40-solaris-x64.tar.gz |
| Windows x86 | 175.71 MB | jdk-8u40-windows-i586.exe |
| Windows x64 | 180.19 MB | jdk-8u40-windows-x64.exe |

5. As you accept the agreement, all the links get activated. Choose the one that best fits your hardware and operating system.

**Java SE Development Kit 8u40**

**You must accept the Oracle Binary Code License Agreement for Java SE to download this software.**

**Thank you for accepting the Oracle Binary Code License Agreement for Java SE; you may now download this software.**

| Product / File Description | File Size | Download |
|---|---|---|
| Linux x86 | 146.84 MB | jdk-8u40-linux-i586.rpm |
| Linux x86 | 166.85 MB | jdk-8u40-linux-i586.tar.gz |
| Linux x64 | 145.14 MB | jdk-8u40-linux-x64.rpm |
| Linux x64 | 165.17 MB | jdk-8u40-linux-x64.tar.gz |
| Mac OS X x64 | 221.91 MB | jdk-8u40-macosx-x64.dmg |
| Solaris SPARC 64-bit (SVR4 package) | 139.09 MB | jdk-8u40-solaris-sparcv9.tar.Z |
| Solaris SPARC 64-bit | 98.68 MB | jdk-8u40-solaris-sparcv9.tar.gz |
| Solaris x64 (SVR4 package) | 130.57 MB | jdk-8u40-solaris-x64.tar.Z |
| Solaris x64 | 89.91 MB | jdk-8u40-solaris-x64.tar.gz |
| Windows x86 | 175.71 MB | jdk-8u40-windows-i586.exe |
| Windows x64 | 180.19 MB | jdk-8u40-windows-x64.exe |

I'm running a Fedora 21 Linux machine, with a 64-bit hardware support, thus I'll use the **jdk-8u40-linux-x64.tar.gz** bundle. I could have used the RPM bundle, but I prefer installing the archive version to better fit my needs in terms of paths; what goes where.

6. Next, we will create a folder named `WFC`, which stands for *WildFly Cookbook* to store the contents of all the necessary software, codes, and files to follow all the recipes of the book. Open your terminal application and run the following command:

```
$ cd && mkdir WFC
```

The `WFC` folder is used just to not interfere with your current environment.

## How to do it...

1. Choose the package archive; once the download is complete, open your command line and extract its contents to the `WFC` folder as follows:

```
$ cd ~/WFC && tar zxvf jdk-8u40-linux-x64.tar.gz
```

This will extract the Oracle JDK software into the `jdk1.8.0_40` folder, inside the `WFC` folder starting from your `home` folder. For convenience, we will use a different folder name, like `jdk8`, to refer to the preceding JDK installation folder. Run the following command:

```
$ cd ~/WFC && mv jdk1.8.0_40 jdk8
```

Now we need to set the `JAVA_HOME` environment variable and make the JDK commands available from our shell (also terminal).

2. Open a text editor of your choice, and add the following directives to the `.bash_profile` file placed in your `home` folder:

```
export JAVA_HOME=~/WFC/jdk8
export PATH=$JAVA_HOME/bin:$PATH
```

The preceding two commands will set the `JAVA_HOME` variable and export the `JAVA_HOME/bin` path into your **PATH** system variable, respectively. The tilde ~ symbol is a shortcut to the user home directory in Unix-like systems.

For the changes to take effect, you can either log out and log back in, or just issue the following command:

```
$ source ~/.bash_profile
```

3. Once you are done with the installation phase, test your new environment by executing the `java -version` command in your terminal application and you should see (more or less) the output as depicted in the following image:

```
[wildfly@foogaro WFC]$ java -version
java version "1.8.0_40"
Java(TM) SE Runtime Environment (build 1.8.0_40-b26)
Java HotSpot(TM) 64-Bit Server VM (build 25.40-b25, mixed mode)
[wildfly@foogaro WFC]$
```

4. Next, we need to install Apache Maven 3. If you haven't downloaded it yet, click on the following link:

   `http://www.us.apache.org/dist/maven/maven-3/3.2.5/binaries/apache-maven-3.2.5-bin.tar.gz`

5. Once the download is complete, open your command line and extract its content to the `WFC` folder:

   **$ cd ~/WFC && tar zxvf apache-maven-3.2.5-bin.tar.gz**

   This will extract the Apache Maven (also known as Maven) software into the `apache-maven-3.2.5` folder, inside the `WFC` folder, starting from your `home` folder. For convenience, we will use a different folder name, like `maven`, to refer to the preceding Maven installation folder. Run the following command:

   **$ cd ~/WFC && mv apache-maven-3.2.5 maven**

   Now we need to set the `M2_HOME` environment variable and make Maven's commands available from our shell (also terminal).

6. Open a text editor of your choice, and add the following directives to the `.bash_profile` file placed in your `home` folder:

   **export M2_HOME=~/WFC/maven**

   **export PATH=$JAVA_HOME/bin:M2_HOME/bin:$PATH**

   The preceding two commands will set the `M2_HOME` variable and export the `M2_HOME/bin` path into your **PATH** system variable, respectively. The tilde ~ symbol is a shortcut to the user home directory, in Unix-like systems.

   For the changes to take effect, you can either log out and log back in, or just issue the following command:

   **$ source ~/.bash_profile**

7. Once you are done with the installation phase, test your new environment by executing the `mvn -version` command in your terminal application and you should see (more or less) the output as depicted in the following image:

```
[wildfly@foogaro WFC]$ mvn -version
Apache Maven 3.2.5 (12a6b3acb947671f09b81f49094c53f426d8cea1; 2014-12-14T12:29:23-05:00)
Maven home: /home/wildfly/WFC/maven
Java version: 1.8.0_40, vendor: Oracle Corporation
Java home: /home/wildfly/WFC/jdk8/jre
Default locale: en_US, platform encoding: ANSI_X3.4-1968
OS name: "linux", version: "3.18.5-tinycore64", arch: "amd64", family: "unix"
[wildfly@foogaro WFC]$
```

8. Last, but not the least, we will need to install the `git`, which is a distributed revision control system. It is mainly used with the source code, but it's also used as a configuration repository. To install the `git` tool, we will rely on the `yum` software manager, which makes the installation process easy. Open a terminal and do as follows:

   ```
   $ sudo yum -y install git
   ```

9. Once done, try to hit the following command:

   ```
   $ git version
   git version 2.1.0
   ```

## There's more...

Now that we have the `git` installed, we can proceed to download the code repository (or repo) used for this book, available on my GitHub account at the following URL: `https://github.com/foogaro/wildfly-cookbook.git`.

You can `git-clone` the repository or just download it as a ZIP archive. Either way, create a folder named `github` into the `WFC` folder and place the source into it.

Using the `git-clone` command, do as follows:

```
$ cd ~/WFC
$ mkdir github
$ cd github
$ git clone https://github.com/foogaro/wildfly-cookbook.git
```

Once the `git` has done cloning the repo, you will find a new folder named `wildfly-cookbook` where you can find all the projects used for the book.

To build a project, just go into the proper folder and execute the `maven-package` command.

For example, to build the project `example`, do as follows:

```
$ cd ~/WFC/github/wildfly-cookbook/example
$ mvn -e clean package
```

The preceding commands builds the project, and generate the web application artifact into a folder named `target`. There you can find the application `example.war`, ready to be deployed.

OK, we have finally finished installing all the software that we will need and use within the book. Just to be sure you are not missing any piece, you should have an environment as depicted in the following image:

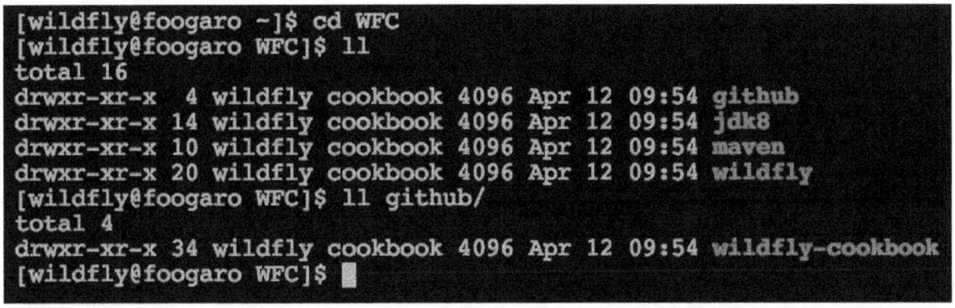

```
[wildfly@foogaro ~]$ cd WFC
[wildfly@foogaro WFC]$ ll
total 16
drwxr-xr-x  4 wildfly cookbook 4096 Apr 12 09:54 github
drwxr-xr-x 14 wildfly cookbook 4096 Apr 12 09:54 jdk8
drwxr-xr-x 10 wildfly cookbook 4096 Apr 12 09:54 maven
drwxr-xr-x 20 wildfly cookbook 4096 Apr 12 09:54 wildfly
[wildfly@foogaro WFC]$ ll github/
total 4
drwxr-xr-x 34 wildfly cookbook 4096 Apr 12 09:54 wildfly-cookbook
[wildfly@foogaro WFC]$
```

# Downloading and installing WildFly

In this recipe, we will learn how to get and install WildFly. As always, in the open source world you can do the same thing in different ways. WildFly can be installed using your preferred software manager or by downloading the bundle provided by the `http://wildfly.org` site. We will choose the second way, as per the JDK.

## Getting ready

Just open your favorite browser and point it to `http://wildfly.org/downloads/`. You should see a page similar to the following screenshot:

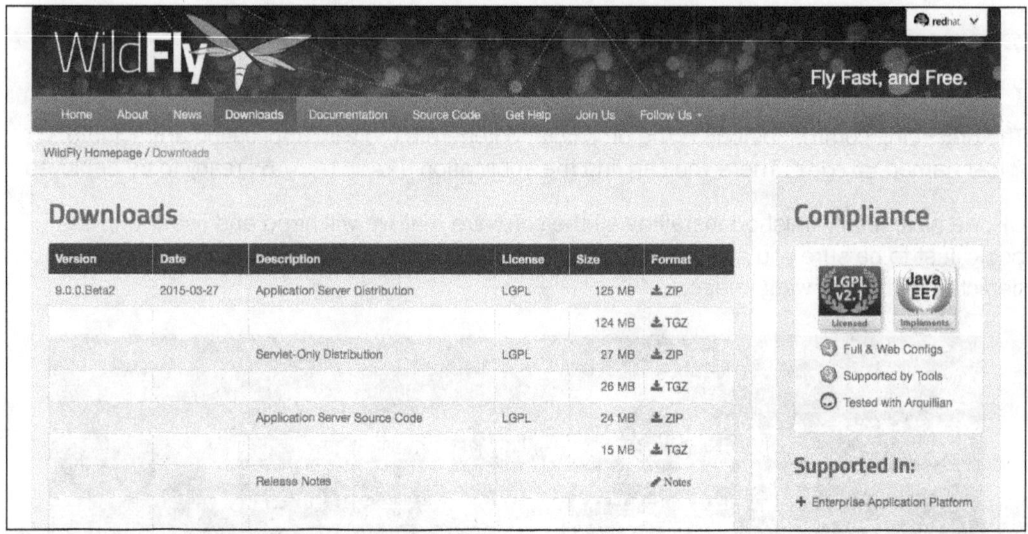


WildFly's download page

At the time of writing this book, the latest WildFly was version 9.0.0.Beta2. The final version is now available and in use.

Now, download the latest version into the `WFC` folder.

## How to do it...

1. Once the download is complete, open a terminal and extract its contents into the `WFC` folder, executing the following commands:

   ```
   $ cd ~/WFC && tar zx wildfly-9.0.0.Beta2.tar.gz
   ```

   The preceding command will first point to our `WildFly Cookbook` folder; it will then extract the WildFly archive from it. Listing our `WFC` folder, we should find the newly created WildFly' folder named `wildfly-9.0.0.Beta2`.

2. To better remember and handle WildFly's installation directory, rename it `wildfly`, as follows:

   ```
   $ cd ~/WFC && mv wildfly-9.0.0.Beta2 wildfly
   ```

   By the way, WildFly can be also installed using the traditional `YUM`, Fedora's software manager.

In a production environment, you will *not* place the WildFly installation directory into the `home` folder of a specific user. Rather, you will be placing it into different paths, relative to the context you are working in.

3. Now we need to create the `JBOSS_HOME` environment variable, which is used by WildFly itself as base directory when it starts up (probably in future releases, this will be updated to `WILDFLY_HOME`). We will also create the `WILDFLY_HOME` environment variable, which we will use throughout the whole book to reference WildFly's installation directory. Thus, open the `.bash_profile` file, placed in your `home` folder, with your favorite text editor and add the following directives:

   ```
   export JBOSS_HOME=~/WFC/wildfly
   export WILDFLY_HOME=$JBOSS_HOME
   ```

4. For the changes to take effect, you can either log out and log back in, or just issue the following command:

   ```
   $ source ~/.bash_profile
   ```

If you followed the first two recipes carefully, your `.bash_profile` file should look like the following image:

```
# .bash_profile

# Get the aliases and functions
if [ -f ~/.bashrc ]; then
        . ~/.bashrc
fi

# User specific environment and startup programs

PATH=$PATH:$HOME/.local/bin:$HOME/bin

export JAVA_HOME=~/WFC/jdk8
export M2_HOME=~/WFC/maven
export JBOSS_HOME=~/WFC/wildfly
export WILDFLY_HOME=$JBOSS_HOME

export PATH=$JAVA_HOME/bin:$M2_HOME/bin:$PATH
```

# Understanding WildFly's directory overview

Now that we have finished installing WildFly, let's look into its folders. This recipe is going to be a little theoretical.

## How to do it...

1. Open your terminal and run the following commands:

   **$ cd $WILDFLY_HOME**

   **$ pwd && ls -la**

2. The output of your commands should be similar to the following image:

```
[wildfly@foogaro ~]$ cd $WILDFLY_HOME
[wildfly@foogaro wildfly]$ pwd && ls -la
/home/wildfly/WFC/wildfly
total 436
drwxr-xr-x 20 wildfly cookbook   4096 Apr 12 09:54 .
drwxr-xr-x 14 wildfly cookbook   4096 Apr 12 10:04 ..
drwxr-xr-x  2 wildfly cookbook   4096 Mar 27 13:57 .installation
-rw-r--r--  1 wildfly cookbook  26530 Mar 27 13:57 LICENSE.txt
-rw-r--r--  1 wildfly cookbook   2531 Mar 27 13:57 README.txt
drwxr-xr-x  4 wildfly cookbook   4096 Apr 12 09:54 appclient
drwxr-xr-x  8 wildfly cookbook   4096 Apr 12 09:54 bin
-rw-r--r--  1 wildfly cookbook   2451 Mar 27 13:57 copyright.txt
drwxr-xr-x  6 wildfly cookbook   4096 Apr 12 09:54 docs
drwxr-xr-x  9 wildfly cookbook   4096 Apr 12 09:54 domain
-rw-r--r--  1 wildfly cookbook 366296 Mar 27 13:57 jboss-modules.jar
drwxr-xr-x  4 wildfly cookbook   4096 Apr 12 09:54 modules
drwxr-xr-x 11 wildfly cookbook   4096 Apr 12 09:54 standalone
drwxr-xr-x  2 wildfly cookbook   4096 Apr 12 09:54 welcome-content
[wildfly@foogaro wildfly]$
```

WildFly's folders overview

## How it works...

The preceding image depicts WildFly's folders in the filesystem. Each is outlined in the following table:

| **Folder name** | **Description** |
| --- | --- |
| `appclient` | Configuration files, deployment content, and writable areas used by the application client container run from this installation. |
| `bin` | Start up scripts, start up configuration files, and various command line utilities like Vault, add-user, and Java diagnostic report available for Unix and Windows environments. |

| Folder name | Description |
|---|---|
| `bin/client` | Contains a client jar for use by non-maven based clients. |
| `docs/schema` | XML schema definition files. |
| `docs/examples/configs` | Example configuration files representing specific use cases. |
| `domain` | Configuration files, deployment content, and writable areas used by the domain mode processes run from this installation. |
| `modules` | WildFly is based on a modular class loading architecture. The various modules used in the server are stored here. |
| `standalone` | Configuration files, deployment content, and writable areas used by the single standalone server run from this installation. |
| `welcome-content` | Default Welcome Page content. |

In the preceding table, I've emphasized the "domain" and the "standalone" folders which are those that determine the mode which WildFly will run in: standalone or domain. In the next few recipes, we will have an overview of them, and get a deep insight later in the book.

Hereby, whenever mentioned, WildFly's home will be intended as `$WILDFLY_HOME`.

# Running WildFly in standalone mode

WildFly in the standalone mode means a WildFly instance is launched and managed on its own. You can have as many standalone WildFly instances as you like, but you will have to manage them separately. This means that every configuration, datasource, deployment, and module has to be managed once per instance.

The main difference between the standalone and domain modes is about management and not about capabilities. Capabilities are determined by the profile you choose to run WildFly with.

## Getting ready

Let's have a look into the standalone folder:

| Folder's name | Description |
|---|---|
| `configuration` | Configuration files used by the single standalone server run from this installation. |
| `deployments` | Deployments content used by the single standalone server run from this installation. |

| Folder's name | Description |
|---|---|
| `lib` | Libraries used by the single standalone server run from this installation. |
| `log` | Log files created by the single standalone server run from this installation. |

So, the configuration folder contains all the configuration files. Yes, you can have more than one, but you will have to choose which one to run with. The `deployments` folder contains all your applications to deploy, deployed and undeployed (as we will see later, there is even a marker for failed deployments). The folder `lib` contains all the library jars referenced by your applications using the Extension-List mechanism. Lastly, the `log` folder contains WildFly's `server.log` file.

As previously mentioned, in the `configuration` folder you will find the following files:

| File name | Description |
|---|---|
| `standalone.xml` (`default`) | Java Enterprise Edition 7 web profile certified configuration with the required technologies. |
| `standalone-ha.xml` | Java Enterprise Edition 7 web profile certified configuration with high availability. |
| `standalone-full.xml` | Java Enterprise Edition 7 full profile certified configuration including all the required EE 7 technologies, including messaging—JMS. |
| `standalone-full-ha.xml` | Java Enterprise Edition 7 full profile certified configuration with high availability. |

Along the lines of Java EE 7 profiles, WildFly defines its own profiles. For the standalone mode, each file corresponds to a WildFly profile, that is, `standalone.xml` corresponds to the default profile, `standalone-ha.xml` corresponds to the `ha` profile, `standalone-full.xml` corresponds to the `full` profile, and `standalone-full-ha.xml` corresponds to the `full-ha` profile. The same WildFly profiles will be found in the domain mode as well.

## How to do it...

Let's try running WildFly in the standalone mode with its default settings, as follows:

```
$ cd $WILDFLY_HOME
$ ./bin/standalone.sh =========================================================================


  JBoss Bootstrap Environment


  JBOSS_HOME: /home/wildfly/WFC/wildfly
```

```
  JAVA: /home/wildfly/WFC/jdk8/bin/java


  JAVA_OPTS:  -server -XX:+UseCompressedOops  -server
-XX:+UseCompressedOops -Xms64m -Xmx512m -XX:MaxPermSize=256m -Djava.
net.preferIPv4Stack=true -Djboss.modules.system.pkgs=org.jboss.byteman
-Djava.awt.headless=true


=========================================================================


Java HotSpot(TM) 64-Bit Server VM warning: ignoring option
MaxPermSize=256m; support was removed in 8.0

08:43:50,658 INFO  [org.jboss.modules] (main) JBoss Modules version
1.4.2.Final

08:43:50,799 INFO  [org.jboss.msc] (main) JBoss MSC version 1.2.4.Final

08:43:50,850 INFO  [org.jboss.as] (MSC service thread 1-6) WFLYSRV0049:
WildFly Full 9.0.0.Beta2 (WildFly Core 1.0.0.Beta2) starting

08:43:51,543 INFO  [org.jboss.as.controller.management-deprecated]
(ServerService Thread Pool -- 26) WFLYCTL0028: Attribute enabled is
deprecated, and it might be removed in future version!

08:43:51,564 INFO  [org.jboss.as.server] (Controller Boot Thread)
WFLYSRV0039: Creating http management service using socket-binding
(management-http)

08:43:51,592 INFO  [org.xnio] (MSC service thread 1-11) XNIO version
3.3.0.Final

08:43:51,601 INFO  [org.xnio.nio] (MSC service thread 1-11) XNIO NIO
Implementation Version 3.3.0.Final

08:43:51,627 WARN  [org.jboss.as.txn] (ServerService Thread Pool -- 54)
WFLYTX0013: Node identifier property is set to the default value. Please
make sure it is unique.

08:43:51,626 INFO  [org.jboss.as.security] (ServerService Thread Pool --
53) WFLYSEC0002: Activating Security Subsystem

08:43:51,631 INFO  [org.wildfly.extension.io] (ServerService Thread Pool
-- 37) WFLYIO001: Worker 'default' has auto-configured to 16 core threads
with 128 task threads based on your 8 available processors

08:43:51,635 INFO  [org.jboss.as.security] (MSC service thread 1-10)
WFLYSEC0001: Current PicketBox version=4.9.0.Beta2

08:43:51,649 INFO  [org.jboss.as.jsf] (ServerService Thread Pool -- 44)
WFLYJSF0007: Activated the following JSF Implementations: [main]

08:43:51,650 INFO  [org.jboss.as.clustering.infinispan] (ServerService
Thread Pool -- 38) WFLYCLINF0001: Activating Infinispan subsystem.

08:43:51,680 INFO  [org.jboss.as.naming] (ServerService Thread Pool --
46) WFLYNAM0001: Activating Naming Subsystem
```

```
08:43:51,686 INFO  [org.jboss.remoting] (MSC service thread 1-11) JBoss
Remoting version 4.0.8.Final

08:43:51,687 INFO  [org.jboss.as.webservices] (ServerService Thread Pool
-- 56) WFLYWS0002: Activating WebServices Extension

08:43:51,704 INFO  [org.jboss.as.connector.subsystems.datasources]
(ServerService Thread Pool -- 33) WFLYJCA0004: Deploying JDBC-compliant
driver class org.h2.Driver (version 1.3)

08:43:51,707 INFO  [org.wildfly.extension.undertow] (MSC service thread
1-5) WFLYUT0003: Undertow 1.2.0.Beta10 starting

08:43:51,707 INFO  [org.wildfly.extension.undertow] (ServerService Thread
Pool -- 55) WFLYUT0003: Undertow 1.2.0.Beta10 starting

08:43:51,714 INFO  [org.jboss.as.connector] (MSC service thread 1-3)
WFLYJCA0009: Starting JCA Subsystem (IronJacamar 1.2.3.Final)

08:43:51,725 INFO  [org.jboss.as.connector.deployers.jdbc] (MSC service
thread 1-5) WFLYJCA0018: Started Driver service with driver-name = h2

08:43:51,813 INFO  [org.jboss.as.naming] (MSC service thread 1-5)
WFLYNAM0003: Starting Naming Service

08:43:51,814 INFO  [org.jboss.as.mail.extension] (MSC service thread 1-7)
WFLYMAIL0001: Bound mail session [java:jboss/mail/Default]

08:43:51,876 INFO  [org.wildfly.extension.undertow] (ServerService Thread
Pool -- 55) WFLYUT0014: Creating file handler for path /Users/foogaro/
wildfly9/wildfly-9.0.0.Beta2/welcome-content

08:43:51,904 INFO  [org.wildfly.extension.undertow] (MSC service thread
1-16) WFLYUT0012: Started server default-server.

08:43:51,926 INFO  [org.wildfly.extension.undertow] (MSC service thread
1-2) WFLYUT0018: Host default-host starting

08:43:51,990 INFO  [org.wildfly.extension.undertow] (MSC service
thread 1-12) WFLYUT0006: Undertow HTTP listener default listening on
/127.0.0.1:8080

08:43:52,122 INFO  [org.jboss.as.connector.subsystems.datasources]
(MSC service thread 1-12) WFLYJCA0001: Bound data source [java:jboss/
datasources/ExampleDS]

08:43:52,166 INFO  [org.jboss.as.server.deployment.scanner] (MSC service
thread 1-5) WFLYDS0013: Started FileSystemDeploymentService for directory
/Users/foogaro/wildfly9/wildfly-9.0.0.Beta2/standalone/deployments

08:43:52,244 INFO  [org.jboss.ws.common.management] (MSC service thread
1-11) JBWS022052: Starting JBoss Web Services - Stack CXF Server
5.0.0.Beta3

08:43:52,403 INFO  [org.jboss.as] (Controller Boot Thread) WFLYSRV0060:
Http management interface listening on http://127.0.0.1:9990/management
```

```
08:43:52,403 INFO  [org.jboss.as] (Controller Boot Thread) WFLYSRV0051:
Admin console listening on http://127.0.0.1:9990
08:43:52,403 INFO  [org.jboss.as] (Controller Boot Thread) WFLYSRV0025:
WildFly Full 9.0.0.Beta2 (WildFly Core 1.0.0.Beta2) started in 1970ms -
Started 202 of 379 services (210 services are lazy, passive or on-demand)
```

## How it works...

The first few lines tell you where WildFly is located and the JVM options. What follows is the Undertow HTTP Listener, which is the component that processes the HTTP request, listening on `http://127.0.0.1:8080`. As a matter of fact, you can test that WildFly is running correctly by pointing to the previous address, and you should see something like the following image:

WildFly's welcome content

Next are the logs about WildFly's management listeners which I have emphasized. The first listener is the HTTP management listener, which is actually an HTTP API used to invoke commands over HTTP. The second one is the Admin Console, which provides you with a Web Console to simplify most of WildFly's configuration. The HTTP management interface and the Admin Console are listening respectively on `http://127.0.0.1:9990/management` and `http://127.0.0.1:9990`.

To access the Admin Console, open a browser and point it to `http://127.0.0.1:9990/`. What you should see is a page as depicted in the following image:

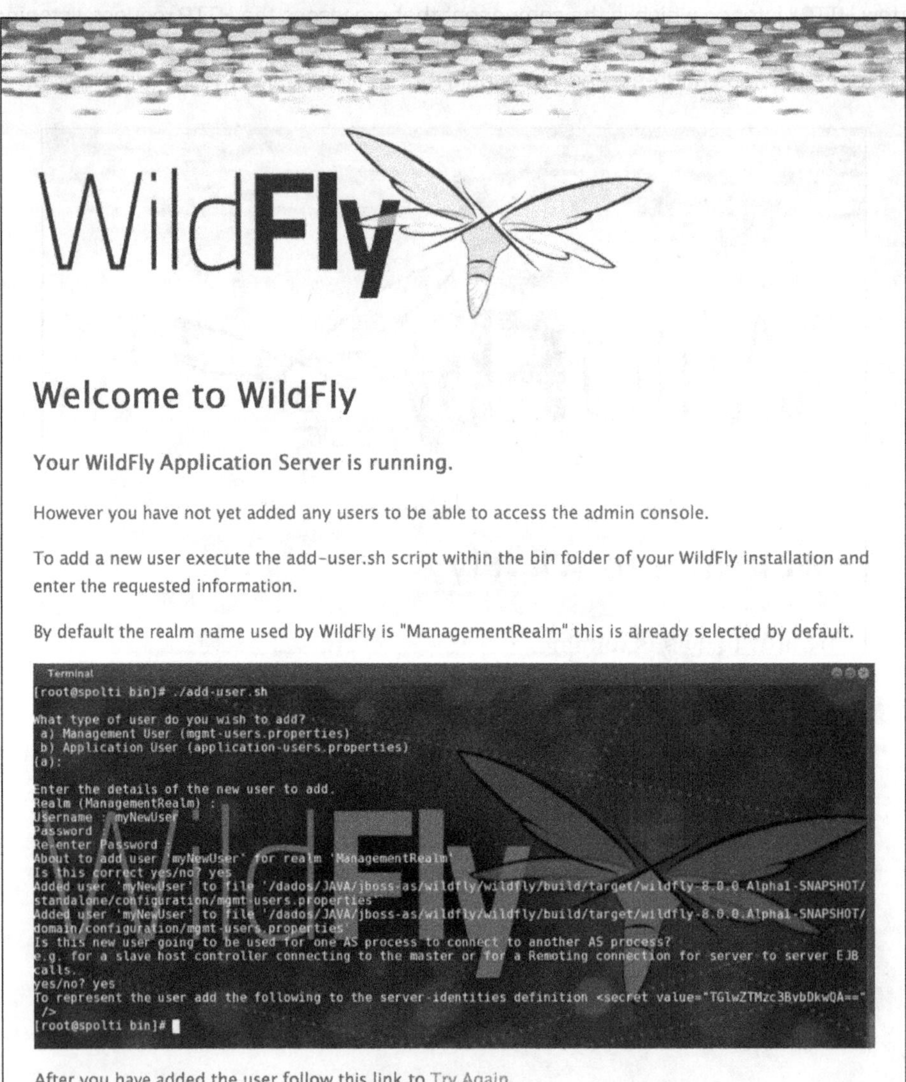

WildFly
Welcome to WildFly
Your WildFly Application Server is running.
However you have not yet added any users to be able to access the admin console.
To add a new user execute the add-user.sh script within the bin folder of your WildFly installation and enter the requested information.
By default the realm name used by WildFly is "ManagementRealm" this is already selected by default.
Terminal
[root@spolti bin]# ./add-user.sh
What type of user do you wish to add?
a) Management User (mgmt-users.properties)
b) Application User (application-users.properties)
(a):
Enter the details of the new user to add.
Realm (ManagementRealm) :
Username : myNewUser
Password :
Re-enter Password :
About to add user 'myNewUser' for realm 'ManagementRealm'
Is this correct yes/no? yes
Added user 'myNewUser' to file '/dados/JAVA/jboss-as/wildfly/wildfly/build/target/wildfly-8.0.0.Alpha1-SNAPSHOT/standalone/configuration/mgmt-users.properties'
Added user 'myNewUser' to file '/dados/JAVA/jboss-as/wildfly/wildfly/build/target/wildfly-8.0.0.Alpha1-SNAPSHOT/domain/configuration/mgmt-users.properties'
Is this new user going to be used for one AS process to connect to another AS process?
e.g. for a slave host controller connecting to the master or for a Remoting connection for server to server EJB calls.
yes/no? yes
To represent the user add the following to the server-identities definition <secret value="TGlwZTMzc3BvbDkwQA==" />
[root@spolti bin]#
After you have added the user follow this link to Try Again.


WildFly's management error page

WildFly is up and running, but the Admin Console is not visible at the moment because there is no user registered to the "security context" (the proper WildFly term is Realm) that the Admin Console belongs to. We will talk about security and realms later in this recipe and in the upcoming chapters.

Hereby, whenever I use the term Admin Console or Web Console, they are to intend the same thing.

Furthermore, the preceding screenshot tells you how to create a user to access the Admin Console. We need to create the admin user by using the `add-user.sh` script provided by WildFly in its `bin` folder.

Once again, open your command line (you should never close it, unless you are shutting down your PC) and execute the following command:

```
$ cd $WILDFLY
$ ./bin/add-user.sh
```

The following screenshot is the result of the preceding code:

```
[wildfly@foogaro wildfly]$ ./bin/add-user.sh

What type of user do you wish to add?
 a) Management User (mgmt-users.properties)
 b) Application User (application-users.properties)
(a):

Enter the details of the new user to add.
Using realm 'ManagementRealm' as discovered from the existing property files.
Username : wildfly
Password recommendations are listed below. To modify these restrictions edit the add-user.properties configuration file.
 - The password should be different from the username
 - The password should not be one of the following restricted values {root, admin, administrator}
 - The password should contain at least 8 characters, 1 alphabetic character(s), 1 digit(s), 1 non-alphanumeric symbol(s)
Password :
Re-enter Password :
What groups do you want this user to belong to? (Please enter a comma separated list, or leave blank for none)[  ]:
About to add user 'wildfly' for realm 'ManagementRealm'
Is this correct yes/no? yes
Added user 'wildfly' to file '/home/wildfly/WFC/wildfly/standalone/configuration/mgmt-users.properties'
Added user 'wildfly' to file '/home/wildfly/WFC/wildfly/domain/configuration/mgmt-users.properties'
Added user 'wildfly' with groups  to file '/home/wildfly/WFC/wildfly/standalone/configuration/mgmt-groups.properties'
Added user 'wildfly' with groups  to file '/home/wildfly/WFC/wildfly/domain/configuration/mgmt-groups.properties'
Is this new user going to be used for one AS process to connect to another AS process?
e.g. for a slave host controller connecting to the master or for a Remoting connection for server to server EJB calls.
yes/no? no
[wildfly@foogaro wildfly]$
```

Examining the script and its interaction:

- In the preceding screenshot, the script first asks for a user type; in our case we need a management user. So just hit *Enter* or type `a` and then hit *Enter*. We do not need to create a user at the application level, used to create security context.
- We specify the username, for example `wildfly`.
- Then we need to enter the password following the specified policy. So we type `cookbook.2015` and hit *Enter*.
- We confirm the password provided in the previous step by re-entering it.

- We confirm that we want to add our user "wildfly" to the `ManagementRealm` realm. So we type `yes` and hit *Enter*.
- In the final step, the script asks if the user will be used to connect one of the WildFly process to another one, or used to authenticate to an EJB. In this case, we type `no` and hit *Enter*.

Now, let's point to the admin address `http://127.0.0.1:9990` again. The page now asks you to enter the username and the password. Specify `wildfly` as username and `cookbook.2015` as password, and you should see the WildFly Admin Console as follows:

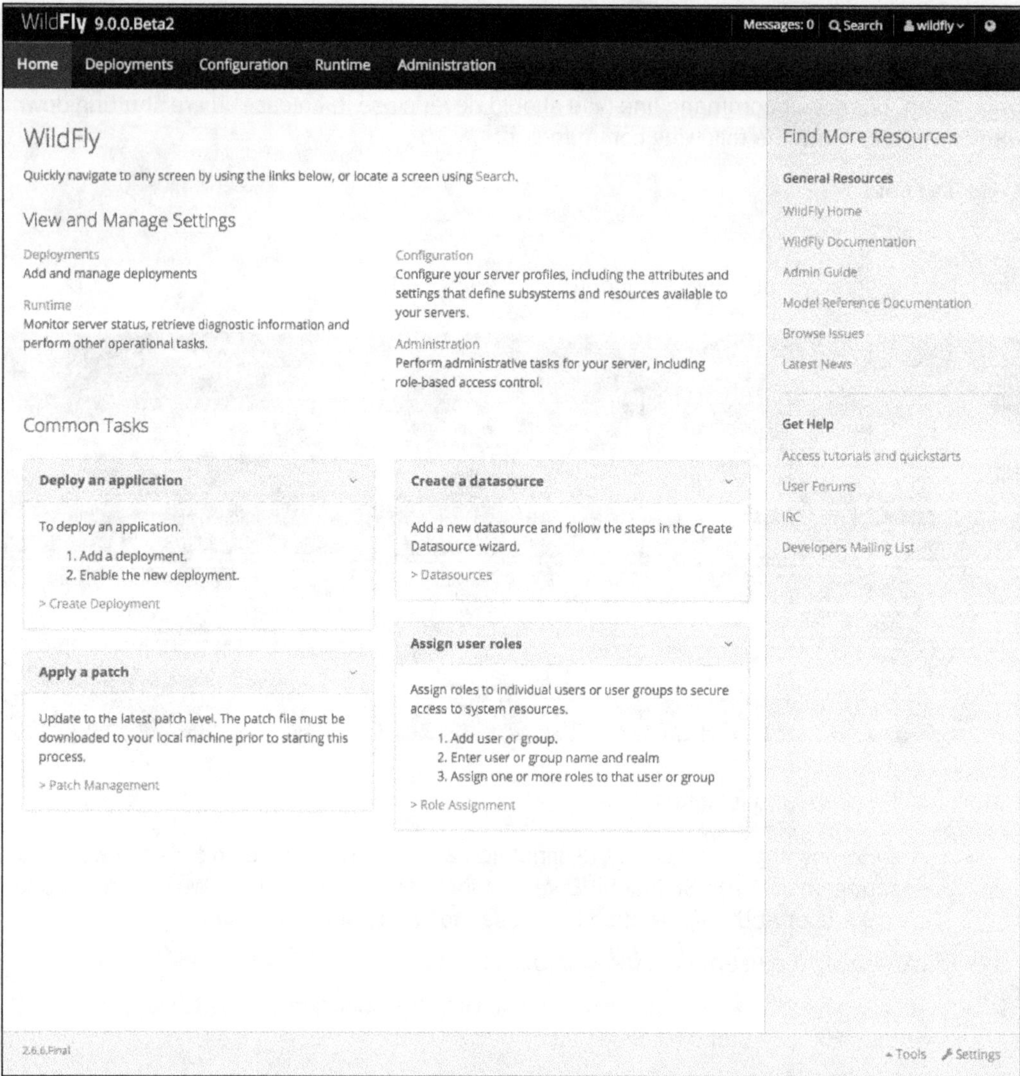


WildFly's Web Console

### See also

We will take a deep dive into the standalone mode soon. In *Chapter 2, Running WildFly in Standalone Mode*, there will be described in detail all the configuration files, which one you should use, and how to manage your instance with both the Admin Console and the CLI. We will also deploy both the management tools.

## Running WildFly in domain mode

The Domain mode is something totally new since JBoss AS 4, 5, and 6. It was first introduced in JBoss AS 7.

It's about grouping several WildFly instances into one single group, a server-group using the WildFly nomenclature. In fact, we group the WildFly server into one logical server-group, and all the WildFly instances will share the same configuration. By this we intend that they share the same WildFly profile (`default`, `ha`, `full`, and `full-ha`), same deployments, and so on. What will not be shared is specific instance configuration such as IP bind address, ports, and others.

Suppose you have an application and you want it to deploy on four servers of your infrastructure (or test rather than preproduction or production). You will need to configure a server-group, associate the four server instances to it, and you are done. Dealing just with the server-group, all your settings and changes will be spread to all the related server instances. This was definitely a big miss in JBoss AS, but now we have it.

Remember that a server-group does *not* form a cluster in any way.

### Getting ready

When dealing with domain mode, there are two new terms to know and understand: **domain controller** (**DC**) and **host controller** (**HC**).

The first one, the DC, acts as the parent process, the "gran maestro" of an orchestra. Every single change is provided by the DC towards all the HCs of all server-groups. The DC configuration file is named `domain.xml`, whilst the HC configuration file is named `host.xml`.

To avoid confusion, it's better to clarify the terminology that we will use in the book. We might refer to the server running the domain controller as the "master" or the "domain". Alternatively, we might refer to a running WildFly instance that is not the domain, as the "host", or "slave".

One more thing to know is that contrary to the standalone mode where you have different files for different profiles, in the domain mode you end up with just one file (there is another one named `host.xml`, but we will talk about it soon) having all the profiles configured in for you. Profiles are the same as for the standalone mode. We will learn how to associate a profile to a server-group in the chapter dedicated to the domain mode.

Let's have a look at the `domain` folder:

| **Folder's name** | **Description** |
|---|---|
| `configuration` | Configuration files for the domain and for the host controller and any servers running off this installation. All configuration information for the servers managed within the domain is located here and is the single place for configuration information. |
| `content` | An internal working area for the host controller that controls this installation. This is where it internally stores the deployment content. This directory is generated by WildFly when it starts and is not meant to be manipulated by the end users. Note that the domain mode does not support deploying content based on scanning a file system. |
| `lib/ext` | Location for the installed library jars referenced by applications using the Extension-List mechanism. |
| `log` | Location where the host controller process writes its logs. The process controller, a small lightweight process that actually spawns the other host controller processes and any application server processes also writes a log here. |
| `servers` | Writable area used by each application server instance that runs from this installation. Each application server instance will have its own subdirectory, created when the server is first started. In each server's subdirectory there will be the following subdirectories:<br>▸ `data`: Information written by the server that needs to survive a restart of the server<br>▸ `log`: The server's log files<br>▸ `tmp`: Location for temporary files written by the server |
| `tmp` | Location for temporary files written by the server |
| `tmp/auth` | Special location used to exchange authentication tokens with local clients so they can confirm that they are local to the running AS process. |

So, the `configuration` folder contains all the configuration files. Let's have a look at all of them:

| File name | Description |
|---|---|
| `domain.xml` (default name) | This is the main configuration file that includes all WildFly profiles plus all other configurations needed to run the AS. When WildFly starts, it will look for a file named `domain.xml` if not differently specified. |
| `host.xml` (default name) | This is the host controller configuration file provided by the WildFly installation. In this you will find the entire specific configurations about server instances. When WildFly starts, it will look for a file named `host.xml` if not differently specified. |
| `host-master.xml` | This is a host controller configuration example file provided by the WildFly installation. It shows you how to configure WildFly running only the domain controller. |
| `host-slave.xml` | This is a host controller configuration example file provided by the WildFly installation used to configure WildFly running as slave and connecting to the domain controller. |

## How to do it...

Let's try running WildFly in the domain mode with its default settings (two server-groups—first one with two instances named `server-one` and `server-two`, last one with one instance named `server-three` with auto-start disabled). Do as follows:

```
$ CD $WILDFLY_HOME
$ ./bin/domain.sh -b 0.0.0.0 -bmanagement 0.0.0.0
=========================================================================

  JBoss Bootstrap Environment

  JBOSS_HOME: /home/wildfly/WFC/wildfly

  JAVA: /home/wildfly/WFC/jdk8/bin/java

  JAVA_OPTS: -Xms64m -Xmx512m -XX:MaxPermSize=256m -Djava.net.
preferIPv4Stack=true -Djboss.modules.system.pkgs=org.jboss.byteman
-Djava.awt.headless=true
```

```
==============================================================

Java HotSpot(TM) 64-Bit Server VM warning: ignoring option
MaxPermSize=256m; support was removed in 8.0

08:50:53,715 INFO  [org.jboss.modules] (main) JBoss Modules version
1.4.2.Final

08:50:53,804 INFO  [org.jboss.as.process.Host Controller.status] (main)
WFLYPC0018: Starting process 'Host Controller'

[Host Controller] Java HotSpot(TM) 64-Bit Server VM warning: ignoring
option MaxPermSize=256m; support was removed in 8.0

[Host Controller] 08:50:54,154 INFO  [org.jboss.modules] (main) JBoss
Modules version 1.4.2.Final

[Host Controller] 08:50:54,841 INFO  [org.jboss.msc] (main) JBoss MSC
version 1.2.4.Final

[Host Controller] 08:50:54,869 INFO  [org.jboss.as] (MSC service thread
1-7) WFLYSRV0049: WildFly Full 9.0.0.Beta2 (WildFly Core 1.0.0.Beta2)
starting

[Host Controller] 08:50:55,326 INFO  [org.xnio] (MSC service thread 1-7)
XNIO version 3.3.0.Final

[Host Controller] 08:50:55,328 INFO  [org.jboss.as] (Controller Boot
Thread) WFLYHC0003: Creating http management service using network
interface (management) port (9990) securePort (-1)

[Host Controller] 08:50:55,332 INFO  [org.xnio.nio] (MSC service thread
1-7) XNIO NIO Implementation Version 3.3.0.Final

[Host Controller] 08:50:55,391 INFO  [org.jboss.remoting] (MSC service
thread 1-7) JBoss Remoting version 4.0.8.Final

[Host Controller] 08:50:55,415 INFO  [org.jboss.as.remoting] (MSC service
thread 1-1) WFLYRMT0001: Listening on 0.0.0.0:9999

[Host Controller] 08:50:56,189 INFO  [org.jboss.as.host.controller]
(Controller Boot Thread) WFLYHC0023: Starting server server-one

08:50:56,199 INFO  [org.jboss.as.process.Server:server-one.status]
(ProcessController-threads - 3) WFLYPC0018: Starting process
'Server:server-one'
```

```
[Server:server-one] 08:50:56,527 INFO  [org.jboss.modules] (main) JBoss
Modules version 1.4.2.Final

[Server:server-one] 08:50:56,692 INFO  [org.jboss.msc] (main) JBoss MSC
version 1.2.4.Final

[Server:server-one] 08:50:56,753 INFO  [org.jboss.as] (MSC service thread
1-7) WFLYSRV0049: WildFly Full 9.0.0.Beta2 (WildFly Core 1.0.0.Beta2)
starting

...

[Host Controller] 08:50:57,401 INFO  [org.jboss.as.domain.controller.
mgmt] (Remoting "master:MANAGEMENT" task-4) WFLYHC0021: Server
[Server:server-one] connected using connection [Channel ID 56504cde
(inbound) of Remoting connection 0f0a1d33 to /192.168.59.3:50968]

[Host Controller] 08:50:57,420 INFO  [org.jboss.as.host.controller]
(Controller Boot Thread) WFLYHC0023: Starting server server-two

08:50:57,423 INFO  [org.jboss.as.process.Server:server-two.status]
(ProcessController-threads - 3) WFLYPC0018: Starting process
'Server:server-two'

[Host Controller] 08:50:57,430 INFO  [org.jboss.as.host.controller]
(server-registration-threads - 1) WFLYHC0020: Registering server server-
one

...

[Server:server-two] 08:50:58,213 INFO  [org.jboss.modules] (main) JBoss
Modules version 1.4.2.Final

[Server:server-two] 08:50:58,513 INFO  [org.jboss.msc] (main) JBoss MSC
version 1.2.4.Final

[Server:server-two] 08:50:58,621 INFO  [org.jboss.as] (MSC service thread
1-6) WFLYSRV0049: WildFly Full 9.0.0.Beta2 (WildFly Core 1.0.0.Beta2)
starting
```

## How it works...

The domain controller is responsible for initiating all local host controllers along with the configured instances. Now, opening the WildFly Admin Console, you can see an overview of the details of both your instances:

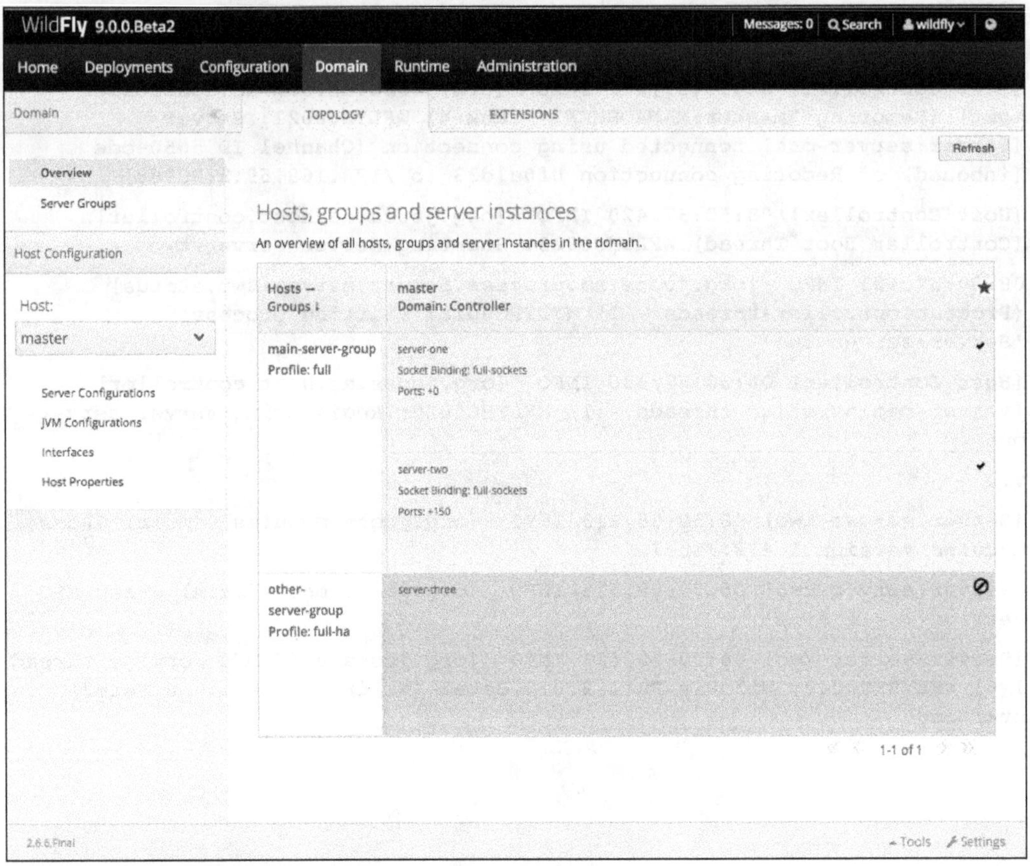

WildFly's runtime domain overview

From the domain perspective, you can see two server-groups named **main-server-group** with `full` profile and the **other-server-group** with `full-ha` profile. The latter is not running because its auto-start property is set to false.

> This time, even if running in the domain mode for the first time, we did *not* have to create a new user, because we already did so while setting up the standalone mode.

### See also

We will take a deep dive into the domain mode soon. In *Chapter 3, Running WildFly in Domain Mode*, all configuration files will be described in detail apart from learning how to choose the correct profile and how to manage your instance with both the Admin Console and the CLI. We will analyze the domain and host controller processes. We will create various examples of server groups, running locally and in pseudo-different machines. We will also deploy both the management tools and analyze how this behaves in the domain mode.

## Running WildFly as a service

In this recipe, you will learn how to install WildFly as a service, actually having WildFly run automatically when the OS starts. If you want to run Wildfly manually on demand, you can skip this recipe, unless for knowledge purpose.

Most Unix-like systems have different "runlevels" (think about them as steps) for various stages of the system running phase. At the operating system level, a service can be activated only if other services have been successfully activated. Thus if you activate a service that needs network before this one is up and running, it gets faulty or useless. This is essentially what "runlevels" are for.

The following is a list of runlevels:

- **rc1.d**: Single user mode
- **rc2.d**: Single user mode with networking
- **rc3.d**: Multi-user mode—boot up in text mode
- **rc4.d**: Undefined
- **rc5.d**: Multi-user mode—boot up in X Windows
- **rc6.d**: Shutdown

Most production Linux systems boot using runlevel 3 (UI is not needed and it will be a waste of resources), but to reach all audiences, we will use level 2, 3 and 5.

### How to do it...

WildFly comes with a predefined script, which can be used to run WildFly as a service. This script is located in the `bin/init.d` folder of the WildFly installation folder. So we just need to copy the file inside the `/etc/init.d` system folder and set it as a service, as follows:

```
$ sudo cp $WILDFLY_HOME/bin/init.d/wildfly-init-redhat.sh /etc/init.d/wildfly
$ sudo chkconfig --add wildfly
$ sudo chkconfig wildfly on --level 235
```

There is also one more file that we need to take a look at, and it is the `wildfly.conf`, placed into the same `bin/init.d` directory of the WildFly installation folder. The following is the file as is:

```
# General configuration for the init.d scripts,
# not necessarily for JBoss AS itself.
# default location: /etc/default/wildfly

## Location of JDK
# JAVA_HOME="/usr/lib/jvm/default-java"

## Location of WildFly
# JBOSS_HOME="/opt/wildfly"

## The username who should own the process.
# JBOSS_USER=wildfly

## The mode WildFly should start, standalone or domain
# JBOSS_MODE=standalone

## Configuration for standalone mode
# JBOSS_CONFIG=standalone.xml

## Configuration for domain mode
# JBOSS_DOMAIN_CONFIG=domain.xml
# JBOSS_HOST_CONFIG=host-master.xml

## The amount of time to wait for startup
# STARTUP_WAIT=60

## The amount of time to wait for shutdown
# SHUTDOWN_WAIT=60

## Location to keep the console log
# JBOSS_CONSOLE_LOG="/var/log/wildfly/console.log"
```

The previous configuration file basically sets a series of parameters that tell `init-script` which WildFly mode to use, which configuration file, which user WildFly should run with, and so on. Any update should be placed into that file.

For the moment, we will rely on the defaults, except for the user that we will mention explicitly by uncommenting the line `# JBOSS_USER=wildfly`, by removing the hash # symbol. You may have noticed that you can also specify the mode which WildFly will run with: domain or standalone.

We now need to create the `wildfly` user, and give the ownership of the WildFly `home` folder to the `wildfly` user. Do as follows:

```
$ sudo groupadd -r wildfly
$ sudo useradd -r -g wildfly -s /sbin/nologin -c "WildFly user" wildfly
$ sudo passwd -d wildfly
$ sudo chown -R :wildfly $WILDFLY_HOME/*
```

Now if you reboot your system, you will have WildFly up and running as a service with the default settings, launched by the `wildfly` user.

# 2

# Running WildFly in Standalone Mode

In this chapter, we will cover the following topics:

- Running WildFly from a custom configuration folder
- Binding WildFly onto a custom port
- Binding WildFly onto a custom IP
- Configuring multiple WildFly instances to run on the same machine with different ports
- Configuring multiple WildFly instances to run on the same machine with different IPs
- Managing applications using the deployments folder
- Connecting to the CLI
- Checking the server-state via the CLI
- Deploying an application via the CLI
- Undeploying an application via the CLI
- Executing commands in batch mode via the CLI
- Reloading a server configuration via the CLI
- Shutting down and restarting an instance via the CLI
- Suspending and resuming an instance via the CLI
- Backing up your configuration file via the CLI

# Introduction

In this chapter, you will learn how to manage WildFly running in the standalone mode. First we will discuss which profile fits our needs, and then we will cover how to run WildFly with a specific configuration file, navigate through the Web Console, and the CLI.

You will also learn how to get multiple WildFly instances running on the same machine, both with different ports and IPs, in case you have only one network interface. You will learn how to connect to the CLI, retrieve server information, reload server configuration, and shut down, deploy, and undeploy an application.

# Running WildFly from a custom configuration folder

In this recipe, you will learn how to run WildFly from a custom configuration folder. This can be handy if you want to use the same WildFly installation folder, but run two or more WildFly instances with different configurations.

## How to do it…

1. What you have to do is to just copy the `standalone` folder to a path of your choice.
2. That's it! Now just run WildFly as usual, specifying your configuration folder by passing the `-Djboss.server.base.dir` directive:

```
$ cd $WILDFLY_HOME
$ ./bin/standalone.sh -Djboss.server.base.dir=/your/config/path
```

## How it works…

On specification of a different `jboss.server.base.dir` directory, WildFly tries to pick up the `standalone.xml` file from the expected folder. In fact, your configuration path has to maintain the same folder structure. WildFly lets you override different paths, in case you need to.

The following is a table summarizing all such paths:

| Property name | Usage | Default value |
|---|---|---|
| `java.ext.dirs` | The JDK extension directory paths | Null |
| `jboss.home.dir` | The root directory of the WildFly installation | Set by `standalone.sh to $JBOSS_HOME` |

| Property name | Usage | Default value |
| --- | --- | --- |
| jboss.server.base.dir | The base directory for server content | jboss.home.dir/standalone |
| jboss.server.config.dir | The base configuration directory | jboss.server.base.dir/configuration |
| jboss.server.data.dir | The directory used for persistent data file storage | jboss.server.base.dir/data |
| jboss.server.log.dir | The directory containing the server.log file | jboss.server.base.dir/log |
| jboss.server.temp.dir | The directory used for temporary file storage | jboss.server.base.dir/tmp |
| jboss.server.deploy.dir | The directory used to store the deployed content | jboss.server.data.dir/content |

## There's more...

Furthermore, you can use a different configuration file by specifying it via the `--server-config` directive, as follows:

```
$ $WILDFLY_HOME/bin/standalone.sh --server-config=standalone-ha.xml
```

# Binding WildFly onto a custom port

Why would you bind WildFly onto a custom port? This is because you might have a different service running on the same IP:PORT (that is, another WildFly or JBoss instance, Tomcat, or GlassFish).

## How to do it...

Just open your command line and launch your WildFly standalone instance as follows:

```
$ cd $WILDFLY_HOME
$ ./bin/standalone.sh
```

Now you can change the port using either the Web Console or the CLI:

## Using the Web Console

1. Point your browser to the following address: `http://127.0.0.1:8080/console`.
2. Log in by entering the credentials specified in *Chapter 1, Welcome to WildFly!* while adding the management user; we entered `wildfly` as the username and `cookbook.2015` as the password.
3. Select the **Configuration** tab and select from the menu on the left side under general configuration, the voice **Socket Binding**, and select **View** as shown in the following screenshot:

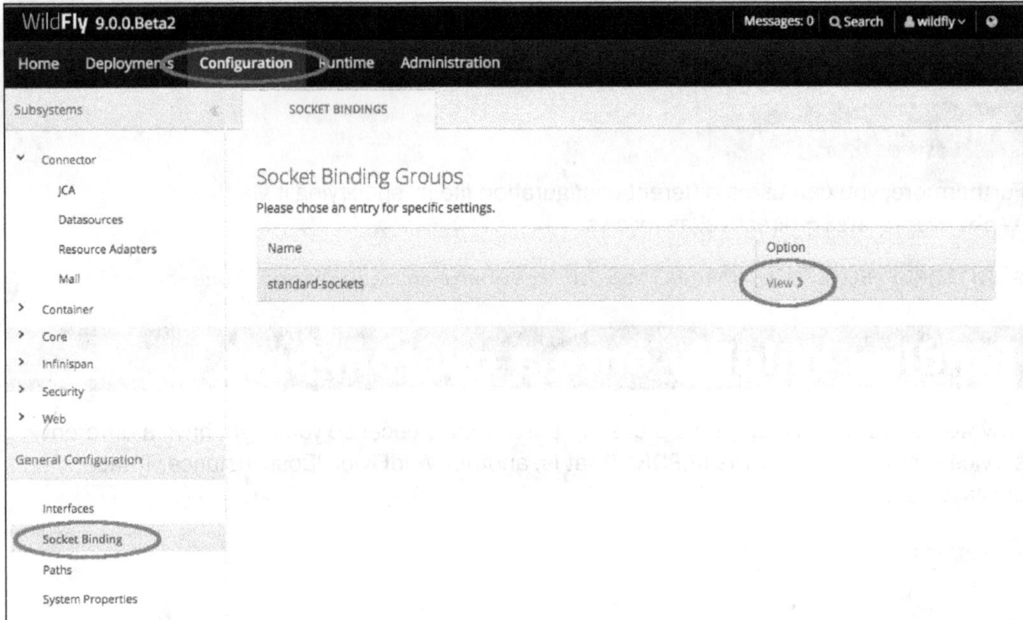

4. Select the `http` property and scroll down the page to edit the port number, as shown in the following screenshot:

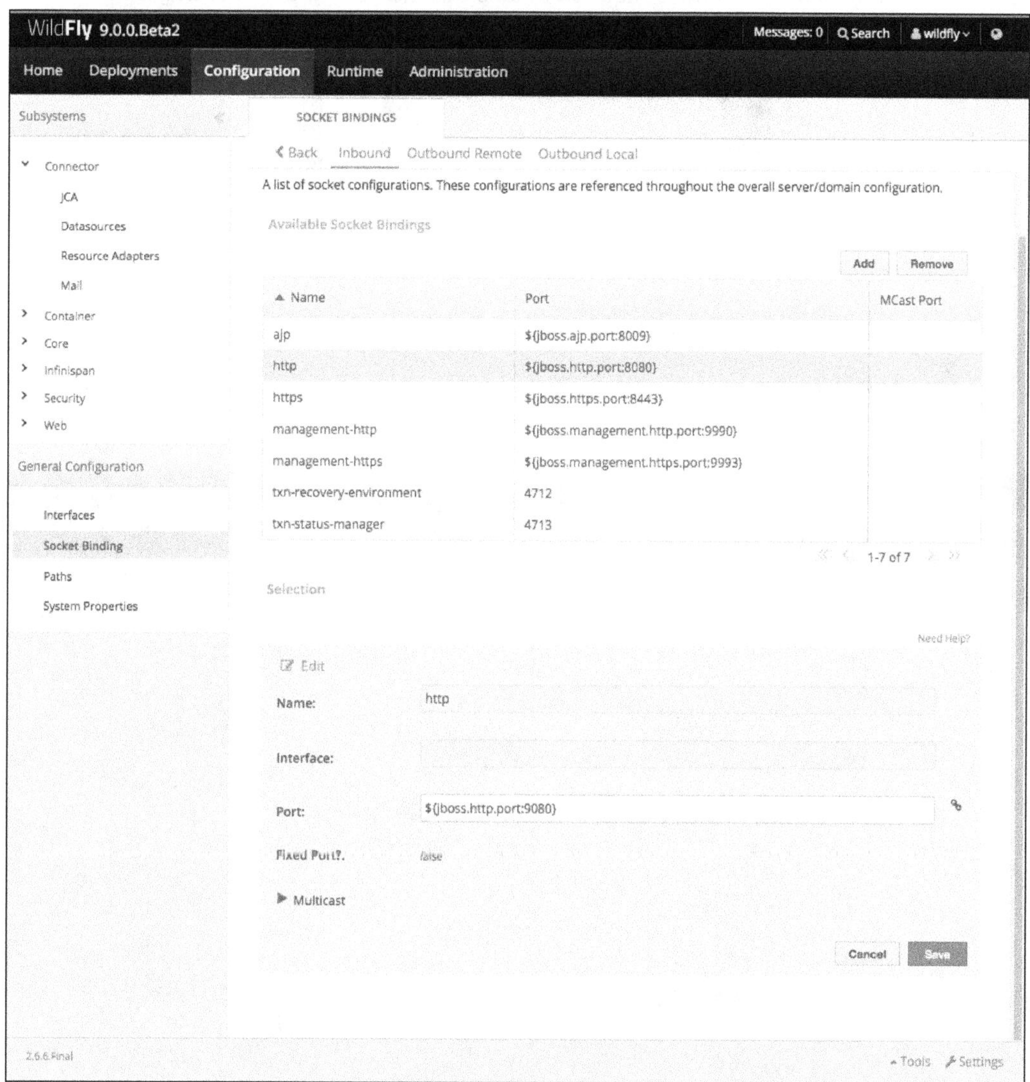

5. Now, change the port number from `8080` to `9080` and click on the button labeled **Save**. You will be notified, but the GUI will denote that the update was successful and that a server reload is required to take advantage of the new changes.

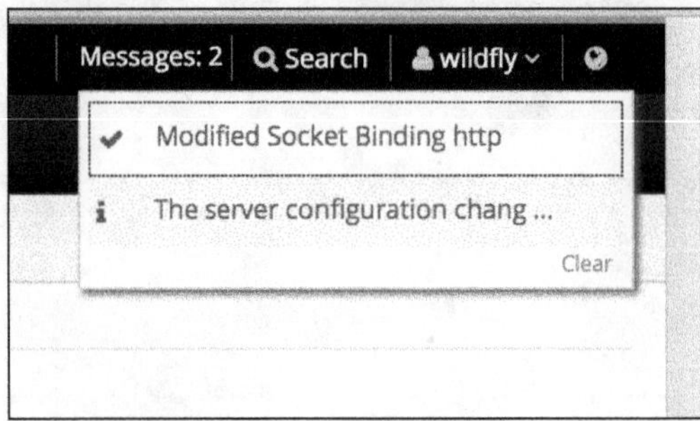


6. Go to the **Runtime** tab. You should see a button labeled **Reload**, click on it and confirm, as shown in the following screenshot:

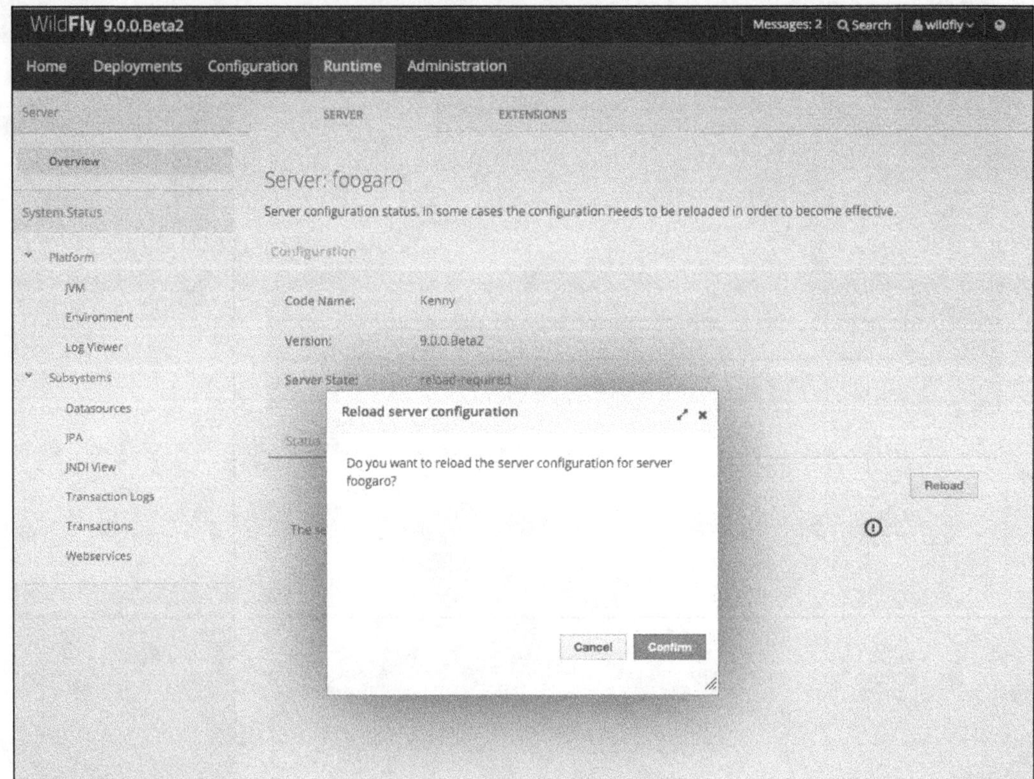


7. Now open your Web Console using the new port number as follows: `http://localhost:9080/console`.

## Using the CLI

In a different terminal, connect to the CLI and do as follows:

```
$ ./bin/jboss-cli.sh
```

You are disconnected at the moment; type `connect` to connect to the server or `help` for the list of supported commands:

```
[disconnected /] connect
[standalone@localhost:9990 /] /socket-binding-group=standard-sockets/
socket-binding=http:read-attribute(name=port)
{
    "outcome" => "success",
    "result" => expression "${jboss.http.port:8080}"
}
[standalone@localhost:9990 /] /socket-binding-group=standard-sockets/
socket-binding=http:read-attribute(name=bound-port)
{
    "outcome" => "success",
    "result" => 8080
}
[standalone@localhost:9990 /] /socket-binding-group=standard-sockets/
socket-binding=http:write-attribute(name=port,value=9080)
{
    "outcome" => "success",
    "response-headers" => {
        "operation-requires-reload" => true,
        "process-state" => "reload-required"
    }
}
[standalone@localhost:9990 /] reload
[standalone@localhost:9990 /] /socket-binding-group=standard-sockets/
socket-binding=http:read-attribute(name=port)
{
    "outcome" => "success",
    "result" => 9080
}
[standalone@localhost:9990 /]
```

## There's more...

Actually there is another method to change the port number, which is by passing `standalone.sh`, a Java parameter (which starts with a capital "D") as follows:

```
$ cd $WILDFLY_HOME
$ ./bin/standalone.sh -Djboss.http.port=9080
```

This will match the property named `http` specified in the `socket-binding` tag, for the attribute `port` in `standalone.xml`.

If you are coming from JBoss AS 5 or 6, you might have used `port-offset`, which still changes the port number by adding the offset to the default value (which is `8080`), but also changes other port numbers. In WildFly, it would also change the management port.

So we specify the port-offset to `1000` as follows :

```
$ ./bin/standalone.sh -Djboss.socket.binding.port-offset=1000
```

We would end up with WildFly listening on port 9080 (that is, 8080+1000) and the WildFly management port would be 10990 (that is, 9090+1000).

# Binding WildFly onto a custom IP

As for the port number, you might want to bind WildFly to an address different from the default one; for example, your public IP.

## How to do it...

To achieve this kind of customization, you can use both the Web Console and the CLI. Nevertheless, it is common to have SSH access to the servers running WildFly, or worse (better for security reasons), you might have SSH on different servers before landing on the WildFly one. In this case, you will only be able to use the CLI, that's why from now on we will mainly use the CLI to manage the server.

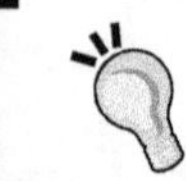

Getting used to the CLI will give you a deeper knowledge of WildFly's configuration setting and it will be more mnemonic so you won't forget it.

Let's change the IP address as follows:

```
$ cd $WILDFLY_HOME
$ ./bin/standalone.sh -Djboss.bind.address=10.0.0.1
...
22:56:05,531 INFO  [org.wildfly.extension.undertow] (MSC service
thread 1-3) WFLYUT0006: Undertow HTTP listener default listening on
/10.0.0.1:8080
...
```

## How it works...

If you look at `standalone.xml`, you will notice properties within the following { } and preceded by the dollar sign `$`. This property will be replaced by the value of the namesake parameter, specified when launching the server with the script.

## There's more...

Furthermore, the same logic applies when you want to modify the management interface address. In that case, you will have to pass the `jboss.bind.address.management` parameter.

By the way, both parameters can be specified with shortcuts, such as `-b 10.0.0.1` for the `jboss.bind.address` parameter, and `-bmanagement 10.0.0.1` for the `jboss.bind.address.management`.

# Configuring multiple WildFly instances to run on the same machine with different ports

In some cases, mostly because of architectural reasons, you may need to run multiple WildFly instances on a single server. You can do this by isolating each instance and giving it a different binding port.

## Getting ready

First of all, we need to create a standalone configuration for each instance that we want to set up and run. All we need to do is replicate the concept explained in the *Running WildFly from a custom configuration folder* recipe. Suppose we want two running nodes/instances, we use the following commands:

```
$ cd $WILDFLY_HOME
$ cp -a standalone node-1
$ cp -a standalone node-2
```

Now we are ready to configure each instance.

## How to do it...

To achieve such a requirement, you can use either of the methods explained earlier in the *Binding WildFly on a custom port* recipe. Let's take a look at each of them.

### Using jboss.http.port

The first thing to try is to run the two WildFly instances by passing the parameter `jboss.http.port`, obviously with different values. Actually, one of them could have the default value:

```
$ cd $WILDFLY_HOME
$ ./bin/standalone.sh -Djboss.server.base.dir=$WILDFLY_HOME//node-1
-Djboss.http.port=8180
...
10:30:23,924 INFO  [org.wildfly.extension.undertow] (MSC service
thread 1-7) WFLYUT0006: Undertow HTTP listener default listening on
/127.0.0.1:8180
...
```

Now we are going to run another WildFly instance by passing a different `jboss.http.port` parameter in a different terminal window:

```
$ cd $WILDFLY_HOME
$ ./bin/standalone.sh -Djboss.server.base.dir=$WILDFLY_HOME$WILDFLY_HOME/
node-2 -Djboss.http.port=8280
...
10:30:34,205 INFO  [org.wildfly.extension.undertow] (MSC service
thread 1-6) WFLYUT0006: Undertow HTTP listener default listening on
/127.0.0.1:8280
...
```

```
10:30:34,473 ERROR [org.jboss.msc.service.fail] (MSC service thread 1-8)
MSC000001: Failed to start service jboss.serverManagement.controller.
management.http: org.jboss.msc.service.StartException in service jboss.
serverManagement.controller.management.http: WFLYSRV0083: Failed to start
the http-interface service

...

10:30:34,685 INFO  [org.jboss.as] (Controller Boot Thread) WFLYSRV0054:
Admin console is not enabled

10:30:34,685 ERROR [org.jboss.as] (Controller Boot Thread) WFLYSRV0026:
WildFly Full 9.0.0.Beta2 (WildFly Core 1.0.0.Beta2) started (with errors)
in 3252ms - Started 196 of 377 services (2 services failed or missing
dependencies, 210 services are lazy, passive or on-demand)
```

Ouch! Something went wrong!

As you can see from the log, `http-interface` couldn't start properly because of the **Address already in use** message. This is because we changed `jboss.http.port`, but not the analogous one for the management interface, which is `http-interface` defined in `standalone.xml`:

```
<management>
    <security-realms>
    </security-realms>
    <audit-log>
    </audit-log>
    <management-interfaces>
        <http-interface security-realm="ManagementRealm" http-upgrade-enabled="true">
            <socket-binding http="management-http"/>
        </http-interface>
    </management-interfaces>
    <access-control provider="simple">
    </access-control>
</management>
```

"http-interface" defined in the standalone.xml

Every standalone instance has its own management interface, thus we need to change its binding as well. Let's fix it:

```
$ cd $WILDFLY_HOME

$ ./bin/standalone.sh -Djboss.server.base.dir=$WILDFLY_HOME//node-1
-Djboss.http.port=8180 -Djboss.management.http.port=9991

...

11:11:05,862 INFO  [org.wildfly.extension.undertow] (MSC service
thread 1-4) WFLYUT0006: Undertow HTTP listener default listening on
/127.0.0.1:8180

...

11:11:06,405 INFO  [org.jboss.as] (Controller Boot Thread) WFLYSRV0060:
Http management interface listening on http://127.0.0.1:9991/management
```

```
11:11:06,406 INFO  [org.jboss.as] (Controller Boot Thread) WFLYSRV0051:
Admin console listening on http://127.0.0.1:9991
...
```

This is in a different terminal window:

```
$ cd $WILDFLY_HOME
$ ./bin/standalone.sh -Djboss.server.base.dir=$WILDFLY_HOME$WILDFLY_HOME/
node-2 -Djboss.http.port=8280 -Djboss.management.http.port=9992
...
11:11:59,777 INFO  [org.wildfly.extension.undertow] (MSC service
thread 1-3) WFLYUT0006: Undertow HTTP listener default listening on
/127.0.0.1:8280
...
11:12:00,358 INFO  [org.jboss.as] (Controller Boot Thread) WFLYSRV0060:
Http management interface listening on http://127.0.0.1:9992/management
11:12:00,359 INFO  [org.jboss.as] (Controller Boot Thread) WFLYSRV0051:
Admin console listening on http://127.0.0.1:9992
...
```

There you go! Now if you check the open sockets at the OS level, filtering by the java process, you will see the following:

```
[luigi@foogaro wildfly]$ netstat -tulpn | grep java
(Not all processes could be identified, non-owned process info
 will not be shown, you would have to be root to see it all.)
tcp        0      0 127.0.0.1:9991          0.0.0.0:*               LISTEN      20051/java
tcp        0      0 127.0.0.1:9992          0.0.0.0:*               LISTEN      20263/java
tcp        0      0 127.0.0.1:8180          0.0.0.0:*               LISTEN      20051/java
tcp        0      0 127.0.0.1:8280          0.0.0.0:*               LISTEN      20263/java
[luigi@foogaro wildfly]$
```

## Using jboss.socket.binding.port-offset

Okay, let's try using the `port-offset` directive:

```
$ cd $WILDFLY_HOME
$ ./bin/standalone.sh -Djboss.serever.base.dir=$WILDFLY_HOME/node-1
-Djboss.socket.binding.port-offset=100
...
11:35:05,783 INFO  [org.wildfly.extension.undertow] (MSC service
thread 1-3) WFLYUT0006: Undertow HTTP listener default listening on
/127.0.0.1:8180
...
11:35:06,512 INFO  [org.jboss.as] (Controller Boot Thread)
WFLYSRV0060: Http management interface listening on
http://127.0.0.1:10090/management
```

```
11:35:06,513 INFO  [org.jboss.as] (Controller Boot Thread)
WFLYSRV0051: Admin console listening on http://127.0.0.1:10090
11:35:06,513 INFO  [org.jboss.as] (Controller Boot Thread)
WFLYSRV0025: WildFly Full 9.0.0.Beta2 (WildFly Core 1.0.0.Beta2)
started in 3228ms - Started 202 of 379 services (210 services are
lazy, passive or on-demand)
```

The following is keyed in a different terminal window:

```
$ cd $WILDFLY_HOME
$ ./bin/standalone.sh -Djboss.serever.base.dir=$WILDFLY_HOME/node-2
-Djboss.socket.binding.port-offset=200
...
11:35:23,389 INFO  [org.wildfly.extension.undertow] (MSC service
thread 1-5) WFLYUT0006: Undertow HTTP listener default listening on
/127.0.0.1:8280
...
11:35:24,030 INFO  [org.jboss.as] (Controller Boot Thread)
WFLYSRV0060: Http management interface listening on
http://127.0.0.1:10190/management
11:35:24,030 INFO  [org.jboss.as] (Controller Boot Thread)
WFLYSRV0051: Admin console listening on http://127.0.0.1:10190
11:35:24,031 INFO  [org.jboss.as] (Controller Boot Thread)
WFLYSRV0025: WildFly Full 9.0.0.Beta2 (WildFly Core 1.0.0.Beta2)
started in 3191ms - Started 202 of 379 services (210 services are
lazy, passive or on-demand)
```

As you have noticed, both servers start up regularly without any additional configuration or precaution. Lastly, just check the socket at the OS level:

```
[luigi@foogaro wildfly]$ netstat -tulpn | grep java
(Not all processes could be identified, non-owned process info
 will not be shown, you would have to be root to see it all.)
tcp        0      0 127.0.0.1:10090         0.0.0.0:*               LISTEN      20647/java
tcp        0      0 127.0.0.1:10190         0.0.0.0:*               LISTEN      20853/java
tcp        0      0 127.0.0.1:8180          0.0.0.0:*               LISTEN      20647/java
tcp        0      0 127.0.0.1:8280          0.0.0.0:*               LISTEN      20853/java
[luigi@foogaro wildfly]$
```

## There's more...

Using the `jboss.socket.binding.port-offset` directive facilitates all configuration needs, in contrast to every single configuration update needed when using `jboss.http.port`.

Furthermore, with WildFly, you could benefit even more by using the `port-offset` configuration, as you would also need to adjust the remoting socket.

# Configuring multiple WildFly instances to run on the same machine with different IPs

In some cases, mostly due to architectural reasons, you may need to run multiple WildFly instances on a single server. You can do this by isolating each instance and giving it different binding IPs. The IPs might be virtual or effectively provided by the physical network interfaces installed on your system. Either way is good.

## Getting ready

If you decide on virtual IPs, you can do this as follows:

```
$ sudo ifconfig YOUR_NIC:1 10.0.1.1 netmask 255.255.255.0
$ sudo ifconfig YOUR_NIC:2 10.0.1.2 netmask 255.255.255.0
```

Here `YOUR_NIC` might be `eth0`. Now, if you list all the available interfaces in your server, you will also see the following new ones:

```
$ ifconfig
eth0: flags=4099<UP,BROADCAST,MULTICAST>  mtu 1500
        ether f0:de:f1:99:b2:94  txqueuelen 1000  (Ethernet)
        RX packets 0  bytes 0 (0.0 B)
        RX errors 0  dropped 0  overruns 0  frame 0
        TX packets 0  bytes 0 (0.0 B)
        TX errors 0  dropped 0 overruns 0  carrier 0  collisions 0
        device interrupt 20  memory 0xf2600000-f2620000
eth0:1: flags=4099<UP,BROADCAST,MULTICAST>  mtu 1500
        inet 10.0.1.1  netmask 255.255.255.0  broadcast 10.0.1.255
        ether f0:de:f1:99:b2:94  txqueuelen 1000  (Ethernet)
        device interrupt 20  memory 0xf2600000-f2620000
eth0:2: flags=4099<UP,BROADCAST,MULTICAST>  mtu 1500
        inet 10.0.1.2  netmask 255.255.255.0  broadcast 10.0.1.255
        ether f0:de:f1:99:b2:94  txqueuelen 1000  (Ethernet)
        device interrupt 20  memory 0xf2600000-f2620000
```

After that, we need to create a standalone configuration for each instance that we want to set up and run. If you have already done so from the previous recipe (*Configuring multiple WildFly instances to run on the same machine with different ports*), you can jump to the *How to do it...* section. Otherwise, all we need to do is replicate the concept explained in the *Binding WildFly onto a custom IP* recipe. Suppose we want two running nodes/instances, the command is as follows:

```
$ cd $WILDFLY_HOME
$ cp -a standalone node-1
$ cp -a standalone node-2
```

Now we are ready to configure each instance.

## How to do it...

Open a terminal window and type in the following commands:

```
$ cd $WILDFLY_HOME
$ ./bin/standalone.sh -Djboss.server.base.dir=$WILDFLY_HOME/node-1
-Djboss.bind.address=10.0.1.1
...
22:32:34,259 INFO  [org.wildfly.extension.undertow] (MSC service
thread 1-6) WFLYUT0006: Undertow HTTP listener default listening on
/10.0.1.1:8080
22:32:34,549 INFO  [org.jboss.as.server.deployment.scanner] (MSC service
thread 1-3) WFLYDS0013: Started FileSystemDeploymentService for directory
/home/luigi/WFC/wildfly/node-1/deployments
22:32:34,623 INFO  [org.jboss.as.connector.subsystems.datasources]
(MSC service thread 1-7) WFLYJCA0001: Bound data source [java:jboss/
datasources/ExampleDS]
22:32:34,729 INFO  [org.jboss.ws.common.management] (MSC service
thread 1-6) JBWS022052: Starting JBoss Web Services - Stack CXF Server
5.0.0.Beta3
22:32:35,022 INFO  [org.jboss.as] (Controller Boot Thread) WFLYSRV0060:
Http management interface listening on http://127.0.0.1:9990/management
22:32:35,023 INFO  [org.jboss.as] (Controller Boot Thread) WFLYSRV0051:
Admin console listening on http://127.0.0.1:9990
22:32:35,024 INFO  [org.jboss.as] (Controller Boot Thread) WFLYSRV0025:
WildFly Full 9.0.0.Beta2 (WildFly Core 1.0.0.Beta2) started in 3260ms -
Started 202 of 379 services (210 services are lazy, passive or on-demand)
```

Type the following in a different terminal window:

```
$ cd $WILDFLY_HOME
./bin/standalone.sh -Djboss.server.base.dir=$WILDFLY_HOME/node-2 -Djboss.
bind.address=10.0.1.2
...
22:33:02,522 INFO  [org.wildfly.extension.undertow] (MSC service
thread 1-8) WFLYUT0006: Undertow HTTP listener default listening on
/10.0.1.2:8080
22:33:02,735 INFO  [org.jboss.as.server.deployment.scanner] (MSC service
thread 1-8) WFLYDS0013: Started FileSystemDeploymentService for directory
/home/luigi/WFC/wildfly/node-2/deployments
22:33:02,830 ERROR [org.jboss.msc.service.fail] (MSC service thread 1-1)
MSC000001: Failed to start service jboss.serverManagement.controller.
management.http: org.jboss.msc.service.StartException in service jboss.
serverManagement.controller.management.http: WFLYSRV0083: Failed to start
the http-interface service
  at org.jboss.as.server.mgmt.UndertowHttpManagementService.start(Underto
wHttpManagementService.java:269)
  at org.jboss.msc.service.ServiceControllerImpl$StartTask.startService(S
erviceControllerImpl.java:1948)
  at org.jboss.msc.service.ServiceControllerImpl$StartTask.
run(ServiceControllerImpl.java:1881)
  at java.util.concurrent.ThreadPoolExecutor.
runWorker(ThreadPoolExecutor.java:1142)
  at java.util.concurrent.ThreadPoolExecutor$Worker.
run(ThreadPoolExecutor.java:617)
  at java.lang.Thread.run(Thread.java:745)
Caused by: java.lang.RuntimeException: java.net.BindException: Address
already in use
  at org.jboss.as.domain.http.server.ManagementHttpServer.
start(ManagementHttpServer.java:160)
  at org.jboss.as.server.mgmt.UndertowHttpManagementService.start(Underto
wHttpManagementService.java:235)
  ... 5 more
Caused by: java.net.BindException: Address already in use
  at sun.nio.ch.Net.bind0(Native Method)
  at sun.nio.ch.Net.bind(Net.java:436)
  at sun.nio.ch.Net.bind(Net.java:428)
  at sun.nio.ch.ServerSocketChannelImpl.bind(ServerSocketChannelImpl.
java:214)
```

```
  at sun.nio.ch.ServerSocketAdaptor.bind(ServerSocketAdaptor.java:74)
  at sun.nio.ch.ServerSocketAdaptor.bind(ServerSocketAdaptor.java:67)
  at org.xnio.nio.NioXnioWorker.createTcpConnectionServer(NioXnioWorker.
java:182)
  at org.xnio.XnioWorker.createStreamConnectionServer(XnioWorker.
java:243)
  at org.jboss.as.domain.http.server.ManagementHttpServer.
start(ManagementHttpServer.java:147)
  ... 6 more


22:33:02,858 INFO  [org.jboss.as.connector.subsystems.datasources]
(MSC service thread 1-7) WFLYJCA0001: Bound data source [java:jboss/
datasources/ExampleDS]
22:33:02,907 INFO  [org.jboss.ws.common.management] (MSC service
thread 1-3) JBWS022052: Starting JBoss Web Services - Stack CXF Server
5.0.0.Beta3
22:33:02,911 ERROR [org.jboss.as.controller.management-operation]
(Controller Boot Thread) WFLYCTL0013: Operation ("add") failed - address:
([
    ("core-service" => "management"),
    ("management-interface" => "http-interface")
]) - failure description: {"WFLYCTL0080: Failed services" => {"jboss.
serverManagement.controller.management.http" => "org.jboss.msc.service.
StartException in service jboss.serverManagement.controller.management.
http: WFLYSRV0083: Failed to start the http-interface service
    Caused by: java.lang.RuntimeException: java.net.BindException:
Address already in use
    Caused by: java.net.BindException: Address already in use"}}
22:33:02,969 INFO  [org.jboss.as.controller] (Controller Boot Thread)
WFLYCTL0183: Service status report
WFLYCTL0186:   Services which failed to start:      service jboss.
serverManagement.controller.management.http: org.jboss.msc.service.
StartException in service jboss.serverManagement.controller.management.
http: WFLYSRV0083: Failed to start the http-interface service


22:33:03,253 INFO  [org.jboss.as] (Controller Boot Thread) WFLYSRV0063:
Http management interface is not enabled
22:33:03,254 INFO  [org.jboss.as] (Controller Boot Thread) WFLYSRV0054:
Admin console is not enabled
```

```
22:33:03,254 ERROR [org.jboss.as] (Controller Boot Thread)
WFLYSRV0026: WildFly Full 9.0.0.Beta2 (WildFly Core 1.0.0.Beta2)
started (with errors) in 3277ms - Started 196 of 377 services (2
services failed or missing dependencies, 210 services are lazy,
passive or on-demand)
```

Ouch! Another fail!

What's wrong now? Pretty much the same thing we had in the previous recipe. We didn't change any binding parameter (IP address or port number) for the management interface.

As a matter of fact, as you can see from the log of the `node-1` instance, the management and HTTP interface are bound to the local address, which is the default one. Thus, the `node-2` instance will have the same settings, hence the error: **Address already in use**.

Let's fix this error:

```
$ ./bin/standalone.sh -Djboss.server.base.dir=$WILDFLY_HOME/node-1
-Djboss.bind.address=10.0.1.1 -Djboss.bind.address.management=10.0.1.1

...

22:38:41,054 INFO  [org.wildfly.extension.undertow] (MSC service
thread 1-6) WFLYUT0006: Undertow HTTP listener default listening on
/10.0.1.1:8080

22:38:41,313 INFO  [org.jboss.as.server.deployment.scanner] (MSC service
thread 1-6) WFLYDS0013: Started FileSystemDeploymentService for directory
/home/luigi/WFC/wildfly/node-1/deployments

22:38:41,372 INFO  [org.jboss.as.connector.subsystems.datasources]
(MSC service thread 1-2) WFLYJCA0001: Bound data source [java:jboss/
datasources/ExampleDS]

22:38:41,450 INFO  [org.jboss.ws.common.management] (MSC service
thread 1-8) JBWS022052: Starting JBoss Web Services - Stack CXF Server
5.0.0.Beta3

22:38:41,792 INFO  [org.jboss.as] (Controller Boot Thread) WFLYSRV0060:
Http management interface listening on http://10.0.1.1:9990/management

22:38:41,793 INFO  [org.jboss.as] (Controller Boot Thread) WFLYSRV0051:
Admin console listening on http://10.0.1.1:9990

22:38:41,794 INFO  [org.jboss.as] (Controller Boot Thread) WFLYSRV0025:
WildFly Full 9.0.0.Beta2 (WildFly Core 1.0.0.Beta2) started in 3224ms -
Started 202 of 379 services (210 services are lazy, passive or on-demand)
```

Type the following in a different terminal window:

```
$ ./bin/standalone.sh -Djboss.server.base.dir=$WILDFLY_HOME/node-2
-Djboss.bind.address=10.0.1.2 -Djboss.bind.address.management=10.0.1.2

...
```

```
22:39:55,815 INFO  [org.wildfly.extension.undertow] (MSC service
thread 1-1) WFLYUT0006: Undertow HTTP listener default listening on
/10.0.1.2:8080
22:39:56,054 INFO  [org.jboss.as.server.deployment.scanner] (MSC service
thread 1-4) WFLYDS0013: Started FileSystemDeploymentService for directory
/home/luigi/WFC/wildfly/node-2/deployments
22:39:56,176 INFO  [org.jboss.as.connector.subsystems.datasources]
(MSC service thread 1-8) WFLYJCA0001: Bound data source [java:jboss/
datasources/ExampleDS]
22:39:56,241 INFO  [org.jboss.ws.common.management] (MSC service
thread 1-7) JBWS022052: Starting JBoss Web Services - Stack CXF Server
5.0.0.Beta3
22:39:56,567 INFO  [org.jboss.as] (Controller Boot Thread) WFLYSRV0060:
Http management interface listening on http://10.0.1.2:9990/management
22:39:56,567 INFO  [org.jboss.as] (Controller Boot Thread) WFLYSRV0051:
Admin console listening on http://10.0.1.2:9990
22:39:56,568 INFO  [org.jboss.as] (Controller Boot Thread) WFLYSRV0025:
WildFly Full 9.0.0.Beta2 (WildFly Core 1.0.0.Beta2) started in 3271ms -
Started 202 of 379 services (210 services are lazy, passive or on-demand)
```

There you go! We have two WildFly instances running at the same time, each using a dedicated IP, even if they are both using the same PORT. Let's check it at OS level:

```
[luigi@foogaro wildfly]$ netstat -tulpn | grep java
(Not all processes could be identified, non-owned process info
 will not be shown, you would have to be root to see it all.)
tcp        0      0 10.0.1.2:9990           0.0.0.0:*               LISTEN      22633/java
tcp        0      0 10.0.1.1:9990           0.0.0.0:*               LISTEN      22418/java
tcp        0      0 10.0.1.2:8080           0.0.0.0:*               LISTEN      22633/java
tcp        0      0 10.0.1.1:8080           0.0.0.0:*               LISTEN      22418/java
[luigi@foogaro wildfly]$
```

## There's more...

As you have noticed in this recipe and in the previous one, we can customize the WildFly binding relative to the IP address and port number, both for the service components (which is your application) and the management components (which are the Admin Console and the CLI).

Obviously, we can even mix customization and thus change both the IP and the port, and change the port number for the service components and the IP address for the management interface. You can do whatever you want as long as you don't make equals binding.

A typical configuration has the services components bound to a public interface (that is, an IP address that's visible externally) and the management interface bound to a private interface (that is, an IP address that's only visible locally or within your network).

# Managing applications using the deployments folder

After configuring and customizing the WildFly standalone, it's time to deploy our first application. WildFly provides a lot of methods to deploy applications, one of them being via the deployment scanner (well known to those of you who come from the JBoss AS version). Basically, all you need to do is to copy your artifact into the `deployments` folder of your standalone instance.

In a production environment, you had better turn off the deployment scanner to avoid replacing a deployment accidentally—you would be in very big trouble. Do use the proper "deploy" operation using either the CLI or the Admin Console. We will see both in this chapter.

## Getting ready

In this recipe, we will need a Java web application. If you want, you can use one of my projects from my GitHub account, at the following address: `https://github.com/foogaro/wildfly-cookbook.git`.

You can `git-clone` the repository or just download it as a ZIP archive. Either way, create a folder named `github` into the `WFC` folder, and place the source into it.

Using the `git-clone` command, do as follows:

```
$ cd ~/WFC
$ mkdir github
$ cd github
$ git clone https://github.com/foogaro/wildfly-cookbook.git
```

Once `git` has done with cloning the repo, you can find a project called `example`. To compile the project, do as follows:

```
$ cd ~/WFC/github/wildfly-cookbook/example
$ mvn -e clean package
```

The preceding commands compile the project and generate the web application artifact into a folder named `target`. There you can find the application `example.awar`, ready to be deployed.

There is also the official WildFly quickstarts repository, which has plenty of precious resources to look at, and it is also available for contribution at the following address: `https://github.com/wildfly/quickstart`.

Now, assume that we are going to use the default `standalone` folder as the base configuration path of our instance. To see everything in action, it's better to first run WildFly and then start managing the application itself using the `deployments` folder.

## How to do it...

1. First, let's start up WildFly:

   ```
   $ cd $WILDFLY_HOME
   $ ./bin/standalone.sh
   ...
   WFLYSRV0025: WildFly Full 9.0.0.Beta2 (WildFly Core 1.0.0.Beta2) started in 3087ms - Started 202 of 379 services (210 services are lazy, passive or on-demand)
   ```

2. Now keeping your terminal windows visible, open your favorite file manager tool, and copy `example.war` into the `deployments` folder.

   Alternatively, you can copy the web application using a new terminal, using the following command:

   ```
   $ cp ~/WFC/github/wildfly-cookbook/example/target/example.war $WILDFLY_HOME/standalone/deployments
   ```

3. A few seconds later (the timer interval is set for every 5 seconds, so you may wait a few milliseconds or 5 seconds), we'll get the following output:

   ```
   22:51:31,396 INFO  [org.jboss.as.repository] (DeploymentScanner-threads - 1) WFLYDR0001: Content added at location /home/luigi/WFC/wildfly/standalone/data/content/21/7dd6250d5bc4afcabdffb0b25c99db92239b5a/content

   22:51:31,447 INFO  [org.jboss.as.server.deployment] (MSC service thread 1-3) WFLYSRV0027: Starting deployment of "example.war" (runtime-name: "example.war")

   22:51:31,986 INFO  [org.wildfly.extension.undertow] (MSC service thread 1-4) WFLYUT0021: Registered web context: /example

   22:51:32,046 INFO  [org.jboss.as.server] (DeploymentScanner-threads - 1) WFLYSRV0010: Deployed "example.war" (runtime-name : "example.war")
   ```

   And you should also get a new file in the `deployments` folder named `example.war.deployed`. This is a marker saying that the application has been successfully deployed. In case of an error, any operation would have been rolled back and a new file named `example.war.failed` would have been created.

4. Now, can you guess how to undeploy it? Yes... rename the marker file extension with `.undeploy` as follows:

```
22:55:17,702 INFO  [org.wildfly.extension.undertow] (MSC service thread 1-7) WFLYUT0022: Unregistered web context: /example
22:55:17,736 INFO  [org.hibernate.validator.internal.util.Version] (MSC service thread 1-4) HV000001: Hibernate Validator 5.1.3.Final
22:55:17,801 INFO  [org.jboss.as.server.deployment] (MSC service thread 1-3) WFLYSRV0028: Stopped deployment example.war (runtime-name: example.war) in 109ms
22:55:17,817 INFO  [org.jboss.as.repository] (DeploymentScanner-threads - 1) WFLYDR0002: Content removed from location /home/luigi/WFC/wildfly/standalone/data/content/21/7dd6250d5bc4afcabdffb0b25c99db92239b5a/content
22:55:17,817 INFO  [org.jboss.as.server] (DeploymentScanner-threads - 1) WFLYSRV0009: Undeployed "example.war" (runtime-name: "example.war")
```

And in the `deployments` folder, a new file named `example.war.undeployed` has been created. How do we redeploy it now? Delete the two marker files, or create a new one named `example.war.dodeploy`.

## How it works...

To recap what we've learned so far, marker files always have the same name as the application plus the suffix. The following table summarizes all the available markers:

| Suffix | Description |
|---|---|
| `.dodeploy` | User generated to indicate that the given content should be deployed. |
| `.skipdeploy` | User generated to indicate that the given content should skip auto-deploy as long as the file is present. This allows you to modify the exploded content without having the scanner initiate redeploy in the middle of the update. Same is true for zipped content. |
| `.isdeploying` | Placed by the deployment scanner service to indicate that it has noticed a `.dodeploy` file or new or updated auto-deploy mode content and is in the process of deploying the content. This marker file will be deleted when the deployment process completes, so you may not see it for small size artifacts. |
| `.deployed` | Placed by the deployment scanner service to indicate that the given content has been deployed. If you delete this file, the content will be undeployed. |

| Suffix | Description |
|---|---|
| `.failed` | Placed by the deployment scanner service to indicate that the given content has failed in its deploying process. In the file, you will find information about what went wrong during deployment. Note that with auto-deploy mode, removing this file will make the deployment eligible for deployment again. |
| `.isundeploying` | Placed by the deployment scanner service to indicate that it has noticed that a `.deployed` file has been deleted and the content is being undeployed. This marker file will be deleted when the undeployment process completes, so you may not see it for small size artifacts. |
| `.undeployed` | Placed by the deployment scanner service to indicate that the given content has been undeployed. If you delete this file, there will be no impact at all. |
| `.pending` | Placed by the deployment scanner service to indicate that it has noticed the need to deploy content but has not yet instructed the server to deploy it.<br><br>This file is created if the scanner detects that some auto-deploy content is still in the process of being copied or if there is some problem that prevents auto-deployment. The scanner will not instruct the server to deploy or undeploy any content (not just the directly affected content) as long as this condition holds. |

# Connecting to the CLI

There are three ways to manage your WildFly, that is, by editing the XML file, the Console and the CLI.

- First of all, editing the XML directly can be error-prone, as it can waste you precious seconds; moreover, every change requires a server restart.
- The Console gives you visual editing features, but it's not complete. The Web Console can perform just a subset of all the available actions that you can execute using the CLI.
- CLI stands for Command Line Interface, and it is a tool that you are recommended to use to manage your WildFly application server.

Why the CLI? Most of the time, for security reasons, you connect to enterprise environments via SSH and are thus not able to see the Web Console at all. CLI WildFly comes in handy for this purpose.

CLI is a powerful tool that gives you full control over WildFly; you can deploy and undeploy applications, create and manage data sources, manage logging, change system properties, stop and start instances, and more. Working with the CLI also helps you understand the WildFly core logic so you can really become an expert WildFly administrator. Nevertheless, if you really want a GUI as well, you can have the CLI in GUI version; just execute the following command while you have your WildFly running:

```
$ cd $WILDFLY_HOME
$ ./bin/jboss-cli.sh --gui
```

The following screenshot depicts the CLI GUI tool:

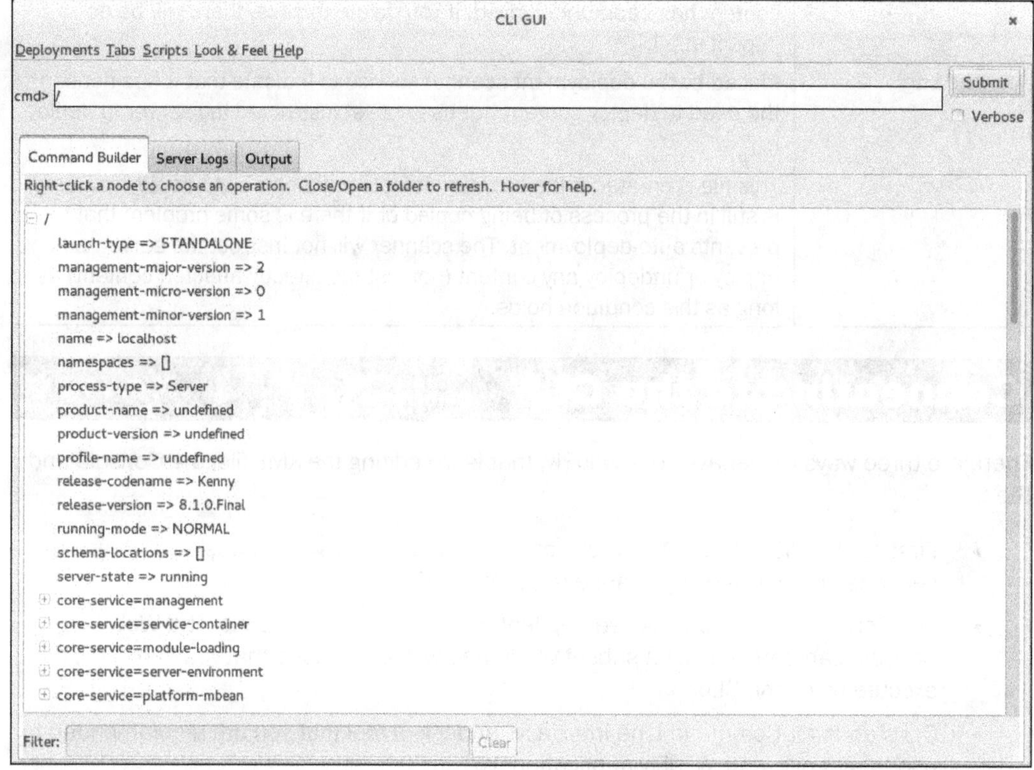


CLI GUI tool

Now, it's time to play around with the CLI. Let's see what you can do!

## Getting ready

As the CLI is a management tool, you will need to have your WildFly instance up and running. In this case too, we will use the default standalone configuration.

Open a terminal window and start WildFly:

```
$ cd $WILDFLY_HOME
$ ./bin/standalone.sh
...
22:12:23,600 INFO  [org.jboss.as] (Controller Boot Thread) WFLYSRV0025:
WildFly Full 9.0.0.Beta2 (WildFly Core 1.0.0.Beta2) started in 3087ms -
Started 202 of 379 services (210 services are lazy, passive or on-demand)
```

## How to do it...

1. Let's open a terminal window:

   ```
   $ cd $WILDFLY_HOME
   $ ./bin/jboss-cli.sh
   You are disconnected at the moment. Type connect to connect to the
   server or help for the list of supported commands.
   [disconnected /]
   ```

2. Once in, we need to connect to the running instance. By typing the command `connect`, the tool connects to the instance with the default parameters, which is `localhost:9990`.

   ```
   [disconnected /] connect
   [standalone@localhost:9990 /]
   ```

3. You can also connect to the CLI directly from the command line by passing the –connect parameter as follows:

   ```
   $ cd $WILDFLY_HOME
   $ ./bin/jboss-cli.sh --connect
   [standalone@localhost:9990 /]
   ```

   From now on, we will connect directly to the CLI without having to connect to it from the inside.

4. Now try the command listing `ls` (as you would do in Linux):

```
[standalone@localhost:9990 /] ls
core-service             subsystem                     namespaces=[]                    running-mode=NORMAL
deployment               system-property               process-type=Server              schema-locations=[]
deployment-overlay       launch-type=STANDALONE        product-name=WildFly Full        server-state=running
extension                management-major-version=3    product-version=9.0.0.Beta2      suspend-state=RUNNING
interface                management-micro-version=0    profile-name=undefined
path                     management-minor-version=0    release-codename=Kenny
socket-binding-group     name=foogaro                  release-version=1.0.0.Beta2
[standalone@localhost:9990 /]
```

5. The list command gives you all the components that you can operate on, pretty much what you can see editing the `standalone.xml`. In fact, listing the subsystems, you will see all the subsystems present declared in `standalone.xml`:

```
[standalone@localhost:9990 /] ls subsystem=
batch                ejb3          jdr        mail                 resource-adapters  undertow
bean-validation      infinispan    jmx        naming               sar                webservices
datasources          io            jpa        pojo                 security           weld
deployment-scanner   jaxrs         jsf        remoting             security-manager
ee                   jca           logging    request-controller   transactions
[standalone@localhost:9990 /]
```

## There's more...

Remember that the *Tab* key on your keyboard is your friend. If you don't remember a command, just hit *Tab*. If you don't remember how to complete a command, just hit *Tab*. Hitting the *Tab* key will show all the possible solutions within your current context.

There are two others special characters within the CLI: / (the forward slash) and : (the colon). The forward slash is used to navigate through the contexts, while the colon is used to invoke method operation within the last selected context. Check the next recipe for an example.

# Checking the server-state via the CLI

In this recipe, we will learn how to check the server status. WildFly may have different status depending on its phase: starting, stopping, started, and stopped. Sometimes, just checking its status at the OS level by looking for its process might not be enough.

## Getting ready

As the CLI is a management tool, you will need to have your WildFly instance up and running. Also for this recipe, we will rely on the default standalone configuration.

Open a terminal window and start WildFly:

```
$ cd $WILDFLY_HOME
$ ./bin/standalone.sh
...
22:12:23,600 INFO  [org.jboss.as] (Controller Boot Thread) WFLYSRV0025: WildFly Full 9.0.0.Beta2 (WildFly Core 1.0.0.Beta2) started in 3226ms - Started 202 of 379 services (210 services are lazy, passive or on-demand)
```

## How to do it...

In a new terminal window, type in the following:

```
$ ./bin/jboss-cli.sh
You are disconnected at the moment. Type 'connect' to connect to the
server or 'help' for the list of supported commands.
[disconnected /] connect
[standalone@localhost:9990 /] :read-attribute(name=server-state)
{
    "outcome" => "success",
    "result" => "running"
}
[standalone@localhost:9990 /]
```

## How it works...

As you connect to the host-controller, you are just in the root of your configuration. Thus, you can invoke an operation on it, and to do that, you need to start with the `:` (colon) symbol.

In our example we used the `read-attribute` method, but you could have any of the available ones. To see them is as easy as hitting the *Tab* key right after the colon symbol, as follows:

```
[standalone@localhost:9990 /] :
add-namespace              map-get                       read-operation-names           suspend
add-schema-location        map-put                       read-resource                  take-snapshot
clean-obsolete-content     map-remove                    read-resource-description      undefine-attribute
delete-snapshot            read-attribute                reload                         upload-deployment-bytes
full-replace-deployment    read-attribute-group          remove-namespace               upload-deployment-stream
list-add                   read-attribute-group-names    remove-schema-location         upload-deployment-url
list-clear                 read-children-names           replace-deployment             validate-address
list-get                   read-children-resources       resolve-expression             validate-operation
list-remove                read-children-types           resolve-internet-address       whoami
list-snapshots             read-config-as-xml            resume                         write-attribute
map-clear                  read-operation-description    shutdown
[standalone@localhost:9990 /] :
```

Getting back to our server state, we received two responses: one saying that our invocation was successful, and the second one reporting the result, **running**.

# Deploying an application via the CLI

In this recipe, we will learn how to deploy an application using the CLI. Here we will use just the basic options but keep in mind that you have several options during deployments, which we will analyze deeply in the chapter dedicated to the CLI.

## Getting ready

In this recipe, and in the following one as well, we will need an application to test our configuration. For this recipe, we will need the application named `example` that you can find in my GitHub repository. If you skipped the *Managing applications using the deployments folder* recipe, please refer to it to download the source code and the projects that you will need.

## How to do it...

1. With your WildFly instance up and running, open up a terminal and connect to the CLI as usual:

```
$ ./bin/jboss-cli.sh --connect
[standalone@localhost:9990 /]
```

2. Now we need to tell the CLI to deploy our application as follows:

```
[standalone@localhost:9990 /] deploy example.war
[standalone@localhost:9990 /]
```

3. And let's have a look at the `server.log` files:

```
23:02:29,511 INFO  [org.jboss.as.repository] (management-handler-thread - 3) WFLYDR0001: Content added at location /home/luigi/WFC/wildfly/standalone/data/content/21/7dd6250d5bc4afcabdffb0b25c99db92239b5a/content
23:02:29,517 INFO  [org.jboss.as.server.deployment] (MSC service thread 1-6) WFLYSRV0027: Starting deployment of "example.war" (runtime-name: "example.war")
23:02:29,613 INFO  [org.wildfly.extension.undertow] (MSC service thread 1-3) WFLYUT0021: Registered web context: /example
23:02:29,641 INFO  [org.jboss.as.server] (management-handler-thread - 3) WFLYSRV0010: Deployed "example.war" (runtime-name : "example.war")
```

4. Now, let's check it for deployment from the CLI:

```
[standalone@localhost:9990 /] deployment-info --name=example.war
NAME         RUNTIME-NAME PERSISTENT ENABLED STATUS
example.war example.war  true       true    OK
[standalone@localhost:9990 /]
```

## How it works...

I emphasized a log line to take your attention. As you can see, WildFly automatically saves its artifacts into its `data/content` folder. In that folder, you will find a lot of folders with hashed names that contain the artifact. The artifact is then renamed as `content`.

If you try to see the `content` file information using the `unzip` command, you will find your artifact structure as seen in the following screenshot:

```
[luigi@foogaro wildfly]$ unzip -l standalone/data/content/21/7dd6250d5bc4afcabdffb0b25c99db92239b5a/content
Archive:  standalone/data/content/21/7dd6250d5bc4afcabdffb0b25c99db92239b5a/content
  Length      Date    Time    Name
---------  ---------- -----   ----
        0  04-13-2015 22:49   META-INF/
      130  04-13-2015 22:49   META-INF/MANIFEST.MF
        0  04-13-2015 22:49   WEB-INF/
        0  04-13-2015 22:49   WEB-INF/classes/
      371  03-02-2015 22:41   index.jsp
      348  04-13-2015 22:49   WEB-INF/classes/log4j.properties
      189  03-02-2015 22:41   WEB-INF/jboss-deployment-structure.xml
      615  03-02-2015 22:41   WEB-INF/web.xml
     1020  03-02-2015 22:41   META-INF/maven/com.packtpub.wildfly-cookbook/example/pom.xml
      120  04-13-2015 22:49   META-INF/maven/com.packtpub.wildfly-cookbook/example/pom.properties
---------                     -------
     2793                     10 files
[luigi@foogaro wildfly]$
```

## There's more...

You can also deploy an artifact disabled, with status stopped, and enable it at your convenience as follows:

```
[standalone@localhost:9990 /] deploy example.war --disabled
```

This will just add the artifact into the `data/content` folder of WildFly in your running-mode, to enable it later:

```
[standalone@localhost:9990 /] deploy --name=example.war
```

There is also a reference to the deployment inside the `standalone.xml` configuration file; open it and scroll down to the end.

```
<deployments>
    <deployment name="example.war" runtime-name="example.war">
        <content sha1="217dd6250d5bc4afcabdffb0b25c99db92239b5a"/>
    </deployment>
</deployments>
```

Standalone.xml updated after a deploy

Yes, you will find the `name` and the `runtime-name` along with the hash. In the *How it works...* section, I showed you where the deployment really persists, and in that case, it was stored into the `$WILDFLY_HOME/standalone/data/content/` folder.

Did you notice it? The first two characters of the `sha1` value denote the first folder, the rest of the `sha1` hash is the subfolder that contains the artifact renamed as `content`.

> Getting the original deployment file can sometimes save your life, especially when dealing with a production environment, where last minute works are not "integrated" that much. Be safe with your backup.

Let's have a look at the `deployments` folder now. It's empty. That is because everything goes into the runtime `data/content` folder. Try to stop the instance and copy the `example.war` application into the `deployments` folder.

Now start the instance again. What do you get? Something similar to the following:

```
23:16:54,708 INFO  [org.jboss.modules] (main) JBoss Modules version 1.4.2.Final

23:16:54,934 INFO  [org.jboss.msc] (main) JBoss MSC version 1.2.4.Final

23:16:55,003 INFO  [org.jboss.as] (MSC service thread 1-6) WFLYSRV0049: WildFly Full 9.0.0.Beta2 (WildFly Core 1.0.0.Beta2) starting

23:16:56,170 INFO  [org.jboss.as.controller.management-deprecated] (ServerService Thread Pool -- 20) WFLYCTL0028: Attribute enabled is deprecated, and it might be removed in future version!

23:16:56,243 ERROR [org.jboss.as.controller.management-operation] (Controller Boot Thread) WFLYCTL0013: Operation ("add") failed - address: ([("deployment" => "example.war")]) - failure description: "WFLYCTL0212: Duplicate resource [(\"deployment\" => \"example.war\")]"

23:16:56,249 FATAL [org.jboss.as.server] (Controller Boot Thread) WFLYSRV0056: Server boot has failed in an unrecoverable manner; exiting. See previous messages for details.

23:16:56,260 INFO  [org.jboss.as.server] (Thread-2) WFLYSRV0220: Server shutdown has been requested.

23:16:56,285 INFO  [org.jboss.as] (MSC service thread 1-3) WFLYSRV0050: WildFly Full 9.0.0.Beta2 (WildFly Core 1.0.0.Beta2) stopped in 16ms
```

This is because you tried to deploy the same artifact twice, once using the CLI and once using the `deployment` folder. There is a listener called `deployment-scanner` that is triggered whenever you modify the content of the `deployment` folder. By the way, you can solve the preceding problem using the CLI, or by removing the auto-generated XML code into `standalone.xml` and leaving the artifact in the `deployments` folder.

# Undeploying an application via the CLI

In this recipe, we will learn how to undeploy an application using the CLI. As per the `deploy` command, we will use just the basic available options. We will analyze the `undeploy` command deeply, later in the book.

## Getting ready

This recipe follows the previous one, which is *Deploying an application via CLI*. This means that we will find the `example` application ready to be `undeployed`. If you skipped the previous recipe, follow the instructions that it provides, or alternatively provide yourself with an application to undeploy.

## How to do it...

1. With your WildFly instance up and running, open a terminal and connect to the CLI as usual:

```
$ ./bin/jboss-cli.sh --connect
[standalone@localhost:9990 /]
```

2. Now we need to tell the CLI to undeploy our application as follows:

```
[standalone@localhost:9990 /] undeploy example.war
[standalone@localhost:9990 /]
```

3. And the `server.log` logs the following:

```
23:19:50,912 INFO  [org.wildfly.extension.undertow] (MSC service
thread 1-4) WFLYUT0022: Unregistered web context: /example
23:19:50,961 INFO  [org.hibernate.validator.internal.util.Version]
(MSC service thread 1-2) HV000001: Hibernate Validator 5.1.3.Final
23:19:51,010 INFO  [org.jboss.as.server.deployment] (MSC service
thread 1-5) WFLYSRV0028: Stopped deployment example.war (runtime-
name: example.war) in 115ms
```

```
23:19:51,058 INFO  [org.jboss.as.repository] (management-handler-
thread - 1) WFLYDR0002: Content removed from location /home/luigi/
WFC/wildfly/standalone/data/content/21/7dd6250d5bc4afcabdffb0b25c9
9db92239b5a/content
23:19:51,059 INFO  [org.jboss.as.server] (management-handler-
thread - 1) WFLYSRV0009: Undeployed "example.war" (runtime-name:
"example.war")
```

## There's more...

If you did a copy and paste of the previous command, you wouldn't have noticed a helpful feature of the `undeploy` command.

You can tell the CLI to list all the deployments first, so you can choose the right one to undeploy using the following command:

```
[standalone@localhost:9990 /] undeploy -l
NAME        RUNTIME-NAME ENABLED STATUS
example.war example.war  true    OK

[standalone@localhost:9990 /]
```

# Executing commands in batch mode via the CLI

In this recipe, we will learn how to invoke commands in the batch mode. Actually, you can declare and prepare a list of commands to execute, and execute them sequentially at once. The batch mode gives you consistency among your operations and configuration.

## Getting ready

Get our WildFly instance up and running; from the folder where we downloaded the GitHub repository, `WFC/github/wildfly-cookbook`, copy the `example.war` and `simple.war` applications into the `$JBOSS_HOME` folder and connect to the CLI.

If you can find the applications, you probably need to compile the projects. I'll show you how to do it for the `simple` application, and the same applies to the others. Open a terminal and do as follows:

```
$ cd ~/WFC/github/wildfly-cookbook
$ cd simple
$ mvn -e clean package

$ cp target/simple.war ~/WFC/wildfly/
```

## How to do it...

We are going to do the following operation in sequence:

1. Deploy `example.war`.
2. Deploy `simple.war`.
3. Let's go to the CLI:

   ```
   $ cd ~/WFC/wildfly
   $ ./bin/jboss-cli.sh --connect
   [standalone@localhost:9990 /] batch
   [standalone@localhost:9990 / #] deploy example.war
   [standalone@localhost:9990 / #] deploy simple.war
   [standalone@localhost:9990 / #] run-batch
   The batch executed successfully
   [standalone@localhost:9990 /]
   ```

4. And the `server.log` logs the following:

   ```
   ...
   07:33:02,191 INFO  [org.jboss.as.repository] (management-
   handler-thread - 4) JBAS014900: Content added at location
   /home/lfugaro/wildfly/standalone/data/content/7a/
   a7c67cb54e0affa9d60cf98230e0c17efd1119/content
   07:33:02,205 INFO  [org.jboss.as.repository] (management-handler-
   thread - 4) JBAS014900: Content added at location /home/lfugaro/
   wildfly/standalone/data/content/e0/2abb62b1b29f97f532ef1501910d64a
   f194b21/content
   07:33:02,227 INFO  [org.jboss.as.server.deployment] (MSC service
   thread 1-2) JBAS015876: Starting deployment of "simple.war"
   (runtime-name: "simple.war")
   07:33:02,227 INFO  [org.jboss.as.server.deployment] (MSC service
   thread 1-7) JBAS015876: Starting deployment of "example.war"
   (runtime-name: "example.war")
   07:33:02,689 INFO  [org.wildfly.extension.undertow] (MSC service
   thread 1-1) JBAS017534: Registered web context: /simple
   07:33:02,689 INFO  [org.wildfly.extension.undertow] (MSC service
   thread 1-6) JBAS017534: Registered web context: /example
   07:33:02,746 INFO  [org.jboss.as.server] (management-handler-
   thread - 4) JBAS018559: Deployed "simple.war" (runtime-name :
   "simple.war")
   07:33:02,746 INFO  [org.jboss.as.server] (management-handler-
   thread - 4) JBAS018559: Deployed "example.war" (runtime-name :
   "example.war")
   ```

## Reloading a server configuration via the CLI

In this recipe, we will learn how to reload the server configuration, without the need for a full restart. Often, there are changes that need the server to be reloaded. Most of the time you realize that a specific setting needs a different value just after a server startup or during tests. So, instead of stopping and starting the all application server, you can just reload the configuration, unless the change involves the JVM or settings that are needed at boot time.

### Getting ready

We have already seen how to reload a server while playing with IPs and port binding, but it's worth mentioning again.

### How to do it...

The command itself is pretty easy:

```
$ ./bin/jboss-cli.sh --connect
[standalone@localhost:9990 /] reload
[standalone@localhost:9990 /]
```

### How it works...

Basically, the `reload` command issues, in sequence, a `stop` for all the WildFly active services and a `start`, which starts up the services again. This should give you important information. The JVM remains the same. If you test the active process at the OS level before and after issuing the `reload` command, you will notice that the processes' IDs are the same.

```
$ ps -efa | grep java | grep -v grep
luigi     4915  4879 80 16:07 pts/3    00:00:11 /home/luigi/WFC/jdk8/bin/java -D[Standalone] -server -Xms64m -Xmx512m -XX:MaxPermSize=256m -Djava.net.preferIPv4Stack=true -Djboss.modules.system.pkgs=org.jboss.byteman -Djava.awt.headless=true -Dorg.jboss.boot.log.file=/home/luigi/WFC/wildfly/standalone/log/server.log -Dlogging.configuration=file:/home/luigi/WFC/wildfly/standalone/configuration/logging.properties -jar /home/luigi/WFC/wildfly/jboss-modules.jar -mp /home/luigi/WFC/wildfly/modules org.jboss.as.standalone -Djboss.home.dir=/home/luigi/WFC/wildfly -Djboss.server.base.dir=/home/luigi/WFC/wildfly/standalone
luigi     5031  5023 36 16:07 pts/2    00:00:01 /home/luigi/WFC/jdk8/bin/java -Djboss.modules.system.pkgs=com.sun.java.swing -Dlogging.configuration=file:/home/luigi/WFC/wildfly/bin/jboss-cli-logging.properties -jar /home/luigi/WFC/wildfly/jboss-modules.jar -mp /home/luigi/WFC/wildfly/modules org.jboss.as.cli --connect
```

Last but not least, your CLI does not disconnect.

# Shutting down and restarting an instance via the CLI

In this recipe, we will learn how to stop a WildFly instance via the CLI, or alternatively, restart it via the CLI.The restart option is in contrast to the `reload` command of the previous recipe.

## Getting ready

Start up your WildFly so that we can directly connect to it via the CLI, as follows:

```
$ cd ~/WFC/wildfly
$ ./bin/standalone.sh
```

## How to do it...

The command itself is pretty easy:

```
$ ./bin/jboss-cli.sh --connect
[standalone@localhost:9990 /] shutdown
[disconnected /]
```

## How it works...

The preceding command stops everything and drops you off from the CLI. Hence, in case you need to restart your WildFly instance, you need to execute the `standalone.sh` script again, along with any parameter previously defined.

## There's more...

Alternatively, if what you really need is a full stop and start, you can rely on the `--restart=true` option for the `shutdown` command.

Before executing the `shutdown` command with the `restart` option, take note of the process ID (PID) of the WildFly instance, as follows:

```
$ ps -efa | grep java | grep -v grep
luigi     5031  5023  0 16:07 pts/2    00:00:03 /home/luigi/WFC/jdk8/
bin/java -Djboss.modules.system.pkgs=com.sun.java.swing -Dlogging.
configuration=file:/home/luigi/WFC/wildfly/bin/jboss-cli-logging.
properties -jar /home/luigi/WFC/wildfly/jboss-modules.jar -mp /home/
luigi/WFC/wildfly/modules org.jboss.as.cli --connect
```

```
luigi      5285  5249 99 16:29 pts/3     00:00:09 /home/luigi/WFC/jdk8/
bin/java -D[Standalone] -server -Xms64m -Xmx512m -XX:MaxPermSize=256m
-Djava.net.preferIPv4Stack=true -Djboss.modules.system.pkgs=org.jboss.
byteman -Djava.awt.headless=true -Dorg.jboss.boot.log.file=/home/luigi/
WFC/wildfly/standalone/log/server.log -Dlogging.configuration=file:/home/
luigi/WFC/wildfly/standalone/configuration/logging.properties -jar /home/
luigi/WFC/wildfly/jboss-modules.jar -mp /home/luigi/WFC/wildfly/modules
org.jboss.as.standalone -Djboss.home.dir=/home/luigi/WFC/wildfly -Djboss.
server.base.dir=/home/luigi/WFC/wildfly/standalone
```

Okay, now go back into the CLI and do as follows:

```
[standalone@localhost:9990 /] shutdown --restart=true
[standalone@localhost:9990 /]
```

The first visible difference is that your CLI doesn't disconnect. Now let's go back to the terminal and list the available processes at the OS level, as done previously:

```
$ ps -efa | grep java | grep -v grep
luigi      5421  5413 10 16:29 pts/2     00:00:01 /home/luigi/WFC/jdk8/
bin/java -Djboss.modules.system.pkgs=com.sun.java.swing -Dlogging.
configuration=file:/home/luigi/WFC/wildfly/bin/jboss-cli-logging.
properties -jar /home/luigi/WFC/wildfly/jboss-modules.jar -mp /home/
luigi/WFC/wildfly/modules org.jboss.as.cli --connect
luigi      5482  5249 99 16:29 pts/3     00:00:10 /home/luigi/WFC/jdk8/
bin/java -D[Standalone] -server -Xms64m -Xmx512m -XX:MaxPermSize=256m
-Djava.net.preferIPv4Stack=true -Djboss.modules.system.pkgs=org.jboss.
byteman -Djava.awt.headless=true -Dorg.jboss.boot.log.file=/home/luigi/
WFC/wildfly/standalone/log/server.log -Dlogging.configuration=file:/home/
luigi/WFC/wildfly/standalone/configuration/logging.properties -jar /home/
luigi/WFC/wildfly/jboss-modules.jar -mp /home/luigi/WFC/wildfly/modules
org.jboss.as.standalone -Djboss.home.dir=/home/luigi/WFC/wildfly -Djboss.
server.base.dir=/home/luigi/WFC/wildfly/standalone
```

This is probably the most important difference with the `reload` command. You get a completely new JVM, a different process ID at the OS level. The preceding command executed into the CLI completely shuts down the current instance and starts up a new one, as shown in the following log entries:

```
...
10:43:31,997 INFO  [org.jboss.as.server] (management-handler-thread - 2)
WFLYSRV0211: Suspending server
10:43:32,002 INFO  [org.jboss.as.server] (Thread-2) WFLYSRV0220: Server
shutdown has been requested.
10:43:32,016 INFO  [org.wildfly.extension.undertow] (MSC service thread
1-10) WFLYUT0019: Host default-host stopping
```

```
10:43:32,017 INFO  [org.jboss.as.connector.subsystems.datasources]
(MSC service thread 1-1) WFLYJCA0010: Unbound data source [java:jboss/
datasources/ExampleDS]
10:43:32,025 INFO  [org.jboss.as.connector.deployers.jdbc] (MSC service
thread 1-11) WFLYJCA0019: Stopped Driver service with driver-name = h2
10:43:32,058 INFO  [org.wildfly.extension.undertow] (MSC service thread
1-1) WFLYUT0008: Undertow HTTP listener default suspending
10:43:32,065 INFO  [org.wildfly.extension.undertow] (MSC service thread
1-1) WFLYUT0007: Undertow HTTP listener default stopped, was bound to
/0.0.0.0:8080
10:43:32,066 INFO  [org.wildfly.extension.undertow] (MSC service thread
1-5) WFLYUT0004: Undertow 1.2.0.Beta10 stopping
10:43:32,152 INFO  [org.jboss.as] (MSC service thread 1-2) WFLYSRV0050:
WildFly Full 9.0.0.Beta2 (WildFly Core 1.0.0.Beta2) stopped in 130ms
Restarting JBoss...
Java HotSpot(TM) 64-Bit Server VM warning: ignoring option
MaxPermSize=256m; support was removed in 8.0
10:43:32,639 INFO  [org.jboss.modules] (main) JBoss Modules version
1.4.2.Final
10:43:32,858 INFO  [org.jboss.msc] (main) JBoss MSC version 1.2.4.Final
10:43:32,936 INFO  [org.jboss.as] (MSC service thread 1-7) WFLYSRV0049:
WildFly Full 9.0.0.Beta2 (WildFly Core 1.0.0.Beta2) starting
10:43:34,064 INFO  [org.jboss.as.controller.management-deprecated]
(ServerService Thread Pool -- 22) WFLYCTL0028: Attribute enabled is
deprecated, and it might be removed in future version!
10:43:34,088 INFO  [org.jboss.as.server] (Controller Boot Thread)
WFLYSRV0039: Creating http management service using socket-binding
(management-http)
10:43:34,120 INFO  [org.xnio] (MSC service thread 1-2) XNIO version
3.3.0.Final
10:43:34,130 INFO  [org.xnio.nio] (MSC service thread 1-2) XNIO NIO
Implementation Version 3.3.0.Final
10:43:34,186 INFO  [org.jboss.as.clustering.infinispan] (ServerService
Thread Pool -- 38) WFLYCLINF0001: Activating Infinispan subsystem.
10:43:34,185 INFO  [org.wildfly.extension.io] (ServerService Thread Pool
-- 37) WFLYIO001: Worker 'default' has auto-configured to 16 core threads
with 128 task threads based on your 8 available processors
10:43:34,193 INFO  [org.jboss.remoting] (MSC service thread 1-2) JBoss
Remoting version 4.0.8.Final
10:43:34,220 INFO  [org.jboss.as.naming] (ServerService Thread Pool --
46) WFLYNAM0001: Activating Naming Subsystem
```

```
10:43:34,230 INFO  [org.jboss.as.security] (ServerService Thread Pool --
53) WFLYSEC0002: Activating Security Subsystem
10:43:34,228 INFO  [org.jboss.as.connector.subsystems.datasources]
(ServerService Thread Pool -- 33) WFLYJCA0004: Deploying JDBC-compliant
driver class org.h2.Driver (version 1.3)
10:43:34,242 WARN  [org.jboss.as.txn] (ServerService Thread Pool -- 54)
WFLYTX0013: Node identifier property is set to the default value. Please
make sure it is unique.
10:43:34,242 INFO  [org.jboss.as.security] (MSC service thread 1-10)
WFLYSEC0001: Current PicketBox version=4.9.0.Beta2
10:43:34,245 INFO  [org.jboss.as.jsf] (ServerService Thread Pool -- 44)
WFLYJSF0007: Activated the following JSF Implementations: [main]
10:43:34,294 INFO  [org.jboss.as.webservices] (ServerService Thread Pool
-- 56) WFLYWS0002: Activating WebServices Extension
10:43:34,311 INFO  [org.wildfly.extension.undertow] (ServerService Thread
Pool -- 55) WFLYUT0003: Undertow 1.2.0.Beta10 starting
10:43:34,328 INFO  [org.wildfly.extension.undertow] (MSC service thread
1-3) WFLYUT0003: Undertow 1.2.0.Beta10 starting
10:43:34,305 INFO  [org.jboss.as.connector] (MSC service thread 1-7)
WFLYJCA0009: Starting JCA Subsystem (IronJacamar 1.2.3.Final)
10:43:34,350 INFO  [org.jboss.as.connector.deployers.jdbc] (MSC service
thread 1-9) WFLYJCA0018: Started Driver service with driver-name = h2
10:43:34,421 INFO  [org.jboss.as.naming] (MSC service thread 1-12)
WFLYNAM0003: Starting Naming Service
10:43:34,421 INFO  [org.jboss.as.mail.extension] (MSC service thread
1-14) WFLYMAIL0001: Bound mail session [java:jboss/mail/Default]
10:43:34,616 INFO  [org.wildfly.extension.undertow] (ServerService Thread
Pool -- 55) WFLYUT0014: Creating file handler for path /home/wildfly/WFC/
wildfly/welcome-content
10:43:34,651 INFO  [org.wildfly.extension.undertow] (MSC service thread
1-16) WFLYUT0012: Started server default-server.
10:43:34,670 INFO  [org.wildfly.extension.undertow] (MSC service thread
1-16) WFLYUT0018: Host default-host starting
10:43:34,749 INFO  [org.wildfly.extension.undertow] (MSC service
thread 1-11) WFLYUT0006: Undertow HTTP listener default listening on
/0.0.0.0:8080
10:43:34,882 INFO  [org.jboss.as.connector.subsystems.datasources]
(MSC service thread 1-2) WFLYJCA0001: Bound data source [java:jboss/
datasources/ExampleDS]
10:43:34,948 INFO  [org.jboss.as.server.deployment.scanner] (MSC service
thread 1-5) WFLYDS0013: Started FileSystemDeploymentService for directory
/home/wildfly/WFC/wildfly/standalone/deployments
```

```
10:43:35,080 INFO  [org.jboss.ws.common.management] (MSC service
thread 1-2) JBWS022052: Starting JBoss Web Services - Stack CXF Server
5.0.0.Beta3

[standalone@localhost:9990 /] 10:43:35,314 INFO  [org.jboss.as]
(Controller Boot Thread) WFLYSRV0060: Http management interface listening
on http://0.0.0.0:9990/management

10:43:35,320 INFO  [org.jboss.as] (Controller Boot Thread) WFLYSRV0051:
Admin console listening on http://0.0.0.0:9990

10:43:35,321 INFO  [org.jboss.as] (Controller Boot Thread) WFLYSRV0025:
WildFly Full 9.0.0.Beta2 (WildFly Core 1.0.0.Beta2) started in 2990ms -
Started 202 of 379 services (210 services are lazy, passive or on-demand)
```

Remember that the PID changes, so if you are monitoring your instance per PID, consider updating your monitoring tool/script as well!

# Suspending and resuming an instance via the CLI

In this recipe, we will learn how to suspend an instance without killing active requests. Once the running requests are completed, the next ones will not be accepted. This is a new feature available in WildFly 9.

## Getting ready

To test this recipe, we will need the application named `grace` that you can find in my GitHub repository. If you skipped the *Managing applications using the deployments folder* recipe, please refer to it to download all the source code and the projects that you will need.

Start up your WildFly so we can directly connect to it via the CLI, as follows:

```
$ cd ~/WFC/wildfly
$ ./bin/standalone.sh
```

## How to do it...

1. First of all, deploy the application `grace.war`. Once the application has been deployed, open it using a browser at the following URL `http://127.0.0.1:8080/grace`

   This will hit the `index.jsp` page which increments a counter and then sleeps for 10 seconds, just to simulate a long running request.

2. While running, open a terminal window and connect to the CLI as usual. Once there, do as follows:

```
$ ./bin/jboss-cli.sh --connect
[standalone@localhost:9990 /] :suspend
```

3. Now, going back on the browser, your request should be done and you should see a page similar to the following one:

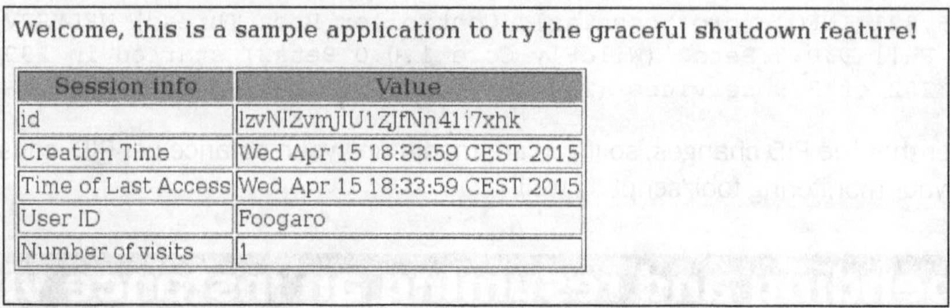

**Welcome, this is a sample application to try the graceful shutdown feature!**

| Session info | Value |
|---|---|
| id | lzvNIZvmJIU1ZJfNn41i7xhk |
| Creation Time | Wed Apr 15 18:33:59 CEST 2015 |
| Time of Last Access | Wed Apr 15 18:33:59 CEST 2015 |
| User ID | Foogaro |
| Number of visits | 1 |

4. On the other hand, to resume the instance, just invoke the following command:

```
[standalone@localhost:9990 /] :resume
```

## How it works...

The command itself is pretty easy. What you should know is what happens to the next user's requests. The next user would get the following page:

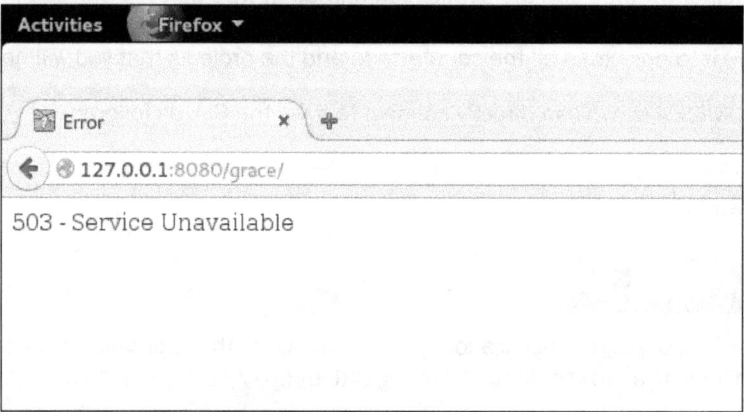


Obviously, you could handle the HTTP **503** code using a special page to warn the users about the technical problems due to the system's upgrade.

On the WildFly logs you should catch the following entry:

```
16:38:05,374 INFO  [org.jboss.as.server] (management-handler-thread - 7)
WFLYSRV0211: Suspending server
```

The `resume` command is pretty easy as well. What needs to be noticed is that the user will not lose his current and active session, which is a really great feature from the user's point of view.

On the WildFly logs, you should catch the following entry:

```
16:38:25,347 INFO  [org.jboss.as.server] (management-handler-thread - 8)
WFLYSRV0212: Resuming server
```

Now if you go back to the application and refresh the page, you should see the counter increasing from where it stopped, as depicted in the following image:

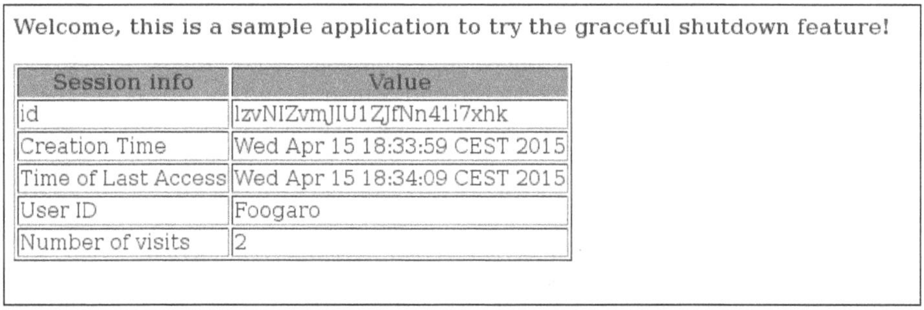

Welcome, this is a sample application to try the graceful shutdown feature!

| Session info | Value |
|---|---|
| id | lzvNIZvmJIU1ZJfNn41i7xhk |
| Creation Time | Wed Apr 15 18:33:59 CEST 2015 |
| Time of Last Access | Wed Apr 15 18:34:09 CEST 2015 |
| User ID | Foogaro |
| Number of visits | 2 |

# Backing up your configuration file via the CLI

In this recipe, we will learn how to backup our configuration via the CLI. Essentially, the CLI backs up the `standalone.xml` file by copying it into the `snapshot`.

## Getting ready

Start up your WildFly so that we can directly connect to it via the CLI, as follows:

```
$ cd ~/WFC/wildfly
$ ./bin/standalone.sh
```

## How to do it...

The command itself is pretty easy:

```
$ ./bin/jboss-cli.sh --connect
[standalone@localhost:9990 /] :take-snapshot
{
    "outcome" => "success",
    "result" => "/home/luigi/WFC/wildfly/standalone/configuration/
standalone_xml_history/snapshot/20150301-165737562standalone.xml"
}
```

That's it! A backup of the `standalone.xml` file gets copied into the `snapshot` folder, named by prefixing the file with the current date and time.

> Always back up your configuration, especially when operating in a production environment.

# 3
# Running WildFly in Domain Mode

In this chapter, you will learn the following recipes:

- Running domain mode
- Connecting the host controller to the domain controller
- Stopping and starting server groups via the Web Console
- Stopping and starting your server groups via the CLI
- Stopping and starting your servers via the CLI
- Deploying and undeploying an application to a specific server group via Web Console
- Deploying and undeploying an application to a specific server group via the CLI
- Checking server status via the CLI

## Introduction

In this chapter, you will learn how to manage WildFly running in the domain mode. You will also learn how to configure and manage it, via both CLI and Web Console. We will also recap some topics covered in the standalone chapter adapted for the domain mode. If you want to know about the following topics, you can refer to the *Appendix* section of this book:

- Domain mode and the server groups
- Understanding the structure of `domain.xml`
- Understanding the structure of `host.xml`

In this chapter, all examples and recipes use the WildFly installation described in *Chapter 1, Welcome to WildFly!*, which is linked to the `$WILDFLY_HOME` variable.

# Running domain mode

In this recipe, we will learn how to run WildFly in the domain mode. There are a few concepts that you need to be aware of—domain controller, host controller and server group. However, those concepts are all explained in the *Appendix* section of this book.

## Getting ready

WildFly comes with pre-configured `domain.xml` and `host.xml` files. There are two defined server groups: one named `main-server-group` referencing the `full` profile; the other one named `other-server-group` referencing the `full-ha` profile.

```
<server-groups>
    <server-group name="main-server-group" profile="full">
        <jvm name="default">
            <heap size="64m" max-size="512m"/>
        </jvm>
        <socket-binding-group ref="full-sockets"/>
    </server-group>
    <server-group name="other-server-group" profile="full-ha">
        <jvm name="default">
            <heap size="64m" max-size="512m"/>
        </jvm>
        <socket-binding-group ref="full-ha-sockets"/>
    </server-group>
</server-groups>
```

Server groups in domain.xml

Each server group is then referenced into the `host.xml` file by a list of servers or hosts.

```
<servers>
    <server name="server-one" group="main-server-group">
        <jvm name="default">
            <heap size="64m" max-size="256m"/>
        </jvm>
    </server>
    <server name="server-two" group="main-server-group" auto-start="true">
        <socket-bindings port-offset="150"/>
    </server>
    <server name="server-three" group="other-server-group" auto-start="false">
        <socket-bindings port-offset="250"/>
    </server>
</servers>
```

Servers declared in host.xml

As you can see from the preceding XML code snippet, each server definition references the server-group membership using the attribute `group`. Also, the `auto-start` attribute defines whether the server will start automatically, or whether it needs a manual startup from the Admin Console or via CLI.

## How to do it...

Just open your command line and launch WildFly in the domain mode as follows:

```
$ cd $WILDFLY_HOME
$ ./bin/domain.sh
...
22:22:53,403 INFO  [org.jboss.modules] (main) JBoss Modules version 1.4.2.Final
22:22:53,525 INFO  [org.jboss.as.process.Host Controller.status] (main) WFLYPC0018: Starting process 'Host Controller'
[Host Controller] Java HotSpot(TM) 64-Bit Server VM warning: ignoring option MaxPermSize=256m; support was removed in 8.0
[Host Controller] 22:22:53,960 INFO  [org.jboss.modules] (main) JBoss Modules version 1.4.2.Final
[Host Controller] 22:22:54,131 INFO  [org.jboss.msc] (main) JBoss MSC version 1.2.4.Final
[Host Controller] 22:22:54,168 INFO  [org.jboss.as] (MSC service thread 1-7) WFLYSRV0049: WildFly Full 9.0.0.Beta2 (WildFly Core 1.0.0.Beta2) starting
...
22:22:56,441 INFO  [org.jboss.as.process.Server:server-one.status] (ProcessController-threads - 3) WFLYPC0018: Starting process 'Server:server-one'
...
[Host Controller] 22:22:58,352 INFO  [org.jboss.as.domain.controller.mgmt] (Remoting "master:MANAGEMENT" task-4) WFLYHC0021: Server [Server:server-one] connected using connection [Channel ID 075c2e34 (inbound) of Remoting connection 2865b4ba to /127.0.0.1:37199]
[Host Controller] 22:22:58,407 INFO  [org.jboss.as.host.controller] (Controller Boot Thread) WFLYHC0023: Starting server server-two
[Host Controller] 22:22:58,444 INFO  [org.jboss.as.host.controller] (server-registration-threads - 1) WFLYHC0020: Registering server server-one
22:22:58,457 INFO  [org.jboss.as.process.Server:server-two.status] (ProcessController-threads - 3) WFLYPC0018: Starting process 'Server:server-two'
```

```
...
[Server:server-one] 22:23:04,175 INFO  [org.jboss.as] (Controller Boot
Thread) WFLYSRV0025: WildFly Full 9.0.0.Beta2 (WildFly Core 1.0.0.Beta2)
started in 7642ms - Started 229 of 405 services (217 services are lazy,
passive or on-demand)
...
[Server:server-two] 22:23:07,024 INFO  [org.jboss.as] (Controller Boot
Thread) WFLYSRV0025: WildFly Full 9.0.0.Beta2 (WildFly Core 1.0.0.Beta2)
started in 8229ms - Started 229 of 405 services (217 services are lazy,
passive or on-demand)
```

Accessing the Admin Console you can see **server-one** and **server-two** up and running, while **server-three** is still stopped, as depicted in the following image:

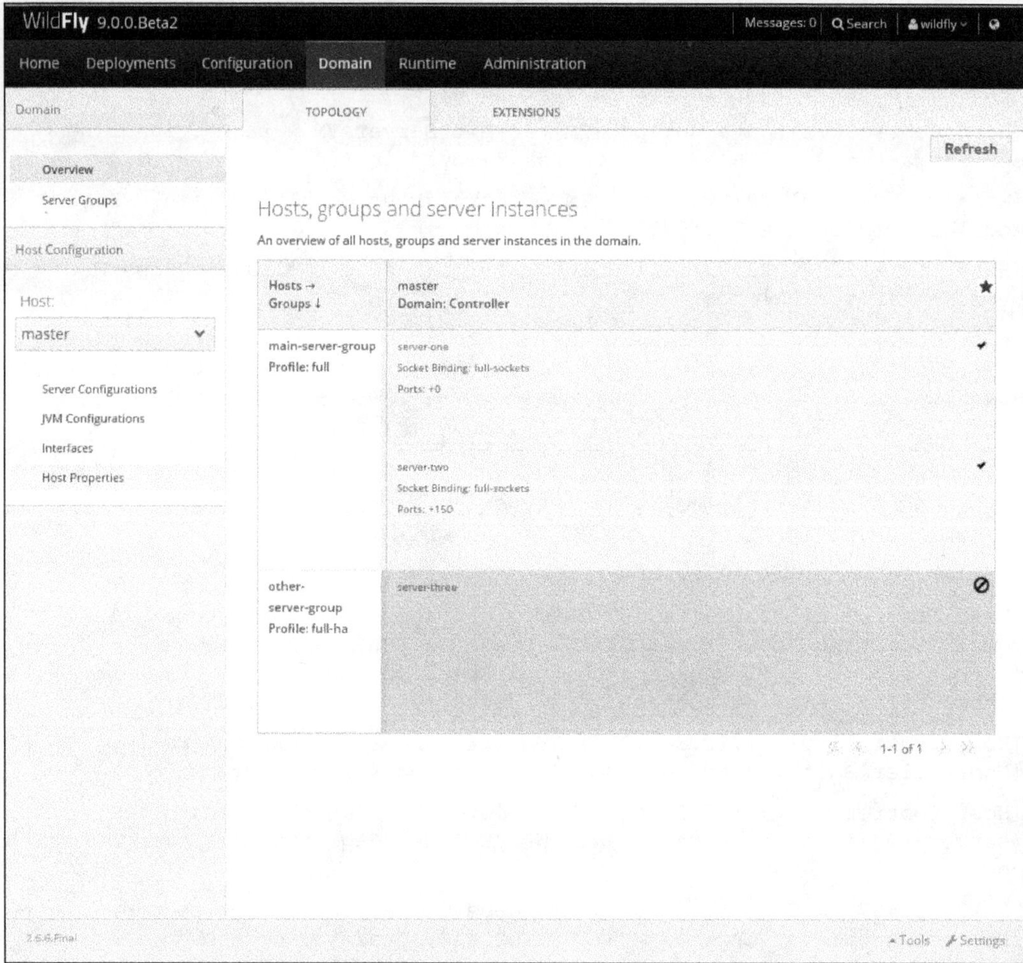

## How it works...

When you start WildFly in the domain mode, the script starts WildFly which looks for its default configuration files. By default, it looks for the `domain.xml` and the `host.xml` files. When WildFly finds those two files, it parses them, and it starts taking up all the services needed and declared by the configuration files.

At the OS level, when you start WildFly in the domain mode, you are actually starting a process called `Process Controller`, which has to start another process called `Host Controller`. The `Host Controller` is responsible for managing the server configuration and for starting the WildFly instances, the servers, declared in the `host.xml` file.

As per `https://weblogs.java.net/blog/arungupta/archive/2014/05/30/wildfly-managed-domain-raspberry-pi-tech-tip-27`,

> *One Host Controller instance is configured to act as the Domain Controller. The Host Controller on each host, meant as remote server (either physical or virtual), interacts with the Domain Controller to control the lifecycle of the application server instances running on its host and to assist the Domain Controller in managing them.*

If you check the processes running at the OS level, you can see the following:

```
wildfly    1525  1429  7 08:26 ?        00:00:01 /home/wildfly/
WFC/jdk8/bin/java -D[Process Controller] -server -Xms64m -Xmx512m
-XX:MaxPermSize=256m -Djava.net.preferIPv4Stack=true -Djboss.modules.
system.pkgs=org.jboss.byteman -Djava.awt.headless=true -Dorg.jboss.
boot.log.file=/home/wildfly/WFC/wildfly/domain/log/process-controller.
log -Dlogging.configuration=file:/home/wildfly/WFC/wildfly/domain/
configuration/logging.properties -jar /home/wildfly/WFC/wildfly/
jboss-modules.jar -mp /home/wildfly/WFC/wildfly/modules org.jboss.
as.process-controller -jboss-home /home/wildfly/WFC/wildfly -jvm /
home/wildfly/WFC/jdk8/bin/java -mp /home/wildfly/WFC/wildfly/modules
-- -Dorg.jboss.boot.log.file=/home/wildfly/WFC/wildfly/domain/log/
host-controller.log -Dlogging.configuration=file:/home/wildfly/WFC/
wildfly/domain/configuration/logging.properties -server -Xms64m -Xmx512m
-XX:MaxPermSize=256m -Djava.net.preferIPv4Stack=true -Djboss.modules.
system.pkgs=org.jboss.byteman -Djava.awt.headless=true -- -default-jvm /
home/wildfly/WFC/jdk8/bin/java

wildfly    1542  1525 62 08:26 ?        00:00:10 /home/wildfly/WFC/jdk8/
bin/java -D[Host Controller] -Dorg.jboss.boot.log.file=/home/wildfly/WFC/
wildfly/domain/log/host-controller.log -Dlogging.configuration=file:/
home/wildfly/WFC/wildfly/domain/configuration/logging.properties -server
-Xms64m -Xmx512m -XX:MaxPermSize=256m -Djava.net.preferIPv4Stack=true
-Djboss.modules.system.pkgs=org.jboss.byteman -Djava.awt.headless=true
-jar /home/wildfly/WFC/wildfly/jboss-modules.jar -mp /home/wildfly/WFC/
wildfly/modules org.jboss.as.host-controller -mp /home/wildfly/WFC/
wildfly/modules --pc-address 127.0.0.1 --pc-port 56310 -default-jvm /
home/wildfly/WFC/jdk8/bin/java -Djboss.home.dir=/home/wildfly/WFC/wildfly
```

```
wildfly    1611  1525 99 08:26 ?        00:00:22 /home/wildfly/WFC/
jdk8/bin/java -D[Server:server-one] -Xms64m -Xmx512m -server -Djava.
awt.headless=true -Djava.net.preferIPv4Stack=true -Djboss.home.dir=/
home/wildfly/WFC/wildfly -Djboss.modules.system.pkgs=org.jboss.byteman
-Djboss.server.log.dir=/home/wildfly/WFC/wildfly/domain/servers/server-
one/log -Djboss.server.temp.dir=/home/wildfly/WFC/wildfly/domain/servers/
server-one/tmp -Djboss.server.data.dir=/home/wildfly/WFC/wildfly/domain/
servers/server-one/data -Dlogging.configuration=file:/home/wildfly/WFC/
wildfly/domain/servers/server-one/data/logging.properties -jar /home/
wildfly/WFC/wildfly/jboss-modules.jar -mp /home/wildfly/WFC/wildfly/
modules org.jboss.as.server
wildfly    1657  1525 99 08:26 ?        00:00:22 /home/wildfly/WFC/
jdk8/bin/java -D[Server:server-two] -Xms64m -Xmx512m -server -Djava.
awt.headless=true -Djava.net.preferIPv4Stack=true -Djboss.home.dir=/
home/wildfly/WFC/wildfly -Djboss.modules.system.pkgs=org.jboss.byteman
-Djboss.server.log.dir=/home/wildfly/WFC/wildfly/domain/servers/server-
two/log -Djboss.server.temp.dir=/home/wildfly/WFC/wildfly/domain/servers/
server-two/tmp -Djboss.server.data.dir=/home/wildfly/WFC/wildfly/domain/
servers/server-two/data -Dlogging.configuration=file:/home/wildfly/WFC/
wildfly/domain/servers/server-two/data/logging.properties -jar /home/
wildfly/WFC/wildfly/jboss-modules.jar -mp /home/wildfly/WFC/wildfly/
modules org.jboss.as.server
```

In the previous console output, I emphasized the process IDs and their JVM names, summarizing the following:

| Process ID | Parent PID | JVM name | Description |
|---|---|---|---|
| 1525 | 1429 | Process Controller | This is the main process responsible for creating the host controller and launching the servers. It is also responsible for recreating the host controller, in case it crashes.<br>Its parent PID is the `domain.sh` bash script process, that originated it. |
| 1542 | 1525 | Host Controller | This is the process that manages all the hosts defined within the `host.xml` file. |
| 1611 | 1525 | Server:server-one | This is the JVM for the host named `server-one`. |
| 1657 | 1525 | Server:server-two | This is the JVM for the host named `server-two`. |

## There's more...

As described in the description of the JVM named `Process Controller`, this is the main process that generates the host controller and the WildFly instances, named `server-one` and `server-two`. At the OS level, this means that if the PC crashes, all its child processes will also go down.

Instead, if the `Host Controller` crashes, nothing happens to the real WildFly instances, they just keep on running and serving your clients. Furthermore, when the `Host Controller` crashes, the `Process Controller` is responsible to start it up again. Let me show you.

Within a different terminal, kill the process with the ID that matches the `Host Controller`, which in this case is `1542`:

```
$ kill -9 1542
```

Within the terminal where you launched WildFly in the domain mode, you should see log entries as follows:

```
[Host Controller]

08:30:41,738 INFO  [org.jboss.as.process.Host Controller.status] (reaper for Host Controller) WFLYPC0011: Process 'Host Controller' finished with an exit status of 137

08:30:41,740 INFO  [org.jboss.as.process-controller.server] (reaper for Host Controller) WFLYPC0021: Waiting 1 seconds until trying to restart process Host Controller.

08:30:42,742 INFO  [org.jboss.as.process.Host Controller.status] (reaper for Host Controller) WFLYPC0018: Starting process 'Host Controller'

[Host Controller] Java HotSpot(TM) 64-Bit Server VM warning: ignoring option MaxPermSize=256m; support was removed in 8.0

[Host Controller] 08:30:43,205 INFO  [org.jboss.modules] (main) JBoss Modules version 1.4.2.Final

[Host Controller] 08:30:43,376 INFO  [org.jboss.msc] (main) JBoss MSC version 1.2.4.Final

[Host Controller] 08:30:43,414 INFO  [org.jboss.as] (MSC service thread 1-7) WFLYSRV0049: WildFly Full 9.0.0.Beta2 (WildFly Core 1.0.0.Beta2) starting

[Host Controller] 08:30:44,005 INFO  [org.xnio] (MSC service thread 1-1) XNIO version 3.3.0.Final

[Host Controller] 08:30:44,007 INFO  [org.jboss.as] (Controller Boot Thread) WFLYHC0003: Creating http management service using network interface (management) port (9990) securePort (-1)

[Host Controller] 08:30:44,014 INFO  [org.xnio.nio] (MSC service thread 1-1) XNIO NIO Implementation Version 3.3.0.Final
```

```
[Host Controller] 08:30:44,146 INFO  [org.jboss.remoting] (MSC service thread 1-1) JBoss Remoting version 4.0.8.Final

[Host Controller] 08:30:44,178 INFO  [org.jboss.as.remoting] (MSC service thread 1-6) WFLYRMT0001: Listening on 127.0.0.1:9999

[Host Controller] 08:30:45,096 INFO  [org.jboss.as.controller.management-deprecated] (Controller Boot Thread) WFLYCTL0028: Attribute enabled is deprecated, and it might be removed in future version!

[Host Controller] 08:30:45,151 INFO  [org.jboss.as.controller.management-deprecated] (Controller Boot Thread) WFLYCTL0028: Attribute enabled is deprecated, and it might be removed in future version!

[Host Controller] 08:30:45,159 INFO  [org.jboss.as.controller.management-deprecated] (Controller Boot Thread) WFLYCTL0028: Attribute default-stack is deprecated, and it might be removed in future version!

[Host Controller] 08:30:45,167 INFO  [org.jboss.as.controller.management-deprecated] (Controller Boot Thread) WFLYCTL0028: Attribute enabled is deprecated, and it might be removed in future version!

[Host Controller] 08:30:45,181 INFO  [org.jboss.as.controller.management-deprecated] (Controller Boot Thread) WFLYCTL0028: Attribute enabled is deprecated, and it might be removed in future version!

[Host Controller] 08:30:45,185 INFO  [org.jboss.as.controller.management-deprecated] (Controller Boot Thread) WFLYCTL0028: Attribute default-stack is deprecated, and it might be removed in future version!

[Host Controller] 08:30:45,485 INFO  [org.jboss.as.host.controller] (Controller Boot Thread) WFLYHC0018: Reconnecting server server-one

[Host Controller] 08:30:45,486 INFO  [org.jboss.as.host.controller] (Controller Boot Thread) WFLYHC0020: Registering server server-one

[Host Controller] 08:30:45,492 INFO  [org.jboss.as.host.controller] (Controller Boot Thread) WFLYHC0018: Reconnecting server server-two

[Host Controller] 08:30:45,492 INFO  [org.jboss.as.host.controller] (Controller Boot Thread) WFLYHC0020: Registering server server-two

[Host Controller] 08:30:45,507 INFO  [org.jboss.as] (Controller Boot Thread) WFLYSRV0060: Http management interface listening on http://127.0.0.1:9990/management

[Host Controller] 08:30:45,509 INFO  [org.jboss.as] (Controller Boot Thread) WFLYSRV0051: Admin console listening on http://127.0.0.1:9990

[Host Controller] 08:30:45,509 INFO  [org.jboss.as] (Controller Boot Thread) WFLYSRV0025: WildFly Full 9.0.0.Beta2 (WildFly Core 1.0.0.Beta2) (Host Controller) started in 2668ms - Started 50 of 52 services (15 services are lazy, passive or on-demand)

[Host Controller] 08:30:45,982 INFO  [org.jboss.as.domain.controller.mgmt] (Remoting "master:MANAGEMENT" task-7) WFLYHC0021: Server [Server:server-two] connected using connection [Channel ID 3d3f3eed (inbound) of Remoting connection 067bd212 to /127.0.0.1:43342]
```

```
[Host Controller] 08:30:45,982 INFO  [org.jboss.as.domain.controller.
mgmt] (Remoting "master:MANAGEMENT" task-8) WFLYHC0021: Server
[Server:server-one] connected using connection [Channel ID 1448766c
(inbound) of Remoting connection 4261cbff to /127.0.0.1:42083]
```

So, the `Process Controller` noticed that the `Host Controller` crashed, and it started a new `Host Controller`. The running WildFly instances reconnected successfully to their `Host Controller`.

Executing the command `ps -efa | grep java` again, you will get a list of processes like the previous ones, except for the `Host Controller` process, which will be new, as follows:

```
wildfly    1525  1429  1 08:26 ?        00:00:07 /home/wildfly/
WFC/jdk8/bin/java -D[Process Controller] -server -Xms64m -Xmx512m
-XX:MaxPermSize=256m -Djava.net.preferIPv4Stack=true -Djboss.modules.
system.pkgs=org.jboss.byteman -Djava.awt.headless=true -Dorg.jboss.
boot.log.file=/home/wildfly/WFC/wildfly/domain/log/process-controller.
log -Dlogging.configuration=file:/home/wildfly/WFC/wildfly/domain/
configuration/logging.properties -jar /home/wildfly/WFC/wildfly/
jboss-modules.jar -mp /home/wildfly/WFC/wildfly/modules org.jboss.
as.process-controller -jboss-home /home/wildfly/WFC/wildfly -jvm /
home/wildfly/WFC/jdk8/bin/java -mp /home/wildfly/WFC/wildfly/modules
-- -Dorg.jboss.boot.log.file=/home/wildfly/WFC/wildfly/domain/log/
host-controller.log -Dlogging.configuration=file:/home/wildfly/WFC/
wildfly/domain/configuration/logging.properties -server -Xms64m -Xmx512m
-XX:MaxPermSize=256m -Djava.net.preferIPv4Stack=true -Djboss.modules.
system.pkgs=org.jboss.byteman -Djava.awt.headless=true -- -default-jvm /
home/wildfly/WFC/jdk8/bin/java

wildfly    1611  1525  6 08:26 ?        00:00:29 /home/wildfly/WFC/
jdk8/bin/java -D[Server:server-one] -Xms64m -Xmx512m -server -Djava.
awt.headless=true -Djava.net.preferIPv4Stack=true -Djboss.home.dir=/
home/wildfly/WFC/wildfly -Djboss.modules.system.pkgs=org.jboss.byteman
-Djboss.server.log.dir=/home/wildfly/WFC/wildfly/domain/servers/server-
one/log -Djboss.server.temp.dir=/home/wildfly/WFC/wildfly/domain/servers/
server-one/tmp -Djboss.server.data.dir=/home/wildfly/WFC/wildfly/domain/
servers/server-one/data -Dlogging.configuration=file:/home/wildfly/WFC/
wildfly/domain/servers/server-one/data/logging.properties -jar /home/
wildfly/WFC/wildfly/jboss-modules.jar -mp /home/wildfly/WFC/wildfly/
modules org.jboss.as.server

wildfly    1657  1525  6 08:26 ?        00:00:29 /home/wildfly/WFC/
jdk8/bin/java -D[Server:server-two] -Xms64m -Xmx512m -server -Djava.
awt.headless=true -Djava.net.preferIPv4Stack=true -Djboss.home.dir=/
home/wildfly/WFC/wildfly -Djboss.modules.system.pkgs=org.jboss.byteman
-Djboss.server.log.dir=/home/wildfly/WFC/wildfly/domain/servers/server-
two/log -Djboss.server.temp.dir=/home/wildfly/WFC/wildfly/domain/servers/
server-two/tmp -Djboss.server.data.dir=/home/wildfly/WFC/wildfly/domain/
servers/server-two/data -Dlogging.configuration=file:/home/wildfly/WFC/
wildfly/domain/servers/server-two/data/logging.properties -jar /home/
wildfly/WFC/wildfly/jboss-modules.jar -mp /home/wildfly/WFC/wildfly/
modules org.jboss.as.server
```

```
wildfly    2887  1525  7 08:30 ?        00:00:15 /home/wildfly/WFC/jdk8/
bin/java -D[Host Controller] -Dorg.jboss.boot.log.file=/home/wildfly/WFC/
wildfly/domain/log/host-controller.log -Dlogging.configuration=file:/
home/wildfly/WFC/wildfly/domain/configuration/logging.properties -server
-Xms64m -Xmx512m -XX:MaxPermSize=256m -Djava.net.preferIPv4Stack=true
-Djboss.modules.system.pkgs=org.jboss.byteman -Djava.awt.headless=true
-jar /home/wildfly/WFC/wildfly/jboss-modules.jar -mp /home/wildfly/WFC/
wildfly/modules org.jboss.as.host-controller -mp /home/wildfly/WFC/
wildfly/modules --pc-address 127.0.0.1 --pc-port 56310 -default-jvm /
home/wildfly/WFC/jdk8/bin/java -Djboss.home.dir=/home/wildfly/WFC/wildfly
--process-restarted
```

# Connecting the host controller to the domain controller

In this recipe, you will learn how to connect the host controller to the domain controller. We will refer to the domain controller as `master`, while we will refer to the host controllers as `slave`.

## Getting ready

The purpose of this recipe is to show how to run a domain controller, and a series of other host controllers (we will use two host controllers) that connect to it. Whether the domain controller is on the same machine or on a different one, the connection type is meant to be "remote".

For the recipe, we will simulate two machines defining different configuration folders for each server that we are going to use. This is also a good practice for the development environment, as you can test a pseudo production scenario. Nevertheless, as we will have a `Host Controller` process running along with a `Domain Controller` process, and because both are responsible for remote management, with the management interfaces settled by default to listen on `localhost:9990`, we will have to bind them differently for each host controller.

In *Chapter 2, Running WildFly in Standalone Mode*, we saw how to run multiple WildFly instances on the same machine but with different IPs or port numbers. Here we have to do the same thing. For brevity, we will see just how to bind the host controllers on different ports.

Lastly, the host controller that connects to the domain controller needs to be authenticated. For this reason, we will need to create a new user by running the `add-user.sh` script, providing the information as depicted in the following screenshot:

```
[luigi@foogaro wildfly]$ cat hostcontroller.user
[luigi@foogaro wildfly]$ ./bin/add-user.sh

What type of user do you wish to add?
 a) Management User (mgmt-users.properties)
 b) Application User (application-users.properties)
(a):

Enter the details of the new user to add.
Using realm 'ManagementRealm' as discovered from the existing property files.
Username : hostcontroller
Password recommendations are listed below. To modify these restrictions edit the add-user.properties configuration file.
 - The password should be different from the username
 - The password should not be one of the following restricted values {root, admin, administrator}
 - The password should contain at least 8 characters, 1 alphabetic character(s), 1 digit(s), 1 non-alphanumeric symbol(s)
Password : hostcontroller.2015
Re-enter Password : hostcontroller.2015
What groups do you want this user to belong to? (Please enter a comma separated list, or leave blank for none)[  ]:
About to add user 'hostcontroller' for realm 'ManagementRealm'
Is this correct yes/no? yes
Added user 'hostcontroller' to file '/home/luigi/WFC/wildfly/standalone/configuration/mgmt-users.properties'
Added user 'hostcontroller' to file '/home/luigi/WFC/wildfly/domain/configuration/mgmt-users.properties'
Added user 'hostcontroller' with groups  to file '/home/luigi/WFC/wildfly/standalone/configuration/mgmt-groups.properties'
Added user 'hostcontroller' with groups  to file '/home/luigi/WFC/wildfly/domain/configuration/mgmt-groups.properties'
Is this new user going to be used for one AS process to connect to another AS process?
e.g. for a slave host controller connecting to the master or for a Remoting connection for server to server EJB calls.
yes/no? yes
To represent the user add the following to the server-identities definition <secret value="aG9zdGNvbnRyb2xsZXIuMjAxNQ==" />
[luigi@foogaro wildfly]$
```

This user belongs to the **ManagementRealm**, the same that was used in *Chapter 1, Welcome to WildFly!* to create the `wildfly` user in order to access the Web Console.

Keep note of the last line, the characters in red, that we will use later in the recipe.

## How to do it...

First we need to create the `Domain Controller` and two `Host Controller` configuration folders. Let's create the structure of our directories:

1. Open your terminal and type as follows:

```
$ cd $WILDFLY_HOME
$ cp -a domain master
$ cp -a domain slave-1
$ cp -a domain slave-2
$ mv slave-1/configuration/domain.xml slave-1/configuration/domain.xml.unused
$ mv slave-2/configuration/domain.xml slave-2/configuration/domain.xml.unused
```

2. Now open the `domain.xml` file of the master directory and replace the `server-groups` declaration with the following XML code snippet:

```
<server-groups>
    <server-group name="server-group-REST-app" profile="default">
        <jvm name="default">
            <heap size="64m" max-size="512m"/>
        </jvm>
        <socket-binding-group ref="standard-sockets"/>
    </server-group>
    <server-group name="server-group-SOAP-app" profile="default">
        <jvm name="default">
            <heap size="64m" max-size="512m"/>
        </jvm>
        <socket-binding-group ref="standard-sockets"/>
    </server-group>
</server-groups>
```

3. Here we are simulating a server group dedicated to host applications targeting the RESTful technology, and another server group dedicated to host applications targeting the SOAP technology. This is just an example. A server group might match with a particular application, or a technology (thus more applications); the choice is up to you. My suggestion is to be as consistent as possible when making such decisions.

4. Edit the `host.xml` file of the `master` directory and remove the entire `servers` declaration. Once done, run the master as follows:

```
$ ./bin/domain.sh -Djboss.domain.base.dir=master
```

5. The log should look as follows:

```
08:44:53,589 INFO  [org.jboss.modules] (main) JBoss Modules
version 1.4.2.Final

08:44:53,730 INFO  [org.jboss.as.process.Host Controller.status]
(main) WFLYPC0018: Starting process 'Host Controller'

[Host Controller] Java HotSpot(TM) 64-Bit Server VM warning:
ignoring option MaxPermSize=256m; support was removed in 8.0

[Host Controller] 08:44:54,319 INFO  [org.jboss.modules] (main)
JBoss Modules version 1.4.2.Final

[Host Controller] 08:44:54,503 INFO  [org.jboss.msc] (main) JBoss
MSC version 1.2.4.Final

[Host Controller] 08:44:54,543 INFO  [org.jboss.as] (MSC service
thread 1-7) WFLYSRV0049: WildFly Full 9.0.0.Beta2 (WildFly Core
1.0.0.Beta2) starting

[Host Controller] 08:44:55,145 INFO  [org.xnio] (MSC service
thread 1-5) XNIO version 3.3.0.Final
```

```
[Host Controller] 08:44:55,147 INFO  [org.jboss.as] (Controller
Boot Thread) WFLYHC0003: Creating http management service using
network interface (management) port (9990) securePort (-1)

[Host Controller] 08:44:55,155 INFO  [org.xnio.nio] (MSC service
thread 1-5) XNIO NIO Implementation Version 3.3.0.Final

[Host Controller] 08:44:55,262 INFO  [org.jboss.remoting] (MSC
service thread 1-5) JBoss Remoting version 4.0.8.Final

[Host Controller] 08:44:55,301 INFO  [org.jboss.as.remoting] (MSC
service thread 1-1) WFLYRMT0001: Listening on 127.0.0.1:9999

[Host Controller] 08:44:56,312 INFO  [org.jboss.as.controller.
management-deprecated] (Controller Boot Thread) WFLYCTL0028:
Attribute enabled is deprecated, and it might be removed in future
version!

[Host Controller] 08:44:56,381 INFO  [org.jboss.as.controller.
management-deprecated] (Controller Boot Thread) WFLYCTL0028:
Attribute enabled is deprecated, and it might be removed in future
version!

[Host Controller] 08:44:56,387 INFO  [org.jboss.as.controller.
management-deprecated] (Controller Boot Thread) WFLYCTL0028:
Attribute default-stack is deprecated, and it might be removed in
future version!

[Host Controller] 08:44:56,400 INFO  [org.jboss.as.controller.
management-deprecated] (Controller Boot Thread) WFLYCTL0028:
Attribute enabled is deprecated, and it might be removed in future
version!

[Host Controller] 08:44:56,413 INFO  [org.jboss.as.controller.
management-deprecated] (Controller Boot Thread) WFLYCTL0028:
Attribute enabled is deprecated, and it might be removed in future
version!

[Host Controller] 08:44:56,419 INFO  [org.jboss.as.controller.
management-deprecated] (Controller Boot Thread) WFLYCTL0028:
Attribute default-stack is deprecated, and it might be removed in
future version!

[Host Controller] 08:44:56,710 INFO  [org.jboss.as] (Controller
Boot Thread) WFLYSRV0060: Http management interface listening on
http://127.0.0.1:9990/management

[Host Controller] 08:44:56,710 INFO  [org.jboss.as] (Controller
Boot Thread) WFLYSRV0051: Admin console listening on
http://127.0.0.1:9990

[Host Controller] 08:44:56,711 INFO  [org.jboss.as] (Controller
Boot Thread) WFLYSRV0025: WildFly Full 9.0.0.Beta2 (WildFly Core
1.0.0.Beta2) (Host Controller) started in 2825ms - Started 50 of
52 services (15 services are lazy, passive or on-demand)
```

There are no running servers at all.

Now it's time to configure our first slave, `slave-1`.

6. Edit the `slave-1/configuration/host.xml` file and do the following:
    - Name the host as `slave-1`: `<host name="slave-1" xmlns="urn:jboss:domain:3.0">`
    - Add the `hostcontroller` user's secret values inside the `ManagementRealm` definition:

    ```
    <server-identities>
        <secret value="aG9zdGNvbnRyb2xsZXIuMjAxNQ=="/>
    </server-identities>
    ```

    - Change the port number for the management-interfaces:

    ```
    <management-interfaces>
      <native-interface security-realm="ManagementRealm">
      <socket interface="management"
      port="${jboss.management.native.port:19999}"/>
        </native-interface>
          <http-interface security-realm="ManagementRealm"
          http-upgrade-enabled="true">
            <socket interface="management"
            port="${jboss.management.http.port:19990}"/>
         </http-interface>
    </management-interfaces>
    ```

    - Use a remote `domain-controller`:

    ```
    <domain-controller>
        <remote host="${jboss.domain.master.address}"
        port="${jboss.domain.master.port:9999}" security-
        realm="ManagementRealm" username="hostcontroller"/>
    </domain-controller>
    ```

    - Define the hosts:

    ```
    <servers>
      <server name="REST-server-one" group="server-group-REST-
      app">
        <jvm name="default">
          <heap size="64m" max-size="256m"/>
        </jvm>
      </server>
    </servers>
    ```

7. You should end up with a file that looks like the following XML code snippet:

```
<?xml version='1.0' encoding='UTF-8'?>
<host name="slave-1" xmlns="urn:jboss:domain:3.0">
  <extensions>
    <extension module="org.jboss.as.jmx"/>
  </extensions>
  <management>
    <security-realms>
      <security-realm name="ManagementRealm">
        <server-identities>
          <secret value="aG9zdGNvbnRyb2xsZXIuMjAxNQ=="/>
        </server-identities>
        <authentication>
          <local default-user="$local" skip-group-
            loading="true"/>
          <properties path="mgmt-users.properties"
          relative-
            to="jboss.domain.config.dir"/>
        </authentication>
        <authorization map-groups-to-roles="false">
          <properties path="mgmt-groups.properties"
          relative-to="jboss.domain.config.dir"/>
        </authorization>
      </security-realm>
      <security-realm name="ApplicationRealm">
        <authentication>
          <local default-user="$local" allowed-users="*"
          skip-group-loading="true"/>
          <properties path="application-users.properties"
          relative-to="jboss.domain.config.dir"/>
        </authentication>
        <authorization>
          <properties path="application-roles.properties"
          relative-to="jboss.domain.config.dir"/>
        </authorization>
      </security-realm>
    </security-realms>
    <audit-log>
      <formatters>
        <json-formatter name="json-formatter"/>
      </formatters>
      <handlers>
```

```
            <file-handler name="host-file" formatter="json-
            formatter" relative-to="jboss.domain.data.dir"
            path="audit-log.log"/>
            <file-handler name="server-file" formatter="json-
            formatter" relative-to="jboss.server.data.dir"
            path="audit-log.log"/>
          </handlers>
          <logger log-boot="true" log-read-only="false"
          enabled="false">
            <handlers>
              <handler name="host-file"/>
            </handlers>
          </logger>
          <server-logger log-boot="true" log-read-only="false"
          enabled="false">
            <handlers>
              <handler name="server-file"/>
            </handlers>
          </server-logger>
        </audit-log>
        <management-interfaces>
          <native-interface security-realm="ManagementRealm">
            <socket interface="management"
            port="${jboss.management.native.port:19999}"/>
          </native-interface>
          <http-interface security-realm="ManagementRealm"
          http-upgrade-enabled="true">
            <socket interface="management"
            port="${jboss.management.http.port:19990}"/>
          </http-interface>
        </management-interfaces>
      </management>
      <domain-controller>
        <remote protocol="remote" host="${jboss.domain.master.
    address}" port="${jboss.domain.master.port:9999}" security-
    realm="ManagementRealm" username="hostcontroller" />
      </domain-controller>
      <interfaces>
        <interface name="management">
          <inet-address
          value="${jboss.bind.address.management:127.0.0.1}"/>
        </interface>
        <interface name="public">
          <inet-address
          value="${jboss.bind.address:127.0.0.1}"/>
        </interface>
```

```
    <interface name="unsecure">
      <!-- Used for IIOP sockets in the standard
      configuration.
        To secure JacORB you need to setup SSL -->
      <inet-address
      value="${jboss.bind.address.unsecure:127.0.0.1}"/>
    </interface>
  </interfaces>
  <jvms>
    <jvm name="default">
      <heap size="64m" max-size="256m"/>
      <permgen size="256m" max-size="256m"/>
      <jvm-options>
        <option value="-server"/>
      </jvm-options>
    </jvm>
  </jvms>
  <servers>
  <server name="REST-server-one" group="server-group-REST-
  app">
  <jvm name="default">
  <heap size="64m" max-size="256m"/>
  </jvm>
  </server>
  </servers>
  <profile>
  <subsystem xmlns="urn:jboss:domain:jmx:1.3">
  <expose-resolved-model/>
  <expose-expression-model/>
  <remoting-connector/>
  </subsystem>
  </profile>
</host>
```

8. Now we are ready to run our `slave-1` host:

   ```
   $ ./bin/domain.sh -Djboss.domain.base.dir=slave-1 -Djboss.domain.
   master.address=127.0.0.1
   ```

9. If you check the log output from master, you will notice that `slave-1` registered itself to the `Domain Controller`:

   ```
   [Host Controller] 23:45:58,523 INFO  [org.jboss.as.domain] (Host
   Controller Service Threads - 32) WFLYHC0019: Registered remote
   slave host "slave-1", JBoss WildFly Full 9.0.0.Beta2 (WildFly
   1.0.0.Beta2)
   ```

10. Repeat the same changes for the second slave. Set the host name to `slave-2` and add the following servers definition:

```
<servers>
  <server name="SOAP-server-one" group="server-group-SOAP-
  app">
    <socket-bindings port-offset="150"/>
  </server>
  <server name="SOAP-server-two" group="server-group-SOAP-
  app">
    <socket-bindings port-offset="250"/>
  </server>
</servers>
```

11. Also, set the `jboss.management.native.port` and `jboss.management.http.port` property default values, to `29999` and `29990` respectively. You should end up with a file that looks like the following XML code snippet:

```
<?xml version='1.0' encoding='UTF-8'?>
<host name="slave-2" xmlns="urn:jboss:domain:3.0">
  <extensions>
    <extension module="org.jboss.as.jmx"/>
  </extensions>
  <management>
    <security-realms>
      <security-realm name="ManagementRealm">
        <server-identities>
          <secret value="aG9zdGNvbnRyb2xsZXIuMjAxNQ=="/>
        </server-identities>
        <authentication>
          <local default-user="$local" skip-group-
          loading="true"/>
          <properties path="mgmt-users.properties"
          relative-to="jboss.domain.config.dir"/>
        </authentication>
        <authorization map-groups-to-roles="false">
          <properties path="mgmt-groups.properties"
          relative-to="jboss.domain.config.dir"/>
        </authorization>
      </security-realm>
      <security-realm name="ApplicationRealm">
        <authentication>
          <local default-user="$local" allowed-users="*"
          skip-group-loading="true"/>
          <properties path="application-users.properties"
          relative-to="jboss.domain.config.dir"/>
        </authentication>
```

```
        <authorization>
          <properties path="application-roles.properties"
          relative-to="jboss.domain.config.dir"/>
        </authorization>
      </security-realm>
    </security-realms>
    <audit-log>
      <formatters>
        <json-formatter name="json-formatter"/>
      </formatters>
      <handlers>
        <file-handler name="host-file" formatter="json-
        formatter" relative-to="jboss.domain.data.dir"
        path="audit-log.log"/>
        <file-handler name="server-file" formatter="json-
        formatter" relative-to="jboss.server.data.dir"
        path="audit-log.log"/>
      </handlers>
      <logger log-boot="true" log-read-only="false"
      enabled="false">
        <handlers>
          <handler name="host-file"/>
        </handlers>
      </logger>
      <server-logger log-boot="true" log-read-only="false"
      enabled="false">
        <handlers>
          <handler name="server-file"/>
        </handlers>
      </server-logger>
    </audit-log>
    <management-interfaces>
      <native-interface security-realm="ManagementRealm">
        <socket interface="management"
        port="${jboss.management.native.port:29999}"/>
      </native-interface>
      <http-interface security-realm="ManagementRealm"
      http-upgrade-enabled="true">
        <socket interface="management"
        port="${jboss.management.http.port:29990}"/>
      </http-interface>
    </management-interfaces>
  </management>
  <domain-controller>
```

```
      <remote protocol="remote"
      host="${jboss.domain.master.address}"
      port="${jboss.domain.master.port:9999}" security-
      realm="ManagementRealm" username="hostcontroller" />
    </domain-controller>
    <interfaces>
      <interface name="management">
        <inet-address value="${jboss.bind.address.
management:127.0.0.1}"/>
      </interface>
      <interface name="public">
        <inet-address
        value="${jboss.bind.address:127.0.0.1}"/>
      </interface>
      <interface name="unsecure">
        <!-- Used for IIOP sockets in the standard
        configuration.
          To secure JacORB you need to setup SSL -->
        <inet-address
        value="${jboss.bind.address.unsecure:127.0.0.1}"/>
      </interface>
    </interfaces>
    <jvms>
      <jvm name="default">
        <heap size="64m" max-size="256m"/>
        <permgen size="256m" max-size="256m"/>
        <jvm-options>
          <option value="-server"/>
        </jvm-options>
      </jvm>
    </jvms>
    <servers>
    <server name="SOAP-server-one" group="server-group-SOAP-
    app">
    <socket-bindings port-offset="150"/>
    </server>
    <server name="SOAP-server-two" group="server-group-SOAP-
    app">
    <socket-bindings port-offset="250"/>
    </server>
    </servers>
    <profile>
    <subsystem xmlns="urn:jboss:domain:jmx:1.3">
    <expose-resolved-model/>
    <expose-expression-model/>
```

```
    <remoting-connector/>
    </subsystem>
    </profile>
</host>
```

12. Now we are ready to run our `slave-2` host:

    ```
    $ ./bin/domain.sh -Djboss.domain.base.dir=slave-2 -Djboss.domain.
    master.address=127.0.0.1
    ```

13. If you check the log output from `master`, you will notice that `slave-2` registered itself to the `Domain Controller`:

    ```
    [Host Controller] 23:51:34,134 INFO  [org.jboss.as.domain] (Host
    Controller Service Threads - 34) WFLYHC0019: Registered remote
    slave host "slave-2", JBoss WildFly Full 9.0.0.Beta2 (WildFly
    1.0.0.Beta2)
    ```

## How it works...

Let's first talk about the master and then about the two slaves.

### Master

Within the master, you define the entire configuration needed to run your WildFly instances. You choose a profile depending on your requirements, set IPs, ports, server, and groups. Everything is persisted into the `domain.xml`, or whatever file you choose to persist to.

As you launch the `domain.sh` script, the process by default looks for a `domain.xml` file and `host.xml` file to read the configuration, starting from the `jboss.home.dir` (whatever `$WILDFLY_HOME` is) appending `domain` and `configuration`, unless you specify differently.

We specify differently by adding the `jboss.domain.base.dir` property valued to `master`. So WildFly, starting from `jboss.home.dir` appends `master` and the `configuration`. As per the standalone mode, WildFly in the domain mode lets you override different paths if necessary.

The following table summarizes all the properties:

| Property name | Usage | Default value |
|---|---|---|
| `jboss.home.dir` | The root directory of the WildFly installation. | Set by `domain.sh` to `$JBOSS_HOME` |
| `jboss.domain.base.dir` | The base directory for domain content. | `jboss.home.dir/domain` |
| `jboss.domain.config.dir` | The base configuration directory. | `jboss.domain.base.dir/configuration` |

| Property name | Usage | Default value |
|---|---|---|
| jboss.domain.data.dir | The directory used for persistent data file storage. | jboss.domain.base.dir/data |
| jboss.domain.log.dir | The directory containing the host-controller.log and process-controller.log files | jboss.domain.base.dir/log |
| jboss.domain.temp.dir | The directory used for temporary file storage. | jboss.domain.base.dir/tmp |
| jboss.domain.deployment.dir | The directory used to store deployed content. | jboss.domain.data.dir/content |
| jboss.domain.servers.dir | The directory containing the output for the managed server instances. | jboss.domain.data.dir/servers |

The master should run alone, without any servers.

## Slaves

As stated in the previous paragraph, when you launch WildFly in the domain mode, it looks, by default, for the `domain.xml` and `host.xml` files. As we are running the slaves, we do not want to load the `domain.xml`, that's why we moved it away (actually we renamed it as `domain.xml.unused`). So the start up process only picks up the `host.xml` file where we defined our servers and the server groups they belong to.

So basically, within the `host.xml` file we just defined our servers and the domain controller that they should connect to.

Furthermore, in the host `slave-2` we needed to specify a `port-offset`, because we already have a running instance on our local machine. Both `SOAP-server-one` and `SOAP-server-two` will increment their port bindings to 150 and 250, hence `8230` for the first http-connector and `8330` for the second http-connector. Also, we had to change the port number for the management-interfaces.

Lastly, we had to specify the domain controller which the slave will connect to, by passing the `-Djboss.domain.master.address=127.0.0.1` parameter.

The domain overview from the Admin Console looks like the following screenshot:

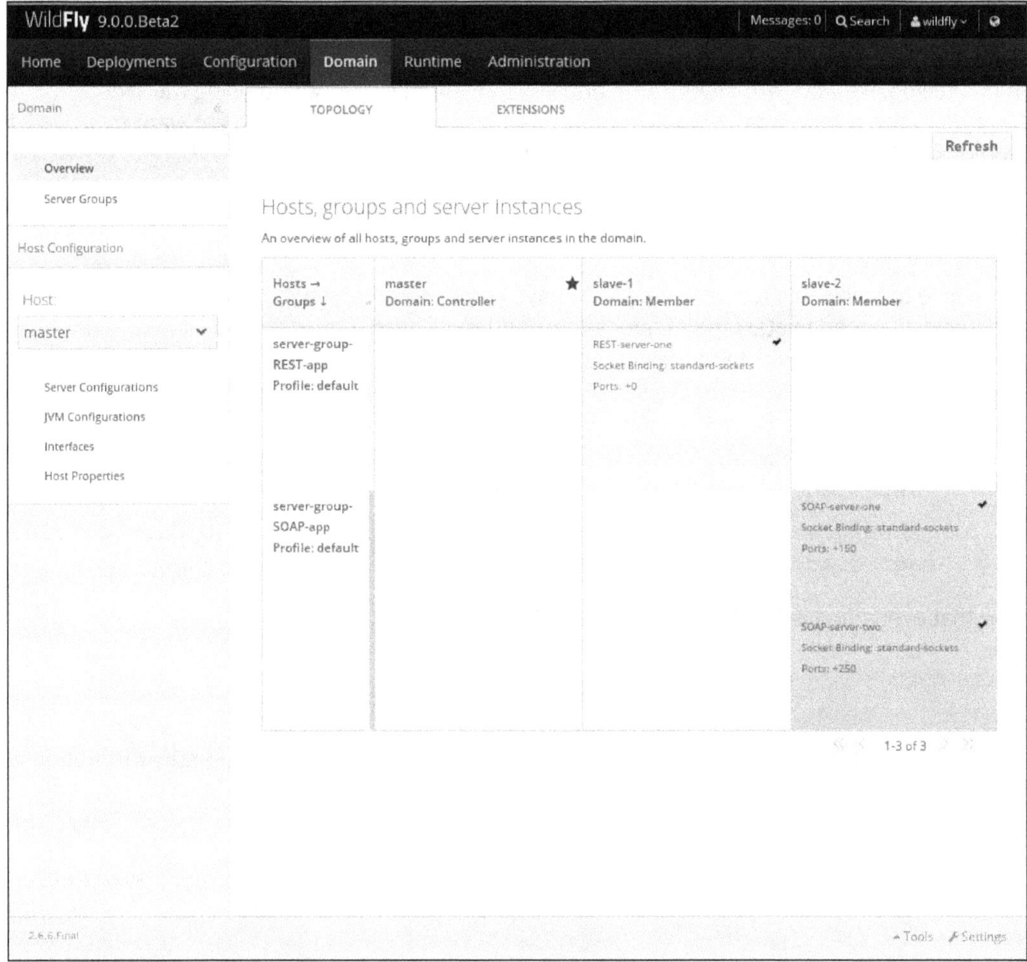


Admin Console—domain overview

# Stopping and starting server groups via the Web Console

In this recipe, we will learn how to stop and start an entire server group using the Web Console. Since a server can belong to more than one server group, you might want to stop or start all servers at once, and thus stop or start the server group.

## Getting ready

To be able to follow this recipe, we need to have completed the previous one. Thus, before we can begin, we need to start the master server and the slaves `slave-1` and `slave-2`. In three different terminals, navigate to the `$WILDFLY_HOME`, and run the following commands:

1. `$ ./bin/domain.sh -Djboss.domain.base.dir=master.`
2. `./bin/domain.sh -Djboss.domain.base.dir=slave-1 -Djboss.domain.master.address=127.0.0.1.`
3. `./bin/domain.sh -Djboss.domain.base.dir=slave-2 -Djboss.domain.master.address=127.0.0.1.`

Now that everything is up and running, let's move ahead.

## How to do it...

1. Open your browser and point it to the Admin Console: `http://localhost:9990`.

2. Enter the username and password (`wildfly` and `cookbook.2015` respectively) and go to the **Domain** tab. You should see a page similar to the following screenshot:

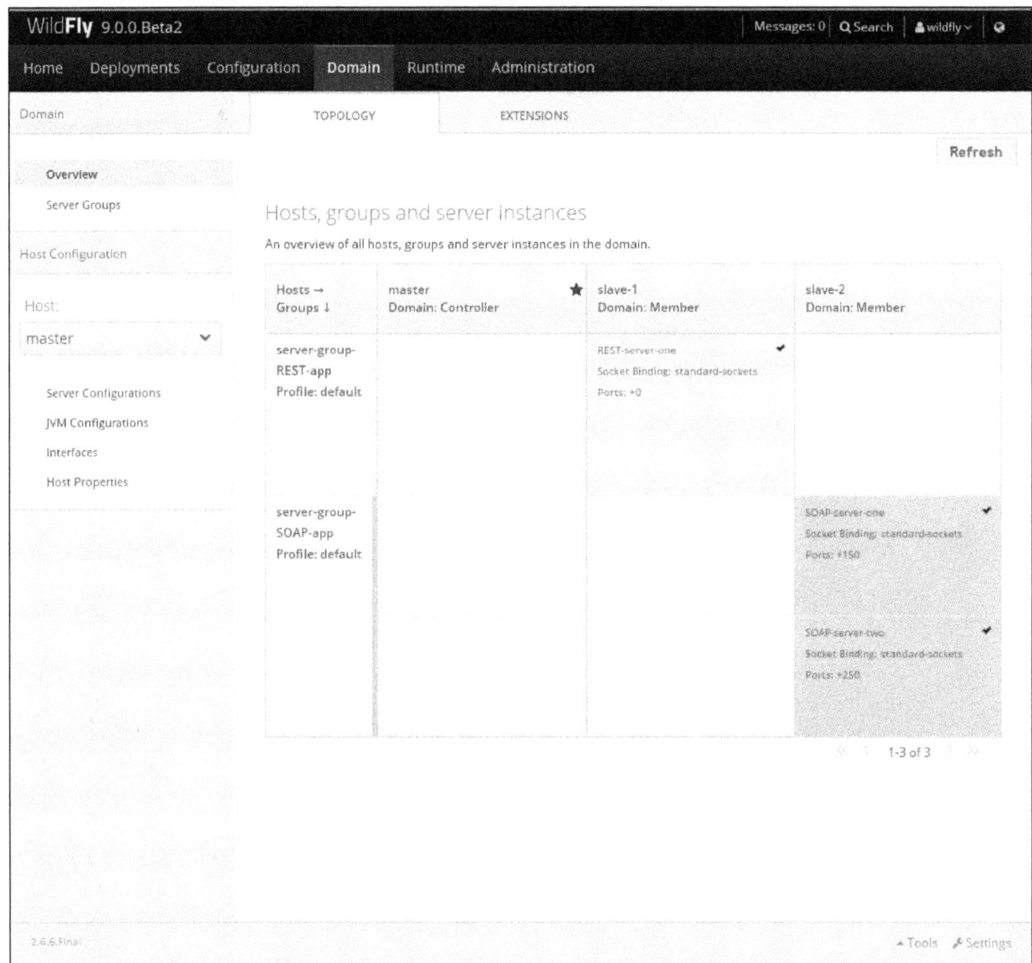


Admin Console—domain overview

3. Now, on hovering the mouse over the **Groups** box, the command links will appear as follows:

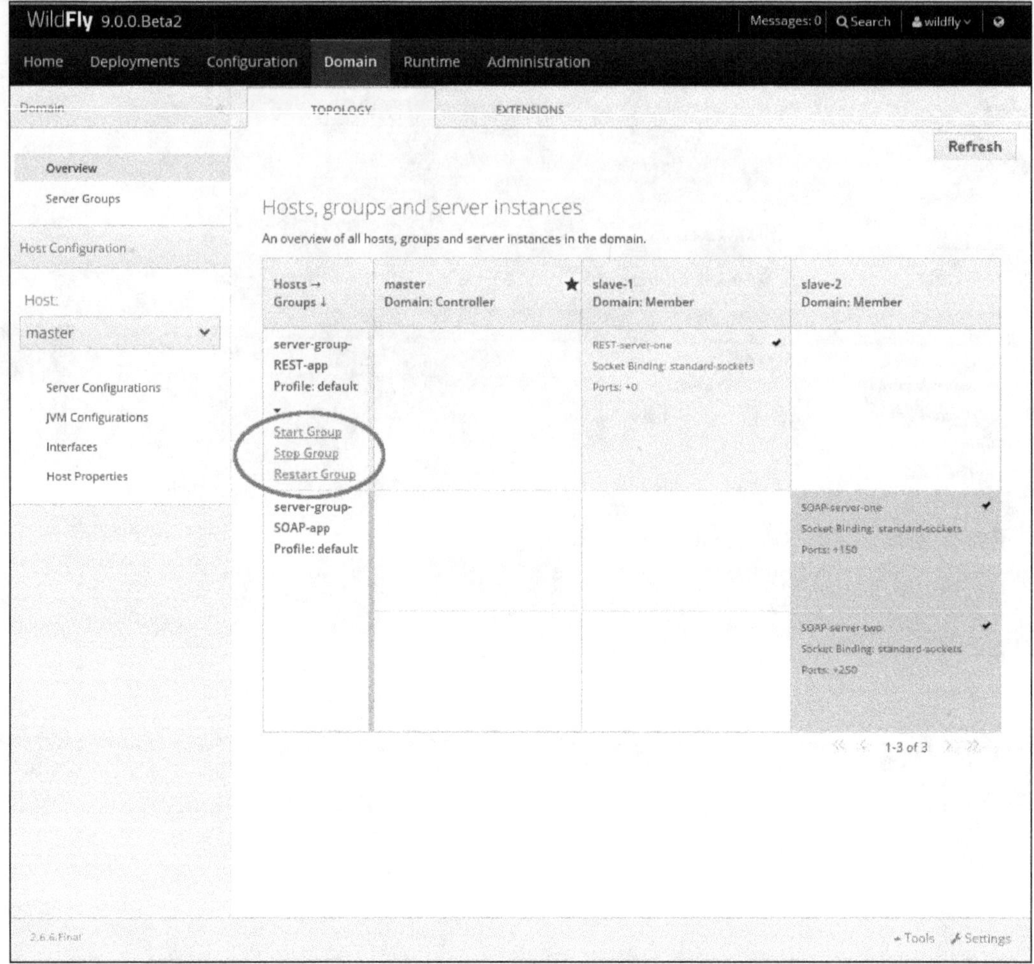


Server Group: Start, Stop and Restart

4. Also, hovering on a server-box, the command links will appear as follows:

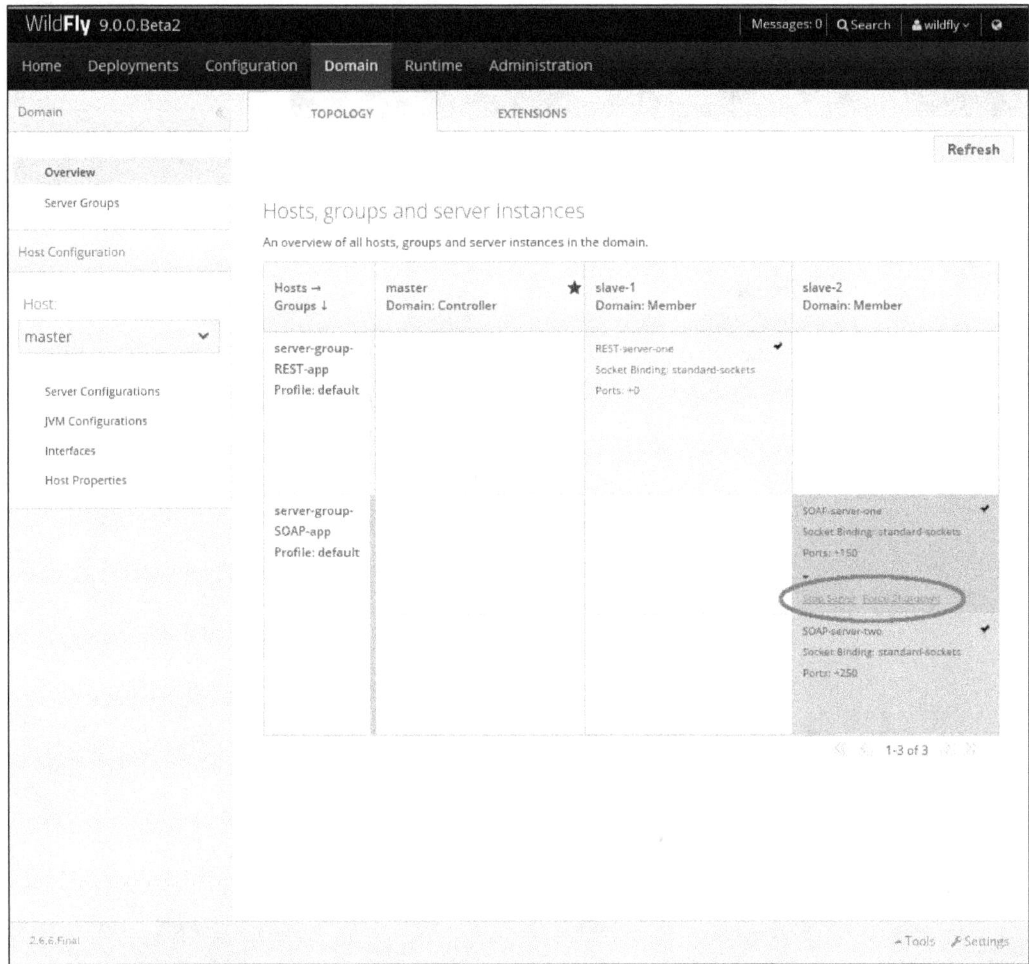

Start server group

5. Now try hitting the **Stop Group** command link and confirm the operation!

6. Tadaaaa... pretty easy huh! The page updates the server instance icon and displays **Operation successful** in the message board:

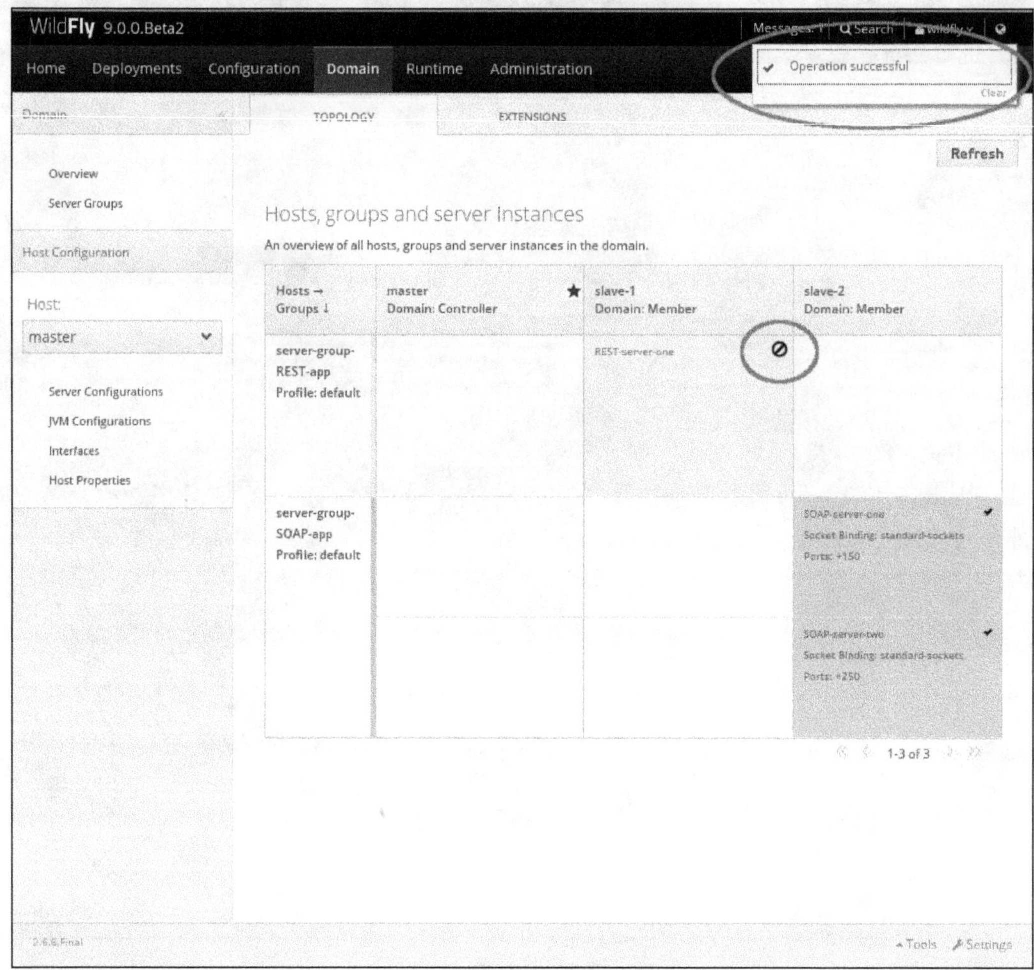


Stopping Server Group

7. In the log, you should see entries similar to the following:

```
[Host Controller] 09:05:52,656 INFO  [org.jboss.as.host.
controller] (Host Controller Service Threads - 9) WFLYHC0024:
Stopping server REST-server-one

[Server:REST-server-one] 09:05:52,692 INFO  [org.jboss.as.server]
(ServerService Thread Pool -- 59) WFLYSRV0211: Suspending server

09:05:52,706 INFO  [org.jboss.as.process.Server:REST-server-one.
status] (ProcessController-threads - 4) WFLYPC0019: Stopping
process 'Server:REST-server-one'

[Server:REST-server-one] 09:05:52,714 INFO  [org.jboss.as.server]
(Thread-2) WFLYSRV0220: Server shutdown has been requested.

[Server:REST-server-one] 09:05:52,732 INFO  [org.jboss.
as.connector.subsystems.datasources] (MSC service thread 1-13)
WFLYJCA0010: Unbound data source [java:jboss/datasources/
ExampleDS]

[Server:REST-server-one] 09:05:52,735 INFO  [org.jboss.
as.connector.deployers.jdbc] (MSC service thread 1-9) WFLYJCA0019:
Stopped Driver service with driver-name = h2

[Server:REST-server-one] 09:05:52,736 INFO  [org.wildfly.
extension.undertow] (MSC service thread 1-16) WFLYUT0019: Host
default-host stopping

[Server:REST-server-one] 09:05:52,745 INFO  [org.wildfly.
extension.undertow] (MSC service thread 1-3) WFLYUT0008: Undertow
HTTP listener default suspending

[Server:REST-server-one] 09:05:52,750 INFO  [org.wildfly.
extension.undertow] (MSC service thread 1-3) WFLYUT0007: Undertow
HTTP listener default stopped, was bound to /127.0.0.1:8080

[Server:REST-server-one] 09:05:52,752 INFO  [org.wildfly.
extension.undertow] (MSC service thread 1-3) WFLYUT0004: Undertow
1.2.0.Beta10 stopping

[Host Controller] 09:05:52,783 INFO  [org.jboss.as.host.
controller] (Remoting "slave-1:MANAGEMENT" task-11) WFLYHC0027:
Unregistering server REST-server-one

[Server:REST-server-one] 09:05:52,853 INFO  [org.jboss.as] (MSC
service thread 1-4) WFLYSRV0050: WildFly Full 9.0.0.Beta2 (WildFly
Core 1.0.0.Beta2) stopped in 112ms

[Server:REST-server-one]

09:05:52,902 INFO  [org.jboss.as.process.Server:REST-server-one.
status] (reaper for Server:REST-server-one) WFLYPC0011: Process
'Server:REST-server-one' finished with an exit status of 0

[Host Controller] 09:05:52,941 INFO  [org.jboss.as.host.
controller] (ProcessControllerConnection-thread - 2) WFLYHC0027:
Unregistering server REST-server-one
```

8. Let's restart the server group, by hitting the **Start Group** command link, as follows:

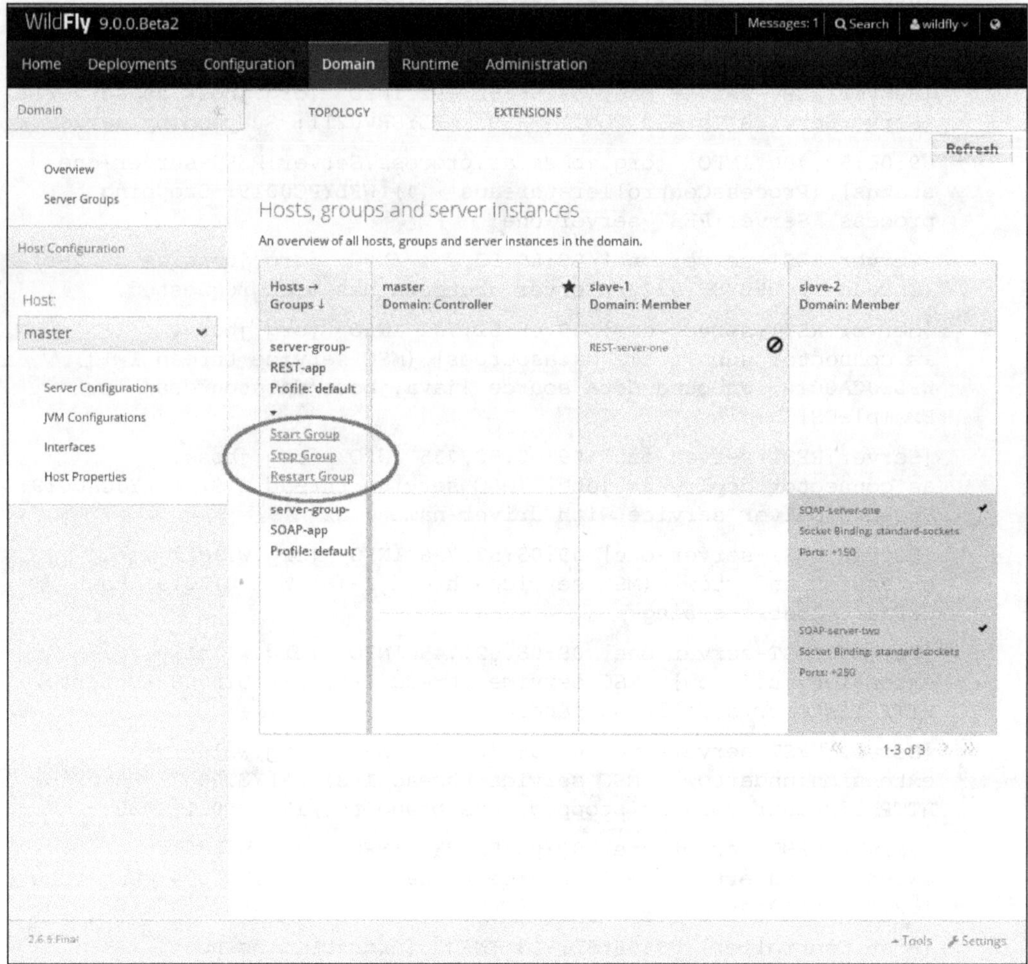

9. Once restarted, WildFly confirms the successful operation by providing you with a message feedback and by updating the status icon associated to the servers belonging to the server group, as follows:

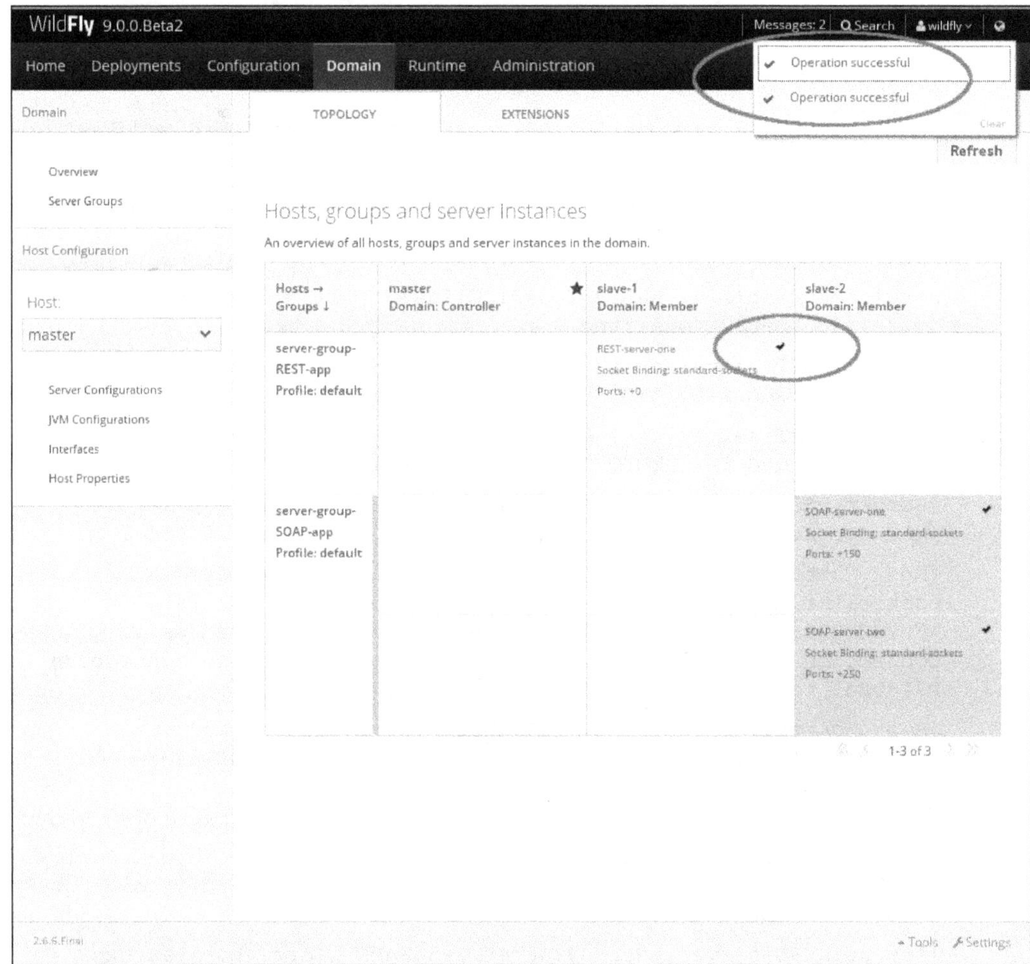


Start Sever Group

10. The entries in the log of `slave-1` are as follows:

```
[Host Controller] 09:08:46,327 INFO  [org.jboss.as.host.
controller] (Host Controller Service Threads - 13) WFLYHC0023:
Starting server REST-server-one

09:08:46,404 INFO  [org.jboss.as.process.Server:REST-server-one.
status] (ProcessController-threads - 5) WFLYPC0018: Starting
process 'Server:REST-server-one'

[Server:REST-server-one] 09:08:46,859 INFO  [org.jboss.modules]
(main) JBoss Modules version 1.4.2.Final

[Server:REST-server-one] 09:08:47,135 INFO  [org.jboss.msc] (main)
JBoss MSC version 1.2.4.Final

[Server:REST-server-one] 09:08:47,243 INFO  [org.jboss.as] (MSC
service thread 1-8) WFLYSRV0049: WildFly Full 9.0.0.Beta2 (WildFly
Core 1.0.0.Beta2) starting

[Server:REST-server-one] 09:08:47,347 INFO  [org.xnio] (MSC
service thread 1-4) XNIO version 3.3.0.Final

[Server:REST-server-one] 09:08:47,356 INFO  [org.xnio.nio] (MSC
service thread 1-4) XNIO NIO Implementation Version 3.3.0.Final

[Server:REST-server-one] 09:08:47,383 INFO  [org.jboss.remoting]
(MSC service thread 1-4) JBoss Remoting version 4.0.8.Final

[Host Controller] 09:08:48,065 INFO  [org.jboss.as.domain.
controller.mgmt] (Remoting "slave-1:MANAGEMENT" task-13)
WFLYHC0021: Server [Server:REST-server-one] connected using
connection [Channel ID 312ade53 (inbound) of Remoting connection
277898d9 to /127.0.0.1:34603]

[Host Controller] 09:08:48,103 INFO  [org.jboss.as.host.
controller] (server-registration-threads - 1) WFLYHC0020:
Registering server REST-server-one

[Server:REST-server-one] 09:08:48,749 INFO  [org.jboss.
as.controller.management-deprecated] (ServerService Thread Pool --
28) WFLYCTL0028: Attribute enabled is deprecated, and it might be
removed in future version!

[Server:REST-server-one] 09:08:48,845 WARN  [org.jboss.as.txn]
(ServerService Thread Pool -- 33) WFLYTX0013: Node identifier
property is set to the default value. Please make sure it is
unique.

[Server:REST-server-one] 09:08:48,845 INFO  [org.jboss.
as.security] (ServerService Thread Pool -- 35) WFLYSEC0002:
Activating Security Subsystem

[Server:REST-server-one] 09:08:48,846 INFO  [org.jboss.
as.webservices] (ServerService Thread Pool -- 19) WFLYWS0002:
Activating WebServices Extension
```

```
[Server:REST-server-one] 09:08:48,850 INFO  [org.jboss.
as.security] (MSC service thread 1-15) WFLYSEC0001: Current
PicketBox version=4.9.0.Beta2

[Server:REST-server-one] 09:08:49,427 INFO  [org.jboss.
as.clustering.infinispan] (ServerService Thread Pool -- 49)
WFLYCLINF0001: Activating Infinispan subsystem.

[Server:REST-server-one] 09:08:49,434 INFO  [org.jboss.as.naming]
(ServerService Thread Pool -- 41) WFLYNAM0001: Activating Naming
Subsystem

[Server:REST-server-one] 09:08:49,443 INFO  [org.jboss.
as.connector] (MSC service thread 1-13) WFLYJCA0009: Starting JCA
Subsystem (IronJacamar 1.2.3.Final)

[Server:REST-server-one] 09:08:49,464 INFO  [org.jboss.as.jsf]
(ServerService Thread Pool -- 43) WFLYJSF0007: Activated the
following JSF Implementations: [main]

[Server:REST-server-one] 09:08:49,498 INFO  [org.wildfly.
extension.io] (ServerService Thread Pool -- 50) WFLYIO001: Worker
'default' has auto-configured to 16 core threads with 128 task
threads based on your 8 available processors

[Server:REST-server-one] 09:08:49,537 INFO  [org.wildfly.
extension.undertow] (ServerService Thread Pool -- 32) WFLYUT0003:
Undertow 1.2.0.Beta10 starting

[Server:REST-server-one] 09:08:49,537 INFO  [org.wildfly.
extension.undertow] (MSC service thread 1-14) WFLYUT0003: Undertow
1.2.0.Beta10 starting

[Server:REST-server-one] 09:08:49,550 INFO  [org.jboss.
as.connector.subsystems.datasources] (ServerService Thread Pool
-- 53) WFLYJCA0004: Deploying JDBC-compliant driver class org.
h2.Driver (version 1.3)

[Server:REST-server-one] 09:08:49,566 INFO  [org.jboss.
as.connector.deployers.jdbc] (MSC service thread 1-8) WFLYJCA0018:
Started Driver service with driver-name = h2

[Server:REST-server-one] 09:08:49,686 INFO  [org.jboss.as.naming]
(MSC service thread 1-15) WFLYNAM0003: Starting Naming Service

[Server:REST-server-one] 09:08:49,698 INFO  [org.jboss.as.mail.
extension] (MSC service thread 1-7) WFLYMAIL0001: Bound mail
session [java:jboss/mail/Default]

[Server:REST-server-one] 09:08:49,777 INFO  [org.wildfly.
extension.undertow] (ServerService Thread Pool -- 32) WFLYUT0014:
Creating file handler for path /home/wildfly/WFC/wildfly/welcome-
content

[Server:REST-server-one] 09:08:49,916 INFO  [org.wildfly.
extension.undertow] (MSC service thread 1-3) WFLYUT0012: Started
server default-server.
```

```
[Server:REST-server-one] 09:08:49,933 INFO  [org.wildfly.
extension.undertow] (MSC service thread 1-3) WFLYUT0018: Host
default-host starting

[Server:REST-server-one] 09:08:50,029 INFO  [org.wildfly.
extension.undertow] (MSC service thread 1-4) WFLYUT0006: Undertow
HTTP listener default listening on /127.0.0.1:8080

[Server:REST-server-one] 09:08:50,170 INFO  [org.jboss.
as.connector.subsystems.datasources] (MSC service thread 1-16)
WFLYJCA0001: Bound data source [java:jboss/datasources/ExampleDS]

[Server:REST-server-one] 09:08:50,440 INFO  [org.jboss.ws.common.
management] (MSC service thread 1-10) JBWS022052: Starting JBoss
Web Services - Stack CXF Server 5.0.0.Beta3

[Server:REST-server-one] 09:08:50,733 INFO  [org.jboss.as]
(Controller Boot Thread) WFLYSRV0025: WildFly Full 9.0.0.Beta2
(WildFly Core 1.0.0.Beta2) started in 4228ms - Started 193 of 370
services (207 services are lazy, passive or on-demand)
```

## There's more...

The same operations apply while stopping and starting a single server instance.

In the `host.xml` file you can define the `auto-start` attribute, the default value of which is `true`. Setting it to `false` will not start the server, and you will have to start it manually via the Admin Console or via CLI.

```
<server name="REST-server-one" group="server-group-REST-app" auto-
start="true">
    <jvm name="default">
    <heap size="64m" max-size="256m"/>
</jvm>
</server>
```

In this regard, let's try the CLI which is more fascinating!

# Stopping and starting your server groups via the CLI

In this recipe, we will learn how to stop and start an entire server group using the CLI. Since a server can belong to more than one server group, you might want to stop or start all the servers at once, and thus stop or start the server group.

## Getting ready

For this recipe, both the domain controller and host controllers should be up and running. For their configuration, refer to the recipe *Connecting the host controller to the domain controller* in this chapter.

## How to do it...

1. Open your terminal and do as follows:

```
[luigi@foogaro wildfly]$ ./bin/jboss-cli.sh --connect
[domain@localhost:9990 /] ls
core-service                        local-host-name=master
deployment                          management-major-version=3
deployment-overlay                  management-micro-version=0
extension                           management-minor-version=0
host                                name=Unnamed Domain
interface                           namespaces=[]
management-client-content           process-type=Domain Controller
path                                product-name=WildFly Full
profile                             product-version=9.0.0.Beta2
server-group                        release-codename=Kenny
socket-binding-group                release-version=1.0.0.Beta2
system-property                     schema-locations=[]
launch-type=DOMAIN
[domain@localhost:9990 /]
```

2. With the command `ls`, you can list the entire context that you walk through. What we want to do is to "stop" the entire server group named `server-group-REST-app`:

```
[domain@localhost:9990 /] /server-group=server-group-REST-app:stop-servers()
{
    "outcome" => "success",
    "result" => undefined,
    "server-groups" => undefined
}
[domain@localhost:9990 /]
```

3. Now let's start the server-group again, by invoking the `start-servers` method:

```
[domain@localhost:9990 /] /server-group=server-group-REST-
app:start-servers()
{
    "outcome" => "success",
    "result" => undefined,
    "server-groups" => undefined
}
[domain@localhost:9990 /]
```

## How it works...

In the CLI, you have basically remapped the entire configuration, hence, if you look at the `domain.xml` or `host.xml` files, you find pretty much the same hierarchy.

In our recipe we wanted to stop a server group, so if you look at the `domain.xml` you can determine the contexts and commands - you can see the available commands by hitting the *Tab* key next to `:` or `/`.

# Stopping and starting your servers via the CLI

In this recipe, we will learn how to stop and start a single server that belongs to a server group using the CLI. Because servers that belong to a server group might be spread over a series of different machines, with different resources available, you might need to stop a single server, without stopping the entire server group to add more resources and start it up back again. Fortunately, WildFly provides such granularity with regards to stop servers.

## Getting ready

For this recipe, both the domain controller and host controllers should be up and running. For their configuration, refer to the recipe *Connecting the host controller to the domain controller* in this chapter.

## How to do it...

1. Open your terminal and do as follows:

```
$ ./bin/jboss-cli.sh --connect

[domain@localhost:9990 /]
```

2. What we want to do is to "stop" the server named `REST-server-one`, which belongs to the `Host Controller` named `slave-1`. This is done as follows:

```
[domain@localhost:9990 /] /host=slave-1/server-config=REST-server-one:stop()
{
    "outcome" => "success",
    "result" => "STOPPING"
}
[domain@localhost:9990 /]
```

As you can see, the server is in the `STOPPING` state; this means it may take a while depending on how many resources you have bound and/or deployed.

3. To check if it is done, try the following command:

```
[domain@localhost:9990 /] /host=slave-1/server-config=REST-server-one:read-resource(include-runtime=true)
{
    "outcome" => "success",
    "result" => {
        "auto-start" => true,
        "cpu-affinity" => undefined,
        "group" => "server-group-REST-app",
        "name" => "REST-server-one",
        "priority" => undefined,
        "socket-binding-group" => undefined,
        "socket-binding-port-offset" => 0,
        "status" => "STOPPED",
        "interface" => undefined,
        "jvm" => {"default" => undefined},
        "path" => undefined,
        "system-property" => undefined
    }
}
[domain@localhost:9990 /]
```

4. Now let's start the server again by invoking the `start` method:

```
[domain@localhost:9990 /] /host=slave-1/server-config=REST-server-one:start()
{
    "outcome" => "success",
    "result" => "STARTING"
}
[domain@localhost:9990 /]
```

## How it works...

The `stop` command itself is pretty easy, and does not need much explanation. What is worth mentioning is that to be able to stop a server, you first need to know which host/slave it belongs to. What you can do is navigate through WildFly's structure, as follows:

```
[domain@localhost:9990 /] ls host=
master   slave-1  slave-2
[domain@localhost:9990 /] ls host=slave-1/server
REST-server-one
[domain@localhost:9990 /] ls host=slave-2/server
SOAP-server-one  SOAP-server-two
[domain@localhost:9990 /]
```

Once you have located the server you want/need to stop, you can issue the `stop` command.

## There's more...

When dealing with the `stop` and `start` commands, on both `server-group` and `server`, you can add the `blocking=true` option which basically hangs the commands until it's done. The command would be as follows:

```
[domain@localhost:9990 /] /host=slave-1/server-config=REST-server-one:start(blocking=true)
```

In this way we know when the server completes the operation. Imagine a case where you are executing multiple CLI commands in sequence, and a command needs the previous operations to be carried out. Without the blocking flag enabled, the command will not work.

# Deploying and undeploying an application to a specific server group via Web Console

In this recipe, we will learn how to deploy and undeploy an application via the Web Console, and assign it to a server group.

## Getting ready

For this recipe, both the domain controller and the host controllers should be up and running. For their configuration, refer to the recipe *Connecting the host controller to the domain controller* in this chapter.

In this and the following recipe, we will need an application to test our configuration. For this recipe, we will need the application named `example` which you can find in my GitHub repository. If you skipped the "*Managing applications using the deployments folder* recipe in *Chapter 2, Running WildFly in Standalone Mode*, please refer to it to download all the source code and projects that you will need.

To build the application, type as follows:

```
$ cd $WILDFLY_HOME/github/wildfly-cookbook
$ cd example
$ mvn -e clean package
```

## How to do it...

1. Open your browser and point it to the Admin Console: `http://localhost:9990`.
2. Enter the username and password (`wildfly` and `cookbook.2015` respectively) and go to **Deployments**. You should get a page similar to the following screenshot:

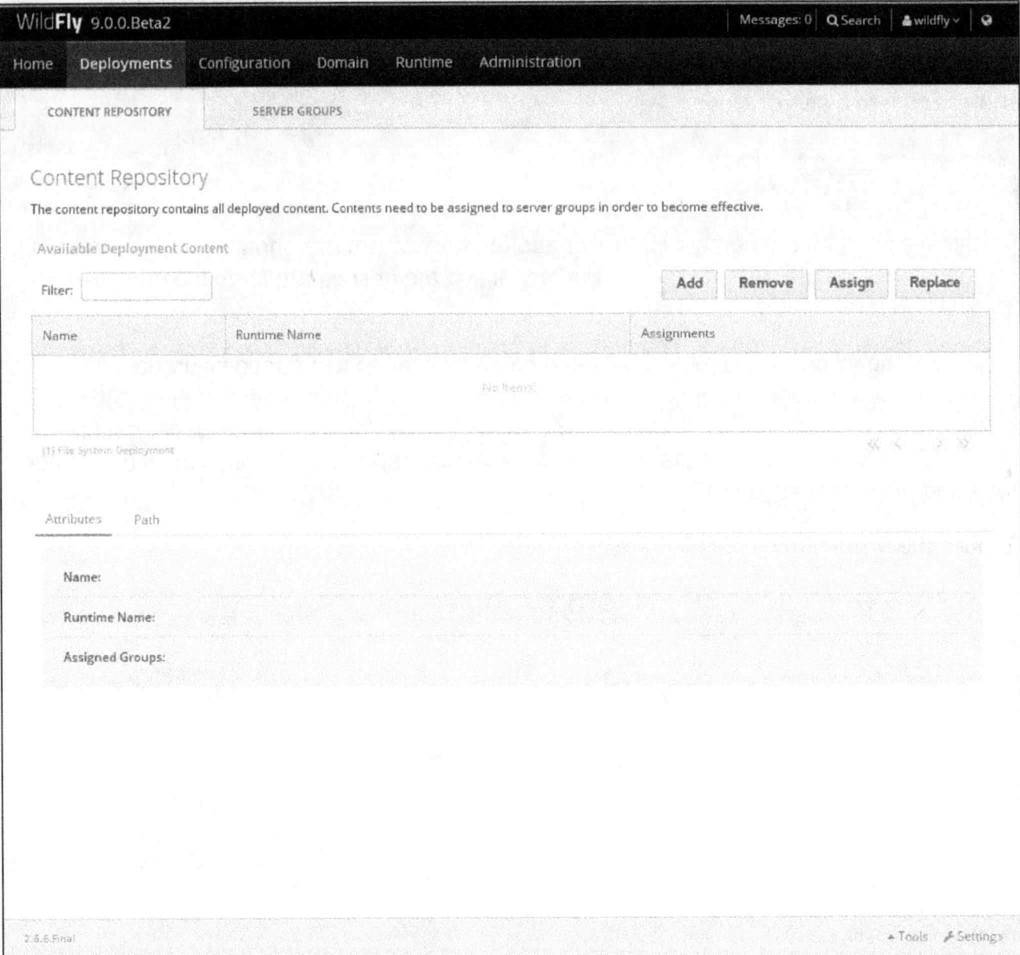


The manage deployments window

3. Now to deploy an application, we first need to add it by clicking the **Add** button and choosing your artifact, as shown in the following image:

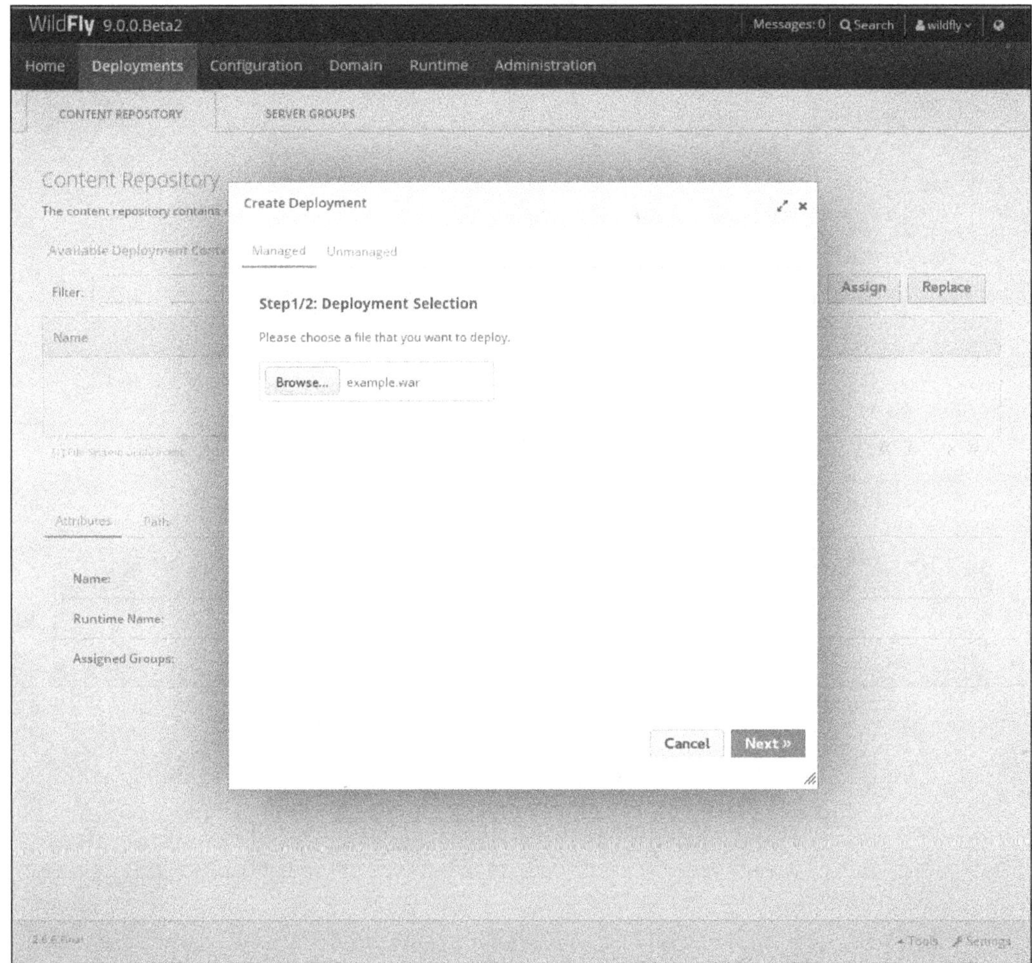


Deploying the example.war application

4. Now just follow the wizard instructions. You should end up with your artifact deployed, but not assigned to a **SERVER GROUPS**, as shown in the following screenshot:

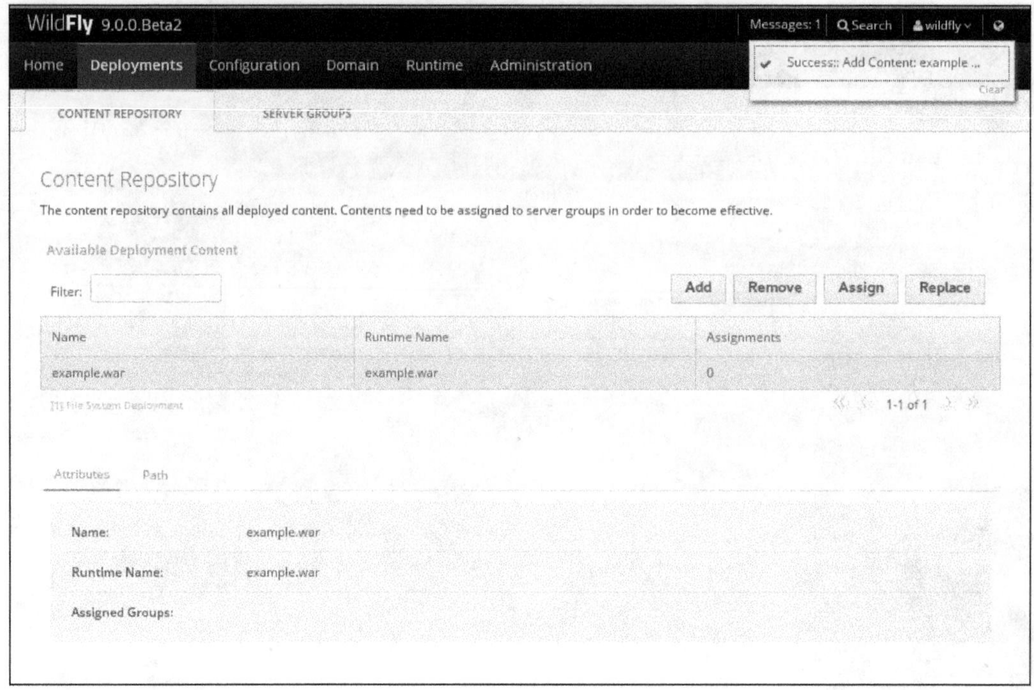


Application deployed but not assigned to any server-group

Within the domain controller's log you should see a log like the following:

```
[Host Controller] 17:02:19,737 INFO  [org.jboss.as.repository]
(XNIO-1 task-1) WFLYDR0001: Content added at location /home/luigi/
WFC/wildfly/master/data/content/21/7dd6250d5bc4afcabdffb0b25c99db9
2239b5a/content
```

5. But you don't see any logs at the `Host Controller` log side. This is because we haven't assigned the application to any server group yet. To assign the application to a server group, just hit the **Assign** button and choose the server group, as shown in the following screenshot:

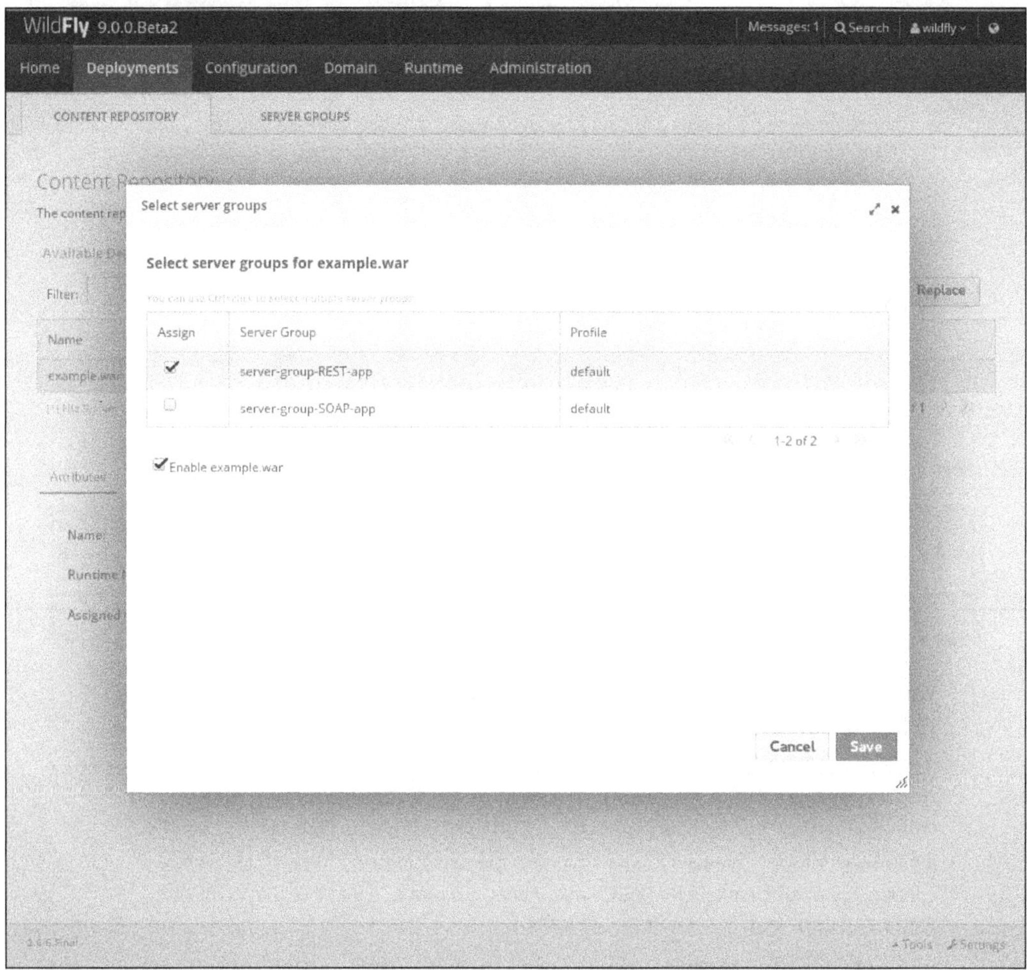


Assigning a deployment to a server-group

6. Save it and the domain controller should spread the deployment to the servers that belong to the selected server group, as shown in the following screenshot:

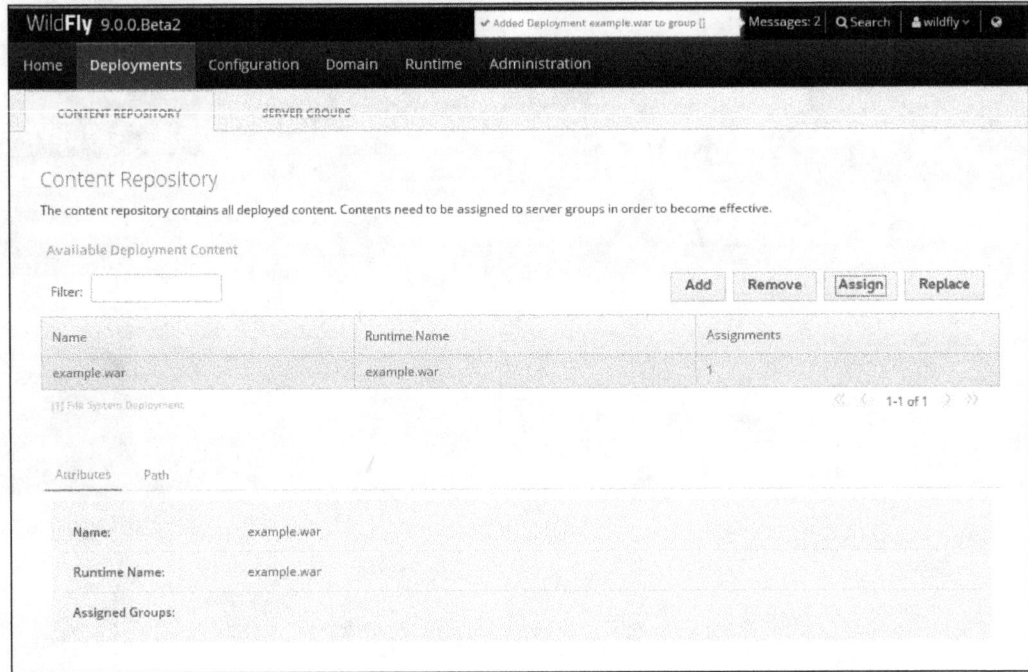


Deployment assigned to a server-group

You can check it from the host controller's log, by looking for entries similar to the following:

```
[Server:REST-server-one] 17:09:13,813 INFO  [org.jboss.as.server.
deployment] (MSC service thread 1-2) WFLYSRV0027: Starting
deployment of "example.war" (runtime-name: "example.war")

[Server:REST-server-one] 17:09:14,406 INFO  [org.wildfly.
extension.undertow] (MSC service thread 1-1) WFLYUT0021:
Registered web context: /example

[Server:REST-server-one] 17:09:14,478 INFO  [org.jboss.as.server]
(ServerService Thread Pool -- 59) WFLYSRV0010: Deployed "example.
war" (runtime-name : "example.war")
```

No more entries will be found on the domain controller side.

7. If you need to check which deployments belong to what server group, go to the **Deployments** tab, select the **Server Groups** tab and click the appropriate **View** command link, as shown in the next screenshot:

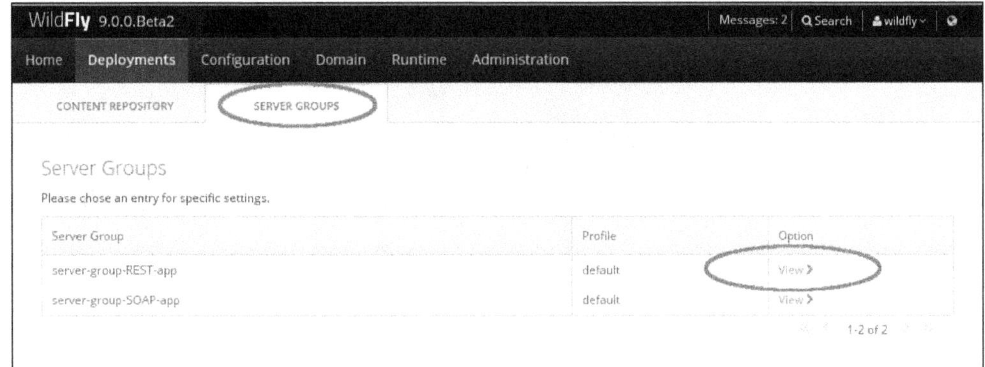


Selecting a server-group

8. You should see all the successful deployments, as shown in the following screenshot:

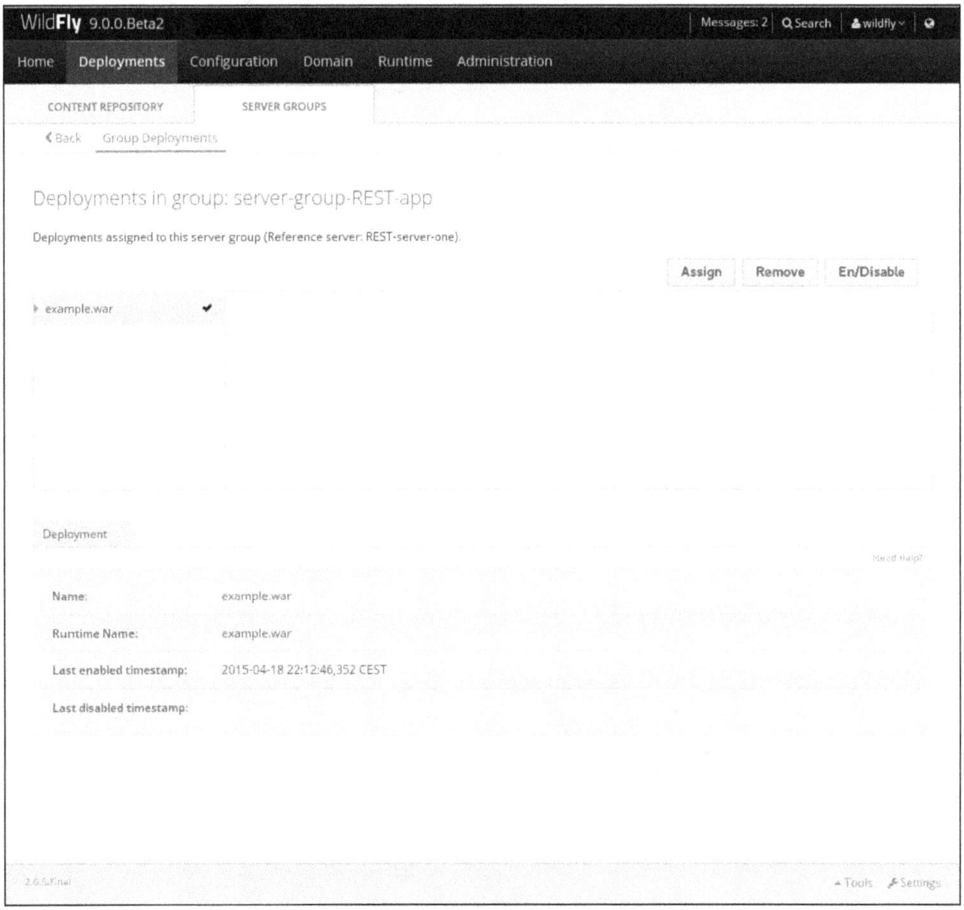

Deployments for a specific server-group

9. Okay, now it's time to undeploy our application. As the Web Console suggests, from the **Deployments** overview you can remove it ( undeploy it in GUI terms) by selecting the artifact and clicking the **Remove** button, as shown in the next screenshot:

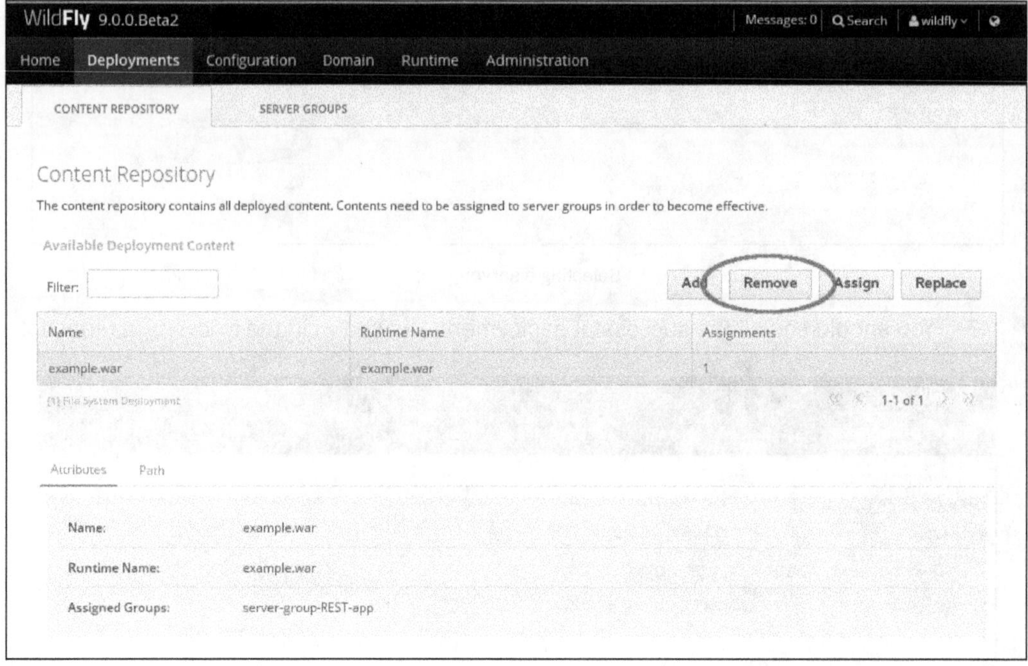


Undeploying the artifact

10. Confirm your operation as follows:

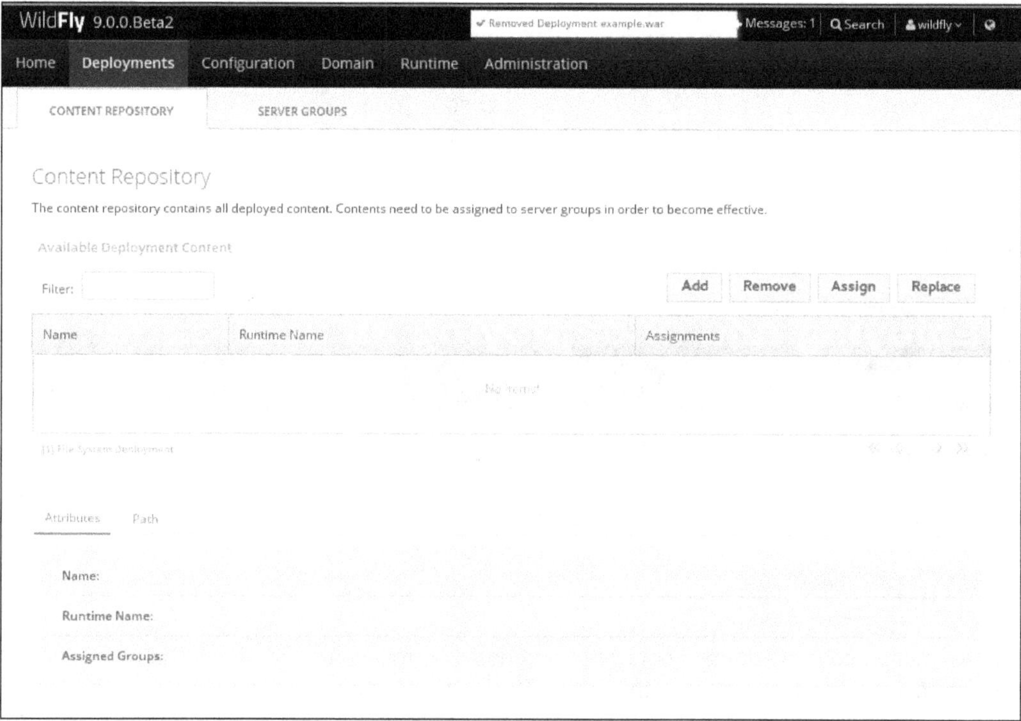


Artifact undeployed

Now looking at the logs, you should find the following entries (first the `Domain Controller` log followed by the `Host Controller` log):

```
[Server:REST-server-one] 22:17:05,544 INFO  [org.wildfly.
extension.undertow] (MSC service thread 1-2) WFLYUT0022:
Unregistered web context: /example

[Server:REST-server-one] 22:17:05,573 INFO  [org.hibernate.
validator.internal.util.Version] (MSC service thread 1-4)
HV000001: Hibernate Validator 5.1.3.Final

[Server:REST-server-one] 22:17:05,612 INFO  [org.jboss.as.server.
deployment] (MSC service thread 1-4) WFLYSRV0028: Stopped
deployment example.war (runtime-name: example.war) in 72ms

[Server:REST-server-one] 22:17:05,659 INFO  [org.jboss.as.server]
(ServerService Thread Pool -- 70) WFLYSRV0009: Undeployed
"example.war" (runtime-name: "example.war")
```

```
[Server:REST-server-one] 22:17:05,663 INFO  [org.
jboss.as.repository] (ServerService Thread Pool -- 70)
WFLYDR0002: Content removed from location /home/luigi/
WFC/wildfl/domain/servers/REST-server-one/data/content/8d/
b8b9b1cda547c7ec3fb493dbd5940cdb378ec0/content
[Host Controller] 22:17:05,666 INFO  [org.jboss.
as.repository] (XNIO-1 task-8) WFLYDR0002: Content removed
from location /home/luigi/WFC/wildfly/domain/data/content/8d/
b8b9b1cda547c7ec3fb493dbd5940cdb378ec0/content
```

Now let's recap all these things and more in the next recipe using the CLI.

# Deploying and undeploying an application to a specific server group via the CLI

In this recipe, we will learn how to deploy and undeploy an application using the CLI, and assign it to a specific server group. This recipe follows pretty much the same operation as executed in the previous recipe, but is specific to the CLI.

## Getting ready

For this recipe, both the domain controller and host controllers should be up and running. For their configuration, please refer to the recipe *Connecting the host controller to the domain controller* in this chapter.

In this and the following recipe, we will need an application to test our configuration. For this recipe, we require the application named `example` which you can find in my GitHub repository. If you skipped the *Managing applications using the deployments folder* recipe in *Chapter 2, Running WildFly in Standalone Mode*, please refer to it in order download all the source code and projects that you will need.

To build the application, type as follows:

```
$ cd $WILDFLY_HOME/github/wildfly-cookbook
$ cd example
$ mvn -e clean package
```

Once you build the application, copy it into the `$WILDFLY_HOME` folder for convenience.

## How to do it...

1. Open your terminal and connect to the DC as usual:

   ```
   $ ./bin/jboss-cli.sh --connect
   ```

2. Now just hit *Tab* to see the available commands:

```
[domain@localhost:9990 /]
alias                  deployment-info        ls                  shutdown
batch                  deployment-overlay     patch               try
cd                     echo                   pwd                 undeploy
clear                  echo-dmr               quit                unset
command                help                   read-attribute      version
connect                history                read-operation      xa-data-source
connection-factory     if                     reload              :
connection-info        jdbc-driver-info       rollout-plan
data-source            jms-queue              run-batch
deploy                 jms-topic              set
[domain@localhost:9990 /]
```

3. There is a `deploy` command available, and it is the one we need. Let's deploy our artifact to both server groups, `server-group-REST-app` and `server-group-SOAP-app`.

   ```
   [domain@localhost:9990 /] deploy example.war --server-groups=server-group-SOAP-app,server-group-REST-app
   [domain@localhost:9990 /]
   ```

Keep in mind that the application's path is relative to the path used to access the CLI. So in case you are in your user home, the path to specify to the `deploy` command would have been `WFC/github/wildfly-cookbook/example/target/example.war`.

4. Let's check what happened to each server group singularly:

   ```
   [domain@localhost:9990 /] deployment-info --server-group=server-group-REST-app
   NAME         RUNTIME-NAME STATE
   example.war  example.war  enabled
   [domain@localhost:9990 /] deployment-info --server-group=server-group-SOAP-app
   NAME         RUNTIME-NAME STATE
   example.war  example.war  enabled
   [domain@localhost:9990 /]
   ```

- If you don't trust the CLI, check what happened to the various logs:

  The `master` log is as follows:

  ```
  [Host Controller] 22:56:08,289 INFO  [org.jboss.
  as.repository] (management-handler-thread - 2) WFLYDR0001:
  Content added at location /home/luigi/WFC/wildfly/master/
  data/content/21/7dd6250d5bc4afcabdffb0b25c99db92239b5a/
  content
  ```

  The `Slave-1` log is as follows:

  ```
  [Server:REST-server-one] 22:56:08,557 INFO  [org.jboss.
  as.server.deployment] (MSC service thread 1-7) WFLYSRV0027:
  Starting deployment of "example.war" (runtime-name:
  "example.war")

  [Server:REST-server-one] 22:56:08,779 INFO  [org.wildfly.
  extension.undertow] (MSC service thread 1-2) WFLYUT0021:
  Registered web context: /example

  [Server:REST-server-one] 22:56:10,121 INFO  [org.jboss.
  as.server] (ServerService Thread Pool -- 65) WFLYSRV0010:
  Deployed "example.war" (runtime-name : "example.war")
  ```

  The `Slave-2` log is as follows:

  ```
  [Server:SOAP-server-one] 22:56:08,725 INFO  [org.jboss.
  as.server.deployment] (MSC service thread 1-6) WFLYSRV0027:
  Starting deployment of "example.war" (runtime-name:
  "example.war")

  [Server:SOAP-server-two] 22:56:08,741 INFO  [org.jboss.
  as.server.deployment] (MSC service thread 1-3) WFLYSRV0027:
  Starting deployment of "example.war" (runtime-name:
  "example.war")

  [Server:SOAP-server-one] 22:56:09,906 INFO  [org.wildfly.
  extension.undertow] (MSC service thread 1-3) WFLYUT0021:
  Registered web context: /example

  [Server:SOAP-server-two] 22:56:10,004 INFO  [org.wildfly.
  extension.undertow] (MSC service thread 1-7) WFLYUT0021:
  Registered web context: /example

  [Server:SOAP-server-one] 22:56:10,121 INFO  [org.jboss.
  as.server] (ServerService Thread Pool -- 59) WFLYSRV0010:
  Deployed "example.war" (runtime-name : "example.war")

  [Server:SOAP-server-two] 22:56:10,134 INFO  [org.jboss.
  as.server] (ServerService Thread Pool -- 59) WFLYSRV0010:
  Deployed "example.war" (runtime-name : "example.war")
  ```

  As you can see from the logs, our artifact has been deployed to all the declared server groups. `Slave-2` has two running instances, each one with its own copy of the artifact.

5. Now to undeploy the artifact; it's as easy as pie:

```
[domain@localhost:9990 /] undeploy example.war -server-
groups=server-group-REST-app,server-group-SOAP-app
```

   - Let's check via CLI if we have effectively undeployed our artifact:

```
[domain@localhost:9990 /] deployment-info --server-
group=server-group-REST-app
[domain@localhost:9990 /] deployment-info --server-
group=server-group-SOAP-app
[domain@localhost:9990 /]
```

Again, check the logs to see what happened:

- The `master` log is as follows:

```
[Host Controller] 22:59:35,225 INFO  [org.jboss.
as.repository] (management-handler-thread - 9) WFLYDR0002:
Content removed from location /home/luigi/WFC/wildfly/
master/data/content/21/7dd6250d5bc4afcabdffb0b25c99db92239b
5a/content
```

- The `slave-1` log is as follows:

```
[Server:REST-server-one] 22:59:35,005 INFO  [org.wildfly.
extension.undertow] (MSC service thread 1-7) WFLYUT0022:
Unregistered web context: /example
[Server:REST-server-one] 22:59:35,044 INFO  [org.jboss.
as.server.deployment] (MSC service thread 1-8) WFLYSRV0028:
Stopped deployment example.war (runtime-name: example.war)
in 40ms
[Server:REST-server-one] 22:59:35,201 INFO  [org.jboss.
as.repository] (ServerService Thread Pool -- 69) WFLYDR0002:
Content removed from location /home/luigi/WFC/wildfly/
slave-1/servers/REST-server-one/data/content/21/7dd6250d5bc4
afcabdffb0b25c99db92239b5a/content
[Server:REST-server-one] 22:59:35,201 INFO  [org.jboss.
as.server] (ServerService Thread Pool -- 69) WFLYSRV0009:
Undeployed "example.war" (runtime-name: "example.war")
[Host Controller] 22:59:35,221 INFO  [org.jboss.
as.repository] (Host Controller Service Threads - 14)
WFLYDR0002: Content removed from location /home/luigi/WFC/
wildfly/slave-1/data/content/21/7dd6250d5bc4afcabdffb0b25c99
db92239b5a/content
[Host Controller] 22:59:42,048 INFO  [org.jboss.
as.repository] (Host Controller Service Threads - 4)
WFLYDR0009: Content /home/luigi/WFC/wildfly/slave-1/data/
content/8d/b8b9b1cda547c7ec3fb493dbd5940cdb378ec0 is
obsolete and will be removed
```

```
[Host Controller] 22:59:42,050 INFO  [org.jboss.
as.repository] (Host Controller Service Threads
- 4) WFLYDR0002: Content removed from location /
home/luigi/WFC/wildfly/slave-1/data/content/8d/
b8b9b1cda547c7ec3fb493dbd5940cdb378ec0/content
[Server:REST-server-one] 22:59:46,550 INFO  [org.jboss.
as.repository] (ServerService Thread Pool -- 59) WFLYDR0009:
Content /home/luigi/WFC/wildfly/slave-1/servers/REST-server-
one/data/content/8d/b8b9b1cda547c7ec3fb493dbd5940cdb378ec0
is obsolete and will be removed
[Server:REST-server-one] 22:59:46,552 INFO  [org.
jboss.as.repository] (ServerService Thread Pool -- 59)
WFLYDR0002: Content removed from location /home/luigi/WFC/
wildfly/slave-1/servers/REST-server-one/data/content/8d/
b8b9b1cda547c7ec3fb493dbd5940cdb378ec0/content
```

- The `Slave-2` log is as follows:

```
[Server:SOAP-server-two] 22:59:35,004 INFO  [org.wildfly.
extension.undertow] (MSC service thread 1-3) WFLYUT0022:
Unregistered web context: /example
[Server:SOAP-server-one] 22:59:35,017 INFO  [org.wildfly.
extension.undertow] (MSC service thread 1-2) WFLYUT0022:
Unregistered web context: /example
[Server:SOAP-server-two] 22:59:35,072 INFO  [org.hibernate.
validator.internal.util.Version] (MSC service thread 1-3)
HV000001: Hibernate Validator 5.1.3.Final
[Server:SOAP-server-one] 22:59:35,093 INFO  [org.hibernate.
validator.internal.util.Version] (MSC service thread 1-5)
HV000001: Hibernate Validator 5.1.3.Final
[Server:SOAP-server-two] 22:59:35,127 INFO  [org.jboss.
as.server.deployment] (MSC service thread 1-6) WFLYSRV0028:
Stopped deployment example.war (runtime-name: example.war)
in 127ms
[Server:SOAP-server-one] 22:59:35,141 INFO  [org.jboss.
as.server.deployment] (MSC service thread 1-8) WFLYSRV0028:
Stopped deployment example.war (runtime-name: example.war)
in 128ms
[Server:SOAP-server-two] 22:59:35,203 INFO  [org.jboss.
as.repository] (ServerService Thread Pool -- 64) WFLYDR0002:
Content removed from location /home/luigi/WFC/wildfly/
slave-2/servers/SOAP-server-two/data/content/21/7dd6250d5bc4
afcabdffb0b25c99db92239b5a/content
[Server:SOAP-server-two] 22:59:35,204 INFO  [org.jboss.
as.server] (ServerService Thread Pool -- 64) WFLYSRV0009:
Undeployed "example.war" (runtime-name: "example.war")
```

```
[Server:SOAP-server-one] 22:59:35,209 INFO  [org.jboss.
as.repository] (ServerService Thread Pool -- 63) WFLYDR0002:
Content removed from location /home/luigi/WFC/wildfly/
slave-2/servers/SOAP-server-one/data/content/21/7dd6250d5bc4
afcabdffb0b25c99db92239b5a/content

[Server:SOAP-server-one] 22:59:35,212 INFO  [org.jboss.
as.server] (ServerService Thread Pool -- 63) WFLYSRV0009:
Undeployed "example.war" (runtime-name: "example.war")

[Host Controller] 22:59:35,219 INFO  [org.jboss.
as.repository] (Host Controller Service Threads - 15)
WFLYDR0002: Content removed from location /home/luigi/WFC/
wildfly/slave-2/data/content/21/7dd6250d5bc4afcabdffb0b25c99
db92239b5a/content

[Host Controller] 22:59:49,597 INFO  [org.jboss.
as.repository] (Host Controller Service Threads - 7)
WFLYDR0009: Content /home/luigi/WFC/wildfly/slave-2/data/
content/8d/b8b9b1cda547c7ec3fb493dbd5940cdb378ec0 is
obsolete and will be removed

[Host Controller] 22:59:49,598 INFO  [org.jboss.
as.repository] (Host Controller Service Threads
- 7) WFLYDR0002: Content removed from location /
home/luigi/WFC/wildfly/slave-2/data/content/8d/
b8b9b1cda547c7ec3fb493dbd5940cdb378ec0/content
```

### There's more...

Actually, you can deploy the artifact to all the server groups with the following directive:

```
[domain@localhost:9990 /] deploy example.war --all-server-groups
```

There is a shortcut for undeploying too:

```
[domain@localhost:9990 /] undeploy example.war --all-relevant-server-
groups
```

It basically undeploys the artifact from all the server groups that it is assigned to.

## Checking server status via the CLI

In this recipe, we will learn how to check the status of the server using the CLI. Using the standalone, there is no need for such a check, because you wouldn't be able to connect to the CLI at all. Thus, in the domain mode, you might need to know if a certain server is up or not before doing some operations.

## Getting ready

For this recipe, both the domain controller and host controllers should be up and running. For their configuration, please refer to the recipe *Connecting the host controller to the domain controller* in this chapter.

## How to do it...

Open your terminal and connect to the domain controller as usual:

```
$ ./bin/jboss-cli.sh --connect

[domain@localhost:9990 /] /host=slave-1/server-config=REST-server-one:read-resource(include-runtime=true)
{
    "outcome" => "success",
    "result" => {
        "auto-start" => true,
        "cpu-affinity" => undefined,
        "group" => "server-group-REST-app",
        "name" => "REST-server-one",
        "priority" => undefined,
        "socket-binding-group" => undefined,
        "socket-binding-port-offset" => 0,
        "status" => "STARTED",
        "interface" => undefined,
        "jvm" => {"default" => undefined},
        "path" => undefined,
        "system-property" => undefined
    }
}
[domain@localhost:9990 /]
```

# 4

# Managing the Logging Subsystem with the CLI

In this chapter, you will cover the following topics:

- Creating a file-handler logging
- Creating a periodic-rotating file-handler
- Creating a size-rotating file-handler
- Defining asynchronous handlers
- Creating a syslog-handler
- Listing and reading log files
- Using a different logging implementation

## Introduction

The logging subsystem is where you can configure the information statements of WildFly and your application, for debugging and auditing purposes.

WildFly comes with a default configuration, which can be found in the `configuration` folder of both the standalone and domain directories. The default configuration automatically logs the information on the console and on a file named `server.log`.

As you will learn in this chapter, WildFly has seven different handlers to help you persist with your application logs:

- **Console**: Writes application logs to the standard output
- **File**: Writes application logs to a file

- **Periodic**: Writes application logs to a file by rotating it on the basis of time
- **Size**: Writes application logs to a file by rotating it on the basis of size
- **Async**: Wraps one or more handler to give asynchronous behavior
- **Custom**: Lets you use your own handler, as long as it extends the `java.util.logging.Handler` class
- **Syslog**: Writes application logs to the default OS logger

Depending on the operation mode of your WildFly, you have different settings concerning the default log file paths.

## Domain mode

In a managed domain, we have two types of log files: Controller and server logs.

Starting with the default configuration of `domain.xml`, both the domain controller components and the servers are located on the same host:

| **Process** | **Log File** |
|---|---|
| `[Host Controller]` | `jboss.domain.log.dir/host-controller.log` |
| `[Process Controller]` | `jboss.domain.log.dir/process-controller.log` |
| `[Server One]` | `jboss.domain.servers.dir/server-one/log/server.log` |
| `[Server Two]` | `jboss.domain.servers.dir/server-two/log/server.log` |
| `[Server Three]` | `jboss.domain.servers.dir/server-three/log/server.log` |

If you want to change one of the previously mentioned properties, you can set a different value, as follows:

```
$ ./bin/domain.sh -Djboss.domain.log.dir=/home/luigi/wildfly-domain-logs
```

## Standalone mode

The default log files for a standalone server is in the log subdirectory of the `jboss.server.base.dir` folder of the WildFly home:

| **Process** | **Log File** |
|---|---|
| `[Server]` | `jboss.server.log.dir/server.log` |

If you want to change the previously mentioned property, you can set a different value, as follows:

```
$ ./bin/standalone.sh -Djboss.server.log.dir=/home/luigi/wildfly-
standalone-logs
```

# Creating a file-handler logging

The logging subsystem is where you configure the output information statements of your application and/or WildFly cores, for debugging or auditing purposes. In this recipe, we will learn how to target the log statement output of your application to a file-handler.

For the sake of simplicity, we will try our recipe with WildFly running in the standalone mode.

## Getting ready

First of all, let's create a standalone configuration for our recipe, as follows:

```
$ cd $WILDFLY_HOME
$ cp -a standalone std-logging
```

To test our logging configuration, we will need an application to log some statements. In this case, we will use the application named `logging`. To obtain the artifact to deploy, please refer to the *Software prerequisites* recipe in *Chapter 1*, *Welcome to WildFly!*.

Now, let's start WildFly, as follows:

```
$ cd $WILDFLY_HOME
$ ./bin/standalone.sh -Djboss.server.base.dir=$WILDFLY_HOME/std-logging
```

## How to do it…

1. With a running WildFly server, open your command-line tool and connect to the CLI:

   ```
   $ ./bin/jboss-cli.sh --connect

   [standalone@localhost:9990 /]
   ```

2. Now execute the following commands:

   ```
   [standalone@localhost:9990 /] /subsystem=logging/file-
   handler=wildflycookbook-fh:add(level=INFO, file={"relative-
   to"=>"jboss.server.log.dir", "path"=>"wildflycookbook-fh.log"},
   append=false, autoflush=true)
   ```

```
[standalone@localhost:9990 /] /subsystem=logging/logger=com.
packtpub.wildflycookbook:add(use-parent-handlers=false,handlers=["
wildflycookbook-fh"],level=INFO)
```

3. Now deploy the `logging.war` application, and take a look at the `log` folder to see if the file `wildflycookbook-fh.log` is present. The corresponding test URL is as follows `http://127.0.0.1:8080/logging`.

Now check your logs and you should see something like this:

```
[luigi@foogaro wildfly]$ tail -f $WILDFLY_HOME/std-logging/log/wildflycookbook-fh.log
15:29:03,380 FATAL [com.packtpub.wildflycookbook.subsystems.logging.Logging] (default task-1) Fatal message
15:29:03,381 ERROR [com.packtpub.wildflycookbook.subsystems.logging.Logging] (default task-1) Error message
15:29:03,381 WARN  [com.packtpub.wildflycookbook.subsystems.logging.Logging] (default task-1) Warning message
15:29:03,381 INFO  [com.packtpub.wildflycookbook.subsystems.logging.Logging] (default task-1) Information message
```

Log statements with wildflycookbook-fh file handler.

## How it works...

We first need to add the file-handler, and then create a category to map the proper application packages to our new file-handler, `wildflycookbook-fh`.

Application package can be any, even the WildFly internal package, that you might be interested in and want to store in a separate file.

Anyway, once you've created the file-handler, you can check it's configuration within the CLI, as follows:

```
[standalone@localhost:9990 /] /subsystem=logging/file-handler=wildflycookbook-fh:read-resource(include-runtime=true)
{
    "outcome" => "success",
    "result" => {
        "append" => false,
        "autoflush" => true,
        "enabled" => true,
        "encoding" => undefined,
        "file" => {
            "relative-to" => "jboss.server.log.dir",
            "path" => "wildflycookbook-fh.log"
        },
        "filter" => undefined,
        "filter-spec" => undefined,
        "formatter" => "%d{HH:mm:ss,SSS} %-5p [%c] (%t) %s%e%n",
        "level" => "INFO",
        "name" => "wildflycookbook-fh",
        "named-formatter" => undefined
    }
}
[standalone@localhost:9990 /]
```

Looking at the `standalone.xml file`, the new file-handler configuration looks as follows:

```
<file-handler name="wildflycookbook-fh" autoflush="true">
  <level name="INFO"/>
  <file relative-to="jboss.server.log.dir" path="wildflycookbook-
  fh.log"/>
```

```
    <append value="false"/>
  </file-handler>
  <logger category="com.packtpub.wildflycookbook" use-parent-
  handlers="false">
    <level name="INFO"/>
    <handlers>
      <handler name="wildflycookbook-fh"/>
    </handlers>
  </logger>
```

## There's more...

Typically, every environment has its own peculiarities, even for the logging subsystem. In a test environment, you will probably need more information to view, so you want developer information to be traced into the log file. We can achieve this behavior by enabling the `DEBUG` level on both, handler and category. Let's see both the instructions.

First we enable the `DEBUG` level on the file handler itself:

```
[standalone@localhost:9990 /] /subsystem=logging/file-
handler=wildflycookbook-fh:write-attribute(name=level,value=DEBUG)
```

Then we enable the `DEBUG` level on the category:

```
[standalone@localhost:9990 /] /subsystem=logging/logger=com.packtpub.
wildflycookbook:write-attribute(name=level,value=DEBUG)
```

# Creating a periodic-rotating file-handler

In this recipe, we will learn how to target the log statement output of your application to a periodic file handler. This is different from the file-handler, in that when the running system reaches a pre-defined time (that is, hour change, day change, and so on), the log file rolls, backing up itself and creating a new file with the same characteristics.

For the sake of simplicity, we will try our recipe with WildFly running in the standalone mode.

## Getting ready

If you didn't follow the previous recipe, we will need to create a standalone configuration for our recipe, as follows:

```
$ cd $WILDFLY_HOME
$ cp -a standalone std-logging
```

To test our logging configuration, we will need an application to log some statements. In this case, we will use the application named `logging`. To obtain the artifact to deploy, please refer to the *Software prerequisites* recipe in *Chapter 1, Welcome to WildFly!*.

Now, let's start WildFly, as follows:

```
$ cd $WILDFLY_HOME
$ ./bin/standalone.sh -Djboss.server.base.dir=$WILDFLY_HOME/std-logging
```

## How to do it...

1. With a running WildFly server, open your command-line tool and connect to the CLI:

   ```
   $ ./bin/jboss-cli.sh --connect

   [standalone@localhost:9990 /]
   ```

2. Now execute the following commands:

   ```
   [standalone@localhost:9990 /] /subsystem=logging/periodic-rotating-file-handler=wildflycookbook-prfh:add(level=INFO, file={"relative-to"=>"jboss.server.log.dir", "path"=>"wildflycookbook-prfh.log"}, append=false, autoflush=true, suffix=".yyyy-MM-dd-HH-mm")
   ```

   In the preceding configuration, we settled the suffix, the rotating algorithm, to minutes just to give an example.

   In a production environment, you should use a daily rotating algorithm and schedule an `olding` mechanism to back up the files somewhere else in order to avoid file system fullfilling.

   Nevertheless, if you followed the previous recipe, you just need to add the `periodic.rotating-file-handler` to the category as follows:

   ```
   [standalone@localhost:9990 /] /subsystem=logging/logger=com.packtpub.wildflycookbook:add-handler(name=wildflycookbook-prfh)
   ```

3. Instead, if you skipped the *Creating a file-handler logging* recipe, you need to create a new category and reference the handler to it, as follows:

   ```
   [standalone@localhost:9990 /] /subsystem=logging/logger=com.packtpub.wildflycookbook:add(use-parent-handlers=false,handlers=["wildflycookbook-prfh"], level=INFO)
   ```

4. Now deploy the `logging.war`, if you haven't done it yet, and take a look at the `log` folder to check if the file `wildflycookbook-prfh.log` is present. To trigger the log statements into the new file, hit the following address: `http://127.0.0.1:8080/logging`.

   Now wait a minute, and refresh the page a couple of times. What you should notice in the `jboss.server.base.dir/log` folder is at least another `*-prfh*` log file, as follows:

```
[luigi@foogaro wildfly]$ ll std-logging/log/*-prfh.*
-rw-rw-r--. 1 luigi luigi 440 Apr 19 15:40 std-logging/log/wildflycookbook-prfh.log
-rw-rw-r--. 1 luigi luigi   0 Apr 19 15:34 std-logging/log/wildflycookbook-prfh.log.2015-04-19-15-34
[luigi@foogaro wildfly]$
```

As you can see, our log file has rotated once.

## How it works...

We first need to create the file-handler and then create a category to map the proper application packages to our new periodic-rotating-file-handler `wildflycookbook-prfh`. Application package can be any, even the WildFly internal package, that you might be interested in and want to store in a separate file.

What about the "zero" byte file? That file was created just after the creation of the handler. In my case, I waited for a few minutes before running the `logging` application, so when it was time to write on the file, the handler first checked if the minute was changed (it was), then rolled the file. It then created the new file and wrote into it.

Anyway, once you've created the periodic-rotating-file-handler, you can check it's configuration within the CLI, as follows:

```
[standalone@localhost:9990 /] /subsystem=logging/periodic-rotating-file-handler=wildflycookbook-prfh:read-resource(include-runtime=true)
{
    "outcome" => "success",
    "result" => {
        "append" => false,
        "autoflush" => true,
        "enabled" => true,
        "encoding" => undefined,
        "file" => {
            "relative-to" => "jboss.server.log.dir",
            "path" => "wildflycookbook-prfh.log"
        },
        "filter" => undefined,
        "filter-spec" => undefined,
        "formatter" => "%d{HH:mm:ss,SSS} %-5p [%c] (%t) %s%e%n",
        "level" => "INFO",
        "name" => "wildflycookbook-prfh",
        "named-formatter" => undefined,
        "suffix" => ".yyyy-MM-dd-HH-mm"
    }
}
[standalone@localhost:9990 /]
```

Looking at `standalone.xml`, the new periodic-rotating-file-handler configuration looks like the following:

```
<periodic-rotating-file-handler name="wildflycookbook-prfh"
autoflush="true">
  <level name="INFO"/>
  <file relative-to="jboss.server.log.dir" path="wildflycookbook-
  prfh.log"/>
  <suffix value=".yyyy-MM-dd-HH-mm"/>
  <append value="false"/>
</periodic-rotating-file-handler>
<logger category="com.packtpub.wildflycookbook" use-parent-
handlers="false">
  <level name="INFO"/>
  <handlers>
    <handler name="wildflycookbook-fh"/>
    <handler name="wildflycookbook-prfh"/>
  </handlers>
</logger>
```

The `wildflycookbook-fh` handler is present because of the previous recipe.

# Creating a size-rotating file-handler

In this recipe, we will learn how to target the log statement output of your application to a size-rotating-file-handler. It is different from a file-handler in that when the file itself reaches a specific size in terms of bytes, it rolls backing up itself and creates a new file with the same characteristics. This mechanism is, by default, settled to have only one backup file. This is to prevent your hard disks running out of space quickly, in case you forget the setting.

For the sake of simplicity, we will try our recipe with WildFly running in the standalone mode.

## Getting ready

If you didn't follow the previous recipe, we will need to create a standalone configuration for our recipe, as follows:

```
$ cd $WILDFLY_HOME
$ cp -a standalone std-logging
```

To test our logging configuration, we will need an application to log some statements. In this case, we will use the application named `logging`. To obtain the artifact to deploy, please refer to the *Software prerequisites* recipe in *Chapter 1, Welcome to WildFly!*.

Now, let's start WildFly, as follows:

```
$ cd $WILDFLY_HOME
$ ./bin/standalone.sh -Djboss.server.base.dir=$WILDFLY_HOME/std-logging
```

## How to do it...

1. With a running WildFly server, open your command-line tool and connect to the CLI:

   ```
   $ ./bin/jboss-cli.sh--connect
   [standalone@localhost:9990 /]
   ```

2. Now execute the following commands:

   ```
   [standalone@localhost:9990 /] /subsystem=logging/size-rotating-file-handler=wildflycookbook-srfh:add(level=INFO, file={"relative-to"=>"jboss.server.log.dir", "path"=>"wildflycookbook-srfh.log"}, append=false, autoflush=true, rotate-size=1k, max-backup-index=5)
   ```

   In the preceding configuration, we settled the `rotate-size` to `1` KB. When the file reaches that size, the handler closes the current file and creates a new one. The old one will be renamed with an index suffix. The property `max-backup-index` specifies exactly how many files the handler has to maintain; in our case it is `five`.

3. Nevertheless, in the *Creating a file-handler logging* recipe we created a logger category. Thus, if you followed that recipe, you just need to add the `size-rotating-file-handler` handler to the category as follows:

   ```
   [standalone@localhost:9990 /] /subsystem=logging/logger=com.packtpub.wildflycookbook:add-handler(name=wildflycookbook-srfh)
   ```

4. Instead, if you skipped the `Creating a file-handler logging` recipe, you need to create a new category and reference the handler to it, as follows:

   ```
   [standalone@localhost:9990 /] /subsystem=logging/logger=com.packtpub.wildflycookbook:add(use-parent-handlers=false,handlers=["wildflycookbook-srfh"], level=INFO)
   ```

5. Now deploy the `logging.war`, if you haven't done it yet, and take a look at the `log` folder to check if the file `wildflycookbook-srfh.log` is present. To trigger the log statements into the new file, hit the following address: `http://127.0.0.1:8080/logging`.

6. Do it three to four times, so that our log file increases in size. What you should notice is a couple of `*-srfh.log` log files in the `jboss.server.base.dir/log` folder, as follows:

```
[luigi@foogaro wildfly]$ ll std-logging/log/*-srfh.*
-rw-rw-r--. 1 luigi luigi  664 Apr 19 16:47 std-logging/log/wildflycookbook-srfh.log
-rw-rw-r--. 1 luigi luigi 1096 Apr 19 16:47 std-logging/log/wildflycookbook-srfh.log.1
[luigi@foogaro wildfly]$
```

## How it works...

We first need to create the size-rotating-file-handler and then create/choose a category to map the proper application packages to our new size-rotating-file-handler, `wildflycookbook-srfh`. Application package can be any, even the WildFly internal package, that you might be interested in and want to store in a separate file.

What happens if we reach `max-backup-index`?

Suppose we already switched our current log file five times, so in our `log` folder we have the following files:

- `wildflycookbook-srfh.log`
- `wildflycookbook-srfh.log.1`
- `wildflycookbook-srfh.log.2`
- `wildflycookbook-srfh.log.3`
- `wildflycookbook-srfh.log.4`
- `wildflycookbook-srfh.log.5`

Indexed files are all about 1 KB in size, while the current one, `wildflycookbook-srfh.log` needs only a few more bytes to roll.

As we hit our application once again, the current file rolls with the index suffix 1, the old `.1` becomes `.2`, the old `.2` becomes `.3` and so on.. What happens to the `.5` file? It gets removed and the `.4` file takes its place.

Anyway, once you've created the size-rotating-file-handler, you can check its configuration within the CLI, as follows:

```
[standalone@localhost:9990 /] /subsystem=logging/size-rotating-file-handler=wildflycookbook-srfh:read-resource(include-runtime=true)
{
    "outcome" => "success",
    "result" => {
        "append" => false,
        "autoflush" => true,
        "enabled" => true,
        "encoding" => undefined,
        "file" => {
            "relative-to" => "jboss.server.log.dir",
            "path" => "wildflycookbook-srfh.log"
        },
        "filter" => undefined,
        "filter-spec" => undefined,
        "formatter" => "%d{HH:mm:ss,SSS} %-5p [%c] (%t) %s%e%n",
        "level" => "INFO",
        "max-backup-index" => 5,
        "name" => "wildflycookbook-srfh",
        "named-formatter" => undefined,
        "rotate-on-boot" => false,
        "rotate-size" => "1k",
        "suffix" => undefined
    }
}
[standalone@localhost:9990 /]
```

Looking at `standalone.xml`, the new size-rotating-file-handler configuration looks like this:

```
<size-rotating-file-handler name="wildflycookbook-srfh"
autoflush="true">
  <level name="INFO"/>
  <file relative-to="jboss.server.log.dir" path="wildflycookbook-
  srfh.log"/>
  <rotate-size value="1k"/>
  <max-backup-index value="5"/>
  <append value="false"/>
</size-rotating-file-handler>
<logger category="com.packtpub.wildflycookbook" use-parent-
handlers="false">
  <level name="INFO"/>
  <handlers>
    <handler name="wildflycookbook-fh"/>
    <handler name="wildflycookbook-prfh"/>
    <handler name="wildflycookbook-srfh"/>
  </handlers>
</logger>
```

The handlers, `wildflycookbook-fh` and `wildflycookbook-prfh`, are present because of the previous recipes.

# Defining asynchronous handlers

In this recipe, you will learn how to target the log statement output of your application to a handler of your choice and have it logging in an asynchronous way. For the sake of simplicity, we will try our recipe with WildFly running in the standalone mode.

## Getting ready

To test our logging configuration, we will need an application to log some statements. In this case, we will use the application named `logging`. To obtain the artifact to deploy, please refer to the *Software prerequisites* recipe in *Chapter 1, Welcome to WildFly!*.

Furthermore, this recipe relies on the configuration made while explaining the *Creating a file-handler logging* and *Creating a periodic-rotating file-handler* recipes of this chapter.

## How to do it...

1. With a running WildFly server, open your command-line tool and connect to the CLI:

```
$ ./bin/jboss-cli.sh--connect
[standalone@localhost:9990 /]
```

2. Now execute the following commands:

```
[standalone@localhost:9990 /] /subsystem=logging/async-handler=wildflycookbook-afh:add(level=INFO, queue-length=1024, overflow-action=BLOCK)
{"outcome" => "success"}
[standalone@localhost:9990 /] /subsystem=logging/async-handler=wildflycookbook-afh:assign-subhandler(name=wildflycookbook-prfh)
{"outcome" => "success"}
[standalone@localhost:9990 /] /subsystem=logging/async-handler=wildflycookbook-afh:assign-subhandler(name=wildflycookbook-fh)
{"outcome" => "success"}
[standalone@localhost:9990 /]
```

3. To check the new configuration, just issue the following command:

```
[standalone@localhost:9990 /] /subsystem=logging/async-handler=wildflycookbook-afh:read-resource(recursive=true,include-runtime=true,include-defaults=true)
{
  "outcome" => "success",
```

```
    "result" => {
        "enabled" => true,
        "filter" => undefined,
        "filter-spec" => undefined,
        "level" => "INFO",
        "name" => "wildflycookbook-afh",
        "overflow-action" => "BLOCK",
        "queue-length" => 1024,
        "subhandlers" => [
            "wildflycookbook-prfh",
            "wildflycookbook-fh"
        ]
    }
}
[standalone@localhost:9990 /]
```

4. Okay, now we have our new async-handler managing two other handlers in an asynchronous way. To check if the async-handler is properly configured, open the browser and point it to the following URL: `http://127.0.0.1:8080/logging`

## How it works...

The files managed by the `wildflycookbook-fh` and `wildflycookbook-prfh` handlers, still write into their own log files. The async-handler itself does not generate any additional files at all; it only adds asynchronous behavior to the other handlers.

The async-handler is used to improve the logging throughput.

It grabs application log statements, puts them into a buffer, and then logs them using the handlers that you defined. Also, this buffer is not unbounded—it has a limit. As a matter of fact, from the commands shown in the *How to do it* section, I've emphasized some of the key points: `queue-length` and `overflow-action`.

Simply speaking, we told the async-handler how many log statements the buffers can hold, and what it should do when there is no more room in them.

We settled `1024` as the number of the log statements for the buffer, and we settled a `block` action as an exceeded limit behavior. This means that the log statement is in a hold state until it finds room in the buffer. You can otherwise choose the `discard` action, with the consequence of losing your logs.

You can use whatever action you want, but keep in mind that for the `block` action, you should tune the size of your buffer to not hold too many or too few logs.

Looking at `standalone.xml`, the new async-handler configuration looks like this:

```
<async-handler name="wildflycookbook-afh">
  <level name="INFO"/>
  <queue-length value="1024"/>
  <overflow-action value="block"/>
  <subhandlers>
    <handler name="wildflycookbook-prfh"/>
    <handler name="wildflycookbook-fh"/>
  </subhandlers>
</async-handler>
```

## There's more...

The async-handler is faster, so why wouldn't you always use that? Well, not always; sometimes you can get a worse performance by using the async-handler.

If your application makes intense use of I/O operations, then you can benefit from it. On the other hand, if your application makes intense use of the CPU, you will definitely not benefit from using the async-handler, as it will increase context-switching.

# Creating a syslog-handler

In this recipe, we will learn how to use "syslog". The syslog is a standard protocol used for message logging. This standard has been implemented for different operating systems, such as Linux, Unix, and Windows. In 2009, the **Internet Engineering Task Force** (**IETF**) standardized the "syslog" protocol specification, which can be viewed at the following address:

`http://tools.ietf.org/html/rfc5424`

You will probably use `syslog-handler` in environments where a centralized logging system is used to collect all system information.

Lastly, for this recipe I will use a syslog server named `syslog-ng`.

1. To install into a Fedora 21 system, do as follows:

   ```
   $ sudo yum -y install rsyslog
   ```

2. Once done, enable the following directives into `/etc/rsyslog.conf`,:

   ```
   $ModLoad imudp.so
   $UDPServerRun 514
   ```

3. Then start the `rsyslogd` daemon with the following command:

   ```
   $ sudo /usr/sbin/rsyslogd
   ```

Its detailed installation and configuration is out of the scope of this book. By the way, you can refer to the official documentation at the following site:

`https://syslog-ng.org`

## Getting ready

If you didn't follow the previous recipe, we will need to create a standalone configuration for our recipe, as follows:

```
$ cd $WILDFLY_HOME
$ cp -a standalone std-logging
```

To test our logging configuration, we will need an application to log some statements. In this case, we will use the application named `logging`. To obtain the artifact to deploy, please refer to the *Software prerequisites* recipe in *Chapter 1, Welcome to WildFly!*.

Now, let's start WildFly, as follows:

```
$ cd $WILDFLY_HOME
$ ./bin/standalone.sh -Djboss.server.base.dir=$WILDFLY_HOME/std-logging
```

## How to do it...

1. With a running WildFly server, open your command-line tool and connect to the CLI:

   ```
   $ ./bin/jboss-cli.sh--connect
   [standalone@localhost:9990 /]
   ```

2. Now execute the following commands:

   ```
   [standalone@localhost:9990 /] /subsystem=logging/syslog-handler=wildfly-slh:add(server-address=localhost,hostname=foogaro,port=514,syslog-format=RFC5424,facility=user-level,level=INFO,app-name=wildfly-logging,enabled=true)
   {"outcome" => "success"}
   ```

3. Now we need to associate the handler to a logger, and we will use `com.packtpub.wildflycookbook` (used in the previous recipes of this chapter), as follows:

   ```
   [standalone@localhost:9990 /] /subsystem=logging/logger=com.packtpub.wildflycookbook:add-handler(name=wildfly-slh)
   {"outcome" => "success"}
   [standalone@localhost:9990 /]
   ```

4. Before we can test our new configuration, open a new terminal window and `tail` the `syslog`, by issuing the following command:

   ```
   $ journalctl -f
   ```

   This will work in Fedora 21; in a different Linux system, you may find your `SysLog` server logging into the `/var/log/messages` file. However, point to the file with regard to your OS.

5. Once ready, deploy the logging application, if you haven't done so yet, and open your browser to the following URL: `http://localhost:8080/logging`.
6. You should see something similar to the following:

   ```
   Message from syslogd@localhost at Apr 19 17:56:36 ...
   wildfly-logging[15343] Fatal message
   ```

   It's our logging application's fatal message catched by the syslog. You know this because it refers to the `wildfly-logging` which corresponds to the value of the attribute `app-name`, when defining the `syslog-handler`. It worked!

## How it works...

First of all, it's better to repeat that "syslog" is a protocol, thus it has many implementations depending on the hardware and software. In other words, it is OS dependent. In our first command, while creating the `syslog-handler`, we specified a lot of parameters.

Let's summarize them in the following table:

| **Attribute** | **Description** |
|---|---|
| `server-address` | This is where the syslog server is—default is `localhost`. |
| `hostname` | This is the hostname of the sever sending the messages. |
| `port` | This is the port that the syslog server listens to—default is `514`. |
| `syslog-format` | The format used to log the message based on the RFC5424 specification—default is `RFC5424`. |
| `facility` | This is the "category" of the message, still based on the RFC5425 specification—default is `user-level`. |
| `level` | This is the log level—default is `ALL`. |
| `app-name` | This should correspond to the application generating the message. It's basically used for filtering. |
| `enabled` | When set to false, disables the `syslog-handler`—default value is `true`. |

However, whenever you create a handler, you will always have to reference it into a logger. Otherwise you will not see any messages at all.

Going into much detail about the "syslog" protocol is out of the scope of this book. For more information about it, please refer to its specification, available at the following site:

http://tools.ietf.org/html/rfc5424

# Listing and reading log files

In this recipe, we will learn how to list and read log files. This can be helpful when you have access only to the CLI (which might be a remote one), and not to the server itself or the file system hosting the log files.

## Getting ready

To fully understand this recipe, you should have followed one of the previous recipes, which have created the various log files. However, the standard WildFly log file `server.log` would be present and it's enough.

## How to do it...

1. With a running WildFly server, open your command-line tool and connect to the CLI:

```
$ ./bin/jboss-cli.sh --connect
[standalone@localhost:9990 /]
```

2. Before reading a file, we need to know which log files are present. To list them all, execute the following commands:

```
[standalone@localhost:9990 /] /subsystem=logging:list-log-files
{
  "outcome" => "success",
  "result" => [
    {
      "file-name" => "server.log",
      "file-size" => 24879L,
      "last-modified-date" => "2015-05-
      24T15:14:29.000+0200"
    },
    {
      "file-name" => "wildflycookbook-fh.log",
      "file-size" => 0L,
```

```
        "last-modified-date" => "2015-05-
        24T15:14:13.000+0200"
      },
      {
        "file-name" => "wildflycookbook-prfh.log",
        "file-size" => 0L,
        "last-modified-date" => "2015-05-
        24T15:14:13.000+0200"
      },
      {
        "file-name" => "wildflycookbook-prfh.log.2015-
        05-24-14-42",
        "file-size" => 0L,
        "last-modified-date" => "2015-05-
        24T14:42:14.000+0200"
      },
      {
        "file-name" => "wildflycookbook-prfh.log.2015-
        05-24-14-43",
        "file-size" => 440L,
        "last-modified-date" => "2015-05-
        24T14:43:06.000+0200"
      },
      {
        "file-name" => "wildflycookbook-srfh.log",
        "file-size" => 0L,
        "last-modified-date" => "2015-05-
        24T15:14:13.000+0200"
      },
      {
        "file-name" => "wildflycookbook-srfh.log.1",
        "file-size" => 1096L,
        "last-modified-date" => "2015-05-
        24T14:44:17.000+0200"
      }
      ]
  }
  [standalone@localhost:9990 /]
```

3. Because of our previous recipes, we have a lot of files to look at. For the purpose of this recipe, we will use the default log file, `server.log`. To read the file, we can try the following command:

```
[standalone@localhost:9990 /] /subsystem=logging:read-log-file(name=server.log)
{
    "outcome" => "success",
    "result" => [
        "2015-05-24 15:14:14,813 INFO  [org.wildfly.extension.undertow] (MSC service thread 1-9) WFLYUT0006: Undertow HTTP listener default listening on /127.0.0.1:8080",
        "2015-05-24 15:14:14,964 INFO  [org.jboss.as.connector.subsystems.datasources] (MSC service thread 1-15) WFLYJCA0001: Bound data source [java:jboss/datasources/ExampleDS]",
        "2015-05-24 15:14:15,021 INFO  [org.jboss.as.server.deployment.scanner] (MSC service thread 1-5) WFLYDS0013: Started FileSystemDeploymentService for directory /Users/foogaro/wildfly-9.0.0.Beta2/std-logging/deployments",
        "2015-05-24 15:14:15,025 INFO  [org.jboss.as.server.deployment] (MSC service thread 1-8) WFLYSRV0027: Starting deployment of \"logging.war\" (runtime-name: \"logging.war\")",
        "2015-05-24 15:14:15,116 INFO [org.jboss.ws.common.management] (MSC service thread 1-4) JBWS022052: Starting JBoss Web Services - Stack CXF Server 5.0.0.Beta3",
        "2015-05-24 15:14:15,363 INFO  [org.wildfly.extension.undertow] (MSC service thread 1-11) WFLYUT0021: Registered web context: /logging",
        "2015-05-24 15:14:15,405 INFO  [org.jboss.as.server] (ServerService Thread Pool -- 34) WFLYSRV0010: Deployed \"logging.war\" (runtime-name : \"logging.war\")",
        "2015-05-24 15:14:15,545 INFO  [org.jboss.as] (Controller Boot Thread) WFLYSRV0060: Http management interface listening on http://127.0.0.1:9990/management",
        "2015-05-24 15:14:15,546 INFO  [org.jboss.as] (Controller Boot Thread) WFLYSRV0051: Admin console listening on http://127.0.0.1:9990",
        "2015-05-24 15:14:15,546 INFO  [org.jboss.as] (Controller Boot Thread) WFLYSRV0025: WildFly Full 9.0.0.Beta2 (WildFly Core 1.0.0.Beta2) started in 2328ms - Started 269 of 451 services (221 services are lazy, passive or on-demand)"
    ]
}
[standalone@localhost:9990 /]
```

As you can see, the output shows just the last few lines of the content.

4. If you want to read from the beginning, you can specify the `tail=false` parameter (by default, it is set to `true`), along with the `name` parameter, as follows:

```
[standalone@localhost:9990 /] /subsystem=logging:read-log-file(name=server.log,tail=false)
{
    "outcome" => "success",
    "result" => [
        "2015-05-24 14:38:38,059 INFO  [org.jboss.modules]
         (main) JBoss Modules version 1.4.2.Final",
        "2015-05-24 14:38:38,216 INFO  [org.jboss.msc]
         (main) JBoss MSC version 1.2.4.Final",
        "2015-05-24 14:38:38,266 INFO  [org.jboss.as] (MSC
        service thread 1-6) WFLYSRV0049: WildFly Full
        9.0.0.Beta2 (WildFly Core 1.0.0.Beta2) starting",
        "2015-05-24 14:38:38,267 DEBUG
         [org.jboss.as.config] (MSC service thread 1-6)
        Configured system properties:",
        "[Standalone] = ",
        "awt.toolkit = sun.lwawt.macosx.LWCToolkit",
        "file.encoding = UTF-8",
        "file.encoding.pkg = sun.io",
        "file.separator = /",
        "ftp.nonProxyHosts =
        local|*.local|169.254/16|*.169.254/16"
    ]
}
[standalone@localhost:9990 /]
```

5. If you want to see more lines of the log file, just specify the number of lines you want, and add the `lines` parameter as follows:

```
[standalone@localhost:9990 /] /subsystem=logging:read-log-file(name=server.log,lines=15)
{
  "outcome" => "success",
  "result" => [
    "2015-05-24 15:14:14,642 INFO  [org.jboss.as.naming] (MSC
    service thread 1-16) WFLYNAM0003: Starting Naming
    Service",
```

```
"2015-05-24 15:14:14,642 INFO
[org.jboss.as.mail.extension] (MSC service thread 1-14)
WFLYMAIL0001: Bound mail session
 [java:jboss/mail/Default]",
"2015-05-24 15:14:14,703 INFO
[org.wildfly.extension.undertow] (ServerService Thread
Pool -- 55) WFLYUT0014: Creating file handler for path
/Users/foogaro/wildfly-9.0.0.Beta2/welcome-content",
"2015-05-24 15:14:14,728 INFO
[org.wildfly.extension.undertow] (MSC service thread 1-5)
WFLYUT0012: Started server default-server.",
"2015-05-24 15:14:14,745 INFO
[org.wildfly.extension.undertow] (MSC service thread 1-3)
WFLYUT0018: Host default-host starting",
"2015-05-24 15:14:14,813 INFO
[org.wildfly.extension.undertow] (MSC service thread 1-9)
WFLYUT0006: Undertow HTTP listener default listening on
/127.0.0.1:8080",
"2015-05-24 15:14:14,964 INFO
[org.jboss.as.connector.subsystems.datasources] (MSC
service thread 1-15) WFLYJCA0001: Bound data source
[java:jboss/datasources/ExampleDS]",
"2015-05-24 15:14:15,021 INFO
[org.jboss.as.server.deployment.scanner] (MSC service
thread 1-5) WFLYDS0013: Started
FileSystemDeploymentService for directory
/Users/foogaro/wildfly-9.0.0.Beta2/std-
logging/deployments",
"2015-05-24 15:14:15,025 INFO
[org.jboss.as.server.deployment] (MSC service thread 1-8)
WFLYSRV0027: Starting deployment of \"logging.war\"
(runtime-name: \"logging.war\")",
"2015-05-24 15:14:15,116 INFO
[org.jboss.ws.common.management] (MSC service thread 1-4)
JBWS022052: Starting JBoss Web Services - Stack CXF Server
5.0.0.Beta3",
"2015-05-24 15:14:15,363 INFO
[org.wildfly.extension.undertow] (MSC service thread 1-11)
WFLYUT0021: Registered web context: /logging",
"2015-05-24 15:14:15,405 INFO  [org.jboss.as.server]
(ServerService Thread Pool -- 34) WFLYSRV0010: Deployed
\"logging.war\" (runtime-name : \"logging.war\")",
"2015-05-24 15:14:15,545 INFO  [org.jboss.as] (Controller
Boot Thread) WFLYSRV0060: Http management interface
listening on http://127.0.0.1:9990/management",
```

```
        "2015-05-24 15:14:15,546 INFO  [org.jboss.as] (Controller
        Boot Thread) WFLYSRV0051: Admin console listening on
        http://127.0.0.1:9990",
        "2015-05-24 15:14:15,546 INFO  [org.jboss.as] (Controller
        Boot Thread) WFLYSRV0025: WildFly Full 9.0.0.Beta2
        (WildFly Core 1.0.0.Beta2) started in 2328ms - Started
        269 of 451 services (221 services are lazy, passive or on-
        demand)"
        ]
    }
    [standalone@localhost:9990 /]
```

Obviously, a continuous `tail -f` like command would be very useful, but there isn't one, at least not for the moment.

## There's more...

There is one more option worth mentioning, that is, the `skip` parameter. It basically shifts your lines up or down, depending on whether you are starting from the head or the tail of the file.

Let's give it a try using a skip by 5 lines:

```
[standalone@localhost:9990 /] /subsystem=logging:read-log-
file(name=server.log,skip=5)
{
  "outcome" => "success",
  "result" => [
    "2015-05-24 15:14:14,642 INFO  [org.jboss.as.naming] (MSC service
    thread 1-16) WFLYNAM0003: Starting Naming Service",
    "2015-05-24 15:14:14,642 INFO  [org.jboss.as.mail.extension] (MSC
    service thread 1-14) WFLYMAIL0001: Bound mail session
    [java:jboss/mail/Default]",
    "2015-05-24 15:14:14,703 INFO  [org.wildfly.extension.undertow]
    (ServerService Thread Pool -- 55) WFLYUT0014: Creating file
    handler for path /Users/foogaro/wildfly-9.0.0.Beta2/welcome-
    content",
    "2015-05-24 15:14:14,728 INFO  [org.wildfly.extension.undertow]
    (MSC service thread 1-5) WFLYUT0012: Started server default-
    server.",
    "2015-05-24 15:14:14,745 INFO  [org.wildfly.extension.undertow]
    (MSC service thread 1-3) WFLYUT0018: Host default-host starting",
```

```
    "2015-05-24 15:14:14,813 INFO  [org.wildfly.extension.undertow]
    (MSC service thread 1-9) WFLYUT0006: Undertow HTTP listener
    default listening on /127.0.0.1:8080",
    "2015-05-24 15:14:14,964 INFO
    [org.jboss.as.connector.subsystems.datasources] (MSC service
    thread 1-15) WFLYJCA0001: Bound data source
    [java:jboss/datasources/ExampleDS]",
    "2015-05-24 15:14:15,021 INFO
    [org.jboss.as.server.deployment.scanner] (MSC service thread 1-5)
    WFLYDS0013: Started FileSystemDeploymentService for directory
    /Users/foogaro/wildfly-9.0.0.Beta2/std-logging/deployments",
    "2015-05-24 15:14:15,025 INFO  [org.jboss.as.server.deployment]
    (MSC service thread 1-8) WFLYSRV0027: Starting deployment of
    \"logging.war\" (runtime-name: \"logging.war\")",
    "2015-05-24 15:14:15,116 INFO  [org.jboss.ws.common.management]
    (MSC service thread 1-4) JBWS022052: Starting JBoss Web Services
    - Stack CXF Server 5.0.0.Beta3"
    ]
}
[standalone@localhost:9990 /]
```

The command just dropped the last 5 lines of the file, but it started displaying the output 5 lines earlier. By default, the total number of lines displayed is 10—this is because, by default, it starts reading the tail of the file.

Since WildFly version 8.2, the logging subsystem earned a new resource called `log-file`. The resource lists all log files defined in the `jboss.server.log.dir` (or `jboss.domain.log.dir` depending on the operational mode), which are defined in the subsystem. With WildFly 9, now you can download a log file by using the management interface.

1. Open a browser and point it to `http://localhost:9990/management/subsystem/logging/log-file/server.log?operation=attribute&name=stream&useStreamAsResponse`.
2. Alternatively, you can use HTTP tools such as `curl`. With the `curl` tool, you can get a log file content, as follows:

   ```
   $ curl --digest -o server.log -L -D - http://127.0.0.1:9990/
   management?useStreamAsResponse --header "Content-Type:
   application/json" -u wildfly:cookbook.2015 -d '{"operation":"read-
   attribute","address":[{"subsystem":"logging"},{"log-file":"server.
   log"}],"name":"stream"}'
   ```

   The preceding example gets the stream of the `server.log` and stores it into a homonymous file (the `-o server.log` directive effectively stores the output).

3. Meanwhile, with the new release of WildFly 9, you can read the log file directly from the Web Console. You can see all the available files by clicking on **Runtime** and by selecting the **Log viewer** menu item on the left, as depicted in the following image:

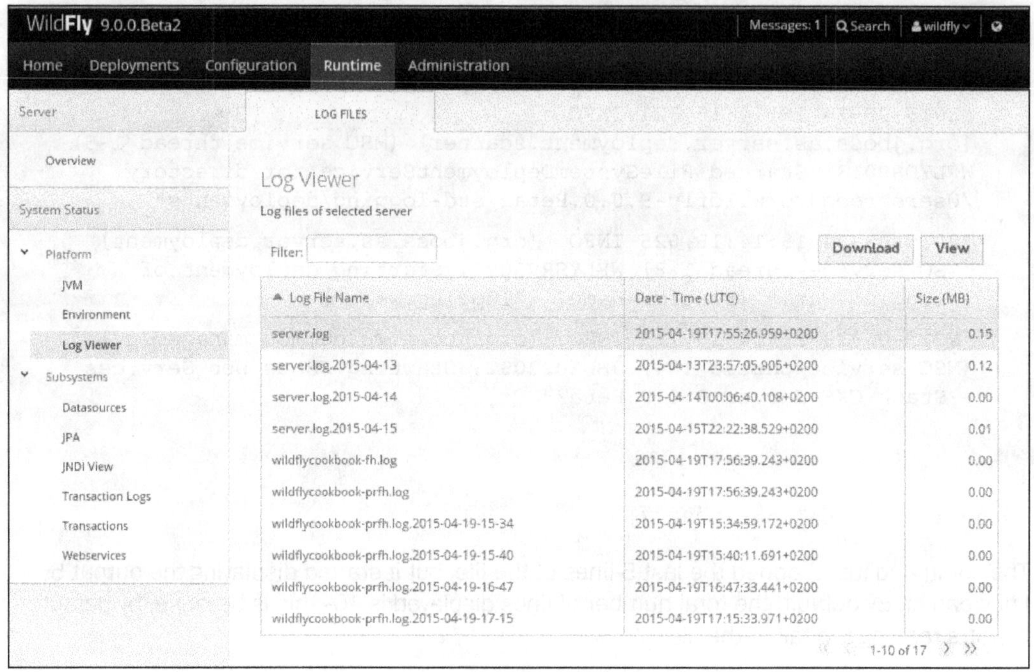

4. Once you select the log file to view, the **Download** and **View** buttons, are enabled. The following screenshot is how a log file looks like in the Web Console:

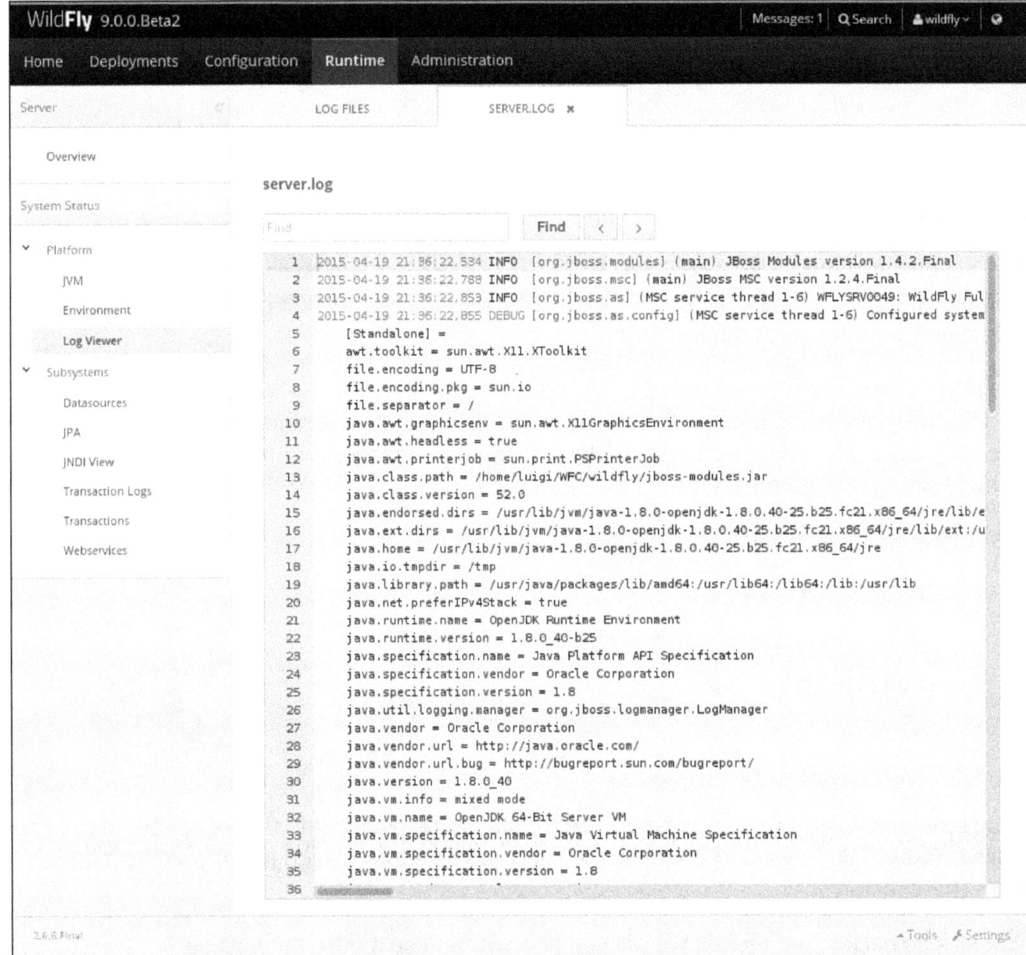


How nice and elegant!

# Using a different logging implementation

In this final recipe about logging, we will learn how to use a different logging implementation. In the earlier version of JBoss AS, you could have relied on the `java.util.logging` (also JUL) or the `log4j` implementation. WildFly relies on the JUL logging implementation.

## Getting ready

To manage which logging implementation you can use, WildFly gives you a couple of attributes.

The first one is named `add-logging-api-dependencies`, which can be set to `true` (default value) or to `false`. When it's true, the WildFly logging default implementation is automatically added to all deployments.

The other attribute is named `use-deployment-logging-config`, which can be set to `true` (default value) or to `false`. When set to `true`, it gives to deployments the `per-deployment logging` feature, which essentially enables your application to carry its own logging configuration file.

The following configuration files are allowed:

- `logging.properties`
- `jboss-logging.properties`
- `log4j.properties`
- `log4j.xml`
- `jboss-log4j.xml`

If you are deploying an EAR application, the file should be placed into the `META-INF` directory. While in case of WAR and JAR bundles, the file could be either placed into the `META-INF` or `WEB-INF` directory.

Now let's go back to our recipe. We will see how we can use a different logging implementation. We will use the `log4j` implementation.

To test our logging configuration, we will need an application to log some statements. In this case, we will use the application named `log4j`. To obtain the artifact to deploy, please refer to the *Software prerequisites* recipe in *Chapter 1, Welcome to WildFly!*.

Now it's time to create a custom standalone configuration folder to test our recipe, as follows:

```
$ cd $WILDFLY_HOME
$ cp -a standalone std-log4j
$ ./bin/standalone.sh -Djboss.server.base.dir=$WILDFLY_HOME/std-log4j
```

## How to do it...

1. With a running WildFly server, open your command-line tool and connect to the CLI:

```
$ ./bin/jboss-cli.sh --connect
[standalone@localhost:9990 /]
```

2. Now we remove the automatic logging dependency of our application. Keep in mind that this setting would be general to all other applications that are running on the same WildFly instance, as shown in the following command:

```
[standalone@localhost:9990 /] /subsystem=logging:write-
attribute(name=add-logging-api-dependencies,value=false)
{"outcome" => "success"}
```

3. Now the application to be deployed needs to declare a dependency to `log4j`, which is already provided to you as a module in the WildFly home `modules/system/layers/base/org/apache/log4j/main` folder. To do this, you need to add a file called `jboss-deployment-structure.xml` into your `META-INF` or `WEB-INF` folder (depending if you got an EAR or a WAR application), which looks like the following:

```
<?xml version="1.0"?>
<jboss-deployment-structure xmlns="urn:jboss:deployment-
structure:1.2">
  <deployment>
    <dependencies>
      <module name="org.apache.log4j" />
     </dependencies>
  </deployment>
</jboss-deployment-structure>
Now, let's go back to the CLI to tell WildFly that we have our own
configuration file, which looks like the following:
<log4j:configuration debug="true" xmlns:log4j='http://jakarta.
apache.org/log4j/'>
  <appender name="fileAppender"
    class="org.apache.log4j.RollingFileAppender">
      <param name="append" value="false" />
      <param name="file" value="log4j.log" />

      <layout class="org.apache.log4j.PatternLayout">
        <param name="ConversionPattern" value="%d{ABSOLUTE}
        %-5p [%c{1}] %m%n" />
      </layout>
```

```
    </appender>
    <root>
      <level value="DEBUG" />
      <appender-ref ref="fileAppender" />
    </root>
</log4j:configuration>
```

4. As previously mentioned, the `per-deployment-logging` feature is enabled by default. However, here is the CLI command to enable it:

```
[standalone@localhost:9990 /] /subsystem=logging:write-attribute(name=use-deployment-logging-config,value=true)
{
  "outcome" => "success",
  "response-headers" => {
    "operation-requires-reload" => true,
    "process-state" => "reload-required"
  }
}
```

Remember to `reload` the server once done.

5. Also, as pointed out in the *Getting ready* section, you can provide your own logging configuration file. The following is the `log4j.xml` file that comes with my `log4j` application:

```
<log4j:configuration debug="true" xmlns:log4j='http://jakarta.apache.org/log4j/'>
  <appender name="fileAppender"
  class="org.apache.log4j.RollingFileAppender">
    <param name="append" value="false" />
    <param name="file" value="log4j.log" />

    <layout class="org.apache.log4j.PatternLayout">
      <param name="ConversionPattern" value="%d{ABSOLUTE}
      %-5p [%c{1}] %m%n" />
    </layout>
  </appender>
    <root>
      <level value="DEBUG" />
      <appender-ref ref="fileAppender" />
    </root>
</log4j:configuration>
```

6. Now we can build and deploy the application. While deploying the application, keep an eye on the logs in the `log4j.log` file ( defined in the above XML code snippet), available in the `£WILDFLY_HOME` folder. You should see the following entries:

```
15:32:20,835 ERROR [Startup] Error message
15:32:20,837 WARN  [Startup] Warning message
15:32:20,837 INFO  [Startup] Information message
15:32:20,837 DEBUG [Startup] Debug message
```

## There is more...

There is another way to achieve the same result. You can maintain the `add-logging-api-dependencies` to `true`, and exclude the `logging` subsystem to avoid implicit dependencies within the `jboss-deployment-structure.xml` file, as follows:

```
<?xml version="1.0"?>
<jboss-deployment-structure xmlns="urn:jboss:deployment-structure:1.2">
  <deployment>
    <exclude-subsystems>
      <subsystem name="logging"/>
      </exclude-subsystems>
      <dependencies>
        <module name="org.apache.log4j" />
      </dependencies>
  </deployment>
</jboss-deployment-structure>
```

This approach is too conservative, as it won't affect other applications which may rely on the logging subsystem.

Furthermore, the dependencies can be written in the standard Java way, which is via the `MANIFEST.MF` file placed in the `META-INF` folder, as follows:

```
Manifest-Version: 1.0
Dependencies: org.apache.log4j
<empty line>
```

Remember to include an empty line at the end of the line, to have a valid `MANIFEST.MF` file. You can also have more dependencies modules, by separating them with a comma `,`.

## See also

More information about how logging works in WildFly 9, can be viewed at `https://docs.jboss.org/author/display/WFLY9/Logging+Configuration`.

# 5

# Managing the Datasource Subsystems with the CLI

In this chapter, you will cover the following topics:

- Preparing a non JDBC-4 compliant driver
- Creating and removing a datasource
- Checking the datasource connection
- Reading the datasource's statistics
- Setting a connection pool
- Creating and removing XA-Datasource

## Introduction

In this chapter, you will learn how to manage WildFly datasource subsystems with the CLI. This is independent of the WildFly operation mode. For this reason and to facilitate the configuration, we will be running WildFly in the standalone mode.

A datasource is the component used by applications to connect to the database. The datasource, in turn, uses a driver to communicate with the underlying database properly. Hence, for WildFly to provide database integration, it needs a driver and a datasource.

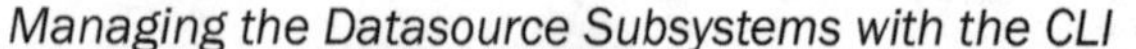

WildFly comes with a default configuration, which is the `ExampleDS` datasource, bound to the "H2" driver. H2 is a Java SQL database, used mainly as an in-memory DB for testing purpose with SQL support.

WildFly automatically recognizes any JDBC 4 compliant driver. For this reason, a driver can be installed as a module (that is, static deployment) or it can be deployed as any normal application.

In the first method, you will have to replicate the driver module installation in all the hosts where the applications and configuration require such a driver. On the other hand, by using dynamic deployment in the domain mode, the driver can be spread to all server groups, and thus to all available hosts, with just one command or a click.

A datasource can also be deployed in the old fashioned way by using a `-ds.xml` file. Even though this alternative is very helpful when migrating from JBoss 5 and JBoss 6, it is not the best choice when configuring a production environment. That's because the datasource cannot be altered via a management interface, such as CLI and Web Admin Console. Also, the datasource cannot be configured to take advantage of the security concerns, such as security domains and password vaults (we will discuss these topics later in the book).

# Preparing a non JDBC-4 compliant driver

In this recipe, we will learn how to make a JDBC driver compliant to version 4. This is needed to install the driver and to make it available for your datasources, and hence to your applications.

## Getting ready

If you already have a JDBC 4 compliant driver, you can skip this recipe; otherwise, I assume that you do not have a JDBC driver and I'll refer to it as `non-jdbc-4-driver.jar`, throughout the recipe.

## How to do it...

To make your driver JDBC 4 compliant, you just need to add a file into it, as described in the following steps:

1. Create a temporary folder and navigate into it.
2. Place your `non-jdbc-4-driver.jar` driver file into it.
3. Create a `META-INF/services` directory.
4. Create a file named `java.sql.Driver` and place it into the folder specified in step 3.
5. Edit the file `java.sqlDriver` and enter one line containing the fully qualified name of the class implementing the driver.

6. Starting from the empty folder as per step 1, update the file non-jdbc-4-driver.jar using the JAR tool as follows:

   ```
   jar -uf non-jdbc-4-driver.jar META-INF/services/java.sql.Driver
   ```

You are now ready to install or deploy your new JDBC 4 compliant driver.

# Creating and removing a datasource

One of the most used features that an application comes with is the possibility to persist states (such as user information, orders, and so on) into a database. In this recipe, we will learn how to configure datasources and a JDBC 4 compliant driver.

## Getting ready

Before we begin, we need to have a running database installed on our computer, or on a remote server. In this recipe, we will use a MySQL database running locally and listening on port 3306—the installation and configuration of the MySQL database server is beyond the scope of this book.

Declaring a new datasource consists of two separate steps:

1. Installing the JDBC driver.
2. Configuring the datasource itself.

The first step can be done in two different ways. You can install a JDBC driver by deploying it as a normal artifact, or you can install it as a WildFly module.

First, download the latest version (which, as per this writing, is "5.1.35") of the MySQL JDBC connector from http://dev.mysql.com/downloads/connector/j/, and place it into your WildFly Cookbook directory WFC, under your home folder.

To install a JDBC driver as a WildFly module, we need to perform the following actions:

1. Go into the modules folder $WILDFLY_HOME/modules/system/layers/base and create a subfolder structure that matches your module name as follows:

   ```
   $ cd $WILDFLY_HOME/modules/system/layers/base
   $ mkdir -p jdbc/mysql/main
   ```

2. Place the ~/WFC/mysql-connector-java-5.1.35-bin.jar file, that you downloaded previously, into the main folder .
3. Within the main folder, create a file named module.xml with the following content:

   ```
   <module xmlns="urn:jboss:module:1.3" name="jdbc.mysql">
     <resources>
   ```

```
        <resource-root path="mysql-connector-java-5.1.35-
        bin.jar"/>
      </resources>
      <dependencies>
        <module name="javax.api"/>
        <module name="javax.transaction.api"/>
      </dependencies>
    </module>
```

As you can see, I've emphasized the name of the module which matched the subfolders structure—except for the main folder which just corresponds to the `version`.

Great! Now we are ready to add the driver to the datasource subsystem.

4. Start WildFly and do the following:

```
$ ./bin/jboss-cli.sh --connect
[standalone@localhost:9990 /] /subsystem=datasources/jdbc-driver=mysql:add(driver-module-name=jdbc.mysql, driver-name=mysql)
{"outcome" => "success"}
[standalone@localhost:9990 /]
```

5. Before we can continue, please create a database on your running MySQL server instance named `wildflycookbook`, as follows:

```
CREATE DATABASE IF NOT EXISTS wildflycookbook
```

Now that we have the JDBC driver installed, we are ready to configure our datasource.

## How to do it...

1. With a running WildFly server, open your command-line tool and connect to the CLI:

```
$ ./bin/jboss-cli.sh
You are disconnected at the moment. Type 'connect' to connect to the server or 'help' for the list of supported commands.
[disconnected /] connect
[standalone@localhost:9990 /]
```

2. Now execute the following commands:

```
[standalone@localhost:9990 /] /subsystem=datasources/data-source=WildFlyCookbookDS:add(jndi-name="java:jboss/datasources/WildFlyCookbookDS", connection-url="jdbc:mysql://localhost:3306/wildflycookbook", driver-name="mysql", user-name="wildflymysql", password="wildfly-mysql-password", prepared-statements-cache-size=128, share-prepared-statements=true, blocking-timeout-wait-millis=60000, idle-timeout-minutes=20)
```

```
{"outcome" => "success"}
[standalone@localhost:9990 /]
```

3. Now, on listing the available datasources, you should find our newly created one:

```
[standalone@localhost:9990 /] ls /subsystem=datasources/data-
source
ExampleDS                WildFlyCookbookDS
[standalone@localhost:9990 /]
```

4. If you need to remove a datasource, invoke `remove` next to it, as follows:

```
[standalone@localhost:9990 /] /subsystem=datasources/data-source=W
ildFlyCookbookDS:remove()
{"outcome" => "success"}
[standalone@localhost:9990 /] ls /subsystem=datasources/data-
source
ExampleDS
[standalone@localhost:9990 /]
```

## How it works...

As you can see, configuring a datasource is not that tough, but what it needs to get there is a lot of work. The datasource itself is just a reference to the database, which involves a connector, that is, the driver. In fact, in the DS configuration, I emphasized the `driver-name` attribute that matches the driver that we defined in the *Getting ready* section. Furthermore, I emphasized the `password` attribute that you should change with regard to your database configuration.

## There's more...

Datasource configuration comes with more parameters such as defining and sizing a connection pool, but we will see that later in this chapter with a dedicated recipe. You will also learn that you can have an XA-Datasource, which actually enables distributed transaction across different transactional systems.

# Checking the datasource connection

Sometimes, you might see errors in your log's application because of something going wrong with your persistence storage. The first thing to do in that case, is to check if the database is up and running by testing its connection; you may even realize that you are pointing to a wrong one or you misspelled the connection URL.

## Getting ready

This recipe is based on the previous one, where we have configured a datasource which connects to a local MySQL database, so we will test our database connection with the WildFlyCookBookDS datasource. You can test the connection with a datasource of your choice as long as you provide the correct configuration as well.

## How to do it...

1. With a running WildFly server, open your command-line tool and connect to the CLI:

```
$ ./bin/jboss-cli.sh --connect
[standalone@localhost:9990 /]
```

2. Now execute the following commands:

```
[standalone@localhost:9990 /] /subsystem=datasources/data-source=WildFlyCookbookDS:test-connection-in-pool()
{
    "outcome" => "success",
    "result" => [true]
}
[standalone@localhost:9990 /]
```

That's it! Wasn't it easy?

# Reading the datasource's statistics

In this recipe, you will learn how to enable the statistics of the datasource to check whether we are getting the most out of it, or if we need to tune something with the datasource, or at worst, scale with the database.

## Getting ready

To get an idea of what is going on with our datasource, let's generate some traffic towards the database. In this case, we will use the application named `datasource-traffic-generator`. To obtain the artifact to deploy, please refer to the *Software prerequisites* recipe in *Chapter 1, Welcome to WildFly!*. Furthermore, in the source code of the application, you can find an Apache JMeter (also JMeter) project, available at the following path: `datasource-traffic-generator/src/main/resources/HTTP Request Defaults.jmx`.

Briefly, Apache JMeter is a testing tool used to make a stress test; as a matter of fact, we will stress the `datasource-traffic-generator` application, which inserts some data into the DB.

You can download the Apache JMeter binary, from `http://jmeter.apache.org/download_jmeter.cgi`.

The installation is quite easy:

1. Just unzip the downloaded package `apache-jmeter-2.13.zip`, into the `~/WFC` folder.
2. To run it, from the command line, navigate to the JMeter folder and issue the following command:

   ```
   $ ./bin/jmeter.sh
   ```

   If everything goes well, you should see the JMeter tool as depicted in the following image:

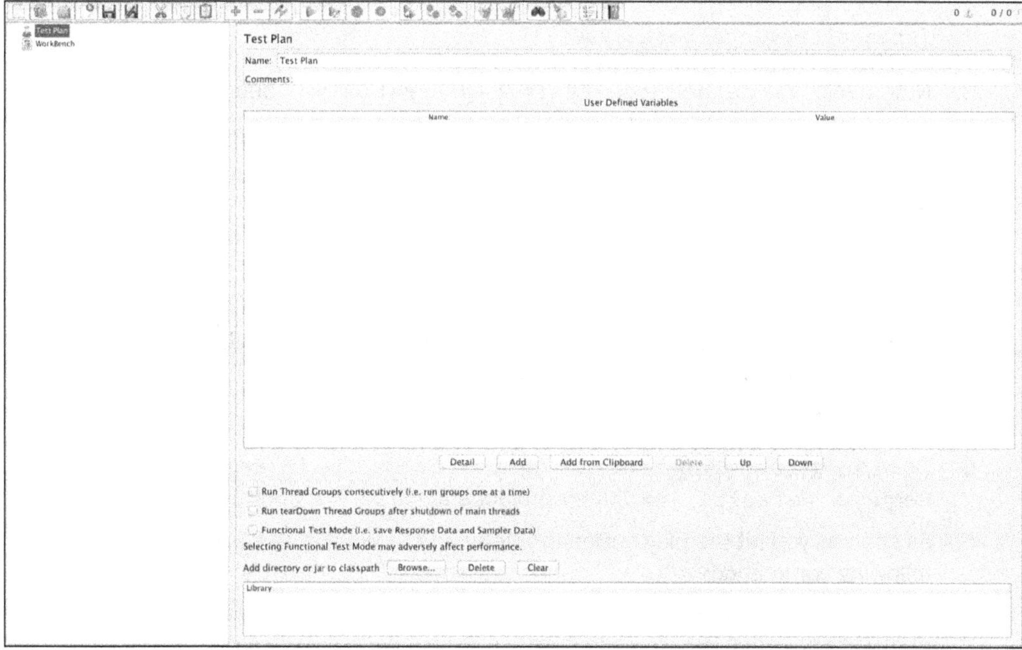


Apache JMeter

3. Furthermore, the database that we are going to use is MySQL. In that, create a database named `wildflycookbook`.
4. Lastly, create a table named `USER`, as follows:

   ```
   CREATE DATABASE IF NOT EXISTS wildflycookbook
   CREATE TABLE
     wildflycookbook.user
     (
       id BIGINT NOT NULL AUTO_INCREMENT,
   ```

```
      firstname VARCHAR(100) NOT NULL,
      lastname VARCHAR(100) NOT NULL,
      email VARCHAR(255) NOT NULL,
      phone VARCHAR(50),
      nickname VARCHAR(50),
      PRIMARY KEY (id),
      CONSTRAINT user_email UNIQUE (email)
    )
    ENGINE=InnoDB DEFAULT CHARSET=latin1
```

## How to do it...

1. With a running WildFly server, open your command-line tool and connect to the CLI:

   ```
   $ ./bin/jboss-cli.sh --connect
   [standalone@localhost:9990 /]
   ```

2. Now, deploy the `datasource-traffic-generator.war` bundle as usual.
3. Enable JDBC and Pool statistics with the following commands on the CLI:

   ```
   [standalone@localhost:9990 /] /subsystem=datasources/
   data-source=WildFlyCookbookDS/statistics=jdbc:write-
   attribute(name=statistics-enabled,value=true)
   {"outcome" => "success"}
   [standalone@localhost:9990 /] /subsystem=datasources/
   data-source=WildFlyCookbookDS/statistics=pool:write-
   attribute(name=statistics-enabled,value=true)
   {"outcome" => "success"}
   ```

4. Open the `datasource-traffic-generator/src/main/resources/HTTP Request Defaults.jmx` JMeter project and hit the start button.
5. As soon as you hit the play button in JMeter, in the WIldFLy CLI, execute the following commands:

   ```
   /subsystem=datasources/data-source=WildFlyCookbookDS/
   statistics=jdbc:read-resource(include-runtime=true)
   /subsystem=datasources/data-source=WildFlyCookbookDS/
   statistics=pool:read-resource(include-runtime=true)
   ```

The result is depicted in the following image:

```
[standalone@localhost:9990 /] /subsystem=datasources/data-source=WildFlyCookbookDS/statistics=jdbc:read-resource(include-runtime=true)
{
    "outcome" => "success",
    "result" => {
        "PreparedStatementCacheAccessCount" => 1500L,
        "PreparedStatementCacheAddCount" => 15L,
        "PreparedStatementCacheCurrentSize" => 15,
        "PreparedStatementCacheDeleteCount" => 0L,
        "PreparedStatementCacheHitCount" => 1485L,
        "PreparedStatementCacheMissCount" => 0L,
        "statistics-enabled" => true
    }
}
[standalone@localhost:9990 /] /subsystem=datasources/data-source=WildFlyCookbookDS/statistics=pool:read-resource(include-runtime=true)
{
    "outcome" => "success",
    "result" => {
        "ActiveCount" => 5,
        "AvailableCount" => 20,
        "AverageBlockingTime" => 1L,
        "AverageCreationTime" => 31L,
        "AverageGetTime" => 4L,
        "AveragePoolTime" => 21L,
        "AverageUsageTime" => 14L,
        "BlockingFailureCount" => 0,
        "CreatedCount" => 5,
        "DestroyedCount" => 0,
        "IdleCount" => 5,
        "InUseCount" => 0,
        "MaxCreationTime" => 39L,
        "MaxGetTime" => 39L,
        "MaxPoolTime" => 15967L,
        "MaxUsageTime" => 334L,
        "MaxUsedCount" => 5,
        "MaxWaitCount" => 0,
        "MaxWaitTime" => 9L,
        "TimedOut" => 0,
        "TotalBlockingTime" => 20L,
        "TotalCreationTime" => 158L,
        "TotalGetTime" => 218L,
        "TotalPoolTime" => 19001L,
        "TotalUsageTime" => 15027L,
        "WaitCount" => 0,
        "XACommitAverageTime" => 9L,
        "XACommitCount" => 1000L,
        "XACommitMaxTime" => 19L,
        "XACommitTotalTime" => 9882L,
        "XAEndAverageTime" => 0L,
        "XAEndCount" => 0L,
        "XAEndMaxTime" => 0L,
        "XAEndTotalTime" => 0L,
        "XAForgetAverageTime" => 0L,
        "XAForgetCount" => 0L,
        "XAForgetMaxTime" => 0L,
        "XAForgetTotalTime" => 0L,
        "XAPrepareAverageTime" => 0L,
        "XAPrepareCount" => 0L,
        "XAPrepareMaxTime" => 0L,
        "XAPrepareTotalTime" => 0L,
        "XARecoverAverageTime" => 0L,
        "XARecoverCount" => 0L,
        "XARecoverMaxTime" => 0L,
        "XARecoverTotalTime" => 0L,
        "XARollbackAverageTime" => 0L
        "XARollbackCount" => 0L,
        "XARollbackMaxTime" => 0L,
        "XARollbackTotalTime" => 0L,
        "XAStartAverageTime" => 0L,
        "XAStartCount" => 1000L,
        "XAStartMaxTime" => 6L,
        "XAStartTotalTime" => 14L,
        "statistics-enabled" => true
    }
}
[standalone@localhost:9990 /]
```

## How it works...

As you can see, we executed two commands, one to retrieve information at the `jdbc` level, and one to retrieve information about the `pool` configured within the datasource.

## There's more...

Instead of executing two commands within the CLI, you can use just one command to retrieve a lot more information. This can be helpful in parsing the data outside the CLI; also keep in mind that the output is very similar to the JSON format.

As a matter of fact, you can execute a CLI command outside the CLI using a bash-script, python, or Java and then parse the result to retrieve just the information you need.

To execute a CLI command using the bash-shell, type the following command:

```
$ ./bin/jboss-cli.sh -c --command="/subsystem=datasources/
data-source=WildFlyCookbookDS:read-resource(include-
runtime=true,recursive=true)"
```

# Setting a connection pool

As in the previous recipe, sometimes we need to extract some information regarding the behavior of database integration. Many times, when your application's concurrent users are in the order of hundreds or thousands, you have to serve multiple DB connections at a time. This is exactly what we will learn in this recipe, using the CLI.

## Getting ready

Think of a connection pool like a bucket pre-filled with a minimum number of ready-to-use connections for your application. There is also an upper bound limit that defines the maximum number of connections that the pool can hold. The default values for the minimum and maximum size of the pool are `0` and `20` respectively, with the `prefill` attribute set to `false` by default. This means that when a datasource is started up, its connection pool is created with `0` active and valid connections, and that it can hold up to 20 connections.

Why would you use a connection pool? Because creating a connection involves a lot of things under the hood, so having it ready helps you with the performance.

## How to do it...

1. With a running WildFly server, open your command line tool and connect to the CLI:

   ```
   $ ./bin/jboss-cli.sh
   You are disconnected at the moment. Type 'connect' to connect to the server or 'help' for the list of supported commands.
   [disconnected /] connect
   [standalone@localhost:9990 /]
   ```

2. Now execute the following commands:

   ```
   [standalone@localhost:9990 /] /subsystem=datasources/data-source=WildFlyCookbookDS:write-attribute(name="min-pool-size", value="10")
   {"outcome" => "success"}
   [standalone@localhost:9990 /] /subsystem=datasources/data-source=WildFlyCookbookDS:write-attribute(name="max-pool-size", value="20")
   {"outcome" => "success"}
   [standalone@localhost:9990 /]
   ```

## How it works...

The previously mentioned commands created a pool for our connections, so that we can count to a series of available connections that goes from 10 to 20.

## There's more...

One more option that we can use to boost our database connection is to have our connection pool pre-filled with connections.

1. To achieve this, we need set the `pool-prefill` attribute to `true`, as follows:

```
[standalone@localhost:9990 /] /subsystem=datasources/data-source=WildFlyCookbookDS:write-attribute(name="pool-prefill", value="true")
{
  "outcome" => "success",
  "response-headers" => {
    "operation-requires-reload" => true,
    "process-state" => "reload-required"
  }
}
[standalone@localhost:9990 /]
```

2. As you can see, not all changes are made at runtime; we often need to reload the WildFly configuration, like in this case. To reload the server (we had a recipe for that, both standalone and domain mode), execute the following command:

```
[standalone@localhost:9990 /] :reload
{
  "outcome" => "success",
  "result" => undefined
}
[standalone@localhost:9990 /]
```

The following image shows the `WildFlyCookbookDS` datasource with its new Pool configuration:

```
[standalone@localhost:9990 /] /subsystem=datasources/data-source=WildFlyCookbookDS:read-resource(attributes-only=true,include-runtime=true,include-defaults=true)
{
    "outcome" => "success",
    "result" => {
        "allocation-retry" => undefined,
        "allocation-retry-wait-millis" => undefined,
        "allow-multiple-users" => false,
        "background-validation" => undefined,
        "background-validation-millis" => undefined,
        "blocking-timeout-wait-millis" => 60000L,
        "capacity-decrementer-class" => undefined,
        "capacity-decrementer-properties" => undefined,
        "capacity-incrementer-class" => undefined,
        "capacity-incrementer-properties" => undefined,
        "check-valid-connection-sql" => undefined,
        "connectable" => false,
        "connection-listener-class" => undefined,
        "connection-listener-property" => undefined,
        "connection-properties" => undefined,
        "connection-url" => "jdbc:mysql://localhost:3306/wildflycookbook",
        "datasource-class" => undefined,
        "driver-class" => undefined,
        "driver-name" => "mysql",
        "enabled" => true,
        "exception-sorter-class-name" => undefined,
        "exception-sorter-properties" => undefined,
        "flush-strategy" => undefined,
        "idle-timeout-minutes" => 20L,
        "initial-pool-size" => undefined,
        "jndi-name" => "java:jboss/datasources/WildFlyCookbookDS",
        "jta" => true,
        "max-pool-size" => 20,
        "min-pool-size" => 10,
        "new-connection-sql" => undefined,
        "password" => "root",
        "pool-prefill" => true,
        "pool-use-strict-min" => undefined,
        "prepared-statements-cache-size" => 128L,
        "query-timeout" => undefined,
        "reauth-plugin-class-name" => undefined,
        "reauth-plugin-properties" => undefined,
        "security-domain" => undefined,
        "set-tx-query-timeout" => false,
        "share-prepared-statements" => true,
        "spy" => false,
        "stale-connection-checker-class-name" => undefined,
        "stale-connection-checker-properties" => undefined,
        "statistics-enabled" => false,
        "track-statements" => "NOWARN",
        "tracking" => false,
        "transaction-isolation" => undefined,
        "url-delimiter" => undefined,
        "url-selector-strategy-class-name" => undefined,
        "use-ccm" => true,
        "use-fast-fail" => false,
        "use-java-context" => true,
        "use-try-lock" => undefined,
        "user-name" => "root",
        "valid-connection-checker-class-name" => undefined,
        "valid-connection-checker-properties" => undefined,
        "validate-on-match" => undefined
    }
}
[standalone@localhost:9990 /]
```

There is also one more important aspect, which is worth mentioning about the datasource connection pool.

What happens if you pre-fill your pool with valid connections and then the database crashes or it gets restarted? Well, your connections might look valid in the pool, but the reference to the underlying database has changed, thus they will not be able to query your data. Fortunately, there are a few parameters that can help you solve this problem.

First of all, you need to choose a mechanism to validate your connection. You can opt for a time based approach, or decide to check your connection every time it is used.

The first approach consists of setting the following attributes:

- background-validation=true
- background-validation-millis=30000—default is 0

On the other hand, the second approach consists of setting the following attribute:

- validate-on-match=true

Whichever approach you use, always set the other one to false.

Once you have chosen the validation mechanism, you need to specify how to check if the connection is valid. You can achieve this by using one of the following attributes:

- check-valid-connection-sql
- valid-connection-checker-class

Both the attributes are database specific. The first one must contain a valid SQL code (for example SELECT 1 or SELECT 1 FROM DUAL). The second one delegates its check algorithm to a class. WildFly provides checker classes for the most used databases, which are as follows:

| Checker class |
| --- |
| org.jboss.jca.adapters.jdbc.extensions.db2.DB2ValidConnectionChecker |
| org.jboss.jca.adapters.jdbc.extensions.mssql.MSSQLValidConnectionChecker |
| org.jboss.jca.adapters.jdbc.extensions.mysql.MySQLReplicationValidConnectionChecker |
| org.jboss.jca.adapters.jdbc.extensions.mysql.MySQLValidConnectionChecker |
| org.jboss.jca.adapters.jdbc.extensions.novendor.GoodForSecondsValidConnectionChecker |
| org.jboss.jca.adapters.jdbc.extensions.novendor.JDBC4ValidConnectionChecker |
| org.jboss.jca.adapters.jdbc.extensions.novendor.NullValidConnectionChecker |
| org.jboss.jca.adapters.jdbc.extensions.novendor.SQLExceptionValidConnectionChecker |
| org.jboss.jca.adapters.jdbc.extensions.oracle.OracleValidConnectionChecker |
| org.jboss.jca.adapters.jdbc.extensions.postgres.PostgreSQLValidConnectionChecker |
| org.jboss.jca.adapters.jdbc.extensions.sybase.SybaseValidConnectionChecker |

Last, but not the least, you can count on two other attributes that help you clean up connections: `stale-connection-checker-class-name` and `exception-sorter-class-name`.

The first one provides you with an easy way to clean up stale connections; you can rely on a generic class, and DB2 and Oracle specific classes, as the following:

| Generic/specific class |
|---|
| `org.jboss.jca.adapters.jdbc.extensions.novendor.AlwaysStaleConnectionChecker` |
| `org.jboss.jca.adapters.jdbc.extensions.novendor.NullStaleConnectionChecker` |
| `org.jboss.jca.adapters.jdbc.extensions.db2.DB2StaleConnectionChecker` |
| `org.jboss.jca.adapters.jdbc.extensions.oracle.OracleStaleConnectionChecker` |

The second attribute provides you with an easy way to clean up connections that threw a `FATAL` exception, and relative to your database, you can rely on the following classes:

| Class |
|---|
| `org.jboss.jca.adapters.jdbc.extensions.db2.DB2ExceptionSorter` |
| `org.jboss.jca.adapters.jdbc.extensions.informix.InformixExceptionSorter` |
| `org.jboss.jca.adapters.jdbc.extensions.mysql.MySQLExceptionSorter` |
| `org.jboss.jca.adapters.jdbc.extensions.mssql.MSSQLExceptionSorter` |
| `org.jboss.jca.adapters.jdbc.extensions.novendor.AlwaysExceptionSorter` |
| `org.jboss.jca.adapters.jdbc.extensions.novendor.NullExceptionSorter` |
| `org.jboss.jca.adapters.jdbc.extensions.oracle.OracleExceptionSorter` |
| `org.jboss.jca.adapters.jdbc.extensions.postgres.PostgreSQLExceptionSorter` |
| `org.jboss.jca.adapters.jdbc.extensions.sybase.SybaseExceptionSorter` |

# Creating and removing XA-Datasource

XA-Datasources are just like normal datasources, except that they need a different `driver-class-name` and they support distributed transaction across heterogeneous transactional systems.

Imagine the classical example of an online store: a user buys an item, the item is removed from the stock database and an amount of money is subtracted from the user's bank account, which is an external system. Both the operations must succeed in order to proceed with payment and shipment.

This was just an example to give you the idea; we will not go any further.

## Getting ready

The prerequisite of this recipe is the *Getting ready* section of the *Creating and removing a datasource* recipe.

## How to do it...

1. With a running WildFly server, open your command-line tool and connect to the CLI:

   ```
   $ ./bin/jboss-cli.sh --connect
   [standalone@localhost:9990 /]
   ```

2. Now execute the following commands:

   ```
   [standalone@localhost:9990 /] batch
   [standalone@localhost:9990 / #] /subsystem=datasources/xa-data-source=XAWildFlyCookBookDS:add(driver-name=mysql,jndi-name=java:jboss/datasources/XAWildFlyCookBookDS,use-java-context=true,new-connection-sql="select 1 from dual",no-tx-separate-pool=true,valid-connection-checker-class-name="org.jboss.jca.adapters.jdbc.extensions.mysql.MySQLValidConnectionChecker",stale-connection-checker-class-name="org.jboss.jca.adapters.jdbc.extensions.mysql.MySQLStaleConnectionChecker",min-pool-size=10,max-pool-size=25,track-statements=true,prepared-statements-cache-size=25, xa-datasource-class="com.mysql.jdbc.jdbc2.optional.MysqlXADataSource")
   [standalone@localhost:9990 / #] /subsystem=datasources/xa-data-source=XAWildFlyCookBookDS/xa-datasource-properties=URL:add(value="jdbc:mysql://localhost:3306/wildflycookbook")
   [standalone@localhost:9990 / #] /subsystem=datasources/xa-data-source=XAWildFlyCookBookDS/xa-datasource-properties=User:add(value="root")
   ```

```
[standalone@localhost:9990 / #] /subsystem=datasources/xa-data-source=XAWildFlyCookBookDS/xa-datasource-properties=Password:add(value="password-root")
[standalone@localhost:9990 / #] run-batch
The batch executed successfully
[standalone@localhost:9990 /]
```

3. Now, on listing the available datasources you should find our newly created one:

```
[standalone@localhost:9990 /] ls /subsystem=datasources/xa-data-source
XAWildFlyCookBookDS
[standalone@localhost:9990 /]
```

4. If you need to remove a datasource, invoke `remove` next to it, as depicted in the following image:

```
[standalone@localhost:9990 /] /subsystem=datasources/xa-data-source=XAWildFlyCookBookDS:remove
{"outcome" => "success"}
[standalone@localhost:9990 /] ls /subsystem=datasources/xa-data-source
[standalone@localhost:9990 /]
```

## How it works...

We first created an XA-DataSource with just the required information and then added the other ones, all in batch mode. By doing this, we are able to split the configuration process and eventually see where we are going wrong.

Additionally, we specified the `xa-datasource-class` class, because XA-DataSource needs a special class that implements and supports distributed transactions. The driver is the same, just specify a different driver class implementation.

# 6
# Clustering WildFly

In this chapter, we will cover the following topics:

- Creating a cluster in standalone mode
- Creating separate clusters in standalone mode
- Creating a cluster in domain mode
- Creating separate clusters in domain mode
- Creating a cluster via TCP
- Testing the UDP protocol with the JGroups tool

## Introduction

In this chapter, you will learn how to create a cluster for a web application spread across two or more WildFly nodes. Clustering is the capability to continue serving a client, even in case of failures (that is, a server crash), and is also known as failover.

Clustering is meant to be at the application level and not at the OS level.

For example, suppose you are filling in a long form, in a large number of steps (where steps are meant to be pages). Now suppose that in the last step, the server or the WildFly node crashes, you would have to refill all the information again. Surely, you will not use that site anymore, if you can choose to do so. By the way, how would you address such a problem? Clustering is the answer.

In clustering, you get the user's session replicated to your cluster nodes. So in case of a failure, in the next HTTP request, you will land on a different server/node, which will continue serving you just as though nothing happened—obviously, the end user will not see that his/her request has been served by a different server/node.

In WildFly, we have two components (from a configuration file point of view, they are subsystems) that accomplish this job; they are *infinispan* (for caching the data session) and *JGroups* (to spread HTTP sessions across cluster nodes). Infinispan is the component that stores the data, whilst JGroups is the component that orchestrates the communication between the nodes forming the application cluster.

We will see how clustering can be achieved using different protocols: UDP (multicast and also the default one) and TCP (unicast). This can be configured in the `jgroups` subsystem. The default one is UDP.

For the sake of completeness, we will try our configuration in both the operational modes: standalone and domain.

Remember that clustering is a service provided by WildFly, as such, it is activated on demand. Thus, you will need to provide a `cluster-aware` application in order to activate clustering. That means having the `<distributable/>` XML tag inside your `web.xml` file.

Within this chapter, you will need a standard WildFly installation and a settled management user. If you are starting from here, take a look at *Chapter 1, Welcome to WildFly!*

# Creating a cluster in standalone mode

In this recipe, you will learn how to cluster two WildFly nodes locally, that is, on your PC. We will try this using the standalone mode and the `ha` profile.

## Getting ready

For this recipe, we will need the `cluster-aware` application named `cluster-test`, that you can find in my GitHub repository. If you skipped the *Managing applications using the deployments folder* recipe in *Chapter 2, Running WildFly in Standalone Mode*, please refer to it to download all the source code and projects that you will need.

To build the application, give the following commands:

```
$ cd ~/WFC/github/wildfly-cookbook
$ cd cluster-test
$ mvn -e clean package
```

## How to do it...

From the WildFly installation directory `$WILDFLY_HOME`, let's create two folders, each one representing a server node:

1. Open a terminal and execute the following commands:

   ```
   $ cd $WILDFLY_HOME
   $ cp -a standalone cl-std-node-1
   $ cp -a standalone cl-std-node-2
   ```

2. Now, let's copy the `cluster-test.war` application into the `deployments` folder of each node that we have just created. Execute the following commands:

   ```
   $ cp ~/WFC/github/wildfly-cookbook/cluster-test/target/cluster-test.war cl-std-node-1/deployments/
   $ cp ~/WFC/github/wildfly-cookbook/cluster-test/target/cluster-test.war cl-std-node-2/deployments/
   ```

3. We are almost ready to test our cluster. We need some configuration, but without editing much, we will just pass a command-line parameter to the `standalone.sh` script. Let's do it:

   ```
   $ ./bin/standalone.sh -Djboss.server.base.dir=cl-std-node-1
   --server-config=standalone-ha.xml -Djboss.socket.binding.port-offset=100 -Djboss.node.name=node-1
   ...
   02:26:22,755 INFO  [org.jboss.as.server.deployment] (MSC service thread 1-14) WFLYSRV0027: Starting deployment of "cluster-test.war" (runtime-name: "cluster-test.war")
   02:26:22,910 INFO  [org.jboss.ws.common.management] (MSC service thread 1-2) JBWS022052: Starting JBoss Web Services - Stack CXF Server 5.0.0.Beta3
   02:26:23,843 INFO  [stdout] (MSC service thread 1-6)
   02:26:23,843 INFO  [stdout] (MSC service thread 1-6) -------------------------------------------------------------------
   02:26:23,843 INFO  [stdout] (MSC service thread 1-6) GMS: address=node-1, cluster=ee, physical address=127.0.0.1:55300
   02:26:23,843 INFO  [stdout] (MSC service thread 1-6) -------------------------------------------------------------------
   02:26:27,145 INFO  [org.infinispan.remoting.transport.jgroups.JGroupsTransport] (ServerService Thread Pool -- 64) ISPN000078: Starting JGroups channel web
   ```

```
02:26:27,154 INFO  [org.infinispan.remoting.transport.jgroups.
JGroupsTransport] (ServerService Thread Pool -- 64) ISPN000094:
Received new cluster view for channel web: [node-1|0] (1) [node-1]
02:26:27,155 INFO  [org.infinispan.remoting.transport.jgroups.
JGroupsTransport] (ServerService Thread Pool -- 64) ISPN000079:
Channel web local address is node-1, physical addresses are
[127.0.0.1:55300]

02:26:27,163 INFO  [org.infinispan.factories.
GlobalComponentRegistry] (ServerService Thread Pool -- 64)
ISPN000128: Infinispan version: Infinispan 'Hoptimus Prime'
7.1.1.Final

02:26:27,706 INFO  [org.jboss.as.clustering.infinispan]
(ServerService Thread Pool -- 64) WFLYCLINF0002: Started dist
cache from web container

02:26:27,706 INFO  [org.jboss.as.clustering.infinispan]
(ServerService Thread Pool -- 62) WFLYCLINF0002: Started cluster-
test.war cache from web container

02:26:27,970 INFO  [org.wildfly.extension.undertow] (MSC service
thread 1-16) WFLYUT0021: Registered web context: /cluster-test
02:26:28,006 INFO  [org.jboss.as.server] (ServerService Thread
Pool -- 36) WFLYSRV0010: Deployed "cluster-test.war" (runtime-name
: "cluster-test.war")
02:26:28,182 INFO  [org.jboss.as] (Controller Boot Thread)
WFLYSRV0060: Http management interface listening on
http://127.0.0.1:10090/management

02:26:28,183 INFO  [org.jboss.as] (Controller Boot Thread)
WFLYSRV0051: Admin console listening on http://127.0.0.1:10090

02:26:28,183 INFO  [org.jboss.as] (Controller Boot Thread)
WFLYSRV0025: WildFly Full 9.0.0.Beta2 (WildFly Core 1.0.0.Beta2)
started in 8645ms - Started 334 of 516 services (285 services are
lazy, passive or on-demand)
```

In the preceding command, I've emphasized only the relevant outputs; this is to give you a clear view of the clustering service.

4. Let's open a browser and point it to the URL `http://127.0.0.1:8180/cluster-test`. Now refresh the page a few times. You should see something like the following screenshot:

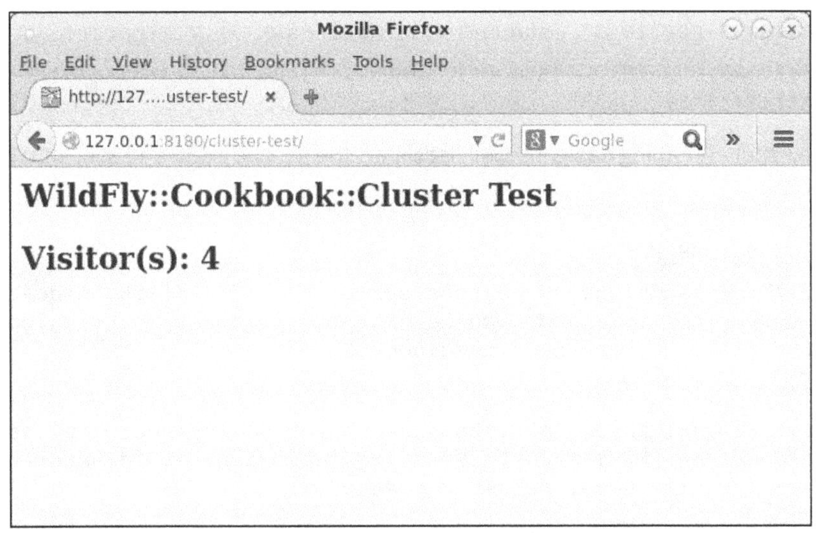


"cluster-test" application running on "node-1"

In the log, you should find the following statements:

```
15:20:25,118 INFO  [stdout] (default task-3) ********************
***********+
15:20:25,119 INFO  [stdout] (default task-3) Visitor(s): 0
15:20:25,119 INFO  [stdout] (default task-3) ********************
***********+
15:20:25,228 INFO  [stdout] (default task-4) ********************
***********+
15:20:25,229 INFO  [stdout] (default task-4) Visitor(s): 1
15:20:25,229 INFO  [stdout] (default task-4) ********************
***********+
15:20:25,291 INFO  [stdout] (default task-5) ********************
***********+
15:20:25,291 INFO  [stdout] (default task-5) Visitor(s): 2
15:20:25,291 INFO  [stdout] (default task-5) ********************
***********+
15:20:25,315 INFO  [stdout] (default task-6) ********************
***********+
15:20:25,315 INFO  [stdout] (default task-6) Visitor(s): 3
```

```
15:20:25,316 INFO  [stdout] (default task-6) ********************
***********+
15:20:25,608 INFO  [stdout] (default task-7) ********************
***********+
15:20:25,609 INFO  [stdout] (default task-7) Visitor(s): 4
15:20:25,609 INFO  [stdout] (default task-7) ********************
***********+
```

Now that everything has gone well, let's start the second node and see what happens.

5. In a new terminal, execute the following commands:

```
$ cd $JBOSS_HOME
$ ./bin/standalone.sh -Djboss.server.base.dir=cl-std-node-2
--server-config=standalone-ha.xml -Djboss.socket.binding.port-
offset=200 -Djboss.node.name=node-2
...
03:13:44,381 INFO  [org.jboss.as.server.deployment] (MSC service
thread 1-14) WFLYSRV0027: Starting deployment of "cluster-test.
war" (runtime-name: "cluster-test.war")
03:13:44,548 INFO  [org.jboss.ws.common.management] (MSC service
thread 1-15) JBWS022052: Starting JBoss Web Services - Stack CXF
Server 5.0.0.Beta3
03:13:45,075 INFO  [stdout] (MSC service thread 1-6)
03:13:45,075 INFO  [stdout] (MSC service thread 1-6) ------------
-------------------------------------------------------
03:13:45,075 INFO  [stdout] (MSC service thread 1-6) GMS:
address=node-2, cluster=ee, physical address=127.0.0.1:55400
03:13:45,077 INFO  [stdout] (MSC service thread 1-6) ------------
-------------------------------------------------------
03:13:45,153 INFO  [org.infinispan.remoting.transport.jgroups.
JGroupsTransport] (Incoming-2,ee,node-1) ISPN000094: Received new
cluster view for channel web: [node-1|1] (2) [node-1, node-2]
03:13:45,675 INFO  [org.infinispan.remoting.transport.jgroups.
JGroupsTransport] (ServerService Thread Pool -- 62) ISPN000078:
Starting JGroups channel web
03:13:45,679 INFO  [org.infinispan.remoting.transport.jgroups.
JGroupsTransport] (ServerService Thread Pool -- 62) ISPN000094:
Received new cluster view for channel web: [node-1|1] (2) [node-1,
node-2]
03:13:45,680 INFO  [org.infinispan.remoting.transport.jgroups.
JGroupsTransport] (ServerService Thread Pool -- 62) ISPN000079:
Channel web local address is node-2, physical addresses are
[127.0.0.1:55400]
```

```
03:13:45,747 INFO  [org.infinispan.factories.
GlobalComponentRegistry] (ServerService Thread Pool -- 62)
ISPN000128: Infinispan version: Infinispan 'Hoptimus Prime'
7.1.1.Final

03:13:46,187 INFO  [org.infinispan.CLUSTER] (remote-thread--p3-t1)
ISPN000310: Starting cluster-wide rebalance for cache cluster-
test.war, topology CacheTopology{id=1, rebalanceId=1, currentCH=De
faultConsistentHash{ns = 80, owners = (1)[node-1: 80+0]}, pendingC
H=DefaultConsistentHash{ns = 80, owners = (2)[node-1: 40+40, node-
2: 40+40]}, unionCH=null, actualMembers=[node-1, node-2]}

03:13:46,187 INFO  [org.infinispan.CLUSTER] (remote-thread--
p3-t2) ISPN000310: Starting cluster-wide rebalance for cache dist,
topology CacheTopology{id=1, rebalanceId=1, currentCH=DefaultCon
sistentHash{ns = 80, owners = (1)[node-1: 80+0]}, pendingCH=Def
aultConsistentHash{ns = 80, owners = (2)[node-1: 40+40, node-2:
40+40]}, unionCH=null, actualMembers=[node-1, node-2]}

03:13:46,204 INFO  [org.infinispan.CLUSTER] (transport-thread--
p2-t10) ISPN000328: Finished local rebalance for cache cluster-
test.war on node node-1, topology id = 1

03:13:46,209 INFO  [org.infinispan.CLUSTER] (transport-thread-
-p2-t11) ISPN000328: Finished local rebalance for cache dist on
node node-1, topology id = 1

03:13:46,416 INFO  [org.infinispan.CLUSTER] (remote-thread--p3-t1)
ISPN000328: Finished local rebalance for cache dist on node node-
2, topology id = 1

03:13:46,431 INFO  [org.infinispan.CLUSTER] (remote-thread--p3-t2)
ISPN000328: Finished local rebalance for cache cluster-test.war on
node node-2, topology id = 1

03:13:46,461 INFO  [org.jboss.as.clustering.infinispan]
(ServerService Thread Pool -- 62) WFLYCLINF0002: Started dist
cache from web container

03:13:46,461 INFO  [org.jboss.as.clustering.infinispan]
(ServerService Thread Pool -- 64) WFLYCLINF0002: Started cluster-
test.war cache from web container

03:13:46,662 INFO  [org.wildfly.extension.undertow] (MSC service
thread 1-3) WFLYUT0021: Registered web context: /cluster-test

03:13:46,700 INFO  [org.jboss.as.server] (ServerService Thread
Pool -- 36) WFLYSRV0010: Deployed "cluster-test.war" (runtime-name
: "cluster-test.war")

03:13:46,863 INFO  [org.jboss.as] (Controller Boot Thread)
WFLYSRV0060: Http management interface listening on
http://127.0.0.1:10190/management
```

```
03:13:46,864 INFO  [org.jboss.as] (Controller Boot Thread)
WFLYSRV0051: Admin console listening on http://127.0.0.1:10190
03:13:46,864 INFO  [org.jboss.as] (Controller Boot Thread)
WFLYSRV0025: WildFly Full 9.0.0.Beta2 (WildFly Core 1.0.0.Beta2)
started in 5424ms - Started 334 of 516 services (285 services are
lazy, passive or on-demand)
```

In the preceding command-line output, I've emphasized only the relevant outputs; this is to give you a clear view of the clustering service. Unlike `node-1`, we can see that now the cluster is composed of two members: `node-1` and `node-2`.

6. Now, let's try pointing the same browser window to the URL `http://127.0.0.1:8280/cluster-test`. You should see something like this:

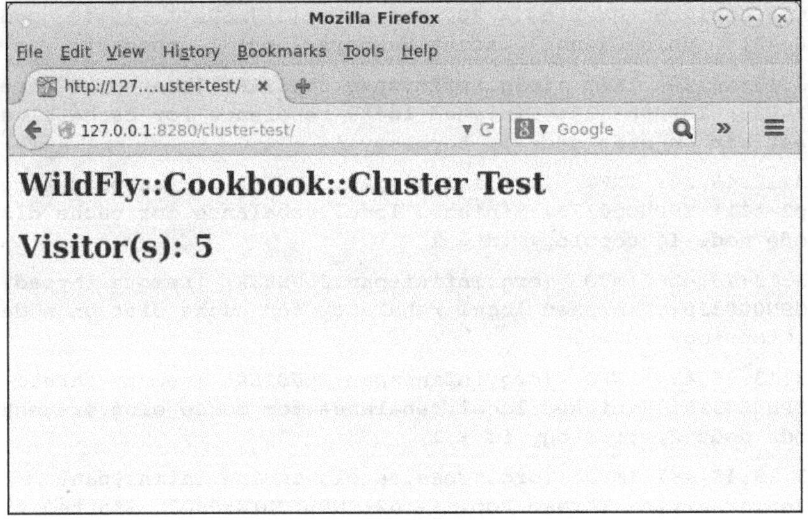


"cluster-test" application running on "node-2"

As you can see, the second node continued counting exactly from where we stopped in `node-1`. Great, our cluster is working!!

## How it works...

Let's analyze what we have done and why it is working without much configuration. Along with `standalone.sh` script for `node-1`, we specified a few parameters such as:

- `jboss.server.base.dir=cl-std-node-1`: Needed to specify our base directory as a starting folder to retrieve all the configuration files.
- `--server-config=standalone-ha.xml`: Needed to specify the server configuration file with `ha` profile.

- `jboss.socket.binding.port-offset=100`: Needed to specify the port offset (`200` for `node-2`). We could have skipped this for the first node, but I like seeing the series: `1,2,3,4..n`, which in this case would have been `8180`, `8280`, `8380`, and so on.
- `jboss.node.name=node-1`: Needed to uniquely identify the node within the cluster (obviously, `node-2` for the second node).

That's all we need to do to make our cluster. This is because of the default WildFly's configuration, especially the configuration of the subsystem, `jgroups`. Let's see its defaults:

```
<subsystem xmlns="urn:jboss:domain:jgroups:3.0">
    <channels default="ee">
        <channel name="ee"/>
    </channels>
    <stacks default="udp">
        <stack name="udp">
            <transport type="UDP" socket-binding="jgroups-udp"/>
            <protocol type="PING"/>
            <protocol type="MERGE3"/>
            <protocol type="FD_SOCK" socket-binding="jgroups-udp-
            fd"/>
            <protocol type="FD_ALL"/>
            <protocol type="VERIFY_SUSPECT"/>
            <protocol type="pbcast.NAKACK2"/>
            <protocol type="UNICAST3"/>
            <protocol type="pbcast.STABLE"/>
            <protocol type="pbcast.GMS"/>
            <protocol type="UFC"/>
            <protocol type="MFC"/>
            <protocol type="FRAG2"/>
            <protocol type="RSVP"/>
        </stack>
        <stack name="tcp">
            <transport type="TCP" socket-binding="jgroups-tcp"/>
            <protocol type="MPING" socket-binding="jgroups-
            mping"/>
            <protocol type="MERGE3"/>
            <protocol type="FD_SOCK" socket-binding="jgroups-tcp-
            fd"/>
            <protocol type="FD"/>
            <protocol type="VERIFY_SUSPECT"/>
            <protocol type="pbcast.NAKACK2"/>
            <protocol type="UNICAST3"/>
            <protocol type="pbcast.STABLE"/>
            <protocol type="pbcast.GMS"/>
```

```
            <protocol type="MFC"/>
            <protocol type="FRAG2"/>
            <protocol type="RSVP"/>
        </stack>
    </stacks>
</subsystem>
```

So, the default protocol used for cluster transportation is the UDP (see the emphasized code). This UDP setting has additional configuration within the `socket-binding-group` specified in the `standalone-ha.xml` file, as follows:

```
<socket-binding-group name="standard-sockets" default-
interface="public" port-offset="${jboss.socket.binding.port-
offset:0}">
    <socket-binding name="management-http" interface="management"
    port="${jboss.management.http.port:9990}"/>
    <socket-binding name="management-https" interface="management"
    port="${jboss.management.https.port:9993}"/>
    <socket-binding name="ajp" port="${jboss.ajp.port:8009}"/>
    <socket-binding name="http" port="${jboss.http.port:8080}"/>
    <socket-binding name="https" port="${jboss.https.port:8443}"/>
    <socket-binding name="jgroups-mping" port="0" multicast-
    address="${jboss.default.multicast.address:230.0.0.4}"
    multicast-port="45700"/>
    <socket-binding name="jgroups-tcp" port="7600"/>
    <socket-binding name="jgroups-tcp-fd" port="57600"/>
    <socket-binding name="jgroups-udp" port="55200" multicast-
    address="${jboss.default.multicast.address:230.0.0.4}"
    multicast-port="45688"/>
    <socket-binding name="jgroups-udp-fd" port="54200"/>
    <socket-binding name="modcluster" port="0" multicast-
    address="224.0.1.105" multicast-port="23364"/>
    <socket-binding name="txn-recovery-environment" port="4712"/>
    <socket-binding name="txn-status-manager" port="4713"/>
    <outbound-socket-binding name="mail-smtp">
        <remote-destination host="localhost" port="25"/>
    </outbound-socket-binding>
</socket-binding-group>
```

So, by default, every member of the cluster advertises itself at the `230.0.0.4` address. Also, every port specified in the configuration is altered along with the `jboss.socket.binding.port-offset` parameter specified by the command-line script.

## There's more...

We could have made our cluster without the `port-offset` directive, and by using different IPs for each node instead, but this wouldn't have worked properly. This is because of the HTTP session reference stored in a cookie. Generally speaking, a cookie consists of a name (typically `JSESSIONID`), a value (which is an ID used to reference the HTTP session on the server), a domain, and a context path.

All these properties must be the same in order to send requests to the same HTTP session on the server, which will not be the case with nodes bound to different IPs. The IP is the domain of the cookie, thus it will not work—unless you balance all the properties—but that's the subject of the next chapter.

## See also

If you have any problem with this configuration, you might have network problems, which you can troubleshoot with the last recipe of this chapter.

# Creating separate clusters in standalone mode

In this recipe, you will learn how to configure different and isolated clusters, running locally. We will try this using the standalone mode and the `ha` profile.

## Getting ready

For this recipe, we will need the `cluster-aware` application named `cluster-test`, that you can find in my GitHub repository. If you skipped the *Managing applications using the deployments folder* recipe of *Chapter 2, Running WildFly in Standalone Mode*, please refer to it to download all the source code and projects that you will need.

To build the application, execute the following commands:

```
$ cd ~/WFC/github/wildfly-cookbook
$ cd cluster-test
$ mvn -e clean package
```

From the WildFly installation directory `$WILDFLY_HOME`, let's create four folders, each one representing a server node.

1. Open a terminal and execute the following commands:

```
$ cd $WILDFLY_HOME
$ cp -a standalone cl-std-node-A1
$ cp -a standalone cl-std-node-A2
$ cp -a standalone cl-std-node-B1
$ cp -a standalone cl-std-node-B2
```

2. Now, let's copy the `cluster-test.war` application into the `deployments` folder of each node that we have just created. Give the following commands:

```
$ cp ~/WFC/github/wildfly-cookbook/cluster-test/target/cluster-test.war cl-std-node-A1/deployments/
$ cp ~/WFC/github/wildfly-cookbook/cluster-test/target/cluster-test.war cl-std-node-A2/deployments/
$ cp ~/WFC/github/wildfly-cookbook/cluster-test/target/cluster-test.war cl-std-node-B1/deployments/
$ cp ~/WFC/github/wildfly-cookbook/cluster-test/target/cluster-test.war cl-std-node-B2/deployments/
```

We are almost ready to test our cluster. We just need some configuration to pass to the `standalone.sh` script, through the command line.

## Node-A1

In the following log output, you can see that a cluster was formed and a member named `node-A1` joined it:

```
$ ./bin/standalone.sh -Djboss.server.base.dir=cl-std-node-A1 --server-config=standalone-ha.xml -Djboss.socket.binding.port-offset=100 -Djboss.node.name=node-A1
...
03:41:27,703 INFO  [stdout] (MSC service thread 1-13)
03:41:27,703 INFO  [stdout] (MSC service thread 1-13) -------------------------------------------------------------------
03:41:27,703 INFO  [stdout] (MSC service thread 1-13) GMS: address=node-A1, cluster=ee, physical address=127.0.0.1:55300
03:41:27,704 INFO  [stdout] (MSC service thread 1-13) -------------------------------------------------------------------
03:41:31,065 INFO  [org.infinispan.remoting.transport.jgroups.JGroupsTransport] (ServerService Thread Pool -- 62) ISPN000078: Starting JGroups channel web
```

```
03:41:31,073 INFO  [org.infinispan.remoting.transport.jgroups.
JGroupsTransport] (ServerService Thread Pool -- 62) ISPN000094: Received
new cluster view for channel web: [node-A1|0] (1) [node-A1]
03:41:31,075 INFO  [org.infinispan.remoting.transport.jgroups.
JGroupsTransport] (ServerService Thread Pool -- 62) ISPN000079: Channel
web local address is node-A1, physical addresses are [127.0.0.1:55300]
...
```

## Node-A2

In the following log output, you can see that a member named `node-A2` joined a cluster along with the other member named `node-A1`:

```
$ ./bin/standalone.sh -Djboss.server.base.dir=cl-std-node-A2 --server-
config=standalone-ha.xml -Djboss.socket.binding.port-offset=200 -Djboss.
node.name=node-A2
...
03:43:27,309 INFO  [stdout] (MSC service thread 1-5)
03:43:27,309 INFO  [stdout] (MSC service thread 1-5) -------------------
-----------------------------------------------
03:43:27,310 INFO  [stdout] (MSC service thread 1-5) GMS:
address=node-A2, cluster=ee, physical address=127.0.0.1:55400
03:43:27,310 INFO  [stdout] (MSC service thread 1-5) -------------------
-----------------------------------------------
03:43:27,672 INFO  [org.infinispan.remoting.transport.jgroups.
JGroupsTransport] (ServerService Thread Pool -- 62) ISPN000078: Starting
JGroups channel web
03:43:27,681 INFO  [org.infinispan.remoting.transport.jgroups.
JGroupsTransport] (ServerService Thread Pool -- 62) ISPN000094: Received
new cluster view for channel web: [node-A1|1] (2) [node-A1, node-A2]
03:43:27,683 INFO  [org.infinispan.remoting.transport.jgroups.
JGroupsTransport] (ServerService Thread Pool -- 62) ISPN000079: Channel
web local address is node-A2, physical addresses are [127.0.0.1:55400]
...
```

## Node-B1

In the following log output, you can see that a cluster was formed and a member named `node-B1` joined it. We do not see any `node-Ax` members, so we have formed a different cluster:

```
$ ./bin/standalone.sh -Djboss.server.base.dir=cl-std-node-B1 --server-
config=standalone-ha.xml -Djboss.socket.binding.port-offset=300 -Djboss.
node.name=node-B1 -Djboss.default.multicast.address=230.0.0.5
...
03:44:59,778 INFO  [stdout] (MSC service thread 1-3)
```

```
03:44:59,778 INFO  [stdout] (MSC service thread 1-3) -------------------
----------------------------------------------

03:44:59,779 INFO  [stdout] (MSC service thread 1-3) GMS:
address=node-B1, cluster=ee, physical address=127.0.0.1:55500

03:44:59,779 INFO  [stdout] (MSC service thread 1-3) -------------------
----------------------------------------------

03:45:03,810 INFO  [org.infinispan.remoting.transport.jgroups.
JGroupsTransport] (ServerService Thread Pool -- 62) ISPN000078: Starting
JGroups channel web

03:45:03,818 INFO  [org.infinispan.remoting.transport.jgroups.
JGroupsTransport] (ServerService Thread Pool -- 62) ISPN000094: Received
new cluster view for channel web: [node-B1|0] (1) [node-B1]

03:45:03,819 INFO  [org.infinispan.remoting.transport.jgroups.
JGroupsTransport] (ServerService Thread Pool -- 62) ISPN000079: Channel
web local address is node-B1, physical addresses are [127.0.0.1:55500]

...
```

## Node-B2

In the following log output, you can see that a member named `node-B2` joined a cluster along with the other member named `node-B1`:

```
$ ./bin/standalone.sh -Djboss.server.base.dir=cl-std-node-B2 --server-
config=standalone-ha.xml -Djboss.socket.binding.port-offset=400 -Djboss.
node.name=node-B2 -Djboss.default.multicast.address=230.0.0.5

...

03:46:32,480 INFO  [stdout] (MSC service thread 1-14)

03:46:32,481 INFO  [stdout] (MSC service thread 1-14) ------------------
-----------------------------------------------

03:46:32,481 INFO  [stdout] (MSC service thread 1-14) GMS:
address=node-B2, cluster=ee, physical address=127.0.0.1:55600

03:46:32,481 INFO  [stdout] (MSC service thread 1-14) ------------------
-----------------------------------------------

03:46:35,068 INFO  [org.infinispan.remoting.transport.jgroups.
JGroupsTransport] (ServerService Thread Pool -- 62) ISPN000078: Starting
JGroups channel web

03:46:35,081 INFO  [org.infinispan.remoting.transport.jgroups.
JGroupsTransport] (ServerService Thread Pool -- 62) ISPN000094: Received
new cluster view for channel web: [node-B1|1] (2) [node-B1, node-B2]

03:46:35,082 INFO  [org.infinispan.remoting.transport.jgroups.
JGroupsTransport] (ServerService Thread Pool -- 62) ISPN000079: Channel
web local address is node-B2, physical addresses are [127.0.0.1:55600]

...
```

## How to do it...

Now that we have launched all the WildFly nodes and formed two different clusters, let's test them with our great `cluster-test` application:

1. Open your browser and point it to the following location: `http://127.0.0.1:8180/cluster-test`.
2. Refresh the page a few times. In the browser window, you should see something similar to the following screenshot:

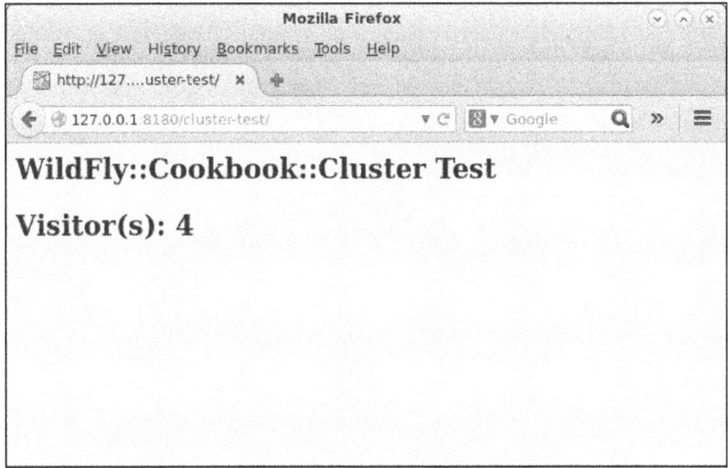


"cluster-test" application running on "node-A1"

In the `node-A1` log, you should find the following statements:

```
17:07:15,429 INFO  [stdout] (default task-1) ********************
***********+

17:07:15,429 INFO  [stdout] (default task-1) Visitor(s): 0

17:07:15,430 INFO  [stdout] (default task-1) ********************
***********+

17:07:16,853 INFO  [stdout] (default task-2) ********************
***********+

17:07:16,854 INFO  [stdout] (default task-2) Visitor(s): 1

17:07:16,854 INFO  [stdout] (default task-2) ********************
***********+

17:07:17,271 INFO  [stdout] (default task-3) ********************
***********+

17:07:17,273 INFO  [stdout] (default task-3) Visitor(s): 2

17:07:17,273 INFO  [stdout] (default task-3) ********************
***********+
```

```
17:07:17,693 INFO  [stdout] (default task-4) ********************
***********+
17:07:17,694 INFO  [stdout] (default task-4) Visitor(s): 3
17:07:17,695 INFO  [stdout] (default task-4) ********************
***********+
17:07:18,208 INFO  [stdout] (default task-5) ********************
***********+
17:07:18,209 INFO  [stdout] (default task-5) Visitor(s): 4
17:07:18,209 INFO  [stdout] (default task-5) ********************
***********+
```

3. Now, let's try pointing the same browser window to the URL `http://127.0.0.1:8280/cluster-test`. You should see something like the following screenshot:

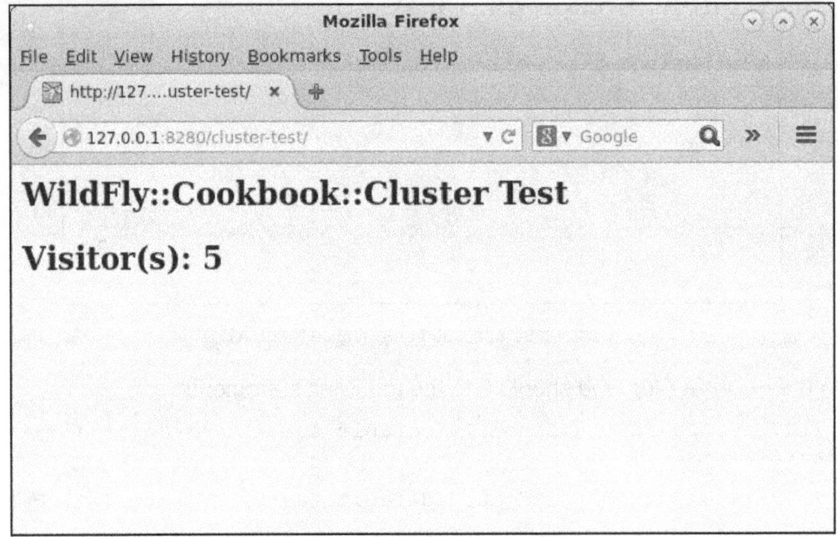


"cluster-test" application running on "node-A2"

As you can see, the second node continued counting exactly from where we stopped in `node-A1`. In the `node-A2` log, you should find the following statements:

```
17:10:29,776 INFO  [stdout] (default task-1) ********************
***********+
17:10:29,777 INFO  [stdout] (default task-1) Visitor(s): 5
17:10:29,777 INFO  [stdout] (default task-1) ********************
***********+
```

OK, cluster `A` is working.

Now let's try the other URLs for nodes `B`:

1. Within the same browser window, point to the address `http://127.0.0.1:8380/cluster-test`. In the browser window, you should see something similar to the following image:

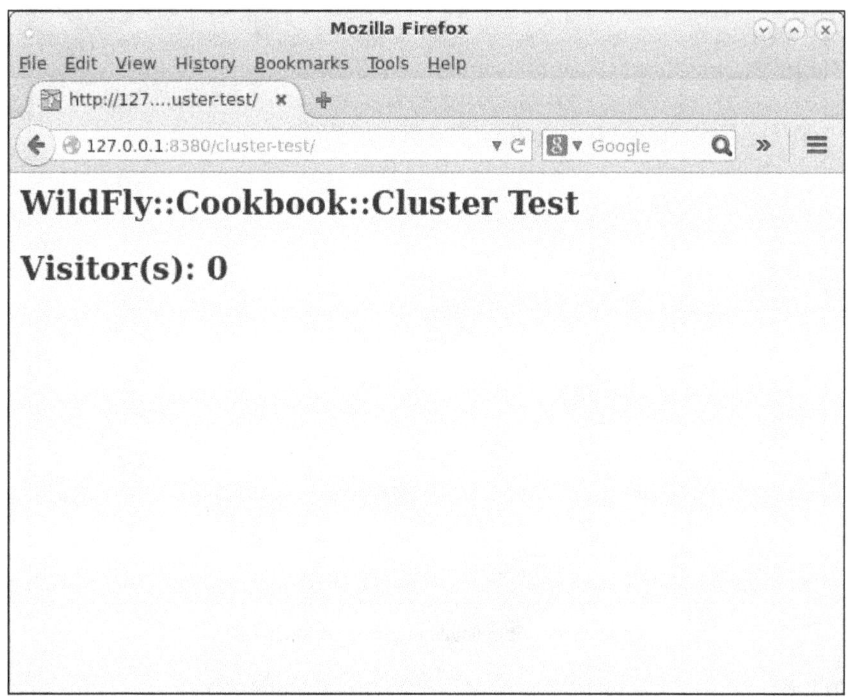


"cluster-test" application running on "node-B1"

As you can see, the application started counting from `0` (zero). The `node-B1` log should have the following statements:

```
17:12:59,978 INFO  [stdout] (default task-1) ********************
***********+
17:12:59,979 INFO  [stdout] (default task-1) Visitor(s): 0
17:12:59,980 INFO  [stdout] (default task-1) ********************
***********+
```

2. Now, let's try pointing the same browser window to the following URL: `http://127.0.0.1:8480/cluster-test`. You should see the following screenshot:

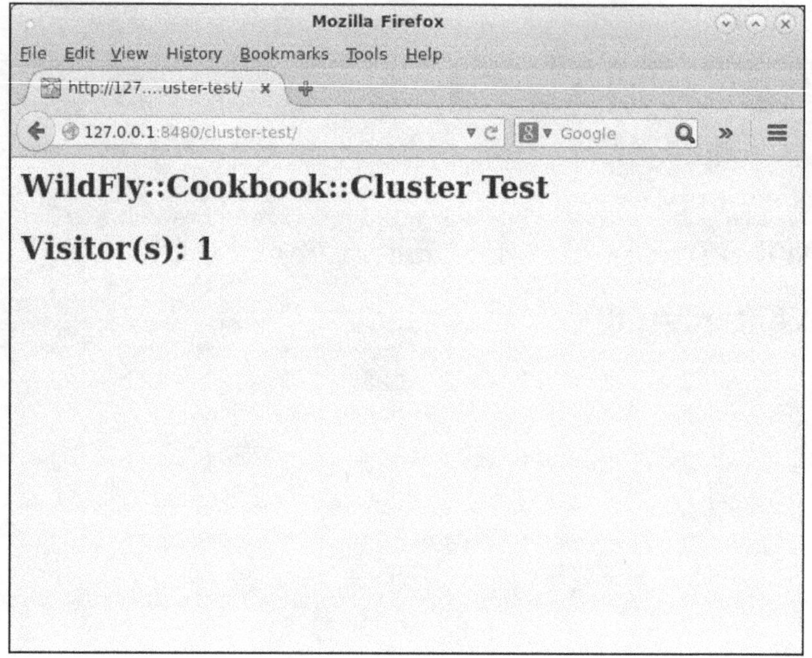


"cluster-test" application running on "node-B2"

In the `node-B2` log, you should find the following statements:

```
17:13:52,841 INFO  [stdout] (default task-1) ********************
***********+
17:13:52,841 INFO  [stdout] (default task-1) Visitor(s): 1
17:13:52,842 INFO  [stdout] (default task-1) ********************
***********+
```

Great, cluster `B` is working too! Now, try switching from one URL to another and see if the cluster responds correctly.

## How it works...

Let's analyze what we have done and why it is working without much configuration. Along with the `standalone.sh` script for `node-A1` and `node-A2`, we specified a few parameters:

- `jboss.server.base.dir=cl-std-node-A1`: Needed to specify our base directory as a starting folder to retrieve all the configuration files (`cl-std-node-A2` for `node-A2`)

- `--server-config=standalone-ha.xml`: Needed to specify the server configuration file with `ha` profile
- jboss.socket.binding.port-offset=100: Needed to specify the port offset (200 for "node-2")
- `jboss.node.name=node-A1`: Needed to uniquely identify the node within the cluster (obviously `node-A2` for the second `A` node)

That's all we need to do to make the cluster for nodes `A`.

To create the nodes `B` cluster, we needed to specify pretty much the same parameters, plus the `jboss.default.multicast.address` one, valued to `230.0.0.5`. The default multicast address value is `230.0.0.4`, which is then used by the `A` nodes. This enabled us to create two different clusters: members of cluster `A` will communicate through the `230.0.0.4` address, while members of cluster `B` will communicate through the *230.0.0.5* address.

# Creating a cluster in domain mode

In this recipe, you will learn how to cluster two WildFly nodes locally, that is, on your PC. We will try this using the domain mode and the `ha` profile.

## Getting ready

For this recipe, we will need the `cluster-aware` application named `cluster-test`, that you can find in my GitHub repository. If you skipped the *Managing applications using the deployments folder* recipe in *Chapter 2, Running WildFly in Standalone Mode*, please refer to it to download all the source code and projects that you will need.

To build the application, run the following commands:

```
$ cd ~/WFC/github/wildfly-cookbook
$ cd cluster-test
$ mvn -e clean package
```

## How to do it...

From the WildFly installation directory `$WILDFLY_HOME`, let's create two folders; one representing the `domain-controller` and the other one representing the hosts (we will have two instances running within the same host).

Open a terminal and execute the following commands:

```
$ cd $WILDFLY_HOME
$ cp -a domain cl-dmn-master
$ cp -a domain cl-dmn-host-1
```

## Master

Now, let's configure our domain controller using the `domain.xml` and `host.xml` files placed in the `cl-dmn-master` folder.

Edit the `domain.xml` file and replace the `<server-groups>...</server-groups>` tag definition with the following:

```
<server-groups>
    <server-group name="cluster-REST-app" profile="ha">
        <jvm name="default">
            <heap size="512m" max-size="512m"/>
        </jvm>
        <socket-binding-group ref="ha-sockets"/>
    </server-group>
</server-groups>
```

Again, to use cluster, we need to use the `ha` profile, which I referenced within the `profile` attribute of `server-group`. Also, we need to reference the appropriate `socket-binding-group` by the `ref` attribute, in this case valued to `ha-sockets`.

Follow this rule: always name server groups properly; do not name them "server-A", "*server-1*", or similar or you will get confused as soon as you start managing more and more servers.

Now let's edit the `host.xml` file in order to just have `domain-controller` without any running hosts.

Following are the steps that are to be taken:

1. Name the host as `master`:

   ```
   <host name="master" xmlns="urn:jboss:domain:3.0">
   ```

2. Replace the `<domain-controller>...</domain-controller>` tag definition with the following:

   ```
   <domain-controller>
     <local/>
   </domain-controller>
   ```

3. Remove the `<servers>` tag definition.

   OK, we are done with `domain-controller`. Let's have a run.

4. Open a terminal and execute the following commands:

   ```
   $ cd $WILDFLY_HOME
   $ ./bin/domain.sh -Djboss.domain.base.dir=cl-dmn-master
   ```

Now we can configure our hosts that will form a part of the cluster.

## Host-1

First of all, let's disable `domain.xml`, present in the `cl-dmn-host-1` folder.

Open a terminal and execute the following commands:

```
$ cd $WILDFLY_HOME
$ cd cl-dmn-host-1
$ mv configuration/domain.xml configuration/domain.xml.unused
```

By doing so, the file will not be read at startup. Now, let's configure our host controller using the `host.xml` file placed in the `cl-dmn-host-1` folder.

Edit the `host.xml` file and follow the steps listed next:

1. Name the host as `host-1`:

   ```
   <host name="host-1" xmlns="urn:jboss:domain:3.0">
   ```

2. Replace the `<management-interfaces>...</management-interfaces>` tag definition, inside the `<management>` tag, with the following:

   ```
   <management-interfaces>
     <native-interface security-realm="ManagementRealm">
       <socket interface="management"
       port="${jboss.management.native.port:19999}"/>
     </native-interface>
     <http-interface security-realm="ManagementRealm" http-
       upgrade-enabled="true">
       <socket interface="management"
       port="${jboss.management.http.port:19990}"/>
     </http-interface>
   </management-interfaces>
   ```

3. Replace the `<domain-controller>...</domain-controller>` tag definition with the following:

   ```
   <domain-controller>
     <remote security-realm="ManagementRealm">
       <discovery-options>
         <static-discovery name="primary"
         protocol="${jboss.domain.master.protocol:remote}"
         host="${jboss.domain.master.address}"
         port="${jboss.domain.master.port:9999}"/>
       </discovery-options>
     </remote>
   </domain-controller>
   ```

4. Replace the `<servers>...</servers>` tag definition with the following:

   ```
   <servers>
     <server name="REST-server-1" group="cluster-REST-app">
       <jvm name="default">
          <heap size="384m" max-size="384m"/>
       </jvm>
         <socket-bindings port-offset="100"/>
     </server>
     <server name="REST-server-2" group="cluster-REST-app">
       <jvm name="default">
         <heap size="384m" max-size="384m"/>
       </jvm>
         <socket-bindings port-offset="200"/>
     </server>
   </servers>
   ```

In this case, naming the servers with an indexed prefix helps because it gives you more information. For example, if you have five servers, each one running two instances, and you catch an error statement within your log files about `REST-server-7`, then you know you have to look into the machine number `4`, right?

Open a terminal and execute the following commands:

```
$ cd $WILDFLY_HOME
$ ./bin/domain.sh -Djboss.domain.base.dir=cl-dmn-host-1 -Djboss.domain.
master.address=127.0.0.1
```

Now, if you looked at the `host-1` log output, you should have noticed that there is nothing about our cluster. Why? (You should know; anyway, the answer will be explained in a little while.)

Now that everything is up and running, let's deploy our application (did you get the answer?).

1. Open a terminal and execute the following commands:

   ```
   $ cd $WILDFLY_HOME
   $ ./bin/jboss-cli.sh
   You are disconnected at the moment. Type 'connect' to connect to
   the server or 'help' for the list of supported commands.
   [disconnected /] connect
   [domain@localhost:9990 /] deploy cluster-test.war --server-
   groups=cluster-REST-app
   ```

2. Let's first check the logs. In `domain-controller`, you should see a statement asserting that the content has been uploaded, as follows:

```
[Host Controller] 20:52:54,502 INFO  [org.jboss.as.repository]
(management-handler-thread - 7) WFLYDR0001: Content added at
location /Users/foogaro/wildfly-9.0.0.Beta2/cl-dmn-master/data/
content/ee/f4c936445881ec81ccb497cd2e7a500b95a92c/content
```

In **host-1** you should see the following statements:

```
[Server:REST-server-2] 21:09:41,157 INFO  [stdout] (MSC service
thread 1-11)

[Server:REST-server-2] 21:09:41,157 INFO  [stdout] (MSC service
thread 1-11) -----------------------------------------------------
--------------

[Server:REST-server-2] 21:09:41,157 INFO  [stdout] (MSC service
thread 1-11) GMS: address=REST-server-2, cluster=ee, physical
address=127.0.0.1:55400

[Server:REST-server-2] 21:09:41,157 INFO  [stdout] (MSC service
thread 1-11) -----------------------------------------------------
--------------

[Server:REST-server-1] 21:09:41,167 INFO  [stdout] (MSC service
thread 1-14)

[Server:REST-server-1] 21:09:41,167 INFO  [stdout] (MSC service
thread 1-14) -----------------------------------------------------
--------------

[Server:REST-server-1] 21:09:41,168 INFO  [stdout] (MSC service
thread 1-14) GMS: address=REST-server-1, cluster=ee, physical
address=127.0.0.1:55300

[Server:REST-server-1] 21:09:41,168 INFO  [stdout] (MSC service
thread 1-14) -----------------------------------------------------
--------------

[Server:REST-server-2] 21:09:44,576 INFO  [org.infinispan.
remoting.transport.jgroups.JGroupsTransport] (ServerService Thread
Pool -- 21) ISPN000078: Starting JGroups channel web

[Server:REST-server-1] 21:09:44,576 INFO  [org.infinispan.
remoting.transport.jgroups.JGroupsTransport] (ServerService Thread
Pool -- 21) ISPN000078: Starting JGroups channel web

[Server:REST-server-1] 21:09:44,580 INFO  [org.infinispan.
remoting.transport.jgroups.JGroupsTransport] (ServerService Thread
Pool -- 21) ISPN000094: Received new cluster view for channel web:
[REST-server-1|0] (1) [REST-server-1]

[Server:REST-server-1] 21:09:44,581 INFO  [org.infinispan.
remoting.transport.jgroups.JGroupsTransport] (ServerService
Thread Pool -- 21) ISPN000079: Channel web local address is REST-
server-1, physical addresses are [127.0.0.1:55300]
```

```
[Server:REST-server-2] 21:09:44,581 INFO  [org.infinispan.
remoting.transport.jgroups.JGroupsTransport] (ServerService Thread
Pool -- 21) ISPN000094: Received new cluster view for channel web:
[REST-server-2|0] (1) [REST-server-2]

[Server:REST-server-2] 21:09:44,582 INFO  [org.infinispan.
remoting.transport.jgroups.JGroupsTransport] (ServerService
Thread Pool -- 21) ISPN000079: Channel web local address is REST-
server-2, physical addresses are [127.0.0.1:55400]

[Server:REST-server-1] 21:09:44,588 INFO  [org.infinispan.
factories.GlobalComponentRegistry] (ServerService Thread Pool --
21) ISPN000128: Infinispan version: Infinispan 'Hoptimus Prime'
7.1.1.Final

[Server:REST-server-2] 21:09:44,589 INFO  [org.infinispan.
factories.GlobalComponentRegistry] (ServerService Thread Pool --
21) ISPN000128: Infinispan version: Infinispan 'Hoptimus Prime'
7.1.1.Final

[Server:REST-server-1] 21:09:44,793 INFO  [org.jboss.
as.clustering.infinispan] (ServerService Thread Pool -- 31)
WFLYCLINF0002: Started cluster-test.war cache from web container

[Server:REST-server-1] 21:09:44,793 INFO  [org.jboss.
as.clustering.infinispan] (ServerService Thread Pool -- 21)
WFLYCLINF0002: Started dist cache from web container

[Server:REST-server-2] 21:09:44,798 INFO  [org.jboss.
as.clustering.infinispan] (ServerService Thread Pool -- 29)
WFLYCLINF0002: Started cluster-test.war cache from web container

[Server:REST-server-2] 21:09:44,798 INFO  [org.jboss.
as.clustering.infinispan] (ServerService Thread Pool -- 21)
WFLYCLINF0002: Started dist cache from web container

[Server:REST-server-1] 21:09:45,050 INFO  [org.wildfly.extension.
undertow] (MSC service thread 1-7) WFLYUT0021: Registered web
context: /cluster-test

[Server:REST-server-2] 21:09:45,052 INFO  [org.wildfly.extension.
undertow] (MSC service thread 1-12) WFLYUT0021: Registered web
context: /cluster-test

[Server:REST-server-1] 21:09:45,119 INFO  [org.jboss.as.server]
(ServerService Thread Pool -- 60) WFLYSRV0010: Deployed "cluster-
test.war" (runtime-name : "cluster-test.war")

[Server:REST-server-2] 21:09:45,119 INFO  [org.jboss.as.server]
(ServerService Thread Pool -- 24) WFLYSRV0010: Deployed "cluster-
test.war" (runtime-name : "cluster-test.war")
```

See, now that we've got a statements log about the cluster, we know the the answer: the cluster will be activated once an application requires it.

Time to test our cluster using our application!

3. Open you browser and point it to the following location: `http://127.0.0.1:8180/cluster-test`. Refresh the page a few times. In the browser window, you should see something similar to the following screenshot:

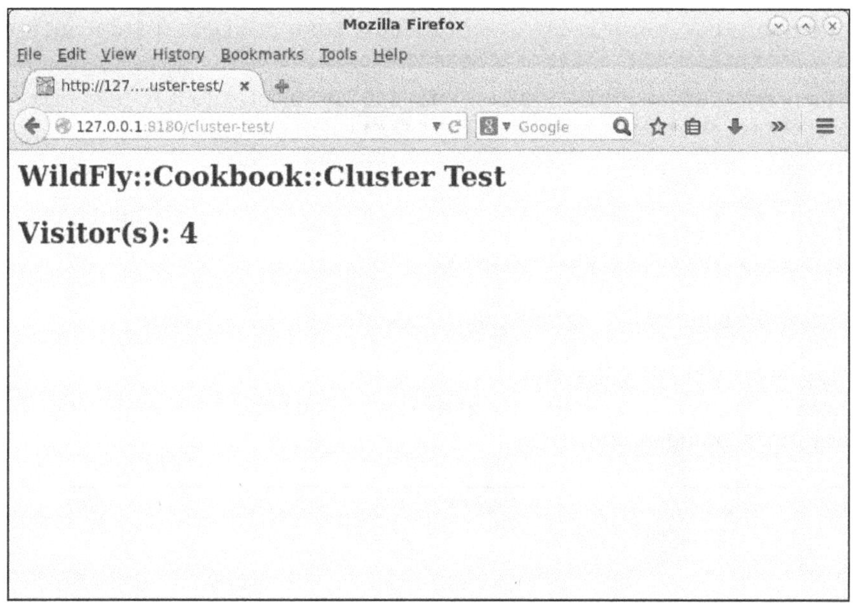


"cluster-test" application running on "host-1" with "REST-server-1"

In the `host-1` log, you should find the following statements:

```
[Server:REST-server-1] 16:05:47,393 INFO  [stdout] (default task-1) *********************************+

[Server:REST-server-1] 16:05:47,394 INFO  [stdout] (default task-1) Visitor(s): 0

[Server:REST-server-1] 16:05:47,394 INFO  [stdout] (default task-1) *********************************+

[Server:REST-server-1] 16:05:50,266 INFO  [stdout] (default task-3) *********************************+

[Server:REST-server-1] 16:05:50,267 INFO  [stdout] (default task-3) Visitor(s): 1

[Server:REST-server-1] 16:05:50,267 INFO  [stdout] (default task-3) *********************************+

[Server:REST-server-1] 16:05:50,529 INFO  [stdout] (default task-4) *********************************+

[Server:REST-server-1] 16:05:50,530 INFO  [stdout] (default task-4) Visitor(s): 2

[Server:REST-server-1] 16:05:50,531 INFO  [stdout] (default task-4) *********************************+
```

```
[Server:REST-server-1] 16:05:50,800 INFO  [stdout] (default task-
5) ********************************+

[Server:REST-server-1] 16:05:50,800 INFO  [stdout] (default task-
5) Visitor(s): 3

[Server:REST-server-1] 16:05:50,801 INFO  [stdout] (default task-
5) ********************************+

[Server:REST-server-1] 16:05:51,405 INFO  [stdout] (default task-
6) ********************************+

[Server:REST-server-1] 16:05:51,406 INFO  [stdout] (default task-
6) Visitor(s): 4

[Server:REST-server-1] 16:05:51,407 INFO  [stdout] (default task-
6) ********************************+
```

Notice the suffix of the log statements indicating the server name.

4. Now, let's try pointing the same browser window to the URL `http://127.0.0.1:8280/cluster-test`. You should see something like the following screenshot:

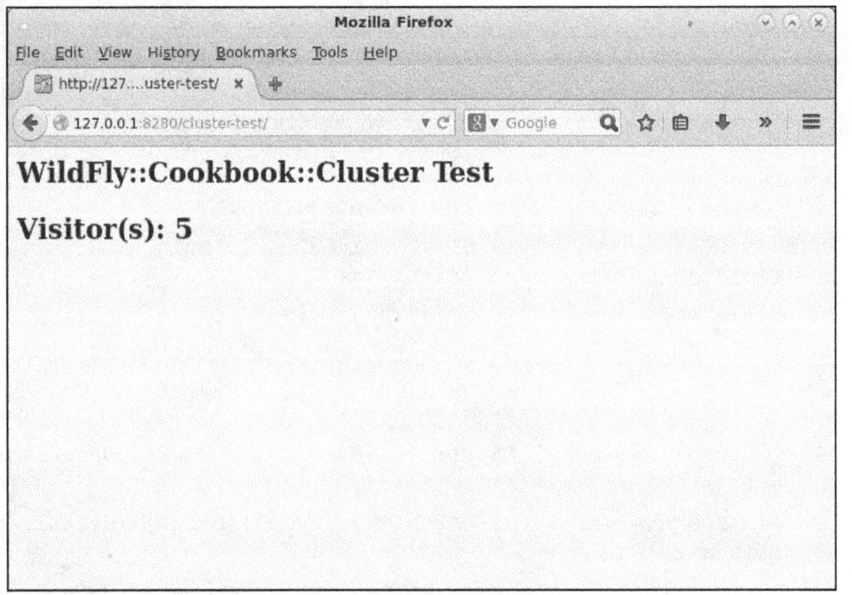


"cluster-test" application running on "host-1" with "REST-server-2"

As you can see, the second node continued counting exactly from where we stopped in `REST-server-1`. In the `host-1` log, you should find the following statements:

```
[Server:REST-server-2] 16:11:27,734 INFO  [stdout]
(default task-1) ********************************+
[Server:REST-server-2] 16:11:27,734 INFO  [stdout]
(default task-1) Visitor(s): 5
[Server:REST-server-2] 16:11:27,734 INFO  [stdout]
(default task-1) ********************************+
```

The suffix of the log changed to `REST-server-2`. OK, our cluster is working properly.

## How it works...

Skipping the details of domain mode configuration (see *Chapter 3, Running WildFly in Domain Mode*), let's analyze what we have done and why it is working without much configuration. Along with the `domain.sh` script for the `master` node, we specified the `-Djboss.domain.base.dir=cl-dmn-master` parameter, indicating our base directory as a starting folder to retrieve the entire configuration file.

Furthermore, within `domain.xml` we specified a reference to the `ha` profile and `ha-sockets`, in the definition of `server-groups`. These configurations enabled clustering capabilities. Remember, only the `ha` and `full-ha` profiles enable the clustering feature.

Looking at the `host-1` side, along with `domain.sh` script, we specified the `-Djboss.domain.base.dir=cl-dmn-host-1` and `-Djboss.domain.master.address=127.0.0.1` properties, setting our base directory as a starting folder to retrieve the entire configuration file, and the address of `domain-controller`, relatively.

Remember, the domain-controller pushes out the configuration to the hosts, through the host-controller. That's why we don't have a configuration counterpart in `host-1`.

That's all we needed to do to make our cluster. This is because of the default WildFly configuration, especially the configuration of the subsystem, `jgroups`. Let's see its defaults:

```
<subsystem xmlns="urn:jboss:domain:jgroups:3.0">
    <channels default="ee">
        <channel name="ee"/>
    </channels>
    <stacks default="udp">
        <stack name="udp">
            <transport type="UDP" socket-binding="jgroups-udp"/>
```

```
                <protocol type="PING"/>
                <protocol type="MERGE3"/>
                <protocol type="FD_SOCK" socket-binding="jgroups-udp-
                    fd"/>
                <protocol type="FD_ALL"/>
                <protocol type="VERIFY_SUSPECT"/>
                <protocol type="pbcast.NAKACK2"/>
                <protocol type="UNICAST3"/>
                <protocol type="pbcast.STABLE"/>
                <protocol type="pbcast.GMS"/>
                <protocol type="UFC"/>
                <protocol type="MFC"/>
                <protocol type="FRAG2"/>
                <protocol type="RSVP"/>
            </stack>
            <stack name="tcp">
                <transport type="TCP" socket-binding="jgroups-tcp"/>
                <protocol type="MPING" socket-binding="jgroups-
                    mping"/>
                <protocol type="MERGE3"/>
                <protocol type="FD_SOCK" socket-binding="jgroups-tcp-
                    fd"/>
                <protocol type="FD"/>
                <protocol type="VERIFY_SUSPECT"/>
                <protocol type="pbcast.NAKACK2"/>
                <protocol type="UNICAST3"/>
                <protocol type="pbcast.STABLE"/>
                <protocol type="pbcast.GMS"/>
                <protocol type="MFC"/>
                <protocol type="FRAG2"/>
                <protocol type="RSVP"/>
            </stack>
        </stacks>
    </subsystem>
```

So, the default protocol used for cluster transportation is the UDP (see the emphasized code). This UDP setting has additional configuration, within `socket-binding-group` named `ha-sockets`, specified in the `domain.xml` file as follows:

```
<socket-binding-group name="ha-sockets" default-interface="public">
    <socket-binding name="ajp" port="${jboss.ajp.port:8009}"/>
    <socket-binding name="http" port="${jboss.http.port:8080}"/>
    <socket-binding name="https" port="${jboss.https.port:8443}"/>
```

```
        <socket-binding name="jgroups-mping" port="0" multicast-
        address="${jboss.default.multicast.address:230.0.0.4}"
        multicast-port="45700"/>
        <socket-binding name="jgroups-tcp" port="7600"/>
        <socket-binding name="jgroups-tcp-fd" port="57600"/>
        <socket-binding name="jgroups-udp" port="55200" multicast-
        address="${jboss.default.multicast.address:230.0.0.4}"
        multicast-port="45688"/>
        <socket-binding name="jgroups-udp-fd" port="54200"/>
        <socket-binding name="modcluster" port="0" multicast-
        address="224.0.1.105" multicast-port="23364"/>
        <socket-binding name="txn-recovery-environment" port="4712"/>
        <socket-binding name="txn-status-manager" port="4713"/>
        <outbound-socket-binding name="mail-smtp">
            <remote-destination host="localhost" port="25"/>
        </outbound-socket-binding>
    </socket-binding-group>
```

So, by default, every member of the cluster advertises itself at the `230.0.0.4` address. Also, every port specified in the configuration is altered along with the `<socket-bindings port-offset="XXX"/>` settings specified in the `host.xml` file in the `host-1` server.

## There's more...

We could have made our cluster without the `port-offset` directive, and by using different IPs for each node instead, but this wouldn't have worked properly. This is because of the HTTP-session reference stored in a cookie. Generally speaking, a cookie consists of a name (typically `JSESSIONID`), a value (which is an ID used to reference the HTTP session on the server), a domain, and a context path.

All these properties must be the same in order to make a request to the same HTTP session on the server, which will not be the case with nodes bound to different IPs. The IP is the domain of the cookie, thus it will not work—unless you balance— but that's covered in the next chapter.

## See also

If you have any problem with this configuration, you might have network problems, which you can troubleshoot with the *Testing the UDP protocol with the JGroups tool* recipe of this chapter.

# Creating separate clusters in domain mode

In the previous recipe, we learned how to create a cluster. What if we need to manage more applications, each one having its own cluster? This is exactly what you will learn in this recipe. We will learn to manage more applications using the `ha` profile.

## Getting ready

For this recipe, we will need the `cluster-aware` application named `example`, that you can find in my GitHub repository. If you skipped the *Managing applications using the deployments folder* recipe in *Chapter 2, Running WildFly in Standalone Mode*, please refer to it to download all the source code and projects that you will need.

To build the application, execute the following commands:

```
$ cd ~/WFC/github/wildfly-cookbook
$ cd example
$ mvn -e clean package
```

## How to do it...

From the WildFly installation directory `$WILDFLY_HOME`, let's create three folders, one for the domain-controller (always run the domain-controller per se, without any other hosts), and two folders representing two different hosts with their own `host-controller`.

Open a terminal and execute the following commands (if you followed the steps in the previous recipe, you can skip the first two `cp` commands):

```
$ cd $WILDFLY_HOME
$ cp -a domain cl-dmn-master
$ cp -a domain cl-dmn-host-1
$ cp -a domain cl-dmn-host-2
```

### Master

Now, let's configure our domain controller using the `domain.xml` and `host.xml` files placed in the `cl-dmn-master` folder. This will be exactly the same as the previous recipe, just in case.

Edit the `domain.xml` file and replace the `<server-groups>...</server-groups>` tag definition with the following:

```
<server-groups>
    <server-group name="cluster-REST-app" profile="ha">
```

```
        <jvm name="default">
            <heap size="512m" max-size="512m"/>
        </jvm>
        <socket-binding-group ref="ha-sockets"/>
    </server-group>
    <server-group name="cluster-SOAP-app" profile="ha">
        <jvm name="default">
            <heap size="512m" max-size="512m"/>
        </jvm>
        <socket-binding-group ref="ha-sockets"/>
    </server-group>
</server-groups>
```

Again, to use cluster, we need to use the ha profile, which I referenced within the profile attribute of the server-group element. Also, we need to reference the appropriate socket-binding-group by the ref attribute, in this case valued to ha-sockets.

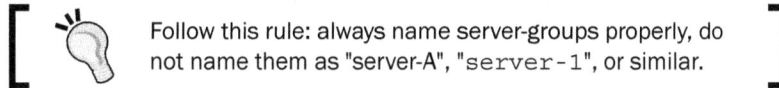

Follow this rule: always name server-groups properly, do not name them as "server-A", "server-1", or similar.

Now let's edit the host.xml file in order to just have domain-controller without any running hosts.

Here are the steps that are to be followed:

1. Name the host as master:

   ```
   <host name="master" xmlns="urn:jboss:domain:3.0">
   ```

2. Replace the <domain-controller>...</domain-controller> tag definition with the following:

   ```
   <domain-controller>
     <local/>
   </domain-controller>
   ```

3. Remove the <servers> tag definition.

   Okay, we are done with the domain-controller. Let's have a run.

4. Open a terminal and execute the following commands:

   ```
   $ cd $WILDFLY_HOME
   $ ./bin/domain.sh -Djboss.domain.base.dir=cl-dmn-master
   ```

Now we can configure our hosts that will be a part of the cluster.

### Host-1

First of all, let's disable the `domain.xml` file present in the `cl-dmn-host-1` folder.

Open a terminal and execute the following commands:

```
$ cd $WILDFLY_HOME
$ cd cl-dmn-host-1
$ mv configuration/domain.xml configuration/domain.xml.unused
```

By doing so, the file will not be read at startup. Now, let's configure our host controller using `host.xml` placed in the `cl-dmn-host-1` folder.

Edit the `host.xml` file and follow the steps listed next:

1. Name the host as `host-1`:

   ```
   <host name="host-1" xmlns="urn:jboss:domain:3.0">
   ```

2. Replace the `<management-interfaces>...</management-interfaces>` tag definition inside the `<management>` tag, with the following:

   ```
   <management-interfaces>
     <native-interface security-realm="ManagementRealm">
       <socket interface="management"
       port="${jboss.management.native.port:19999}"/>
       </native-interface>
       <http-interface security-realm="ManagementRealm" http-
       upgrade-enabled="true">
           <socket interface="management"
       port="${jboss.management.http.port:19990}"/>
       </http-interface>
   </management-interfaces>
   ```

   This is only needed when more management interfaces are running on the same server.

3. Replace the `<domain-controller>...</domain-controller>` tag definition with the following:

   ```
   <domain-controller>
     <remote security-realm="ManagementRealm">
       <discovery-options>
         <static-discovery name="primary"
         protocol="${jboss.domain.master.protocol:remote}"
         host="${jboss.domain.master.address}"
         port="${jboss.domain.master.port:9999}"/>
       </discovery-options>
     </remote>
   </domain-controller>
   ```

As you can see, there is no default for the `jboss.domain.master.address` property, so we need to pass it somehow.

4. Replace the `<servers>...</servers>` tag definition with the following:

```
<servers>
  <server name="REST-server-1" group="cluster-REST-app">
    <socket-bindings port-offset="100"/>
  </server>
  <server name="SOAP-server-1" group="cluster-SOAP-app">
    <socket-bindings port-offset="200"/>
  </server>
</servers>
```

5. Open a terminal and execute the following commands:

```
$ cd $WILDFLY_HOME
$ ./bin/domain.sh -Djboss.domain.base.dir=cl-dmn-host-1 -Djboss.domain.master.address=127.0.0.1
```

Remember that a cluster is activated on demand, that is, after we installed a `cluster-aware` application.

## Host-2

Let's do exactly the same thing for `host-2` with just a few adjustments.

Open a terminal and execute the following commands:

```
$ cd $WILDFLY_HOME
$ cd cl-dmn-host-2
$ mv configuration/domain.xml configuration/domain.xml.unused
```

Edit the `host.xml` file and follow the steps listed below:

1. Name the host as `host-2`:

```
<host name="host-2" xmlns="urn:jboss:domain:3.0">
```

2. Replace the `<management-interfaces>...</management-interfaces>` tag definition inside the `<management>` tag, with the following:

```
<management-interfaces>
    <native-interface security-realm="ManagementRealm">
        <socket interface="management"
        port="${jboss.management.native.port:29999}"/>
    </native-interface>
```

```
    <http-interface security-realm="ManagementRealm" http-
    upgrade-enabled="true">
        <socket interface="management"
        port="${jboss.management.http.port:29990}"/>
    </http-interface>
</management-interfaces>
```

3. Replace the `<domain-controller>...</domain-controller>` tag definition with the following:

```
<domain-controller>
    <remote security-realm="ManagementRealm">
        <discovery-options>
            <static-discovery name="primary"
            protocol="${jboss.domain.master.
            protocol:remote}"
            host="${jboss.domain.master.address}"
            port="${jboss.domain.master.port:9999}"/>
        </discovery-options>
    </remote>
</domain-controller>
```

4. Replace the `<servers>...</servers>` tag definition with the following:

```
<servers>
    <server name="REST-server-2" group="cluster-REST-app">
        <socket-bindings port-offset="300"/>
    </server>
    <server name="SOAP-server-2" group="cluster-SOAP-app">
        <socket-bindings port-offset="400"/>
    </server>
</servers>
```

5. Open a terminal and execute the following commands:

```
$ cd $WILDFLY_HOME
$ ./bin/domain.sh -Djboss.domain.base.dir=cl-dmn-host-2 -Djboss.
domain.master.address=127.0.0.1
```

Remember that cluster is activated on demand, that is, after we installed a `cluster-aware` application.

6. Let's deploy the application as follows:

```
$ cd $WILDFLY_HOME
$ ./bin/jboss-cli.sh
You are disconnected at the moment. Type 'connect' to connect to
the server or 'help' for the list of supported commands.
[disconnected /] connect
[domain@localhost:9990 /] deploy cluster-test.war --all-server-
groups
```

## Testing the clusters

Now that all the hosts are up and running, let's test our two clusters!

Open a browser and point to the following URLs, using different windows:

- The URL `http://127.0.0.1:8180/cluster-test` will depict the following output:

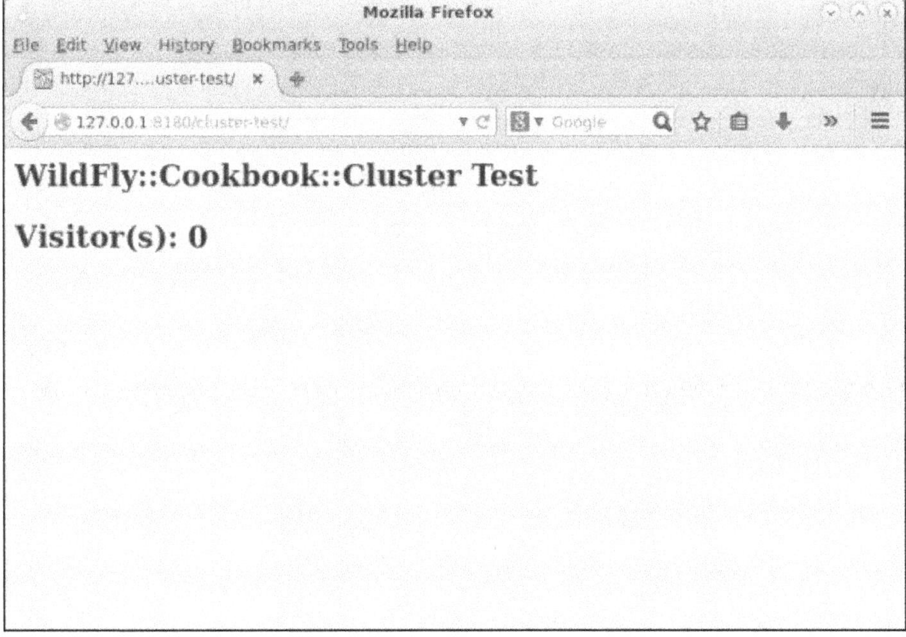

- The URL `http://127.0.0.1:8280/cluster-test` will depict the following output:

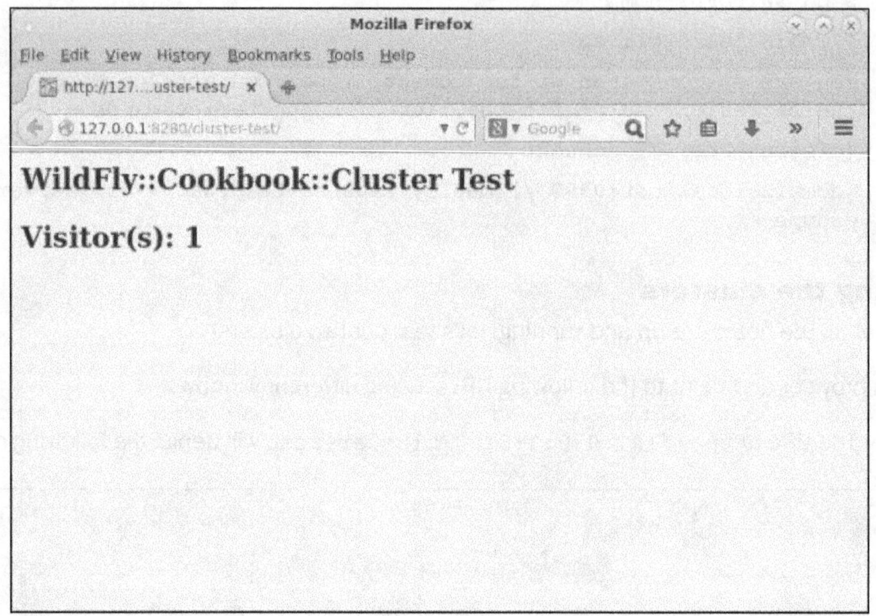


- The URL `http://127.0.0.1:8380/cluster-test` will depict the following output:

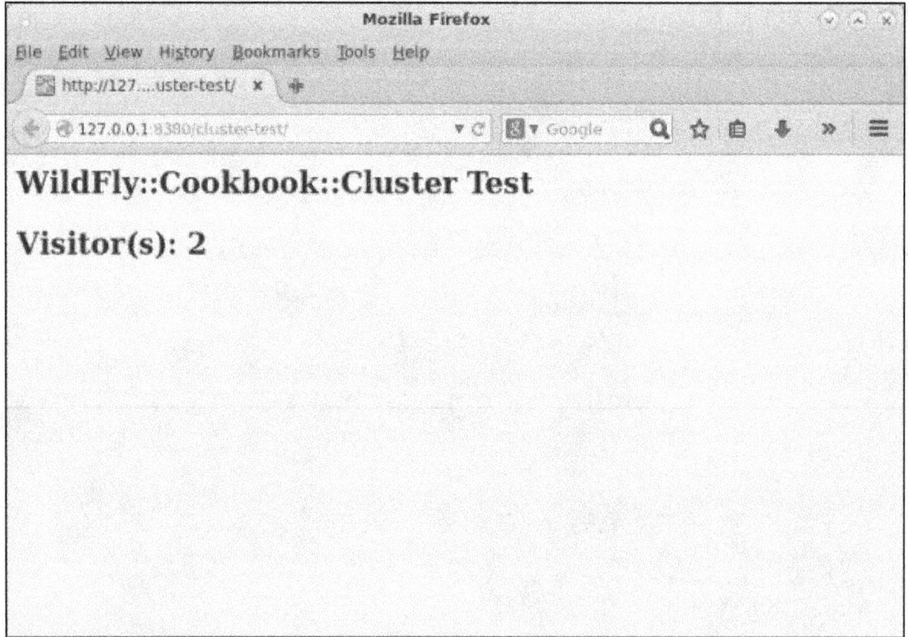

- The URL `http://127.0.0.1:8480/cluster-test` will depict the following output:

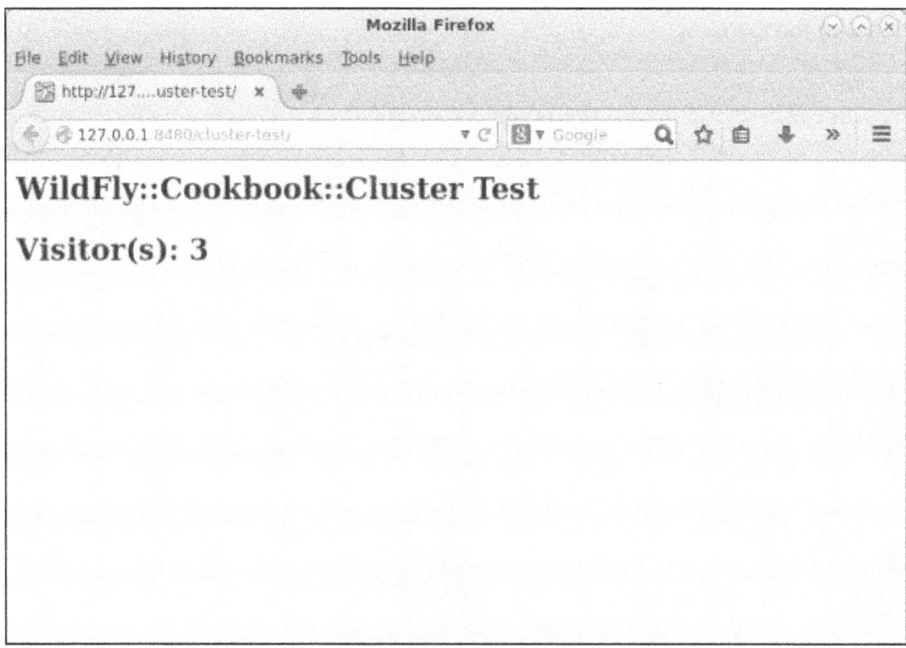


Oops! We were not expecting this, were we? What did we miss?

- Okay, we got the same application, but still, the cluster should have worked. I mean two separate clusters. We got different ports for all the hosts. So what's wrong?
- A server group does not define a cluster. A cluster is defined at the network level. To have a second cluster, thus a separate cluster, we need to specify a different multicast address for the servers we want to form a second cluster with. Both server-groups are sharing the same socket-binding-group `ha-sockets`, so all the information, cache, and cluster pings go onto the same network.

How do we do that? Passing the multicast address as a parameter along with the `domain.sh` script for the `host-2`? Nope! That way, we set a different multicast address for the `REST-server-2` server, which should be present in the first cluster, `cluster-REST-app`.

We need to define a multicast address for the first cluster and another one for the second cluster. Our clusters are logically represented by the `cluster-REST-app` server group and the `cluster-SOAP-app` server group, we can just define those multicast addresses at the server group level, hence in `domain.xml`.

Now, stop everything!

### Master

Edit the `domain.xml` file and replace the `<server-groups>...</server-groups>` tag definition with the following:

```
<server-groups>
    <server-group name="cluster-REST-app" profile="ha">
        <jvm name="default">
            <heap size="512m" max-size="512m"/>
        </jvm>
        <socket-binding-group ref="ha-sockets"/>
        <system-properties>
         <property name="jboss.default.multicast.address"
         value="${rest.multicast.address}" />
        </system-properties>
        <deployments>
            <deployment name="cluster-test.war" runtime-
         name="cluster-test.war"/>
        </deployments>
    </server-group>
    <server-group name="cluster-SOAP-app" profile="ha">
        <jvm name="default">
            <heap size="512m" max-size="512m"/>
        </jvm>
        <socket-binding-group ref="ha-sockets"/>
        <system-properties>
         <property name="jboss.default.multicast.address"
         value="${soap.multicast.address}" />
        </system-properties>
        <deployments>
            <deployment name="cluster-test.war" runtime-
         name="cluster-test.war"/>
        </deployments>
    </server-group>
</server-groups>
```

Open a terminal and execute the following commands:

```
$ cd $WILDFLY_HOME
$ ./bin/domain.sh -Djboss.domain.base.dir=cl-dmn-master
```

### Host-1

Open a terminal and execute the following commands:

```
$ cd $WILDFLY_HOME
$ ./bin/domain.sh -Djboss.domain.base.dir=cl-dmn-host-1 -Djboss.domain.
master.address=127.0.0.1 -Drest.multicast.address=230.0.0.4 -Dsoap.
multicast.address=230.0.0.5
```

### Host-2

Open a terminal and execute the following commands:

```
$ cd $WILDFLY_HOME
$ ./bin/domain.sh -Djboss.domain.base.dir=cl-dmn-host-2 -Djboss.domain.
master.address=127.0.0.1 -Drest.multicast.address=230.0.0.4 -Dsoap.
multicast.address=230.0.0.5
```

## Re-testing the clusters

Let's open two windows of the same browser and point them to the following URLs:

- The URL `http://127.0.0.1:8180/cluster-test` will depict the following output:

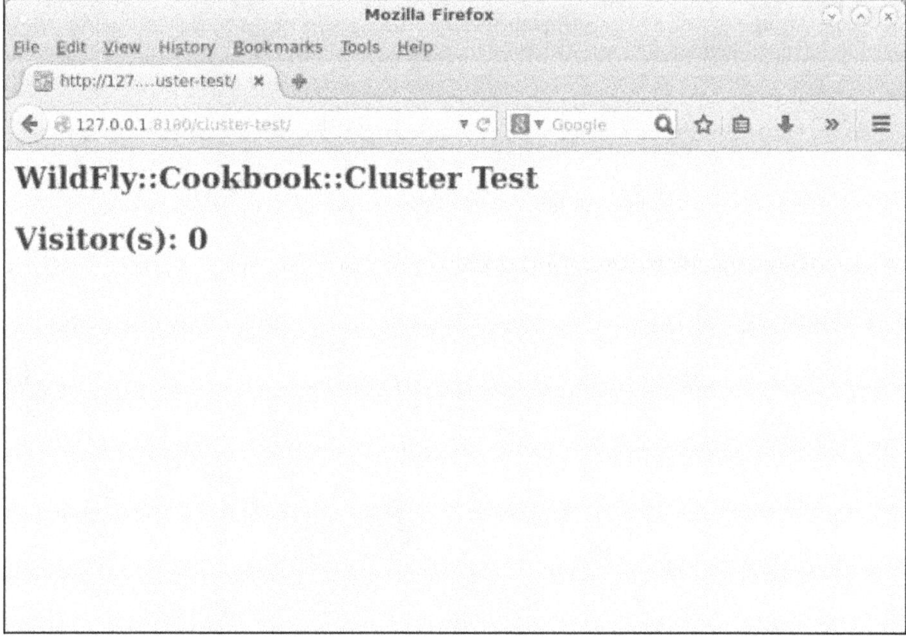

- The URL `http://127.0.0.1:8380/cluster-test` will depict the following output:

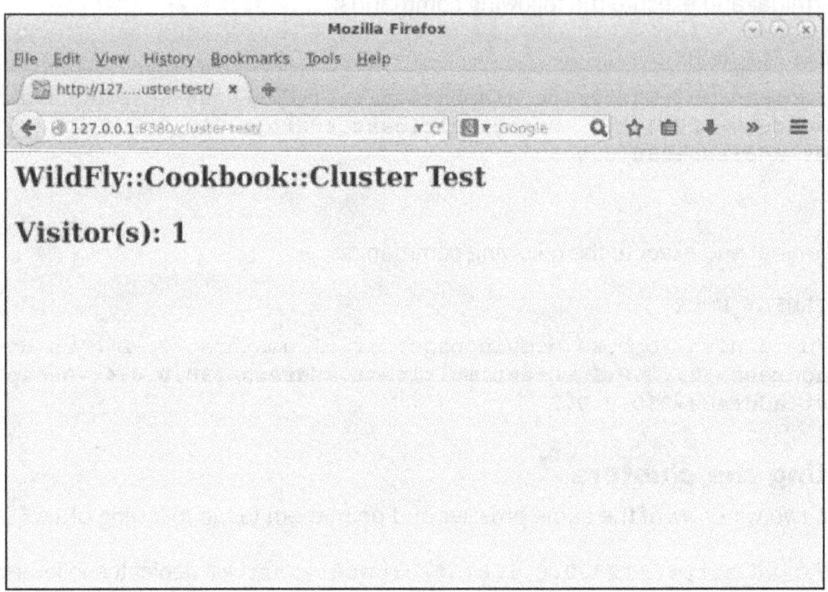


Now open two other windows of a different browser and point them to the following URLs:

- The URL `http://127.0.0.1:8280/cluster-test` will depict the following output:

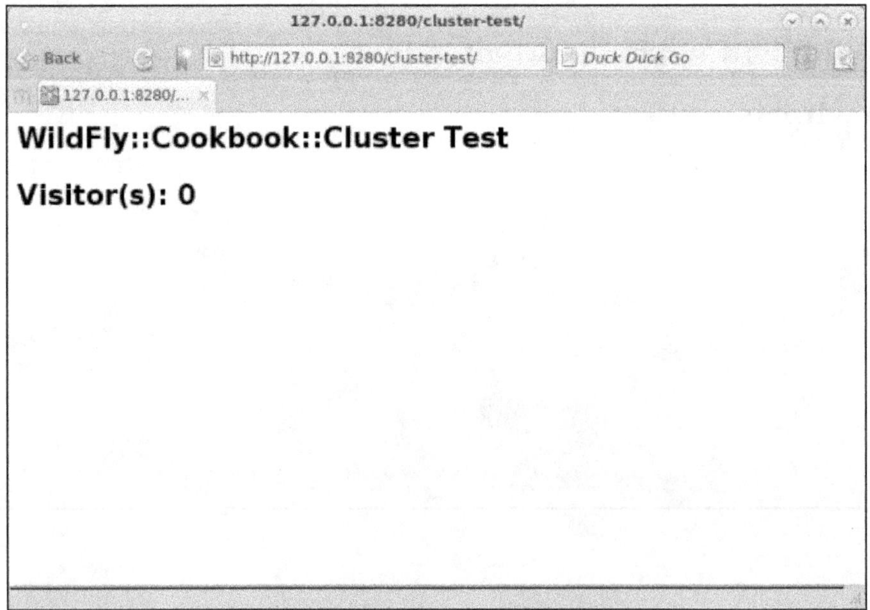

- The URL `http://127.0.0.1:8480/cluster-test` will depict the following output:

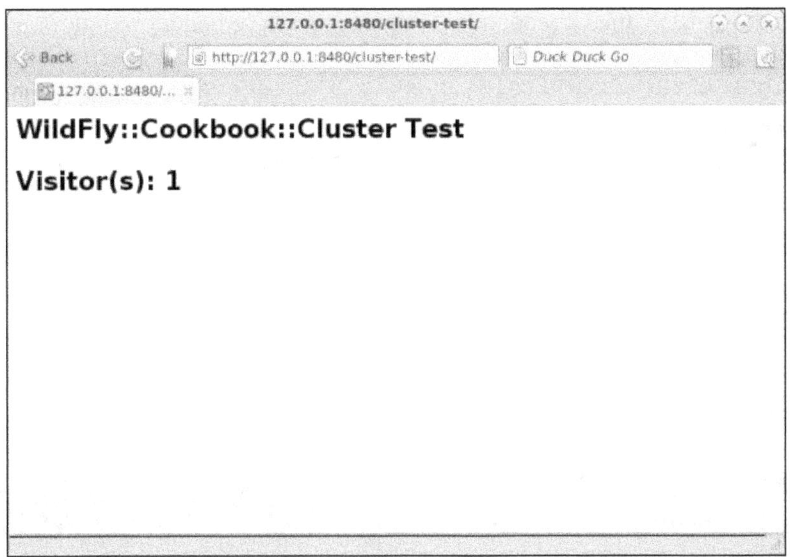


There we go!

## How it works...

We explained what was wrong in the first test, along the way. The second test, though, is a bit different; it seems that having different browsers does the magic. Well, kind of.

First of all, we effectively split the cluster in two, each one with its own network, which is right by design and implementation.

The different browser is needed for just one reason— because we are testing on the same IP (but different ports), and because the hostname (that is, the IP) matches the domain of the session cookie on the browser, having all four windows sharing the same cookie would end up in a totally wrong behavior—from our point of view.

Let's describe the "same-four-windows-browser" scenario and see if it fits our thinking:

- **Client makes a request on server 8180**: This responds with a `set-cookie` header with name `JSESSIONID`, domain `127.0.0.1`, path `/cluster-test` and a value `0o0hPhIZ73unAtIMDCb0zR2h.host-1:REST-server-1`. Visitor number `0`.
- **Client makes a request on server 8380**: This responds without a `set-cookie` header, because the browser finds the cookie on itself and sends it to the server, along with the request. As the server `8180` and `8380` are in the same cluster, and the HTTP session is replicated across them, the server finds the session and increments our visitors number. Visitor number `1`.

- **Client makes a request on the server 8280**: This we configured to be on a separate cluster. The browser sends the cookie along with the request itself. The server can't find the session, thus it responds with a `set-cookie` header with newly created values: name `JSESSIONID`, domain `127.0.0.1`, path `/cluster-test` and a value `8X1gLkCbr5RsmELxwTlI0izj.host-1:SOAP-server-1`. Visitor number `0`.
- **Client makes a request on the server 8480**: The browser sends the cookie along with the request itself. The server can't find the session, thus it responds with a `set-cookie` header with newly created values.

As you can see, using the same browser— at least the same session's browser— could not work.

## See also

If you have any problem with this configuration, you might have network problems, which you can troubleshoot with the last recipe of this chapter.

# Creating a cluster via TCP

Often times, especially in enterprise and cloud environments where there are several restrictions among networks, you are not able to use multicast addresses, even in the same network. Fortunately, the `jgroups` subsystem helps you out with this by providing an easy way to switch between UDP and TCP clustering, and this is exactly what you will learn in this recipe. We will work using the standalone mode with the `ha` profile.

## Getting ready

For this recipe, we will need the "cluster-aware" application named "example", that you can find in my GitHub repository. If you skipped the *Managing applications using the deployments folder* recipe in *Chapter 2, Running WildFly in Standalone Mode*, please refer to it to download all the source code and projects that you will need.

To build the application, do as follows:

```
$ cd ~/WFC/github/wildfly-cookbook
$ cd example
$ mvn -e clean package
```

## How to do it...

From the WildFly installation directory `$WILDFLY_HOME`, let's create two folders, each one representing a server node.

1. Open a terminal and execute the following commands:

   ```
   $ cd $WILDFLY_HOME
   $ cp -a standalone cl-std-tcp-node-1
   $ cp -a standalone cl-std-tcp-node-2
   ```

2. Now, let's copy the `cluster-test.war` application into the `deployments` folder of each node that we have just created. Run the following commands:

   ```
   $ cp cluster-test.war cl-std-tcp-node-1/deployments/
   $ cp cluster-test.war cl-std-tcp-node-2/deployments/
   ```

We are almost ready to test our cluster. We just need some configuration.

### Node-1

Edit the `standalone-ha.xml` file and replace the `jgroups` subsystem with the following definition:

```
<subsystem xmlns="urn:jboss:domain:jgroups:3.0">
    <channels default="ee">
        <channel name="ee"/>
    </channels>
    <stacks default="tcp">
        <stack name="udp">
            <transport type="UDP" socket-binding="jgroups-udp"/>
            <protocol type="PING"/>
            <protocol type="MERGE3"/>
            <protocol type="FD_SOCK" socket-binding="jgroups-udp-
            fd"/>
            <protocol type="FD_ALL"/>
            <protocol type="VERIFY_SUSPECT"/>
            <protocol type="pbcast.NAKACK2"/>
            <protocol type="UNICAST3"/>
            <protocol type="pbcast.STABLE"/>
            <protocol type="pbcast.GMS"/>
            <protocol type="UFC"/>
            <protocol type="MFC"/>
            <protocol type="FRAG2"/>
            <protocol type="RSVP"/>
        </stack>
```

```
        <stack name="tcp">
            <transport type="TCP" socket-binding="jgroups-tcp"/>
              <protocol type="TCPPING">
                <property name="initial_hosts">
                  127.0.0.1[7700],127.0.0.1[7800]
                </property>
                <property name="num_initial_members">
                  2
                </property>
                <property name="port_range">
                  0
                </property>
                <property name="timeout">
                  2000
                </property>
              </protocol>
            <protocol type="MPING" socket-binding="jgroups-
            mping"/>
            <protocol type="MERGE3"/>
            <protocol type="FD_SOCK" socket-binding="jgroups-tcp-
            fd"/>
            <protocol type="FD"/>
            <protocol type="VERIFY_SUSPECT"/>
            <protocol type="pbcast.NAKACK2"/>
            <protocol type="UNICAST3"/>
            <protocol type="pbcast.STABLE"/>
            <protocol type="pbcast.GMS"/>
            <protocol type="MFC"/>
            <protocol type="FRAG2"/>
            <protocol type="RSVP"/>
        </stack>
    </stacks>
</subsystem>
```

Open a terminal and execute the following commands:

```
$ cd $WILDFLY_HOME
$ ./bin/standalone.sh -Djboss.server.base.dir=cl-std-tcp-node-1 --server-config=standalone-ha.xml -Djboss.socket.binding.port-offset=100 -Djboss.node.name=node-1
```

## Node-2

Edit the `standalone-ha.xml` file and replace the `jgroups` subsystem as we have done for `node-1`.

Open a terminal and execute the following commands:

```
$ cd $WILDFLY_HOME
$ ./bin/standalone.sh -Djboss.server.base.dir=cl-std-tcp-node-2 --server-config=standalone-ha.xml -Djboss.socket.binding.port-offset=200 -Djboss.node.name=node-2
```

## Testing the TCP cluster

Now that all the nodes are up and running, let's test our TCP cluster!

1. Open a browser and point to `http://127.0.0.1:8180/cluster-test`. Refresh the page a few times and you should see something like the following image:

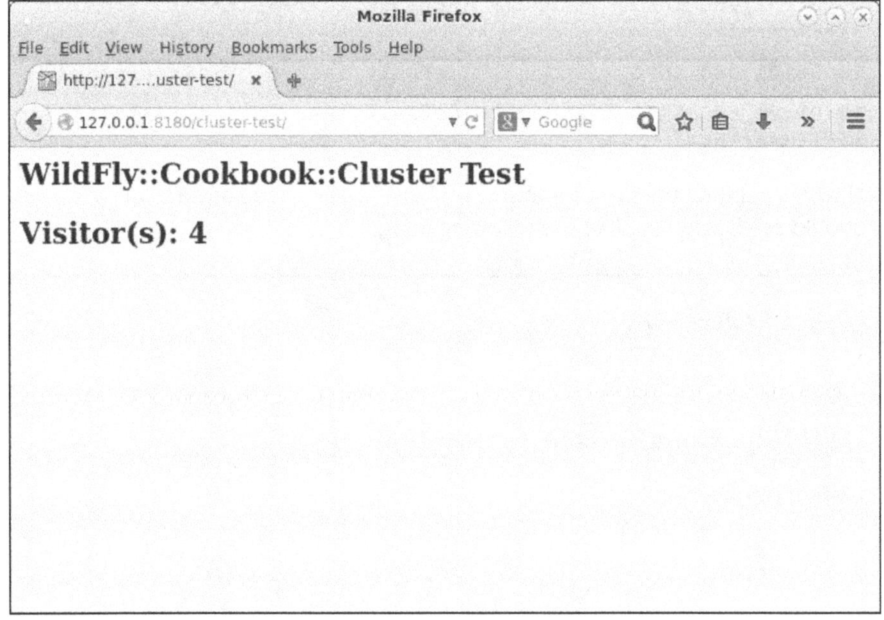


"cluster-test" application running on "node-1" in the TCP cluster—standalone mode with "ha" profile

In the `node-1` logs, you should catch the following statements:

```
15:04:57,966 INFO  [stdout] (default task-1) ********************
***********+
15:04:57,967 INFO  [stdout] (default task-1) Visitor(s): 0
15:04:57,967 INFO  [stdout] (default task-1) ********************
***********+
```

```
15:04:59,762 INFO  [stdout] (default task-3) ********************
***********+
15:04:59,763 INFO  [stdout] (default task-3) Visitor(s): 1
15:04:59,763 INFO  [stdout] (default task-3) ********************
***********+
15:05:00,105 INFO  [stdout] (default task-4) ********************
***********+
15:05:00,105 INFO  [stdout] (default task-4) Visitor(s): 2
15:05:00,105 INFO  [stdout] (default task-4) ********************
***********+
15:05:00,462 INFO  [stdout] (default task-5) ********************
***********+
15:05:00,462 INFO  [stdout] (default task-5) Visitor(s): 3
15:05:00,463 INFO  [stdout] (default task-5) ********************
***********+
15:05:01,080 INFO  [stdout] (default task-6) ********************
***********+
15:05:01,080 INFO  [stdout] (default task-6) Visitor(s): 4
15:05:01,080 INFO  [stdout] (default task-6) ********************
***********+
```

2. Now, try pointing the browser to `http://127.0.0.1:8280/cluster-test`. You should see something like the following image:

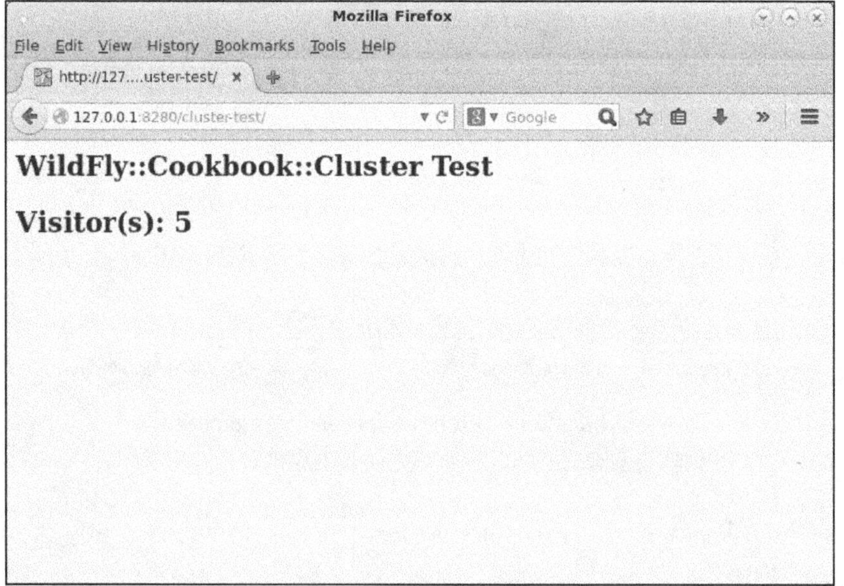


"cluster-test" application running on "node-2" in the TCP cluster—standalone mode with "ha" profile

And in the node-2 logs, you should catch the following statements:

```
15:05:28,122 INFO  [stdout] (default task-1) ********************
***********+
15:05:28,123 INFO  [stdout] (default task-1) Visitor(s): 5
15:05:28,123 INFO  [stdout] (default task-1) ********************
***********+
```

Our TCP cluster is working! Let's also try and see if it scales well:

1. Open a terminal and execute the following commands:

   ```
   $ cd $WILDFLY_HOME
   $ cp -a standalone cl-std-tcp-node-3
   ```

2. Now, let's copy the cluster-test.war application into the deployments folder of node-3, as follows:

   ```
   $ cp cluster-test.war cl-std-tcp-node-3/deployments/
   ```

3. Edit the standalone-ha.xml file and replace the jgroups subsystem as we have done for node-1 and node-2.
4. Open a terminal and execute the following commands:

   ```
   $ cd $JBOSS_HOME
   $ ./bin/standalone.sh -Djboss.server.base.dir=cl-std-tcp-node-3
   --server-config=standalone-ha.xml -Djboss.socket.binding.port-
   offset=300 -Djboss.node.name=node-3
   ```

In the logs of the first two nodes, you should see the following entries:

- 23:14:24,466 INFO [org.infinispan.remoting.transport.jgroups.JGroupsTransport] (Incoming-8,ee,node-1) ISPN000094: Received new cluster view for channel web: [node-1|2] (3) [node-1, node-2, node-3]
- 23:14:24,468 INFO [org.infinispan.remoting.transport.jgroups.JGroupsTransport] (Incoming-9,ee,node-2) ISPN000094: Received new cluster view for channel web: [node-1|2] (3) [node-1, node-2, node-3]

Let's test it in the browser by pointing it to `http://127.0.0.1:8380/cluster-test`. You should see something like the following screenshot:

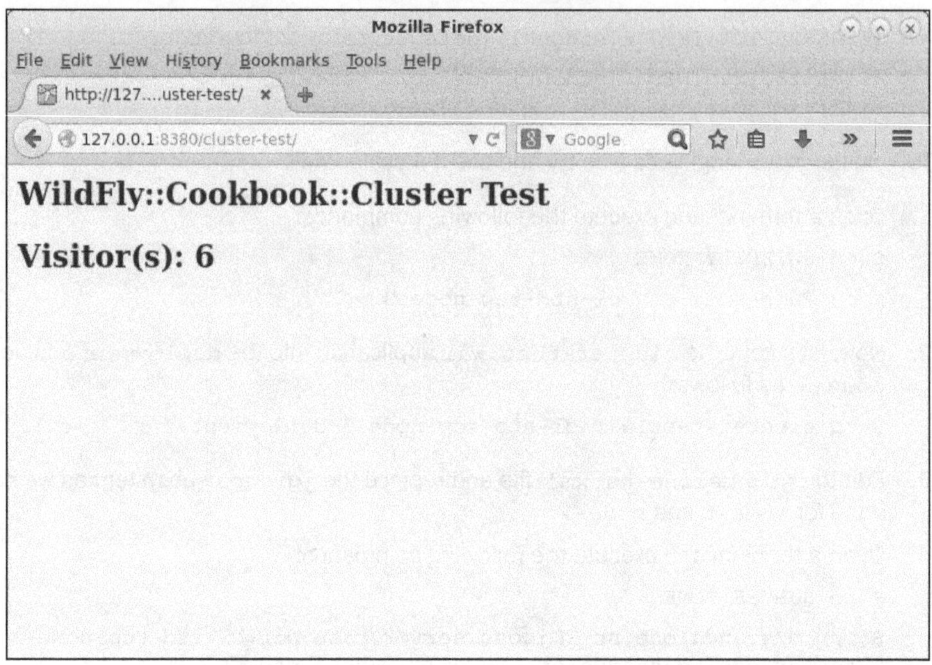


Scaling "cluster-test" application running on "node-3" in the TCP cluster—standalone mode with "ha" profile

Okay, everything worked as expected!

## How it works...

Let's analyze what we have done.

The main configuration, despite few parameters for the `standalone.sh` script, consists of properly setting the `default` attribute of the `stack` element for the JGroups subsystem, to TCP. Furthermore, we had to set how cluster members ping each other. Default is the `MPING` protocol (the `M` stands for multicast). Hence, we defined the ping protocol, named `TCPPING`, and defined the well-known hosts (the `initial_hosts` property).

The concept is that every host which wants to join the cluster will ask the well-known hosts for membership information. If those are not running, the new node cannot join the cluster. By the way, if all cluster members are up and the well-known hosts go down, nothing happens to the cluster; they are just seen as two members who left the cluster.

As a matter of fact, while testing the TCP cluster scaling by adding `node-3` and stopping the first two nodes, we would have just seen those entries in the `node-3` logs:

```
23:21:54,480 INFO  [org.infinispan.remoting.transport.jgroups.
JGroupsTransport] (Incoming-8,ee,node-3) ISPN000094: Received new cluster
view for channel web: [node-3|5] (2) [node-3, node-2]
23:21:57,473 INFO  [org.infinispan.remoting.transport.jgroups.
JGroupsTransport] (Incoming-10,ee,node-3) ISPN000094: Received new
cluster view for channel web: [node-3|6] (1) [node-3]
```

The properties we defined with regard to the `<protocol type="TCPPING">...</protocol>` are as follows:

- `num_initial_members`: The number of nodes before the cluster is considered as complete.
- `port_range`: The port range to try in case a well-known host is not responding. For example, with a `port_range` of `50` and a well-known host `10.0.0.1[7600]`, a new member would try with port `7600`, `7601`, 7602 to port `7650`.
- `timeout`: The timeout which a member will wait before joining the cluster.

# Testing the UDP protocol with the JGroups tool

Often times, you need to validate and/or certify a configuration, and in case of issues regarding UDP clustering, the first thing to check is if the UDP is working properly.

In this recipe, you will learn how to check if the UDP is working, testing it with a graphical tool and using java applications (thus without UI—which is the case of enterprise environment).

## How to do it...

First of all, let's check if we have the JGroups library in our WildFly installation folder.

Open your command-line tool and execute the following command:

```
$ find . -name "jgroups*.jar"
./modules/system/layers/base/org/jgroups/main/jgroups-3.6.2.Final.jar
```

Great! Now we can test it.

## Graphical test

Open your command-line tool.

1. Now execute the following command:

```
$ java -cp modules/system/layers/base/org/jgroups/main/jgroups-
3.6.2.Final.jar org.jgroups.demos.Draw
...
-------------------------------------------------------------------
--
GMS: address=0-44172, cluster=draw-cluster, physical address=fe80:
0:0:0:f2de:f1ff:fe99:b294%2:35420
-------------------------------------------------------------------
--
** View=[0-44172|0] (1) [0-44172]
```

You should see an application like the following image:

First JGroups draw application

2. If you get a network problem because of the IPv6, try forcing IPv4 by adding the following parameter:

```
-Djava.net.preferIPv4Stack=true
```

3. Now in a different terminal, execute the same command as mentioned previously:

```
$ java -cp $WILDFLY_HOME/modules/system/layers/base/org/jgroups/
main/jgroups-3.6.2.Final.jar org.jgroups.demos.Draw
...
-------------------------------------------------------------------
--
```

```
GMS: address=0-3647, cluster=draw-cluster, physical address=fe80:0
:0:0:f2de:f1ff:fe99:b294%2:40803
------------------------------------------------------------------
--
** View=[0-44172|1] (2) [0-44172, 0-3647]
```

From this second command, I emphasized the cluster view which is counting two members, and you now see the same application running (the number within parenthesis also indicates cluster members):

Second JGroups draw application

4. Draw something on it, and if your UDP works, your sketch should come up on the other canvas, just like mine:

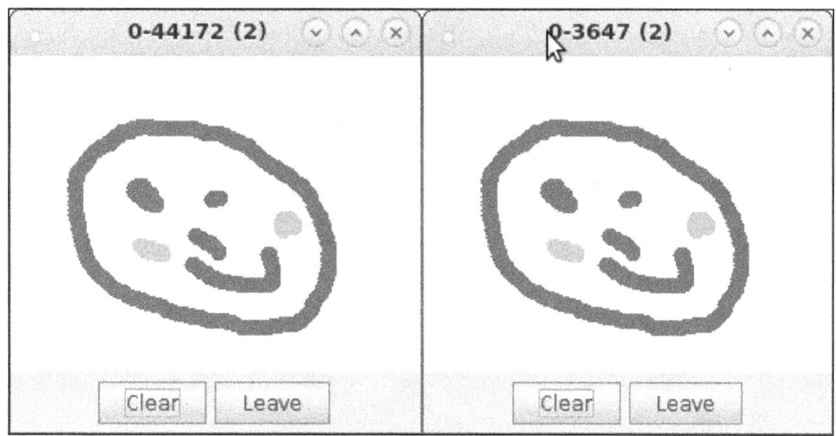


JGroups draw application reflecting changes

If you have problems with the graphical test, try to test the UDP via command line, as explained in the next section.

## Shell test

Open your command-line tool:

1. Now execute the following command:

```
$ java -cp $WILDFLY_HOME/modules/system/layers/base/org/jgroups/
main/jgroups-3.6.2.Final.jar org.jgroups.tests.McastReceiverTest
Socket=0.0.0.0/0.0.0.0:5555, bind interface=/172.17.42.1
Socket=0.0.0.0/0.0.0.0:5555, bind interface=/10.0.1.6
Socket=0.0.0.0/0.0.0.0:5555, bind interface=/10.0.1.5
Socket=0.0.0.0/0.0.0.0:5555, bind interface=/10.0.1.4
Socket=0.0.0.0/0.0.0.0:5555, bind interface=/10.0.1.3
Socket=0.0.0.0/0.0.0.0:5555, bind interface=/fe80:0:0:0:f2de:f1ff:
fe99:b294%em1
Socket=0.0.0.0/0.0.0.0:5555, bind interface=/10.0.254.33
Socket=0.0.0.0/0.0.0.0:5555, bind interface=/0:0:0:0:0:0:0:1%lo
Socket=0.0.0.0/0.0.0.0:5555, bind interface=/127.0.0.1
```

   This will start a JGroups application as a receiver, so it will be listening for incoming messages.

2. Again, if you get a network problem because of the IPv6, try forcing IPv4 by adding the following parameter:

```
-Djava.net.preferIPv4Stack=true
```

3. Now, in a different terminal, let's call it `sender`, execute the following commands:

```
$ java -cp $WILDFLY_HOME/modules/system/layers/base/org/jgroups/
main/jgroups-3.6.2.Final.jar org.jgroups.tests.McastSenderTest
Socket #1=0.0.0.0/0.0.0.0:5555, ttl=32, bind
interface=/172.17.42.1
Socket #2=0.0.0.0/0.0.0.0:5555, ttl=32, bind interface=/10.0.1.6
Socket #3=0.0.0.0/0.0.0.0:5555, ttl=32, bind interface=/10.0.1.5
Socket #4=0.0.0.0/0.0.0.0:5555, ttl=32, bind interface=/10.0.1.4
Socket #5=0.0.0.0/0.0.0.0:5555, ttl=32, bind interface=/10.0.1.3
Socket #6=0.0.0.0/0.0.0.0:5555, ttl=32, bind interface=/fe80:0:0:0
:f2de:f1ff:fe99:b294%em1
Socket #7=0.0.0.0/0.0.0.0:5555, ttl=32, bind
interface=/10.0.254.33
Socket #8=0.0.0.0/0.0.0.0:5555, ttl=32, bind
interface=/0:0:0:0:0:0:0:1%lo
Socket #9=0.0.0.0/0.0.0.0:5555, ttl=32, bind interface=/127.0.0.1
>
```

4. This second terminal will wait for standard input. As I didn't specify any interface or multicast address, it will bind to any available interface, which in my case is more than a couple. By the way, let's try typing something and hitting *Enter*, as follows:

   ```
   > Ciao!
   >
   ```

5. Now look at the first terminal, the one where we launched the `receiver` application:

   ```
   Ciao! [sender=172.17.42.1:5555]
   Ciao! [sender=10.0.1.6:5555]
   Ciao! [sender=10.0.1.5:5555]
   Ciao! [sender=10.0.1.4:5555]
   Ciao! [sender=10.0.1.3:5555]
   Ciao! [sender=10.0.254.33:5555]
   Ciao! [sender=10.0.254.33:5555]
   Ciao! [sender=127.0.0.1:5555]
   Ciao! [sender=127.0.0.1:5555]
   ```

Yeah! We received everything, from all available and configured interfaces.

# 7

# Load Balancing WildFly

In this chapter, we will cover the following topics:

- Installing and configuring Apache HTTPD
- Installing and configuring mod_cluster for Apache
- Balancing WildFly using auto advertising – UDP
- Balancing WildFly using a list of available balancers – TCP
- Balancing using the HTTP connector instead of AJP
- Preserve WildFly workers while restarting Apache
- Balancing the same context for different applications
- Rolling updates

## Introduction

In this chapter, you will learn how to load balance your WildFly instances. Load balancing is the capability to distribute the workload across multiple nodes, in our case, WildFly nodes. This technique is used for optimizing resources, minimizing the response time, and maximizing the application throughput.

To achieve load balancing, we need a component which fronts our WildFly nodes, and distributes the workload across them. A common pattern of distributing the workload is to forward client requests in a round-robin manner, so that every node serves the same number of requests.

What about the real workload that a request can generate into a node? For example, a long-running request or a request which involves heavy tasks would make the node much busier than the others that are handling just static page requests.

This is not a fair workload distribution! We need something to better calibrate this workload distribution, depending on how busy the nodes really are.

We've already got the Apache HTTP Server (also known as HTTPD), that can balance towards our WildFly nodes. We also have a component called `mod_cluster` in both HTTPD and WildFly, to get the real workload distribution.

The `mod_cluster` component for Apache HTTP Server is a set of modules, as we will see later in this chapter, while `mod_cluster` for WildFly is a subsystem named `mod_cluster`.

The `mod_cluster` component decouples the frontend from the backend. Basically, the Apache HTTP Server doesn't have any reference to the WildFly nodes, and WildFly doesn't have any reference to the HTTPD balancers—as long as multicast advertisement is used. Furthermore, `mod_cluster` supports AJP, HTTP, and HTTPS protocols. More information can be obtained by reading the official documentation, at the following URL: `http://docs.jboss.org/mod_cluster/1.2.0/html/`.

Load balancing does not affect WildFly's operational mode that you are running it in (domain or standalone). You can do load balancing between instances running in both domain mode and standalone mode. For our purpose, we will first start using the standalone mode, and then we will switch to the domain mode.

# Installing and configuring Apache HTTPD

In this recipe, you will learn how to install and configure Apache HTTPD. We will first download the software and then install it to the source. If you want, you can choose to obtain the Apache HTTP Server by using a package manager such as `YUM`, but I think understanding and learning how to build it from source is much more interesting.

We will be using Apache HTTPD Version 2.2.29 because the 2.2.x version is one of the most used versions in the production environment to run with `mod_cluster`. It already comes with the APR and APR-Util lib, along with the PCRE.

## Getting ready

To download the Apache HTTP Server, visit `http://httpd.apache.org/download.cgi`. When you first visit this site, you can choose between two stable versions: 2.2 and 2.4. Obviously, version 2.4 is newer and it has some new features. It also has a different syntax for its configuration files.

On the other hand, version 2.2 has been around for a long time and it might be more stable. Nonetheless, the 2.2 bundle provides the APR, APR-Util, and the PCRE packages, so you don't have to download and install them separately, as in version 2.4.

Having said that, we will be using the Apache HTTP Server version 2.2.29. Furthermore, we will need the `openssl-devel` (development) version installed in your system. To install it:

- For Fedora 21, use the following command:

```
sudo yum-y install gcc openssl openssl-devel wget tar unzip
```

- For Fedora 22, use the following command:

```
sudo yum-y install gcc openssl openssl-devel wget tar unzip
findutils
```

Download all the software into the `~/WFC/` folder.

## How to do it...

1. Once the download is complete, open a terminal and execute the following commands:

```
$ cd ~/WFC
$ sudo tar zxvf httpd-2.2.29.tar.gz
```

   Now that we have all the software unpacked, we are ready to configure, compile, and build our Apache HTTPD.

2. Execute the following commands for Fedora 21/22:

```
$ cd httpd-2.2.29
sudo ./configure --prefix=/home/<USER>/WFC/httpd --with-mpm=worker
--enable-mods-shared=most --enable-maintainer-mode --with-
expat=builtin --enable-ssl --enable-proxy --enable-proxy-http
--enable-proxy-ajp --disable-proxy-balancer --with-included-apr
```

   Here, `<USER>` must be replaced with your username. In my case, this is `luigi`; thus the `--prefix` directive will be `--prefix=/home/luigi/WFC/httpd`. So, let's start executing the following commands:

```
...
$ sudo make
...
$ sudo make install
...
Installing configuration files
mkdir /home/luigi/WFC/httpd/conf
mkdir /home/luigi/WFC/httpd/conf/extra
mkdir /home/luigi/WFC/httpd/conf/original
mkdir /home/luigi/WFC/httpd/conf/original/extra
Installing HTML documents
```

```
mkdir /home/luigi/WFC/httpd/htdocs
Installing error documents
mkdir /home/luigi/WFC/httpd/error
Installing icons
mkdir /home/luigi/WFC/httpd/icons
mkdir /home/luigi/WFC/httpd/logs
Installing CGIs
mkdir /home/luigi/WFC/httpd/cgi-bin
Installing header files
Installing build system files
Installing man pages and online manual
mkdir /home/luigi/WFC/httpd/man
mkdir /home/luigi/WFC/httpd/man/man1
mkdir /home/luigi/WFC/httpd/man/man8
mkdir /home/luigi/WFC/httpd/manual
```

3. Okay, now we are ready to launch our Apache. Navigate to its `bin` folder and execute it, as shown in the following commands:

```
$ cd ~/WFC/httpd/bin
$ ./httpd -k start -f ~/WFC/httpd/conf/httpd.conf
httpd: Could not reliably determine the server's fully qualified domain name, using mylaptop for ServerName
(13)Permission denied: make_sock: could not bind to address [::]:80
(13)Permission denied: make_sock: could not bind to address 0.0.0.0:80
no listening sockets available, shutting down
Unable to open logs
```

4. Ouch... Apache listens on port `80`, which is a privileged port; we got to the root. Let's try again with `sudo`:

```
$ sudo ./httpd -k start -f /opt/httpd/conf/httpd.conf
httpd: Could not reliably determine the server's fully qualified domain name, using mylaptop for ServerName
```

Bear in mind that in a production environment, the Apache HTTP Server should not be run as a root user for security reasons. It goes now, even if we have a warning complaining about a `ServerName` directive not settled. Let's get rid of this now.

5. Edit the `/opt/httpd/conf/httpd.conf` file and look for the following comment line `#ServerName www.example.com:80`. Replace it with the following entry:

```
ServerName balancer-one.com:80
```

6. Now, as a root user, open and edit the `/etc/hosts` file and add the following directive:

```
127.0.0.1 balancer-one.com
```

7. Now going back to the Apache `bin` folder, run the `httpd` script again:

```
$ sudo ./httpd -k restart -f /opt/httpd/conf/httpd.conf
```

8. The warning disappears. Let's test if everything is working by opening a browser and pointing it to `http://balancer-one.com`. You should see the following page:

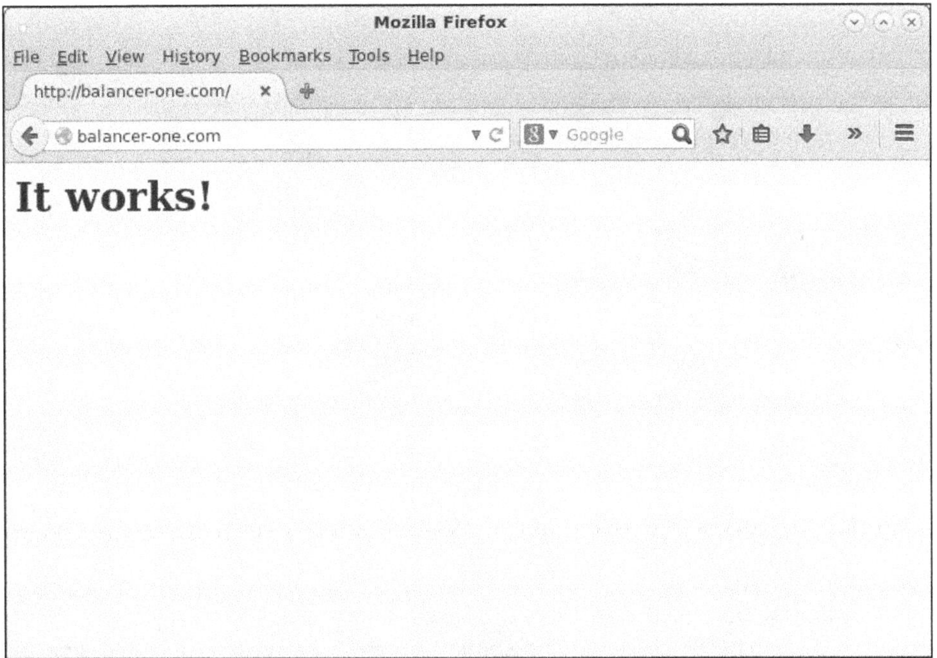


Apache HTTPD working and serving its default page

## See also

Every issue you find while installing the Apache HTTPD software can be mitigated by reading the Apache documentation at the following site `http://httpd.apache.org/docs/2.2/`.

# Installing and configuring mod_cluster for Apache

In this recipe, we will learn how to install and configure `mod-cluster` within your Apache HTTPD installation. This recipe requires a working Apache HTTPD and it assumes that its installation directory is `/opt/httpd`. If you do not have Apache installed in your environment, please follow the instructions in the previous recipe.

## Getting ready

1. First of all, download mod-cluster modules from the following site `http://mod-cluster.jboss.org/downloads/1-2-6-Final-bin`.
2. Download all the software into the `/opt/httpd/modules` folder.
3. If you prefer, you can install `mod_cluster` via your OS package manager which, in a Fedora-like system, is as follows:

```
sudo yum install mod_cluster
```

## How to do it...

1. Once the download is complete, open a terminal and execute the following commands:

```
$ cd /opt/httpd/modules
$ tar zxvf mod_cluster-1.2.6.Final-linux2-x64-so.tar.gz
mod_advertise.so
mod_manager.so
mod_proxy_cluster.so
mod_slotmem.so
```

Now that we have all the software unpacked, we are ready to configure `mod_cluster`. To better configure and administer `mod_cluster`, let's create a private network interface for internal communication, that is between Apache and WildFly.

2. Open a terminal window and execute the following commands:

```
$ sudo ifconfig eth0:1 10.0.0.1 netmask 255.255.255.0
```

If you didn't follow the previous recipe, you may need to edit the `httpd.conf` file and disable the `proxy-balancer` module, which conflicts with `mod_cluster` modules.

3. Edit the `/opt/httpd/conf/httpd.conf` file and look for the following comment line `LoadModule proxy_balancer_module modules/mod_proxy_balancer.so`. Replace it with the following entry:

```
#LoadModule proxy_balancer_module modules/mod_proxy_balancer.so
```

4. In the terminal window, create a new file named `mod_cluster.conf` and place it into the `opt/httpd/conf/extra` folder as follows:

```
$ touch /opt/httpd/conf/extra/mod_cluster.conf
$ vim /opt/httpd/conf/extra/mod_cluster.conf
```

5. Now add the following code:

```
LoadModule slotmem_module modules/mod_slotmem.so
LoadModule manager_module modules/mod_manager.so
LoadModule proxy_cluster_module modules/mod_proxy_cluster.so
LoadModule advertise_module modules/mod_advertise.so

Listen 10.0.0.1:80
Listen 10.0.0.1:6666

<VirtualHost 10.0.0.1:80>
  <Location /mcm>
    SetHandler mod_cluster-manager
    Order deny,allow
    Deny from all
    Allow from 10.0.0.1
  </Location>
</VirtualHost>

<VirtualHost 10.0.0.1:6666>
  <Directory />
    Order deny,allow
    Deny from all
    Allow from 10.0.0.1
  </Directory>
  ServerAdvertise on http://10.0.0.1:6666
  EnableMCPMReceive
</VirtualHost>
```

6. Now, let's edit the `httpd.conf` file again and add the following directive at the end. It is pretty much self-explanatory:

```
# mod_cluster settings
Include conf/extra/mod_cluster.conf
```

This will load the preceding file, featuring all our `mod_cluster` configuration.

7. Let's start our Apache with the following commands:

```
$ cd /opt/httpd/bin
$ sudo ./httpd -k start -f /opt/httpd/conf/httpd.conf
```

8. Now point your browser to the following URLs:
   - `http://10.0.0.1`
   - `http://10.0.0.1/mcm`

   You should see pages as depicted in the following screenshots:

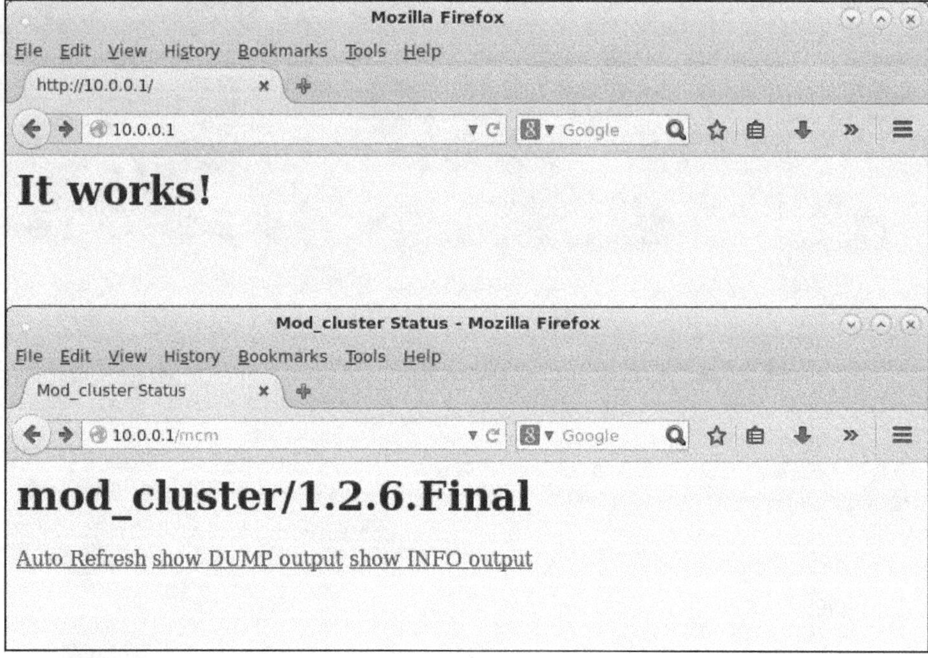


Apache HTTPD and mod_cluster manager serving on a private network interface

## How it works...

Let's analyze what we have done so far:

- First, we copied all the `mod_cluster` modules into Apache's `modules` directory. Then we referenced them by adding a `LoadModule` directive into the `mod_cluster.conf` file, in order to load the modules. Furthermore, we referenced the `mod_cluster.conf` file into the default Apache configuration file `httpd.conf`, with the `Include` directive.

  This gave us the glue to stick Apache and `mod_cluster` together.

- Why did we create a private network interface? It's due to design and security reasons. Design might be a good practice, but security is a must. Internal communication should be exposed to a private network, but not to a public network. Nevertheless, in an enterprise environment, you are very likely to have servers with two network interfaces to accomplish exactly this purpose. Thus, to simulate an enterprise environment and give you a good design, we just created another network interface.
- So, due to the the reason stated in the previous point, we bound the private interface between the `mod_cluster` management page `/mcm` and all the communications between Apache and WildFly. It is, essentially, about exchanging messages between the `mod_cluster` on Apache and the `mod_cluster` component on WildFly.
- This basically provides balancing; a WildFly `mod_cluster` sends a signal to the `10.0.0.1:6666` multicast address, `Hi there, I'm here`. On the other side, at Apache, the `mod_cluster` component reads the message and enables that WildFly node by balancing it for new requests.

Later in this chapter, we will need to change some of the preceding settings, adding more directives. The ones discussed here are just the basics to get started with.

# Balancing WildFly using auto advertising – UDP

In this recipe, we will learn how to balance two WildFly nodes running in the standalone mode. Default `mod_cluster` settings provide auto advertising as enabled, using a multicast address. Furthermore, in this recipe we will use a cluster configuration also to provide a better test feeling. If you need more information about clustering with WildFly, read *Chapter 6, Clustering WildFly*.

The entire WildFly configuration used for this recipe will not relay on any previous one. On the contrary, we assume that the Apache HTTPD installation and configuration are based on the first two recipes of this chapter.

## Getting ready

For this recipe, we will need an application named `balancing-test`, that you can find in my GitHub repository. If you skipped the *Managing applications using the deployments folder* recipe in *Chapter 2, Running WildFly in Standalone Mode*, please refer to it to download all the source code and projects that you will need.

To build the application, give the following commands:

```
$ cd ~/WFC/github/wildfly-cookbook
$ cd balancing-test
$ mvn clean package
```

## How to do it...

Let's create two folders from the WildFly installation directory `$WILDFLY_HOME`, each one representing a server node.

1. Open a terminal and execute the following commands:

   ```
   $ cd $WILDFLY_HOME
   $ cp -a standalone bl-std-node-1
   $ cp -a standalone bl-std-node-2
   ```

2. Now, let's copy the `balancing-test.war` application into the `deployments` folder of each node that we have just created. Do as follows:

   ```
   $ cp balancing-test.war bl-std-node-1/deployments/
   $ cp balancing-test.war bl-std-node-2/deployments/
   ```

   Now, let's generate a virtual IP for each of the nodes:

   ```
   $ sudo ifconfig eth0:2 10.0.1.1 netmask 255.255.255.0
   $ sudo ifconfig eth0:3 10.0.1.2 netmask 255.255.255.0
   ```

3. If it's not already running, let's launch the Apache and its logs, by executing the following commands:

   ```
   $ cd /opt/httpd/bin
   $ sudo ./httpd -k start -f /opt/httpd/conf/httpd.conf
   $ tail -f ../logs/{access,error}_log
   ==> ../logs/access_log <==


   ==> ../logs/error_log <==
   [Sun Oct 12 16:10:29 2014] [notice] SIGHUP received.  Attempting
   to restart
   [Sun Oct 12 16:10:29 2014] [notice] Digest: generating secret for
   digest authentication ...
   [ Sun Oct 12 16:10:29 2014] [notice] Digest: done
   [ Sun Oct 12 16:10:29 2014] [warn] httpd version 2.2.29 mismatch
   detected
   [ Sun Oct 12 16:10:29 2014] [notice] Advertise initialized for
   process 26675
   [ Sun Oct 12 16:10:29 2014] [notice] Apache/2.2.29 (Unix) mod_
   ssl/2.2.29 OpenSSL/1.0.1e-fips DAV/2 mod_cluster/1.2.6.Final
   configured -- resuming normal operations
   ```

4. Okay, now Apache is up. Let's start our first node by issuing the following command into a new terminal window:

```
$ ./bin/standalone.sh -Djboss.server.base.dir=bl-std-node-1
--server-config=standalone-ha.xml -Djboss.bind.address=10.0.1.1
-Djboss.management.http.port=19990 -Djboss.node.name=node-1
...
16:13:58,472 INFO  [org.jboss.as] (Controller Boot Thread)
JBAS015874: WildFly 8.1.0.Final "Kenny" started in 6531ms -
Started 289 of 400 services (179 services are lazy, passive or on-
demand)
```

5. Now, a few seconds after `node-1` starts you should see the following entries in `access_log` of the Apache logs:

```
==> ../logs/access_log <==
10.0.0.1 - - [12/Oct/2014:16:14:05 +0200] "INFO / HTTP/1.1" 200 -
10.0.0.1 - - [12/Oct/2014:16:14:05 +0200] "CONFIG / HTTP/1.1" 200
-
10.0.0.1 - - [12/Oct/2014:16:14:05 +0200] "ENABLE-APP / HTTP/1.1"
200 -
10.0.0.1 - - [12/Oct/2014:16:14:05 +0200] "STATUS / HTTP/1.1" 200
46
10.0.0.1 - - [12/Oct/2014:16:14:15 +0200] "STATUS / HTTP/1.1" 200
46
```

Those are `mod_cluster` logs stating that they received an information message, a configuration message, and then it enabled the application provided by WildFly `node-1`.

6. Now, open the `mod_cluster-manager` page that we defined in the file `mod_cluster.conf`—Apache side—at the following URL:

```
http://10.0.0.1/mcm
```

You should see the following page:

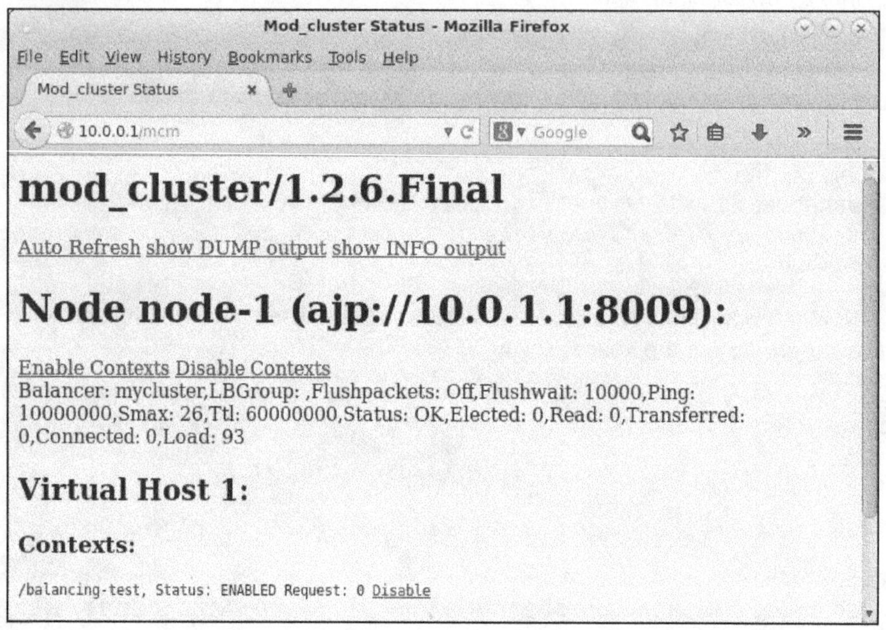


mod_cluster manager page displaying a running node and its contexts.

7. Let's start the other node `node-2` in a new terminal window, as follows:

```
$ ./bin/standalone.sh -Djboss.server.base.dir=bl-std-node-2
--server-config=standalone-ha.xml -Djboss.bind.address=10.0.1.2
-Djboss.management.http.port=29990 -Djboss.node.name=node-2

...

16:13:58,472 INFO  [org.jboss.as] (Controller Boot Thread)
JBAS015874: WildFly 8.1.0.Final "Kenny" started in 6531ms -
Started 289 of 400 services (179 services are lazy, passive or on-
demand)
```

Now, a few seconds after `node-2` starts, you should see the following entries in the Apache logs, that is, in `access_log`:

```
...

10.0.0.1 - - [12/Oct/2014:16:23:45 +0200] "STATUS / HTTP/1.1" 200
46

10.0.0.1 - - [12/Oct/2014:16:23:55 +0200] "STATUS / HTTP/1.1" 200
46

10.0.0.1 - - [12/Oct/2014:16:24:05 +0200] "STATUS / HTTP/1.1" 200
46

10.0.0.1 - - [12/Oct/2014:16:24:15 +0200] "STATUS / HTTP/1.1" 200
46
```

```
10.0.0.1 - - [12/Oct/2014:16:24:21 +0200] "INFO / HTTP/1.1" 200
331
10.0.0.1 - - [12/Oct/2014:16:24:21 +0200] "CONFIG / HTTP/1.1" 200
-
10.0.0.1 - - [12/Oct/2014:16:24:21 +0200] "ENABLE-APP / HTTP/1.1"
200 -
10.0.0.1 - - [12/Oct/2014:16:24:21 +0200] "STATUS / HTTP/1.1" 200
46
10.0.0.1 - - [12/Oct/2014:16:24:25 +0200] "STATUS / HTTP/1.1" 200
46
```

8. Let's refresh the `mcm` page:

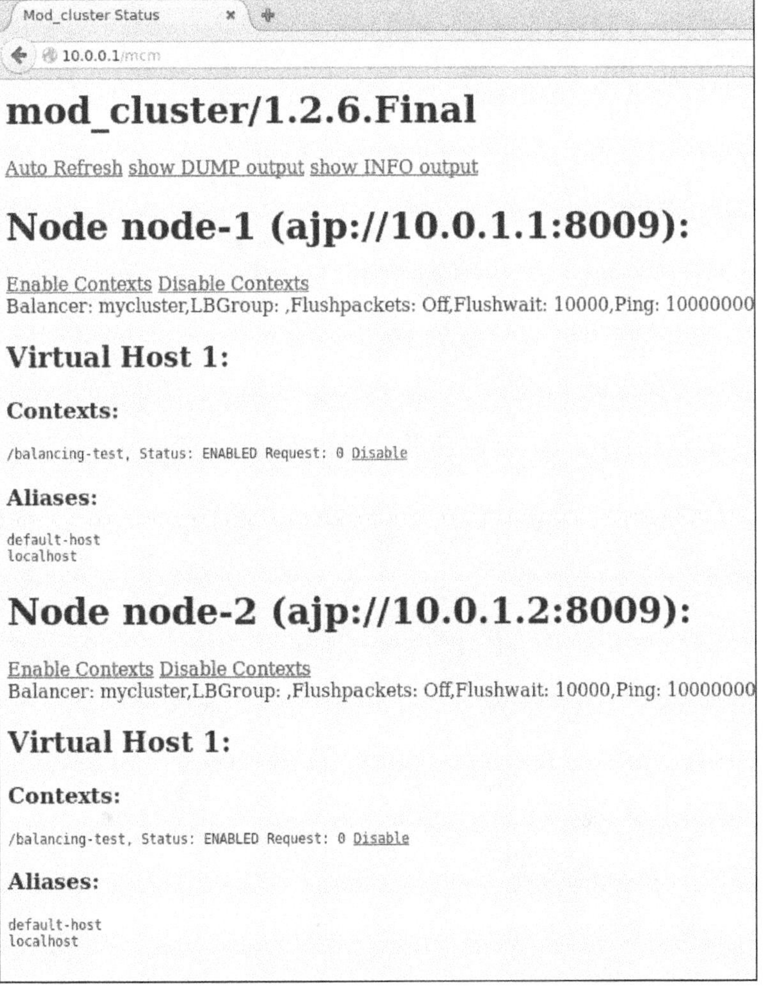


mod_cluster manager page displaying both running nodes and their contexts.

Now that everything is up and running, let's play with our marvelous application.

9. Point your browser to the following URL and refresh the page a few times:

   `http://10.0.0.1/balancing-test`

   You should see a page like the following:

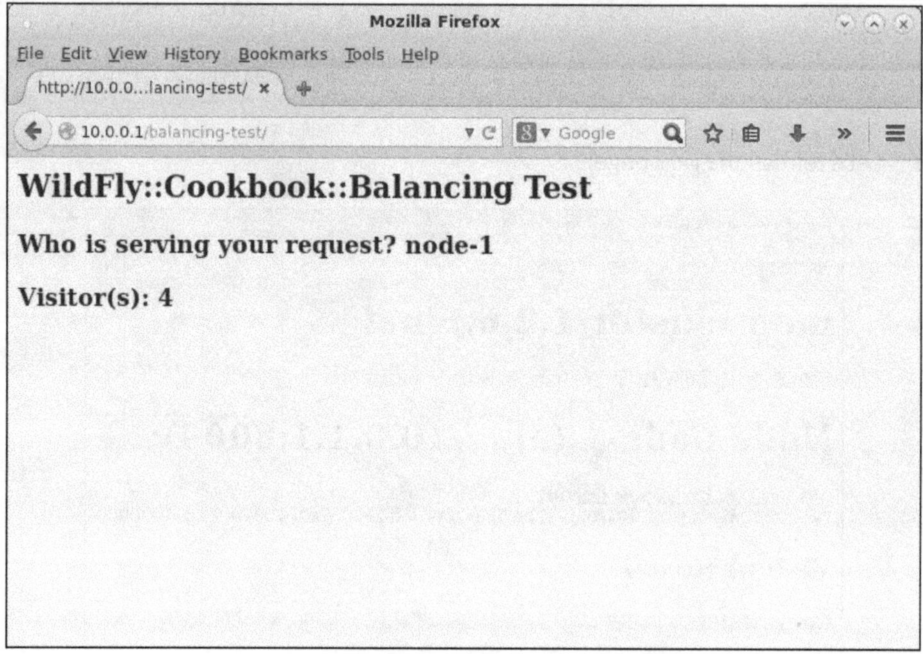


Apache serving balancing-test application on node-1

In my case, the request landed on server `node-1`; yours might land on `node-2`. Also, keep in mind that the WildFly `mod_cluster` comes with some balancing default settings such as:

- `sticky-session="true"`: which sticks subsequent requests for the same session, to the same node, if still alive
- `sticky-session-force="true"`: which forces Apache to respond with an error in case subsequent requests cannot be routed to the same node;
- `sticky-session-remove="false"`: which indicates if Apache should remove sticky behavior in case subsequent requests cannot be routed to the same node.

That's why, while refreshing the page, the node name never changes. By the way, let's stop the serving node and refresh the page one more time. If everything worked as expected, you should end up with a page like the one seen in the following screenshot:

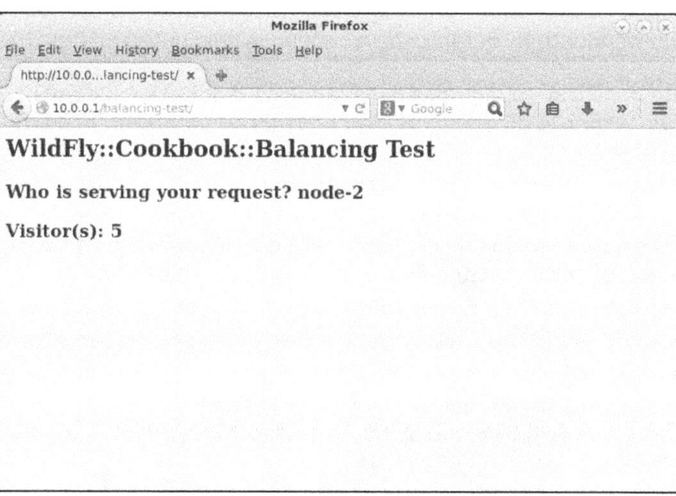


Apache serving balancing-test application on node-2

Yes, we got it!

## How it works...

If you noticed, we didn't change any particular `mod_cluster` setting on WildFly, in both nodes. This is because the WildFly `mod_cluster` configuration relays on defaults that are the same as on the Apache side. The entire configuration resides in the `mod_cluster` subsystem and in the socket-binding-group. Follow this configuration:

```
<subsystem xmlns="urn:jboss:domain:mod_cluster:1.2">
    <mod-cluster-config advertise-socket="mod_cluster"
    advertise="true" connector="ajp">
        <dynamic-load-provider>
            <load-metric type="cpu"/>
        </dynamic-load-provider>
    </mod-cluster-config>
</subsystem>
```

The preceding code describes how `mod_cluster` should inform its counterpart in Apache, concerning its workload. By default, the workload is calculated against the CPU.

```
<socket-binding-group name="standard-sockets" default-
interface="public" port-offset="${jboss.socket.binding.port-
offset:0}">
    <socket-binding name="management-http" interface="management"
    port="${jboss.management.http.port:9990}"/>
    <socket-binding name="management-https" interface="management"
    port="${jboss.management.https.port:9993}"/>
    <socket-binding name="ajp" port="${jboss.ajp.port:8009}"/>
    <socket-binding name="http" port="${jboss.http.port:8080}"/>
    <socket-binding name="https" port="${jboss.https.port:8443}"/>
    <socket-binding name="jgroups-mping" port="0" multicast-
    address="${jboss.default.multicast.address:230.0.0.4}"
    multicast-port="45700"/>
    <socket-binding name="jgroups-tcp" port="7600"/>
    <socket-binding name="jgroups-tcp-fd" port="57600"/>
    <socket-binding name="jgroups-udp" port="55200" multicast-
    address="${jboss.default.multicast.address:230.0.0.4}"
    multicast-port="45688"/>
    <socket-binding name="jgroups-udp-fd" port="54200"/>
    <socket-binding name="modcluster" port="0" multicast-
    address="224.0.1.105" multicast-port="23364"/>
    <socket-binding name="txn-recovery-environment" port="4712"/>
    <socket-binding name="txn-status-manager" port="4713"/>
    <outbound-socket-binding name="mail-smtp">
        <remote-destination host="localhost" port="25"/>
    </outbound-socket-binding>
</socket-binding-group>
```

The preceding code describes how `mod_cluster` communicates with its counterpart in Apache, concerning its availability and workload. By default, the multicast address is settled to `224.0.1.105`.

If you need to change the multicast address, for any reason, remember to change its counterpart setting in Apache, with the following directive:

```
AdvertiseGroup http://MULTICAST_ADDR:PORT
```

## Dissecting processes

A list of processes where you can check IPs and port bindings, provided by the `netstat` tool, is shown in the following image:

```
$ sudo netstat -tulpn | grep 'java\|httpd'
tcp        0      0 10.0.1.2:8080         0.0.0.0:*          LISTEN      9853/java
tcp        0      0 10.0.1.1:8080         0.0.0.0:*          LISTEN      9674/java
tcp        0      0 10.0.0.1:80           0.0.0.0:*          LISTEN      9524/./httpd
tcp        0      0 127.0.0.1:19990       0.0.0.0:*          LISTEN      9674/java
tcp        0      0 10.0.1.2:54200        0.0.0.0:*          LISTEN      9853/java
tcp        0      0 10.0.1.1:54200        0.0.0.0:*          LISTEN      9674/java
tcp        0      0 127.0.0.1:29990       0.0.0.0:*          LISTEN      9853/java
tcp        0      0 10.0.1.2:8009         0.0.0.0:*          LISTEN      9853/java
tcp        0      0 10.0.1.1:8009         0.0.0.0:*          LISTEN      9674/java
tcp        0      0 10.0.0.1:6666         0.0.0.0:*          LISTEN      9524/./httpd
udp        0      0 224.0.1.105:23364     0.0.0.0:*                      9853/java
udp        0      0 224.0.1.105:23364     0.0.0.0:*                      9674/java
udp    60160      0 0.0.0.0:23364         0.0.0.0:*                      9524/./httpd
udp        0      0 230.0.0.4:45688       0.0.0.0:*                      9853/java
udp        0      0 230.0.0.4:45688       0.0.0.0:*                      9674/java
udp        0      0 10.0.1.2:55200        0.0.0.0:*                      9853/java
udp        0      0 10.0.1.1:55200        0.0.0.0:*                      9674/java
$
```

The netstat tool showing IPs and ports binding by processes

When Apache starts, a process is actually being executed—PID `9524` (as depicted in the `netstat` figure)—which listens on ports `80` and `6666` for the `10.0.0.1` IP; the process also listens on port `23364` for any interface (`0.0.0.0`).

When the WildFly node `node-1` starts, a process is actually being executed—PID `9674` (as depicted in the `netstat` figure)—which listens on various ports and IPs:

- port `8080`, bound to IP `10.0.1.1`, is used by the HTTP connector
- port `19990`, bound to IP `127.0.0.1`, is used by the host-controller to allow remote management
- port `8009`, bound to IP `10.0.1.1`, is used by the AJP connector
- port `23364`, bound to IP `224.0.1.105`, is used by `mod_cluster`
- port `45688`, bound to IP `230.0.0.4`, is used by `jgroups` to form the cluster

When WildFly node `node-2` starts, a process is actually being executed—PID `9853` (as depicted in the `netstat` figure)—which listens on various ports and IPs:

- port `8080`, bound to IP `10.0.1.2`, is used by the HTTP connector
- port `29990`, bound to IP `127.0.0.1`, is used by the host-controller to allow remote management
- port `8009`, bound to IP `10.0.1.2`, is used by the AJP connector
- port `23364`, bound to IP `224.0.1.105`, is used by `mod_cluster`
- port `45688`, bound to IP `230.0.0.4`, is used by `jgroups` to form the cluster

There are bindings that are not relevant for the moment, so we will not discuss them. What you should notice, is that there are identical bindings for both WildFly nodes.

- `224.0.1.105:23364` is used by both to advertise themselves to the `mod_cluster` on the Apache side.
- `230.0.0.4:45688` is used by both to create the UDP cluster, so having the same binding allows them to join the same cluster.

## Dissecting communications

Let's analyze how all the components involved in load balancing communicate to each other. First, look at the following image that is worth a thousand words:

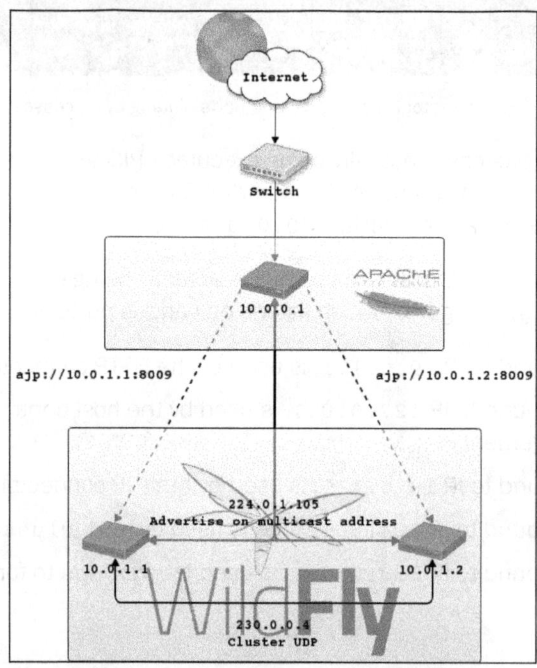


Architecture diagram showing balancing and clustering communication configuration with UDP

Skipping the steps when the clients/users ask for a resource, and when the request hits the switch which routes it to the Apache balancer, let's concentrate on the sequence of events in the communication between Apache and WildFly and see what happens in the middle.

The sequence of events is as follows:

- Apache listens on `224.0.1.105:23364` for workers to balance
- When the WildFly nodes get started, they advertise themselves to `224.0.1.105:23364`
- Apache receives the following messages:

```
10.0.0.1 - - [12/Oct/2014:16:24:21 +0200] "INFO / HTTP/1.1" 200
331
10.0.0.1 - - [12/Oct/2014:16:24:21 +0200] "CONFIG / HTTP/1.1" 200
-
10.0.0.1 - - [12/Oct/2014:16:24:21 +0200] "ENABLE-APP / HTTP/1.1"
200 -
10.0.0.1 - - [12/Oct/2014:16:24:21 +0200] "STATUS / HTTP/1.1" 200
46
```

- Apache starts balancing the nodes, via the AJP protocol, to `10.0.1.1/2:8009` depending on the workload received with the `STATUS` message
- WildFly nodes receive the requests and elaborate them responding back to Apache
- Meantime, `jgroups` serialize and de-serialize the http sessions between cluster members
- Simultaneously, the WildFly nodes send `STATUS` messages to Apache concerning the actual workload, and so on

This is pretty much what's beyond balancing a cluster of WildFly, via UDP.

You can easily balance a non-clustered environment, which is fine for stateless services; the configuration is the same, except that you will have to use a "non-ha" profile.

## There's more...

As previously mentioned, the WildFly `mod_cluster` manages the calculation of workload, which is CPU by default.

The following are some other types of load metrics:

| **Type** | **Load metric** |
|---|---|
| `cpu` | Returns the system CPU load |
| `mem` | Returns the system memory usage |
| `heap` | Returns the heap memory usage as a percentage of max heap size |
| `sessions` | Given a capacity, returns the percentage based on activeSessions/ Capacity |
| `requests` | Returns the number of requests/sec |
| `send-traffic` | Returns the outgoing request traffic in KB/sec |
| `receive-traffic` | Returns the incoming request POST traffic in KB/sec |
| `busyness` | Returns the percentage of connector threads from the thread pool that are busy servicing requests |
| `connection-pool` | Returns the percentage of connections from a connection pool that are in use |

You can add a load-metric to the mod-cluster subsystem for `node-1` as follows:

```
$ ./bin/jboss-cli.sh
You are disconnected at the moment. Type 'connect' to connect to the
server or 'help' for the list of supported commands.
[disconnected /] connect 127.0.0.1:19990
[standalone@127.0.0.1:19990 /] /subsystem=modcluster/mod-cluster-
config=configuration:add-metric(type=mem, weight=2, capacity=1)
{
    "outcome" => "success",
    "response-headers" => {
        "operation-requires-reload" => true,
        "process-state" => "reload-required"
    }
}
[standalone@127.0.0.1:19990 /] :reload()
{
    "outcome" => "success",
    "result" => undefined
}
[standalone@127.0.0.1:19990 /]
```

This basically adds a new load-metric for system memory usage. If we look into the `standalone-ha.xml` file, we will find the following:

```
<subsystem xmlns="urn:jboss:domain:modcluster:2.0">
    <mod-cluster-config advertise-socket="modcluster"
    advertise="true" connector="ajp">
```

```
            <dynamic-load-provider>
                <load-metric type="cpu"/>
                <load-metric type="mem" weight="2" capacity="1"/>
            </dynamic-load-provider>
        </mod-cluster-config>
    </subsystem>
```

Hereby, `mod_cluster` will inform its Apache counterpart with a load factor based on both metrics. This can be quite helpful if you have WildFly installed in a heterogeneous environment, say a server with different resource capabilities—a server might have less RAM than others, or less cores then others. Thus, adding and removing metrics gives you the freedom to adjust your workload distribution properly.

## See also

For cluster configuration, please refer to *Chapter 5, Managing the Datasource Subsystems with the CLI*, of this book.

# Balancing WildFly using a list of available balancers – TCP

In this recipe, we will learn how to balance two WildFly nodes running in the standalone mode, using TCP balancing. Instead of sending information messages to a multicast address, the WildFly `mod_cluster` sends everything directly to Apache.

Furthermore, in this recipe we will also use a cluster configuration, to provide a better test feeling. If you need more information about clustering with WildFly, refer to *Chapter 5, Managing the Datasource Subsystems with the CLI*. By the way, the entire WildFly configuration used for this recipe will not relay on any previous one. On the contrary, we assume that Apache HTTPD installation and configuration are based on the first two recipes of this chapter.

## Getting ready

For this recipe, we will need an application named `balancing-test`, that you can find in my GitHub repository. If you skipped the *Managing applications using the deployments folder* recipe in *Chapter 2, Running WildFly in Standalone Mode*, please refer to it to download all the source code and projects that you will need.

To build the application, give the following commands:

```
$ cd ~/WFC/github/wildfly-cookbook
$ cd balancing-test
$ mvn clean package
```

## How to do it...

From the WildFly installation directory `$WILDFLY_HOME`, let's create two folders, each one representing a server node.

1. Open a terminal and execute the following commands:

```
$ cd $WILDFLY_HOME
$ cp -a standalone bl-tcp-std-node-1
$ cp -a standalone bl-tcp-std-node-2
```

2. Now, let's copy the `balancing-test.war` application into the `deployments` folder of each node that we have just created. Do as follows:

```
$ cp balancing-test.war bl-tcp-std-node-1/deployments/
$ cp balancing-test.war bl-tcp-std-node-2/deployments/
```

3. Now, let's generate a virtual IP for each of the nodes:

```
$ sudo ifconfig eth0:2 10.0.1.1 netmask 255.255.255.0
$ sudo ifconfig eth0:3 10.0.1.2 netmask 255.255.255.0
```

4. Now, let's go back to the Apache configuration and edit `mod_cluster.conf`, disabling advertising as follows:

```
<VirtualHost 10.0.0.1:6666>
        <Directory />
                Order deny,allow
                Deny from all
                Allow from 10.0.0.1
        </Directory>
        ServerAdvertise off
        EnableMCPMReceive
</VirtualHost>
```

5. If it's not already running, let's launch Apache and its logs by executing the following commands:

```
$ cd /opt/httpd/bin
$ sudo ./httpd -k start -f /opt/httpd/conf/httpd.conf
$ tail -f ../logs/{access,error}_log
==> ../logs/access_log <==

==> ../logs/error_log <==
[Sat Oct 18 23:10:29 2014] [notice] SIGHUP received.  Attempting
to restart
```

```
[Sat Oct 18 23:10:29 2014] [notice] Digest: generating secret for
digest authentication ...

[Sat Oct 18 23:10:29 2014] [notice] Digest: done

[Sat Oct 18 23:10:29 2014] [warn] httpd version 2.2.29 mismatch
detected

[Sat Oct 18 23:10:29 2014] [notice] Advertise initialized for
process 26675

[Sat Oct 18 23:10:29 2014] [notice] Apache/2.2.29 (Unix) mod_
ssl/2.2.29 OpenSSL/1.0.1e-fips DAV/2 mod_cluster/1.2.6.Final
configured -- resuming normal operations
```

6. Now we need to tell the WildFly `mod_cluster` to communicate directly with Apache by adding some attributes to the `mod_cluster` subsystem of the `standalone-ha.xml` file, as follows:

```
<subsystem xmlns="urn:jboss:domain:modcluster:2.0">
    <mod-cluster-config advertise-socket="modcluster"
    advertise="false" proxy-list="10.0.0.1:6666"
    connector="ajp">
        <dynamic-load-provider>
            <load-metric type="cpu"/>
        </dynamic-load-provider>
    </mod-cluster-config>
</subsystem>
```

7. As emphasized in the preceding code, we are telling `mod_cluster` to disable autoadvertising, and to advertise itself to the proxy specified in the `proxy-list` attribute. To specify more than one proxy, use a comma , as a delimiter:

```
proxy-list="10.0.0.1:6666,10.0.0.2:6666"
```

8. Now that Apache is up and running, and that we have configured our node, let's start it by issuing the following command in a new terminal window:

```
$ cd $WILDFLY_HOME

$ ./bin/standalone.sh -Djboss.server.base.dir=bl-tcp-std-node-1
--server-config=standalone-ha.xml -Djboss.bind.address=10.0.1.1
-Djboss.management.http.port=19990 -Djboss.node.name=node-1

...

23:13:58,472 INFO  [org.jboss.as] (Controller Boot Thread)
JBAS015874: WildFly 8.1.0.Final "Kenny" started in 6531ms -
Started 289 of 400 services (179 services are lazy, passive or on-
demand)
```

9. A few seconds after `node-1` starts you should see the following entries in the Apache logs, the `access_log`:

```
==> ../logs/access_log <==
```

```
10.0.0.1 - - [18/Oct/2014:23:14:05 +0200] "INFO / HTTP/1.1" 200 -

10.0.0.1 - - [18/Oct/2014:23:14:05 +0200] "CONFIG / HTTP/1.1" 200
-

10.0.0.1 - - [18/Oct/2014:23:14:05 +0200] "ENABLE-APP / HTTP/1.1"
200 -

10.0.0.1 - - [18/Oct/2014:23:14:05 +0200] "STATUS / HTTP/1.1" 200
46

10.0.0.1 - - [18/Oct/2014:23:14:15 +0200] "STATUS / HTTP/1.1" 200
46
```

Those are `mod_cluster` logs stating that it received an information message, a configuration message, and then it enabled the application provided by WildFly `node-1`.

10. Replicate the WildFly `mod_cluster` configuration for `node-2` as well, and then start it in a new terminal window, as follows:

```
$ ./bin/standalone.sh -Djboss.server.base.dir=bl-tcp-std-node-2
--server-config=standalone-ha.xml -Djboss.bind.address=10.0.1.2
-Djboss.management.http.port=29990 -Djboss.node.name=node-2

...

23:13:58,472 INFO  [org.jboss.as] (Controller Boot Thread)
JBAS015874: WildFly 8.1.0.Final "Kenny" started in 6531ms -
Started 289 of 400 services (179 services are lazy, passive or on-
demand)
```

11. A few seconds after `node-2` starts, you should see the following entries in the Apache logs, the `access_log`:

```
...

10.0.0.1 - - [18/Oct/2014:23:23:45 +0200] "STATUS / HTTP/1.1" 200
46

10.0.0.1 - - [18/Oct/2014:23:23:55 +0200] "STATUS / HTTP/1.1" 200
46

10.0.0.1 - - [18/Oct/2014:23:24:05 +0200] "STATUS / HTTP/1.1" 200
46

10.0.0.1 - - [18/Oct/2014:23:24:15 +0200] "STATUS / HTTP/1.1" 200
46

10.0.0.1 - - [18/Oct/2014:23:24:21 +0200] "INFO / HTTP/1.1" 200
331

10.0.0.1 - - [18/Oct/2014:23:24:21 +0200] "CONFIG / HTTP/1.1" 200
-

10.0.0.1 - - [18/Oct/2014:23:24:21 +0200] "ENABLE-APP / HTTP/1.1"
200 -
```

```
10.0.0.1 - - [18/Oct/2014:23:24:21 +0200] "STATUS / HTTP/1.1" 200
46
10.0.0.1 - - [18/Oct/2014:23:24:25 +0200] "STATUS / HTTP/1.1" 200
46
```

12. Now, open the `mod_cluster-manager` page that we defined in the file `mod_cluster.conf`—Apache side—at the following URL:

    `http://10.0.0.1/mcm`

    You should see the following page:

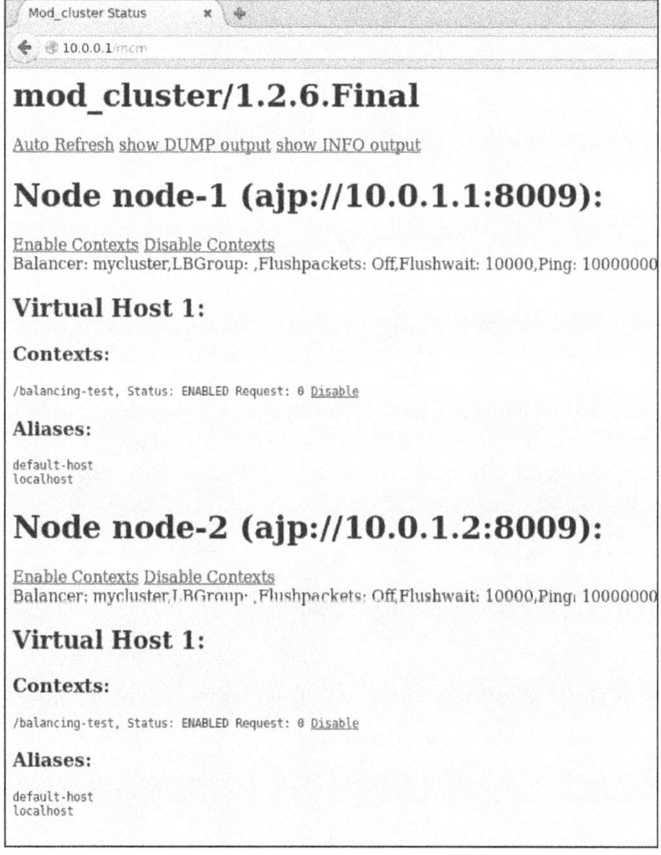


mod_cluster manager page displaying both running nodes and their contexts—TCP

Now that everything is up and running, let's play with our marvelous application.

13. Point your browser to the following URL and refresh the page a few times:

    `http://10.0.0.1/balancing-test`

    You should see a page like the following screenshot:

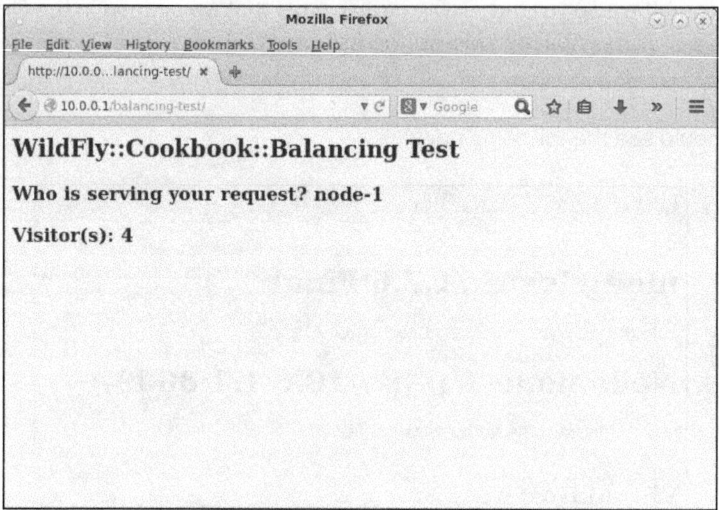


Apache serving balancing-test application on node-1

14. In my case, the request landed on the server `node-1`, yours might land on `node-2`. Let's stop the serving node and refresh the page one more time. If everything works as expected, you should end up with a page like the one seen in the following screenshot:

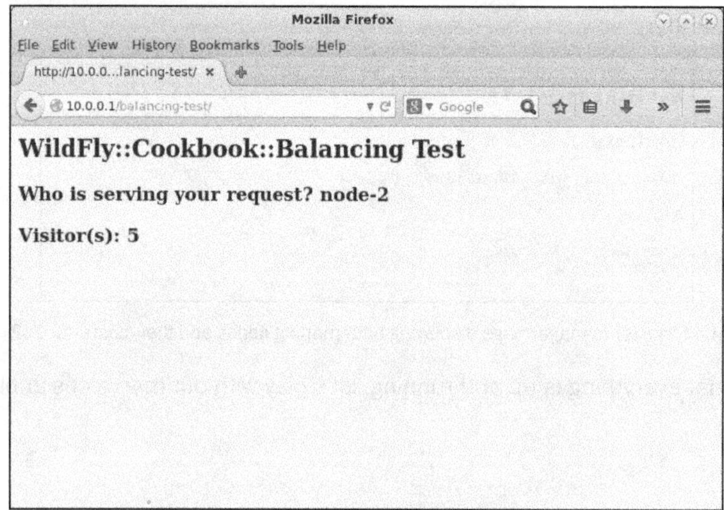


Apache serving balancing-test application on node-2

We got it to work exactly as it worked for balancing with auto-advertising.

## How it works...

What is different in this case, from balancing with auto-advertising enabled, is that `mod_cluster` connects directly to Apache to communicate its `STATUS` information, as depicted in the following image:

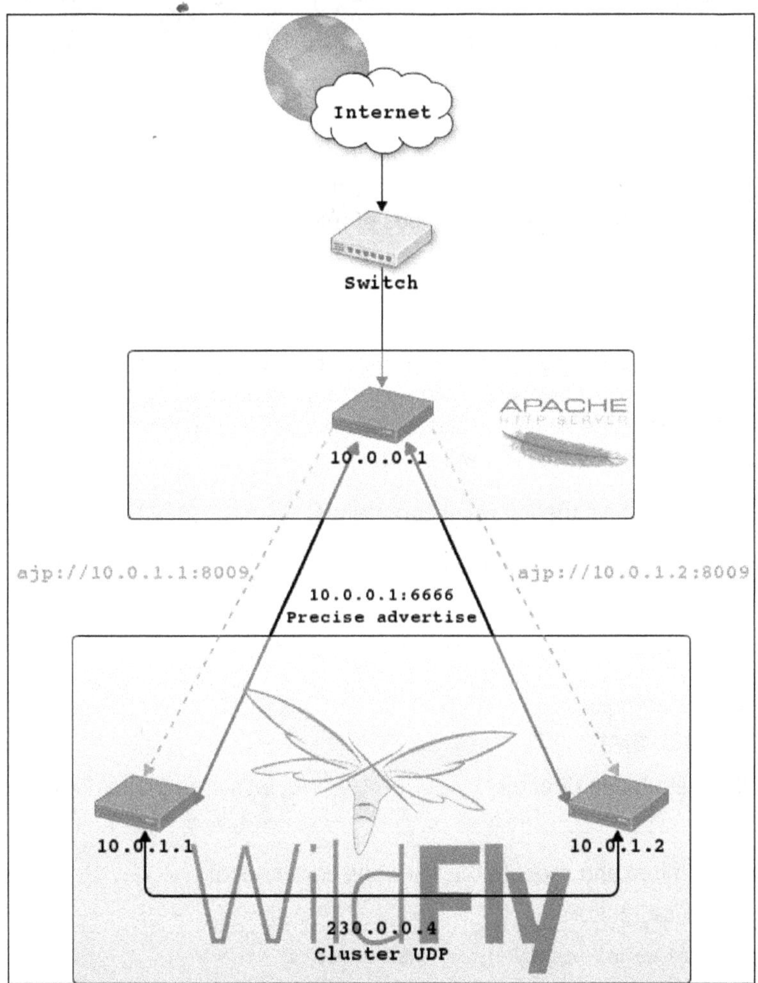


Architecture diagram showing balancing and clustering communication configuration with TCP

Nevertheless, WildFly scales out in the same way; you can add as many WildFly nodes as you want, and they will automatically be balanced by Apache. The drawback is that if you add another Apache instance, you need to add its reference into the WildFly `mod_cluster` configuration through the `proxy-list` attribute of the `mod_cluster` subsystem; the change eventually requires a server reload.

# Balancing using the HTTP connector instead of AJP

In this recipe, we will learn how to balance a WildFly node using an HTTP connector instead of the binary protocol, AJP. The purpose of this recipe is to show you how to use a different connector, not how to really balance a service provided by WildFly. For this reason, we will use just a WildFly node, fronted by Apache. We also assume that Apache HTTPD installation and configuration are based on the first two recipes of this chapter.

## Getting ready

For this recipe, we will need an application named `balancing-test`, that you can find in my GitHub repository. If you skipped the *Managing applications using the deployments folder* recipe in *Chapter 2, Running WildFly in Standalone Mode*, please refer to it to download all the source code and projects that you will need.

To build the application, give the following commands:

```
$ cd ~/WFC/github/wildfly-cookbook
$ cd balancing-test
$ mvn clean package
```

## How to do it...

From the WildFly installation directory `$WILDFLY_HOME`, let's create a folder representing a server node.

1. Open a terminal and execute the following commands:

   ```
   $ cd $WILDFLY_HOME
   $ cp -a standalone bl-http-std-node-1
   ```

2. Now, let's copy the `balancing-test.war` application into the `deployments` folder of the node that we have just created. Type the following command:

   ```
   $ cp balancing-test.war bl-http-std-node-1/deployments/
   ```

3. Now, let's generate a virtual IP for the node:

   ```
   $ sudo ifconfig eth0:1 10.0.1.1 netmask 255.255.255.0
   ```

4. If it's not running already, let's launch Apache and its logs, by executing the following commands:

```
$ cd /opt/httpd/bin
$ sudo ./httpd -k start -f /opt/httpd/conf/httpd.conf
$ tail -f ../logs/{access,error}_log
==> ../logs/access_log <==

==> ../logs/error_log <==
[Sun Oct 12 16:10:29 2014] [notice] SIGHUP received.  Attempting to restart
[Sun Oct 12 16:10:29 2014] [notice] Digest: generating secret for digest authentication ...
[Sun Oct 12 16:10:29 2014] [notice] Digest: done
[Sun Oct 12 16:10:29 2014] [warn] httpd version 2.2.29 mismatch detected
[Sun Oct 12 16:10:29 2014] [notice] Advertise initialized for process 26675
[Sun Oct 12 16:10:29 2014] [notice] Apache/2.2.29 (Unix) mod_ssl/2.2.29 OpenSSL/1.0.1e-fips DAV/2 mod_cluster/1.2.6.Final configured -- resuming normal operations
```

5. Now it's time to configure our WildFly node `node-1`. Edit the `standalone-ha.xml` file in the `bl-http-std-node-1/configuration` folder, and configure the undertow subsystem as follows:

```
<subsystem xmlns="urn:jboss:domain:undertow:2.0">
    <buffer-cache name="default"/>
    <server name="default-server">
        <http-listener name="http" socket-binding="http"
        enabled="true"/>
        <ajp-listener name="ajp" socket-binding="ajp"
        enabled="false"/>
        <host name="default-host" alias="localhost">
            <location name="/" handler="welcome-content"/>
            <filter-ref name="server-header"/>
            <filter-ref name="x-powered-by-header"/>
        </host>
    </server>
    <servlet-container name="default">
        <jsp-config/>
    </servlet-container>
    <handlers>
        <file name="welcome-content"
```

```
        path="${jboss.home.dir}/welcome-content"/>
    </handlers>
    <filters>
        <response-header name="server-header" header-
        name="Server" header-value="WildFly/8"/>
        <response-header name="x-powered-by-header" header-
        name="X-Powered-By" header-value="Undertow/1"/>
    </filters>
</subsystem>
```

6. We disabled the AJP listener by adding the attribute `enabled` and setting it to `false`. Based on these changes, we need to update the `mod_cluster` subsystem as follows:

```
<subsystem xmlns="urn:jboss:domain:modcluster:2.0">
    <mod-cluster-config advertise-socket="modcluster"
    connector="http">
        <dynamic-load-provider>
            <load-metric type="cpu"/>
        </dynamic-load-provider>
    </mod-cluster-config>
</subsystem>
```

7. We changed the connector reference from AJP to HTTP. Now we need to update the connector reference in the remoting subsystem which references the connector with its default name, which is `default`. Apply the following changes:

```
<subsystem xmlns="urn:jboss:domain:remoting:3.0">
    <endpoint worker="default"/>
    <http-connector name="http-remoting-connector"
    connector-ref="default" security-realm="ApplicationRealm"/>
</subsystem>
```

8. That's it; we are done with our configuration. Let's start our node by issuing the following command into a new terminal window:

```
$ ./bin/standalone.sh -Djboss.server.base.dir=bl-http-std-node-1
--server-config=standalone-ha.xml -Djboss.bind.address=10.0.1.1
-Djboss.management.http.port=19990 -Djboss.node.name=node-1
...
18:03:57,734 INFO  [org.jboss.as] (Controller Boot Thread)
JBAS015874: WildFly 8.1.0.Final "Kenny" started in 6670ms -
Started 287 of 399 services (179 services are lazy, passive or on-
demand)
```

9. Now, a few seconds after `node-1` starts, you should see the following entries in the Apache logs, that is, in `access_log`:

```
==> ../logs/access_log <==
...
10.0.0.1 - - [16/Oct/2014:18:04:03 +0200] "INFO / HTTP/1.1" 200 -
10.0.0.1 - - [16/Oct/2014:18:04:03 +0200] "CONFIG / HTTP/1.1" 200
-
10.0.0.1 - - [16/Oct/2014:18:04:03 +0200] "ENABLE-APP / HTTP/1.1"
200 -
10.0.0.1 - - [16/Oct/2014:18:04:03 +0200] "STATUS / HTTP/1.1" 200
46
10.0.0.1 - - [16/Oct/2014:18:04:13 +0200] "STATUS / HTTP/1.1" 200
46
```

   Those are mod-cluster logs stating that it received an information message and a configuration message, and then it enabled the application provided by WildFly `node-1`.

10. Let's test our application by opening a browser and pointing it to the following URL:

    `http://10.0.0.1/balancing-test`

    You should see a page like the following screenshot:

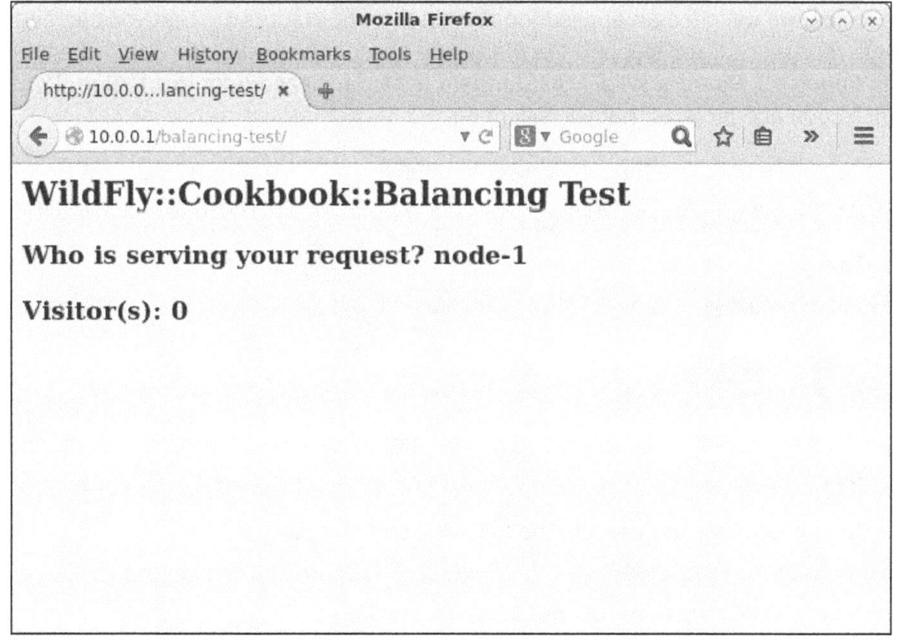


Apache serving balancing-test application on node-1 via HTTP connector

### How it works...

If you were expecting to change something on the Apache side, you were wrong. WildFly `mod_cluster` connects to Apache and says `Hi there, I need to be balanced. Here is how I'm reachable`. So when Apache receives all the information about applications, topology, and the communication strategy, it starts dispatching requests to WildFly.

This is exactly what we have done. We configured the new communication channel through the HTTP connector, disabled the AJP connector, and that's it! Pretty easy, isn't it?

## Preserve WildFly workers while restarting Apache

Many times, you need to restart Apache and all your WildFly instances become unavailable for a few seconds. So, this annoying **404** error may be a problem. In this recipe, we will learn how to mitigate this problem in a simple way. We also assume that the Apache HTTPD installation and configuration are based on the first two recipes of this chapter.

### Getting ready

For this recipe, we will need an application named `balancing-test`, that you can find in my GitHub repository. If you skipped the *Managing applications using the deployments folder* recipe in *Chapter 2, Running WildFly in Standalone Mode*, please refer to it to download all the source code and projects that you will need.

To build the application, give the following commands:

```
$ cd ~/WFC/github/wildfly-cookbook
$ cd balancing-test
$ mvn clean package
```

### How to do it...

From the WildFly installation directory `$WILDFLY_HOME`, let's create a folder representing a server node.

1. Open a terminal and execute the following commands:

   ```
   $ cd $WILDFLY_HOME
   $ cp -a standalone bl-persist-std-node-1
   ```

2. Now, let's copy the `balancing-test.war` application into the `deployments` folder of the node that we have just created. Type the following command:

```
$ cp balancing-test.war bl-persist-std-node-1/deployments/
```

3. Now, let's generate a virtual IP for the node:

```
$ sudo ifconfig eth0:1 10.0.1.1 netmask 255.255.255.0
```

4. If it's not running already, let's launch Apache and its logs, by executing the following commands:

```
$ cd /opt/httpd/bin
$ sudo ./httpd -k start -f /opt/httpd/conf/httpd.conf
$ tail -f ../logs/{access,error}_log
==> ../logs/access_log <==

==> ../logs/error_log <==
[Thu Oct 16 18:51:51 2014] [warn] Init: Session Cache is not
configured [hint: SSLSessionCache]
[Thu Oct 16 18:51:51 2014] [warn] httpd version 2.2.29 mismatch
detected
[Thu Oct 16 18:51:51 2014] [notice] Digest: generating secret for
digest authentication ...
[Thu Oct 16 18:51:51 2014] [notice] Digest: done
[Thu Oct 16 18:51:51 2014] [warn] httpd version 2.2.29 mismatch
detected
[Thu Oct 16 18:51:51 2014] [notice] Advertise initialized for
process 15525
[Thu Oct 16 18:51:51 2014] [notice] Apache/2.2.29 (Unix) mod_
ssl/2.2.29 OpenSSL/1.0.1e-fips DAV/2 mod_cluster/1.2.6.Final
configured -- resuming normal operations
```

5. Let's start our node, by issuing the following command in a new terminal window:

```
$ ./bin/standalone.sh -Djboss.server.base.dir=bl-persist-
std-node-1 --server-config=standalone-ha.xml -Djboss.bind.
address=10.0.1.1 -Djboss.management.http.port=19990 -Djboss.node.
name=node-1
...
18:55:37,613 INFO  [org.jboss.as] (Controller Boot Thread)
JBAS015874: WildFly 8.1.0.Final "Kenny" started in 6723ms -
Started 289 of 400 services (179 services are lazy, passive or on-
demand)
```

Now, a few seconds after `node-1` starts, you should see the following entries in the Apache logs, that is, `access_log`:

```
==> ./logs/access_log <==
...
10.0.0.1 - - [16/Oct/2014:18:55:43 +0200] "INFO / HTTP/1.1" 200 -
10.0.0.1 - - [16/Oct/2014:18:55:43 +0200] "CONFIG / HTTP/1.1" 200
-
10.0.0.1 - - [16/Oct/2014:18:55:43 +0200] "ENABLE-APP / HTTP/1.1"
200 -
10.0.0.1 - - [16/Oct/2014:18:55:43 +0200] "STATUS / HTTP/1.1" 200
54
10.0.0.1 - - [16/Oct/2014:18:55:53 +0200] "STATUS / HTTP/1.1" 200
54
```

Those are `mod_cluster` logs stating that it received an information message and a configuration message, and then it enabled the application provided by WildFly `node-1`.

6. Now let's restart Apache by executing the following command:

```
$ cd /opt/httpd/bin
$ ./httpd -k restart -f /opt/httpd/conf/httpd.conf
```

In the Apache logs, you should see statements similar to the following:

```
==> ../logs/error_log <==
...
[Thu Oct 16 18:57:23 2014] [warn] manager_handler STATUS error:
MEM: Can't read node


==> ../logs/access_log <==
10.0.0.1 - - [16/Oct/2014:18:57:23 +0200] "STATUS / HTTP/1.1" 500
535
```

In the WildFly logs, you should see the following log entry:

```
18:57:23,879 ERROR [org.jboss.modcluster]
(UndertowEventHandlerAdapter - 1) MODCLUSTER000042: Error MEM
sending STATUS command to 10.0.0.1/10.0.0.1:6666, configuration
will be reset: MEM: Can't read node
```

Wait for just a few seconds, and now you should see WildFly sending its messages to Apache as follows:

```
==> ../logs/access_log <==
10.0.0.1 - - [16/Oct/2014:18:57:23 +0200] "STATUS / HTTP/1.1" 500
535
```

```
10.0.0.1 - - [16/Oct/2014:18:57:33 +0200] "INFO / HTTP/1.1" 200 -
10.0.0.1 - - [16/Oct/2014:18:57:33 +0200] "CONFIG / HTTP/1.1" 200
-
10.0.0.1 - - [16/Oct/2014:18:57:33 +0200] "ENABLE-APP / HTTP/1.1"
200 -
10.0.0.1 - - [16/Oct/2014:18:57:33 +0200] "STATUS / HTTP/1.1" 200
46
10.0.0.1 - - [16/Oct/2014:18:57:43 +0200] "STATUS / HTTP/1.1" 200
46
```

While restarting, users would have seen a **NOT FOUND** error page for your application, as follows:

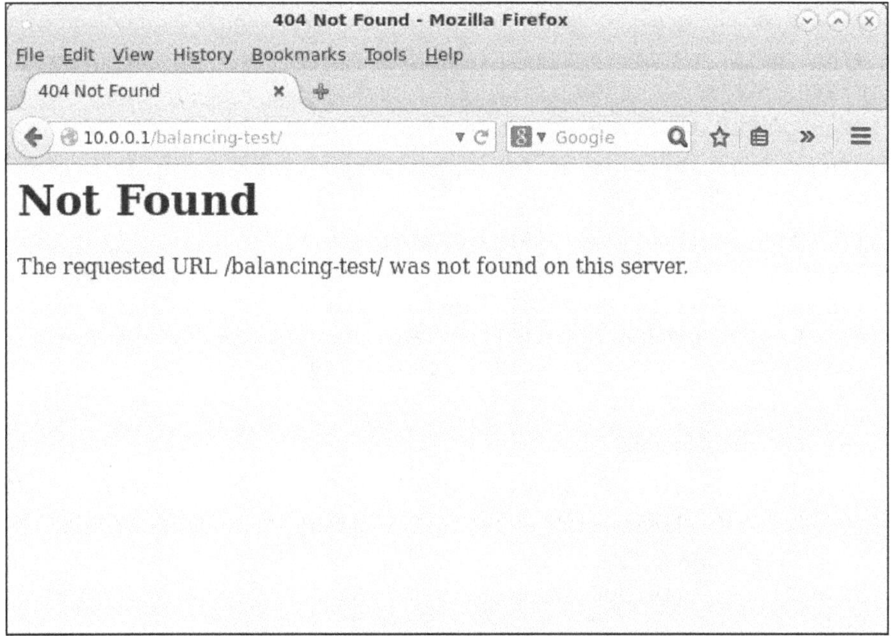


Apache could not find the application context after a restart

7. So, to mitigate this problem, you can tell Apache to persist somehow with the WildFly node information before it shuts down, and then read the information back again at startup.

   Edit the `mod_cluster.conf` file in the `/opt/httpd/conf/extra` folder, and add the following directive outside the virtual hosts declaration:

   ```
   ...
   Listen 10.0.0.1:80
   ```

```
Listen 10.0.0.1:6666

PersistSlots On

<VirtualHost 10.0.0.1:80>
...
```

8. Let's see if it works. Stop both Apache and WildFly, and then restart them. After a few seconds, we should have the following entries:

```
==> ../logs/error_log <==
[Thu Oct 16 19:14:39 2014] [warn] Init: Session Cache is not configured [hint: SSLSessionCache]
[Thu Oct 16 19:14:39 2014] [warn] httpd version 2.2.29 mismatch detected
[Thu Oct 16 19:14:39 2014] [notice] Digest: generating secret for digest authentication ...
[Thu Oct 16 19:14:39 2014] [notice] Digest: done
[Thu Oct 16 19:14:39 2014] [warn] httpd version 2.2.29 mismatch detected
[Thu Oct 16 19:14:39 2014] [notice] Advertise initialized for process 16529
[Thu Oct 16 19:14:39 2014] [notice] Apache/2.2.29 (Unix) mod_ssl/2.2.29 OpenSSL/1.0.1e-fips DAV/2 mod_cluster/1.2.6.Final configured -- resuming normal operations


==> ../logs/access_log <==
10.0.0.1 - - [16/Oct/2014:19:15:01 +0200] "INFO / HTTP/1.1" 200 -
10.0.0.1 - - [16/Oct/2014:19:15:01 +0200] "CONFIG / HTTP/1.1" 200 -
10.0.0.1 - - [16/Oct/2014:19:15:01 +0200] "ENABLE-APP / HTTP/1.1" 200 -
10.0.0.1 - - [16/Oct/2014:19:15:01 +0200] "STATUS / HTTP/1.1" 200 55
```

9. Now restart Apache and look at its logs:

```
==> ../logs/error_log <==
[Thu Oct 16 19:17:05 2014] [notice] SIGHUP received.  Attempting to restart
[Thu Oct 16 19:17:05 2014] [notice] Digest: generating secret for digest authentication ...
[Thu Oct 16 19:17:05 2014] [notice] Digest: done
```

```
[Thu Oct 16 19:17:05 2014] [warn] httpd version 2.2.29 mismatch
detected

[Thu Oct 16 19:17:05 2014] [notice] Advertise initialized for
process 16529

[Thu Oct 16 19:17:05 2014] [notice] Apache/2.2.29 (Unix) mod_
ssl/2.2.29 OpenSSL/1.0.1e-fips DAV/2 mod_cluster/1.2.6.Final
configured -- resuming normal operations

==> ../logs/access_log <==

10.0.0.1 - - [16/Oct/2014:19:17:11 +0200] "STATUS / HTTP/1.1" 200
46

10.0.0.1 - - [16/Oct/2014:19:17:21 +0200] "STATUS / HTTP/1.1" 200
46
```

See, no more `INFO`, `CONFIG`, and `ENABLE-APP` messages from WildFly! The WildFly log didn't catch anything, and our application is served as fast as Apache starts up.

# Balancing the same context for different applications

A large enterprise environment might be composed of several application servers providing lots of applications. Sometimes, it happens that applications have the same context path while running on different nodes (eventually, even different server-groups in the case of WildFly in the domain mode), but they share the same balancer, that is, Apache.

In this recipe, we will learn how to balance the same application context coming from different applications from different nodes.

## Getting ready

For this recipe, we will need an application named `balancing-test`, that you can find in my GitHub repository. If you skipped the *Managing applications using the deployments folder* recipe in *Chapter 2, Running WildFly in Standalone Mode*, please refer to it to download all the source code and projects that you will need.

To build the application, give the following commands:

```
$ cd ~/WFC/github/wildfly-cookbook
$ cd balancing-test
$ mvn clean package
```

## How to do it...

From the WildFly installation directory `$WILDFLY_HOME`, let's create two folders, each one representing a server node.

1. Open a terminal and execute the following commands:

```
$ cd $WILDFLY_HOME
$ cp -a standalone bl-std-node-bar
$ cp -a standalone bl-std-node-foo
```

2. Now, let's copy the two web applications in the `deployments` folder, to their corresponding node. Type the following commands:

```
$ cp app-bar-with-this-context.war bl-std-node-bar/deployments/
$ cp app-foo-with-this-context.war bl-std-node-foo/deployments/
```

3. Now, let's generate a virtual IP for each of the nodes:

```
$ sudo ifconfig eth0:1 10.0.1.1 netmask 255.255.255.0
$ sudo ifconfig eth0:2 10.0.1.2 netmask 255.255.255.0
```

4. Now, let's go back to the Apache configuration and edit `mod_cluster.conf`. We need to replace the entire configuration, as follows:

```
LoadModule slotmem_module modules/mod_slotmem.so
LoadModule manager_module modules/mod_manager.so
LoadModule proxy_cluster_module modules/mod_proxy_cluster.so
LoadModule advertise_module modules/mod_advertise.so

PersistSlots On
ServerAdvertise Off

Listen 10.0.0.3:80
<VirtualHost 10.0.0.3:80>

        ServerName mcm.com

        <Location />
                SetHandler mod_cluster-manager
                Order deny,allow
                Deny from all
                Allow from all
        </Location>

</VirtualHost>

Listen 10.0.0.1:80
```

```
<VirtualHost 10.0.0.1:80>

        ServerName bar.com

        <Directory />
                Order deny,allow
                Deny from all
                Allow from all
        </Directory>

        EnableMCPMReceive On

        CreateBalancers 1
        ProxyPass / balancer://barBalancer/this

</VirtualHost>

Listen 10.0.0.2:80
<VirtualHost 10.0.0.2:80>

        ServerName foo.com

        <Directory />
                Order deny,allow
                Deny from all
                Allow from all
        </Directory>

        EnableMCPMReceive On

        CreateBalancers 1
        ProxyPass / balancer://fooBalancer/this

</VirtualHost>
```

5. As you can see, we changed virtual hosts bindings, so let's create the appropriate virtual IPs for them:

   ```
   $ sudo ifconfig eth0:3 10.0.0.1 netmask 255.255.255.0
   $ sudo ifconfig eth0:4 10.0.0.2 netmask 255.255.255.0
   $ sudo ifconfig eth0:5 10.0.0.3 netmask 255.255.255.0
   ```

6. Now we need to map the `ServerName` directive into the `/etc/hosts` file, as follows:

   ```
   10.0.0.3 mcm.com
   10.0.0.1 bar.com
   10.0.0.2 foo.com
   ```

7. Now, let's check if our configuration is okay—at least the Apache configuration—by starting Apache HTTPD in a new terminal window, as follows:

```
$ cd /opt/httpd/bin
$ ./httpd -k restart -f /opt/httpd/conf/httpd.conf
```

In the Apache logs, you should see entries similar to the following:

```
==> ../logs/access_log <==

==> ../logs/error_log <==
[Fri Oct 17 00:12:57 2014] [warn] Init: Session Cache is not configured [hint: SSLSessionCache]
[Fri Oct 17 00:12:57 2014] [warn] httpd version 2.2.29 mismatch detected
[Fri Oct 17 00:12:57 2014] [notice] Digest: generating secret for digest authentication ...
[Fri Oct 17 00:12:57 2014] [notice] Digest: done
[Fri Oct 17 00:12:57 2014] [warn] httpd version 2.2.29 mismatch detected
[Fri Oct 17 00:12:57 2014] [notice] Advertise initialized for process 23907
[Fri Oct 17 00:12:57 2014] [notice] Apache/2.2.29 (Unix) mod_ssl/2.2.29 OpenSSL/1.0.1e-fips DAV/2 mod_cluster/1.2.6.Final configured -- resuming normal operations
```

8. Open the browser and point it to the following URL:

```
http://mcm.com
```

You should see the `mod_cluster-manager` page, as follows:

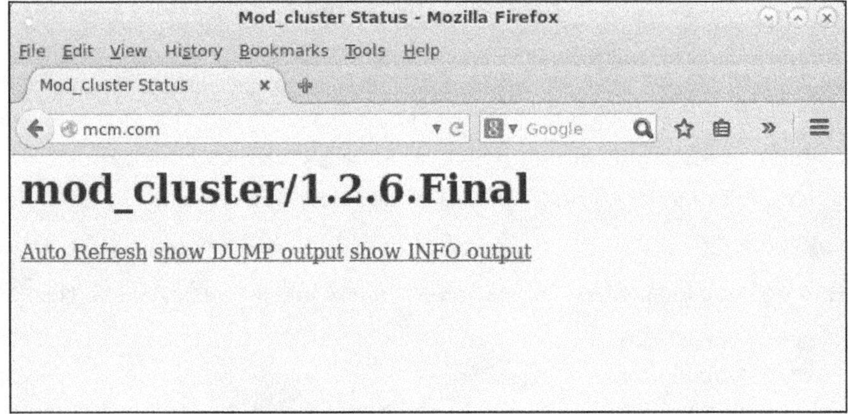


mod_cluster-manager page served by Apache through the mcm.com address

9. Now, let's configure our first node, `node-bar`. We need to adjust our `mod_cluster` subsystem, as follows:

```
<subsystem xmlns="urn:jboss:domain:modcluster:2.0">
    <mod-cluster-config advertise-socket="modcluster"
    advertise="false" proxy-list="${proxy.list}"
    connector="ajp" balancer="${balancer.name}">
        <dynamic-load-provider>
            <load-metric type="cpu"/>
        </dynamic-load-provider>
    </mod-cluster-config>
</subsystem>
```

10. Now we can start our `node-bar` by executing the following commands:

```
$ cd $WILDFLY_HOME
$ ./bin/standalone.sh -Djboss.server.base.dir=bl-std-node-bar
--server-config=standalone-ha.xml -Djboss.bind.address=10.0.1.1
-Djboss.management.http.port=19990 -Djboss.node.name=node-bar
-Dbalancer.name=barBalancer -Dproxy.list=10.0.0.1:80 -Djboss.
default.multicast.address=230.0.1.4
...
00:24:20,643 INFO  [org.wildfly.extension.undertow] (MSC service
thread 1-1) WFLYUT0021: Registered web context: /this
...
```

Apache should have caught the following log entries:

```
10.0.0.1 - - [17/Oct/2014:00:24:16 +0200] "INFO / HTTP/1.1" 200 -
10.0.0.1 - - [17/Oct/2014:00:24:16 +0200] "CONFIG / HTTP/1.1" 200
-
10.0.0.1 - - [17/Oct/2014:00:24:16 +0200] "STATUS / HTTP/1.1" 200
48
10.0.0.1 - - [17/Oct/2014:00:24:20 +0200] "ENABLE-APP / HTTP/1.1"
200 -
10.0.0.1 - - [17/Oct/2014:00:24:20 +0200] "ENABLE-APP / HTTP/1.1"
200 -
10.0.0.1 - - [17/Oct/2014:00:24:26 +0200] "STATUS / HTTP/1.1" 200
48
```

11. Now, apply the same changes that we made to the `mod_cluster` subsystem, to `node-foo` as well. Once done, start the node as follows:

```
$ cd $WILDFLY_HOME
$ ./bin/standalone.sh -Djboss.server.base.dir=bl-std-node-foo
--server-config=standalone-ha.xml -Djboss.bind.address=10.0.1.2
-Djboss.management.http.port=29990 -Djboss.node.name=node-foo
-Dbalancer.name=fooBalancer -Dproxy.list=10.0.0.2:80 -Djboss.
default.multicast.address=230.0.2.4
```

```
...
00:24:39,689 INFO  [org.wildfly.extension.undertow] (MSC service
thread 1-5) WFLYUT0021: Registered web context: /this
...
```

Apache should have caught the following log entries:

```
10.0.0.1 - - [17/Oct/2014:00:24:32 +0200] "INFO / HTTP/1.1" 200
325
10.0.0.1 - - [17/Oct/2014:00:24:32 +0200] "CONFIG / HTTP/1.1" 200
-
10.0.0.1 - - [17/Oct/2014:00:24:32 +0200] "STATUS / HTTP/1.1" 200
48
10.0.0.1 - - [17/Oct/2014:00:24:36 +0200] "STATUS / HTTP/1.1" 200
48

==> ../logs/error_log <==
[Fri Oct 17 00:24:39 2014] [warn] ENABLE: context /this is in
balancer fooBalancer and barBalancer

==> ../logs/access_log <==
10.0.0.1 - - [17/Oct/2014:00:24:39 +0200] "ENABLE-APP / HTTP/1.1"
200 -

==> ../logs/error_log <==
[Fri Oct 17 00:24:39 2014] [warn] ENABLE: context /this is in
balancer fooBalancer and barBalancer

==> ../logs/access_log <==
10.0.0.1 - - [17/Oct/2014:00:24:39 +0200] "ENABLE-APP / HTTP/1.1"
200 -
10.0.0.1 - - [17/Oct/2014:00:24:42 +0200] "STATUS / HTTP/1.1" 200
48
10.0.0.1 - - [17/Oct/2014:00:24:46 +0200] "STATUS / HTTP/1.1" 200
48
```

As you can see, Apache warns you about the context `/this` using the two balancers, which is fine; this is exactly what we wanted.

12. Now let's refresh the `mcm.com` site:

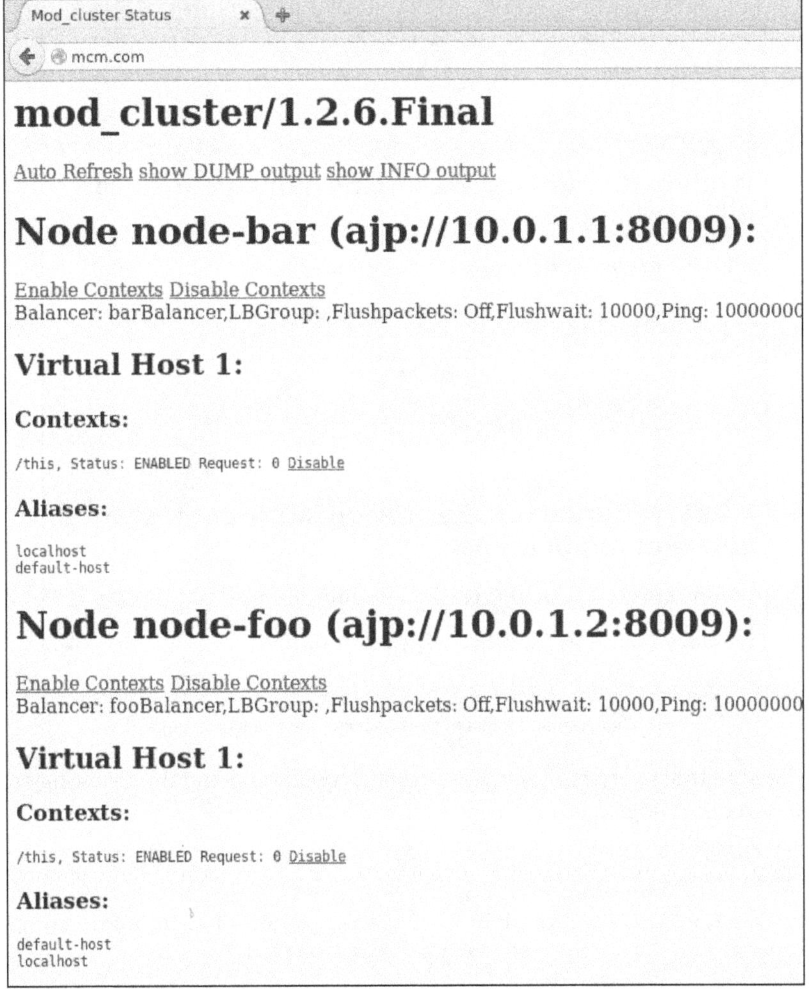


mod_cluster manger page showing both nodes with the same application context path

13. Now it's time to see if our two sites, `bar.com` and `foo.com` are correctly balanced and served by our Apache configuration:

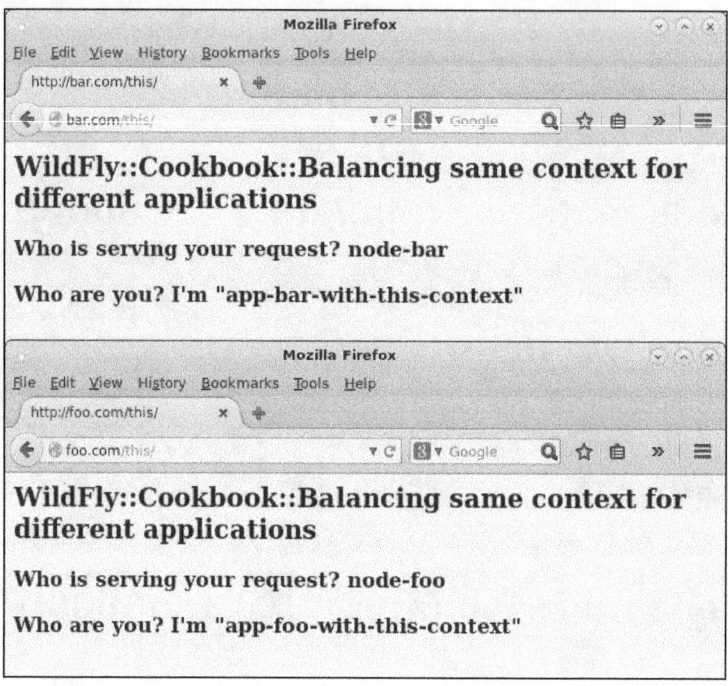


The bar.com and foo.com sites showing their welcome page

To be sure that everything worked correctly, you should find the following entries in the `node-bar` logs:

```
00:37:42,053 INFO  [stdout] (default task-1) ********************
***********+
00:37:42,054 INFO  [stdout] (default task-1) I'm serving your
request and I'm "app-bar-with-this-context"
00:37:42,054 INFO  [stdout] (default task-1) ********************
***********+
```

And for `node-foo`, you should find the following log entries:

```
00:37:43,709 INFO  [stdout] (default task-1) ********************
***********+
00:37:43,709 INFO  [stdout] (default task-1) I'm serving your
request and I'm "app-foo-with-this-context"
00:37:43,709 INFO  [stdout] (default task-1) ********************
***********+
```

Great, everything worked as expected!

## How it works...

Most of the configuration is on the Apache side and is about how we configured our virtual hosts. We needed to specify one `mod_cluster` directive, that is, `CreateBalancers`. They define how balancers are created in the enclosing virtual host, thus you can control which balancer handles your requests (as in our case).

This `mod_cluster` directive can have the following values:

- `0`: Creates balancers in all VirtualHosts defined in the Apache HTTPD
- `1`: Does not create balancers (requires at least one `ProxyPass/ProxyPassMatch` to define the balancer names)
- `2`: Creates only the main balancer named `myclsuter`, and it is the default setting.

As per the preceding definition, for the `bar.com` site, we used the following definition:

```
Listen 10.0.0.1:80
<VirtualHost 10.0.0.1:80>
        ServerName bar.com
        <Directory />
                Order deny,allow
                Deny from all
                Allow from all
        </Directory>
        EnableMCPMReceive On
        CreateBalancers 1
        ProxyPass / balancer://barBalancer/this
</VirtualHost>
```

For the `foo.com` site, we used the following definition:

```
Listen 10.0.0.2:80
<VirtualHost 10.0.0.2:80>
        ServerName foo.com
        <Directory />
                Order deny,allow
                Deny from all
                Allow from all
        </Directory>
        EnableMCPMReceive On
        CreateBalancers 1
        ProxyPass / balancer://fooBalancer/this
</VirtualHost>
```

So we commanded Apache to use the balancer `barBalancer` to handle the `bar.com` requests, and to use `fooBalancer` to handle the `foo.com` requests. On the WildFly side, we had to match the balancer name in the `mod_cluster` subsystem to the relative node.

We achieved this by defining the attribute `balancer` in the `mod_cluster` subsystem. The attribute is valued to a property to pass at start up, named `balancer.name`. The following was our configuration:

```
<subsystem xmlns="urn:jboss:domain:modcluster:2.0">
    <mod-cluster-config advertise-socket="modcluster"
    advertise="false" proxy-list="${proxy.list}" connector="ajp"
    balancer="${balancer.name}">
        <dynamic-load-provider>
            <load-metric type="cpu"/>
        </dynamic-load-provider>
    </mod-cluster-config>
</subsystem>
```

We also needed to specify which Apache was serving our requests, by using the `proxy-list` attribute, settled with a property named `proxy.list`, which we passed at the command line.

## See also

For understanding Apache directives better, check the documentation at the following sites:

- http://docs.jboss.org/mod_cluster/1.2.0/html/native.config.html
- http://httpd.apache.org/docs/2.2/mod/mod_proxy.html#proxypass

# Rolling updates

In this recipe, you will learn how to update your application, using rolling updates, while still providing service availability. To achieve this, we need to configure quite a few things from Apache to WildFly, and code the tester application. We also assume that Apache HTTPD installation and configuration are based on the first two recipes of this chapter.

## Getting ready

For this recipe, we will need the application named `rolling-test`, that you can find in my GitHub repository. If you skipped the *Managing applications using the deployments folder* recipe in *Chapter 2, Running WildFly in Standalone Mode*, please refer to it to download all the source code and projects that you will need.

To build the application, do as follows:

```
$ cd ~/WFC/github/wildfly-cookbook
$ cd rolling-test
$ mvn -e clean package
```

## How to do it...

Let's create four folders from the WildFly installation directory `$WILDFLY_HOME`, each one representing a server node.

1. Open a terminal and execute the following commands:

   ```
   $ cd $WILDFLY_HOME
   $ cp -a standalone bl-rolling-node-1
   $ cp -a standalone bl-rolling-node-2
   $ cp -a standalone bl-rolling-node-3
   $ cp -a standalone bl-rolling-node-4
   ```

2. Now, let's copy the `rolling-test-1.0.war` web application into the `deployments` folder of each node that we just created, as follows:

   ```
   $ cp ~/WFC/github/wildfly-cookbook/rolling-test/target/rolling-test-1.0.war bl-rolling-node-1/deployments/
   $ cp ~/WFC/github/wildfly-cookbook/rolling-test/target/rolling-test-1.0.war bl-rolling-node-2/deployments/
   $ cp ~/WFC/github/wildfly-cookbook/rolling-test/target/rolling-test-1.0.war bl-rolling-node-3/deployments/
   $ cp ~/WFC/github/wildfly-cookbook/rolling-test/target/rolling-test-1.0.war bl-rolling-node-4/deployments/
   ```

3. Now, let's generate a virtual IP for each of the nodes:

   ```
   $ sudo ifconfig eth0:2 10.0.1.1 netmask 255.255.255.0
   $ sudo ifconfig eth0:3 10.0.1.2 netmask 255.255.255.0
   $ sudo ifconfig eth0:4 10.0.1.3 netmask 255.255.255.0
   $ sudo ifconfig eth0:5 10.0.1.4 netmask 255.255.255.0
   ```

4. Edit the file `standalone-ha.xml` of each WildFly node, and replace the `cache-container` XML element named `web` of the `infinispan` subsystem, with the following XML code:

   ```
   <cache-container name="web" default-cache="repl" module="org.wildfly.clustering.web.infinispan">
     <transport lock-timeout="60000"/>
   ```

```
    <replicated-cache name="repl" mode="SYNC"
    batching="true">
      <locking isolation="REPEATABLE_READ"/>
    </replicated-cache>
    <distributed-cache name="dist" mode="ASYNC"
    batching="true" l1-lifespan="0" owners="2">
      <file-store/>
    </distributed-cache>
  </cache-container>
```

5. Now, let's go back to the Apache configuration and edit `mod_cluster.conf`. We need to replace the entire configuration, as follows:

```
LoadModule slotmem_module modules/mod_slotmem.so
LoadModule manager_module modules/mod_manager.so
LoadModule proxy_cluster_module modules/mod_proxy_cluster.so
LoadModule advertise_module modules/mod_advertise.so

Listen 10.0.0.1:80
<VirtualHost 10.0.0.1:80>
        <Location /mcm>
                SetHandler mod_cluster-manager
                Order deny,allow
                Deny from all
                Allow from 10.0.0.1
        </Location>
</VirtualHost>

Listen 10.0.0.1:6666
<VirtualHost 10.0.0.1:6666>
        <Directory />
                Order deny,allow
                Deny from all
                Allow from 10.0.0.1
        </Directory>
        ServerAdvertise on http://10.0.0.1:6666
        EnableMCPMReceive
</VirtualHost>

Listen 10.0.0.2:80
<VirtualHost 10.0.0.2:80>
        ServerName rolling.com
        <Directory />
                Order deny,allow
                Deny from all
```

```
        Allow from all
    </Directory>
    EnableMCPMReceive On

    RewriteEngine On
    RewriteCond %{REQUEST_URI} !^/(rolling/.*)$
    RewriteRule ^/(.*)$ /rolling/$1 [P,L]

    ProxyPass / balancer://mycluster/rolling stickysession=JSE
SSIONID|jsessionid nofailover=Off
    ProxyPassReverse /rolling /
    ProxyPassReverseCookieDomain / rolling.com
    ProxyPassReverseCookiePath /rolling /
</VirtualHost>
```

6. Add another virtual IP for the second virtual host, as follows:

   ```
   $ sudo ifconfig eth0:6 10.0.0.2 netmask 255.255.255.0
   ```

7. Now, as root user, edit the `/etc/hosts` file and add the following directive:

   ```
   10.0.0.2 rolling.com
   ```

8. Now we are ready to start Apache and all four WildFly nodes.

   For Apache, do as follows:

   ```
   $ sudo ./httpd -k restart -f /opt/httpd/conf/httpd.conf
   $ tail -f ../logs/{access,error}_log
   ==> ../logs/access_log <==

   ==> ../logs/error_log <==
   [Fri Oct 17 15:22:34 2014] [warn] Init: Session Cache is not
   configured [hint: SSLSessionCache]
   [Fri Oct 17 15:22:34 2014] [warn] httpd version 2.2.29 mismatch
   detected
   [Fri Oct 17 15:22:34 2014] [notice] Digest: generating secret for
   digest authentication ...
   [Fri Oct 17 15:22:34 2014] [notice] Digest: done
   [Fri Oct 17 15:22:34 2014] [warn] httpd version 2.2.29 mismatch
   detected
   [Fri Oct 17 15:22:34 2014] [notice] Advertise initialized for
   process 26498
   [Fri Oct 17 15:22:34 2014] [notice] Apache/2.2.29 (Unix) mod_
   ssl/2.2.29 OpenSSL/1.0.1e-fips DAV/2 mod_cluster/1.2.6.Final
   configured -- resuming normal operations
   ```

9. For WildFly nodes, open four different terminal windows, and in each of them, do as follows:

   - For `node-1`:

     ```
     ./bin/standalone.sh -Djboss.server.base.dir=bl-rolling-node-1 --server-config=standalone-ha.xml -Djboss.bind.address=10.0.1.1 -Djboss.management.http.port=19990 -Djboss.node.name=node-1
     ```

   - For `node-2`:

     ```
     ./bin/standalone.sh -Djboss.server.base.dir=bl-rolling-node-2 --server-config=standalone-ha.xml -Djboss.bind.address=10.0.1.2 -Djboss.management.http.port=29990 -Djboss.node.name=node-2
     ```

   - For `node-3`:

     ```
     ./bin/standalone.sh -Djboss.server.base.dir=bl-rolling-node-3 --server-config=standalone-ha.xml -Djboss.bind.address=10.0.1.3 -Djboss.management.http.port=39990 -Djboss.node.name=node-3
     ```

   - For `node-4`:

     ```
     ./bin/standalone.sh -Djboss.server.base.dir=bl-rolling-node-4 --server-config=standalone-ha.xml -Djboss.bind.address=10.0.1.4 -Djboss.management.http.port=49990 -Djboss.node.name=node-4
     ```

10. Open the browser and point it to the following site, refreshing the page a couple of times:

    `http://rolling.com`

    You should see the following:

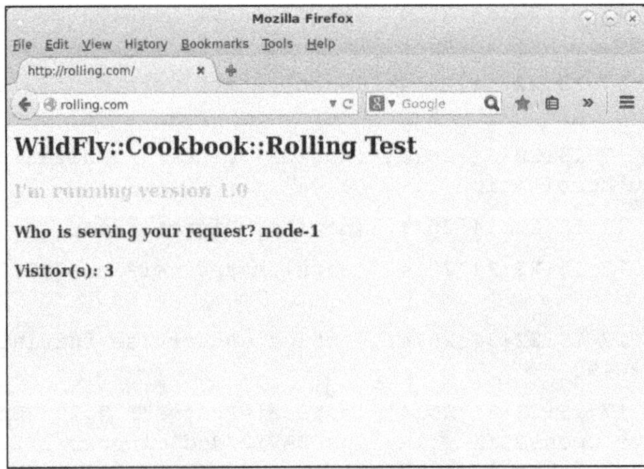


Apache serving the rolling application via the server name rolling.com

11. Without spending too much time watching the logs, let's stop the `node-1`, or whichever node you landed on. Refresh the page a few times:

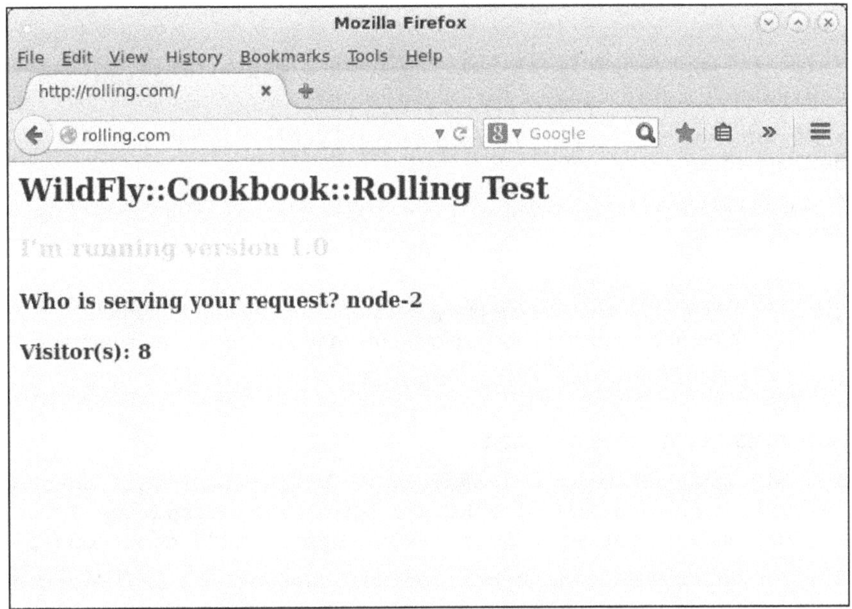


Rolling application provided by another member of the cluster, node-2

OK, it worked. Now suppose that our super boss wants to go into production with the latest version of our great application. Obviously he wants it done for yesterday, and obviously he does not want to give a **Service unavailable** to customers.

You know the answer: **Yes Sir, yes!**.

12. Edit the `index.jsp` file of the `rolling-test` application and change its content by replacing the `<h3>...</h3>` HTML tag with the following one:

```
<h3 style="color:#ccff00;">I'm running version 1.1</h3>
```

13. Now we need to increment the application version; we can do this by editing the `pom.xml` Maven file of the `rolling-test` project, and change its `<version>` tag, as follows:

```
<version>1.1</version>
```

14. Now we can build the project again as follows:

```
$ cd ~/WFC/github/wildfly-cookbook
$ cd rolling-test
$ mvn -e clean package
```

15. Stop node-2 and update the application by removing the old package and copying the new one, to node-1 and node-2 as follows:

```
$ rm -rf /opt/wildfly/bl-rolling-node-1/deployments/rolling-test-1.0.war
$ rm -rf /opt/wildfly/bl-rolling-node-2/deployments/rolling-test-1.0.war
$ cp rolling-test-1.1.war /opt/wildfly/bl-rolling-node-1/deployments/
$ cp rolling-test-1.1.war /opt/wildfly/bl-rolling-node-2/deployments/
```

We can do this as we are using the standalone mode. Nonetheless, remember to disable hot-deployments in the production environment, just in case.

16. Now, restart both nodes as usual:

```
$ ./bin/standalone.sh -Djboss.server.base.dir=bl-rolling-node-1 --server-config=standalone-ha.xml -Djboss.bind.address=10.0.1.1 -Djboss.management.http.port=19990 -Djboss.node.name=node-1
$ ./bin/standalone.sh -Djboss.server.base.dir=bl-rolling-node-2 --server-config=standalone-ha.xml -Djboss.bind.address=10.0.1.2 -Djboss.management.http.port=29990 -Djboss.node.name=node-2
```

17. Go back to the browser and refresh the page; you should get the new functionality desired by our super boss, as follows:

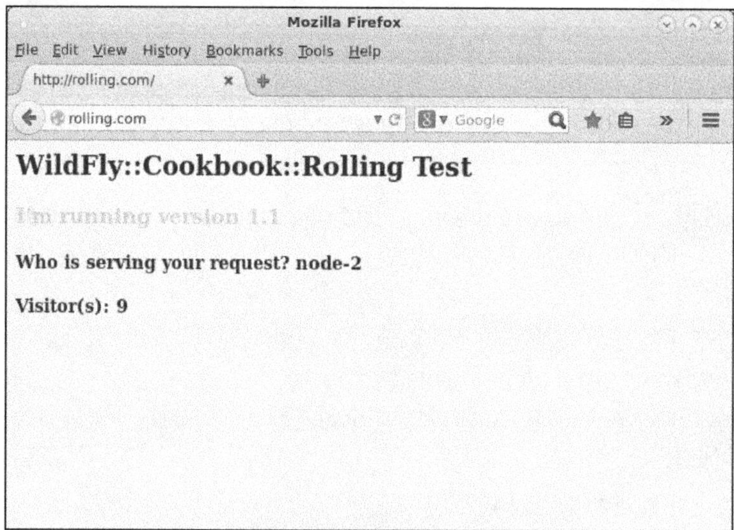


Rolling application with its new functionality

And yes, we didn't even loose the session. Now we need to upgrade the other two nodes, `node-3` and `node-4`, otherwise a user might get the following page by accessing the application:

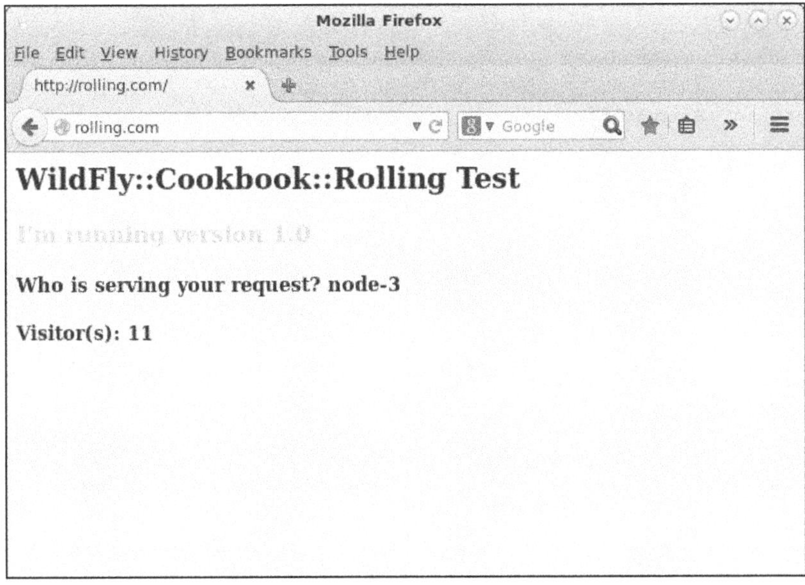


Rolling application needs to be updated in every node of the cluster

18. So, let's stop `node-3` and `node-4`, remove the old artifact, and deploy the new one as follows:

```
$ rm -rf /opt/wildfly/bl-rolling-node-3/deployments/rolling-test-1.0.war
```

```
$ rm -rf /opt/wildfly/bl-rolling-node-4/deployments/rolling-test-1.0.war
```

```
$ cp rolling-test-1.1.war /opt/wildfly/bl-rolling-node-3/deployments/
```

```
$ cp rolling-test-1.1.war /opt/wildfly/bl-rolling-node-4/deployments/
```

19. Now, restart both nodes as usual:

```
$ ./bin/standalone.sh -Djboss.server.base.dir=bl-rolling-node-3
--server-config=standalone-ha.xml -Djboss.bind.address=10.0.1.3
-Djboss.management.http.port=39990 -Djboss.node.name=node-3
```

```
$ ./bin/standalone.sh -Djboss.server.base.dir=bl-rolling-node-4
--server-config=standalone-ha.xml -Djboss.bind.address=10.0.1.4
-Djboss.management.http.port=49990 -Djboss.node.name=node-4
```

20. Now that all nodes have the same application, by stopping one node at a time and refreshing the page, obviously leaving one node up, we should have a scenario as depicted in the following screenshot:

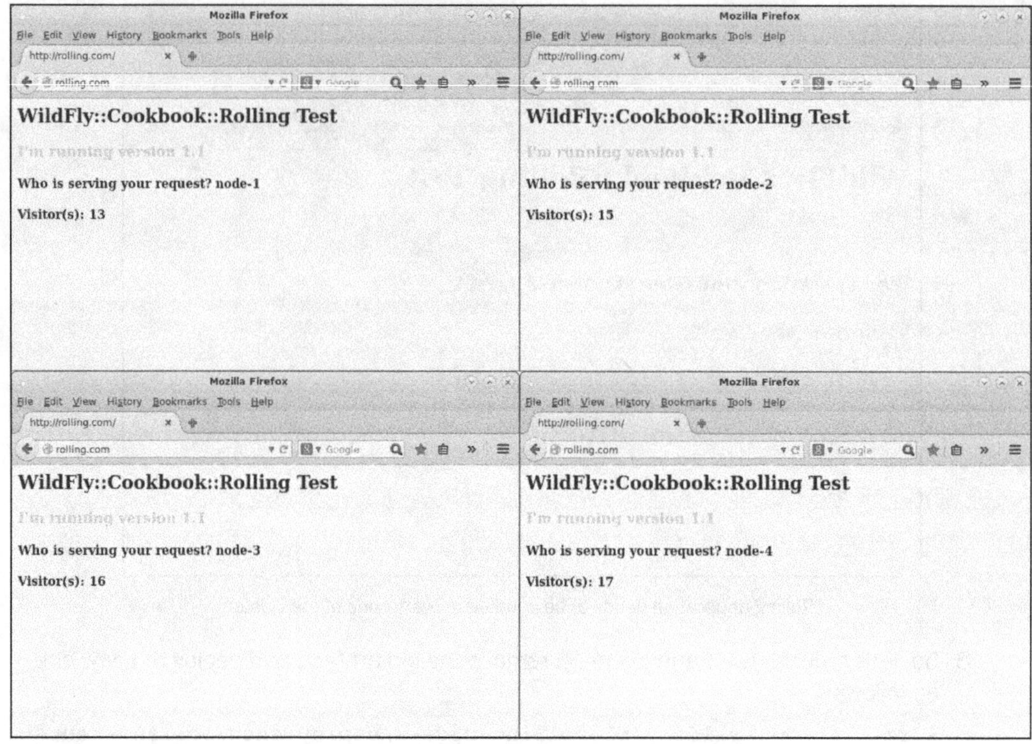


Rolling update completed on all 4 nodes

Perfect! Let's go to the boss's office and tell him we are done!

## How it works...

Well, actually the entire configuration is on the Apache side. In WildFly we didn't do much. As you saw, we configured a replicated-cache, just for demonstration purpose. The difference between a replicated cache and a distributed cache is that in the first one, all information is replicated to all nodes while in the second one, sessions are replicated to just select nodes. Those nodes, if not otherwise specified, are selected randomly.

From the configuration you can tell the cache how many nodes to distribute the session on, by the attribute owners.

- We also relayed on the `standalone-ha` profile, with its defaults, and started it along with some custom bindings for each node.

- We created one cluster composed of four nodes. Each node had its own copy of the application.
- We then stopped two nodes. Stopping two nodes lets the users use our application, as their requests would be balanced on the other available nodes.

> Rolling updates might be much harder; it all depends on the backward compatibility of the application, concerning functionalities, and the domain model, which is what goes into a session. In our example, the data shared across cluster nodes was the same for the first version of the application as well as the last one.

## There's more...

In a domain mode, it's pretty much the same:

- First you need to logically split the cluster in two, as we did during our rolling updates. To do this, we should configure a server-group which would represent the first half of the cluster—let's call it `sg-rolling-1`—and then configure another server-group, naming it `sg-rolling-2`, which in turn would represent the second half of the cluster.
- When doing the first rolling update, you would stop the first server-group, undeploy the old application, and then deploy the new one. Once the deployment has finished, you can restart the server-group.
- When all the nodes are up and running, you can repeat this operation for the second server group. That's pretty much what you should do using the domain mode.

## See also

If you need a deeper understanding of clustering WildFly, refer to *Chapter 5, Managing the Datasource Subsystems with the CLI*.

# 8

# Commanding the CLI

In this chapter, you will learn the following recipes:

- Invoking CLI commands
- Checking the WildFly version
- Checking WildFly operational mode
- Getting the OS version
- Getting the JVM version
- Checking the JVM options
- Checking JVM memories - heap-size and all
- Checking the server status
- Checking the JNDI tree view
- Invoking CLI commands declared in an external file

## Introduction

In this chapter, you will learn how to use the CLI to grab the information that you need. The CLI also provides a method to execute commands outside it, by specifying the WildFly to connect to and the command to be executed. Furthermore, WildFly provides you with an HTTP API, which can be used to perform action and to also retrieve information. Most of this API is used to perform system monitoring.

As WildFly can be run in a standalone or domain mode, whenever it makes sense, we will use both modes because you may access the same information differently.

Within this chapter, we will simulate/use remote WildFly instances, just like the real scenario where you can apply the following recipes to connect to remote servers. It does not make sense trying the recipes in `localhost` without seeing any authentication and authorization issues.

To simulate a remote server, you can eventually use VirtualBox or Docker and then install WildFly as described in the first chapter.

I'm going to use WildFly running on a Linux container using the Docker tool version 1.5. You can obviously use a real remote server, it would be the same; what counts is the WildFly platform being exposed

By the way, the last chapter of this book is all about running WildFly within a Linux container using Docker, so if you are totally new to Docker (where have you been hiding?), have a look at the last chapter of this book, or grab a definitely excellent Docker book, *The Docker Book, James Turnbull* at `http://www.dockerbook.com`

So, my Docker configuration says the following:

```
DOCKER_HOST=tcp://192.168.59.103:2376
```

Thus, my remote WildFly instance will be bound to that IP along with the usual WildFly ports such as `8080`, `9990` and `9999`. The same management user is the one used throughout the book: `wildfly` as username and `cookbook.2015` as password.

# Invoking CLI commands

In this recipe, you will learn how to invoke CLI commands directly from your command line without accessing the CLI itself, let's say not in an interactive way. This technique might be helpful in case you have to script some processes, like stopping and starting servers in a sequence, deploying an application only if another one has already been deployed, and so on. Often times, you also need to monitor some state, thus you just need that number (as typically seen in Nagios).

## Getting ready

Remember I'm running WildFly remotely, bound to `192.168.59.103` as IP. WildFly is already up and running.

## How to do it...

On your local PC, open a new terminal window and run the following commands:

```
$ cd $WILDFLY_HOME
$ ./bin/jboss-cli.sh -c --controller=192.168.59.103:9990 --user=wildfly
--password=cookbook.2015 --command=":read-attribute(name=release-
codename)"
{
    "outcome" => "success",
    "result" => "Kenny"
}
```

Obviously, you can extract just the information you need by using the `awk` command in the output (you can use whichever tool you are comfortable with), as follows:

```
$ ./bin/jboss-cli.sh -c --controller=192.168.59.103:9990 --user=wildfly
--password=cookbook.2015 --command=":read-attribute(name=release-
codename)" | awk 'NR==3 { print $3 }'
"Kenny"
```

In case you are running WildFly in the domain mode, both the invocation and the result are the same.

## How it works...

Actually, there is not much to say or explain, just that the `jboss-cli.sh` script invokes the `org.jboss.as.cli.CommandLineMain` class of the `wildfly-cli-1.0.0.Beta2.jar` library, passing all the arguments. The `command` basically disables the interactive mode, executes the statements, and prints the output in the standard output before returning back to the standard input.

What we have done is basically the following:

```
$ cd $WILDFLY_HOME
$ ./bin/jboss-cli.sh
You are disconnected at the moment. Type 'connect' to connect to the
server or 'help' for the list of supported commands.
[disconnected /] connect 192.168.59.103:9990
Authenticating against security realm: ManagementRealm
Username: wildfly
Password: [cookbook.2015]
```

```
[standalone@192.168.59.103:9990 /] :read-attribute(name=release-codename)
{
    "outcome" => "success",
    "result" => "Kenny"
}
[standalone@192.168.59.103:9990 /]
```

By the way, you cannot manipulate the output.

## There's more...

WildFly provides one more API, which is the HTTP API. Let's try it with some network command-line tools such as `curl`.

### curl

With a running WildFly instance, perform the following steps:

1. On you local PC, open a new terminal window and execute the following commands:

```
$ curl --verbose http://192.168.59.103:9990/management/?operation=
attribute\&name=release–codename
* Hostname was NOT found in DNS cache
*   Trying 192.168.59.103...
* Connected to 192.168.59.103 (192.168.59.103) port 9990 (#0)
> GET /management/?operation=attribute&name=release-codename
HTTP/1.1
> User-Agent: curl/7.37.0
> Host: 192.168.59.103:9990
> Accept: */*
>
< HTTP/1.1 401 Unauthorized
< Connection: keep-alive
< WWW-Authenticate: Digest realm="ManagementRealm",domain="/manage
ment",nonce="it/3pAte8WkNMTQzMDkzNzkzNDYwN+FFS4e5sd6vPqf6T/M4bQI="
,opaque="00000000000000000000000000000000",algorithm=MD5
< Content-Length: 77
< Content-Type: text/html
< Date: Wed, 06 May 2015 18:45:34 GMT
<
* Connection #0 to host 192.168.59.103 left intact
```

```
<html><head><title>Error</title></head><body>401 - Unauthorized</
body></html>
```

As you can see, `curl` complains about a `Digest` authentication for the `ManagementRealm`, which is the one used by WildFly management interfaces.

2. Let's give the username `wildfly` and password `cookbook.2015` to the command, as follows:

```
$ curl --verbose --digest --user wildfly
http://192.168.59.103:9990/management/?operation=attribute\&name=r
elease-codename
Enter host password for user 'wildfly':
* Hostname was NOT found in DNS cache
*   Trying 192.168.59.103...
* Connected to 192.168.59.103 (192.168.59.103) port 9990 (#0)
* Server auth using Digest with user 'wildfly'
> GET /management/?operation=attribute&name=release-codename
HTTP/1.1
> User-Agent: curl/7.37.0
> Host: 192.168.59.103:9990
> Accept: */*
>
< HTTP/1.1 401 Unauthorized
< Connection: keep-alive
< WWW-Authenticate: Digest realm="ManagementRealm",domain="/manage
ment",nonce="6ofpOO62oNsNMTQzMDkzNzk2ODQzORxjucrlmU+bXpQSbl6Mkos="
,opaque="00000000000000000000000000000000",algorithm=MD5
< Content-Length: 77
< Content-Type: text/html
< Date: Wed, 06 May 2015 18:46:08 GMT
<
* Ignoring the response-body
* Connection #0 to host 192.168.59.103 left intact
* Issue another request to this URL: 'http://192.168.59.103:9990/
management/?operation=attribute&name=release-codename'
* Found bundle for host 192.168.59.103: 0x228bb70
* Re-using existing connection! (#0) with host 192.168.59.103
* Connected to 192.168.59.103 (192.168.59.103) port 9990 (#0)
* Initializing NSS with certpath: sql:/etc/pki/nssdb
```

```
* Server auth using Digest with user 'wildfly'
> GET /management/?operation=attribute&name=release-codename
HTTP/1.1
> Authorization: Digest username="wildfly",
realm="ManagementRealm", nonce="6ofpOO62oNsNMTQzMDkzNzk2ODQzORxjuc
rlmU+bXpQSbl6Mkos=", uri="/management/?operation=attribute&name=re
lease-codename", response="e52ce8f429808ef48a76da7193de27e9", opaq
ue="00000000000000000000000000000000", algorithm="MD5"
> User-Agent: curl/7.37.0
> Host: 192.168.59.103:9990
> Accept: */*
>
< HTTP/1.1 200 OK
< Connection: keep-alive
< Authentication-Info: nextnonce="tsPhgznQArENMTQzMDkzNzk2ODU0NSgg
91cYeN3rLKUkBXYRMA8="
< Content-Type: application/json; charset=utf-8
< Content-Length: 7
< Date: Wed, 06 May 2015 18:46:08 GMT
<
* Connection #0 to host 192.168.59.103 left intact
"Kenny"
```

3. Okay, it works; now remove the `--verbose` flag and execute the command again. You should get just `Kenny`, after entering the password.
4. If you do not want to enter the password, you can pass it as an argument as well, with all the security concerns this comes with. For this, do as follows:

```
$ curl --digest --user wildfly:cookbook.2015
http://192.168.59.103:9990/management/?operation=attribute\&name=r
elease-codename
"Kenny"
```

# Checking the WildFly version

In this recipe, you will learn to check the version of WildFly that you are running by invoking a command to the CLI.

## Getting ready

Remember I'm running WildFly remotely, bound to `192.168.59.103` as IP. WildFly is already up and running.

## How to do it...

On your local PC, open a new terminal window and execute the following commands:

```
$ cd $WILDFLY_HOME
$ ./bin/jboss-cli.sh -c --controller=192.168.59.103:9990 --user=wildfly
--password=cookbook.2015 --command=":read-attribute(name=product-
version)"
{
    "outcome" => "success",
    "result" => "9.0.0.Beta2"
}
```

Obviously, you can extract just the information you need by using the `awk` command in the output (you can use whichever tool you are comfortable with), as follows:

```
$ ./bin/jboss-cli.sh -c --controller=192.168.59.103:9990 --user=wildfly
--password=cookbook.2015 --command=":read-attribute(name=product-
version)" | awk 'NR==3 { print $3 }'
"9.0.0.Beta2"
```

In case you are running WildFly in the domain mode, the invocation and result would be the same.

## How it works...

Here we are telling the `jboss-cli.sh` script to execute the command that we define within the `--command` parameter, and to return the result in the standard output.

Using the CLI, it would be as follows:

```
$ cd $WILDFLY_HOME
$ ./bin/jboss-cli.sh
You are disconnected at the moment. Type 'connect' to connect to the
server or 'help' for the list of supported commands.
[disconnected /] connect 192.168.59.103
Authenticating against security realm: ManagementRealm
Username: wildfly
```

```
Password:
[standalone@192.168.59.103:9990 /] :read-attribute(name=product-version)
{
    "outcome" => "success",
    "result" => "9.0.0.Beta2"
}
[standalone@192.168.59.103:9990 /]
```

By the way, you cannot manipulate the output.

## There's more...

WildFly provides one more API, which is the HTTP API. Let's try it with some network command-line tools such as `curl`.

### curl

With a running WildFly instance, perform the following steps:

1. Open a new terminal window and run the following commands:

```
$ curl --verbose http://192.168.59.103:9990/management/?operation=
attribute\&name=product-version
* Hostname was NOT found in DNS cache
*   Trying 192.168.59.103...
* Connected to 192.168.59.103 (192.168.59.103) port 9990 (#0)
> GET /management/?operation=attribute&name=product-version
HTTP/1.1
> User-Agent: curl/7.37.1
> Host: 192.168.59.103:9990
> Accept: */*
>
< HTTP/1.1 401 Unauthorized
< Connection: keep-alive
< WWW-Authenticate: Digest realm="ManagementRealm",domain="/
management",nonce="Z9fm45feS/QNMTQzMTk1ODE4OTA5OXjLOp5ZQcJ+ag+dmE6
jbEM=",opaque="00000000000000000000000000000000",algorithm=MD5
< Content-Length: 77
< Content-Type: text/html
< Date: Mon, 18 May 2015 14:09:49 GMT
<
```

```
* Connection #0 to host 192.168.59.103 left intact
<html><head><title>Error</title></head><body>401 - Unauthorized</
body></html>
```

As you can see `curl` complains about a Digest authentication for the `ManagementRealm`, which is the one used by WildFly management interfaces.

2. Let's give the username `wildfly` and password `cookbook.2015` to the command, as follows:

```
$ curl --verbose --digest --user wildfly
http://192.168.59.103:9990/management/?operation=attribute\&name=p
roduct-version
Enter host password for user 'wildfly':
* Hostname was NOT found in DNS cache
*   Trying 192.168.59.103...
* Connected to 192.168.59.103 (192.168.59.103) port 9990 (#0)
* Server auth using Digest with user 'wildfly'
> GET /management/?operation=attribute&name=product-version
HTTP/1.1
> User-Agent: curl/7.37.1
> Host: 192.168.59.103:9990
> Accept: */*
>
< HTTP/1.1 401 Unauthorized
< Connection: keep-alive
< WWW-Authenticate: Digest realm="ManagementRealm",domain="/manage
ment",nonce="iRU9d5SaQI8NMTQzMTk1ODc1NTY2OAgdi5zSNYp+IAgtpOgBZRU="
,opaque="00000000000000000000000000000000",algorithm=MD5
< Content-Length: 77
< Content-Type: text/html
< Date: Mon, 18 May 2015 14:19:15 GMT
<
* Ignoring the response-body
* Connection #0 to host 192.168.59.103 left intact
* Issue another request to this URL: 'http://192.168.59.103:9990/
management/?operation=attribute&name=product-version'
* Found bundle for host 192.168.59.103: 0x7fc3a0400ed0
* Re-using existing connection! (#0) with host 192.168.59.103
* Connected to 192.168.59.103 (192.168.59.103) port 9990 (#0)
```

```
* Server auth using Digest with user 'wildfly'

> GET /management/?operation=attribute&name=product-version
HTTP/1.1

> Authorization: Digest username="wildfly",
realm="ManagementRealm", nonce="iRU9d5SaQI8NMTQzMTk1ODc1NTY2OAgdi
5zSNYp+IAgtpOgBZRU=", uri="/management/?operation=attribute&name=p
roduct-version", response="e3f7a23441f44992d1d7e2c9fcc00cc2", opaq
ue="00000000000000000000000000000000", algorithm="MD5"

> User-Agent: curl/7.37.1

> Host: 192.168.59.103:9990

> Accept: */*

>

< HTTP/1.1 200 OK

< Connection: keep-alive

< Authentication-Info: nextnonce="45+yNlhzGZ8NMTQzMTk1ODc1NTY4MZP/
ti6JYQlWeum3jKxWEao="

< Content-Type: application/json; charset=utf-8

< Content-Length: 13

< Date: Mon, 18 May 2015 14:19:15 GMT

<

* Connection #0 to host 192.168.59.103 left intact

"9.0.0.Beta2"
```

Okay, it works; now remove the `--verbose` flag and execute the command again. You should get just `9.0.0.Beta2`, after entering the password.

3. If you do not want to enter the password, you can pass it as an argument as well, with all the security concerns this comes with, as follows:

```
$ curl  --digest --user wildfly:cookbook.2015
http://192.168.59.103:9990/management/?operation=attribute\&name=p
roduct-version
"9.0.0.Beta2"
```

# Checking WildFly operational mode

In this recipe, you will learn to check the operational mode that WildFly is running with by invoking a command to the CLI.

## Getting ready

Remember I'm running WildFly remotely, bound to `192.168.59.103` as IP. WildFly is already up and running.

## How to do it...

Open a new terminal window and execute the following commands:

```
$ cd $WILDFLY_HOME
$ ./bin/jboss-cli.sh -c --controller=192.168.59.103:9990 --user=wildfly
--password=cookbook.2015 --command=":read-attribute(name=launch-type)"
{
    "outcome" => "success",
    "result" => "STANDALONE"
}
```

Obviously, you can extract just the information you need using the `awk` command in the output (you can use whichever tool you are comfortable with), as follows:

```
$ ./bin/jboss-cli.sh -c --controller=192.168.59.103:9990 --user=wildfly
--password=cookbook.2015 --command=":read-attribute(name=launch-type)" |
awk 'NR==3 { print $3 }'
"STANDALONE"
```

In case you are running WildFly in the domain mode, the invocation is the same, but the result would be as follows:

```
"DOMAIN"
```

That's it!

## How it works...

Here we are telling the `jboss-cli.sh` script to execute the command that we define within the `--command` parameter, and to return the result in the standard output.

Using the CLI, it would be as follows:

```
$ cd $WILDFLY_HOME
$ ./bin/jboss-cli.sh
You are disconnected at the moment. Type 'connect' to connect to the
server or 'help' for the list of supported commands.
[disconnected /] connect 192.168.59.103:9990
```

```
Authenticating against security realm: ManagementRealm
Username: wildfly
Password:
[standalone@192.168.59.103:9990 /] :read-attribute(name=launch-type)
{
    "outcome" => "success",
    "result" => "STANDALONE"
}
[standalone@192.168.59.103:9990 /]
```

By the way, you cannot manipulate the output.

## There's more...

WildFly provides one more API, which is the HTTP API. Let's try it with some network command-line tools such as `curl`.

### curl

With a running WildFly instance, perform the following steps:

1. Open a new terminal window and execute the following commands:

```
$ curl --verbose http://192.168.59.103:9990/management/?operation=
attribute\&name=launch-type
* Hostname was NOT found in DNS cache
*   Trying 192.168.59.103...
* Connected to 192.168.59.103 (192.168.59.103) port 9990 (#0)
> GET /management/?operation=attribute&name=launch-type HTTP/1.1
> User-Agent: curl/7.37.1
> Host: 192.168.59.103:9990
> Accept: */*
>
< HTTP/1.1 401 Unauthorized
< Connection: keep-alive
< WWW-Authenticate: Digest realm="ManagementRealm",domain="/manage
ment",nonce="oOubmxOIcS0NMTQzMTk1OTg2Mjk4Nqu/YSX7Gh368EZ1XPoG3Eg="
,opaque="00000000000000000000000000000000",algorithm=MD5
< Content-Length: 77
< Content-Type: text/html
< Date: Mon, 18 May 2015 14:37:42 GMT
```

```
<
* Connection #0 to host 192.168.59.103 left intact
<html><head><title>Error</title></head><body>401 - Unauthorized</
body></html>
```

As you can see, `curl` complains about a Digest authentication for `ManagementRealm`, which is the one used by WildFly management interfaces.

2. Let's give the username and password to the command, as follows:

```
$ curl --verbose --digest --user wildfly
http://192.168.59.103:9990/management/?operation=attribute\&name=l
aunch-type
Enter host password for user 'wildfly':
* Hostname was NOT found in DNS cache
*   Trying 192.168.59.103...
* Connected to 192.168.59.103 (192.168.59.103) port 9990 (#0)
* Server auth using Digest with user 'wildfly'
> GET /management/?operation=attribute&name=launch-type HTTP/1.1
> User-Agent: curl/7.37.1
> Host: 192.168.59.103:9990
> Accept: */*
>
< HTTP/1.1 401 Unauthorized
< Connection: keep-alive
< WWW-Authenticate: Digest realm="ManagementRealm",domain="/manage
ment",nonce="ma7nUTWjpCINMTQzMTk2MDA1MjIyOPhpd9+Np6mKrGK9OIhVD1A="
,opaque="00000000000000000000000000000000",algorithm=MD5
< Content-Length: 77
< Content-Type: text/html
< Date: Mon, 18 May 2015 14:40:52 GMT
<
* Ignoring the response-body
* Connection #0 to host 192.168.59.103 left intact
* Issue another request to this URL: 'http://192.168.59.103:9990/
management/?operation=attribute&name=launch-type'
* Found bundle for host 192.168.59.103: 0x7fb833d00c70
* Re-using existing connection! (#0) with host 192.168.59.103
* Connected to 192.168.59.103 (192.168.59.103) port 9990 (#0)
* Server auth using Digest with user 'wildfly'
```

```
> GET /management/?operation=attribute&name=launch-type HTTP/1.1
> Authorization: Digest username="wildfly",
realm="ManagementRealm", nonce="ma7nUTWjpCINMTQzMTk2MDA1MjIyOPhpd
9+Np6mKrGK9OIhVD1A=", uri="/management/?operation=attribute&name
=launch-type", response="3ae09c2aaf9a1c29a0f2c5153d56d485", opaq
ue="00000000000000000000000000000000", algorithm="MD5"
> User-Agent: curl/7.37.1
> Host: 192.168.59.103:9990
> Accept: */*
>
< HTTP/1.1 200 OK
< Connection: keep-alive
< Authentication-Info: nextnonce="xWcBNZToWOoNMTQzMTk2MDA1MjIzNKGJ
WH9tRyHEBw/DEd3VE6w="
< Content-Type: application/json; charset=utf-8
< Content-Length: 12
< Date: Mon, 18 May 2015 14:40:52 GMT
<
* Connection #0 to host 192.168.59.103 left intact
"STANDALONE"
```

3. Okay, it works; now remove the `--verbose` flag and execute the command again. You should get just `STANDALONE`, after entering the password.
4. If you do not want to enter the password, you can pass it as an argument as well, with all the security concerns this comes with, as follows:

```
$ curl --verbose --digest --user wildfly:cookbook.2015
http://192.168.59.103:9990/management/?operation=attribute\&name=l
aunch-type
"STANDALONE"
```

# Getting the OS version

In this recipe, you will learn how to get the OS version that WildFly is running on by invoking a command to the CLI.

## Getting ready

Remember I'm running WildFly remotely, bound to `192.168.59.103` as IP. WildFly is already up and running.

## How to do it...

1. Open a new terminal window and run the following commands:

```
$ cd $WILDFLY_HOME
$ ./bin/jboss-cli.sh -c --controller=192.168.59.103:9990
--user=wildfly --password=cookbook.2015 --command="/
core-service=platform-mbean/type=operating-system:read-
resource(include-runtime=true,include-defaults=true)"
{
    "outcome" => "success",
    "result" => {
        "name" => "Linux",
        "arch" => "amd64",
        "version" => "3.18.5-tinycore64",
        "available-processors" => 8,
        "system-load-average" => 0.0,
        "object-name" => "java.lang:type=OperatingSystem"
    }
}
```

2. Obviously, you can extract just the information you need using the `awk` command in the output (you can use whichever tool you are comfortable with), as follows:

```
$ ./bin/jboss-cli.sh -c --controller=192.168.59.103:9990
--user=wildfly --password=cookbook.2015 --command="/
core-service=platform-mbean/type=operating-system:read-
resource(include-runtime=true,include-defaults=true)" | awk 'NR==4
{ print $3 }'
"Linux",
```

3. In case you are running WildFly in the domain mode, the invocation is done as follows:

```
$ ./bin/jboss-cli.sh -c --controller=192.168.59.103:9990
--user=wildfly --password=cookbook.2015 --command="/host=master/
server=server-one/core-service=platform-mbean/type=operating-
system:read-resource(include-runtime=true,include-defaults=true)"
{
    "outcome" => "success",
    "result" => {
        "name" => "Linux",
        "arch" => "amd64",
        "version" => "3.18.5-tinycore64",
```

```
            "available-processors" => 8,
            "system-load-average" => 0.0,
            "object-name" => "java.lang:type=OperatingSystem"
        }
    }
```

That's it!

## How it works...

Here we are telling the `jboss-cli.sh` script to execute the command that we define within the `--command` parameter, and to return the result in the standard output.

Using the CLI, it would be as follows:

```
$ cd $WILDFLY_HOME
$ ./bin/jboss-cli.sh
You are disconnected at the moment. Type 'connect' to connect to the
server or 'help' for the list of supported commands.
[disconnected /] connect 192.168.59.103:9990
Authenticating against security realm: ManagementRealm
Username: wildfly
Password:
[standalone@192.168.59.103:9990 /] /core-service=platform-mbean/
type=operating-system:read-resource(include-runtime=true,include-
defaults=true)
{
    "outcome" => "success",
    "result" => {
        "name" => "Linux",
        "arch" => "amd64",
        "version" => "3.16.4-tinycore64",
        "available-processors" => 8,
        "system-load-average" => 0.0,
        "object-name" => "java.lang:type=OperatingSystem"
    }
}
[standalone@192.168.59.103:9990 /]
```

By the way, you cannot manipulate the output.

## There's more...

WildFly provides one more API, which is the HTTP API. Let's try it with some network command-line tools such as `curl`.

### curl

With a running WildFly instance, perform the following steps:

1. Open a new terminal window and do as follows:

```
$ curl --verbose http://192.168.59.103:9990/management/core-service/platform-mbean/type/operating-system?operation=resource\&include-runtime=true\&include-defaults=true
* Hostname was NOT found in DNS cache
*   Trying 192.168.59.103...
* Connected to 192.168.59.103 (192.168.59.103) port 9990 (#0)
> GET /management/core-service/platform-mbean/type/operating-system?operation=resource&include-runtime=true&include-defaults=true HTTP/1.1
> User-Agent: curl/7.37.1
> Host: 192.168.59.103:9990
> Accept: */*
>
< HTTP/1.1 401 Unauthorized
< Connection: keep-alive
< WWW-Authenticate: Digest realm="ManagementRealm",domain="/management",nonce="vgtjzIheBzkNMTQzMTk2MDkwMzkyMPnsADViafwy586SMaSftDU=",opaque="00000000000000000000000000000000",algorithm=MD5
< Content-Length: 77
< Content-Type: text/html
< Date: Mon, 18 May 2015 14:55:03 GMT
<
* Connection #0 to host 192.168.59.103 left intact
<html><head><title>Error</title></head><body>401 - Unauthorized</body></html>
```

As you can see, `curl` complains about a Digest authentication for `ManagementRealm`, which is the one used by WildFly management interfaces.

2. Let's give the username and password to the command, as follows:

```
$ curl --verbose --digest --user wildfly
http://192.168.59.103:9990/management/core-service/platform-
mbean/type/operating-system?operation=resource\&include-
runtime=true\&include-defaults=true

Enter host password for user 'wildfly':

* Hostname was NOT found in DNS cache

*   Trying 192.168.59.103...

* Connected to 192.168.59.103 (192.168.59.103) port 9990 (#0)

* Server auth using Digest with user 'wildfly'

> GET /management/core-service/platform-mbean/type/operating-syst
em?operation=resource&include-runtime=true&include-defaults=true
HTTP/1.1

> User-Agent: curl/7.37.1

> Host: 192.168.59.103:9990

> Accept: */*

>

< HTTP/1.1 401 Unauthorized

< Connection: keep-alive

< WWW-Authenticate: Digest realm="ManagementRealm",domain="/
management",nonce="Z7R7/j+3b5oNMTQzMTk2MTA3NjQ1N4lD5fc075kCb3a0afe
4pCg=",opaque="00000000000000000000000000000000",algorithm=MD5

< Content-Length: 77

< Content-Type: text/html

< Date: Mon, 18 May 2015 14:57:56 GMT

<

* Ignoring the response-body

* Connection #0 to host 192.168.59.103 left intact

* Issue another request to this URL: 'http://192.168.59.103:9990/
management/core-service/platform-mbean/type/operating-system?opera
tion=resource&include-runtime=true&include-defaults=true'

* Found bundle for host 192.168.59.103: 0x7ff722414af0

* Re-using existing connection! (#0) with host 192.168.59.103

* Connected to 192.168.59.103 (192.168.59.103) port 9990 (#0)

* Server auth using Digest with user 'wildfly'

> GET /management/core-service/platform-mbean/type/operating-syst
em?operation=resource&include-runtime=true&include-defaults=true
HTTP/1.1
```

```
> Authorization: Digest username="wildfly",
realm="ManagementRealm", nonce="Z7R7/j+3b5oNMTQzMTk2MTA3Nj
Q1N4lD5fc075kCb3a0afe4pCg=", uri="/management/core-service/
platform-mbean/type/operating-system?operation=resource&inclu
de-runtime=true&include-defaults=true", response="d71b0f677bfb47
6226880ae0f55b899c", opaque="00000000000000000000000000000000",
algorithm="MD5"
> User-Agent: curl/7.37.1
> Host: 192.168.59.103:9990
> Accept: */*
>
< HTTP/1.1 200 OK
< Connection: keep-alive
< Authentication-Info: nextnonce="xEfjYw89nD8NMTQzMTk2MTA3NjQ3MSkj
dHABRCjFARHS2aR438k="
< Content-Type: application/json; charset=utf-8
< Content-Length: 176
< Date: Mon, 18 May 2015 14:57:56 GMT
<
* Connection #0 to host 192.168.59.103 left intact
{"name" : "Linux", "arch" : "amd64", "version" :
"3.18.5-tinycore64", "available-processors" : 8, "system-load-
average" : 0.0, "object-name" : "java.lang:type=OperatingSystem"}
```

3. Okay, it works; now remove the `--verbose` flag and execute the command again. You should get just the JSON output after entering the password, as follows:

```
{"name" : "Linux", "arch" : "amd64", "version" :
"3.16.4-tinycore64", "available-processors" : 8, "system-load-
average" : 0.0, "object-name" : "java.lang:type=OperatingSystem"}
```

   Neat, but pretty ugly!

4. If you want to prettify the JSON output and you do not want to enter the password (you can pass it as an argument as well, with all the security concerns this comes with), you can do as follows:

```
$ curl --digest --user wildfly:cookbook.2015
http://192.168.59.103:9990/management/core-service/platform-
mbean/type/operating-system?operation=resource\&include-
runtime=true\&include-defaults=true\&json.pretty=true
{
    "name" : "Linux",
    "arch" : "amd64",
```

```
    "version" : "3.18.5-tinycore64",
    "available-processors" : 8,
    "system-load-average" : 0.0,
    "object-name" : "java.lang:type=OperatingSystem"
}
```

That's the way I like it!

# Getting the JVM version

In this recipe, you will learn how to get the JVM WildFly is running with by invoking a command to the CLI.

## Getting ready

Remember I'm running WildFly remotely, bound to `192.168.59.103` as IP. WildFly is already up and running.

## How to do it...

1. Open a new terminal window and execute the following commands:

   ```
   $ cd $WILDFLY_HOME
   $ ./bin/jboss-cli.sh -c --controller=192.168.59.103:9990
   --user=wildfly --password=cookbook.2015 --command="/core-
   service=platform-mbean/type=runtime:read-attribute(name=spec-
   version)"
   {
       "outcome" => "success",
       "result" => "1.8"
   }
   ```

2. Obviously, you can extract just the information you need by using the `awk` command in the output (you can use whichever tool you are comfortable with), as follows:

   ```
   $ ./bin/jboss-cli.sh -c --controller=192.168.59.103:9990
   --user=wildfly --password=cookbook.2015 --command="/core-
   service=platform-mbean/type=runtime:read-attribute(name=spec-
   version)" | awk 'NR==3 { print $3 }'
   "1.8"
   ```

3. In case you are running WildFly in the domain mode, the invocation is as follows:

   ```
   $ ./bin/jboss-cli.sh -c --controller=192.168.59.103:9990
   --user=wildfly --password=cookbook.2015 --command="/host=master/
   server=server-one/core-service=platform-mbean/type=runtime:read-
   attribute(name=spec-version)" | awk 'NR==3 { print $3 }'
   "1.8"
   ```

That's it!

## How it works...

Here we are telling the `jboss-cli.sh` script to execute the command that we define within the `--command` parameter, and to return the result in the standard output.

Using the CLI, it would be as follows:

```
$ cd $WILDFLY_HOME
$ ./bin/jboss-cli.sh
You are disconnected at the moment. Type 'connect' to connect to the
server or 'help' for the list of supported commands.
[disconnected /] connect 192.168.59.103:9990
Authenticating against security realm: ManagementRealm
Username: wildfly
Password:
[standalone@192.168.59.103:9990 /] /core-service=platform-mbean/
type=runtime:read-attribute(name=spec-version)
{
    "outcome" => "success",
    "result" => "1.8"
}
[standalone@192.168.59.103:9990 /]
```

By the way, you cannot manipulate the output.

## There's more...

WildFly provides one more API, which is the HTTP API. Let's try it with some network command-line tools such as `curl`.

## curl

With a running WildFly instance, perform the following steps:

1. Open a new terminal window and run the following commands:

```
$ curl --verbose http://192.168.59.103:9990/management/core-service/platform-mbean/type/runtime?operation=attribute\&name=spec-version

* Hostname was NOT found in DNS cache

*   Trying 192.168.59.103...

* Connected to 192.168.59.103 (192.168.59.103) port 9990 (#0)

> GET /management/core-service/platform-mbean/type/runtime?operation=attribute&name=spec-version HTTP/1.1

> User-Agent: curl/7.37.1

> Host: 192.168.59.103:9990

> Accept: */*

>

< HTTP/1.1 401 Unauthorized

< Connection: keep-alive

< WWW-Authenticate: Digest realm="ManagementRealm",domain="/management",nonce="wvo9g8raGFsNMTQzMTk2MTgwNjk1NE1gqeXx9Q8BkyC5OMS5Dy8=",opaque="00000000000000000000000000000000",algorithm=MD5

< Content-Length: 77

< Content-Type: text/html

< Date: Mon, 18 May 2015 15:10:06 GMT

<

* Connection #0 to host 192.168.59.103 left intact

<html><head><title>Error</title></head><body>401 - Unauthorized</body></html>
```

   As you can see, `curl` complains about a Digest authentication for `ManagementRealm`, which is the one used by WildFly management interfaces.

2. Let's give the username and password to the command, as follows:

```
$ curl --verbose --digest --user wildfly http://192.168.59.103:9990/management/core-service/platform-mbean/type/runtime?operation=attribute\&name=spec-version

Enter host password for user 'wildfly':

* Hostname was NOT found in DNS cache

*   Trying 192.168.59.103...

* Connected to 192.168.59.103 (192.168.59.103) port 9990 (#0)
```

```
* Server auth using Digest with user 'wildfly'
> GET /management/core-service/platform-mbean/type/runtime?operati
on=attribute&name=spec-version HTTP/1.1
> User-Agent: curl/7.37.1
> Host: 192.168.59.103:9990
> Accept: */*
>
< HTTP/1.1 401 Unauthorized
< Connection: keep-alive
< WWW-Authenticate: Digest realm="ManagementRealm",domain="/manage
ment",nonce="lq4EWazA3IUNMTQzMTk2MTgzMjI3NM2iKbJNsltAipmEDWj2zBs="
,opaque="00000000000000000000000000000000",algorithm=MD5
< Content-Length: 77
< Content-Type: text/html
< Date: Mon, 18 May 2015 15:10:32 GMT
<
* Ignoring the response-body
* Connection #0 to host 192.168.59.103 left intact
* Issue another request to this URL: 'http://192.168.59.103:9990/
management/core-service/platform-mbean/type/runtime?operation=attr
ibute&name=spec-version'
* Found bundle for host 192.168.59.103: 0x7fb35ac14a40
* Re-using existing connection! (#0) with host 192.168.59.103
* Connected to 192.168.59.103 (192.168.59.103) port 9990 (#0)
* Server auth using Digest with user 'wildfly'
> GET /management/core-service/platform-mbean/type/runtime?operati
on=attribute&name=spec-version HTTP/1.1
> Authorization: Digest username="wildfly",
realm="ManagementRealm", nonce="lq4EWazA3IUNMTQzMTk2MTgzMj
I3NM2iKbJNsltAipmEDWj2zBs=", uri="/management/core-service/
platform-mbean/type/runtime?operation=attribute&name=spec-
version", response="b91b7944f1c95154b5a0a97e2c87cace", opaq
ue="00000000000000000000000000000000", algorithm="MD5"
> User-Agent: curl/7.37.1
> Host: 192.168.59.103:9990
> Accept: */*
>
< HTTP/1.1 200 OK
< Connection: keep-alive
```

```
< Authentication-Info: nextnonce="EP8IM2uluIcNMTQzMTk2MTgzMjI4NeTU
7FBtoaXVQ/6HR5zlVzw="
< Content-Type: application/json; charset=utf-8
< Content-Length: 5
< Date: Mon, 18 May 2015 15:10:32 GMT
<
* Connection #0 to host 192.168.59.103 left intact
"1.8"
```

3. Okay, it works; now remove the `--verbose` flag and execute the command again. You should get just the output after entering the password, as follows:

   ```
   "1.8"
   ```

4. If you do not want to enter the password, you can pass it as an argument as well, with all the security concerns this comes with, as follows:

   ```
   $ curl --digest --user wildfly:cookbook.2015
   http://192.168.59.103:9990/management/core-service/platform-mbean/
   type/runtime?operation=attribute\&name=spec-version
   "1.8"
   ```

That's the way I like it!

## More about the runtime type

The `runtime` type that we just used in the preceding steps, provides a lot of information that can be very helpful. Here is the complete list of all the information you can have in a pretty JSON format:

```
{    "name" : "1145@e0d713e81636",
    "vm-name" : "Java HotSpot(TM) 64-Bit Server VM",
    "vm-vendor" : "Oracle Corporation",
    "vm-version" : "25.40-b25",
    "spec-name" : "Java Virtual Machine Specification",
    "spec-vendor" : "Oracle Corporation",
    "spec-version" : "1.8",
    "management-spec-version" : "1.2",
    "class-path" : "/home/wildfly/WFC/wildfly/jboss-modules.jar",
    "library-path" :
    "/usr/java/packages/lib/amd64:/
    usr/lib64:/lib64:/lib:/usr/lib",
    "boot-class-path-supported" : true,
```

```
    "boot-class-path" : "/home/wildfly/WFC/jdk8/jre/lib/resources.
jar:/home/wildfly/WFC/jdk8/jre/lib/rt.jar:/home/wildfly/WFC/jdk8/
jre/lib/sunrsasign.jar:/home/wildfly/WFC/jdk8/jre/lib/jsse.jar:/
home/wildfly/WFC/jdk8/jre/lib/jce.jar:/home/wildfly/WFC/jdk8/jre/lib/
charsets.jar:/home/wildfly/WFC/jdk8/jre/lib/jfr.jar:/home/wildfly/WFC/
jdk8/jre/classes",
    "input-arguments" : [
        "-D[Standalone]",
        "-XX:+UseCompressedOops",
        "-XX:+UseCompressedOops",
        "-Xms64m",
        "-Xmx512m",
        "-XX:MaxPermSize=256m",
        "-Djava.net.preferIPv4Stack=true",
        "-Djboss.modules.system.pkgs=org.jboss.byteman",
        "-Djava.awt.headless=true",
        "-
        Dorg.jboss.boot.log.file=/home/wildfly
        /WFC/wildfly/standalone/log/server.log",
        "-Dlogging.configuration=file:/home/wildfly
        /WFC/wildfly/standalone/configuration/logging.properties"
    ],
    "start-time" : 1431960757217,
    "system-properties" : {
        "[Standalone]" : "",
        "awt.toolkit" : "sun.awt.X11.XToolkit",
        "file.encoding" : "ANSI_X3.4-1968",
        "file.encoding.pkg" : "sun.io",
        "file.separator" : "/",
        "java.awt.graphicsenv" : "sun.awt.X11GraphicsEnvironment",
        "java.awt.headless" : "true",
        "java.awt.printerjob" : "sun.print.PSPrinterJob",
        "java.class.path" : "/home/wildfly/WFC/wildfly/jboss-
        modules.jar",
        "java.class.version" : "52.0",
        "java.endorsed.dirs" :
        "/home/wildfly/WFC/jdk8/jre/lib/endorsed",
        "java.ext.dirs" :
        "/home/wildfly/WFC/jdk8/jre/lib/ext:
        /usr/java/packages/lib/ext",
        "java.home" : "/home/wildfly/WFC/jdk8/jre",
        "java.io.tmpdir" : "/tmp",
        "java.library.path" :
        "/usr/java/packages/lib/amd64:/usr/lib64:
        /lib64:/lib:/usr/lib",
```

```
"java.naming.factory.url.pkgs" :
"org.jboss.as.naming.interfaces:
org.jboss.ejb.client.naming",
"java.net.preferIPv4Stack" : "true",
"java.runtime.name" : "Java(TM) SE Runtime Environment",
"java.runtime.version" : "1.8.0_40-b26",
"java.specification.name" : "Java Platform API
Specification",
"java.specification.vendor" : "Oracle Corporation",
"java.specification.version" : "1.8",
"java.util.logging.manager" :
"org.jboss.logmanager.LogManager",
"java.vendor" : "Oracle Corporation",
"java.vendor.url" : "http://java.oracle.com/",
"java.vendor.url.bug" :
"http://bugreport.sun.com/bugreport/",
"java.version" : "1.8.0_40",
"java.vm.info" : "mixed mode",
"java.vm.name" : "Java HotSpot(TM) 64-Bit Server VM",
"java.vm.specification.name" : "Java Virtual Machine
Specification",
"java.vm.specification.vendor" : "Oracle Corporation",
"java.vm.specification.version" : "1.8",
"java.vm.vendor" : "Oracle Corporation",
"java.vm.version" : "25.40-b25",
"javax.management.builder.initial" :
"org.jboss.as.jmx.PluggableMBeanServerBuilder",
"javax.xml.datatype.DatatypeFactory" :
"__redirected.__DatatypeFactory",
"javax.xml.parsers.DocumentBuilderFactory" :
"__redirected.__DocumentBuilderFactory",
"javax.xml.parsers.SAXParserFactory" :
"__redirected.__SAXParserFactory",
"javax.xml.stream.XMLEventFactory" :
"__redirected.__XMLEventFactory",
"javax.xml.stream.XMLInputFactory" :
"__redirected.__XMLInputFactory",
"javax.xml.stream.XMLOutputFactory" :
"__redirected.__XMLOutputFactory",
"javax.xml.transform.TransformerFactory" :
"__redirected.__TransformerFactory",
"javax.xml.validation.SchemaFactory:
http://www.w3.org/2001/XMLSchema" :
"__redirected.__SchemaFactory",
```

```
"javax.xml.xpath.XPathFactory:
http://java.sun.com/jaxp/xpath/dom" :
"__redirected.__XPathFactory",
"jboss.bind.address" : "0.0.0.0",
"jboss.bind.address.management" : "0.0.0.0",
"jboss.home.dir" : "/home/wildfly/WFC/wildfly",
"jboss.host.name" : "e0d713e81636",
"jboss.modules.dir" : "/home/wildfly/WFC/wildfly/modules",
"jboss.modules.system.pkgs" : "org.jboss.byteman",
"jboss.node.name" : "e0d713e81636",
"jboss.qualified.host.name" : "e0d713e81636",
"jboss.server.base.dir" :
"/home/wildfly/WFC/wildfly/standalone",
"jboss.server.config.dir" :
"/home/wildfly/WFC/wildfly/standalone/configuration",
"jboss.server.data.dir" :
"/home/wildfly/WFC/wildfly/standalone/data",
"jboss.server.deploy.dir" :
"/home/wildfly/WFC/wildfly/standalone/data/content",
"jboss.server.log.dir" :
"/home/wildfly/WFC/wildfly/standalone/log",
"jboss.server.name" : "e0d713e81636",
"jboss.server.persist.config" : "true",
"jboss.server.temp.dir" :
"/home/wildfly/WFC/wildfly/standalone/tmp",
"line.separator" : "\n",
"logging.configuration" :
"file:/home/wildfly/WFC/wildfly/standalone
/configuration/logging.properties",
"module.path" : "/home/wildfly/WFC/wildfly/modules",
"org.apache.xml.security.ignoreLineBreaks" : "true",
"org.jboss.boot.log.file" :
"/home/wildfly/WFC/wildfly/standalone/log/server.log",
"org.jboss.resolver.warning" : "true",
"org.jboss.security.context.ThreadLocal" : "true",
"org.xml.sax.driver" : "__redirected.__XMLReaderFactory",
"os.arch" : "amd64",
"os.name" : "Linux",
"os.version" : "3.18.5-tinycore64",
"path.separator" : ":",
"sun.arch.data.model" : "64",
```

```
            "sun.boot.class.path" :
            "/home/wildfly/WFC/jdk8/jre/lib/resources.jar:
            /home/wildfly/WFC/jdk8/jre/lib/rt.jar:
            /home/wildfly/WFC/jdk8/jre/lib/sunrsasign.jar:
            /home/wildfly/WFC/jdk8/jre/lib/jsse.jar:
            /home/wildfly/WFC/jdk8/jre/lib/jce.jar:
            /home/wildfly/WFC/jdk8/jre/lib/charsets.jar:
            /home/wildfly/WFC/jdk8/jre/lib/jfr.jar:
            /home/wildfly/WFC/jdk8/jre/classes",
            "sun.boot.library.path" :
            "/home/wildfly/WFC/jdk8/jre/lib/amd64",
            "sun.cpu.endian" : "little",
            "sun.cpu.isalist" : "",
            "sun.io.unicode.encoding" : "UnicodeLittle",
            "sun.java.command" : "/home/wildfly/WFC/wildfly/jboss-
            modules.jar -mp /home/wildfly/WFC/wildfly/modules
            org.jboss.as.standalone -
            Djboss.home.dir=/home/wildfly/WFC/wildfly -
            Djboss.server.base.dir=/home/wildfly/
            WFC/wildfly/standalone -b 0.0.0.0 -bmanagement 0.0.0.0",
            "sun.java.launcher" : "SUN_STANDARD",
            "sun.jnu.encoding" : "ANSI_X3.4-1968",
            "sun.management.compiler" : "HotSpot 64-Bit Tiered
            Compilers",
            "sun.nio.ch.bugLevel" : "",
            "sun.os.patch.level" : "unknown",
            "user.country" : "US",
            "user.dir" : "/home/wildfly/WFC/wildfly",
            "user.home" : "/home/wildfly",
            "user.language" : "en",
            "user.name" : "wildfly",
            "user.timezone" : "America/New_York"
        },
        "uptime" : 1393273,
        "object-name" : "java.lang:type=Runtime"
    }
```

As you can see, there is a lot of information, and with the `operation=attribute` directive, you can directly grab the attribute that you need. Otherwise use the `awk` command.

# Checking the JVM options

In this recipe, you will learn how to get the JVM options used to run WildFly by invoking a command to the CLI.

## Getting ready

Remember I'm running WildFly remotely, bound to `192.168.59.103` as IP. WildFly is already up and running.

## How to do it...

1. Open a new terminal window and execute the following commands:

```
$ cd WILDFLY_HOME
$ ./bin/jboss-cli.sh -c --controller=192.168.59.103:9990
--user=wildfly --password=cookbook.2015 --command="/core-
service=platform-mbean/type=runtime:read-attribute(name=input-
arguments,include-defaults=true)"
{
    "outcome" => "success",
    "result" => [
        "-D[Standalone]",
        "-Xms64m",
        "-Xmx512m",
        "-XX:MaxPermSize=256m",
        "-Djava.net.preferIPv4Stack=true",
        "-Djboss.modules.system.pkgs=org.jboss.byteman",
        "-Djava.awt.headless=true",
        "-Dorg.jboss.boot.log.file=/home/wildfly/WFC/wildfly/
standalone/log/server.log",
        "-Dlogging.configuration=file:home/wildfly/WFC/wildfly/
standalone/configuration/logging.properties"
    ]
}
```

2. Obviously, you can extract just the information that you need by using the awk command in the output (you can use whichever tool you are comfortable with), as follows:

```
$ ./bin/jboss-cli.sh -c --controller=192.168.59.103:9990
--user=wildfly --password=cookbook.2015 --command="/core-
service=platform-mbean/type=runtime:read-attribute(name=input-
arguments,include-defaults=true)" | awk 'NR==6 { print $1 }'
"-Xmx521m",
```

3. In case you are running WildFly in the domain mode, the invocation is as follows:

```
$ ./bin/jboss-cli.sh -c --controller=192.168.59.103:9990
--user=wildfly --password=cookbook.2015 --command="/host=master/
server=server-one/core-service=platform-mbean/type=runtime:read-
attribute(name=input-arguments,include-defaults=true)" | awk
'NR==6 { print $1 }'
"-Xmx521m",
```

That's it!

## How it works...

Here we are telling the `jboss-cli.sh` script to execute the command that we define within the `--command` parameter, and to return the result in the standard output.

Using the CLI, it would be as follows:

```
$ cd $WILDFLY_HOME
$ ./bin/jboss-cli.sh
You are disconnected at the moment. Type 'connect' to connect to the
server or 'help' for the list of supported commands.
[disconnected /] connect 192.168.59.103:9990
Authenticating against security realm: ManagementRealm
Username: wildfly
Password:
[standalone@192.168.59.103:9990 /] /core-service=platform-mbean/
type=runtime:read-attribute(name=input-arguments,include-defaults=true)

{
    "outcome" => "success",
    "result" => [
        "-D[Standalone]",
        "-Xms64m",
```

```
        "-Xmx512m",
        "-XX:MaxPermSize=256m",
        "-Djava.net.preferIPv4Stack=true",
        "-Djboss.modules.system.pkgs=org.jboss.byteman",
        "-Djava.awt.headless=true",
        "-Dorg.jboss.boot.log.file=/home/wildfly/WFC/wildfly/standalone/
log/server.log",
        "-Dlogging.configuration=file:/home/wildfly/WFC/wildfly/
standalone/configuration/logging.properties"
    ]
}
[standalone@192.168.59.103:9990 /]
```

Remember, you cannot manipulate the output.

## There's more...

WildFly provides one more API, which is the HTTP API. Let's try it with some network command-line tools such as `curl`.

### curl

With a running WildFly instance, perform the following steps:

1. Open a new terminal window and do as follows:

```
$ curl --verbose http://192.168.59.103:9990/management/core-
service/platform-mbean/type/runtime?operation=attribute\&name=inp
ut-arguments\&include-defaults=true
* Hostname was NOT found in DNS cache
*   Trying 192.168.59.103...
* Connected to 192.168.59.103 (192.168.59.103) port 9990 (#0)
> GET /management/core-service/platform-mbean/type/runtime?operati
on=attribute&name=input-arguments&include-defaults=true HTTP/1.1
> User-Agent: curl/7.37.1
> Host: 192.168.59.103:9990
> Accept: */*
>
< HTTP/1.1 401 Unauthorized
< Connection: keep-alive
```

```
< WWW-Authenticate: Digest realm="ManagementRealm",domain="/manage
ment",nonce="Hipx4QD6g24NMTQzMTk2MjY2ODcyNhXQ5pLbS5A/ZruXxypB1gM="
,opaque="00000000000000000000000000000000",algorithm=MD5
< Content-Length: 77
< Content-Type: text/html
< Date: Mon, 18 May 2015 15:24:28 GMT
<
* Connection #0 to host 192.168.59.103 left intact
<html><head><title>Error</title></head><body>401 - Unauthorized</
body></html>
```

As you can see, `curl` complains about a Digest authentication for the `ManagementRealm`, which is the one used by WildFly management interfaces.

2. Let's give the username and password to the command, as follows:

```
$ curl --verbose --digest --user wildfly
http://192.168.59.103:9990/management/core-service/platform-mbean/
type/runtime?operation=attribute\&name=input-arguments\&include-
defaults=true
Enter host password for user 'wildfly':
* Hostname was NOT found in DNS cache
*   Trying 192.168.59.103...
* Connected to 192.168.59.103 (192.168.59.103) port 9990 (#0)
* Server auth using Digest with user 'wildfly'
> GET /management/core-service/platform-mbean/type/runtime?operati
on=attribute&name=input-arguments&include-defaults=true HTTP/1.1
> User-Agent: curl/7.37.1
> Host: 192.168.59.103:9990
> Accept: */*
>
< HTTP/1.1 401 Unauthorized
< Connection: keep-alive
< WWW-Authenticate: Digest realm="ManagementRealm",domain="/manage
ment",nonce="QVV7pMN+yIYNMTQzMTk2Mjg1MzAwNIEcpzHTEA2YeGu3jANV1bI="
,opaque="00000000000000000000000000000000",algorithm=MD5
< Content-Length: 77
< Content-Type: text/html
< Date: Mon, 18 May 2015 15:27:33 GMT
<
```

```
* Ignoring the response-body
* Connection #0 to host 192.168.59.103 left intact
* Issue another request to this URL: 'http://192.168.59.103:9990/
management/core-service/platform-mbean/type/runtime?operation=attr
ibute&name=input-arguments&include-defaults=true'
* Found bundle for host 192.168.59.103: 0x7fd4c0500e00
* Re-using existing connection! (#0) with host 192.168.59.103
* Connected to 192.168.59.103 (192.168.59.103) port 9990 (#0)
* Server auth using Digest with user 'wildfly'
> GET /management/core-service/platform-mbean/type/runtime?operati
on=attribute&name=input-arguments&include-defaults=true HTTP/1.1
> Authorization: Digest username="wildfly",
realm="ManagementRealm", nonce="QVV7pMN+yIYNMTQzMTk2Mjg1MzAwNIEcpz
HTEA2YeGu3jANV1bI=", uri="/management/core-service/platform-mbean/
type/runtime?operation=attribute&name=input-arguments&include-
defaults=true", response="8d550a343d3a56cfcd7afdd6ca0c1664", opaq
ue="00000000000000000000000000000000", algorithm="MD5"
> User-Agent: curl/7.37.1
> Host: 192.168.59.103:9990
> Accept: */*
>
< HTTP/1.1 200 OK
< Connection: keep-alive
< Authentication-Info: nextnonce="UkyiLKmVGuYNMTQzMTk2Mjg1MzAwN08E
KUU+895ECweZBtXoCdQ="
< Content-Type: application/json; charset=utf-8
< Content-Length: 402
< Date: Mon, 18 May 2015 15:27:33 GMT
<
* Connection #0 to host 192.168.59.103 left intact
["-D[Standalone]","-XX:+UseCompressedOops","-
XX:+UseCompressedOops","-Xms64m","-Xmx512m","-
XX:MaxPermSize=256m","-Djava.net.preferIPv4Stack=true","-
Djboss.modules.system.pkgs=org.jboss.byteman","-Djava.awt.
headless=true","-Dorg.jboss.boot.log.file=/home/wildfly/WFC/
wildfly/standalone/log/server.log","-Dlogging.configuration=file:/
home/wildfly/WFC/wildfly/standalone/configuration/logging.
properties"]
```

3. Okay, it works; now remove the `--verbose` flag and execute the command again. You should get just the JSON output, after entering the password, as follows:

```
["-D[Standalone]","-XX:+UseCompressedOops","-
XX:+UseCompressedOops","-Xms64m","-Xmx512m","-
XX:MaxPermSize=256m","-Djava.net.preferIPv4Stack=true","-
Djboss.modules.system.pkgs=org.jboss.byteman","-Djava.awt.
headless=true","-Dorg.jboss.boot.log.file=/home/wildfly/WFC/
wildfly/standalone/log/server.log","-Dlogging.configuration=file:/
home/wildfly/WFC/wildfly/standalone/configuration/logging.
properties"]
```

   Neat, but pretty ugly!

4. If you want to prettify the JSON output and you do not want to enter the password (you can pass it as an argument as well, with all the security concerns this comes with), you can do as follows:

```
$ curl --digest --user wildfly:cookbook.2015
http://192.168.59.103:9990/management/core-service/platform-mbean/
type/runtime?operation=attribute\&name=input-arguments\&include-
defaults=true\&json.pretty=true[
    "-D[Standalone]",
    "-XX:+UseCompressedOops",
    "-XX:+UseCompressedOops",
    "-Xms64m",
    "-Xmx512m",
    "-XX:MaxPermSize=256m",
    "-Djava.net.preferIPv4Stack=true",
    "-Djboss.modules.system.pkgs=org.jboss.byteman",
    "-Djava.awt.headless=true",
    "-Dorg.jboss.boot.log.file=/home/wildfly/WFC/wildfly/
standalone/log/server.log",
    "-Dlogging.configuration=file:/home/wildfly/WFC/wildfly/
standalone/configuration/logging.properties"
]
```

That's the way I like it!

# Checking JVM memories – heap-size and all

In this recipe, we will learn how to get the JVM memory information with regard to heap-size, non heap-size, metaspace size (PermGen until Java 7), eden, old, and survivor, by invoking a command to the CLI. There is a command for each of them.

## Getting ready

Remember I'm running WildFly remotely, bound to `192.168.59.103` as IP. WildFly is already up and running.

## How to do it...

We will walk through the "`heap`", "`non-heap`", "`metaspace`" (PermGen until Java 7), "`eden`", "`old`", and the "`survivor`" area memories, separately.

### Heap

For information on heap memory, perform the following steps:

1. Open a new terminal window and do as follows:

```
$ cd $WILDFLY_HOME
$ ./bin/jboss-cli.sh -c --controller=192.168.59.103:9990
--user=wildfly --password=cookbook.2015 --command="/core-
service=platform-mbean/type=memory:read-attribute(name=heap-
memory-usage,include-defaults=true)"
{
    "outcome" => "success",
    "result" => {
        "init" => 67108864L,
        "used" => 90009368L,
        "committed" => 199753728L,
        "max" => 477626368L
    }
}
```

2. Obviously, you can extract just the information you need using the `awk` command in the output (you can use whichever tool you are comfortable with), as follows:

```
$ ./bin/jboss-cli.sh -c --controller=192.168.59.103:9990
--user=wildfly --password=cookbook.2015 --command="/core-
service=platform-mbean/type=memory:read-attribute(name=heap-
memory-usage,include-defaults=true)" | awk 'NR==7 { print $0 }'
"max" => 477626368L
```

If you just need the number, which is a `long` datatype, use `$3` in the `print` statement.

3. In case you are running WildFly in the domain mode, the invocation is as follows:

```
$ ./bin/jboss-cli.sh --connect --controller=192.168.59.103:9990
--user=wildfly --password=cookbook.2015 --command="/host=master/
server=server-one/core-service=platform-mbean/type=memory:read-
attribute(name=heap-memory-usage,include-defaults=true)"
{
    "outcome" => "success",
    "result" => {
        "init" => 67108864L,
        "used" => 78141544L,
        "committed" => 147324928L,
        "max" => 477626368L
    }
}
```

That's it!

### Non-heap

For information on non-heap memory, perform the following steps:

1. Open a new terminal window and execute the following commands:

```
$ cd $WILDFLY_HOME
$ ./bin/jboss-cli.sh -c --controller=192.168.59.103:9990
--user=wildfly --password=cookbook.2015 --command="/core-
service=platform-mbean/type=memory:read-attribute(name=non-heap-
memory-usage,include-defaults=true)"
{
    "outcome" => "success",
    "result" => {
```

```
        "init" => 2555904L,
        "used" => 55613336L,
        "committed" => 62128128L,
        "max" => -1L
    }
}
```

2. Obviously, you can extract just the information you need by using the `awk` command in the output (you can use whichever tool you are comfortable with), as follows:

   ```
   $ ./bin/jboss-cli.sh -c --controller=192.168.59.103:9990
   --user=wildfly --password=cookbook.2015 --command="/core-
   service=platform-mbean/type=memory:read-attribute(name=non-heap-
   memory-usage,include-defaults=true)" | awk 'NR==5 { print $0 }'
   "used" => 55613336L,
   ```

3. In case you are running WildFly in the domain mode, the invocation is as follows:

   ```
   $ ./bin/jboss-cli.sh -c --controller=192.168.59.103:9990
   --user=wildfly --password=cookbook.2015 --command="/host=master/
   server=server-one/core-service=platform-mbean/type=memory:read-
   attribute(name=non-heap-memory-usage,include-defaults=true)"
   {
       "outcome" => "success",
       "result" => {
           "init" => 2555904L,
           "used" => 65766592L,
           "committed" => 73310208L,
           "max" => -1L
       }
   }
   ```

That's it!

## Metaspace or PermGen

Metaspace is available since Java 1.8, while PermGen was available until Java 1.7. For the metaspace memory information, perform the following steps:

1. Open a new terminal window and do as follows:

   ```
   $ cd $WILDFLY_HOME
   $ ./bin/jboss-cli.sh -c --controller=192.168.59.103:9990
   --user=wildfly --password=cookbook.2015 --command="/core-
   service=platform-mbean/type=memory-pool/name=Metaspace:read-
   resource(include-runtime=true,include-defaults=true)"
   ```

```
{
    "outcome" => "success",
    "result" => {
        "name" => "Metaspace",
        "type" => "NON_HEAP",
        "valid" => true,
        "memory-manager-names" => ["Metaspace_Manager"],
        "usage-threshold-supported" => true,
        "collection-usage-threshold-supported" => false,
        "usage-threshold" => 0L,
        "collection-usage-threshold" => undefined,
        "usage" => {
            "init" => 0L,
            "used" => 42415280L,
            "committed" => 47185920L,
            "max" => -1L
        },
        "peak-usage" => {
            "init" => 0L,
            "used" => 42415280L,
            "committed" => 47185920L,
            "max" => -1L
        },
        "usage-threshold-exceeded" => false,
        "usage-threshold-count" => 0L,
        "collection-usage-threshold-exceeded" => undefined,
        "collection-usage-threshold-count" => undefined,
        "collection-usage" => undefined,
        "object-name" => "java.lang:type=MemoryPool,name=Metaspa
ce"
    }
}
```

2. Obviously, you can extract just the information you need by using the `awk` command in the output (you can use whichever tool you are comfortable with). However, in this case, you should better use the `read-attribute` syntax and then use the `awk` command for the information you want, as follows:

```
$ ./bin/jboss-cli.sh -c --controller=192.168.59.103:9990
--user=wildfly --password=cookbook.2015 --command="/core-
service=platform-mbean/type=memory-pool/name=Metaspace:read-
attribute(name=usage,include-defaults=true)"
{
    "outcome" => "success",
    "result" => {
        "init" => 0L,
        "used" => 42512536L,
        "committed" => 47448064L,
        "max" => -1L
    }
}
```

3. In case you are running WildFly in the domain mode, the invocation is as follows:

```
$ ./bin/jboss-cli.sh --connect --controller=192.168.59.103:9990
--user=wildfly --password=cookbook.2015 --command="/host=master/
server=server-one/core-service=platform-mbean/type=memory-pool/
name=Metaspace:read-resource(include-runtime=true,include-
defaults=true)"
{
    "outcome" => "success",
    "result" => {
        "name" => "Metaspace",
        "type" => "NON_HEAP",
        "valid" => true,
        "memory-manager-names" => ["Metaspace_Manager"],
        "usage-threshold-supported" => true,
        "collection-usage-threshold-supported" => false,
        "usage-threshold" => 0L,
        "collection-usage-threshold" => undefined,
        "usage" => {
            "init" => 0L,
```

```
                "used" => 51111424L,
                "committed" => 56885248L,
                "max" => -1L
            },
            "peak-usage" => {
                "init" => 0L,
                "used" => 51111424L,
                "committed" => 56885248L,
                "max" => -1L
            },
            "usage-threshold-exceeded" => false,
            "usage-threshold-count" => 0L,
            "collection-usage-threshold-exceeded" => undefined,
            "collection-usage-threshold-count" => undefined,
            "collection-usage" => undefined,
            "object-name" => "java.lang:type=MemoryPool,name=Metaspa
ce"
        }
    }
```

That's it!

## Eden

For information on eden memory, perform the following steps:

1. Open a new terminal window and give the following commands:

```
$ cd /opt/wildfly
$ ./bin/jboss-cli.sh -c --controller=192.168.59.103:9990
--user=wildfly --password=cookbook.2015 --command="/core-
service=platform-mbean/type=memory-pool/name=PS_Eden_Space:read-
resource(include-runtime=true,include-defaults=true)"
{
    "outcome" => "success",
    "result" => {
        "name" => "PS_Eden_Space",
        "type" => "HEAP",
        "valid" => true,
        "memory-manager-names" => [
```

```
            "PS_MarkSweep",
            "PS_Scavenge"
        ],
        "usage-threshold-supported" => false,
        "collection-usage-threshold-supported" => true,
        "usage-threshold" => undefined,
        "collection-usage-threshold" => 0L,
        "usage" => {
            "init" => 16777216L,
            "used" => 61270456L,
            "committed" => 147849216L,
            "max" => 147849216L
        },
        "peak-usage" => {
            "init" => 16777216L,
            "used" => 67108864L,
            "committed" => 147849216L,
            "max" => 173539328L
        },
        "usage-threshold-exceeded" => undefined,
        "usage-threshold-count" => undefined,
        "collection-usage-threshold-exceeded" => false,
        "collection-usage-threshold-count" => 0L,
        "collcction usage" -> {
            "init" => 16777216L,
            "used" => 0L,
            "committed" => 147849216L,
            "max" => 147849216L
        },
        "object-name" => "java.lang:type=MemoryPool,name=\"PS
        Eden Space\""
    }
}
```

2. Obviously, you can extract just the information that you need by using the `awk` command in the output (you can use whichever tool you are comfortable with). However, in this case, you should better use the `read-attribute` syntax and then `awk` the information you want, as follows:

```
$ ./bin/jboss-cli.sh --connect --controller=192.168.59.103:9990
--user=wildfly --password=cookbook.2015 --command="/core-
service=platform-mbean/type=memory-pool/name=PS_Eden_Space:read-
attribute(name=usage,include-defaults=true)"
{
    "outcome" => "success",
    "result" => {
        "init" => 16777216L,
        "used" => 70648432L,
        "committed" => 147849216L,
        "max" => 147849216L
    }
}
```

3. In case you are running WildFly in the domain mode, the invocation is as follows:

```
$ ./bin/jboss-cli.sh --connect --controller=192.168.59.103:9990
--user=wildfly --password=cookbook.2015 --command="/host=master/
server=server-one/core-service=platform-mbean/type=memory-pool/
name=PS_Eden_Space:read-resource(include-runtime=true,include-
defaults=true)"
{
    "outcome" => "success",
    "result" => {
        "name" => "PS_Eden_Space",
        "type" => "HEAP",
        "valid" => true,
        "memory-manager-names" => [
            "PS_MarkSweep",
            "PS_Scavenge"
        ],
        "usage-threshold-supported" => false,
        "collection-usage-threshold-supported" => true,
        "usage-threshold" => undefined,
        "collection-usage-threshold" => 0L,
        "usage" => {
```

```
                "init" => 16777216L,
                "used" => 40625992L,
                "committed" => 58720256L,
                "max" => 144703488L
            },
            "peak-usage" => {
                "init" => 16777216L,
                "used" => 58720256L,
                "committed" => 58720256L,
                "max" => 173539328L
            },
            "usage-threshold-exceeded" => undefined,
            "usage-threshold-count" => undefined,
            "collection-usage-threshold-exceeded" => false,
            "collection-usage-threshold-count" => 0L,
            "collection-usage" => {
                "init" => 16777216L,
                "used" => 0L,
                "committed" => 58720256L,
                "max" => 144703488L
            },
            "object-name" => "java.lang:type=MemoryPool,name=\"PS Eden
Space\""
        }
    }
```

That's it!

## Old

For information regarding old memory, perform the following steps:

1. Open a new terminal window and execute the following:

```
$ cd /opt/wildfly
$ ./bin/jboss-cli.sh -c --controller=192.168.59.103:9990
--user=wildfly --password=cookbook.2015 --command="/core-
service=platform-mbean/type=memory-pool/name=PS_Old_Gen:read-
resource(include-runtime=true,include-defaults=true)"{
    "outcome" => "success",
```

```
        "result" => {
            "name" => "PS_Old_Gen",
            "type" => "HEAP",
            "valid" => true,
            "memory-manager-names" => ["PS_MarkSweep"],
            "usage-threshold-supported" => true,
            "collection-usage-threshold-supported" => true,
            "usage-threshold" => 0L,
            "collection-usage-threshold" => 0L,
            "usage" => {
                "init" => 45088768L,
                "used" => 17330048L,
                "committed" => 59244544L,
                "max" => 358088704L
            },
            "peak-usage" => {
                "init" => 45088768L,
                "used" => 17330048L,
                "committed" => 59244544L,
                "max" => 358088704L
            },
            "usage-threshold-exceeded" => false,
            "usage-threshold-count" => 0L,
            "collection-usage-threshold-exceeded" => false,
            "collection-usage-threshold-count" => 0L,
            "collection-usage" => {
                "init" => 45088768L,
                "used" => 17330048L,
                "committed" => 59244544L,
                "max" => 358088704L
            },
            "object-name" => "java.lang:type=MemoryPool,name=\"PS
            Old Gen\""
        }
    }
```

2. Obviously, you can extract just the information you need by using the `awk` command in the output (you can use whichever tool you are comfortable with). However, in this case, you should better use the `read-attribute` syntax and then `awk` the information you want, as follows:

```
$ ./bin/jboss-cli.sh --connect --controller=192.168.59.103:9990
--user=wildfly --password=cookbook.2015 --command="/core-
service=platform-mbean/type=memory-pool/name=PS_Old_Gen:read-
attribute(name=usage,include-defaults=true)"{
    "outcome" => "success",
    "result" => {
        "init" => 45088768L,
        "used" => 17330048L,
        "committed" => 59244544L,
        "max" => 358088704L
    }
}
```

3. In case you are running WildFly in the domain mode, the invocation is as follows:

```
$ ./bin/jboss-cli.sh --connect --controller=192.168.59.103:9990
--user=wildfly --password=cookbook.2015 --command="/host=master/
server=server-one/core-service=platform-mbean/type=memory-pool/
name=PS_Old_Gen:read-resource(include-runtime=true,include-
defaults=true)"
{
    "outcome" => "success",
    "result" => {
        "name" => "PS_Old_Gen",
        "type" => "HEAP",
        "valid" => true,
        "memory-manager-names" => ["PS_MarkSweep"],
        "usage-threshold-supported" => true,
        "collection-usage-threshold-supported" => true,
        "usage-threshold" => 0L,
        "collection-usage-threshold" => 0L,
        "usage" => {
            "init" => 45088768L,
            "used" => 21521968L,
            "committed" => 70254592L,
            "max" => 358088704L
```

```
            },
            "peak-usage" => {
                "init" => 45088768L,
                "used" => 21521968L,
                "committed" => 70254592L,
                "max" => 358088704L
            },
            "usage-threshold-exceeded" => false,
            "usage-threshold-count" => 0L,
            "collection-usage-threshold-exceeded" => false,
            "collection-usage-threshold-count" => 0L,
            "collection-usage" => {
                "init" => 45088768L,
                "used" => 18670576L,
                "committed" => 70254592L,
                "max" => 358088704L
            },
            "object-name" => "java.lang:type=MemoryPool,name=\"PS
            Old Gen\""
        }
    }
```

That's it!

## Survivor

For information regarding survivor memory, perform the following steps:

1. Open a new terminal window and give the following commands:

```
$ cd /opt/wildfly
$ ./bin/jboss-cli.sh -c --controller=192.168.59.103:9990
--user=wildfly --password=cookbook.2015 --command="/core-
service=platform-mbean/type=memory-pool/name=PS_Survivor_
Space:read-resource(include-runtime=true,include-defaults=true)"
{
    "outcome" => "success",
    "result" => {
        "name" => "PS_Survivor_Space",
        "type" => "HEAP",
```

```
        "valid" => true,
        "memory-manager-names" => [
            "PS_MarkSweep",
            "PS_Scavenge"
        ],
        "usage-threshold-supported" => false,
        "collection-usage-threshold-supported" => true,
        "usage-threshold" => undefined,
        "collection-usage-threshold" => 0L,
        "usage" => {
            "init" => 2621440L,
            "used" => 0L,
            "committed" => 15728640L,
            "max" => 15728640L
        },
        "peak-usage" => {
            "init" => 2621440L,
            "used" => 12809608L,
            "committed" => 15728640L,
            "max" => 15728640L
        },
        "usage-threshold-exceeded" => undefined,
        "usage-threshold-count" => undefined,
        "collection-usage-threshold-exceeded" => false,
        "collection-usage-threshold-count" => 0L,
        "collection-usage" => {
            "init" => 2621440L,
            "used" => 0L,
            "committed" => 15728640L,
            "max" => 15728640L
        },
        "object-name" => "java.lang:type=MemoryPool,name=\"PS
Survivor Space\""
    }
}
```

2. Obviously, you can extract just the information you need by using the `awk` command in the output (you can use whichever tool you are comfortable with). However, in this case, you should better use the `read-attribute` syntax and then `awk` the information you want, as follows:

```
$ ./bin/jboss-cli.sh --connect --controller=192.168.59.103:9990
--user=wildfly --password=cookbook.2015 --command="/core-
service=platform-mbean/type=memory-pool/name=PS_Survivor_
Space:read-attribute(name=usage,include-defaults=true)"
{
    "outcome" => "success",
    "result" => {
        "init" => 2621440L,
        "used" => 0L,
        "committed" => 15728640L,
        "max" => 15728640L
    }
}
```

3. In case you are running WildFly in the domain mode, the invocation is as follows:

```
$ ./bin/jboss-cli.sh --connect --controller=192.168.59.103:9990
--user=wildfly --password=cookbook.2015 --command="/host=master/
server=server-one/core-service=platform-mbean/type=memory-pool/
name=PS_Survivor_Space:read-resource(include-runtime=true,include-
defaults=true)"
{
    "outcome" => "success",
    "result" => {
        "name" => "PS_Survivor_Space",
        "type" => "HEAP",
        "valid" => true,
        "memory-manager-names" => [
            "PS_MarkSweep",
            "PS_Scavenge"
        ],
        "usage-threshold-supported" => false,
        "collection-usage-threshold-supported" => true,
        "usage-threshold" => undefined,
        "collection-usage-threshold" => 0L,
        "usage" => {
```

```
                "init" => 2621440L,
                "used" => 15199856L,
                "committed" => 15204352L,
                "max" => 15204352L
            },
            "peak-usage" => {
                "init" => 2621440L,
                "used" => 15199856L,
                "committed" => 15204352L,
                "max" => 15204352L
            },
            "usage-threshold-exceeded" => undefined,
            "usage-threshold-count" => undefined,
            "collection-usage-threshold-exceeded" => false,
            "collection-usage-threshold-count" => 0L,
            "collection-usage" => {
                "init" => 2621440L,
                "used" => 15199856L,
                "committed" => 15204352L,
                "max" => 15204352L
            },
            "object-name" => "java.lang:type=MemoryPool,name=\"PS 
    Survivor Space\""
        }
    }
```

That's it!

## How it works...

Here we are telling the `jboss-cli.sh` script to execute the command that we define within the `--command` parameter, and to return the result in the standard output.

Using the CLI, it would be as follows:

```
$ ./bin/jboss-cli.sh
You are disconnected at the moment. Type 'connect' to connect to the 
server or 'help' for the list of supported commands.
[disconnected /] connect 192.168.59.103:9990
```

```
Authenticating against security realm: ManagementRealm
Username: wildfly
Password:
[standalone@192.168.59.103:9990 /] /core-service=platform-mbean/
type=memory:read-attribute(name=heap-memory-usage,include-defaults=true)
{
    "outcome" => "success",
    "result" => {
        "init" => 67108864L,
        "used" => 76422344L,
        "committed" => 175112192L,
        "max" => 477626368L
    }
}
[standalone@192.168.59.103:9990 /]
```

By the way, you cannot manipulate the output.

You can try the other memory spaces yourself, by replacing the memory name with the one that you are interested in.

## There's more...

WildFly provides one more API, which is the HTTP API. Let's try it with some network command-line tools such as `curl`.

Here we will examine just the JVM heap memory, as an example.

### Curl

Perform the following steps using curl:

1. With a running WildFly instance, open a new terminal window and execute the following commands:

```
$ curl --verbose http://192.168.59.103:9990/management/core-
service/platform-mbean/type/memory?operation=attribute\&name=heap-
memory-usage
* Hostname was NOT found in DNS cache
*   Trying 192.168.59.103...
* Connected to 192.168.59.103 (192.168.59.103) port 9990 (#0)
> GET /management/core-service/platform-mbean/type/memory?operatio
n=attribute&name=heap-memory-usage HTTP/1.1
```

```
> User-Agent: curl/7.37.1
> Host: 192.168.59.103:9990
> Accept: */*
>
< HTTP/1.1 401 Unauthorized
< Connection: keep-alive
< WWW-Authenticate: Digest realm="ManagementRealm",domain="/manage
ment",nonce="SwXvsbP7j0UNMTQzMjAxNjUxODY4Ml1gpwERAQYWFmaOqeygbx4="
,opaque="00000000000000000000000000000000",algorithm=MD5
< Content-Length: 77
< Content-Type: text/html
< Date: Tue, 19 May 2015 06:21:58 GMT
<
* Connection #0 to host 192.168.59.103 left intact
<html><head><title>Error</title></head><body>401 - Unauthorized</
body></html>
```

As you can see, `curl` complains about a Digest authentication for `ManagementRealm`, which is the one used by WildFly management interfaces.

2. Let's give the username and password to the command, as follows:

```
$ curl --verbose --digest --user wildfly
http://192.168.59.103:9990/management/core-service/platform-mbean/
type/memory?operation=attribute\&name=heap-memory-usage
Enter host password for user 'wildfly':
* Hostname was NOT found in DNS cache
*   Trying 192.168.59.103...
* Connected to 192.168.59.103 (192.168.59.103) port 9990 (#0)
* Server auth using Digest with user 'wildfly'
> GET /management/core-service/platform-mbean/type/memory?operatio
n=attribute&name=heap-memory-usage HTTP/1.1
> User-Agent: curl/7.37.1
> Host: 192.168.59.103:9990
> Accept: */*
>
< HTTP/1.1 401 Unauthorized
< Connection: keep-alive
< WWW-Authenticate: Digest realm="ManagementRealm",domain="/manage
ment",nonce="47ky6duDTAANMTQzMjAxNjY2NTc1NDQr1KuuN1GzJ50GQ0PUuCs="
,opaque="00000000000000000000000000000000",algorithm=MD5
```

```
< Content-Length: 77
< Content-Type: text/html
< Date: Tue, 19 May 2015 06:24:25 GMT
<
* Ignoring the response-body
* Connection #0 to host 192.168.59.103 left intact
* Issue another request to this URL: 'http://192.168.59.103:9990/
management/core-service/platform-mbean/type/memory?operation=attri
bute&name=heap-memory-usage'
* Found bundle for host 192.168.59.103: 0x7fa919d00dd0
* Re-using existing connection! (#0) with host 192.168.59.103
* Connected to 192.168.59.103 (192.168.59.103) port 9990 (#0)
* Server auth using Digest with user 'wildfly'
> GET /management/core-service/platform-mbean/type/memory?operatio
n=attribute&name=heap-memory-usage HTTP/1.1
> Authorization: Digest username="wildfly",
realm="ManagementRealm", nonce="47ky6duDTAANMTQzMjAxNjY2NT
c1NDQr1KuuN1GzJ50GQ0PUuCs=", uri="/management/core-service/
platform-mbean/type/memory?operation=attribute&name=heap-memory-
usage", response="f04575d464d4151697dc6468610ec989", opaq
ue="00000000000000000000000000000000", algorithm="MD5"
> User-Agent: curl/7.37.1
> Host: 192.168.59.103:9990
> Accept: */*
>
< HTTP/1.1 200 OK
< Connection: keep-alive
< Authentication-Info: nextnonce="kFsM2zG0/
XANMTQzMjAxNjY2NTc2MP4TtqHrlyzAujuq4ZLn9ek="
< Content-Type: application/json; charset=utf-8
< Content-Length: 82
< Date: Tue, 19 May 2015 06:24:25 GMT
<
* Connection #0 to host 192.168.59.103 left intact
{"init" : 67108864, "used" : 62314024, "committed" : 222298112,
"max" : 477626368}
```

3. Okay, it works; now remove the `--verbose` flag and execute the command again. You should get just the JSON output, after entering the password, as follows:

   ```
   {"init" : 67108864, "used" : 66257248, "committed" : 222298112,
   "max" : 477626368}
   ```

   Neat, but pretty ugly!

4. If you want to prettify the JSON output and you do not want to enter the password (you can pass it as an argument as well, with all the security concerns this comes with), you can execute the following commands:

   ```
   $ curl --digest --user wildfly:cookbook.2015
   http://192.168.59.103:9990/management/core-service/platform-mbean/
   type/memory?operation=attribute\&name=heap-memory-usage\&json.
   pretty=true{
       "init" : 67108864,
       "used" : 67826544,
       "committed" : 222298112,
       "max" : 477626368
   }
   ```

That's the way I like it!

# Checking the server status

In this recipe, we will learn how to check the state of a running WildFly instance, by invoking a command to the CLI.

## Getting ready

Remember I'm running WildFly remotely, bound to `192.168.59.103` as IP. WildFly is already up and running.

## How to do it...

Open a new terminal window and execute the following:

```
$ cd $WILDFLY_HOME
$ ./bin/jboss-cli.sh -c --controller=192.168.59.103:9990 --user=wildfly
--password=cookbook.2015 --command=":read-attribute(name=server-state)"
{
    "outcome" => "success",
    "result" => "running"
}
```

You can extract just the information you need by using the `awk` command in the output (you can use whichever tool you are comfortable with), as follows:

```
$ ./bin/jboss-cli.sh -c --controller=192.168.59.103:9990 --user=wildfly
--password=cookbook.2015 --command=":read-attribute(name=server-state)" |
awk 'NR==3 { print $3 }'
"running"
```

In case you are running WildFly in the domain mode, the invocation is as follows:

```
$ ./bin/jboss-cli.sh -c --controller=192.168.59.103:9990 --user=wildfly
--password=cookbook.2015 --command="/host=master/server=server-one:read-
attribute(name=server-state)" | awk 'NR==3 { print $3 }'
"running"
```

That's it!

## How it works...

Here we are telling the `jboss-cli.sh` script to execute the command that we define within the `--command` parameter, and to return the result in the standard output.

Using the CLI, it would be as follows:

```
$ cd $WILDFLY_HOME
$ ./bin/jboss-cli.sh
You are disconnected at the moment. Type 'connect' to connect to the
server or 'help' for the list of supported commands.
[disconnected /] connect 192.168.59.103:9990
Authenticating against security realm: ManagementRealm
Username: wildfly
Password:
[standalone@192.168.59.103:9990 /] :read-attribute(name=server-state)
{
    "outcome" => "success",
    "result" => "running"
}
[standalone@192.168.59.103:9990 /]
```

By the way, you cannot manipulate the output.

## There's more...

WildFly provides one more API, which is the HTTP API. Let's try it with some network command-line tools such as `curl`.

### curl

With a running WildFly instance, perform the following steps:

1. Open a new terminal window and execute the following commands:

```
$ curl --verbose http://192.168.59.103:9990/management/?operation=
attribute\&name=server-state
* Hostname was NOT found in DNS cache
*   Trying 192.168.59.103...
* Connected to 192.168.59.103 (192.168.59.103) port 9990 (#0)
> GET /management/?operation=attribute&name=server-state HTTP/1.1
> User-Agent: curl/7.37.1
> Host: 192.168.59.103:9990
> Accept: */*
>
< HTTP/1.1 401 Unauthorized
< Connection: keep-alive
< WWW-Authenticate: Digest realm="ManagementRealm",domain="/manage
ment",nonce="kv+FBaxYgDINMTQzMjAxNzUzMTYyNbC9h3WcIBNOnUH1mBkR1vY="
,opaque="00000000000000000000000000000000",algorithm=MD5
< Content-Length: 77
< Content-Type: text/html
< Date: Tue, 19 May 2015 06:38:51 GMT
<
* Connection #0 to host 192.168.59.103 left intact
<html><head><title>Error</title></head><body>401 - Unauthorized</
body></html>
```

   As you can see, `curl` complains about a Digest authentication for `ManagementRealm`, which is the one used by WildFly management interfaces.

2. Let's give the username and password to the command, as follows:

```
$ curl --verbose --digest --user wildfly
http://192.168.59.103:9990/management/?operation=attribute\&name=s
erver-state
Enter host password for user 'wildfly':
```

```
* Hostname was NOT found in DNS cache
*   Trying 192.168.59.103...
* Connected to 192.168.59.103 (192.168.59.103) port 9990 (#0)
* Server auth using Digest with user 'wildfly'
> GET /management/?operation=attribute&name=server-state HTTP/1.1
> User-Agent: curl/7.37.1
> Host: 192.168.59.103:9990
> Accept: */*
>
< HTTP/1.1 401 Unauthorized
< Connection: keep-alive
< WWW-Authenticate: Digest realm="ManagementRealm",domain="/manage
ment",nonce="Pl2q17HyCSsNMTQzMjAxNzU0NTUxOC3ZiDpK6wbWOysSkGTtFd8="
,opaque="00000000000000000000000000000000",algorithm=MD5
< Content-Length: 77
< Content-Type: text/html
< Date: Tue, 19 May 2015 06:39:05 GMT
<
* Ignoring the response-body
* Connection #0 to host 192.168.59.103 left intact
* Issue another request to this URL: 'http://192.168.59.103:9990/
management/?operation=attribute&name=server-state'
* Found bundle for host 192.168.59.103: 0x7f897b500c70
* Re-using existing connection! (#0) with host 192.168.59.103
* Connected to 192.168.59.103 (192.168.59.103) port 9990 (#0)
* Server auth using Digest with user 'wildfly'
> GET /management/?operation=attribute&name=server-state HTTP/1.1
> Authorization: Digest username="wildfly",
realm="ManagementRealm", nonce="Pl2q17HyCSsNMTQzMjAxNzU0NTUxOC3Zi
DpK6wbWOysSkGTtFd8=", uri="/management/?operation=attribute&name
=server-state", response="7b740a1695f01a9041a3d0c61cf35c91", opaq
ue="00000000000000000000000000000000", algorithm="MD5"
> User-Agent: curl/7.37.1
> Host: 192.168.59.103:9990
> Accept: */*
>
< HTTP/1.1 200 OK
< Connection: keep-alive
```

```
< Authentication-Info: nextnonce="3gZb5DbobbENMTQzMjAxNzU0NTUzOD7w
AHJMcsZDujeJP3F/N9M="
< Content-Type: application/json; charset=utf-8
< Content-Length: 9
< Date: Tue, 19 May 2015 06:39:05 GMT
<
* Connection #0 to host 192.168.59.103 left intact
"running"
```

3. Okay, it works; now remove the `--verbose` flag and execute the command again. You should get just `running`, after entering the password.
4. If you do not want to enter the password, you can pass it as an argument as well, with all the security concerns this comes with. For this, execute the following:

```
$ curl --verbose --digest --user wildfly:cookbook.2015
http://192.168.59.103:9990/management/?operation=attribute
\&name=server-state
"running"
```

# Checking the JNDI tree view

In this recipe, we will learn how to get the JNDI tree view of your WildFly instances, by invoking a command to the CLI. This might be useful in case you need to check whether some application context exits, if you need to know a datasource JNDI name, or if you need to lookup for an EJB.

## Getting ready

Remember I'm running WildFly remotely, bound to `192.168.59.103` as IP. WildFly is already up and running.

## How to do it…

1. Open a new terminal window and execute the as following:

```
$ cd $WILDFLY_HOME
$ ./bin/jboss-cli.sh -c --controller=192.168.59.103:9990
--user=wildfly --password=cookbook.2015 -command="/
subsystem=naming:jndi-view"
{
    "outcome" => "success",
    "result" => {
        "java: contexts" => {
```

```
"java:" => {"TransactionManager" => {
    "class-name" =>
    "com.arjuna.ats.jbossatx.jta.
    TransactionManagerDelegate",
    "value" => "com.arjuna.ats.jbossatx.jta.
    TransactionManagerDelegate@16b89a30"
}},
"java:jboss" => {
    "TransactionManager" => {
        "class-name" =>
        "com.arjuna.ats.jbossatx.jta.
        TransactionManagerDelegate",
        "value" => "com.arjuna.ats.jbossatx.jta.
        TransactionManagerDelegate@16b89a30"
    },
    "TransactionSynchronizationRegistry" => {
        "class-name" =>
        "org.jboss.as.txn.service.internal.tsr
        .TransactionSynchronization
        RegistryWrapper",
        "value" =>
        "org.jboss.as.txn.service.internal.tsr.
        TransactionSynchronization
        RegistryWrapper@315ee6c0"
    },
    "UserTransaction" => {
        "class-name" =>
        "javax.transaction.UserTransaction",
        "value" => "UserTransaction"
    },
    "jaas" => {
        "class-name" => "com.sun.proxy.$Proxy11",
        "value" => "java:jboss/jaas/ Context
        proxy"
    },
    "ee" => {
        "class-name" => "javax.naming.Context",
        "children" => {"concurrency" => {
            "class-name" =>
            "javax.naming.Context",
```

```
"children" => {
    "scheduler" => {
        "class-name" =>
        "javax.naming.Context",
        "children" => {"default" => {
            "class-name" =>
            "java.lang.Object",
            "value" => "?"
        }}
    },
    "factory" => {
        "class-name" =>
        "javax.naming.Context",
        "children" => {"default" => {
            "class-name" =>
            "java.lang.Object",
            "value" => "?"
        }}
    },
    "executor" => {
        "class-name" =>
        "javax.naming.Context",
        "children" => {"default" => {
            "class-name" =>
            "java.lang.Object",
            "value" => "?"
        }}
    },
    "context" => {
        "class-name" =>
        "javax.naming.Context",
        "children" => {"default" => {
            "class-name" =>
            "java.lang.Object",
            "value" => "?"
        }}
    }
}
```

```
                        }}
                    },
                    "datasources" => {
                        "class-name" => "javax.naming.Context",
                        "children" => {"ExampleDS" => {
                            "class-name" =>
                            "org.jboss.as.connector.subsystems
                            .datasources.WildFlyDataSource",
                            "value" =>
                            "org.jboss.as.connector
                            .subsystems.datasources
                            .WildFlyDataSource@59b69704"
                        }}
                    },
                    "mail" => {
                        "class-name" => "javax.naming.Context",
                        "children" => {"Default" => {
                            "class-name" => "javax.mail.Session",
                            "value" =>
                            "javax.mail.Session@25c2acd6"
                        }}
                    }
                },
                "java:jboss/exported" => undefined,
                "java:global" => undefined
            },
            "applications" => undefined
        }
    }
```

Obviously, you can extract just the information you need by using the `awk` command in the output (you can use whichever tool you are comfortable with).

2. In case you are running WildFly in the domain mode, the invocation is as follows:

```
$ cd $WILDFLY_HOME
$ ./bin/jboss-cli.sh -c --controller=192.168.59.103:9990
--user=wildfly --password=cookbook.2015 --command='/host=master/
server=server-one/subsystem=naming:jndi-view'
{
    "outcome" => "success",
```

```
        "result" => {
            "java: contexts" => {
                ...
            },
            "applications" => {"example.war" => {
                "java:app" => {
                    "AppName" => {
                        "class-name" => "java.lang.String",
                        "value" => "example"
                    },
                    "env" => {
                        "class-name" =>
                        "org.jboss.as.naming.NamingContext",
                        "value" => "env"
                    }
                },
                "modules" => undefined
            }}
        }
    }
```

That's it!

## How it works...

Here we are telling the `jboss-cli.sh` script to execute the command that we define within the `--command` parameter, and to return the result in the standard output.

Using the CLI, it would be as follows:

```
$ cd $WILDFLY_HOME
$ ./bin/jboss-cli.sh
You are disconnected at the moment. Type 'connect' to connect to the
server or 'help' for the list of supported commands.
[disconnected /] connect 192.168.59.103:9990
Authenticating against security realm: ManagementRealm
Username: wildfly
Password:
[standalone@192.168.59.103:9990 /] /subsystem=naming:jndi-view
....
```

The output would be the same as shown in the image of the *How to do it* section of this recipe.

# Invoking CLI commands declared in an external file

In this recipe, we will learn how to execute commands declared in a separate file, using the `jboss-cli.sh` script.

## Getting ready

Remember I'm running WildFly remotely, bound to `192.168.59.103` as IP. WildFly is already up and running.

Create a file named `wildfly-cookbook.cli`, and insert the listing command `ls` into it. Place the file in your local `$WILDFLY_HOME` folder.

Now it's time to invoke our commands through the CLI!

## How to do it...

Open a new terminal window and execute the following:

```
$ cd $WILDFLY_HOME
$ ./bin/jboss-cli.sh -c --controller=192.168.59.103:9990 --user=wildfly
--password=cookbook.2015 --file=wildfly-cookbook.cli
core-service
deployment
deployment-overlay
extension
interface
path
socket-binding-group
subsystem
system-property
launch-type=STANDALONE
management-major-version=3
management-micro-version=0
management-minor-version=0
name=7536a491dba6
namespaces=[]
```

```
process-type=Server
product-name=WildFly Full
product-version=9.0.0.Beta2
profile-name=undefined
release-codename=Kenny
release-version=1.0.0.Beta2
running-mode=NORMAL
schema-locations=[]
server-state=running
suspend-state=RUNNING
```

## How it works...

Here we are telling the `jboss-cli.sh` script to read the commands defined inside the `wildfly-cookbook.2015` file, by the `--file` directive. The CLI reads our `wildfly-cookbook.cli` file and executes its commands.

Using a file to store the commands needed to configure your WildFly instance is very useful to automate configuration.

Imagine a scenario where you need to scale a system automatically. Suppose you have all your applications' source code in a version-control-software repository such as `git`, along with the `.cli` configuration files. It would be a piece of cake to download your app, build it, configure your WildFly instance using the `.cli` files, deploy the app, and start the server!

In the next chapter, we will discuss how to stop and start a server, deploy an application using the CLI, and much more.

# 9

# Conquering the CLI

In this chapter, you will learn the following recipes:

- Invoking server stop, start, and reload
- Invoking server group stop, start, restart, and reload
- Creating a server group
- Creating a server
- Managing an application – deploy, undeploy

## Introduction

In this chapter, you will learn how to use the CLI to alter the system's state. That is, changing different settings such as deployments and creating new servers. In the previous chapter, we saw how to grab information out of the CLI. The CLI also provides a method to execute the commands outside it, by specifying the WildFly to connect to and the command to execute.

Furthermore, WildFly provides you with an HTTP API, which can be used to perform actions and to retrieve information (most of these APIs are used to perform system monitoring analysis). In the previous chapter, we were using the CLI to grab information; thus via HTTP we have been using the GET verb of the HTTP protocol. In the following recipes, we will alter the state of the server by using the POST verb, along with the parameters that the WildFly HTTP API needs. The HTTP API only accepts JSON data, so we need to send the data that way.

We will use methods within both the operational modes— standalone and domain—whenever it makes sense, because with regard to the operational mode, you may have different entry points.

In this chapter, we will simulate/use remote WildFly instances, just as in the real scenario where you can apply the following recipes to connect to remote servers. It does not make sense to try the recipes in `localhost`, without seeing any authentication and authorization issues.

To simulate a remote server, you can eventually use VirtualBox or Docker, and then install WildFly as described in the first chapter.

I'm going to use WildFly running on a Linux container using the Docker tool version 1.5. You can obviously use a real remote server– it would be the same; what really counts is the WildFly platform being exposed.

By the way, the last chapter of this book is all about running WildFly within a Linux container, using Docker. So if you are totally new to Docker (where have you been hiding?), have a look at the last chapter of this book, or grab the excellent Docker book, *The Docker Book, James Turnbull* at `http://www.dockerbook.com`.

My Docker configuration says the following:

```
DOCKER_HOST=tcp://192.168.59.103:2376
```

Thus, my remote WildFly instance will be bound to that IP along with the usual WildFly ports, such as `8080`, `9990`, and `9999`. The management user is the same throughout the book with `wildfly` as the username and `cookbook.2015` as the password.

# Invoking server stop, start, and reload

In this recipe, we will learn how to stop, start and reload a WildFly instance by invoking a command to the CLI. You may need to stop a server manually to correct a misconfiguration or to redeploy an application. Thus, knowing how to stop, start and reload a server is a must.

## Getting ready

Remember, I'm running WildFly remotely, bound to `192.168.59.103` as IP. WildFly is already up and running.

## How to do it...

We will walk through the `stop`, `start`, `restart`, and `reload` commands separately to better explain their invocation, and eventually, the differences. For example, the `start` command only makes sense when running in the domain mode, as starting WildFly in the standalone mode is a manual operation.

### Stop

Open a new terminal window and execute the following commands:

```
$ cd $WILDFLY_HOME
$ ./bin/jboss-cli.sh -c --controller=192.168.59.103:9990 --user=wildfly
--password=cookbook.2015 --command=":shutdown(restart=false)"
{"outcome" => "success"}
```

Obviously, after this command you need to start up WildFly manually. This is because the host-controller process went down along with the WildFly instance, and therefore, you cannot access the management interface to control your instance.

In case you are running WildFly in the domain mode, you first need to identify the host and the server that you want to stop, and then invoke the stop method, as follows:

```
$ ./bin/jboss-cli.sh --connect --controller=192.168.59.103:9990
--user=wildfly --password=cookbook.2015 --command="/host=master/server-config=server-one:stop()"
{
    "outcome" => "success",
    "result" => "STOPPING"
}
```

### Start

This command only makes sense in the domain mode, where you connect to the domain controller. Then you can push commands to the various active host-controllers, which bring WildFly instances up or down, as shown next.

Open a new terminal window and execute the following commands:

```
$ cd $WILDFLY_HOME
$ ./bin/jboss-cli.sh --connect --controller=192.168.59.103:9990
--user=wildfly --password=cookbook.2015 --command="/host=master/server-config=server-one:start()"
{
    "outcome" => "success",
    "result" => "STARTING"
}
```

## Restart

Open a new terminal window and run the following code:

```
$ cd $WILDFLY_HOME
$ ./bin/jboss-cli.sh -c --controller=192.168.59.103:9990 --user=wildfly
--password=cookbook.2015 --command=":shutdown(restart=true)"
{"outcome" => "success"}
```

As you were probably wondering in the preceding `stop` section, passing the `restart` argument set as `true` to the `shutdown` method would have probably restarted the WildFly instance and, in fact, it did.

By the way, there is no counterpart to the domain mode. It would only be applicable for a server group, which is discussed later in this chapter.

## Reload

Open a new terminal window and execute the following:

```
$ cd $WILDFLY_HOME
$ ./bin/jboss-cli.sh -c --controller=192.168.59.103:9990 --user=wildfly
--password=cookbook.2015 --command=":reload()"
{
    "outcome" => "success",
    "result" => undefined
}
```

The `reload` method just shuts down all active WildFly services, unbinds resources, and then brings them all up back again, reloading the configuration.

If you are running WildFly in the domain mode, the purpose of the invocation remains the same— to reload the server configuration; you can do as follows:

```
$ ./bin/jboss-cli.sh --connect --controller=192.168.59.103:9990
--user=wildfly --password=cookbook.2015 --command=":reload-servers()"
{
    "outcome" => "success",
    "result" => undefined,
    "server-groups" => undefined
}
```

## How it works...

Here, we are telling the `jboss-cli.sh` script to execute the command that we define in the `--command` parameter, and to return the result in the standard output.

## There's more...

WildFly provides one more API, which is the HTTP API. Let's try it with some network command-line tools such as `curl`.

### Curl

1. With a running WildFly instance, open a new terminal window and give the following commands:

   ```
   $ curl --verbose http://192.168.59.103:9990/management/ -X POST -H
   "Content-Type: application/json" -d '{"operation":"reload"}'
   ```

2. You should get the following output:

   ```
   * Hostname was NOT found in DNS cache
   *   Trying 192.168.59.103...
   * Connected to 192.168.59.103 (192.168.59.103) port 9990 (#0)
   > POST /management/ HTTP/1.1
   > User-Agent: curl/7.37.1
   > Host: 192.168.59.103:9990
   > Accept: */*
   > Content-Type: application/json
   > Content-Length: 22
   >
   * upload completely sent off: 22 out of 22 bytes
   < HTTP/1.1 401 Unauthorized
   < Connection: keep-alive
   < WWW-Authenticate: Digest realm="ManagementRealm",domain="/
   management",nonce="//unXxm6vjoNMTQzNTA1MTg1NDUyNtkzOlQPF6rdPZp9cTc
   QnhY=",opaque="00000000000000000000000000000000",algorithm=MD5
   < Content-Length: 77
   < Content-Type: text/html
   < Date: Tue, 23 Jun 2015 09:30:44 GMT
   <
   ```

```
* Connection #0 to host 192.168.59.103 left intact
<html><head><title>Error</title></head><body>401 - Unauthorized</
body></html>
```

As you can see, `curl` complains about a digest authentication for `ManagementRealm`, which is the one used by the WildFly management interfaces.

3. Let's give the username and password to the command, as follows:

```
$ curl --verbose --digest --user wildfly
http://192.168.59.103:9990/management/ -X POST -H "Content-Type:
application/json" -d '{"operation":"reload"}'
```

4. You should get the following output:

```
Enter host password for user 'wildfly':
* Hostname was NOT found in DNS cache
*   Trying 192.168.59.103...
* Connected to 192.168.59.103 (192.168.59.103) port 9990 (#0)
* Server auth using Digest with user 'wildfly'
> POST /management/ HTTP/1.1
> User-Agent: curl/7.37.1
> Host: 192.168.59.103:9990
> Accept: */*
> Content-Type: application/json
> Content-Length: 0
>
< HTTP/1.1 401 Unauthorized
< Connection: keep-alive
< WWW-Authenticate: Digest realm="ManagementRealm",domain="/manage
ment",nonce="urmPLpGMJgkNMTQzNTA1MjEwMTI4NJYIEw20Br2YWefE0GbBBk8="
,opaque="00000000000000000000000000000000",algorithm=MD5
< Content-Length: 77
< Content-Type: text/html
< Date: Tue, 23 Jun 2015 09:30:44 GMT
<
* Ignoring the response-body
* Connection #0 to host 192.168.59.103 left intact
* Issue another request to this URL: 'http://192.168.59.103:9990/
management/'
* Found bundle for host 192.168.59.103: 0x7fc1104149d0
* Re-using existing connection! (#0) with host 192.168.59.103
```

```
* Connected to 192.168.59.103 (192.168.59.103) port 9990 (#0)
* Server auth using Digest with user 'wildfly'
> POST /management/ HTTP/1.1
> Authorization: Digest username="wildfly",
realm="ManagementRealm", nonce="urmPLpGMJgkNMTQzNTA1MjEwMTI4NJYIE
w20Br2YWefE0GbBBk8=", uri="/management/", response="0bbe505bc1af
3907ff3a8ca960387829", opaque="00000000000000000000000000000000",
algorithm="MD5"
> User-Agent: curl/7.37.1
> Host: 192.168.59.103:9990
> Accept: */*
> Content-Type: application/json
> Content-Length: 22
>
* upload completely sent off: 22 out of 22 bytes
< HTTP/1.1 200 OK
< Connection: keep-alive
< Authentication-Info: nextnonce="oIOIlHtymVgNMTQzNTA1MjEwMTI4OZI0
7WcGItS8EhmrBTUgrCU="
< Content-Type: application/json; charset=utf-8
< Content-Length: 40
< Date: Tue, 23 Jun 2015 09:30:44 GMT
<
* Connection #0 to host 192.168.59.103 left intact
{"outcome" : "success", "result" : null}
```

5. Okay, it works; now remove the `--verbose` flag and execute the command again. You should get just the JSON output, after entering the password, as follows:

```
$ curl --digest --user wildfly:cookbook.2015
http://192.168.59.103:9990/management/ -X POST -H "Content-Type:
application/json" -d '{"operation":"reload"}'
{"outcome" : "success", "result" : null}
$
```

I chose the `reload` method just to show you how to do it using the HTTP API.

# Invoking server group stop, start, restart, and reload

In this recipe, we will learn how to stop, start, restart, and reload a WildFly server group, by invoking a command to the CLI. As you should know by now, you can stop, start, restart, and reload a single server belonging to a server group. We will see all these commands using the CLI.

As we are talking about a server group, this recipe only makes sense with WildFly running in the domain mode.

## Getting ready

Remember, I'm running WildFly remotely, bound to `192.168.59.103` as IP. WildFly is already up and running.

## How to do it...

We will walk through the `stop`, `start`, `restart`, and `reload` commands separately to better explain their invocation and eventual differences.

### Stop

Open a new terminal window and execute the following code:

```
$ cd $WILDFLY_HOME
$ ./bin/jboss-cli.sh -c --controller=192.168.59.103:9990 --user=wildfly
--password=cookbook.2015 --command="/server-group=main-server-group:stop-
servers()"
{
    "outcome" => "success",
    "result" => undefined,
    "server-groups" => undefined
}
```

### Start

Open a new terminal window and run the following commands:

```
$ cd $WILDFLY_HOME
$ ./bin/jboss-cli.sh -c --controller=192.168.59.103:9990 --user=wildfly
--password=cookbook.2015 --command="/server-group=main-server-
group:start-servers()"
```

```
{
    "outcome" => "success",
    "result" => undefined,
    "server-groups" => undefined
}
```

### Restart

Open a new terminal window and execute the following commands:

```
$ cd $WILDFLY_HOME
$ ./bin/jboss-cli.sh -c --controller=192.168.59.103:9990 --user=wildfly
--password=cookbook.2015 --command="/server-group=main-server-
group:restart-servers()"
{
    "outcome" => "success",
    "result" => undefined,
    "server-groups" => undefined
}
```

### Reload

Open a new terminal window and run the following code:

```
$ cd $WILDFLY_HOME
$ ./bin/jboss-cli.sh -c --controller=192.168.59.103:9990 --user=wildfly
--password=cookbook.2015 --command="/server-group=main-server-
group:reload-servers()"
{
    "outcome" => "success",
    "result" => undefined,
    "server-groups" => undefined
}
```

## How it works...

Here, we are telling the `jboss-cli.sh` script to execute the command that we define in the `--command` parameter, and to return the result in the standard output.

Using the CLI, it would be as follows:

```
$ ./bin/jboss-cli.sh
You are disconnected at the moment. Type 'connect' to connect to the
server or 'help' for the list of supported commands.
[disconnected /] connect 192.168.59.103:9990
Authenticating against security realm: ManagementRealm
Username: wildfly
Password:
[standalone@192.168.59.103:9990 /] /server-group=main-server-group:stop-
servers()
{
    "outcome" => "success",
    "result" => undefined,
    "server-groups" => undefined
}
[standalone@192.168.59.103:9990 /]
```

The same applies for the other methods: `start-servers()`, `restart-servers()`, and `reload-servers()`.

## There's more...

WildFly provides one more API, which is the HTTP API. Let's try it with some network command-line tools such as `curl`.

### Curl

With a running WildFly instance, open a new terminal window and execute the following code:

```
$ curl --digest --user wildfly:cookbook.2015 http://192.168.59.103:9990/
management/ -X POST -H "Content-Type: application/json" -d
'{"operation":"restart-servers","address":[{"server-group":"main-server-
group"}]}'
{"outcome" : "success", "result" : null, "server-groups" : null}
```

That's it!

# Creating a server group

In this recipe, you will learn how to create a server group, by invoking a command to the CLI. This applies only within the domain mode.

## Getting ready

Remember, I'm running WildFly remotely, bound to `192.168.59.103` as IP. WildFly is already up and running.

## How to do it...

Open a new terminal window and run the following code:

```
$ cd $WILDFLY_HOME
$ ./bin/jboss-cli.sh -c --controller=192.168.59.103:9990 --user=wildfly
--password=cookbook.2015 --command="/server-group=next-server-
group:add(profile=ha,socket-binding-group=ha-sockets)"
{
    "outcome" => "success",
    "result" => undefined,
    "server-groups" => undefined
}
```

> The server group is ready to use without requiring any reload or restart. This means that it can be used to add servers to it. For the moment, it is just an empty server group. Later in this chapter, we will see how to add a server to a server group, using the CLI.

In case you need to remove the server group, just use the `remove` method on it, as follows:

```
$ ./bin/jboss-cli.sh -c --controller=192.168.59.103:9990 --user=wildfly
--password=cookbook.2015 --command="/server-group=next-server-
group:remove()"
{
    "outcome" => "success",
    "result" => undefined,
    "server-groups" => undefined
}
```

## How it works...

Here, we are telling the `jboss-cli.sh` script to execute the command that we define within the `--command` parameter, and to return the result in the standard output.

Using the CLI, it would be as follows:

```
$ ./bin/jboss-cli.sh
You are disconnected at the moment. Type 'connect' to connect to the
server or 'help' for the list of supported commands.
[disconnected /] connect 192.168.59.103:9990
Authenticating against security realm: ManagementRealm
Username: wildfly
Password:
[domain@192.168.59.103:9990 /] /server-group=next-server-
group:add(profile=ha,socket-binding-group=ha-sockets)
{
    "outcome" => "success",
    "result" => undefined,
    "server-groups" => undefined
}
[domain@192.168.59.103:9990 /]
```

## There's more...

WildFly provides one more API, which is the HTTP API. Let's try it with some network command-line tool, such as `curl`.

With a running WildFly instance, open a new terminal window and run the following code:

```
$ curl --digest --user wildfly:cookbook.2015 http://192.168.59.103:9990/
management/ -X POST -H "Content-Type: application/json" -d '{"operation"
: "composite", "address" : [], "steps" : [{"operation" : "add", "address"
: {"server-group" : "next-server-group"}, "profile" : "ha", "socket-
binding-group" : "ha-sockets"}]}'
{"outcome" : "success", "result" : {"step-1" : {"outcome" : "success"}},
"server-groups" : null}
```

# Creating a server

In this recipe, we will learn how to create a server by invoking a command to the CLI. This applies only to the domain mode.

## Getting ready

Remember, I'm running WildFly remotely, bound to `192.168.59.103` as IP. WildFly is already up and running.

## How to do it...

Open a new terminal window and execute the following commands:

```
$ cd $WILDFLY_HOME
$ ./bin/jboss-cli.sh -c --controller=192.168.59.103:9990 --user=wildfly
--password=cookbook.2015 --command="/host=master/server-config=server-
four:add(group=main-server-group, auto-start=true, socket-binding-port-
offset=450)"
{
    "outcome" => "success",
    "result" => undefined,
    "server-groups" => undefined
}
```

Now the server is ready, you just need to start it manually. This can be achieved by starting the servers of the server group that your new server belongs to, in this case, `main-server-group`. Run the following code:

```
$ ./bin/jboss-cli.sh -c --controller=192.168.59.103:9990 --user=wildfly
--password=cookbook.2015 --command=/server-group=main-server-group:start-
servers()
{
    "outcome" => "success",
    "result" => undefined,
    "server-groups" => undefined
}
```

The preceding command just starts the servers in the `STOPPED` state.

## How it works...

Here, we are telling the `jboss-cli.sh` script to execute the command that we define within the `--command` parameter, and to return the result in the standard output.

Using the CLI, it would be as follows:

```
$ ./bin/jboss-cli.sh
You are disconnected at the moment. Type 'connect' to connect to the
server or 'help' for the list of supported commands.
[disconnected /] connect 192.168.59.103:9990
Authenticating against security realm: ManagementRealm
Username: wildfly
Password:
[standalone@192.168.59.103:9990 /] /host=master/server-config=server-
four:add(group=main-server-group, auto-start=true, socket-binding-port-
offset=450)
{
    "outcome" => "success",
    "result" => undefined,
    "server-groups" => undefined
}
[standalone@192.168.59.103:9990 /]
```

## There's more...

WildFly provides one more API, which is the HTTP API. Let's try it with some network command-line tools, such as `curl`.

### Curl

With a running WildFly instance, open a new terminal window and execute the following commands:

```
$ curl --digest --user wildfly:cookbook.2015 http://192.168.59.103:9990/
management/ -X POST -H "Content-Type: application/json" -d '{"operation"
: "composite", "address" : [], "steps" : [{"operation" : "add", "address"
: [{"host" : "master"},{"server-config" : "server-four"}], "group" :
"main-server-group", "auto-start" : "true", "socket-binding-port-offset"
: "450"}]}'
{"outcome" : "success", "result" : {"step-1" : {"outcome" : "success"}},
"server-groups" : null}
```

# Managing an application – deploy, undeploy

In this recipe, we will learn how to deploy and undeploy an application, and to check its status, on a running WildFly instance, by invoking a command to the CLI.

## Getting ready

Remember, I'm running WildFly remotely, bound to `192.168.59.103` as IP. WildFly is already up and running.

For this recipe, we will need the application named `example`, which you can find in my GitHub repository. If you skipped the *Managing applications using the deployments folder* recipe of *Chapter 2, Running WildFly in Standalone Mode*, please refer to it to download all the source code and projects that you will need.

To build the application, give the following commands:

```
$ cd ~/WFC/github/wildfly-cookbook
$ cd example
$ mvn -e clean package
```

Once done, copy the artifact `example.war` into your local `$WILDFLY_HOME` folder.

## How to do it...

We will walk through the `deploy`, `status`, and `undeploy` commands separately to better explain their differences when dealing with the standalone and domain modes.

### Deploy

Open a new terminal window and run the following commands:

```
$ cd $WILDFLY_HOME
$ ./bin/jboss-cli.sh -c --controller=192.168.59.103:9990 --user=wildfly
--password=cookbook.2015 --command="deploy example.war"
```

In case you are running WildFly in the domain mode, the invocation is as follows:

```
$ ./bin/jboss-cli.sh -c --controller=192.168.59.103:9990 --user=wildfly
--password=cookbook.2015 --command="deploy example.war --server-
groups=main-server-group"
```

### Status

If you need to check the deployment, you can execute the following code:

```
$ ./bin/jboss-cli.sh -c --controller=192.168.59.103:9990 --user=wildfly
--password=cookbook.2015 --command="/deployment=example.war:read-
attribute(name=status)"
{
    "outcome" => "success",
    "result" => "OK"
}
```

If you are running WildFly in the domain mode, we first need to know the server group that the application belongs to. We can do that by issuing the following command:

```
$ ./bin/jboss-cli.sh -c --controller=192.168.59.103:9990 --user=wildfly
--password=cookbook.2015 --command="deployment-info --name=example.war"
NAME        RUNTIME-NAME
example.war example.war

SERVER-GROUP        STATE
main-server-group   enabled
other-server-group  not added
```

If you already know the server group, you can check the deployment status directly to check the server it belongs to by invoking the following command:

```
$ ./bin/jboss-cli.sh -c --controller=192.168.59.103:9990 --user=wildfly
--password=cookbook.2015 --command="/host=master/server=server-one/
deployment=example.war:read-attribute(name=status)"
{
    "outcome" => "success",
    "result" => "OK"
}
```

### Undeploy

In case you need to undeploy your application, just hit the following command:

```
$ ./bin/jboss-cli.sh -c --controller=192.168.59.103:9990 --user=wildfly
--password=cookbook.2015 --command="undeploy example.war"
```

In case you are running WildFly in the domain mode, the invocation is as follows:

```
$ ./bin/jboss-cli.sh -c --controller=192.168.59.103:9990 --user=wildfly
--password=cookbook.2015 --command="undeploy example.war --all-relevant-
server-groups"
```

That's it!

## How it works...

Here, we are telling the `jboss-cli.sh` script to execute the command that we define within the `--command` parameter, and to return the result in the standard output.

### Deploy

Use the CLI as follows:

```
$ ./bin/jboss-cli.sh
You are disconnected at the moment. Type 'connect' to connect to the
server or 'help' for the list of supported commands.
[disconnected /] connect 192.168.59.103:9990
Authenticating against security realm: ManagementRealm
Username: wildfly
Password:
[standalone@192.168.59.103:9990 /] deploy example.war
[standalone@192.168.59.103:9990 /]
```

Within the domain mode, you will have the following command:

```
[domain@192.168.59.103:9990 /] deploy example.war --server-groups=main-
server-group
[domain@192.168.59.103:9990 /]
```

By the way, you cannot manipulate the output.

### Status

Use the CLI as follows:

```
$ ./bin/jboss-cli.sh
You are disconnected at the moment. Type 'connect' to connect to the
server or 'help' for the list of supported commands.
[disconnected /] connect 192.168.59.103:9990
Authenticating against security realm: ManagementRealm
Username: wildfly
```

```
Password:
[standalone@192.168.59.103:9990 /] deployment-info example.war
{
    "outcome" => "success",
    "result" => "OK"
}
[standalone@192.168.59.103:9990 /]
Within the domain mode, you will have the following command:
[domain@192.168.59.103:9990 /] /host=master/server=server-one/
deployment=example.war:read-attribute(name=status)
{
    "outcome" => "success",
    "result" => "OK"
}
[domain@192.168.59.103:9990 /]
```

## Undeploy

Use the CLI as follows:

```
$ ./bin/jboss-cli.sh
You are disconnected at the moment. Type 'connect' to connect to the
server or 'help' for the list of supported commands.
[disconnected /] connect 192.168.59.103:9990
Authenticating against security realm: ManagementRealm
Username: wildfly
Password:
[standalone@192.168.59.103:9990 /] undeploy example.war
[standalone@192.168.59.103:9990 /]
```

Within the domain mode, give the following command:

```
[domain@192.168.59.103:9990 /] undeploy example.war --all-relevant-
server-groups
[domain@192.168.59.103:9990 /]
```

By the way, you cannot manipulate the output.

## There's more...

WildFly provides one more API, which is the HTTP API. Let's try it with some network command-line tools, such as `curl`.

### Curl deployment

Let's deploy using `curl`:

1. With a running WildFly instance, open a new terminal window and execute the following command:

   ```
   $ curl --digest --user wildfly:cookbook.2015 -F "file=@example.war" http://192.168.59.103:9990/management/add-content

   {"outcome" : "success", "result" : { "BYTES_VALUE" : "eqfGfLVOCv+p1gz5gjDgwX79ERk=" }}
   ```

The file `example.war` should be placed in the same folder from which you are invoking the command.

2. Okay, it works. But we just uploaded our file, we haven't deployed it yet. To deploy it, we need to grab the hash code that resulted from the `upload` command, and use it in the next one as follows:

   ```
   $ curl --digest --user wildfly:cookbook.2015 http://192.168.59.103:9990/management -X POST -H "Content-Type: application/json" -d '{"content":[{"hash": {"BYTES_VALUE" : "eqfGfLVOCv+p1gz5gjDgwX79ERk="}}], "address": [{"deployment":"example.war"}], "operation":"add", "enabled":"true"}'

   {"outcome" : "success"}
   ```

   There you go! We have successfully deployed our interstellar web application.

3. If you are running WildFly in the domain mode, the upload method is the same; thus, for effectively deploying the application, you can hit the following command:

   ```
   $ curl  --digest --user wildfly:cookbook.2015 http://192.168.59.103:9990/management -X POST -H "Content-Type: application/json" -d '{"content":[{"hash": {"BYTES_VALUE" : "eqfGfLVOCv+p1gz5gjDgwX79ERk="}}], "address": [{"deployment":"example.war"}], "server-groups":"main-server-group", "runtime-name":"example.war", "operation":"add", "enabled":"true"}'
   {"outcome" : "success", "result" : null, "server-groups" : null}
   ```

That's it!

### Status

To check the status of your deployment, execute the following command:

```
$ curl --digest --user wildfly:cookbook.2015 http://192.168.59.103:9990/
management -X POST -H "Content-Type: application/json" -d
'{"address": [{"deployment":"example.war"}],"operation":"read-
attribute","name":"status"}'
{"outcome" : "success", "result" : "OK"}
```

If you are running WildFly in the domain mode, you can run the following code:

```
$ curl --digest --user wildfly:cookbook.2015 http://192.168.59.103:9990/
management -X POST -H "Content-Type: application/json" -d '{"operation"
: "read-resource", "address" : [{"deployment":"example.war"}], "json.
pretty":1}'
{
    "outcome" : "success",
    "result" : {
        "content" : [{"hash" : {
            "BYTES_VALUE" : "eqfGfLVOCv+p1gz5gjDgwX79ERk="
        }}],
        "name" : "example.war",
        "runtime-name" : "example.war"
    }
}
```

And that's all.

### Curl undeployment

Let's undeploy using `curl`:

```
$ curl --digest --user wildfly:cookbook.2015 http://192.168.59.103:9990/
management/ -X POST -H "Content-Type: application/json" -d '{"address" :
[{"deployment":"example.war"}],"operation":"undeploy"}'
{"outcome" : "success"}
```

That's it!

# 10

# Hardening the WildFly Communication

In this chapter, you will learn the following recipes:

- Securing WildFly using HTTPS
- Securing a specific application using HTTPS
- Securing the WildFly console using HTTPS
- Securing domain and host controllers' communication using HTTPS

## Introduction

In this chapter, you will learn how to secure your WildFly systems from a communication channel point of view, which is the HTTPS protocol. If system security is a concern, you will need to provide such a capability. By the way, when securing your system at any layer, keep an eye on performance, because it may cause some overhead.

We will learn how to provide security in a WildFly system at different stages, that is,:

- Securing your application communication access protocol
- Securing the WildFly management console
- Securing the communication between the domain controller and all the host controllers

While the last two points do not impact performance that much as they are administrative tools, the first one may impact your performance. By the way, in an enterprise environment, often times, your WildFly middleware platform is behind a reverse proxy (that is, Apache HTTPD), and into a **Demilitarized Zone** (**DMZ**). For this reason, you should eventually secure the reverse proxy and not the traffic between Apache and WildFly, which will just cause CPU overhead. Avoid HTTPS between Apache and WildFly when your network infrastructure already provides security within a DMZ.

Okay, now that I'm in peace with my conscience, let's start!

# Securing WildFly using HTTPS

In this recipe, we will learn how to use a secure channel to provide your applications with services, which is by using the HTTPS protocol. If privacy is a concern for you, this recipe will show how you can protect your data traffic. By the way, securing your applications needs different considerations and aspects, which should be addressed and resolved by developers and operations team.

## Getting ready

To get started, let's first create an `ad-hoc` folder to run our WildFly. In a terminal window execute the following:

```
$ cd $WILDFLY_HOME
$ cp -a standalone sec-std-node-1
```

Now it's time to create our keystore which is used to encrypt the data traffic. We will be using one password to open the keystore file itself, and one password to load the alias.

1. Open a new terminal window and give the following commands:

   ```
   $ cd $WILDFLY_HOME
   $ cd sec-std-node-1/configuration
   $ keytool -v -genkey -alias wildfly.ssl -keypass alias.2015
   -keyalg RSA -keysize 2048 -sigalg SHA1withRSA -keystore wildfly.
   ssl.keystore -storepass keystore.2015

   What is your first and last name?
     [Unknown]:  WildFly Cookbook
   What is the name of your organizational unit?
     [Unknown]:  Packt Publishing
   What is the name of your organization?
     [Unknown]:  packtpub.com
   ```

```
What is the name of your City or Locality?
  [Unknown]:  Birmingham
What is the name of your State or Province?
  [Unknown]:  GB
What is the two-letter country code for this unit?
  [Unknown]:  UK
Is CN=WildFly Cookbook, OU=Packt Publishing, O=packtpub.com,
L=Birmingham, ST=GB, C=UK correct?
  [no]:  yes

Generating 2,048 bit RSA key pair and self-signed certificate
(SHA1withRSA) with a validity of 90 days
  for: CN=WildFly Cookbook, OU=Packt Publishing,
  O=packtpub.com, L=Birmingham, ST=GB, C=UK

[Storing wildfly.ssl.keystore]
```

2. Okay, now we have created the keystore to encrypt HTTP messages. Let's check its integrity by executing the following command:

```
$ keytool -list -v -keystore wildfly.ssl.keystore
Enter keystore password:

Keystore type: JKS
Keystore provider: SUN

Your keystore contains 1 entry

Alias name: wildfly.ssl
Creation date: Nov 21, 2014
Entry type: PrivateKeyEntry
Certificate chain length: 1
Certificate[1]:
Owner: CN=WildFly Cookbook, OU=Packt Publishing, O=packtpub.com,
L=Birmingham, ST=GB, C=UK
Issuer: CN=WildFly Cookbook, OU=Packt Publishing, O=packtpub.com,
L=Birmingham, ST=GB, C=UK
Serial number: 5514d1d1
```

```
Valid from: Fri Nov 21 10:36:31 CET 2014 until: Thu Feb 19
10:36:31 CET 2015
Certificate fingerprints:
   MD5:  D3:FA:9D:20:6D:79:DF:83:C3:50:B1:AC:23:B2:7D:9F
   SHA1:
   89:AB:67:27:23:A4:89:85:06:10:FF:70:C6:6B:05:3D:14:DA:2D:AD
   SHA256:
   7C:DD:A7:E3:44:B4:C5:9F:05:EE:87:2D:
   75:35:C2:3C:90:00:1B:DF:67:89:9B:13:33:F7:58:55:74:89:F7:7C
   Signature algorithm name: SHA1withRSA
   Version: 3

Extensions:

#1: ObjectId: 2.5.29.14 Criticality=false
SubjectKeyIdentifier [
KeyIdentifier [
0000: 1A F5 F7 EC D8 88 D9 80   DE 34 E7 A9 00 75 6A 74
.........4...ujt
0010: E8 60 56 D4                                        .`V.
]
]



*******************************************
*******************************************
```

Okay, everything is fine!!!

We are now ready to configure WildFly to expose itself and our applications via HTTPS.

## How to do it...

We are now going to make a few changes to the WildFly configuration files in order to achieve our goal. We will see both the operational modes: standalone and domain.

### Standalone

1. First of all, start a WildFly instance as usual:

```
$ cd $WILDFLY_HOME
$ ./bin/standalone.sh -Djboss.server.base.dir=sec-std-node-1
```

2. Within a different terminal window, connect to the WildFly CLI and run the following code:

```
$ ./bin/jboss-cli.sh --connect
[standalone@localhost:9990 /] /core-service=management/security-realm=SSLRealm:add()
{"outcome" => "success"}
[standalone@localhost:9990 /] /core-service=management/security-realm=SSLRealm/server-identity=ssl:add(keystore-path=wildfly.ssl.keystore, keystore-relative-to=jboss.server.config.dir,keystore-password=keystore.2015, alias=wildfly.ssl, key-password=alias.2015)
{
    "outcome" => "success",
    "response-headers" => {
        "operation-requires-reload" => true,
        "process-state" => "reload-required"
    }
}
[standalone@localhost:9990 /] :reload()
{
    "outcome" => "success",
    "result" => undefined
}
[standalone@localhost:9990 /] /subsystem=undertow/server=default-server/https-listener=https:add(socket-binding=https, security-realm=SSLRealm)
{"outcome" => "success"}
[standalone@localhost:9990 /]
```

Okay, we are done with the configuration.

3. Let's test everything by opening a browser and pointing it to `https://localhost:8443/`:

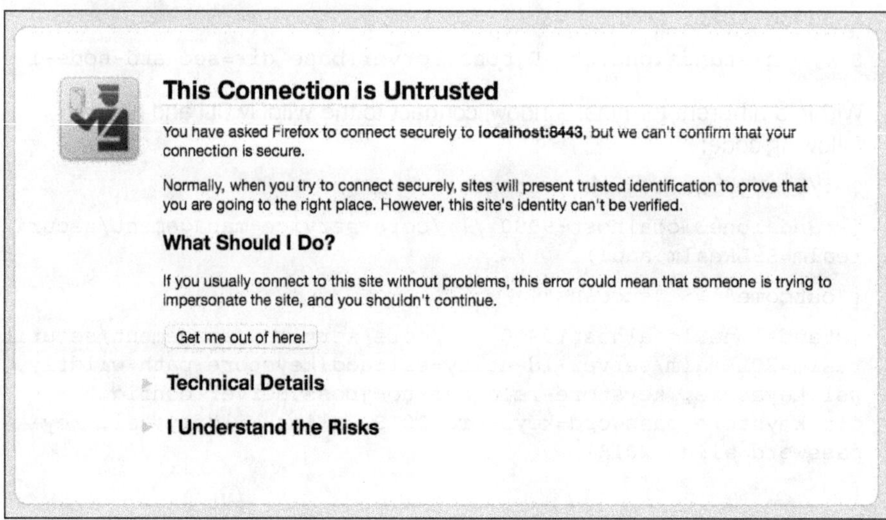

This Connection is Untrusted
You have asked Firefox to connect securely to localhost:8443, but we can't confirm that your connection is secure.
Normally, when you try to connect securely, sites will present trusted identification to prove that you are going to the right place. However, this site's identity can't be verified.
What Should I Do?
If you usually connect to this site without problems, this error could mean that someone is trying to impersonate the site, and you shouldn't continue.
Get me out of here!
Technical Details
I Understand the Risks


Browser warning the user about a self-signed certificate, thus untrusted

4. First the browser will warn you about a security issue; just hit the **Add exception** button, and then, in the next pop-up, hit the **Confirm security exception** button. Once you confirm, the browser displays our WildFy instance running on HTTPS, as follows:

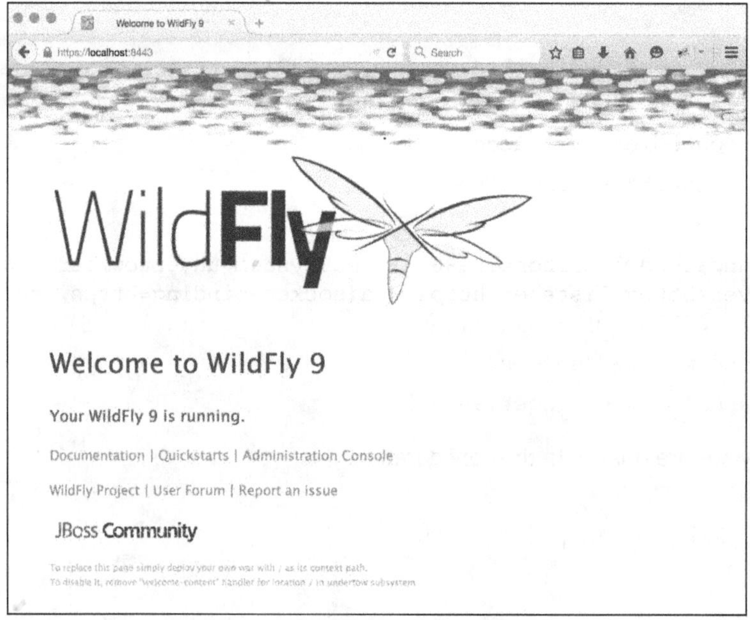


Browser showing WildFly via HTTPS

### Domain

1. First of all, create an `ad-hoc` folder to operate in the domain mode:

   ```
   $ cd $WILDFLY_HOME
   $ cp -a domain sec-dmn-1
   ```

2. From the *Getting ready* section of this recipe, see how you can create a keystore, or copy it from the `sec-std-node-1` folder (if you followed the *Standalone* section steps), as follows:

   ```
   $ cp sec-std-node-1/configuration/wildfly.ssl.keystore sec-dmn-1/configuration
   ```

3. Now start WildFly in the domain mode as follows:

   ```
   $ cd $WILDFLY_HOME
   $ ./bin/domain.sh -Djboss.domain.base.dir=sec-dmn-1
   ```

4. Next, within a different terminal window, connect to the WildFly CLI and execute the following:

   ```
   $ ./bin/jboss-cli.sh --connect
   [domain@localhost:9990 /] /host=master/core-service=management/security-realm=SSLRealm:add()
   {
       "outcome" => "success",
       "result" => undefined,
       "server-groups" => undefined
   }
   [domain@localhost:9990 /] /host=master/core-service=management/security-realm=SSLRealm/server-identity=ssl:add(keystore-path=wildfly.ssl.keystore, keystore-relative-to=jboss.domain.config.dir,keystore-password=keystore.2015, alias=wildfly.ssl, key-password=alias.2015)
   {
       "outcome" => "success",
       "response-headers" => {
           "operation-requires-reload" => true,
           "process-state" => "reload-required"
       },
       "result" => undefined,
       "server-groups" => undefined
   }
   [domain@localhost:9990 /] :reload-servers
   ```

```
{
    "outcome" => "success",
    "result" => undefined,
    "server-groups" => undefined,
    "response-headers" => {"process-state" => "reload-required"}
}
[domain@localhost:9990 /]
```

5. As we know that the WildFly default domain configuration provides two server-groups, one bound to the `full` profile and one bound to the `full-ha` profile (this one without an active server), we can enable the HTTPS protocol for the `full` profile. Within the same CLI console, run the following code:

```
[domain@localhost:9990 /] /profile=full/subsystem=undertow/
server=default-server/https-listener=https:add(socket-
binding=https, security-realm=SSLRealm)
{
    "outcome" => "success",
    "result" => undefined,
    "server-groups" => {"main-server-group" => {"host" =>
{"master" => {
        "server-one" => {"response" => {"outcome" => "success"}},
        "server-two" => {"response" => {"outcome" => "success"}}
    }}}},
    "response-headers" => {"process-state" => "reload-required"}
}
[domain@localhost:9990 /]
```

Keep in mind that acting on the profile, once the configuration has been reloaded, will spread the changes to all servers belonging to the server-group referencing the `full` profile.

Okay, we are done with the configuration.

6. Let's test everything by opening a browser and pointing it to `https://localhost:8443/`:

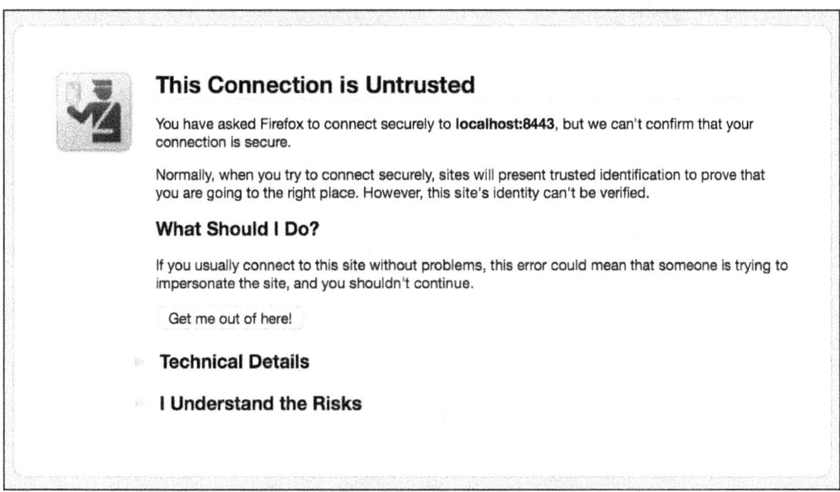
This Connection is Untrusted
You have asked Firefox to connect securely to **localhost:8443**, but we can't confirm that your connection is secure.
Normally, when you try to connect securely, sites will present trusted identification to prove that you are going to the right place. However, this site's identity can't be verified.
What Should I Do?
If you usually connect to this site without problems, this error could mean that someone is trying to impersonate the site, and you shouldn't continue.
Get me out of here!
Technical Details
I Understand the Risks

Browser warning the user about a self-signed certificate, thus untrusted

7. First the browser will warn you about a security issue; just hit the **Add exception** button, and then, in the next pop-up, hit the **Confirm security exception** button. Once you confirm, the browser displays our WildFy instance running on HTTPS, as follows:

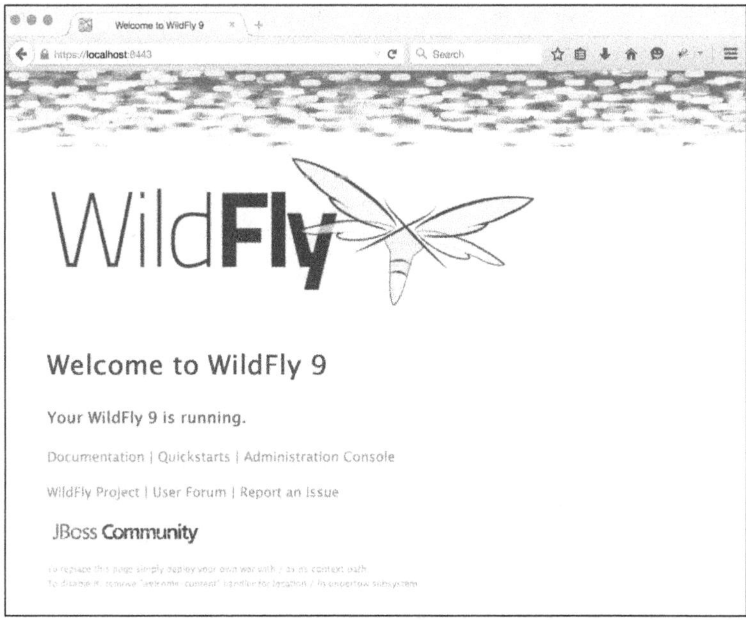
Welcome to WildFly 9
Search
WildFly
Welcome to WildFly 9
Your WildFly 9 is running.
Documentation | Quickstarts | Administration Console
WildFly Project | User Forum | Report an Issue
JBoss Community

Browser showing WildFly via HTTPS

## How it works...

On the WildFly side, we declared a new realm in the `management` section, calling it `SSLRealm`.

Within the new realm, we declared the keystore, which contains the certificates to be used by the HTTPS protocol to encrypt the data.

Lastly, for both the operational modes, we added the `https-listener` to the `Undertow` subsystem, referencing the newly created realm and the `https` socket-binding.

That is all that is needed by WildFly to serve your application via a secure channel, that is, via HTTPS.

## There's more...

As you have noticed from the configuration files `standalone.xml` and `domain.xml`, we left the `http-listener`. As a matter of fact, our applications are also available via HTTP, which is clear, so both the following URLs would provide our WildFly welcome page and our applications, if any:

- `http://localhost:8080`
- `https://localhost:8443`

If you are seeing a page like the following, it is because you entered the hostname and the port correctly (that is, `localhost` and `8443`), but you used the HTTP schema, instead of the HTTPS schema:

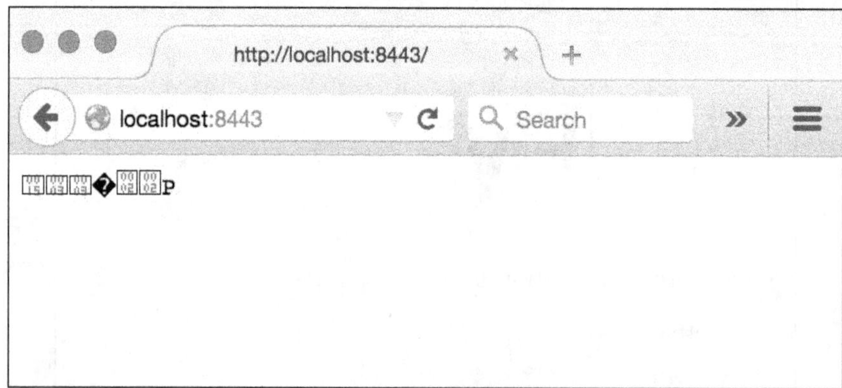


Browser trying to show the encrypted data within US-ASCII encoding

Nevertheless, if you want to provide just the secure channel, remove the `http-listener` declaration from the configuration, and you will be secured.

Bear in mind that disabling the `http-listener` needs a little attention, because it is referenced by other subsystems such as `ejb3` and `webservices` (both related to the `http-remoting-connector`, which is bound to the `http-listener`).

Doing so, your application will not be reachable via HTTP, as seen in the following screenshot:

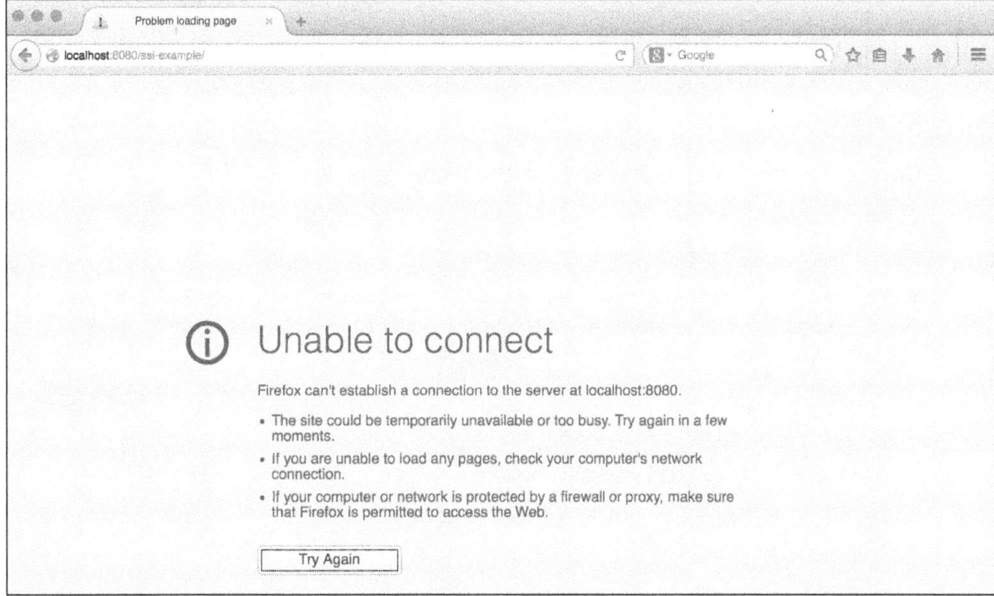


Browser cannot reach the application via HTTP

## See also...

- For a deeper understanding of the keytool command, please refer to the Oracle official documentation at `https://docs.oracle.com/javase/8/docs/technotes/tools/unix/keytool.html`.

# Securing a specific application using HTTPS

In this recipe, we will learn how to use a secure channel for a specific application. This is related to how your application is reached, and not to how to secure your data model, functionality, and all the features that an application comes with. Securing applications needs different considerations and aspects, which should be addressed and resolved mostly on the dev-side.

## Getting ready

To get started, let's first create an `ad-hoc` folder to run our WildFly. In a terminal window execute the following commands:

```
$ cd $WILDFLY_HOME
$ cp -a standalone sec-std-node-2
```

Now it's time to create our keystore, which is used to encrypt data traffic for our specific application:

1. Open a new terminal window and run the following codes:

```
$ cd $WILDFLY_HOME
$ cd sec-std-node-2/configuration
$ keytool -v -genkey -alias wildfly.ssl.app -keyalg RSA -keysize
2048 -sigalg SHA1withRSA -keystore wildfly.ssl.app.keystore
-storepass keystore.2015 -keypass alias.2015

What is your first and last name?
  [Unknown]:  WildFly Cookbook
What is the name of your organizational unit?
  [Unknown]:  Packt Publishing
What is the name of your organization?
  [Unknown]:  packtpub.com
What is the name of your City or Locality?
  [Unknown]:  Birmingham
What is the name of your State or Province?
  [Unknown]:  GB
What is the two-letter country code for this unit?
  [Unknown]:  UK
Is CN=WildFly Cookbook, OU=Packt Publishing, O=packtpub.com,
L=Birmingham, ST=GB, C=UK correct?
  [no]:  yes

Generating 2,048 bit RSA key pair and self-signed certificate
(SHA1withRSA) with a validity of 90 days
  for: CN=WildFly Cookbook, OU=Packt Publishing,
  O=packtpub.com, L=Birmingham, ST=GB, C=UK

[Storing wildfly.ssl.app.keystore]
```

2. Okay, now we have created the keystore to encrypt HTTP messages. Let's check its integrity by executing the following command:

```
$ keytool -list -v -keystore wildfly.ssl.app.keystore
Enter keystore password:

Keystore type: JKS
Keystore provider: SUN

Your keystore contains 1 entry

Alias name: wildfly.ssl.app
Creation date: Nov 21, 2014
Entry type: PrivateKeyEntry
Certificate chain length: 1
Certificate[1]:
Owner: CN=WildFly Cookbook, OU=Packt Publishing, O=packtpub.com,
L=Birmingham, ST=GB, C=UK
Issuer: CN=WildFly Cookbook, OU=Packt Publishing, O=packtpub.com,
L=Birmingham, ST=GB, C=UK
Serial number: 17c96347
Valid from: Fri Nov 21 16:04:21 CET 2014 until: Thu Feb 19
16:04:21 CET 2015
Certificate fingerprints:
   MD5:  17:F1:E5:1D:93:4D:FE:AD:43:5A:7A:D6:79:9E:3A:6A
   SHA1:
90:7B:26:B0:07:6D:B2:E3:AD:A1:81:D2:F1:AA:47:C0:8D:0B:6D:43
   SHA256: C9:F3:AC:23:B7:54:45:AC:84:D7:D6:D7:A7:5D:B9:7C:ED:99:9
5:EC:9C:B9:9C:E0:47:68:30:C0:48:9D:D8:BD
   Signature algorithm name: SHA1withRSA
   Version: 3

Extensions:

#1: ObjectId: 2.5.29.14 Criticality=false
SubjectKeyIdentifier [
KeyIdentifier [
0000: 8C 21 34 9C F6 30 39 BD   21 43 CF 34 C4 31 A1 B7
.!4..09.!C.4.1..
```

```
0010: 81 7E E6 D1                                       ....
]
]




*******************************************
*******************************************
```

Okay, everything is fine!

We are now ready to configure WildFly to expose our specific application via HTTPS.

3. To test the HTTPS configuration, we will need two applications named `ssl-example` and `no-ssl-example`, which you can find in my GitHub repository. If you skipped the *Managing applications using the deployments folder* recipe in *Chapter 2, Running WildFly in Standalone Mode*, please refer to it to download all source code and projects that you will need.
4. To build the application, execute the following:

   ```
   $ cd ~/WFC/github/wildfly-cookbook
   $ mvn -e clean package -f ssl-example/pom.xml
   $ mvn -e clean package -f no-ssl-example/pom.xml
   ```

5. Once done, copy the artifacts `no-ssl-example.war` and `ssl-example.war` (under their relative `target` folder) into your local `$WILDFLY_HOME` folder.

## How to do it...

We are now going to make a few changes to the WildFly configuration files in order to achieve our goal. We will see both the operational modes: standalone and domain.

### Standalone

First of all, start a WildFly instance as follows:

```
$ cd $WILDFLY_HOME
$ ./bin/standalone.sh -Djboss.server.base.dir=sec-std-node-2
```

Within a different terminal window, connect to the WildFly CLI and execute the following:

```
$ cd $WILDFLY_HOME
$ ./bin/jboss-cli.sh --connect
[standalone@localhost:9990 /] /core-service=management/security-realm=AppSSLRealm:add()
```

```
{"outcome" => "success"}
[standalone@localhost:9990 /] /core-service=management/security-
realm=AppSSLRealm/server-identity=ssl:add(keystore-path=wildfly.ssl.
app.keystore, keystore-relative-to=jboss.server.config.dir,keystore-
password=keystore.2015, alias=wildfly.ssl.app, key-password=alias.2015)
{
    "outcome" => "success",
    "response-headers" => {
        "operation-requires-reload" => true,
        "process-state" => "reload-required"
    }
}
[standalone@localhost:9990 /] :reload()
{
    "outcome" => "success",
    "result" => undefined
}
[standalone@localhost:9990 /] /subsystem=undertow/server=secure-
server:add()
{
    "outcome" => "success",
    "response-headers" => {
        "operation-requires-reload" => true,
        "process-state" => "reload-required"
    }
}
[standalone@localhost:9990 /] :reload
{
    "outcome" => "success",
    "result" => undefined
}
[standalone@localhost:9990 /] /subsystem=undertow/server=secure-
server/https-listener=https:add(socket-binding=https, security-
realm=AppSSLRealm)
{"outcome" => "success"}
[standalone@localhost:9990 /] /subsystem=undertow/server=secure-server/
host=secure-host:add()
{"outcome" => "success"}
```

```
[standalone@localhost:9990 /] /subsystem=undertow/server=secure-server:write-attribute(name=default-host,value=secure-host)
{
    "outcome" => "success",
    "response-headers" => {
        "operation-requires-reload" => true,
        "process-state" => "reload-required"
    }
}
[standalone@localhost:9990 /] :reload
{
    "outcome" => "success",
    "result" => undefined
}
[standalone@localhost:9990 /]
```

Okay, we are done with the configuration.

## Testing

1. We now need to deploy our applications using the CLI, as follows:

   ```
   [standalone@localhost:9990 /] deploy no-ssl-example.war
   [standalone@localhost:9990 /] deploy ssl-example.war
   [standalone@localhost:9990 /]
   ```

2. To test the configuration, open your browser and point it to `http://localhost:8080/no-ssl-example`.

3. You should get a page similar to the following:

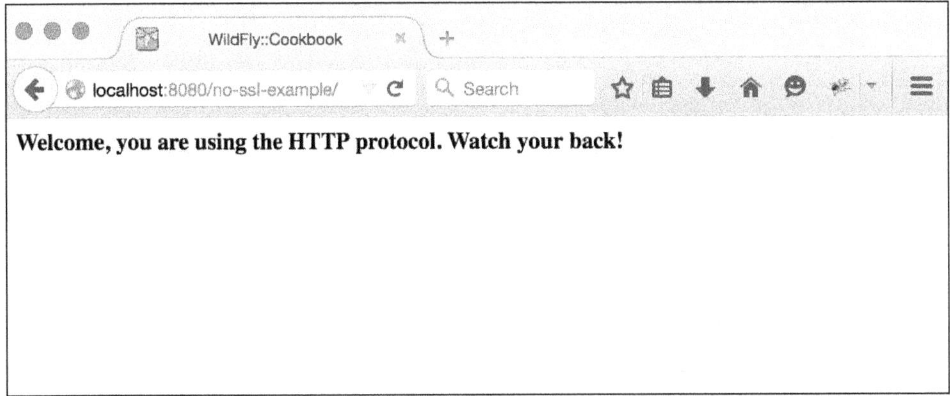


4. Now, point the browser to `https://localhost:8443/ssl-example`.
5. After the security warning, you should get a page similar to the following:

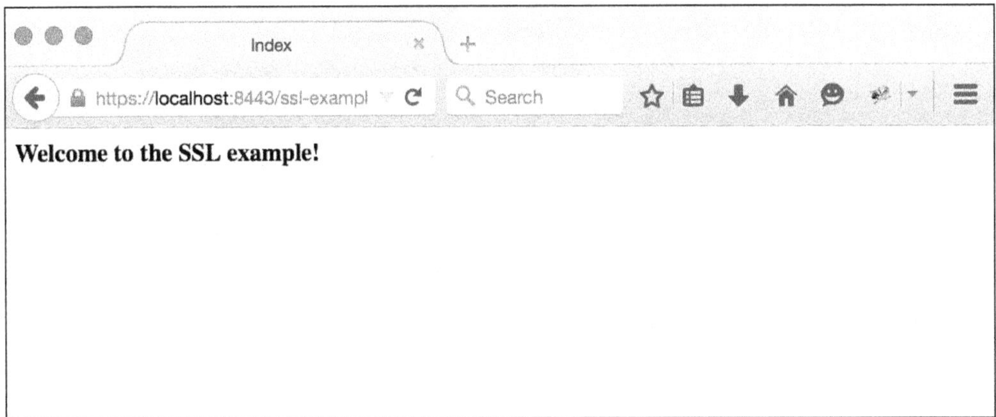


Now if you try to mix the schema and port along with the context application, you will see that the `ssl-example` application is only reachable via HTTPS, and that the `no-ssl-example` is only reachable via HTTP.

## Domain

1. First of all, create an `ad-hoc` folder to operate in the domain mode:

```
$ cd $WILDFLY_HOME
$ cp -a domain sec-dmn-2
```

2. From the *Getting ready* section of this recipe, see how you can create a keystore, or copy it from the `sec-std-node-2` folder (if you followed the *Standalone* section steps), as follows:

```
$ cp sec-std-node-2/configuration/wildfly.ssl.app.keystore sec-dmn-2/configuration
```

3. Now start WildFly in the domain mode, as follows:

```
$ cd $WILDFLY_HOME
$ ./bin/domain.sh -Djboss.domain.base.dir=sec-dmn-2
```

4. Next, within a different terminal window, connect to the WildFly CLI and execute the following command:

```
[domain@localhost:9990 /] /host=master/core-service=management/security-realm=AppSSLRealm:add()
{
    "outcome" => "success",
    "result" => undefined,
    "server-groups" => undefined
}
[domain@localhost:9990 /] /host=master/core-service=management/security-realm=AppSSLRealm/server-identity=ssl:add(keystore-path=wildfly.ssl.app.keystore,keystore-relative-to=jboss.domain.config.dir,keystore-password=keystore.2015,alias=wildfly.ssl.app,key-password=alias.2015)
{
    "outcome" => "success",
    "response-headers" => {
        "operation-requires-reload" => true,
        "process-state" => "reload-required"
    },
    "result" => undefined,
    "server-groups" => undefined
}
[domain@localhost:9990 /] reload --host=master
[domain@localhost:9990 /]
```

As we know that the WildFly default domain configuration provides two server-groups, one bound to the `full` profile and one bound to the `full-ha` profile (this one without an active server), we can enable the HTTPS protocol for the `full` profile.

5. Within the same CLI console, execute the following command:

```
[domain@localhost:9990 /] /profile=full/subsystem=undertow/
server=secure-server:add()
{
    "outcome" => "success",
    "result" => undefined,
    "server-groups" => {"main-server-group" => {"host" =>
    {"master" => {
        "server-one" => {"response" => {
            "outcome" => "success",
            "response-headers" => {
                "operation-requires-reload" => true,
                "process-state" => "reload-required"
            }
        }},
        "server-two" => {"response" => {
            "outcome" => "success",
            "response-headers" => {
                "operation-requires-reload" => true,
                "process-state" => "reload-required"
            }
        }}
    }}}}
}
[domain@localhost:9990 /] reload --host=master
[domain@localhost:9990 /] /profile=full/subsystem=undertow/
server=secure-server/https-listener=https:add(socket-
binding=https,security-realm=AppSSLRealm)
{
    "outcome" => "success",
    "result" => undefined,
    "server-groups" => {"main-server-group" => {"host" =>
    {"master" => {
```

```
        "server-one" => {"response" => {"outcome" =>
        "success"}},
        "server-two" => {"response" => {"outcome" =>
        "success"}}
    }}}}
}
[domain@localhost:9990 /] /profile=full/subsystem=undertow/
server=secure-server/host=secure-host:add()
{
    "outcome" => "success",
    "result" => undefined,
    "server-groups" => {"main-server-group" => {"host" =>
    {"master" => {
        "server-one" => {"response" => {"outcome" =>
        "success"}},
        "server-two" => {"response" => {"outcome" =>
        "success"}}
    }}}}
}
[domain@localhost:9990 /] /profile=full/subsystem=undertow/
server=secure-server:write-attribute(name=default-
host,value=secure-host)
{
    "outcome" => "success",
    "result" => undefined,
    "server-groups" => {"main-server-group" => {"host" =>
{"master" => {
        "server-one" => {"response" => {
            "outcome" => "success",
            "response-headers" => {
                "operation-requires-reload" => true,
                "process-state" => "reload-required"
            }
        }},
        "server-two" => {"response" => {
            "outcome" => "success",
            "response-headers" => {
                "operation-requires-reload" => true,
```

```
                    "process-state" => "reload-required"
                }
            }}
        }}}}
    }
    [domain@localhost:9990 /] reload --host=master
    [domain@localhost:9990 /]
```

Keep in mind that acting on the profile, once the configuration has been reloaded, will spread the changes to all servers belonging to the server-group referencing the `full` profile.

Okay, we are done with the configuration.

### Testing

We now need to deploy our applications using the CLI, as follows:

```
[domain@localhost:9990 /] deploy no-ssl-example.war --server-groups=main-server-group
[domain@localhost:9990 /] deploy ssl-example.war --server-groups=main-server-group
[domain@localhost:9990 /]
```

To test the configuration, open your browser and point it to the following URL:

- `http://localhost:8080/no-ssl-example`
- `https://localhost:8443/ssl-example`

You should follow the same steps as described for the standalone mode, along with the same final pages.

## How it works...

On the WildFly side, using the CLI, we created a new realm in the `management` section, calling it `AppSSLRealm`. Within the new realm, we declared the keystore, which contains the certificates to be used by the HTTPS protocol to encrypt the data.

Working on the `Undertow` subsystem, we added a server named `secure-server`. We then added `https-listener` to it, binding the listener to the `https` socket binding configuration and to the `AppSSLRealm` security realm.

Lastly, we defined a host named `secure-host`, and made it the default host for our `secure-server`.

Wait a minute! How did we match the `ssl-example.war` application to the `secure-host` configuration declared in the `Undertow` subsystem?

Matching happens at the application level. Within the `jboss-web.xml` in the `WEB-INF` folder of our application, you need to declare the following:

```
<?xml version="1.0" encoding="UTF-8"?>
<jboss-web>
    <server-instance>secure-server</server-instance>
    <virtual-host>secure-host</virtual-host>
</jboss-web>
```

The preceding XML code instructs WildFly that the application needs to be bound to the server named `secure-server`, along with the host named `secure-host`.

This way WildFly (actually Undertow) will serve your application using that specific host.

Let's view both the configurations together to better understand the matches:

| WildFly – Undertow | Application |
|---|---|
| <server name="secure-server" default-host="secure-host "><br>    <https-listener name="https" socket-binding="https" security-realm="SSLRealm"/><br>    <host name="secure-host"><br>        <filter-ref name="server-header"/><br>        <filter-ref name="x-powered-by-header"/><br>    </host><br></server> | <?xml version="1.0" encoding="UTF-8"?><br><jboss-web><br>    <server-instance>secure-server</server-instance><br>    <virtual-host>secure-host</virtual-host><br></jboss-web> |

In the `server` declaration, there is also an attribute named `default-host` set to `secure-host`, but it is just used to indicate which host to use if there is more than one.

## There's more...

If you try to mix our configuration via the browser, you will notice that the `ssl-example` application will not be found using the `http-listener` configuration. The same holds true for the `example` application using the `https-listener` configuration.

If you try to open your browser and point it to `http://localhost:8080/ssl-example`, you should land on a **404 – Not Found** page as seen in the following screenshot:

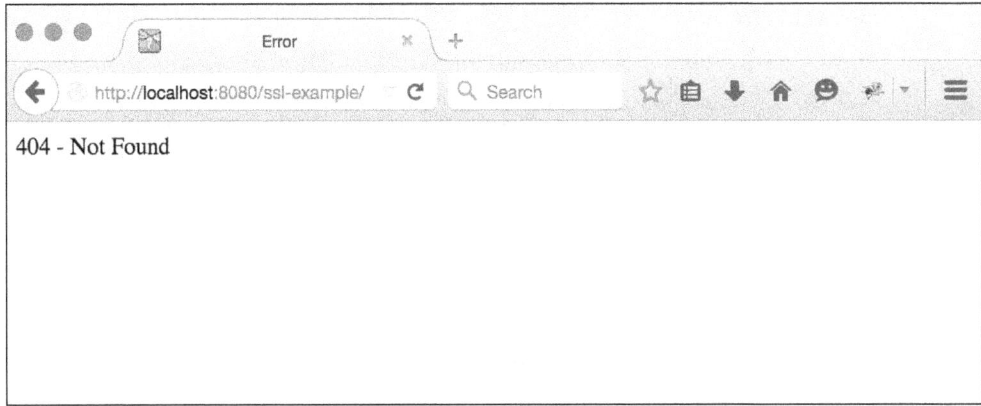


The same applies if you visit `https://localhost:8443/no-ssl-example`.

## See also...

- For a deeper understanding of the `keytool` command, please refer to the Oracle official documentation at `https://docs.oracle.com/javase/8/docs/technotes/tools/unix/keytool.html`.

# Securing the WildFly console using HTTPS

In this recipe, we will learn how to secure your WildFly management console at the communication protocol level. To achieve such a configuration, we will need to create a certificate which will be used to encrypt all the traffic.

## Getting ready

To get started, let's first create an `ad-hoc` folder to run our WildFly. In a terminal window run the following commands:

```
$ cd $WILDFLY_HOME
$ cp -a standalone sec-std-node-mgmt
```

Now it's time to create our keystore which is used to encrypt data traffic.

1. Open a new terminal window and execute the following:

```
$ cd $WILDFLY_HOME
$ cd sec-std-node-mgmt/configuration
$ keytool -v -genkey -alias wildfly.management -keyalg RSA
-keysize 2048 -sigalg SHA1withRSA -keystore wildfly.management.
keystore -storepass keystore.2015 -keypass alias.2015

What is your first and last name?
  [Unknown]:  WildFly Cookbook
What is the name of your organizational unit?
  [Unknown]:  Packt Publishing
What is the name of your organization?
  [Unknown]:  packtpub.com
What is the name of your City or Locality?
  [Unknown]:  Birmingham
What is the name of your State or Province?
  [Unknown]:  GB
What is the two-letter country code for this unit?
  [Unknown]:  UK
Is CN=WildFly Cookbook, OU=Packt Publishing, O=packtpub.com,
L=Birmingham, ST=GB, C=UK correct?
  [no]:  yes

Generating 2,048 bit RSA key pair and self-signed certificate
(SHA1withRSA) with a validity of 90 days
  for: CN=WildFly Cookbook, OU=Packt Publishing,
  O=packtpub.com, L=Birmingham, ST=GB, C=UK

[Storing wildfly.management.keystore]
```

2. Okay, now we have created the keystore to encrypt HTTP messages. Let's check its integrity by executing the following command:

```
$ keytool -list -v -keystore wildfly.management.keystore
Enter keystore password:

Keystore type: JKS
Keystore provider: SUN

Your keystore contains 1 entry

Alias name: wildfly.management
Creation date: Nov 19, 2014
Entry type: PrivateKeyEntry
Certificate chain length: 1
Certificate[1]:
Owner: CN=WildFly Cookbook, OU=Packt Publishing, O=packtpub.com,
L=Birmingham, ST=GB, C=UK
Issuer: CN=WildFly Cookbook, OU=Packt Publishing, O=packtpub.com,
L=Birmingham, ST=GB, C=UK
Serial number: 3bdf9d9
Valid from: Wed Nov 19 15:26:50 CET 2014 until: Tue Feb 17
15:26:50 CET 2015
Certificate fingerprints:
   MD5:  C6:D1:87:5D:93:FC:C4:55:9D:7E:77:A4:9F:94:C1:68
   SHA1:
  DF:B4:E6:96:D4:08:2C:58:A9:62:F1:B7:6F:F8:5E:3E:47:43:06:6F
   SHA256:
  E2:B9:47:D4:22:32:D7:D3:6A:A9:38:FF:E2:1F:FC:
  4E:A3:1A:5D:53:77:95:1E:5C:8E:A7:26:5E:89:6D:BE:44
   Signature algorithm name: SHA1withRSA
   Version: 3

Extensions:

#1: ObjectId: 2.5.29.14 Criticality=false
```

```
SubjectKeyIdentifier [
KeyIdentifier [
0000: 42 20 64 A6 07 50 7D 05   16 0F 21 25 78 1A 66 06  B
d..P....!%x.f.
0010: 97 8C B3 F2                                        ....
]
]



*******************************************
*******************************************
```

Okay, everything is fine!

We are now ready to configure WildFly to expose its management console via HTTPS.

## How to do it...

We are now going to make a few changes to the WildFly configuration files in order to achieve our goal. We will see both the operational modes: standalone and domain.

### Standalone

First of all, as we will create and use a new management realm (named `SecureManagementRealm`), we need to add a new management user (named `securewildfly`) to it.

1. Open a new terminal window and execute the following:

```
$ cd $WILDFLY_HOME
$ java -cp modules/system/layers/base/org/jboss/sasl/main/jboss-sasl-1.0.5.Final.jar org.jboss.sasl.util.UsernamePasswordHashUtil securewildfly SecureManagementRealm cookbook.2015 >> sec-std-node-mgmt/configuration/secure-mgmt-users.properties
```

Be sure to clear the OS history commands after running the preceding command, because the password will be displayed as well. To clear the history, invoke a `history -c` command in the same terminal.

2. Now we can proceed with the effective configuration. Start WildFly as follows:

```
$ cd $WILDFLY_HOME
$ ./bin/standalone.sh -Djboss.server.base.dir=sec-std-node-mgmt
```

3. Now, within a different terminal window, connect to the WildFly CLI and run the following commands:

```
$ cd $WILDFLY_HOME
$ ./bin/jboss-cli.sh --connect
[standalone@localhost:9990 /] batch
[standalone@localhost:9990 / #] /core-service=management/security-realm=SecureManagementRealm:add()
[standalone@localhost:9990 / #] /core-service=management/security-realm=SecureManagementRealm/authentication=local:add(skip-group-loading=true, default-user="$local")
[standalone@localhost:9990 / #] /core-service=management/security-realm=SecureManagementRealm/authentication=properties:add(path=secure-mgmt-users.properties, relative-to=jboss.server.config.dir)
[standalone@localhost:9990 / #] /core-service=management/security-realm=SecureManagementRealm/authorization=properties:add(path=mgmt-groups.properties, relative-to=jboss.server.config.dir)
[standalone@localhost:9990 / #] /core-service=management/security-realm=SecureManagementRealm:write-attribute(name=map-groups-to-roles,value=false)
[standalone@localhost:9990 / #] /core-service=management/security-realm=SecureManagementRealm/server-identity=ssl:add(keystore-path=wildfly.management.keystore,keystore-relative-to=jboss.server.config.dir,keystore-password=keystore.2015,alias=wildfly.management, key-password=alias.2015)
[standalone@localhost:9990 / #] /core-service=management/management-interface=http-interface:write-attribute(name=security-realm,value=SecureManagementRealm)
[standalone@localhost:9990 / #] /core-service=management/management-interface=http-interface:write-attribute(name=secure-socket-binding,value=management-https)
[standalone@localhost:9990 / #] :reload()
[standalone@localhost:9990 / #] run-batch
The batch executed successfully
[standalone@localhost:9990 /]
```

Okay, we are done with the configuration.

## Testing

Open your browser and point it at `https://localhost:9993`:

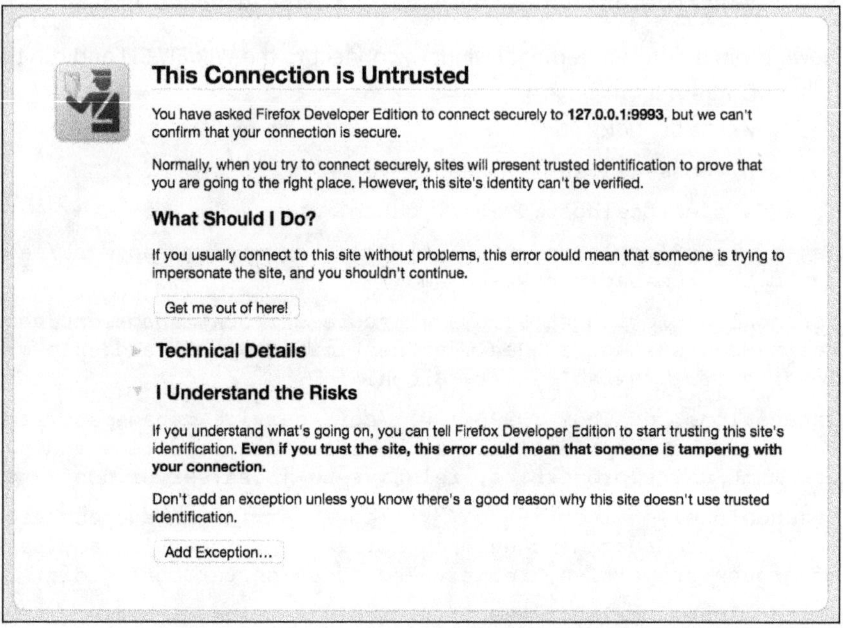

This Connection is Untrusted
You have asked Firefox Developer Edition to connect securely to 127.0.0.1:9993, but we can't confirm that your connection is secure.
Normally, when you try to connect securely, sites will present trusted identification to prove that you are going to the right place. However, this site's identity can't be verified.
What Should I Do?
If you usually connect to this site without problems, this error could mean that someone is trying to impersonate the site, and you shouldn't continue.
Get me out of here!
Technical Details
I Understand the Risks
If you understand what's going on, you can tell Firefox Developer Edition to start trusting this site's identification. Even if you trust the site, this error could mean that someone is tampering with your connection.
Don't add an exception unless you know there's a good reason why this site doesn't use trusted identification.
Add Exception...


Browser warning the user about an untrusted certificate

First, the browser will warn you about a security issue; just hit the **Add exception** button, and then, in the next pop-up, hit the **Confirm security exception** button.

The browser will then prompt you to enter the credentials to access the WildFly management console for the `SecureManagementRealm`; just input `securewildfly` as the username and `cookbook.2015` as the password.

You should now be inside the Web Console, as depicted in the following image:

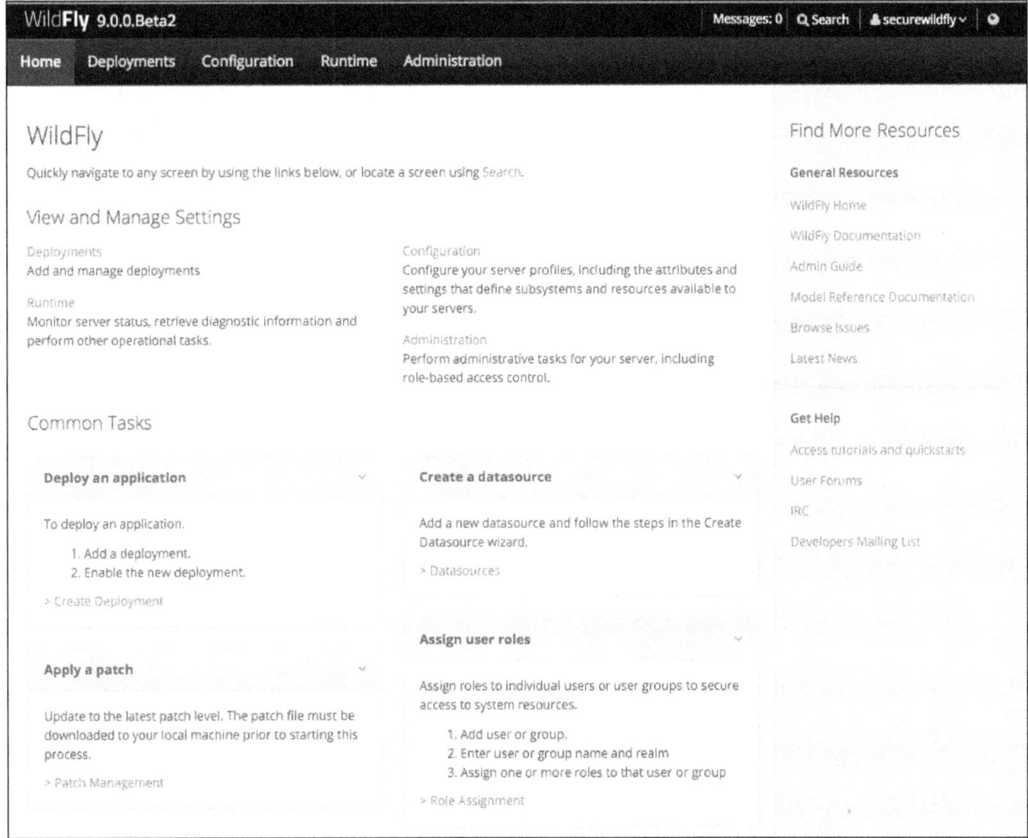

WildFly's management console via HTTPS

Great, we are done!

By the way, securing the console via HTTPS might be okay by itself, but still, people with credentials can log into it, and mess around with it. To better secure your management console, you should concentrate on a **Role Based Access Control** (**RBAC**) feature, available in WildFly and discussed later in this book, which gives you finer control over who can do what.

## Domain

1. First of all, create an `ad-hoc` folder to operate in the domain mode:

   ```
   $ cd $WILDFLY_HOME
   $ cp -a domain sec-dmn-mgmt
   ```

2. From the *Getting ready* section of this recipe, see how you can create a keystore, or copy it from the `sec-std-node-mgmt` folder (if you followed the *Standalone* section steps), as follows:

   ```
   $ cp sec-std-node-mgmt/configuration/wildfly.management.keystore
   sec-dmn-mgmt/configuration/
   ```

   Next, as we will create and use a new management realm (named `SecureManagementRealm`), we need to add a new management user (named `securewildfly`) to it.

3. Open a new terminal window and execute the following commands:

   ```
   $ cd $WILDFLY_HOME
   $ java -cp modules/system/layers/base/org/jboss/sasl/main/jboss-
   sasl-1.0.5.Final.jar org.jboss.sasl.util.UsernamePasswordHashUtil
   securewildfly SecureManagementRealm cookbook.2015 >> sec-dmn-mgmt/
   configuration/secure-mgmt-users.properties
   ```

> Be sure to clear the OS history commands after running the preceding command, because the password will be displayed as well. To clear the history, invoke a `history -c` command in the same terminal.

4. Now start WildFly in the domain mode as follows:

   ```
   $ cd $WILDFLY_HOME
   $ ./bin/domain.sh -Djboss.domain.base.dir=sec-dmn-mgmt
   ```

5. Next, within a different terminal window, connect to the WildFly CLI and run the following:

   ```
   $ ./bin/jboss-cli.sh --connect
   [domain@localhost:9990 /] batch
   [domain@localhost:9990 / #] /host=master/core-service=management/
   security-realm=SecureManagementRealm:add()
   [domain@localhost:9990 / #] /host=master/core-
   service=management/security-realm=SecureManagementRealm/
   authentication=local:add(skip-group-loading=true, default-
   user="$local")
   ```

```
[domain@localhost:9990 / #] /host=master/core-service=management/
security-realm=SecureManagementRealm/authentication=properties:
add(path=secure-mgmt-users.properties, relative-to=jboss.domain.
config.dir)

[domain@localhost:9990 / #] /host=master/core-service=management/
security-realm=SecureManagementRealm/authorization=properties:add(
path=mgmt-groups.properties, relative-to=jboss.domain.config.dir)

[domain@localhost:9990 / #] /host=master/core-service=management/
security-realm=SecureManagementRealm:write-attribute(name=map-
groups-to-roles,value=false)

[domain@localhost:9990 / #] /host=master/core-
service=management/security-realm=SecureManagementRealm/
server-identity=ssl:add(keystore-path=wildfly.management.
keystore,keystore-relative-to=jboss.domain.config.dir,keystore-
password=keystore.2015,alias=wildfly.management, key-
password=alias.2015)

[domain@localhost:9990 / #] /host=master/core-service=management/
management-interface=http-interface:write-attribute(name=security-
realm,value=SecureManagementRealm)

[domain@localhost:9990 / #] /host=master/core-service=management/
management-interface=http-interface:write-attribute(name=secure-
port,value="${jboss.management.https.port:9993}")

[domain@localhost:9990 / #] run-batch

The batch executed successfully

process-state: reload-required

[domain@localhost:9990 /] reload --host=master

Failed to establish connection in 6058ms: WFLYPRT0053: Could not
connect to http-remoting://localhost:9990. The connection failed:
XNIO000816: Redirect encountered establishing connection

[disconnected /]
```

We are kicked out from the console because it is not reachable on port `9990` any more, but on port `9993` (by default) instead.

### Testing

On opening a browser and pointing it to the `https://localhost:9993` URL, you will see the same as is described in the standalone mode: a security warning complaining about a self-signed certificate, the login pop up and finally the WildFly Admin Console.

## How it works...

First, we defined the security realm via CLI and added it to the host, in this case, `master`. Within the new realm, we declared the keystore to be used by the HTTPS protocol to encrypt the data.

Next, we referenced the newly created `SecureManagementRealm` into the `http-interface` section of the `management-interface`. For this, we also had to specify the `secure-port`, otherwise we would have bound the whole management interface to the default port `9990`, which would have led us to a `ssl_error_rx_record_too_long` browser error.

That is all that is needed by WildFly to provide its management console via HTTPS.

## There's more...

Within this recipe, we have created and used a new realm to secure the management console. Nonetheless, we could have used the default `ManagementRealm`, which was fine.

Using a different realm would free us to switch realms as needed. But more importantly, when you create a user using the `add-user.sh` script, the password being generated contains the string's username, the realm name, and the password, all of which are then hashed using MD5 and then decoded in hexadecimal value.

So, within the `*-user.properties` files of your configuration, when you see `username=SOMETHING`, you should read it as follows:

```
username=HEX(MD5('username':'realm':'password'))
```

## See also

- For a deeper understanding of the `keytool` command, please refer to the Oracle official documentation at `https://docs.oracle.com/javase/8/docs/technotes/tools/unix/keytool.html`.

# Securing domain and host controller communication using HTTPS

In this recipe, we will learn how to secure the communication between the domain controller and the host controller. To achieve this, we need to create a keystore and certificate, one for each controller, including the domain.

## Getting ready

To get started, let's first create the ad-hoc folders to run our WildFly instances: one master and two hosts. In a terminal window execute the following:

```
$ cd $WILDFLY_HOME
$ cp -a domain sec-dmn-master
$ cp -a domain sec-dmn-node-1
$ cp -a domain sec-dmn-node-2
```

We also better prepare our configuration folders to have the proper configuration files, using the preinstalled ones as templates and executing the following:

```
$ cd $WILDFLY_HOME
$ mv sec-dmn-master/configuration/host-master.xml sec-dmn-master/
configuration/host.xml
$ mv sec-dmn-node-1/configuration/domain.xml sec-dmn-node-1/
configuration/domain.xml.unused
$ mv sec-dmn-node-1/configuration/host-slave.xml sec-dmn-node-1/
configuration/host.xml
$ mv sec-dmn-node-2/configuration/domain.xml sec-dmn-node-2/
configuration/domain.xml.unused
$ mv sec-dmn-node-2/configuration/host-slave.xml sec-dmn-node-2/
configuration/host.xml
```

Now we can proceed towards creating the certificates.

## How to do it...

We will first create the keystores for each server; we will then extract the certificates out of them, and lastly, we will import the host's certificates into the domain controller keystore and the domain certificate into the host's keystores. It will become clear soon.

1. Open a new terminal window and run the following:

   ```
   $ cd $WILDFLY_HOME
   $ keytool -genkeypair -alias sec-dmn-master -keyalg RSA
   -keysize 1024 -validity 365 -keystore sec-dmn-master.jks
   -dname "CN=sec-dmn-master,OU=Packt Publishing,O=packtpub.
   com,L=Birmingham,ST=GB,C=UK" -keypass "cookbook.2015" -storepass
   "cookbook.2015"
   ```

```
$ keytool -genkeypair -alias sec-dmn-node-1 -keyalg RSA
-keysize 1024 -validity 365 -keystore sec-dmn-node-1.jks
-dname "CN=sec-dmn-node-1,OU=Packt Publishing,O=packtpub.
com,L=Birmingham,ST=GB,C=UK" -keypass "cookbook.2015" -storepass
"cookbook.2015"

$ keytool -genkeypair -alias sec-dmn-node-2 -keyalg RSA
-keysize 1024 -validity 365 -keystore sec-dmn-node-2.jks
-dname "CN=sec-dmn-node-2,OU=Packt Publishing,O=packtpub.
com,L=Birmingham,ST=GB,C=UK" -keypass "cookbook.2015" -storepass
"cookbook.2015"
```

2. Now we need to export the certificate out of each keystore, and store it in a file. Within the same terminal of the previous `keytool` commands, execute the following commands:

```
$ keytool -exportcert  -keystore sec-dmn-master.jks -alias sec-
dmn-master -keypass "cookbook.2015" -storepass "cookbook.2015"
-file sec-dmn-master.cer

$ keytool -exportcert  -keystore sec-dmn-node-1.jks -alias sec-
dmn-node-1 -keypass "cookbook.2015" -storepass "cookbook.2015"
-file sec-dmn-node-1.cer

$ keytool -exportcert  -keystore sec-dmn-node-2.jks -alias sec-
dmn-node-2 -keypass "cookbook.2015" -storepass "cookbook.2015"
-file sec-dmn-node-2.cer
```

3. Now if you look inside the `$WILDFLY_HOME` folder, you should see the following files:
   - `sec-dmn-master.cer`
   - `sec-dmn-master.jks`
   - `sec-dmn-node-1.cer`
   - `sec-dmn-node-1.jks`
   - `sec-dmn-node-2.cer`
   - `sec-dmn-node-2.jks`

4. Now we need to import the host's certificates into the `domain` keystore, as follows:

```
$ keytool -importcert -keystore sec-dmn-master.jks -storepass
"cookbook.2015" -trustcacerts -alias sec-dmn-node-1 -file sec-dmn-
node-1.cer

Owner: CN=sec-dmn-node-1, OU=Packt Publishing, O=packtpub.com,
L=Birmingham, ST=GB, C=UK

Issuer: CN=sec-dmn-node-1, OU=Packt Publishing, O=packtpub.com,
L=Birmingham, ST=GB, C=UK

Serial number: 47cc055

Valid from: Mon Nov 24 15:48:33 CET 2014 until: Tue Nov 24
15:48:33 CET 2015
```

```
Certificate fingerprints:
   MD5:  BB:31:D0:6F:20:78:FB:07:70:B7:E4:68:DB:EC:2C:83
   SHA1:
  83:DE:B0:D5:01:F4:8F:8C:5D:06:5E:6F:78:D1:28:A9:BF:C4:AE:18
   SHA256:
  B4:4C:BC:D0:C6:EC:5E:11:D0:0E:BB:5F:84:74:D4:
  8B:9C:EA:13:17:A6:E2:6E:1B:C2:65:DC:16:9B:F0:0D:D4
   Signature algorithm name: SHA256withRSA
   Version: 3

Extensions:

#1: ObjectId: 2.5.29.14 Criticality=false
SubjectKeyIdentifier [
KeyIdentifier [
0000: F2 12 C7 78 60 40 26 A3   7D 43 E3 14 0F 76 46 B0
...x`@&..C...vF.
0010: 62 A8 52 40                                       b.R@
]
]

Trust this certificate? [no]:  yes
Certificate was added to keystore
```

5. Once done, let's do the same for the other host:

```
$ keytool -importcert -keystore sec-dmn-master.jks -storepass
"cookbook.2015" -trustcacerts -alias sec-dmn-node-2 -file sec-dmn-
node-2.cer
Owner: CN=sec-dmn-node-2, OU=Packt Publishing, O=packtpub.com,
L=Birmingham, ST=GB, C=UK
Issuer: CN=sec-dmn-node-2, OU=Packt Publishing, O=packtpub.com,
L=Birmingham, ST=GB, C=UK
Serial number: 4cc64451
Valid from: Mon Nov 24 15:48:34 CET 2014 until: Tue Nov 24
15:48:34 CET 2015
Certificate fingerprints:
   MD5:  29:CD:32:78:13:CD:63:7E:16:CE:AE:FC:4A:00:48:7D
   SHA1:
  7D:19:1B:C9:B8:61:72:10:C1:9A:80:98:36:6F:8F:D6:B9:87:F9:83
```

```
    SHA256:
  0A:5E:12:4D:EF:41:BC:AB:4C:7F:56:23:7B:80:E0:
  00:6C:D0:AC:7C:37:B8:FA:51:ED:2A:70:98:39:67:F7:4B
    Signature algorithm name: SHA256withRSA
    Version: 3

Extensions:

#1: ObjectId: 2.5.29.14 Criticality=false
SubjectKeyIdentifier [
KeyIdentifier [
0000: 6E 82 DC 55 F3 91 29 55   25 E7 B5 88 96 F5 1F 42  n..U..)
U%.....B
0010: 0A 52 7F 64                                        .R.d
]
]

Trust this certificate? [no]:  yes
Certificate was added to keystore
```

6. Now it's time for the hosts to import the `domain` certificate, as follows:

```
$ keytool -importcert -keystore sec-dmn-node-1.jks -storepass
"cookbook.2015" -trustcacerts -alias sec-dmn-master -file sec-dmn-
master.cer
Owner: CN=sec-dmn-master, OU=Packt Publishing, O=packtpub.com,
L=Birmingham, ST=GB, C=UK
Issuer: CN=sec-dmn-master, OU=Packt Publishing, O=packtpub.com,
L=Birmingham, ST=GB, C=UK
Serial number: 337c6e75
Valid from: Mon Nov 24 15:48:33 CET 2014 until: Tue Nov 24
15:48:33 CET 2015
Certificate fingerprints:
    MD5:  20:B4:7F:FB:E6:E5:6C:A8:29:82:19:2B:F7:56:90:B8
    SHA1:
  1F:1D:64:49:F5:B5:A4:CC:B7:CA:4C:15:3C:E6:75:C4:E6:03:09:F7
  SHA256:
  C0:66:C8:FF:E3:B8:CD:5B:6D:99:61:1D:6B:05:19:
  F0:05:B1:28:D0:4D:96:CB:AC:B4:89:FB:2B:73:01:7D:04
    Signature algorithm name: SHA256withRSA
```

```
    Version: 3

Extensions:

#1: ObjectId: 2.5.29.14 Criticality=false
SubjectKeyIdentifier [
KeyIdentifier [
0000: 3B 84 5D 1C 5D C1 F6 EF   8C 2B AF C6 80 D7 03 89
;.].]....+......
0010: F9 0A 6D CE                                        ..m.
]
]

Trust this certificate? [no]:  yes
Certificate was added to keystore
```

7. Once done, let's do the same for the other host:

```
$ keytool -importcert -keystore sec-dmn-node-2.jks -storepass
"cookbook.2015" -trustcacerts -alias sec-dmn-master -file sec-dmn-
master.cer
Owner: CN=sec-dmn-master, OU=Packt Publishing, O=packtpub.com,
L=Birmingham, ST=GB, C=UK
Issuer: CN=sec-dmn-master, OU=Packt Publishing, O=packtpub.com,
L=Birmingham, ST=GB, C=UK
Serial number: 337c6e75
Valid from: Mon Nov 24 15:48:33 CET 2014 until: Tue Nov 24
15:48:33 CET 2015
Certificate fingerprints:
    MD5:  20:B4:7F:FB:E6:E5:6C:A8:29:82:19:2B:F7:56:90:B8
    SHA1:
1F:1D:64:49:F5:B5:A4:CC:B7:CA:4C:15:3C:E6:75:C4:E6:03:09:F7
    SHA256:
  C0:66:C8:FF:E3:B8:CD:5B:6D:99:61:1D:6B:05:19:F0:05:
  B1:28:D0:4D:96:CB:AC:B4:89:FB:2B:73:01:7D:04
    Signature algorithm name: SHA256withRSA
    Version: 3

Extensions:

#1: ObjectId: 2.5.29.14 Criticality=false
```

```
SubjectKeyIdentifier [
KeyIdentifier [
0000: 3B 84 5D 1C 5D C1 F6 EF   8C 2B AF C6 80 D7 03 89
;.].]....+......
0010: F9 0A 6D CE                                        ..m.
]
]

Trust this certificate? [no]:  yes
Certificate was added to keystore
```

8. Okay, we are done. Let's copy each keystore to its `ad-hoc` configuration folder, as follows:

```
$ cd $WILDFLY_HOME
$ cp sec-dmn-master.jks sec-dmn-master/configuration/
$ cp sec-dmn-node-1.jks sec-dmn-node-1/configuration/
$ cp sec-dmn-node-2.jks sec-dmn-node-2/configuration/
```

9. Now we need to make some adjustments to the default domain configuration. Open the `sec-dmn-master/configuration/domain.xml` file and set the `default` profile to all `server-groups` declared in the file. Also set the `socket-binding-group` reference to `standard-sockets`, again to all the declared server-groups—we are doing this just to avoid complex configuration due to the `full` and `full-ha` profiles, which involve messaging and clustering.

10. Next, open `sec-dmn-node-1/configuration/host.xml` and change the host name as follows:

```
<host name="sec-dmn-node-1" xmlns="urn:jboss:domain:3.0">
```

11. Also make sure to properly set the port-offset attribute for each configured server (default configuration provides two servers named `server-one` and `server-two`), as per the following example:

```
server-one - <socket-bindings port-offset="100"/>
server-two - <socket-bindings port-offset="150"/>
```

12. Let's do the same for the other host. Open `sec-dmn-node-2/configuration/host.xml` and change the host name as follows:

```
<host name="sec-dmn-node-2" xmlns="urn:jboss:domain:3.0">
```

13. Here too, make sure to properly set the port-offset attribute for each configured server, as follows:

```
server-one - <socket-bindings port-offset="200"/>
server-two - <socket-bindings port-offset="250"/>
```

We are not done yet. We need to configure our keystores, and we will use the CLI, so all our servers must be up and running.

14. Let's start them up by executing each of the following commands in a separate terminal window:

```
$ ./bin/domain.sh -Djboss.domain.base.dir=sec-dmn-master
```

```
$ ./bin/domain.sh -Djboss.domain.base.dir=sec-dmn-node-1
-Djboss.management.native.port=19999 -Djboss.domain.master.
address=127.0.0.1
```

```
$ ./bin/domain.sh -Djboss.domain.base.dir=sec-dmn-node-2
-Djboss.management.native.port=29999 -Djboss.domain.master.
address=127.0.0.1
```

15. At this point, we need to declare our keystore into the WildFly configuration files. Again, in a separate terminal window, connect to the CLI as follows:

```
$ cd $WILDFLY_HOME
$ ./bin/jboss-cli.sh -c
batch
/host=master/core-service=management/security-
realm=DCHCSecureRealm:add()
/host=master/core-service=management/security-
realm=DCHCSecureRealm/server-identity=ssl:add(alias=sec-dmn-
master,keystore-relative-to=jboss.domain.config.dir,keystore-
path=sec-dmn-master.jks,keystore-password=cookbook.2015)
/host=master/core-service=management/security-
realm=DCHCSecureRealm/authentication=truststore:add(keystore-
relative-to=jboss.domain.config.dir,keystore-path=sec-dmn-master.
jks,keystore-password=cookbook.2015)
/host=master/core-service=management/security-
realm=DCHCSecureRealm/authentication=local:add(default-
user=\$local)
/host=master/core-service=management/security-
realm=DCHCSecureRealm/authentication=properties:add(relative-
to=jboss.domain.config.dir,path=mgmt-users.properties)
/host=master/core-service=management/management-
interface=native-interface:write-attribute(name=security-
realm,value=DCHCSecureRealm)
/host=sec-dmn-node-1/core-service=management/security-
realm=DCHCSecureRealm:add()
/host=sec-dmn-node-1/core-service=management/security-
realm=DCHCSecureRealm/server-identity=ssl:add(alias=sec-dmn-node-
1,keystore-relative-to=jboss.domain.config.dir,keystore-path=sec-
dmn-node-1.jks,keystore-password=cookbook.2015)
```

```
/host=sec-dmn-node-1/core-service=management/security-realm=DCHCSecureRealm/authentication=truststore:add(keystore-relative-to=jboss.domain.config.dir,keystore-path=sec-dmn-node-1.jks,keystore-password=cookbook.2015)

/host=sec-dmn-node-1/core-service=management/security-realm=DCHCSecureRealm/authentication=local:add(default-user="\$local")

/host=sec-dmn-node-1/core-service=management/security-realm=DCHCSecureRealm/authentication=properties:add(relative-to=jboss.domain.config.dir,path=mgmt-users.properties)

/host=sec-dmn-node-1/core-service=management/management-interface=native-interface:write-attribute(name=security-realm,value=DCHCSecureRealm)

/host=sec-dmn-node-1:write-remote-domain-controller(security-realm=DCHCSecureRealm)

/host=sec-dmn-node-2/core-service=management/security-realm=DCHCSecureRealm:add()

/host=sec-dmn-node-2/core-service=management/security-realm=DCHCSecureRealm/server-identity=ssl:add(alias=sec-dmn-node-2,keystore-relative-to=jboss.domain.config.dir,keystore-path=sec-dmn-node-2.jks,keystore-password=cookbook.2015)

/host=sec-dmn-node-2/core-service=management/security-realm=DCHCSecureRealm/authentication=truststore:add(keystore-relative-to=jboss.domain.config.dir,keystore-path=sec-dmn-node-2.jks,keystore-password=cookbook.2015)

/host=sec-dmn-node-2/core-service=management/security-realm=DCHCSecureRealm/authentication=local:add(default-user="\$local")

/host=sec-dmn-node-2/core-service=management/security-realm=DCHCSecureRealm/authentication=properties:add(relative-to=jboss.domain.config.dir,path=mgmt-users.properties)

/host=sec-dmn-node-2/core-service=management/management-interface=native-interface:write-attribute(name=security-realm,value=DCHCSecureRealm)

/host=sec-dmn-node-2:write-remote-domain-controller(security-realm=DCHCSecureRealm)

run-batch

reload --host=master
```

For the moment, just don't mind about the errors; we need one more step.

16. Stop the domain controller along with the host controllers and start them as follows:

```
$ ./bin/domain.sh -Djboss.domain.base.dir=sec-dmn-master -Djavax.
net.ssl.trustStore=$WILDFLY_HOME/sec-dmn-master/configuration/sec-
dmn-master.jks
```

```
$ ./bin/domain.sh -Djboss.domain.base.dir=sec-dmn-node-1
-Djboss.management.native.port=19999 -Djboss.domain.master.
address=127.0.0.1 -Djavax.net.ssl.trustStore=$WILDFLY_HOME/sec-
dmn-node-1/configuration/sec-dmn-node-1.jks
```

```
$ ./bin/domain.sh -Djboss.domain.base.dir=sec-dmn-node-2
-Djboss.management.native.port=29999 -Djboss.domain.master.
address=127.0.0.1 -Djavax.net.ssl.trustStore=$WILDFLY_HOME/sec-
dmn-node-2/configuration/sec-dmn-node-2.jks
```

Now the domain controller is communicating with the host controllers using HTTPS.

## How it works...

Let's try to explain in words what we needed and we what have done so far.

We needed to encrypt the traffic between the domain controller and the host controllers. To achieve this, we need a certificate. Thus, because communication between the domain and host controllers requires authentication, we also needed to create a kind of trusted communication between them. All this mechanism can be achieved using Java keystores.

We first create the keystore for the domain and the host controllers:

```
$ keytool -genkeypair -alias sec-dmn-master -keyalg RSA -keysize
1024 -validity 365 -keystore sec-dmn-master.jks -dname "CN=sec-dmn-
master,OU=Packt Publishing,O=packtpub.com,L=Birmingham,ST=GB,C=UK"
-keypass "cookbook.2015" -storepass "cookbook.2015"
```

```
$ keytool -genkeypair -alias sec-dmn-node-1 -keyalg RSA -keysize 1024
-validity 365 -keystore sec-dmn-node-1.jks -dname "CN=sec-dmn-node-
1,OU=Packt Publishing,O=packtpub.com,L=Birmingham,ST=GB,C=UK" -keypass
"cookbook.2015" -storepass "cookbook.2015"
```

```
$ keytool -genkeypair -alias sec-dmn-node-2 -keyalg RSA -keysize 1024
-validity 365 -keystore sec-dmn-node-2.jks -dname "CN=sec-dmn-node-
2,OU=Packt Publishing,O=packtpub.com,L=Birmingham,ST=GB,C=UK" -keypass
"cookbook.2015" -storepass "cookbook.2015"
```

We then extract a certificate out of each keystore, and store it in a `cer` file:

```
$ keytool -exportcert  -keystore sec-dmn-master.jks -alias sec-dmn-master
-keypass "cookbook.2015" -storepass "cookbook.2015" -file sec-dmn-master.
cer
```

```
$ keytool -exportcert  -keystore sec-dmn-node-1.jks -alias sec-dmn-node-1
-keypass "cookbook.2015" -storepass "cookbook.2015" -file sec-dmn-node-1.
cer
```

```
$ keytool -exportcert  -keystore sec-dmn-node-2.jks -alias sec-dmn-node-2
-keypass "cookbook.2015" -storepass "cookbook.2015" -file sec-dmn-node-2.
cer
```

As we need the domain controller to remotely connect to the host controllers and vice versa, we needed to create a link within the keystore, thus importing the host controllers' certificates into the domain controller keystore:

```
$ keytool -importcert -keystore sec-dmn-master.jks -storepass
"cookbook.2015" -trustcacerts -alias sec-dmn-node-1 -file sec-dmn-node-1.
cer
$ keytool -importcert -keystore sec-dmn-master.jks -storepass
"cookbook.2015" -trustcacerts -alias sec-dmn-node-2 -file sec-dmn-node-2.
cer
```

This way, the `sec-dmn-master.jks` keystore file would work as a truststore too, having the host controllers' certificates in it. As a matter of fact, on checking the `sec-dmn-master.jks` keystore, we should find three entries in it:

```
$ keytool -list -v -keystore sec-dmn-master.jks
Enter keystore password:

Keystore type: JKS
Keystore provider: SUN

Your keystore contains 3 entries

Alias name: sec-dmn-node-2

...

Alias name: sec-dmn-node-1

...

Alias name: sec-dmn-master
...
```

The same mechanism applies to the host controllers, having them only import the domain controller's certificate:

```
$ keytool -importcert -keystore sec-dmn-node-1.jks -storepass
"cookbook.2015" -trustcacerts -alias sec-dmn-master -file sec-dmn-master.
cer
$ keytool -importcert -keystore sec-dmn-node-2.jks -storepass
"cookbook.2015" -trustcacerts -alias sec-dmn-master -file sec-dmn-master.
cer
```

For brevity, I will not show you the check list for those two keystores; by the way you can issue the commands as follows:

```
keytool -list -v -keystore sec-dmn-node-1.jks
keytool -list -v -keystore sec-dmn-node-2.jks
```

They should both contain two entries.

After all this preparation, we had to start all servers in order to update our configuration. This is because in the domain mode we can only see the running hosts, not the declared ones. We then ran the CLI and executed a bunch of commands in the batch mode.

After the `run-batch` command, which essentially runs each command and commits, we run the `reload` command against the `host=master`, that is the domain controller.

When the domain controller starts, it pushes its configuration to all the connected host controllers, but in this case, our host controllers got disconnected because of the following errors showing up in the `server.log`:

- The following error is for `sec-dmn-master`:

  ```
  [Host Controller] ERROR [org.jboss.remoting.remote.connection]
  JBREM000200: Remote connection failed: javax.net.ssl.SSLException:
  Received fatal alert: certificate_unknown
  ```

- The following error is for `sec-dmn-node-1`:

  ```
  [Host Controller] WARN  [org.jboss.as.host.controller] JBAS010914:
  Connection to remote host-controller closed.
  [Host Controller] INFO  [org.jboss.as.host.controller] JBAS016584:
  Trying to reconnect to master host controller.
  [Host Controller] WARN  [org.jboss.as.host.controller]
  JBAS010900: Could not connect to remote domain controller at
  remote://127.0.0.1:9999 -- java.net.ConnectException: JBAS012174:
  Could not connect to remote://127.0.0.1:9999. The connection
  failed
  [Host Controller] WARN  [org.jboss.as.host.controller] JBAS016581:
  No domain controller discovery options remain.
  [Host Controller] INFO  [org.jboss.as.host.controller] JBAS016584:
  Trying to reconnect to master host controller.
  ```

```
[Host Controller] WARN  [org.jboss.as.host.controller]
JBAS010900: Could not connect to remote domain controller at
remote://127.0.0.1:9999 -- java.lang.IllegalStateException:
JBAS016509: Unable to connect due to SSL failure.
```

- The following error is for `sec-dmn-node-2`:

```
[Host Controller] WARN  [org.jboss.as.host.controller] JBAS010914:
Connection to remote host-controller closed.
[Host Controller] INFO  [org.jboss.as.host.controller] JBAS016584:
Trying to reconnect to master host controller.
[Host Controller] WARN  [org.jboss.as.host.controller]
JBAS010900: Could not connect to remote domain controller at
remote://127.0.0.1:9999 -- java.net.ConnectException: JBAS012174:
Could not connect to remote://127.0.0.1:9999. The connection
failed
[Host Controller] WARN  [org.jboss.as.host.controller] JBAS016581:
No domain controller discovery options remain.
[Host Controller] INFO  [org.jboss.as.host.controller] JBAS016584:
Trying to reconnect to master host controller.
[Host Controller] WARN  [org.jboss.as.host.controller]
JBAS010900: Could not connect to remote domain controller at
remote://127.0.0.1:9999 -- java.lang.IllegalStateException:
JBAS016509: Unable to connect due to SSL failure.
```

The domain controller enabled the SSL communication, and the host controllers are not passing their own certificate because the default JVM `cacert` truststore file is passed instead. That's why we had to stop everything.

When restarting the domain and host controllers, we had to add the `-Djavax.net.ssl.trustStore` property (specifying the proper keystore for the starting controller) so that the SSL Handshake phase would succeed, because at this time each controller would have passed its relative keystore.

Follow the commands to start the domain and host controllers:

```
./bin/domain.sh -Djboss.domain.base.dir=sec-dmn-master -Djavax.net.ssl.
trustStore=$WILDFLY_HOME/sec-dmn-master/configuration/sec-dmn-master.jks

./bin/domain.sh -Djboss.domain.base.dir=sec-dmn-node-1 -Djboss.
management.native.port=19999 -Djboss.domain.master.address=127.0.0.1
-Djavax.net.ssl.trustStore=$WILDFLY_HOME/sec-dmn-node-1/configuration/
sec-dmn-node-1.jks

./bin/domain.sh -Djboss.domain.base.dir=sec-dmn-node-2 -Djboss.
management.native.port=29999 -Djboss.domain.master.address=127.0.0.1
-Djavax.net.ssl.trustStore=$WILDFLY_HOME/sec-dmn-node-2/configuration/
sec-dmn-node-2.jks
```

## See also...

- For a deeper understanding of the `keytool` command, please refer to the Oracle official documentation at `https://docs.oracle.com/javase/8/docs/technotes/tools/unix/keytool.html`.
- For more details on the `SSL` protocol, start looking at `http://en.wikipedia.org/wiki/Transport_Layer_Security`.

# 11
# Hardening the WildFly Configuration

In this chapter, you will learn the following recipes:

- Delivering your configuration using property files
- Securing your configuration hashing passwords
- Securing and protecting passwords using a vault

## Introduction

In this chapter, you will learn how to secure your WildFly system configuration using different methods. Securing the configuration means hiding sensitive data, such as passwords, from other people who might collaborate on your project or system in one way or another.

This goal can be achieved in different ways:

- Using property files to externalize the dynamic parameters, such as bindings, credentials, and so on
- Hashing passwords—this is a quite common technique
- Storing passwords in a vault—this is the most secure method that you can use to protect your passwords

The first approach is not a totally secure one, thus it's a clean method to customize your settings. Still, it can give the freedom to distribute your configuration files without worrying about security concerns because there will just be default settings in it and nothing more. Furthermore, each of your WildFly infrastructure environments can rely on different property files. Configuration is the same; you just deliver a different property file.

The last two approaches are more focused on obfuscating passwords. Hashing uses a hash algorithm to encrypt the password. Thus, whoever sees the password in the XML configuration file will just see its hash value, not the real password.

Storing passwords in a vault is a little more complicated, but gives you better protection since a certificate is used to encrypt and decrypt the password.

# Delivering your configuration using property files

In this recipe, you will learn how to deliver you configuration using property files. This might be handy if you do not want to put all your settings' hardcode into the XML files, thus having to change them for each of your environments. This way, you can provide the general configuration via XML files and provide specific settings for your specific environment via property files.

Thanks to the property substitution feature provided by WildFly, you can use the `${your.property.goes.here}` syntax inside the XML files (that are `standalone.xml` or `domain.xml` and `host.xml`).

## Getting ready

To get started, let's first create an `ad-hoc` folder to run our WildFly. In a terminal window run the following commands:

```
$ cd $WILDFLY_HOME
$ cp -a standalone sec-std-cfg-node-1
```

Now it's time to create some property!

## How to do it...

1. First of all, let's create a property file named `wildflycookbook.properties` and add the following property and value:

   ```
   jboss.bind.address=10.0.0.1
   ```

2. Now create the preceding virtual IP in your system. In Linux, you would do it by opening a terminal window and running the following command:

   ```
   $ sudo ifconfig eth0:1 10.0.0.1 netmask 255.255.255.0
   ```

   where `eth0` is the name of your network interface.

3. Now, in a terminal window, execute the following command:

```
$ cd $WILDFLY_HOME
$ ./bin/standalone.sh -Djboss.server.base.dir=sec-std-cfg-node-1
-P wildflycookbook.properties
...
17:24:05,588 INFO  [org.wildfly.extension.undertow] (MSC service
thread 1-16) WFLYUT0006: Undertow HTTP listener default listening
on /10.0.0.1:8080
...
17:24:06,019 INFO  [org.jboss.as] (Controller Boot Thread)
WFLYSRV0025: WildFly Full 9.0.0.Beta2 (WildFly Core 1.0.0.Beta2)
started in 2822ms - Started 202 of 379 services (210 services are
lazy, passive or on-demand)
```

   As you can see from the log output, the emphasized characters, the property has been read from WildFly and placed into its configuration at runtime. So now our WildFly instance is bound to `http://10.0.0.1:8080`.

## How it works...

This approach is pretty easy and straightforward; there is not much to talk about except its usage. The preceding example gives you just an idea of what you can do with it.

The `-P file.property` directive is a WildFly feature to load a bunch of system properties from a property file. WildFly takes advantage of this mechanism by providing property substitution for its configurations.

Imagine a datasource configuration as follows:

```
<subsystem xmlns="urn:jboss:domain:datasources:1.1">
    <datasources>
    <datasource jndi-name="java:jboss/MySqlDS" pool-
    name="MySqlDS">
      <connection-url>jdbc:mysql://mysql-prod-cluster-node-
      1:3306/store</connection-url>
      <driver>mysql</driver>
      <security>
        <user-name>root</user-name>
        <password>1password</password>
      </security>
    </datasource>
    <drivers/>
    </datasources>
</subsystem>
```

As you can see, parameters to connect to the database, such as server name, server port, database name, and credentials are all hardcoded into the file.

Now suppose you need to replicate your WildFly configuration somewhere else, but the actual work will be done by a person outside your company. Would you give this person all this information? I guess not.

Having a property file can somehow protect you from giving such information, as follows:

```
<subsystem xmlns="urn:jboss:domain:datasources:1.1">
    <datasources>
    <datasource jndi-name="java:jboss/MySqlDS" pool-
    name="MySqlDS">
      <connection-url>${db.prod.conn.url}</connection-url>
      <driver>mysql</driver>
      <security>
        <user-name>${db.prod.uid}</user-name>
        <password>${db.prod.pwd}</password>
      </security>
    </datasource>
    <drivers/>
    </datasources>
</subsystem>
```

Obviously, the preceding property needs to be found and matched into a property file, with the following content:

```
db.prod.conn.url=jdbc:mysql://mysql-uat-cluster-node-1:3306/store
db.prod.uid=uat
dp.prod.pwd=uat-password
```

Much better!

## There's more...

Keep in mind that passing property or property files in Java keeps precedence ordering. Thus, passing a property with `-D` notation after specifying a property file would take precedence over the same property. The last one wins!

# Securing your configuration hashing passwords

In this recipe, you will learn how to mask passwords as configuration files so that they are not visible, or better, are meaningless for people looking at them.

You may have heard about transforming a text that should be secret or private, such as a password. Often times, terms such as encoding, encryption, and hashing are used indiscriminately, but they are not the same. Let's clear these concepts before we go.

Encoding a text is about transforming it to make it readable and acceptable for a different format (like the `&` symbol in HTML should be converted to `&`).

Encryption is about transforming a text to make it secret and meaningless. The transformation is based on a key and an algorithm (like AES, RSA, and Blowfish), such that the mix of the key and the algorithm makes the text completely different from its original content. Just the client who knows the key and the algorithm can revert the encrypted text to its original value.

Hashing is about integrity. This means that it is used to check whether a message (a text, a password, a file, and so on) which has arrived at its destination has been changed during its trip or not. A hash is not reversible. Given an input value, you will always get the same hash output. If you make a tiny change to your source, you will get a totally different hash output. There are several hash function algorithms, like MD5, SHA-3, and so on.

Let's try the MD5 checksum on a small piece of text, as follows:

```
$ md5sum <<< abcdef
5ab557c937e38f15291c04b7e99544ad  -
$ md5sum <<< abcdeF
7ab0aeb4ce14fd8efa00f3c903f72cf5  -
```

As you can see, by just changing the last character from `f` (lowercase) to `F` (uppercase), the MD5 checksum hash function gives a completely different output.

By the way, in this chapter, we will just use the term hash, either on transformed password by encoding, encrypting or hashing.

Okay, I hope I've given you a little more information on such topics that really need a deeper explanation. Other than a load of technical books which you can find for yourself, there is a quite interesting one named *The Code Book, Simon Singh*.

Let's go back to WildFly now.

## Getting ready

To get started, let's first create an `ad-hoc` folder to run our WildFly. In a terminal window execute the following:

```
$ cd $WILDFLY_HOME
$ cp -a standalone sec-std-cfg-node-2
```

Now it's time to create the hash for our password.

## How to do it...

1. Open a new terminal window and run the following commands:

   ```
   $ cd $WILDFLY_HOME
   $ java -cp modules/system/layers/base/org/picketbox/main/
   picketbox-4.9.0.Beta2.jar org.picketbox.datasource.security.
   SecureIdentityLoginModule cookbook.2015
   Encoded password: 2663ecfd3089b80f99cabb669aa2636e
   ```

   The output of the preceding script is your hashed password.

2. To accomplish this task, we rely on security domains. Create a security domain like the following:

   ```
   <security-domain name="encrypted-security-domain" cache-
   type="default">
     <authentication>
       <login-module
       code="org.picketbox.datasource.security.
       SecureIdentityLoginModule" flag="required">
         <module-option name="username" value="root"/>
         <module-option name="password"
         value="2663ecfd3089b80f99cabb669aa2636e"/>
       </login-module>
     </authentication>
   </security-domain>
   ```

3. Now, let's go back to our datasource definition and reference the security domain as follows:

   ```
   <subsystem xmlns="urn:jboss:domain:datasources:3.0">
       <datasources>
       <datasource jndi-name="java:jboss/MySqlDS" pool-
       name="MySqlDS">
         <connection-url>jdbc:mysql://mysql-prod-cluster-node-
         1:3306/store</connection-url>
   ```

```
            <driver>mysql</driver>
            <security>
              <security-domain>encrypted-security-
              domain</security-domain>
            </security>
          </datasource>
          <drivers/>
          </datasources>
      </subsystem>
```

Now it works. Neat!

## How it works...

All you have to do is generate the hash using the Pickbox security framework provided by WildFly and use its `SecurityIdentityLoginModule`.

After that, you need to create a security domain within your WildFly configuration, which uses the same program (that is the `SecurityIdentityLoginModule` class) that generated your password.

Next, whenever you need to provide a hashed password, just reference that security domain and you are done. In doing so, the security domain first generates a hash for the password it is receiving and then matches the generated hash with the one that you stored in your configuration. The rest is just a match/no-match matter.

To be able to use that password hash within our configuration file, we need to define a security domain which uses exactly the same functionality that generated the hash, otherwise it would be difficult to recognize a clear text password with an encrypted one.

For example, in a datasource definition, you cannot have the following XML code snippet:

```
<subsystem xmlns="urn:jboss:domain:datasources:3.0">
    <datasources>
    <datasource jndi-name="java:jboss/MySqlDS" pool-
    name="MySqlDS">
      <connection-url>jdbc:mysql://mysql-prod-cluster-node-
      1:3306/store</connection-url>
      <driver>mysql</driver>
      <security>
        <user-name>root</user-name>
        <password>2663ecfd3089b80f99cabb669aa2636e</password>
      </security>
    </datasource>
    <drivers/>
    </datasources>
</subsystem>
```

That is, using the password hash in place does not work! Who can tell if that password is a clear text one or a hashed one?

## There's more...

This kind of approach can be used not only for datasource, but even for `login-module` itself, JMS queues, and topics.

# Securing and protecting passwords using a vault

In this recipe, you will learn how to secure and protect our password, still providing them to our WildFly configuration. The vault is a place where you store passwords, encrypted using a keystore. For our recipe, we will create a keystore and store a password used to connect to the MySQL database. MySQL installation is out of the scope of this book; if you need more information, refer to the MySQL documentation site at `https://dev.mysql.com/doc/refman/5.5/en/installing.html`.

## Getting ready

To get started, let's first create an `ad-hoc` folder to run our WildFly:

1. In a terminal window run the following commands:

   ```
   $ cd $WILDFLY_HOME
   $ cp -a standalone sec-std-cfg-node-3
   ```

   Now it's time to create our keystore.

2. Within the same terminal window, execute the following:

   ```
   $ cd $WILDFLY_HOME
   $ cd sec-std-cfg-node-3/configuration
   $ mkdir vault
   $ cd vault
   $ keytool -v -genkey -alias wildfly.vault -keyalg RSA -keysize
   2048 -sigalg SHA1withRSA -keystore wildfly.vault.keystore
   Enter keystore password: [vault.2015]
   Re-enter new password: [vault.2015]
   What is your first and last name?
     [Unknown]:  WildFly Cookbook
   What is the name of your organizational unit?
   ```

```
  [Unknown]:  Packt Publishing
What is the name of your organization?
  [Unknown]:  packtpub.com
What is the name of your City or Locality?
  [Unknown]:  Birmingham
What is the name of your State or Province?
  [Unknown]:  GB
What is the two-letter country code for this unit?
  [Unknown]:  UK
Is CN=WildFly Cookbook, OU=Packt Publishing, O=packtpub.com,
L=Birmingham, ST=GB, C=UK correct?
  [no]:  yes

Generating 2,048 bit RSA key pair and self-signed certificate
(SHA1withRSA) with a validity of 90 days
  for: CN=WildFly Cookbook, OU=Packt Publishing,
  O=packtpub.com, L=Birmingham, ST=GB, C=UK
Enter key password for <wildfly.vault>
  (RETURN if same as keystore password):
[Storing wildfly.vault.keystore]
```

3. Okay, now we have created the keystore to encrypt our passwords. Let's check its integrity by executing the following command:

```
$ keytool -list -v -keystore wildfly.vault.keystore
Enter keystore password:

Keystore type: JKS
Keystore provider: SUN

Your keystore contains 1 entry

Alias name: wildfly.vault
Creation date: Dec 6, 2014
Entry type: PrivateKeyEntry
Certificate chain length: 1
Certificate[1]:
Owner: CN=WildFly Cookbook, OU=Packt Publishing, O=packtpub.com,
L=Birmingham, ST=GB, C=UK
```

```
Issuer: CN=WildFly Cookbook, OU=Packt Publishing, O=packtpub.com,
L=Birmingham, ST=GB, C=UK
Serial number: 6cfc82e9
Valid from: Sat Dec 06 14:43:16 CET 2014 until: Fri Mar 06
14:43:16 CET 2015
Certificate fingerprints:
   MD5:  FA:A6:5F:E6:7F:04:70:7E:70:FA:56:E7:9C:8A:B8:95
   SHA1:
  D2:18:BE:44:58:B1:57:54:0A:69:F9:E2:DB:3F:A7:82:7D:DE:DB:6B
   SHA256:
  8D:DF:16:64:3D:F6:08:08:71:8A:5F:4C:16:27:
  82:C8:20:75:FC:67:DD:9D:68:0E:0C:6F:08:7F:FA:E8:5D:18
   Signature algorithm name: SHA1withRSA
   Version: 3

Extensions:

#1: ObjectId: 2.5.29.14 Criticality=false
SubjectKeyIdentifier [
KeyIdentifier [
0000: 68 21 C0 CE C1 A5 A0 11   3D 5B EE E8 18 92 72 ED
h!......=[....r.
0010: C4 28 46 2B                                        .(F+
]
]



*******************************************
*******************************************
```

Okay, everything is fine! We are now ready to encrypt our passwords and store them into a vault.

## How to do it...

To generate a vault, WildFly provides us with a script, `vault.sh`, inside the `bin` folder.

As an example, we will generate a vault that stores a password that will be used to connect to a database:

1. Open a terminal window and execute the following:

```
$ cd $WILDFLY_HOME/sec-std-cfg-node-3/configuration
$ $WILDFLY_HOME/bin/vault.sh -a PASSWORD -x cookbook.2015 -b
DB-PROD -i 50 -k vault/wildfly.vault.keystore -p vault.2015 -s
86427531 -v wildfly.vault

...

Dec 06, 2014 10:28:20 PM org.picketbox.plugins.vault.
PicketBoxSecurityVault init
INFO: PBOX000361: Default Security Vault Implementation
Initialized and Ready
Secured attribute value has been stored in Vault.
Please make note of the following:
********************************************
Vault Block:DB-PROD
Attribute Name:PASSWORD
Configuration should be done as follows:
VAULT::DB-PROD::PASSWORD::1
********************************************
Vault Configuration in WildFly configuration file:
********************************************
...
</extensions>
<vault>
  <vault-option name="KEYSTORE_URL" value="vault/wildfly.vault.
keystore"/>
  <vault-option name="KEYSTORE_PASSWORD" value="MASK-
1cn1ENbx4KLXxve5VvGlPy"/>
  <vault-option name="KEYSTORE_ALIAS" value="wildfly.vault"/>
  <vault-option name="SALT" value="86427531"/>
```

```
    <vault-option name="ITERATION_COUNT" value="50"/>
    <vault-option name="ENC_FILE_DIR" value="vault/"/>
</vault><management> ...
******************************************
```

The preceding script is the `vault.sh` output and it depicts the following points:

- How to reference the password stored in the vault
- A file named `VAULT.dat` inside a `vault` folder
- An XML code snippet to be placed into the `standalone.xml` or `host.xml` file

2. We can now use the vault in our datasource configuration, as follows:

```
<datasource jndi-name="java:jboss/datasources/VaultDS" pool-
name="VaultDS" enabled="true" use-java-context="true">
    <connection-url>jdbc:mysql://192.168.59.103:3306/test
</connection-url>
    <driver>mysql</driver>
    <security>
        <user-name>root</user-name>
        <password>${VAULT::DB-PROD::PASSWORD::1}</password>
    </security>
</datasource>
```

To test our configuration, we need a running MySQL server. In my case, it is bound to a server running at `192.168.59.103:3306`. Furthermore, we need to configure the connection pool in order to instantly put valid connections into it that act as proof.

3. So the datasource configuration is as follows:

```
<datasource jndi-name="java:jboss/datasources/VaultDS" pool-
name="VaultDS" enabled="true">
    <connection-
    url>jdbc:mysql://192.168.59.103:3306/test</connection-
    url>
    <driver>mysql</driver>
    <pool>
        <min-pool-size>5</min-pool-size>
        <max-pool-size>5</max-pool-size>
        <prefill>true</prefill>
    </pool>
    <security>
        <user-name>root</user-name>
        <password>${VAULT::DB-PROD::PASSWORD::1}</password>
    </security>
</datasource>
```

4. Let's start our WildFly instance and take a look at the logs. Run the following command:

```
$ ./bin/standalone.sh -Djboss.server.base.dir=sec-std-cfg-node-3
...
15:32:35,607 INFO  [org.jboss.as.server.deployment.
scanner] (MSC service thread 1-4) JBAS015012: Started
FileSystemDeploymentService for directory /opt/wildfly/sec-std-
cfg-node-2/deployments
15:32:35,636 INFO  [org.jboss.as.connector.subsystems.datasources]
(MSC service thread 1-1) JBAS010400: Bound data source
[java:jboss/datasources/VaultDS]
15:32:35,636 INFO  [org.jboss.as.connector.subsystems.datasources]
(MSC service thread 1-13) JBAS010400: Bound data source
[java:jboss/datasources/ExampleDS]
15:32:35,676 INFO  [org.jboss.ws.common.management] (MSC service
thread 1-12) JBWS022052: Starting JBoss Web Services - Stack CXF
Server 4.2.4.Final
15:32:35,722 INFO  [org.jboss.as] (Controller Boot
Thread) JBAS015961: Http management interface listening on
http://127.0.0.1:9990/management
15:32:35,723 INFO  [org.jboss.as] (Controller Boot Thread)
JBAS015951: Admin console listening on http://127.0.0.1:9990
15:32:35,723 INFO  [org.jboss.as] (Controller Boot Thread)
JBAS015874: WildFly 8.1.0.Final "Kenny" started in 3854ms -
Started 203 of 251 services (81 services are lazy, passive or on-
demand)
```

5. In the log, I've emphasized the statement pointing out the `VaultDS` datasource, which is successfully bounded. Now open a new terminal window and connect to the CLI to check our available connections, as follows:

```
$ ./bin/jboss-cli.sh
You are disconnected at the moment. Type 'connect' to connect to
the server or 'help' for the list of supported commands.
[disconnected /] connect
[standalone@localhost:9990 /] /subsystem=datasources/data-
source=VaultDS/statistics=pool:read-resource(include-runtime=true)
{
    "outcome" => "success",
    "result" => {
        "ActiveCount" => "5",
        "AvailableCount" => "5",
        "AverageBlockingTime" => "0",
```

```
            "AverageCreationTime" => "36",
            "AverageGetTime" => "0",
            "BlockingFailureCount" => "0",
            "CreatedCount" => "5",
            "DestroyedCount" => "0",
            "IdleCount" => "5",
            "InUseCount" => "0",
            "MaxCreationTime" => "43",
            "MaxGetTime" => "0",
            "MaxUsedCount" => "1",
            "MaxWaitCount" => "0",
            "MaxWaitTime" => "0",
            "TimedOut" => "0",
            "TotalBlockingTime" => "0",
            "TotalCreationTime" => "180",
            "TotalGetTime" => "0",
            "WaitCount" => "0"
        }
    }
[standalone@localhost:9990 /]
```

Great! From the preceding output, we can say that the connection pool of our `VaultDS` datasource is filled with five available and active connections.

6. Now, just to prove that we are doing well, let's try adding two more datasources connecting to the same database; one using a password in clear text, the other one using a wrong vault-block definition. Add the following datasource definition:

```
<datasource jndi-name="java:jboss/datasources/UnsecureDS" pool-
name="UnsecureDS" enabled="true">
    <connection-
    url>jdbc:mysql://192.168.59.103:3306/test</connection-
    url>
    <driver>mysql</driver>
    <pool>
        <min-pool-size>2</min-pool-size>
        <max-pool-size>2</max-pool-size>
        <prefill>true</prefill>
    </pool>
    <security>
        <user-name>root</user-name>
```

```
        <password>cookbook.2015</password>
    </security>
</datasource>
<datasource jndi-name="java:jboss/datasources/WrongVaultDS" pool-
name="WrongVaultDS" enabled="true">
    <connection-
    url>jdbc:mysql://192.168.59.103:3306/test</connection-
    url>
    <driver>mysql</driver>
    <pool>
        <min-pool-size>1</min-pool-size>
        <max-pool-size>1</max-pool-size>
        <prefill>true</prefill>
    </pool>
    <security>
        <user-name>root</user-name>
        <password>${VAULT::DB-TEST::PASSWORD::1}</password>
    </security>
</datasource>
```

7. The `UnsecureDS` datasource connects to the database using a clear text password, whilst the `WrongVaultDS` is using a wrong `vault-block`, that is `DB-TEST` which we didn't create. Let's start our WildFly once again and catch the logs for errors. Execute the following command:

```
$ ./bin/standalone.sh -Djboss.server.base.dir=sec-std-cfg-node-3
...
15:52:08,452 ERROR [org.jboss.as.controller.management-operation]
(ServerService Thread Pool -- 27) JBAS014612: Operation ("add")
failed - address: ([
    ("subsystem" => "datasources"),
    ("data-source" => "WrongVaultDS")
]): java.lang.SecurityException: JBAS013311: Security Exception
  at  org.jboss.as.security.vault.RuntimeVaultReader.
  retrieveFromVault(RuntimeVaultReader.java:104)
  at org.jboss.as.server.RuntimeExpressionResolver.
  resolvePluggableExpression
  (RuntimeExpressionResolver.java:45)
...
15:52:08,499 INFO  [org.wildfly.extension.undertow] (MSC service
thread 1-2) JBAS017519: Undertow HTTP listener default listening
on /127.0.0.1:8080
```

```
15:52:08,499 INFO  [org.wildfly.extension.undertow] (MSC service
thread 1-4) JBAS017519: Undertow AJP listener ajp listening on
/127.0.0.1:8009
15:52:08,631 ERROR [org.jboss.as.controller.management-operation]
(Controller Boot Thread) "JBAS014784: Failed executing subsystem
datasources boot operations"
15:52:08,633 ERROR [org.jboss.as.controller.management-operation]
(Controller Boot Thread) JBAS014613: Operation ("parallel-
subsystem-boot") failed - address: ([]) - failure description:
"\"JBAS014784: Failed executing subsystem datasources boot
operations\""
15:52:08,670 INFO  [org.jboss.as.server.deployment.
scanner] (MSC service thread 1-1) JBAS015012: Started
FileSystemDeploymentService for directory /Users/foogaro/wildfly-
8.1.0.Final/sec-std-cfg-node-2/deployments
15:52:08,705 INFO  [org.jboss.ws.common.management] (MSC service
thread 1-5) JBWS022052: Starting JBoss Web Services - Stack CXF
Server 4.2.4.Final
15:52:08,706 ERROR [org.jboss.as.controller.management-operation]
(Controller Boot Thread) JBAS014613: Operation ("add") failed -
address: ([
    ("subsystem" => "datasources"),
    ("data-source" => "WrongVaultDS")
]) - failure description: "JBAS014749: Operation handler failed:
JBAS013311: Security Exception"
15:52:08,748 INFO  [org.jboss.as] (Controller Boot
Thread) JBAS015961: Http management interface listening on
http://127.0.0.1:9990/management
15:52:08,748 INFO  [org.jboss.as] (Controller Boot Thread)
JBAS015951: Admin console listening on http://127.0.0.1:9990
15:52:08,749 INFO  [org.jboss.as] (Controller Boot Thread)
JBAS015874: WildFly 8.1.0.Final "Kenny" started in 3150ms -
Started 183 of 231 services (81 services are lazy, passive or on-
demand)
```

As you can see, the log is showing errors and complaining about a `SecurityException` regarding the `WrongVaultDS`. Thus, all the datasource subsystem is in error and not initialized.

8. Try removing `WrongVaultDS` from the datasource definition, start WildFly once again and you should find the following log entries:

   ```
   15:57:07,585 INFO  [org.jboss.as.connector.subsystems.datasources]
   (MSC service thread 1-11) JBAS010400: Bound data source
   [java:jboss/datasources/VaultDS]
   15:57:07,585 INFO  [org.jboss.as.connector.subsystems.datasources]
   (MSC service thread 1-16) JBAS010400: Bound data source
   [java:jboss/datasources/UnsecureDS]
   ```

As you can see, both `VaultDS` and `UnsecureDS` are properly bound.

## How it works...

The `keytool` command is a tool provided by the Java SE platform, but understanding its usage and parameters is out of the scope of this book. However, a link to the official documentation provided by Oracle has been given in the *See also...* section of this recipe.

Let's analyze the vault script used in this recipe and provided by WildFly for you. Let's first see what option we have with the preceding script, by issuing the following command in a terminal window:

```
$ ./bin/vault.sh --help
usage: vault.sh <empty> |  [-a <arg>] [-b <arg>] -c | -h | -x <arg> [-e
      <arg>]  [-i <arg>] [-k <arg>] [-p <arg>] [-s <arg>] [-v <arg>]
 -a,--attribute <arg>          Attribute name
 -b,--vault-block <arg>        Vault block
 -c,--check-sec-attr           Check whether the secured attribute
                               already exists in the Vault
 -e,--enc-dir <arg>            Directory containing encrypted files
 -h,--help                     Help
 -i,--iteration <arg>          Iteration count
 -k,--keystore <arg>           Keystore URL
 -p,--keystore-password <arg>  Keystore password
 -s,--salt <arg>               8 character salt
 -v,--alias <arg>              Vault keystore alias
 -x,--sec-attr <arg>           Secured attribute value (such as
                               password)to store
```

Now check how we invoked the script:

```
$ cd $WILDFLY_HOME/sec-std-cfg-node-3/configuration
$ $WILDFLY_HOME/bin/vault.sh -a PASSWORD -x cookbook.2015 -b DB-PROD -i
50 -k vault/wildfly.vault.keystore -p vault.2015 -s 86427531 -v wildfly.
vault
```

So, we created an attribute named `PASSWORD` using the `-a` (minus `a`) notation, we then set its value as `cookbook.2015` using the `-x` (minus `x`) notation. Then, we created a vault-block to store the attribute and its value using the `-b` (minus `b`) notation. The rest of the parameters are used to bind the keystore which encrypts the attribute value, which is our password.

The `vault.sh` script generates for us a helpful output to invoke and reference the vault and the vault-block, which maps to our password. Using the information that it needs, WildFly is able to automatically extract the password and pass it to the component that is requesting it.

## There's more...

The vault can store more passwords just by providing a different `vault-block`.

For example, at the end of the *How to do it...* section of this recipe, we tried to bind a datasource (`WrongVaultDS`) using a different `vault-block`; we called it `DB-TEST`. As a result, we couldn't bind that datasource and thus, the whole datasource subsystem was in error. Let's now try to add the same datasource definition, but this time, we will also provide the `DB-TEST` vault-block to our vault file:

1. Open a terminal window, and execute the following command:

```
$ cd $WILDFLY_HOME/sec-std-cfg-node-2/configuration
$ $WILDFLY_HOME/bin/vault.sh -a PASSWORD -x cookbook.2015 -b
DB-TEST -i 50 -k vault/wildfly.vault.keystore -p vault.2015 -s
86427531 -v wildfly.vault
...
Dec 08, 2014 4:20:17 PM org.picketbox.plugins.vault.
PicketBoxSecurityVault init
INFO: PBOX000361: Default Security Vault Implementation
Initialized and Ready
Secured attribute value has been stored in Vault.
Please make note of the following:
********************************************
Vault Block:DB-TEST
Attribute Name:PASSWORD
Configuration should be done as follows:
VAULT::DB-TEST::PASSWORD::1
```

```
******************************************

Vault Configuration in WildFly configuration file:

******************************************

...

</extensions>

<vault>

  <vault-option name="KEYSTORE_URL" value="vault/wildfly.vault.
keystore"/>

  <vault-option name="KEYSTORE_PASSWORD" value="MASK-
1cn1ENbx4KLXxve5VvGlPy"/>

  <vault-option name="KEYSTORE_ALIAS" value="wildfly.vault"/>

  <vault-option name="SALT" value="86427531"/>

  <vault-option name="ITERATION_COUNT" value="50"/>

  <vault-option name="ENC_FILE_DIR" value="vault/"/>

</vault><management> ...

******************************************
```

2. Now edit the `standalone.xml` file and add the following XML code snippet:

```
<datasource jndi-name="java:jboss/datasources/WrongVaultDS" pool-
name="WrongVaultDS" enabled="true">
    <connection-
    url>jdbc:mysql://192.168.59.103:3306/test</connection-
    url>
    <driver>mysql</driver>
    <pool>
        <min-pool-size>1</min-pool-size>
        <max pool-size>1</max-pool-size>
        <prefill>true</prefill>
    </pool>
    <security>
        <user-name>root</user-name>
        <password>${VAULT::DB-TEST::PASSWORD::1}</password>
    </security>
</datasource>
```

3. Now, start WildFly as usual and look at the log. Run the following command:

```
$ ./bin/standalone.sh -Djboss.server.base.dir=sec-std-cfg-node-3

...

16:33:02,063 INFO  [org.jboss.as.connector.subsystems.datasources]
(MSC service thread 1-3) JBAS010400: Bound data source
[java:jboss/datasources/WrongVaultDS]
```

```
16:33:02,063 INFO  [org.jboss.as.connector.subsystems.datasources]
(MSC service thread 1-6) JBAS010400: Bound data source
[java:jboss/datasources/ExampleDS]
16:33:02,063 INFO  [org.jboss.as.connector.subsystems.datasources]
(MSC service thread 1-2) JBAS010400: Bound data source
[java:jboss/datasources/VaultDS]
16:33:02,063 INFO  [org.jboss.as.connector.subsystems.datasources]
(MSC service thread 1-9) JBAS010400: Bound data source
[java:jboss/datasources/UnsecureDS]
16:33:02,064 INFO  [org.jboss.ws.common.management] (MSC service
thread 1-5) JBWS022052: Starting JBoss Web Services - Stack CXF
Server 4.2.4.Final
16:33:02,118 INFO  [org.jboss.as] (Controller Boot
Thread) JBAS015961: Http management interface listening on
http://127.0.0.1:9990/management
16:33:02,119 INFO  [org.jboss.as] (Controller Boot Thread)
JBAS015951: Admin console listening on http://127.0.0.1:9990
16:33:02,120 INFO  [org.jboss.as] (Controller Boot Thread)
JBAS015874: WildFly 8.1.0.Final "Kenny" started in 1992ms -
Started 203 of 251 services (81 services are lazy, passive or on-
demand)
```

It worked! As you can see, you can define and store all passwords that you want in a vault as long as you declare a different vault-block.

## See also

- For a deep understanding of the keytool command, please refer to the Oracle official documentation at `https://docs.oracle.com/javase/8/docs/technotes/tools/unix/keytool.html`

# 12
# Role-based Access Control with WildFly

In this chapter, you will learn the following recipes:

- Switching between simple and RBAC providers
- Managing users, groups, and their role mapping
- Setting a predefined role to all authenticated users
- Granting user access by server group or host - scoped roles
- Integrating with OpenLDAP

## Introduction

In this chapter, you will learn how to improve your WildFly management console by providing a fine-grained access control mechanism. WildFly comes with two built-in providers: one is called simple, which is the default one and the second one is called RBAC—as you guessed, it stands for **role-based access control**.

Switching to the RBAC provider means you can control what a user can do and see, and what kinds of operations the user is allowed to perform. Using the RBAC provider, you are basically sharing responsibility with different users. You might want some users to just make deployments, others to occasionally monitor the overall system, and so on. Furthermore, we will see how to integrate RBAC with an LDAP system (which provides users and groups), and mapping them to the WildFly roles.

WildFly comes with a set of predefined roles, each one having a specific permission. These roles are as follows:

- **Monitor**: As the name may suggest, this role can just view the state of the server, but it cannot see sensitive data, such as passwords.
- **Operator**: This role has the same permissions as those provided by the monitor, plus it can stop and start a server, or pause runtime services such as JMS destinations. You would typically give such a role to people who are responsible for managing a specific server instance. Still, an operator cannot see sensitive data, such as passwords.
- **Maintainer**: This role has the permissions to view and edit all the runtime states and all configurations, besides sensitive data. Users with such a role can manage almost the entire system.
- **Deployer**: This role is like the monitor role, plus it can read and modify the configuration and the state of deployments.
- **Auditor**: This role is like the monitor role, plus it can view sensitive data. It also has access to the audit logging subsystem.
- **Administrator**: This role can do anything, view and modify everything except the audit logging subsystem. The administrator can also configure the RBAC provider.
- **SuperUser**: This is the most powerful role. It can view and modify resources, state, and sensitive data. This role is the one that was used before the RBAC was introduced.

These roles can be combined together to form a group of roles, which can be used by a specific user.

# Switching between simple and RBAC providers

In this recipe, we will learn how to switch from the simple provider to the RBAC provider. RBAC provides a fine-grained access control to our management console.

## Getting ready

To get started, let's first create an `ad-hoc` folder to run our WildFly. In a terminal window, execute the following commands:

```
$ cd $WILDFLY_HOME
$ cp -a standalone rbac-std-node-1
```

Now it's time to run our WildFly!!!

## How to do it...

Perform the following steps:

1. Open a terminal window and enter the following commands:

```
$ cd $WILDFLY_HOME
$ ./bin/standalone.sh -Djboss.server.base.dir=rbac-std-node-1
```

2. Once started, in a new terminal window, connect to the CLI and switch to the RBAC provider, as follows:

```
$ cd $WILDFLY_HOME
$ ./bin/jboss-cli.sh
You are disconnected at the moment. Type 'connect' to connect to the server or 'help' for the list of supported commands.
[disconnected /] connect
[standalone@localhost:9990 /] /core-service=management/access=authorization:write-attribute(name=provider,value=rbac)
{
    "outcome" => "success",
    "response-headers" => {
        "operation-requires-reload" => true,
        "process-state" => "reload-required"
    }
}
[standalone@localhost:9990 /] :reload()
{
    "outcome" => "success",
    "result" => undefined
}
[standalone@localhost:9990 /]
```

Great, we successfully switched to the RBAC provider.

3. In our `standalone.xml` file, we should find the following definition:

```
<access-control provider="rbac">
    <role-mapping>
        <role name="SuperUser">
            <include>
                <user name="$local"/>
            </include>
        </role>
    </role-mapping>
</access-control>
```

4. To switch back to the `simple` provider, do as follows:

```
standalone@localhost:9990 /] /core-service=management/
access=authorization:write-attribute(name=provider,value=simple)
{
    "outcome" => "success",
    "response-headers" => {
        "operation-requires-reload" => true,
        "process-state" => "reload-required"
    }
}
[standalone@localhost:9990 /] :reload()
{
    "outcome" => "success",
    "result" => undefined
}
[standalone@localhost:9990 /]
```

5. In our `standalone.xml` file, we should find the following definition:

```
<access-control provider="simple">
    <role-mapping>
        <role name="SuperUser">
            <include>
                <user name="$local"/>
            </include>
        </role>
    </role-mapping>
</access-control>
```

That's it, pretty easy so far!!!

## How it works...

This approach is pretty easy and straightforward; there is not much to talk about except its usage. The preceding example is just the first step. As a matter of fact, if you try to access the console after you switch to the `RBAC` provider, you are not able to log in.

Try it!!! Open the browser and point it to `http://localhost:9990`. Enter the username and password that we specified at the beginning of the book: `wildfly` as the username and `cookbook.2015` as the password.

See, you cannot log in. How to resolve this?

From the preceding XML code snippet, you should have noticed the directive `include` referring the user named `$local`. In this case, `$local` means the users defined within the `ManagementRealm` and `ApplicationRealm` realms, but with no privileges at all to access the console.

What we should do, is add our `wildfly` user from `ManagementRealm` in the `include` XML element, as follows:

```
[standalone@localhost:9990 /] /core-service=management/
access=authorization/role-mapping=SuperUser/
include=wildfly:add(name=wildfly,realm=ManagementRealm,type=USER)
{"outcome" => "success"}
[standalone@localhost:9990 /]
```

The preceding commands generate the following XML code into our `standalone.xml` file:

```
<access-control provider="rbac">
    <role-mapping>
        <role name="SuperUser">
            <include>
                <user name="$local"/>
                <user alias="wildfly" realm="ManagementRealm"
                name="wildfly"/>
            </include>
        </role>
    </role-mapping>
</access-control>
```

Now if we try to access the console as usual, we should be able to log in successfully.

## There's more...

Regardless the providers that you have chosen, once logged in, you can see the role of your user, by clicking on the username, displayed on the top-right corner of the web console:

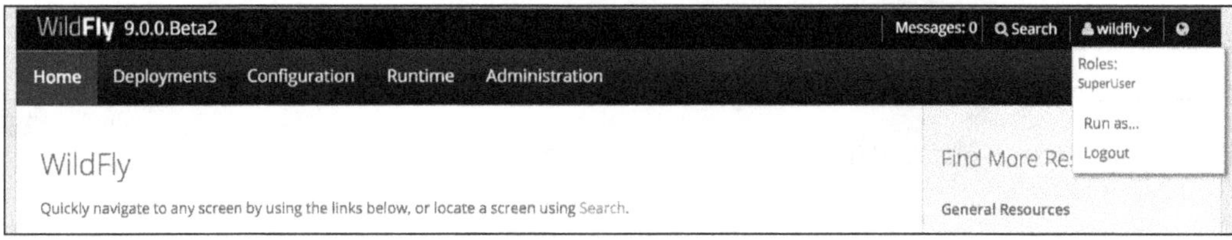


Displaying current logged user's role

As you can see, we have a role called **SuperUser**. Looking a little bit further, there is an interesting link **Run as...** which should intrigue you. Let's click it!

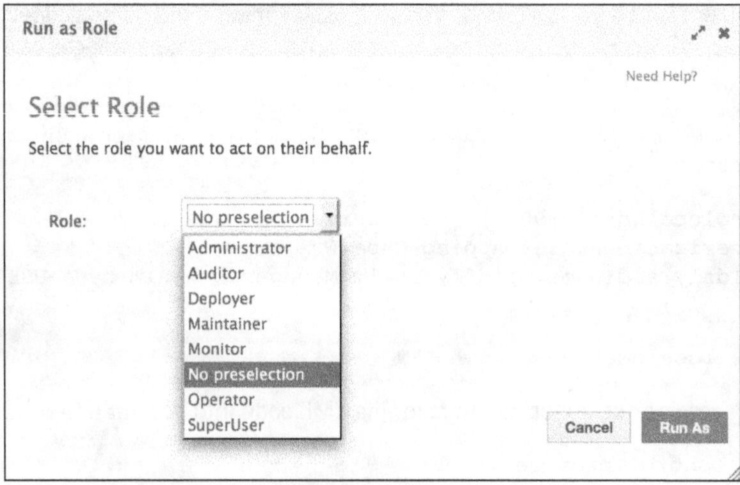


Run as role selection role pop-up

Try to play around with it to better understand the different roles and the permissions you get. For example, try to deploy an application using the **Monitor** role, or check if you can view or edit the username and password of a datasource. Be curious!

# Managing users, groups, and their role mapping

In this recipe, you will learn how to manage users, groups, and their relative mapping to the WildFly roles. We will perform most of the tasks from within the Web Console.

## Getting ready

To get started, let's first create an `ad-hoc` folder to run our WildFly. In a terminal window, execute the following commands:

```
$ cd $WILDFLY_HOME
$ cp -a standalone rbac-std-node-2
```

Now it's time to run our WildFly.

## How to do it...

1. Open a terminal window and enter the following commands:

   ```
   $ cd $WILDFLY_HOME
   $ ./bin/standalone.sh -Djboss.server.base.dir=rbac-std-node-2
   ```

2. Once started, connect to the CLI and switch to the RBAC provider in a new terminal window as we did in the previous recipe:

   ```
   $ cd $WILDFLY_HOME
   $ ./bin/jboss-cli.sh
   You are disconnected at the moment. Type 'connect' to connect to the server or 'help' for the list of supported commands.
   [disconnected /] connect
   [standalone@localhost:9990 /] /core-service=management/access=authorization:write-attribute(name=provider,value=rbac)
   {
       "outcome" => "success",
       "response-headers" => {
           "operation-requires-reload" => true,
           "process-state" => "reload-required"
       }
   }
   [standalone@localhost:9990 /] :reload()
   {
       "outcome" => "success",
       "result" => undefined
   }
   [standalone@localhost:9990 /]
   ```

3. Now that we've successfully switched to the RBAC provider, we need to map our local management user (if you've been following the book, you'll know it is **wildfly**) to the **SuperUser** role, as follows:

   ```
   [standalone@localhost:9990 /] /core-service=management/access=authorization/role-mapping=SuperUser/include=wildfly:add(name=wildfly,realm=ManagementRealm,type=USER)
   {"outcome" => "success"}
   [standalone@localhost:9990 /]
   ```

Okay, we can now access the Web Console, and see how we can manage users, groups, and their relative mappings.

## Users

Let's first add some users:

1. In a new terminal window, execute the following commands:

```
$ cd $WILDFLY_HOME
$ ./bin/add-user.sh --silent=true devguy devguy.2015 -sc rbac-std-node-2/configuration
$ ./bin/add-user.sh --silent=true opsguy opsguy.2015 -sc rbac-std-node-2/configuration
$ ./bin/add-user.sh --silent=true devopsguy devopsguy.2015 -sc rbac-std-node-2/configuration
$ ./bin/add-user.sh --silent=true pmguy pmguy.2015 -sc rbac-std-node-2/configuration
```

2. Okay, now let's open the browser and point it to `http://localhost:9990`.
3. Once logged in as the **wildfly** user, click on the Administration tab and you should see a page like the following:

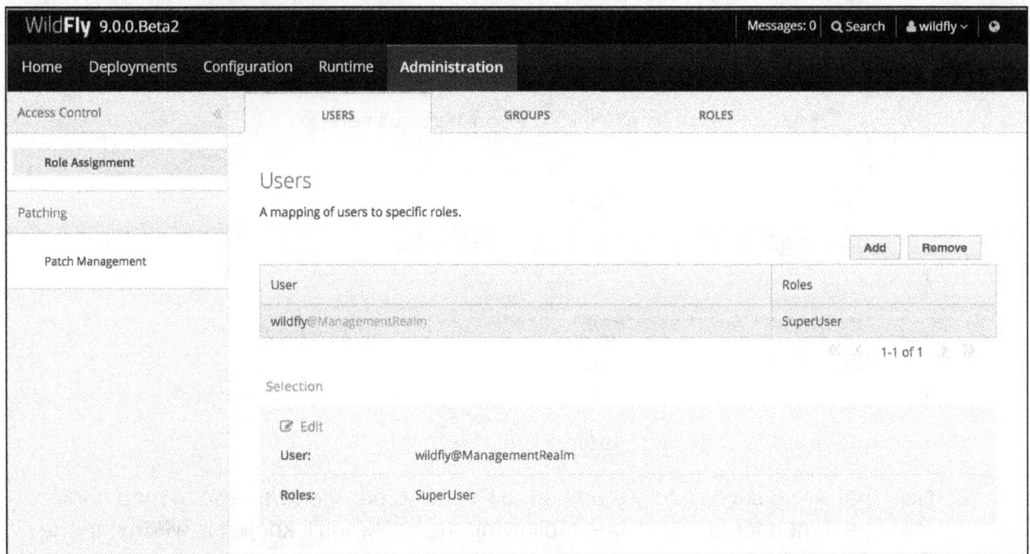


Displaying RBAC users

4. Our **wildfly** user is there. Let's add the user `devguy` by clicking on the button labeled **Add**, and filling in the form as follows:

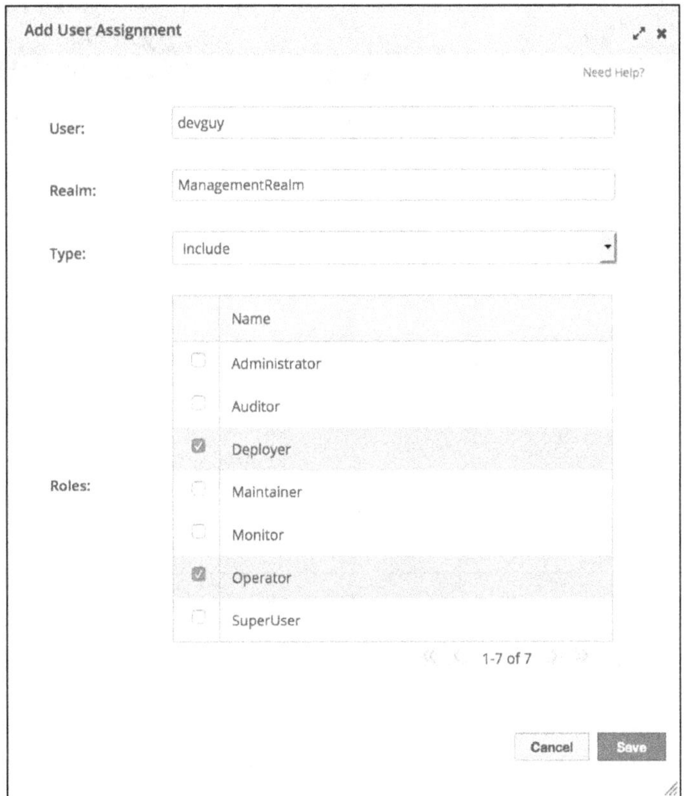


RBAC form for adding a user and its roles

5. Confirm by clicking the **Save** button. Now we should have the new user added to the list, as depicted in the next image:

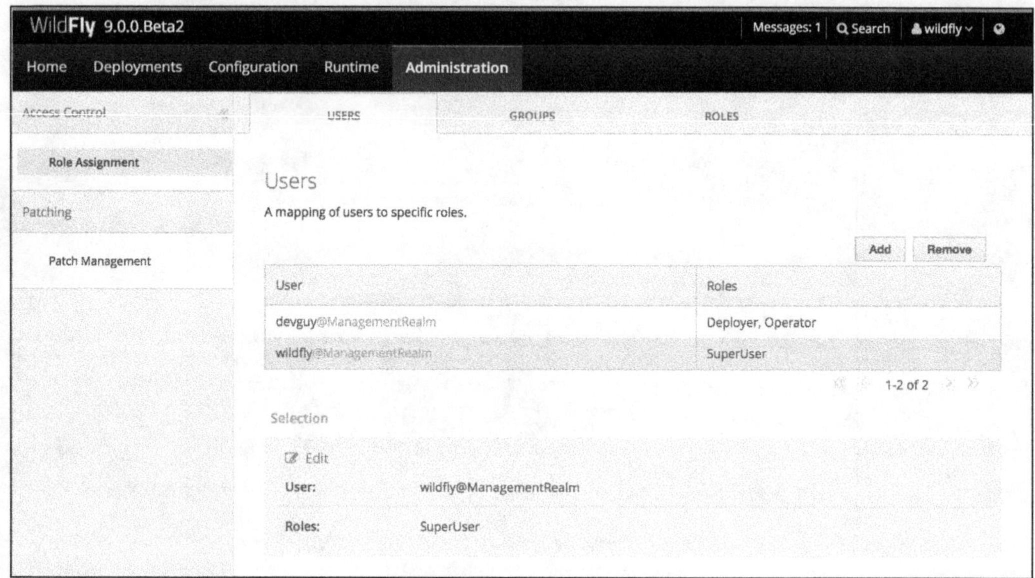


Displaying the newly added user devguy

6. If we cannot access the Web Console for any reason, we can rely on the CLI, and specify the following commands:

```
[standalone@localhost:9990 /] /core-service=management/
access=authorization/role-mapping=Deployer:add
{"outcome" => "success"}
[standalone@localhost:9990 /] /core-service=management/
access=authorization/role-mapping=Deployer/include=devguy:add(name
=devguy,type=USER,realm=ManagementRealm)
{"outcome" => "success"}
[standalone@localhost:9990 /] /core-service=management/
access=authorization/role-mapping=Operator:add
{"outcome" => "success"}
[standalone@localhost:9990 /] /core-service=management/
access=authorization/role-mapping=Operator/include=devguy:add(name
=devguy,type=USER,realm=ManagementRealm)
{"outcome" => "success"}
[standalone@localhost:9990 /]
```

7. Let's add the other users, `opsguy`, `devopsguy`, and `pmguy`, giving them appropriate roles:
    - `opsguy`: Roles of the maintainer and operator
    - `devopsguy`: Role of the administrator
    - `pmguy`: Role of the monitor
8. You should have the following list:

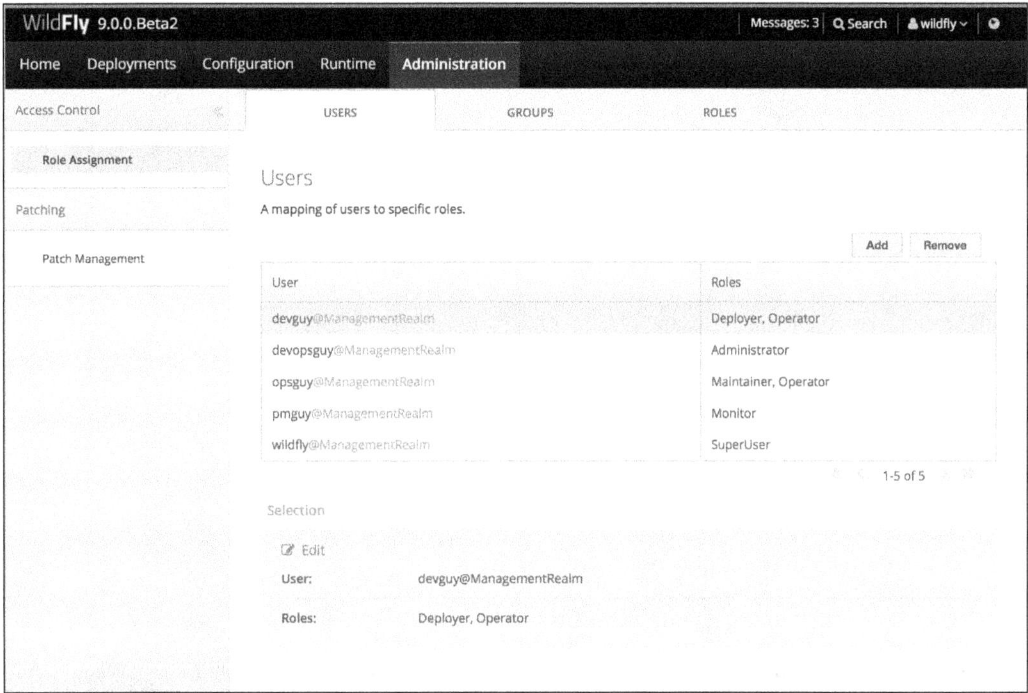


List of users

Now that we've entered all our users, let's try one of them.

9. So log out and log back in with the user `pmguy`. Once we are back in, let's go to the **Deployments** tab. You see a page similar to the following:

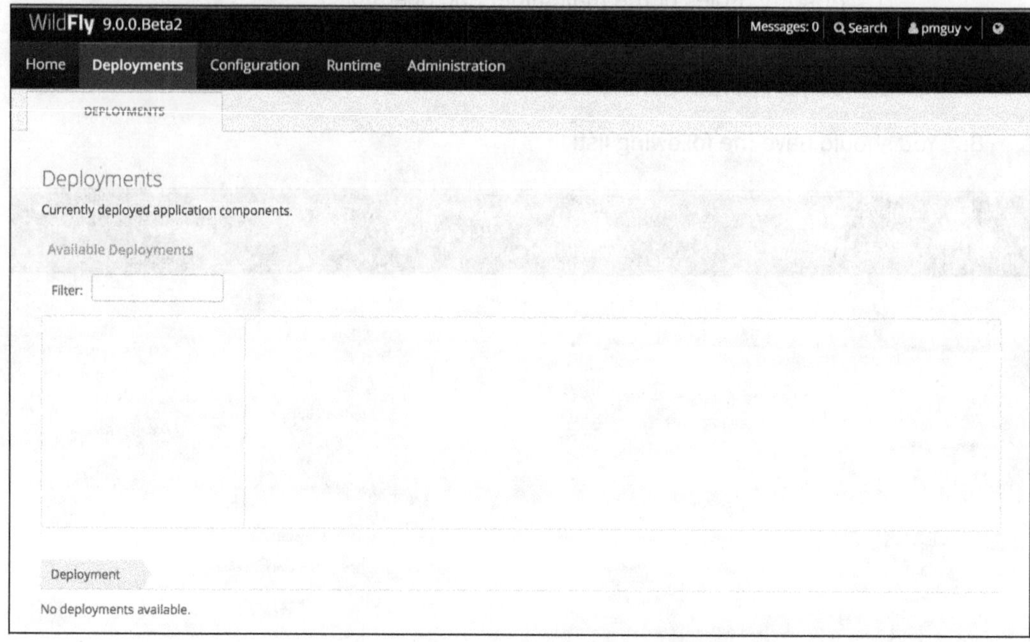


Deployments page without any buttons to alter deployments

As you can see, we cannot manage our deployments, we cannot remove or disable them, nor can we deploy new applications.

10. Let's go back to our **Administration** tab and see if we can add a more powerful role:

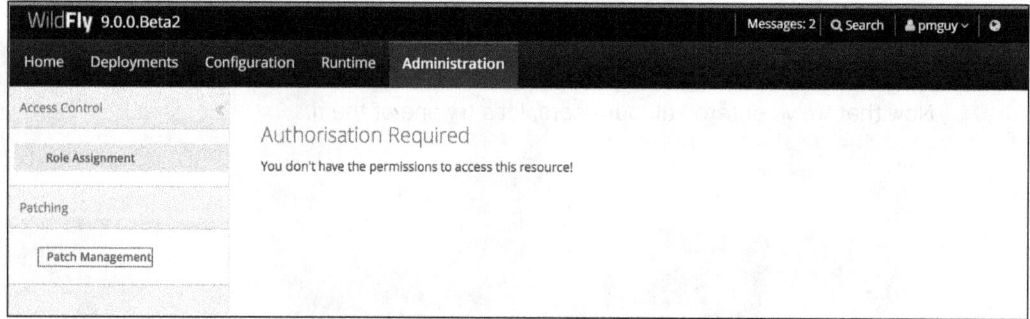


Administration page warning about Authorization Required

We can't; only users with the Administrator and SuperUser roles can.

## Groups

As we saw, every role has specific permissions on what you can and can't do, and on what you can and cannot see. Despite the simple mapping user roles, you can manage and combine multiple roles under a specific group.

Let's create two groups: `development` and `operations`:

1. If you are still logged in as the `pmguy` user, log off and log back in with as the `wildfly` user.
2. Once there, go to the **Administration** tab and click **Groups**:

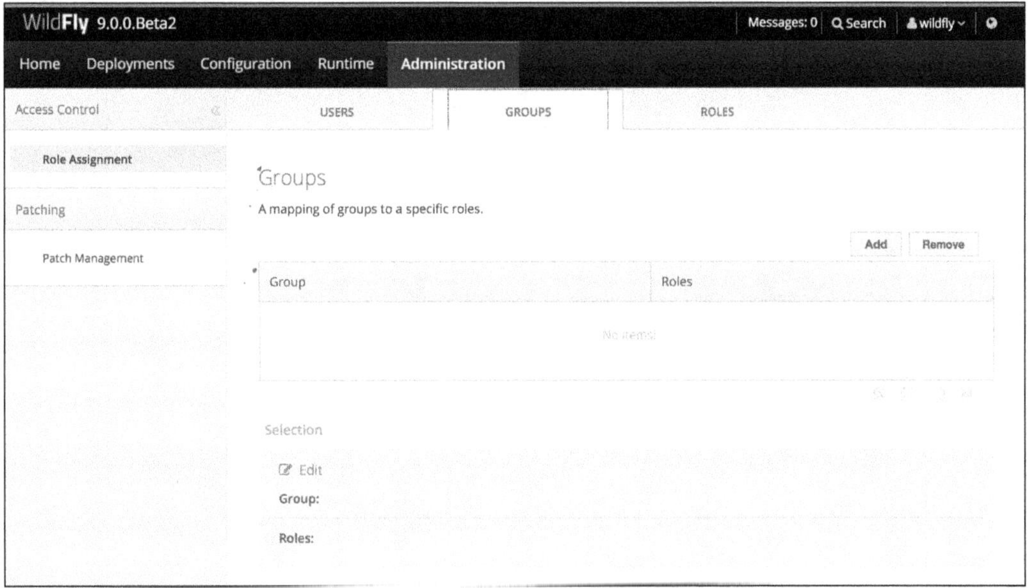


Displaying RBAC groups

3. Add the two groups by clicking the **Add** button, as follows:

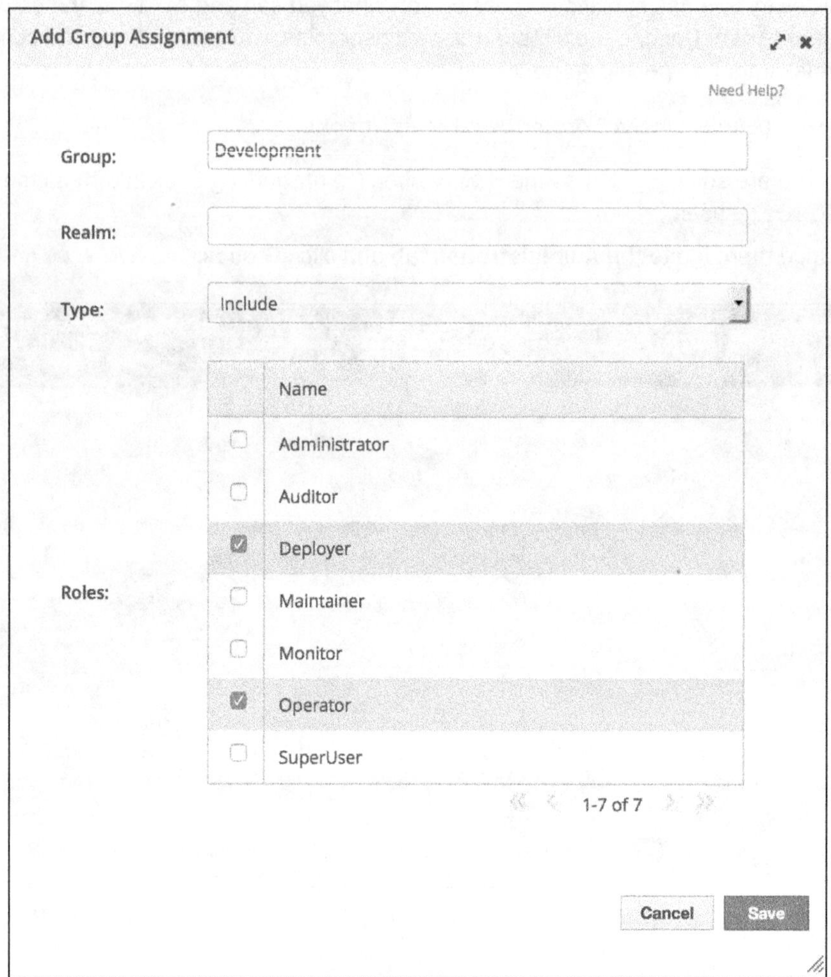


Creating the Development group

4. In the preceding screenshot, we are selecting the **Deployer** and the **Operator** roles from the list of WildFly's built-in roles, and giving them to the **Development** group.

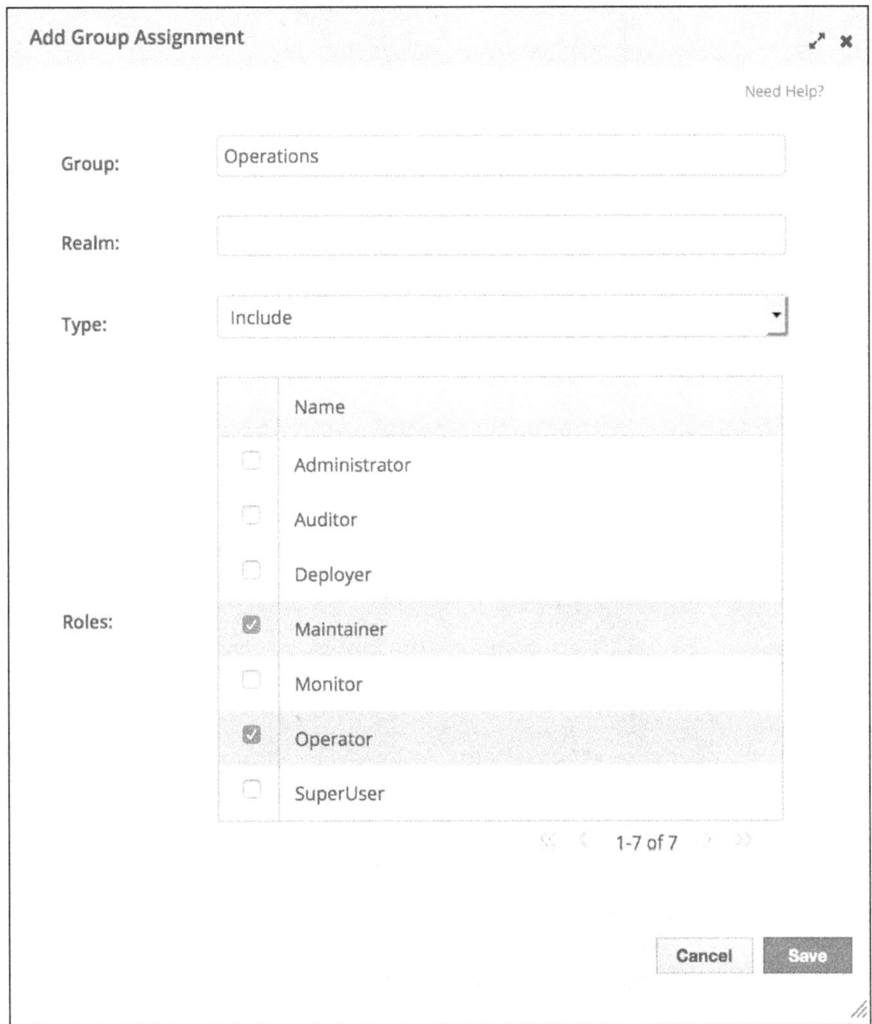


Creating the Operations group

5. In the preceding screenshot, we are selecting the **Maintainer** and the **Operator** roles from the list of WildFly's built-in roles, and giving them to the **Operations** group.

6. Now we should have the following entries in our `group-roles` table:

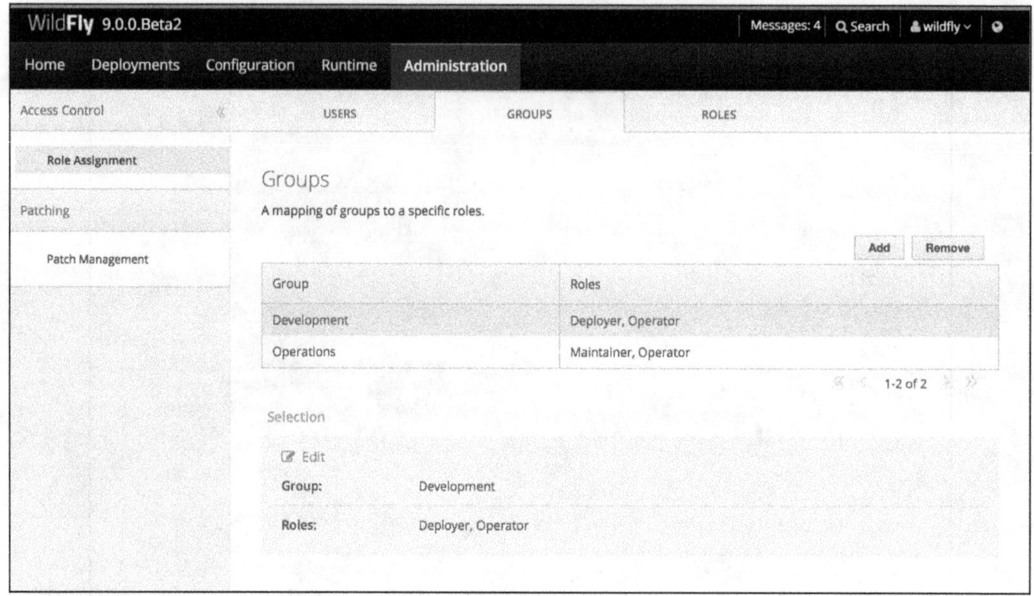

List of groups

7. Our `standalone.xml` file should have the following definition:

```
<access-control provider="rbac">
    <role-mapping>
        <role name="SuperUser">
            <include>
                <user name="$local"/>
                <user alias="wildfly"
                realm="ManagementRealm" name="wildfly"/>
            </include>
        </role>
        <role name="Deployer">
            <include>
                <user realm="ManagementRealm"
                name="devguy"/>
                <group name="Development"/>
            </include>
        </role>
        <role name="Operator">
            <include>
                <user realm="ManagementRealm"
                name="devguy"/>
```

```
                <user realm="ManagementRealm"
                name="opsguy"/>
                <group name="Development"/>
                <group name="Operations"/>
            </include>
        </role>
        <role name="Maintainer">
            <include>
                <user realm="ManagementRealm"
                name="opsguy"/>
                <group name="Operations"/>
            </include>
        </role>
        <role name="Administrator">
            <include>
                <user realm="ManagementRealm"
                name="devopsguy"/>
            </include>
        </role>
        <role name="Monitor">
            <include>
                <user realm="ManagementRealm"
                name="pmguy"/>
            </include>
        </role>
    </role-mapping>
</access-control>
```

As you can see, the groups too have been included in the appropriate role. Now we need to give a group to a user. With our configuration, we could give the **Development** group to the `devguy` user, and the **Operations** group to the `opsguy`.

As we are dealing with users that belong to **ManagementRealm** to accomplish this task from the command line, we can follow two different ways:

1. Insert the user again, using the `add-user.sh` script and passing the group, as follows:

   ```
   $ ./bin/add-user.sh --silent=true devguy devguy.2015 -g
   Development -sc rbac-std-node-2/configuration
   ```

2. Adding the user directly to the `mgmt-groups.properties` file, as follows:

   ```
   $ echo "opsguy=Operations" >> rbac-std-node-2/configuration/mgmt-
   groups.properties
   ```

> Because we could potentially have tens, hundreds, and thousands of users, we probably do not want to map a role for every user, but instead, map a set of roles to a group, and map users to that group. This is the kind of scenario that we find in a corporate having its users stored in an `Active Directory` or LDAP stores—we will dive into integrating the LDAP store later in this chapter.

Having said that, let's remove the role mapping for the users `devguy` and `opsguy`.

1. We can do this from the Web Console, by selecting the user and clicking on the **Remove** button.
2. Once done, we should have the following scenario:

| User | Roles |
|---|---|
| devopsguy@ManagementRealm | Administrator |
| pmguy@ManagementRealm | Monitor |
| wildfly@ManagementRealm | SuperUser |

List of users

3. Now we should be able to log out and log back in with the user `devguy`.
4. Once done, let's click on the `devguy` link on the top-right corner of the page, and we should see his roles, as follows:

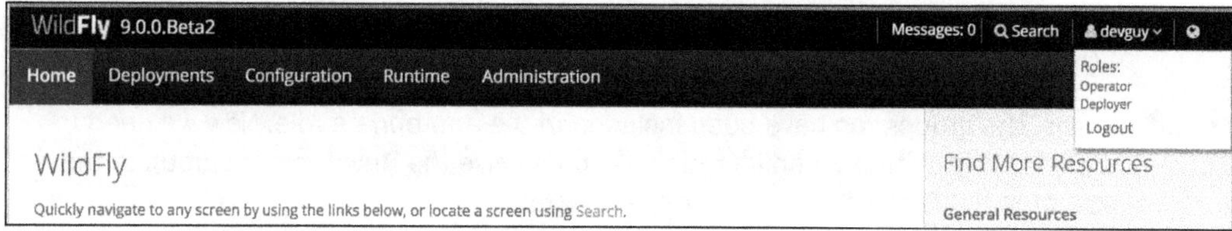


Displaying user's roles

Let's try this with the other user, `opsguy`. If everything is fine, we should see his roles as well.

## How it works...

Users and groups management is simplified by the Web Console; nevertheless, we still need some tasks to be done outside the Web Console, like mapping users to groups. By the way, here is the main process:

- We need a user capable of accessing the RBAC administration page and adding/removing users and groups—just like our WildFly SuperUser
- We need to add users or groups and map them to the appropriate role

- Users have to be present in a store, like the properties file and LDAP (both stores are supported by WildFly); we used the `add-user.sh` script to silently add users, along with their realm

# Setting a predefined role to all authenticated users

In this recipe, you will learn how to set a predefined role to all authenticated users. This setting might be handy when you have a large user base and you don't have a complete view of all users and groups that are present in the the identity store. So instead of not authorizing some users, you may want to give them the simplest and the least privileges.

## Getting ready

To get started, let's first create an `ad-hoc` folder to run our WildFly. In a terminal window execute the following commands:

```
$ cd $WILDFLY_HOME
$ cp -a standalone rbac-std-node-3
```

Now it's time to run our WildFly!

## How to do it...

1. Open a terminal window and enter the following commands:

   ```
   $ cd $WILDFLY_HOME
   $ ./bin/standalone.sh -Djboss.server.base.dir=rbac-std-node-3
   ```

2. Once started, in a new terminal window, connect to the CLI and switch to the RBAC provider as we did in the previous recipe:

   ```
   $ cd $WILDFLY_HOME
   $ ./bin/jboss-cli.sh
   You are disconnected at the moment. Type 'connect' to connect to
   the server or 'help' for the list of supported commands.
   [disconnected /] connect
   [standalone@localhost:9990 /] /core-service=management/
   access=authorization:write-attribute(name=provider,value=rbac)
   {
       "outcome" => "success",
       "response-headers" => {
           "operation-requires-reload" => true,
   ```

```
        "process-state" => "reload-required"
    }
}
[standalone@localhost:9990 /] :reload()
{
    "outcome" => "success",
    "result" => undefined
}
[standalone@localhost:9990 /]
```

3. Now that we've successfully switched to the RBAC provider, we need to map our local management user (if you are following the book, the local management user is `wildfly`) to the **SuperUser** role, as follows:

   ```
   [standalone@localhost:9990 /] /core-service=management/
   access=authorization/role-mapping=SuperUser/
   include=wildfly:add(name=wildfly,realm=ManagementRealm,type=USER)
   {"outcome" => "success"}
   [standalone@localhost:9990 /]
   ```

4. Now we need to add some users, just to simulate the users whom we didn't consider as having access to our system; in a new terminal window, execute the following commands:

   ```
   $ cd $WILDFLY_HOME
   $ ./bin/add-user.sh --silent=true luigi luigi.2015 -sc rbac-std-
   node-3/configuration
   $ ./bin/add-user.sh --silent=true fabio fabio.2015 -sc rbac-std-
   node-3/configuration
   $ ./bin/add-user.sh --silent=true stefano stefano.2015 -sc rbac-
   std-node-3/configuration
   ```

   Okay, we can now access the Web Console and see how we can manage those kinds of users, by giving them the default role.

5. Let's open the browser and point it to `http://localhost:9990`.
6. Authenticate with the `wildfly` user and once there, click on the **Administration** tab and then on the **Roles** section.

7. Then, select the **Monitor** role, click the **Edit** link, and mark the **Include All** check, as follows:

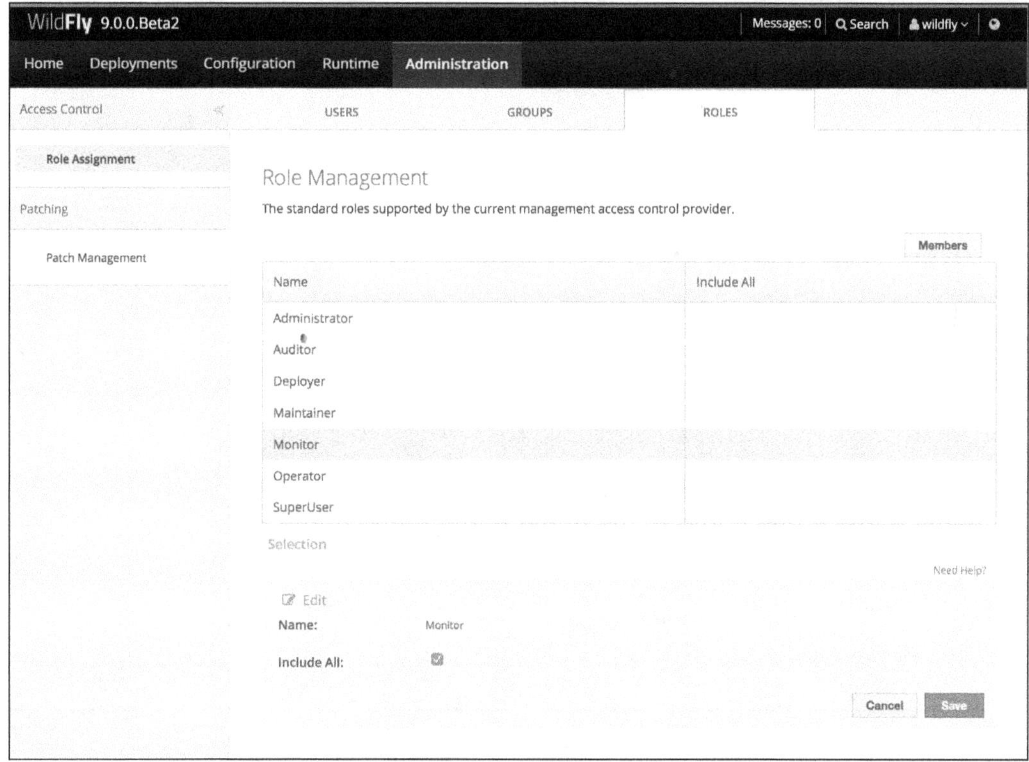


Giving a default role to all authenticated users

8. Once you click **Save**, the selected role will be given as the default one to all authenticated users.

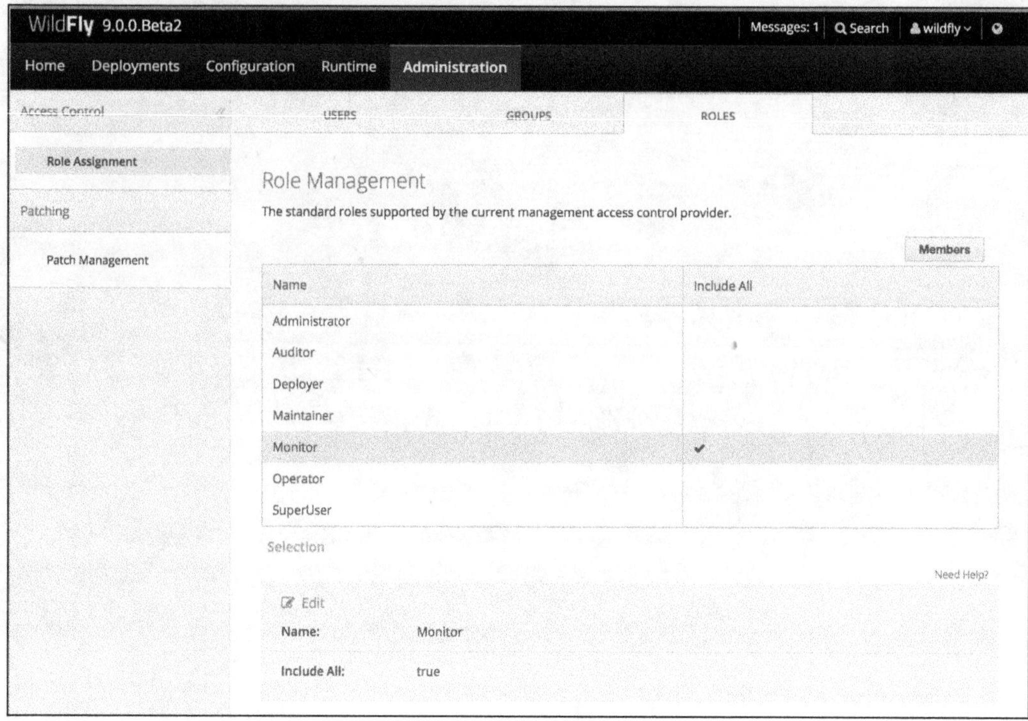


List of roles

9. If we don't have access to the Web Console, we can still rely on our CLI and issue the following commands:

```
[standalone@localhost:9990 /] /core-service=management/
access=authorization/role-mapping=Monitor:write-
attribute(name=include-all,value=true)
{"outcome" => "success"}
[standalone@localhost:9990 /]
```

10. Okay, let's try our settings by logging out and logging back in with the user `luigi`. Open the browser and point it to `http://localhost:9990`.

11. Insert `luigi` as the username and `luigi.2015` as the password; we should end up with the following scenario:

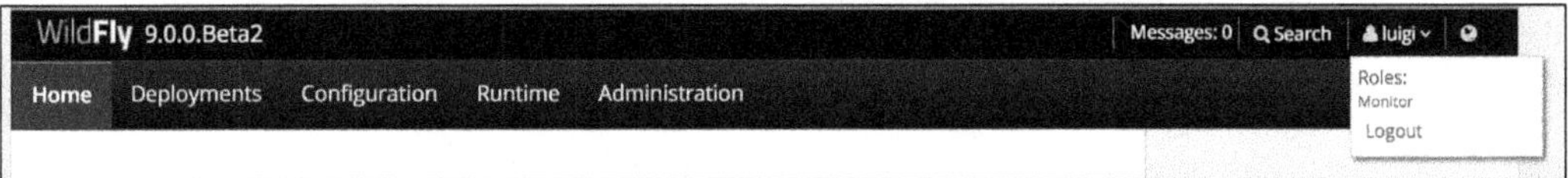


User luigi mapped to the default role Monitor

Neat!

## How it works...

There is not much to talk about as the process is pretty straightforward. Let's recap what we did and how we did it.

First we needed to switch the provider, passing it from `simple` to `rbac` using the CLI.

Secondly, we needed to include our management user `wildfly` to the **SuperUser** role, which resulted in the following configuration:

```
<access-control provider="rbac">
    <role-mapping>
        <role name="SuperUser">
            <include>
                <user name="$local"/>
                <user alias="wildfly" realm="ManagementRealm"
                name="wildfly"/>
            </include>
        </role>
    </role-mapping>
</access-control>
```

Then, we added the potential, unmanaged users to the `ManagementRealm` realm, using the `add-user.sh` script:

```
$ cd $WILDFLY_HOME
$ ./bin/add-user.sh --silent=true luigi luigi.2015 -sc rbac-std-node-3/configuration
$ ./bin/add-user.sh --silent=true fabio fabio.2015 -sc rbac-std-node-3/configuration
$ ./bin/add-user.sh --silent=true stefano stefano.2015 -sc rbac-std-node-3/configuration
```

The `--silent=true` command basically means non-interactive mode; we then passed the username followed by its password, and then we specified the path for storing our users. By default, the store is represented by the `mgmt-users.properties` file, which corresponds to the `ManagementRealm`, on the WildFly side.

If we wanted to store the users in `ApplicationRealm`, we should have passed the option `-a` to the script. Furthermore, if we wanted to store the users' credentials into a different file, we could have passed the option `-up /path/filename.properties`.

For a complete list of available options, issue the `add-user.sh` script passing the `--help` directive, as follows:

```
$ ./bin/add-user.sh -help
```

```
Usage: ./add-user.sh [args...]
where args include:
    -a                                        If set add an application user instead
                                              of a management user

    -dc <value>                               Define the location of the domain
                                              config directory.

    -sc <value>                               Define the location of the server
                                              config directory.

    -up, --user-properties <value>            The file name of the user properties
                                              file which can be an absolute path.

    -g, --group <value>                       Comma-separated list of groups for the
                                              user.

    -gp, --group-properties <value>           The file name of the group properties
                                              file which can be an absolute path. (If
                                              group properties is specified then user
                                              properties MUST also be specified).

    -p, --password <value>                    Password of the user, this will be
                                              checked against the password
                                              requirements defined within the
                                              add-user.properties configuration

    -u, --user <value>                        Name of the user

    -r, --realm <value>                       Name of the realm used to secure the
                                              management interfaces (default is
                                              "ManagementRealm")

    -s, --silent                              Activate the silent mode (no output to
                                              the console)

    -e, --enable                              Enable the user

    -d, --disable                             Disable the user

    -cw, --confirm-warning                    Automatically confirm warning in
                                              interactive mode

    -h, --help                                Display this message and exit
```

Lastly, we made the monitor role the default one for all authenticated users.

# Granting user access by server group or host – scoped roles

In this recipe, you will learn how to grant access to a user only in a specific server-group or host. This is available only in the domain mode, obviously. This feature takes the name of scoped roles, and it comes in very handy when you need to share your environment with multiple teams such as development teams. This way, every team can actually work on its server group or dedicated host, without interfering with the other server groups or hosts.

## Getting ready

To get started, let's first create an `ad-hoc` folder to run our WildFly. In a terminal window enter the following commands:

```
$ cd $WILDFLY_HOME
$ cp -a domain rbac-dmn-scp-roles
```

Now it's time to run our WildFly.

## How to do it...

1. Open a terminal window and execute the following commands:

   ```
   $ cd $WILDFLY_HOME
   $ ./bin/domain.sh -Djboss.domain.base.dir=rbac-dmn-scp-roles
   ```

2. Once started, connect to the CLI in a new terminal window and switch to the RBAC provider, as we did in the previous recipe:

   ```
   $ cd $WILDFLY_HOME
   $ ./bin/jboss-cli.sh
   You are disconnected at the moment. Type 'connect' to connect to
   the server or 'help' for the list of supported commands.
   [disconnected /] connect
   [domain@localhost:9990 /] /core-service=management/
   access=authorization:write-attribute(name=provider,value=rbac)
   {
       "outcome" => "success",
       "response-headers" => {
           "operation-requires-reload" => true,
           "process-state" => "reload-required"
       },
   ```

```
    "result" => undefined,
    "server-groups" => {"main-server-group" => {"host" =>
    {"master" => {
        "server-one" => {"response" => {
            "outcome" => "success",
            "response-headers" => {
                "operation-requires-reload" => true,
                "process-state" => "reload-required"
            }
        }},
        "server-two" => {"response" => {
            "outcome" => "success",
            "response-headers" => {
                "operation-requires-reload" => true,
                "process-state" => "reload-required"
            }
        }}
    }}}}
}
[domain@localhost:9990 /] reload --host=master
[domain@localhost:9990 /]
```

3. Now that we've successfully switched to the RBAC provider, we need to map our `wildfly` user to the **SuperUser** role, as follows:

```
[domain@localhost:9990 /] /core-service=management/
access=authorization/role-mapping=SuperUser/
include=wildfly:add(name=wildfly,realm=ManagementRealm,type=USER)
{
    "outcome" => "success",
    "result" => undefined,
    "server-groups" => {"main-server-group" => {"host" =>
    {"master" => {
        "server-one" => {"response" => {"outcome" =>
    "success"}},
        "server-two" => {"response" => {"outcome" =>
    "success"}}
    }}}}
}
[domain@localhost:9990 /]
```

Now we can log in to our WildFly console and create the so called `scoped-roles`.

4. Log in to the WildFly Web Console and go to the **Administration** tab. Then select the **Roles** sub tab, and select the **Scoped Roles** section. The page is depicted as follows:

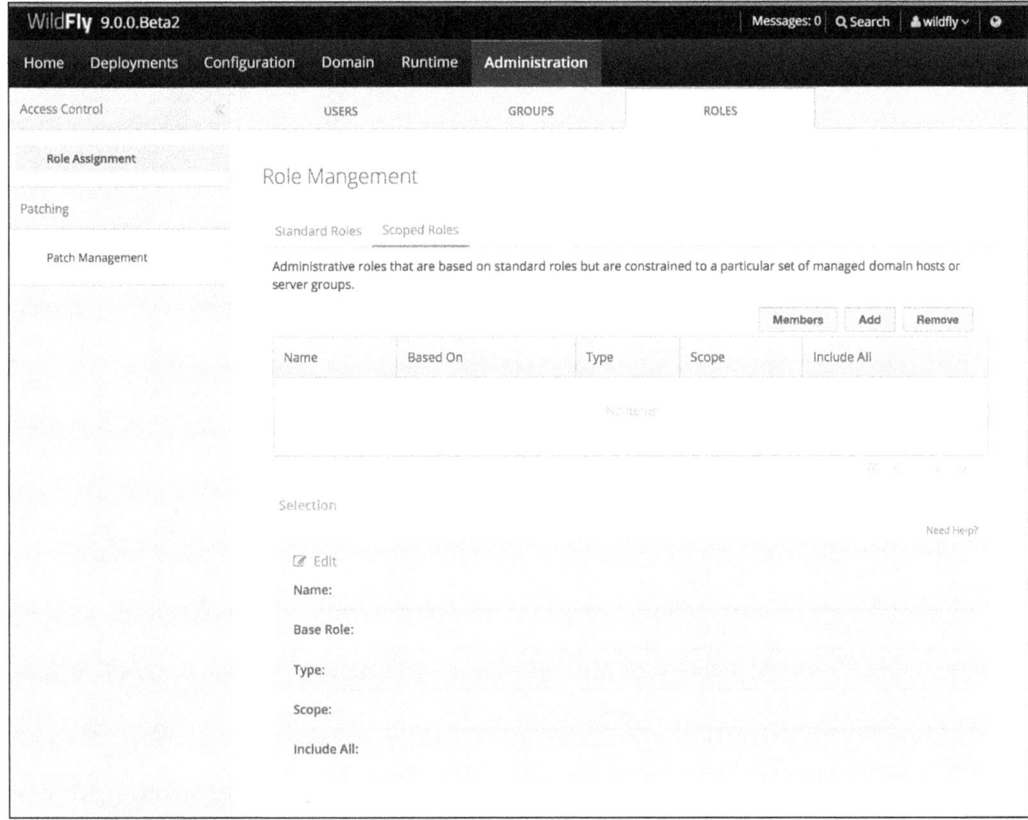


Administrative page of the scoped roles

5. Now click the **Add** button and fill in the form as depicted in the following screenshot:

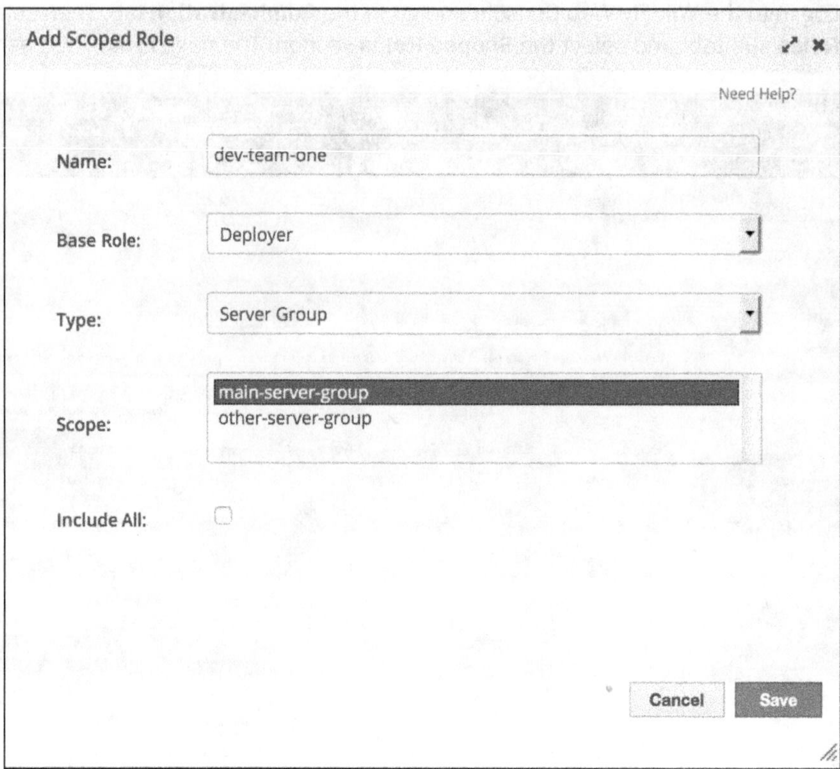


Scoped Role adding form

6. Once you submit the form by clicking on the **Save** button, the scoped role will be inserted and shown as per the following list:

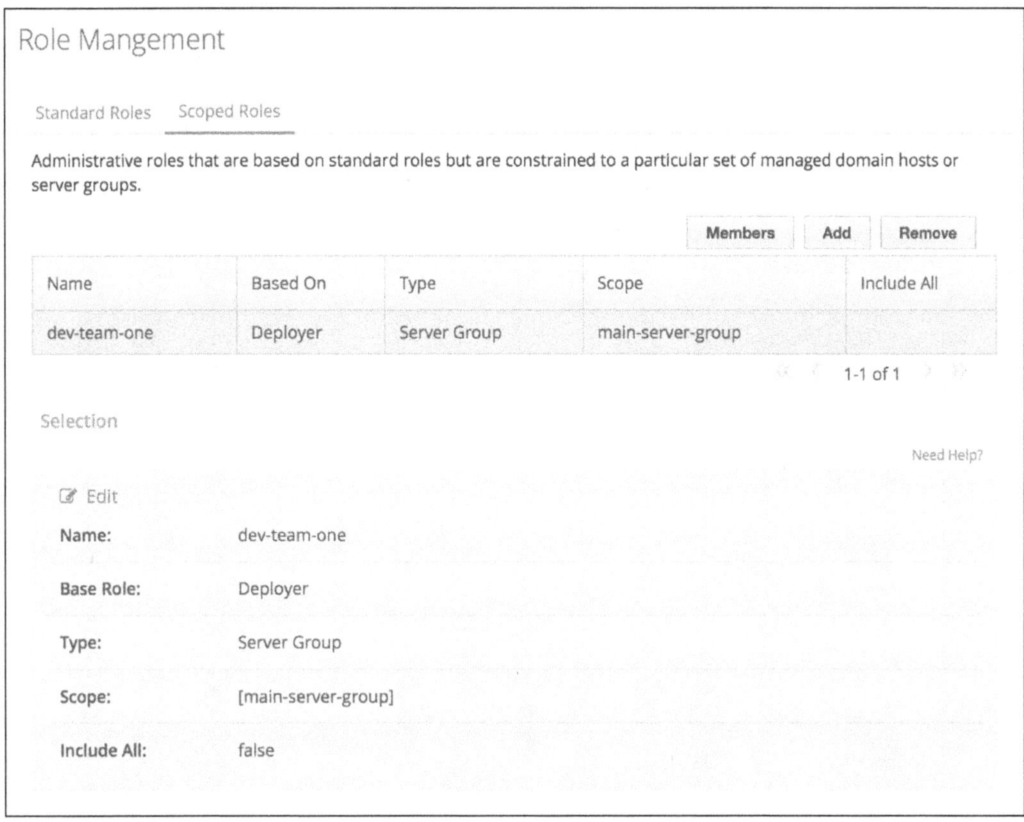


List displaying the dev-team-one scoped role

Now it's time to create a user to map it to the scoped role created in the previous steps.

1. Open a terminal and execute the following commands:

   ```
   $ cd $WILDFLY_HOME
   $ ./bin/add-user.sh --silent=true user-dev-1 devguy.2015 -sc rbac-dmn-scp-roles/configuration
   ```

   Now we can add that user to the `dev-team-one` scoped role.

2. Let's go back to the WildFly Web Console, select the **Administration** tab, then the **Users** sub tab, and click the **Add** button. Fill in the form as depicted in the following image:

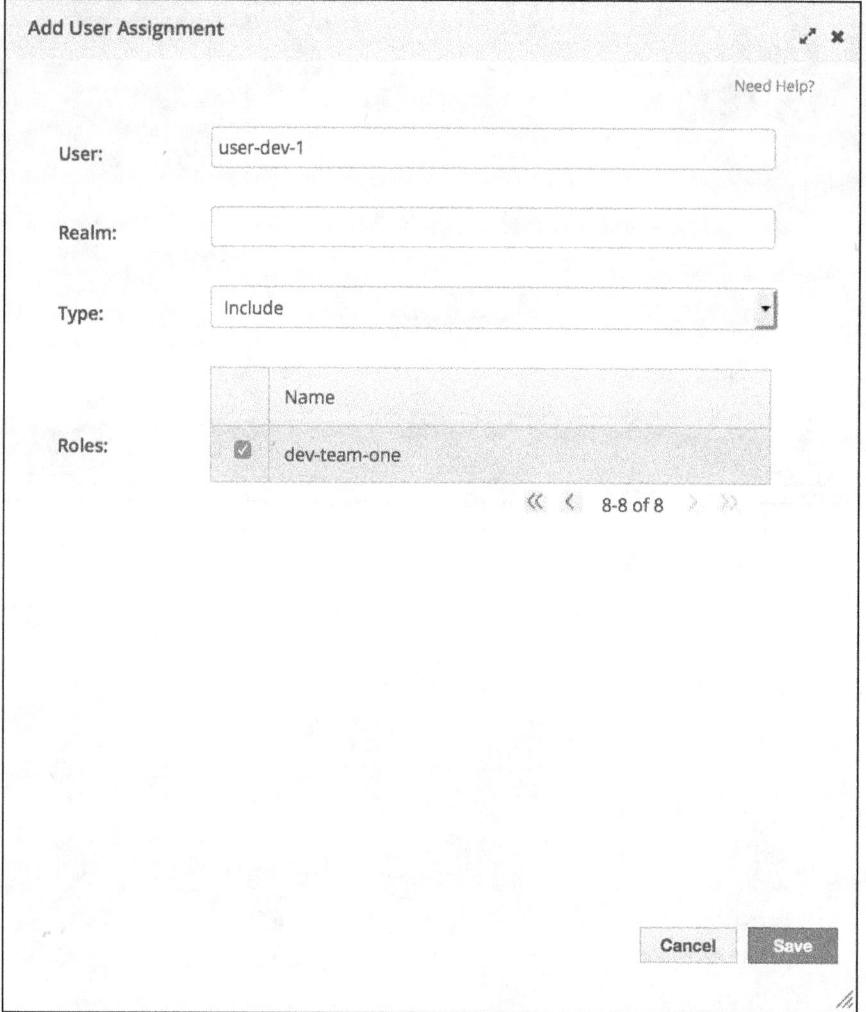

3. Once you save your changes, you should have the following list:

4. Now we can log out and log back in with the `user-dev-1` user and the password `devguy.2015`.

   Now if you go to the **Domain** tab, in the **Overview** section (the menu item on the left), you will only see the topology of the server group that your user belongs to, as depicted in the following screenshot:

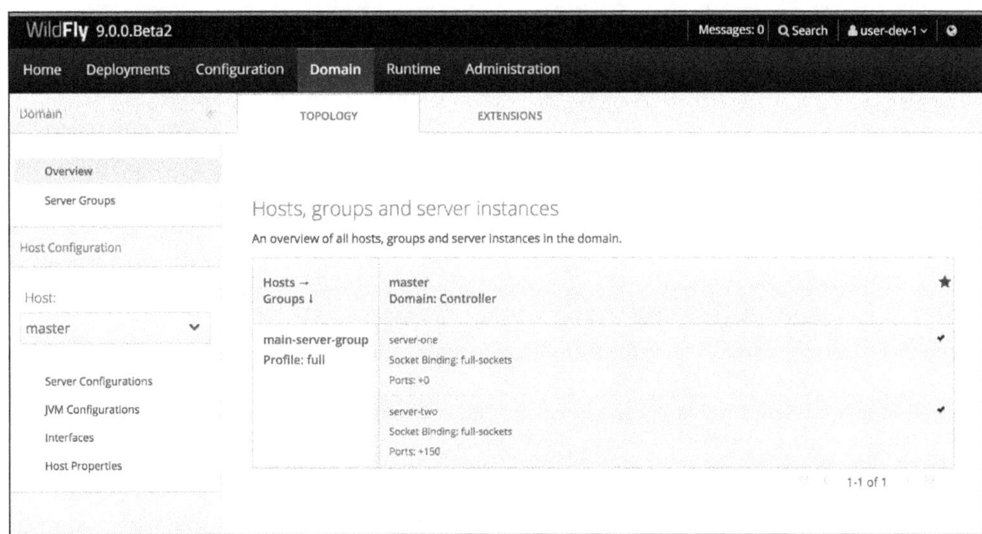


That's it!

## How it works...

There is not much to talk about as the process is pretty straightforward. Let's recap what we did and how we did it.

First we needed to switch the provider, passing from `simple` to the `rbac` provider, using the CLI.

Secondly, we needed to include our management user `wildfly` to the **SuperUser** role, which resulted in the following configuration:

```
<access-control provider="rbac">
  <role-mapping>
    <role name="SuperUser">
      <include>
        <user name="$local"/>
        <user alias="wildfly" realm="ManagementRealm"
        name="wildfly"/>
      </include>
    </role>
  </role-mapping>
</access-control>
```

Then we logged into the WildFly Web Console with the user `wildfly`, and added our first scoped role. We mapped the scoped role to a server group, the one named `main-server-group` with the base role of `Deployer`.

We could have also mapped our scoped role to a host by specifying the `Host` in the **Type** selection component, depicted as follows:

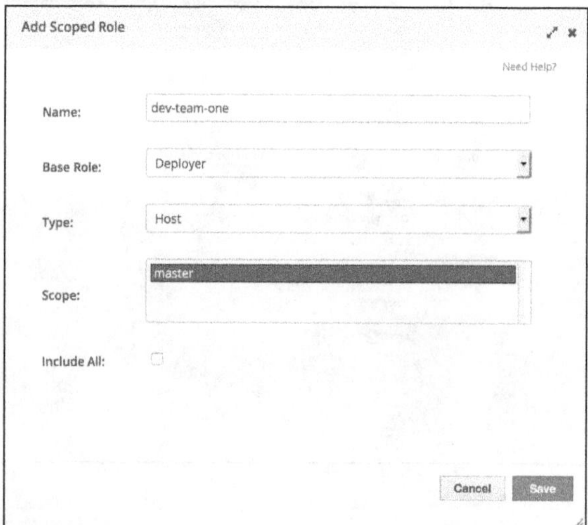

As you can see, the scope of the role would have matched the host names available in our configuration, that is, `master` in our case.

Then, we added a user, using the `add- user.sh` script:

```
$ cd $WILDFLY_HOME
$ ./bin/add-user.sh --silent=true user-dev-1 devguy.2015 -sc rbac-dmn-scp-roles/configuration
```

The `--silent=true` command basically means the non-interactive mode; we then passed the username followed by its password, and then we specified the path for storing users. By default, the store is represented by the `mgmt-users.properties` file, which corresponds to the `ManagementRealm`, on the WildFly side.

Lastly, we mapped the `user-dev-1` to the scoped role, and we logged in with it.

As a result, we had the WildFly Web Console available just to the server group specified in the scoped role, accordingly to the role assigned to it; in our case that was the `Deployer` role.

# Integrating with OpenLDAP

In this recipe, you will learn how to integrate OpenLDAP to provide a user base for our RBAC provider. In an enterprise environment, you usually find databases where companies store their users. Those databases typically have some kind of structure which defines roles, profiles, and/or groups for each user.

For example, people connecting to a server may or may not see certain files or directories. People accessing an application may or may not find a particular functionality; that could be the case of the WildFly Web Console. LDAP is a protocol used by many databases that are used to store those users' grants. There are many of them such as the Microsoft Active Directory, but to keep us on track with the open source world, we will see and use the OpenLDAP tool.

## Getting ready

For this recipe, you will use a ready-to-use OpenLDAP server as the installation of the OpenLDAP server is out of the scope of this book.

Nonetheless, we will use the LDAP structure defined in the following LDIF file:

- `https://raw.githubusercontent.com/foogaro/wildfly-cookbook/master/rbac.ldif`

By the way, if you want a deep dive into OpenLDAP, you can rely on the excellent book *Mastering OpenLDAP: Configuring, Securing and Integrating Directory Services, Matt Butcher, Packt Publishing.*

To get started, let's first create an `ad-hoc` folder to run our WildFly. In a terminal window enter the following commands:

```
$ cd $WILDFLY_HOME
$ cp -a standalone rbac-std-ldap
```

Now it's time to run our WildFly.

## How to do it...

1. Open a terminal window and execute the following commands:

   ```
   $ cd $WILDFLY_HOME
   $ ./bin/standalone.sh -Djboss.server.base.dir=rbac-std-ldap
   ```

2. Once started, in a new terminal window, connect to the CLI and switch to the RBAC provider, as we did in the previous recipes:

   ```
   $ cd $WILDFLY_HOME
   $ ./bin/jboss-cli.sh
   You are disconnected at the moment. Type 'connect' to connect to
   the server or 'help' for the list of supported commands.
   [disconnected /] connect
   [standalone@localhost:9990 /] /core-service=management/
   access=authorization:write-attribute(name=provider,value=rbac)
   {
       "outcome" => "success",
       "response-headers" => {
           "operation-requires-reload" => true,
           "process-state" => "reload-required"
       }
   }
   [standalone@localhost:9990 /] :reload()
   {
       "outcome" => "success",
       "result" => undefined
   }
   [standalone@localhost:9990 /]
   ```

3. Now that we've successfully switched to the RBAC provider, we need to map our local management user (if you are following the book, you'll know it is `wildfly`) to the **SuperUser** role, as follows:

```
[standalone@localhost:9990 /] /core-service=management/
access=authorization/role-mapping=SuperUser/
include=wildfly:add(name=wildfly,realm=ManagementRealm,type=USER)
{"outcome" => "success"}
[standalone@localhost:9990 /]
```

4. Now that we've completely switched to the RBAC provider, we need to configure the LDAP connection and its grouping filter. Stop WildFly, open the `standalone.xml` file, and then add the following `security-realm`:

```
<security-realm name="LDAPRealm">
    <authentication>
        <ldap connection="ldap" base-
        dn="ou=Users,dc=example,dc=com">
            <username-filter attribute="uid"/>
        </ldap>
    </authentication>
    <authorization>
        <ldap connection="ldap">
            <group-search group-name="SIMPLE"
            iterative="true" group-dn-attribute="dn" group-
            name-attribute="cn">
                <group-to-principal base-
                dn="ou=Groups,dc=example,dc=com"
                recursive="true" search-
                by="DISTINGUISHED_NAME">
                    <membership-filter principal-
                    attribute="uniqueMember" />
                </group-to-principal>
            </group-search>
        </ldap>
    </authorization>
</security-realm>
```

5. Now, just right after the `</security-realms>` XML closing tag, add the following:

```
<outbound-connections>
    <ldap name="ldap" url="ldap://localhost:389" search-
    dn="cn=Manager,dc=example,dc=com" search-
    credential="ldap.2015"/>
</outbound-connections>
```

Map distinguish name (the `dn` attribute), to whatever fits your current LDAP system. Do the same for the `search-credential` attribute which represents the password used by the `admin` user, specified at the beginning of the `dn` attribute: `cn=Manager`.

Also keep in mind that in a production environment you would use the LDAP protocol over SSL, which transmit credentials in a secure way. Thus the URL would be `ldaps://secureldap.intranet:636`.

Keep your `standalone.xml` file open and apply the following changes:

1. Find the following definition:

```
<management-interfaces>
    <http-interface security-realm="ManagementRealm" http-
    upgrade-enabled="true">
        <socket-binding http="management-http"/>
    </http-interface>
</management-interfaces>
```

2. Replace it with the following:

```
<management-interfaces>
    <http-interface security-realm="LDAPRealm" http-
    upgrade-enabled="true">
        <socket-binding http="management-http"/>
    </http-interface>
</management-interfaces>
```

That's all we have to do to integrate LDAP with RBAC for our management console.

I've populated the OpenLDAP server with the `rbac.ldif` file, and have referenced `user1` to the custom groups on OpenLDAP itself. The following is an extraction of such a configuration:

```
# Development Group:
dn: cn=Developers,ou=Groups,dc=example,dc=com
cn: Developers
ou: Groups
description: Users who are Developers
uniqueMember: uid=user1,ou=Users,dc=example,dc=com
uniqueMember: uid=user3,ou=Users,dc=example,dc=com
uniqueMember: uid=user5,ou=Users,dc=example,dc=com
objectClass: groupOfUniqueNames

# Operational Group:
dn: cn=Operational,ou=Groups,dc=example,dc=com
cn: Operational
ou: Groups
description: Users who are Operational
```

```
uniqueMember: uid=user1,ou=Users,dc=example,dc=com
uniqueMember: uid=user2,ou=Users,dc=example,dc=com
objectClass: groupOfUniqueNames
```

Now we need to map the OpenLDAP groups to WildFly's built-in roles, as described in the *Managing users, groups, and their role mapping* recipe, such that `user1` would have the roles **Deployers**, **Operators**, and **Maintainer**. Please bind the groups and roles as depicted in the following image:

Now, if you try to log out and log back into the WildFly Web Console with the user `user1`, you will be first prompted for credentials for the LDAPRealm, as depicted in the following image:

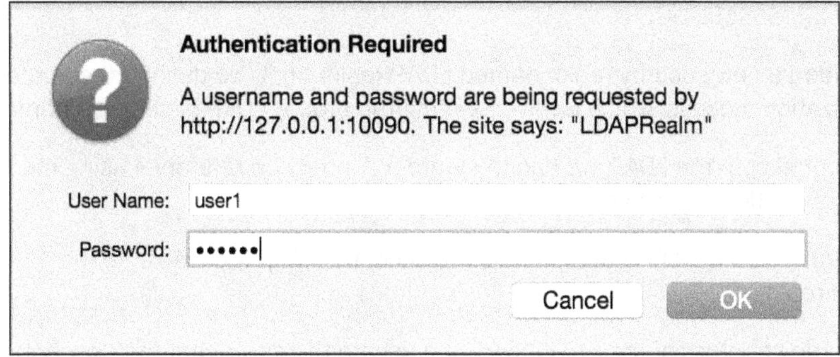

Next, you will login with proper roles, as depicted in the following image:

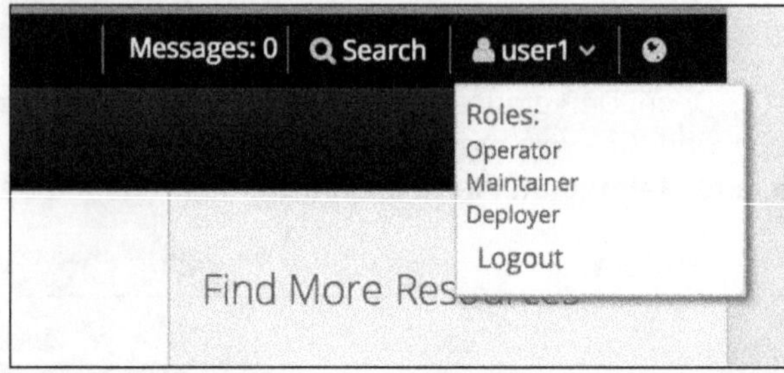


As you can see, the user `user1` is logged in with the roles of **Operator**, **Maintainer**, and **Deployer**.

## How it works...

First we needed to switch the provider, passing from `simple` to `rbac` using the CLI.

Secondly, we needed to include our management user `wildfly` in the `SuperUser` role, which resulted in the following configuration:

```
<access-control provider="rbac">
    <role-mapping>
        <role name="SuperUser">
            <include>
                <user name="$local"/>
                <user alias="wildfly" realm="ManagementRealm"
                name="wildfly"/>
            </include>
        </role>
    </role-mapping>
</access-control>
```

Then we added a new security-realm named LDAPRealm. In it, we defined the authentication and authorization process, which involved setting the proper LDAP distinguish names.

In order to connect to the LDAP, we had to create a connection reference using the outbound-connections directive.

Lastly, we mapped the HTTP management interface, the WildFly console, to the LDAPRealm realm.

Because of the structure of the `rbac.ldif` file, where the group that the user belongs to is mapped into the group itself, we had to instruct the `group-search` element instead of the `user-to-dn` element.

# 13
# Messaging with WildFly

In this chapter, you will learn the following recipes:

- Running the messaging system using HornetQ
- Sending and receiving messages to/from a JMS queue destination
- Clustering HornetQ using a shared store
- Clustering HornetQ using message replication

## Introduction

In this chapter, you will learn how to configure HornetQ embedded in our WildFly in order to provide JMS capabilities to our applications. As WildFly is a Java EE 7-certified application server, it implements the JMS specification version 2.0.

HornetQ is a **Message oriented middleware** (**MOM**) used to exchange messages in clustered and asynchronous systems. It can run standalone (I'm not talking about the WildFly standalone mode) or embedded, that is inside an application server such as WildFly, by using the **Java EE Connector Architecture** (**JCA**).

Because HornetQ uses the JCA to integrate itself with WildFly, it also provides out-of-the-box support for connection pooling, JTA transactions, and container managed security, features that simplify a developer's life. Thus, integrating your EJB application with the JMS system will not need additional work.

HornetQ uses two fundamental concepts, that is, acceptors and connectors. Acceptors determine how the HornetQ server accepts incoming connections, while connectors determine how to make connections with other HornetQ servers or JMS clients.

Two types of acceptors and connectors exist:

- **invm**: The connections within the same JVM (more performance, obviously)
- **netty**: The connections to/from remote JVMs

Each configured connector is used just to reach a server if there is the same type of acceptor configured on the other server. In other words, if we are making a connection with an `invm` connector, the other server must have an `invm` acceptor configured. On the other hand, if we are making a connection with a `netty` connector, the other server must have a `netty` acceptor configured.

HornetQ provides HA capabilities using a live server and a backup server. The backup server is in idle mode; it does not work until the live server fails.

Essentially, all messages are constantly replicated from the live server to the backup server. This synchronization is achieved in two ways: shared store and message replication. Shared store essentially means that both the live and backup servers share the same filesystem where messages are stored. Message replication, on the other hand, works via network traffic. Each server will then persist messages in its own local filesystem.

Only persistent messages are replicated; thus they survive a server crash.

HornetQ has its own persistence, which is based on a high-performance journal filesystem. HornetQ uses three different journals:

- Bindings journal
- JMS journal
- Message journal

HornetQ supports two different configurations for shared stores:

- GFS2 on a SAN, using the AsyncIO journal type
- NFSv4, using either the AsyncIO or NIO journal type

NFS should only be used in a development environment, because of its performance issues.

We can find the HornetQ configuration embedded into our WildFly configuration files, more precisely in the `standalone-full.xml` and `standalone-full-ha.xml`, if we are running in the standalone mode. However, if we are running in the domain mode, we can find the proper HornetQ configuration in the WildFly provided profiles such as `full` and `full-ha`. The `full` configuration enables the messaging systems, while the `full-ha` adds clustering and load-balancing capabilities.

For this chapter, it's assumed that you are familiar with JMS concepts such as Queue, Topic, MDB, DLQ, ExpiryQueue, point-to-point, and publish/subscribe, because we will not go too deep into JMS specification details. If you want to start learning about HornetQ, I really suggest you to read the excellent book *HornetQ Messaging Developer's Guide, Piero Giacomelli, Packt Publishing*, which goes deep into the development aspects of the framework and the JMS specification.

There are also alternatives to HornetQ, such as ActiveMQ. For a deeper look into ActiveMQ, please refer to official documentation at `http://activemq.apache.org`.

Architecting a messaging system is a hard and complex task; it involves a lot of aspects (memory, performance, network, storage, clustering, and so on) and there is no one-fits-all configuration. Every messaging system needs to be configured adhoc, tested and tuned a lot of times before going into production.

# Running the messaging system using HornetQ

In this recipe, you will learn how to configure and run the WildFly messaging system provided by HornetQ. This is a warm-up recipe, just to get you ready.

## Getting ready

To get started, let's first create an `adhoc` folder to run our WildFly. In a terminal window enter the following commands:

```
$ cd $WILDFLY_HOME
$ cp -a standalone jms-std-node-1
```

Now it's time to run our WildFly!!!

## How to do it...

1. Open a terminal window and execute the following:

   ```
   $ cd $WILDFLY_HOME
   $ ./bin/standalone.sh -Djboss.server.base.dir=jms-std-node-1
   --server-config=standalone-full.xml
   ```

2. Now if we open the Web Console, we should find the **Messaging** subsystem as well, as depicted in the following screenshot:

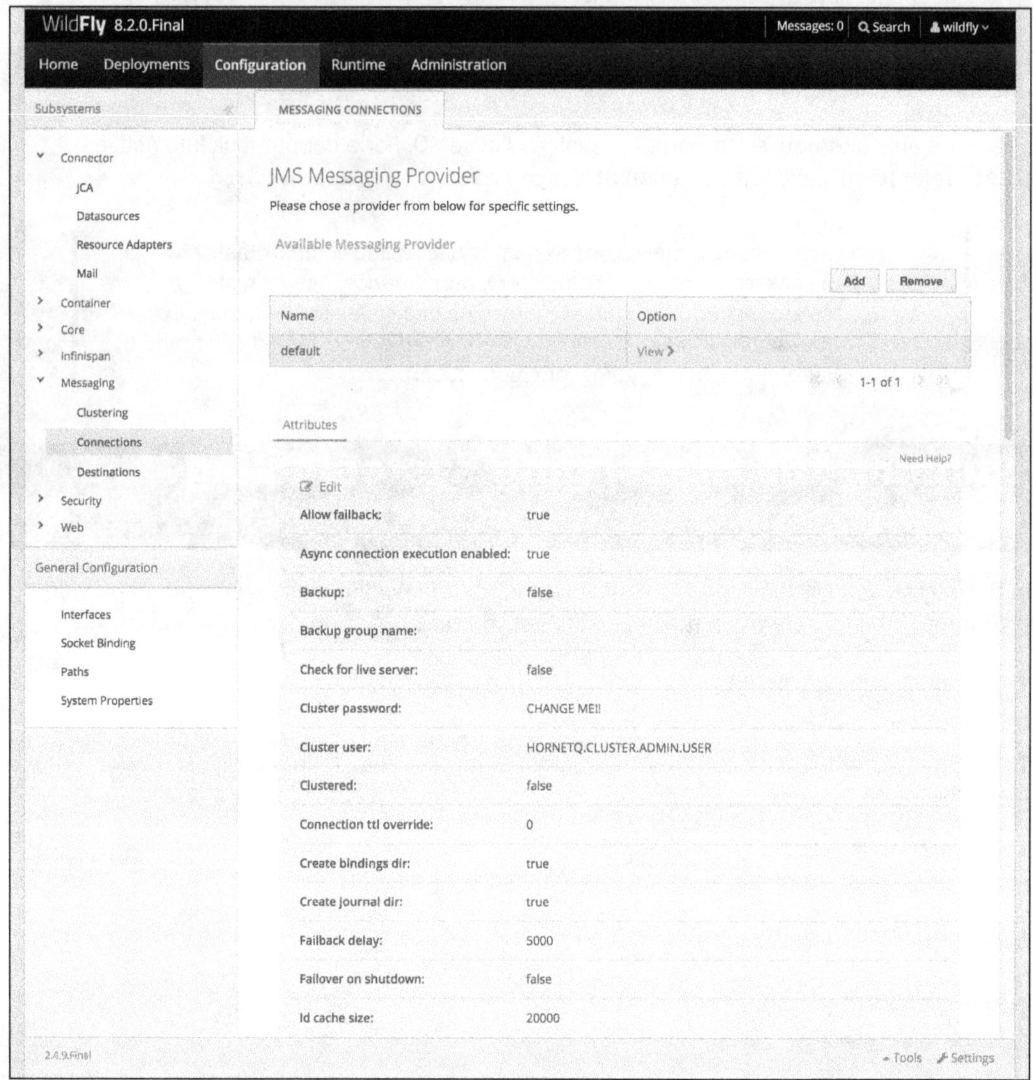


Admin Console showing the Messaging subsystem

Well, that was quite simple! Let's try something more exciting with the following recipes of this chapter.

## How it works...

First of all, you should have noticed that we specified the `--server-config` directive, which overrides the default configuration filename, that is, `standalone.xml` for the standalone mode, and `host.xml` for the domain mode.

The configuration filename specified is the one which has the messaging system pre-configured. If you remember from the earlier recipes of the book, in WildFly (as also in JBoss AS, and JBoss EAP) we have the following for different profiles:

- `default`: This should be used for common web applications (including REST backend)
- `full`: This should be used for applications with JMS capabilities
- `ha`: This should be used for common web applications that require clustering and balancing capabilities
- `full-ha`: This should be used for applications that require JMS, clustering, and balancing capabilities all together

Thus, the `standalone-full.xml` file gives us the proper configuration to run applications with JMS capabilities.

After we launched the start-up script, the log showed us various entries. Take for example the following entry:

```
07:49:49,151 WARN  [org.jboss.as.messaging] (MSC service thread 1-11)
WFLYMSG0075: AIO wasn't located on this platform, it will fall back to
using pure Java NIO. Your platform is Linux, install LibAIO to enable the
AIO journal.
```

It is complaining about the use of the native API to access the filesystem instead of using the Java NIO ones. This is because, as mentioned in the introduction, HornetQ persists JMS messages on the filesystem, so a better performant API is preferred.

Other interesting log entries are the following:

```
07:49:50,249 INFO  [org.hornetq.core.server] (ServerService Thread Pool
-- 68) HQ221043: Adding protocol support CORE
07:49:50,262 INFO  [org.hornetq.core.server] (ServerService Thread Pool
-- 68) HQ221043: Adding protocol support AMQP
07:49:50,268 INFO  [org.hornetq.core.server] (ServerService Thread Pool
-- 68) HQ221043: Adding protocol support STOMP
07:49:50,535 INFO  [org.hornetq.core.server] (ServerService Thread Pool
-- 68) HQ221034: Waiting to obtain live lock
07:49:50,536 INFO  [org.hornetq.core.server] (ServerService Thread Pool
-- 68) HQ221035: Live Server Obtained live lock
```

```
07:49:50,585 INFO  [org.jboss.messaging] (MSC service thread 1-12)
WFLYMSG0016: Registered HTTP upgrade for hornetq-remoting protocol
handled by http-acceptor-throughput acceptor
07:49:50,585 INFO  [org.jboss.messaging] (MSC service thread 1-3)
WFLYMSG0016: Registered HTTP upgrade for hornetq-remoting protocol
handled by http-acceptor acceptor
07:49:50,710 INFO  [org.hornetq.core.server] (ServerService Thread Pool
-- 68) HQ221007: Server is now live
07:49:50,711 INFO  [org.hornetq.core.server] (ServerService Thread Pool
-- 68) HQ221001: HornetQ Server version 2.4.5.FINAL (Wild Hornet, 124)
[48a0b5e3-1b30-11e5-838f-0fbc7481b7aa]
```

The preceding entries are relative to the multi-protocol interoperability that HornetQ provides (it doesn't implement just the JMS specification). They imply that the server (meaning HornetQ) is now ready to produce and consume messages, and all that comes with it.

Last, but not least, the following entries describe the resource that we have preconfigured:

```
07:49:50,740 INFO  [org.jboss.as.messaging] (ServerService Thread Pool --
68) WFLYMSG0002: Bound messaging object to jndi name java:jboss/exported/
jms/RemoteConnectionFactory
07:49:50,765 INFO  [org.hornetq.core.server] (ServerService Thread Pool
-- 70) HQ221003: trying to deploy queue jms.queue.DLQ
07:49:50,849 INFO  [org.jboss.as.messaging] (ServerService Thread
Pool -- 71) WFLYMSG0002: Bound messaging object to jndi name java:/
ConnectionFactory
07:49:50,851 INFO  [org.hornetq.core.server] (ServerService Thread Pool
-- 69) HQ221003: trying to deploy queue jms.queue.ExpiryQueue
07:49:50,878 INFO  [org.jboss.as.connector.deployment] (MSC service
thread 1-7) WFLYJCA0007: Registered connection factory java:/JmsXA
07:49:50,930 INFO  [org.hornetq.ra] (MSC service thread 1-7) HornetQ
resource adaptor started
07:49:50,931 INFO  [org.jboss.as.connector.services.resourceadapters.Reso
urceAdapterActivatorService$ResourceAdapterActivator] (MSC service thread
1-7) IJ020002: Deployed: file://RaActivatorhornetq-ra
07:49:50,937 INFO  [org.jboss.as.connector.deployment] (MSC service
thread 1-13) WFLYJCA0002: Bound JCA ConnectionFactory [java:/JmsXA]
07:49:50,938 INFO  [org.jboss.as.messaging] (MSC service thread
1-16) WFLYMSG0002: Bound messaging object to jndi name java:jboss/
DefaultJMSConnectionFactory
```

We have connection factories, which are used to connect and obtain a session from the server to send and receive messages.

We also have two destinations: `jms.queue.DLQ` and `jms.queue.ExpiryQueue`.

The first one is the *dead letter queue*, where all messages that couldn't be successfully processed (consumed) go to. When something goes wrong while consuming a message with a **Message Driven Bean** (**MDB**), the message gets rolled back and goes directly to the DLQ. Nevertheless, there are redelivery policies that can try to send our message again.

All expired messages go to the queue called `ExpiryQueue`.

If you are running on Mac and using the `full-ha` profile, beware of the following network issue you might meet:

`HQ224033`: Failed to broadcast connector `configs: java.io.IOException`; Can't assign requested address

The `full-ha` profile, because of its additional clustering and balancing capabilities, provides auto-discovery to its HornetQ server, and it does so by using the multicast address. Often, UDP traffic gets dropped, so make sure that the environment you are in accepts UDP traffic.

For example, in our case, we are probably trying the recipe at home, and UDP traffic gets forwarded to the ISP that drops such traffic. What we need to do is create a local route to redirect the UDP traffic to our loopback interface, which is our localhost, `127.0.0.1` IP address.

You can add the multicast route to the loopback interface as follows:

```
sudo route add 224.0.0.0 127.0.0.1 -netmask
240.0.0.0
```

Beware that when running in a production environment, adding this loopback route will prevent any and all multicast messages from reaching other servers.

## See also

- For a deeper understanding of the HornetQ server principles, please refer to the official documentation at `http://hornetq.jboss.org`.

# Sending and receiving messages to/from a JMS queue destination

In this recipe, we will learn how to produce and consume a JMS queue message. We will use two little applications, one that produces messages, and another one that consumes messages.

## Getting ready

1. To get started, let's first create an `adhoc` folder to run our WildFly. In a terminal window enter the following commands:

   ```
   $ cd $WILDFLY_HOME
   $ cp -a standalone jms-std-node-2
   ```

2. In this recipe, we will need an application to test our configuration. For this recipe, we will need the applications named `jms-producer` and `jms-consumer`, which you can find in my GitHub repository. If you skipped the *Managing applications using the deployments folder* recipe of *Chapter 2, Running WildFly in Standalone Mode*, please refer to it to download all the source code and projects that you will need.
3. To build the application, enter the following commands:

   ```
   $ cd $WILDFLY_HOME/github/wildfly-cookbook
   $ cd jms-producer
   $ mvn clean package
   ```

Now it's time to run our WildFly!!!

## How to do it...

First of all, we need to add a user to the `ApplicationRealm` realm, which is the one used by the remoting subsystem and hence, the messaging subsystem.

1. Open a terminal window and execute the following:

   ```
   $ ./bin/add-user.sh -sc jms-std-node-2/configuration

   What type of user do you wish to add?
    a) Management User (mgmt-users.properties)
    b) Application User (application-users.properties)
   (a): b

   Enter the details of the new user to add.
   Using realm 'ApplicationRealm' as discovered from the existing
   property files.
   Username : jmsuser
   Password recommendations are listed below. To modify these
   restrictions edit the add-user.properties configuration file.
    - The password should not be one of the following restricted
   values {root, admin, administrator}
   ```

```
 - The password should contain at least 8 characters, 1 alphabetic
character(s), 1 digit(s), 1 non-alphanumeric symbol(s)
 - The password should be different from the username
Password : [jmsuser.2015]
Re-enter Password : [jmsuser.2015]
What groups do you want this user to belong to? (Please enter a
comma separated list, or leave blank for none)[  ]: guest
About to add user 'jmsuser' for realm 'ApplicationRealm'
Is this correct yes/no? yes
Added user 'jmsuser' to file '/opt/wildfly/jms-std-node-2/
configuration/application-users.properties'
Added user 'jmsuser' with groups guest to file '/opt/wildfly/jms-
std-node-2/configuration/application-roles.properties'
Is this new user going to be used for one AS process to connect to
another AS process?
e.g. for a slave host controller connecting to the master or for a
Remoting connection for server to server EJB calls.
yes/no? no
```

2. Now it's time to run our WildFly as follows:

```
$ cd $WILDFLY_HOME
$ ./bin/standalone.sh -Djboss.server.base.dir=jms-std-node-2
--server-config=standalone-full.xml
```

3. Once started, let's connect to the CLI in a new terminal and create the queue, as follows:

```
$ cd $WILDFLY_HOME
$ ./bin/jboss-cli.sh
You are disconnected at the moment. Type 'connect' to connect to
the server or 'help' for the list of supported commands.
[disconnected /] connect
[standalone@localhost:9990 /] jms-queue add --queue-
address=WildFlyCookbookQueue --entries=queue/test,java:jboss/
exported/jms/queue/test
[standalone@localhost:9990 /]
```

4. In our `server.log`, we should find the following entries:

```
12:02:52,183 INFO  [org.hornetq.core.server] (ServerService
Thread Pool -- 60) HQ221003: trying to deploy queue jms.queue.
WildFlyCookbookQueue
```

Great, we've successfully created our queue destination!!!

5. Now it's time to run our `jms-producer` and send a message to our `WildFlyCookbookQueue` queue. Let's compile it and run it, as follows:

   ```
   $ cd $WILDFLY_HOME/github/wildfly-cookbook/jms-producer
   $ mvn clean compile exec:java
   ```

   The result of the preceding command is depicted in the following image:

```
[INFO] Scanning for projects...
[INFO]
[INFO] ------------------------------------------------------------------------
[INFO] Building jms-producer 1.0
[INFO] ------------------------------------------------------------------------
[INFO]
[INFO] >>> exec-maven-plugin:1.1.1:java (default-cli) > validate @ jms-producer >>>
[INFO]
[INFO] <<< exec-maven-plugin:1.1.1:java (default-cli) < validate @ jms-producer <<<
[INFO]
[INFO] --- exec-maven-plugin:1.1.1:java (default-cli) @ jms-producer ---
Jun 25, 2015 9:58:17 AM org.xnio.Xnio <clinit>
INFO: XNIO version 3.3.0.Final
Jun 25, 2015 9:58:17 AM org.xnio.nio.NioXnio <clinit>
INFO: XNIO NIO Implementation Version 3.3.0.Final
Jun 25, 2015 9:58:17 AM org.jboss.remoting3.EndpointImpl <clinit>
INFO: JBoss Remoting version 4.0.8.Final
Attempting to acquire connection factory "jms/RemoteConnectionFactory"
Found connection factory "jms/RemoteConnectionFactory" in JNDI
Attempting to acquire destination "jms/queue/test"
Found destination "jms/queue/test" in JNDI
Sending messages with content: A message by WildFly Cookbook
[INFO] ------------------------------------------------------------------------
[INFO] BUILD SUCCESS
[INFO] ------------------------------------------------------------------------
[INFO] Total time: 2.522 s
[INFO] Finished at: 2015-06-25T09:58:19-04:00
[INFO] Final Memory: 15M/161M
[INFO] ------------------------------------------------------------------------
[wildfly@boot2docker jms-producer]$
```

   Our producer sent ten text messages containing the following text: `A message by WildFly Cookbook`.

6. So if we now connect to the CLI, we can count the number of messages in our `WildFlyCookbookQueue` destination, as follows:

   ```
   $ cd $WILDFLY_HOME
   $ ./bin/jboss-cli.sh
   You are disconnected at the moment. Type 'connect' to connect to the server or 'help' for the list of supported commands.
   [disconnected /] connect
   [standalone@localhost:9990 /] jms-queue count-messages --queue-address=WildFlyCookbookQueue
   10L
   ```

7. The preceding CLI command shows, effectively, the number of messages we were expecting. Let's try our consumer by executing the following commands:

   ```
   $ cd $WILDFLY_HOME/github/wildfly-cookbook/jms-consumer
   $ mvn clean compile exec:java
   ```

   The result of the preceding command is depicted in the following image:

```
[wildfly@boot2docker jms-consumer]$ mvn exec:java
[INFO] Scanning for projects...
[INFO]
[INFO] ------------------------------------------------------------------------
[INFO] Building jms-consumer 1.0
[INFO] ------------------------------------------------------------------------
[INFO]
[INFO] >>> exec-maven-plugin:1.1.1:java (default-cli) > validate @ jms-consumer >>>
[INFO]
[INFO] <<< exec-maven-plugin:1.1.1:java (default-cli) < validate @ jms-consumer <<<
[INFO]
[INFO] --- exec-maven-plugin:1.1.1:java (default-cli) @ jms-consumer ---
Jun 25, 2015 10:08:59 AM org.xnio.Xnio <clinit>
INFO: XNIO version 3.3.0.Final
Jun 25, 2015 10:08:59 AM org.xnio.nio.NioXnio <clinit>
INFO: XNIO NIO Implementation Version 3.3.0.Final
Jun 25, 2015 10:08:59 AM org.jboss.remoting3.EndpointImpl <clinit>
INFO: JBoss Remoting version 4.0.8.Final
Attempting to acquire connection factory "jms/RemoteConnectionFactory"
Found connection factory "jms/RemoteConnectionFactory" in JNDI
Attempting to acquire destination "jms/queue/test"
Found destination "jms/queue/test" in JNDI
Receiving messages with content: 0A message by WildFly Cookbook
Receiving messages with content: 1A message by WildFly Cookbook
Receiving messages with content: 2A message by WildFly Cookbook
Receiving messages with content: 3A message by WildFly Cookbook
Receiving messages with content: 4A message by WildFly Cookbook
Receiving messages with content: 5A message by WildFly Cookbook
Receiving messages with content: 6A message by WildFly Cookbook
Receiving messages with content: 7A message by WildFly Cookbook
Receiving messages with content: 8A message by WildFly Cookbook
Receiving messages with content: 9A message by WildFly Cookbook
[INFO] ------------------------------------------------------------------------
[INFO] BUILD SUCCESS
[INFO] ------------------------------------------------------------------------
[INFO] Total time: 4.798 s
[INFO] Finished at: 2015-06-25T10:09:03-04:00
[INFO] Final Memory: 15M/156M
[INFO] ------------------------------------------------------------------------
[wildfly@boot2docker jms-consumer]$
```

Great, we successfully consumed the messages that were stored in our queue!!!

Furthermore, when consuming a message with an MDB, if your MDB has a bug, or if it gets an exception for any reason, its process gets rolled back; thus, the message goes to the DLQ.

## How it works...

To be able to understand what we have done and why, we need to look at the default messaging subsystem configuration. For the purpose of this recipe, we will analyze a specific setting such as the `security-setting`:

```
<security-settings>
    <security-setting match="#">
        <permission type="send" roles="guest"/>
        <permission type="consume" roles="guest"/>
        <permission type="createNonDurableQueue" roles="guest"/>
        <permission type="deleteNonDurableQueue" roles="guest"/>
    </security-setting>
</security-settings>
```

The above XML code snippet defines that any ("#" symbol is a wildcard to indicate any) destination needs to have a specific roles for a specific permission, such as sending and consuming a message. Default settings specify the "guest" role for sending and consuming a message from any queue.

That's why we need to add a user, using the `add-user` script with the role, `guest`. Furthermore, why did we need a user at all?

As we are connecting to the destination remotely using the `http-remoting://localhost:8080` address, WildFly uses the remoting subsystem to handle remote connections, which has the following configuration:

```
<subsystem xmlns="urn:jboss:domain:remoting:2.0">
    <endpoint worker="default"/>
    <http-connector name="http-remoting-connector" connector-
    ref="default" security-realm="ApplicationRealm"/>
</subsystem>
```

The remoting subsystem references the `ApplicationRealm` realm, that's why we added the `jmsuser` user to that realm.

On the Java code side, we added the user's reference as follows:

```
final Properties env = new Properties();
env.put(Context.INITIAL_CONTEXT_FACTORY, INITIAL_CONTEXT_FACTORY);
env.put(Context.PROVIDER_URL, System.getProperty(Context.PROVIDER_URL,
PROVIDER_URL));
env.put(Context.SECURITY_PRINCIPAL, System.getProperty("username",
DEFAULT_USERNAME));
env.put(Context.SECURITY_CREDENTIALS, System.getProperty("password",
DEFAULT_PASSWORD));
context = new InitialContext(env);
```

If we hadn't specified a user in the Java code (actually omitting the `SECURITY_PRINCIPAL` and `SECURITY_CREDENTIALS` properties), or even added to the realm, we would have ended up with the following error:

```
Attempting to acquire connection factory "jms/RemoteConnectionFactory"
Found connection factory "jms/RemoteConnectionFactory" in JNDI
Attempting to acquire destination "jms/queue/test"
Found destination "jms/queue/test" in JNDI
javax.jms.JMSSecurityException: HQ119031: Unable to validate user: null
  at org.hornetq.core.protocol.core.impl.ChannelImpl.
  sendBlocking(ChannelImpl.java:394)
  at org.hornetq.core.client.impl.ClientSessionFactoryImpl.
  createSessionInternal(ClientSessionFactoryImpl.java:891)
  at org.hornetq.core.client.impl.ClientSessionFactoryImpl.
  createSessionInternal(ClientSessionFactoryImpl.java:800)
  at org.hornetq.core.client.impl.ClientSessionFactoryImpl.
  createSession(ClientSessionFactoryImpl.java:337)
  at org.hornetq.jms.client.HornetQConnection.
  authorize(HornetQConnection.java:719)
  at org.hornetq.jms.client.HornetQConnectionFactory.
  createConnectionInternal(HornetQConnectionFactory.java:762)
  at org.hornetq.jms.client.HornetQConnectionFactory.
  createConnection(HornetQConnectionFactory.java:112)
  at org.hornetq.jms.client.HornetQConnectionFactory.
  createConnection(HornetQConnectionFactory.java:107)
  at com.packtpub.wildflycookbook.JMSProducer.
  main(JMSProducer.java:59)
  at sun.reflect.NativeMethodAccessorImpl.invoke0(Native Method)
  at sun.reflect.NativeMethodAccessorImpl.
  invoke(NativeMethodAccessorImpl.java:62)
  at sun.reflect.DelegatingMethodAccessorImpl.
  invoke(DelegatingMethodAccessorImpl.java:43)
  at java.lang.reflect.Method.invoke(Method.java:483)
  at org.codehaus.mojo.exec.ExecJavaMojo$1.run(ExecJavaMojo.java:283)
  at java.lang.Thread.run(Thread.java:745)
Caused by: HornetQSecurityException[errorType=SECURITY_EXCEPTION
message=HQ119031: Unable to validate user: null]
  ... 15 more
```

## There's more...

The logic seen in the preceding example, also applies to Topic. Within the CLI, we have pretty much the same commands for adding a `topic`:

```
[standalone@localhost:9990 /] jms-topic add --topic-
address=WildFlyCookbookTopic --entries=topic/test,java:jboss/exported/
jms/topic/test
```

## See also

- Information about the JMS specification can be found at `https://jcp.org/aboutJava/communityprocess/final/jsr343/index.html`
- For a deeper understanding of the HornetQ server principles, please refer to the official documentation at `http://hornetq.jboss.org`

# Clustering HornetQ using a shared store

In this recipe, you will learn how to configure HornetQ to provide clustering features by configuring to WildFly instances; one acting as a **Live** HornetQ server, the other one acting as a **Backup** HornetQ server.

The overall configuration can be represented as seen in the following image:

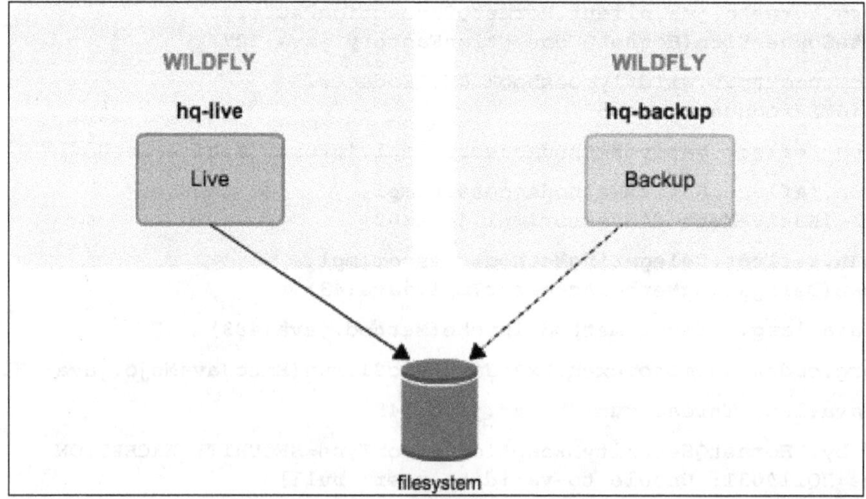


Shared store configuration

Within the recipe, we will use a local shared store by giving each live and backup server pair the same `data` directory. This kind of configuration can also be very useful in both development and test environments to easily simulate high availability and failover capabilities.

In a production environment, you should provide high availability by having more pairs of live and backup servers, and use a proper filesystem as depicted in the following image:

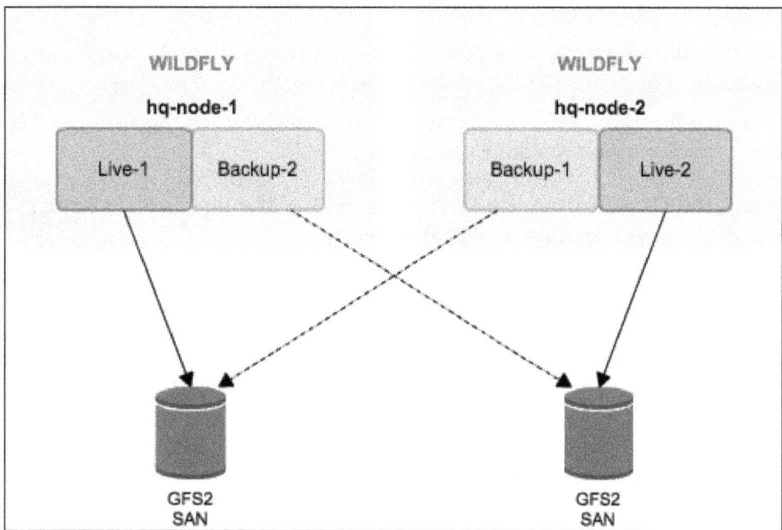


Shared store configuration with high-availability

## Getting ready

To get started, let's first create two `adhoc` folders to run our WildFly.

1. In a terminal window, run the following commands:

```
$ cd $WILDFLY_HOME
$ cp -a standalone hq-live
$ cp -a standalone hq-backup
```

2. For this recipe, we will need two applications named `jms-producer` and `jms-consumer`, which you can find in my GitHub repository. If you skipped the *Managing applications using the deployments folder* recipe of *Chapter 2, Running WildFly in Standalone Mode*, please refer to it to download all the source code and projects that you will need.
3. To build the application, execute the following commands:

```
$ cd $WILDFLY_HOME/github/wildfly-cookbook
$ cd jms-producer
$ mvn clean package
```

## How to do it...

First of all, we need to add a user to the `ApplicationRealm` realm, which is the one used by the remoting subsystem and hence, the messaging subsystem:

1. Open a terminal window and enter the following commands:

```
$ cd $WILDFLY_HOME
$ ./bin/add-user.sh --silent -a -u jmsuser -p jmsuser.2015 -g guest -sc hq-live/configuration
$ ./bin/add-user.sh --silent -a -u jmsuser -p jmsuser.2015 -g guest -sc hq-backup/configuration
```

2. Now edit the file `standalone-full-ha.xml` of the `hq-live server`, and replace the `messaging` subsystem with the following:

```
<subsystem xmlns="urn:jboss:domain:messaging:3.0">
    <hornetq-server>
        <clustered>true</clustered>
        <persistence-enabled>true</persistence-enabled>
        <cluster-user>us3r</cluster-user>
        <cluster-password>p@ssw0rd</cluster-password>
        <backup>false</backup>
        <allow-failback>true</allow-failback>
        <failover-on-shutdown>true</failover-on-shutdown>
        <check-for-live-server>true</check-for-live-server>
        <backup-group-name>backup-group-2</backup-group-
        name>
        <shared-store>true</shared-store>
        <journal-type>NIO</journal-type>
        <journal-min-files>2</journal-min-files>
        <journal-file-size>102400</journal-file-size>
        <paging-directory path="hq-data/paging" relative-
        to="user.home"/>
        <bindings-directory path="hq-data/bindings"
        relative-to="user.home"/>
        <journal-directory path="hq-data/journal" relative-
        to="user.home"/>
        <large-messages-directory path="hq-data/large-
        messages" relative-to="user.home"/>
        <connectors>
            <http-connector name="http-connector" socket-
            binding="http">
                <param key="http-upgrade-endpoint"
                value="http-acceptor"/>
            </http-connector>
```

```
    <http-connector name="http-connector-
    throughput" socket-binding="http">
        <param key="http-upgrade-endpoint"
        value="http-acceptor-throughput"/>
        <param key="batch-delay" value="50"/>
    </http-connector>
    <in-vm-connector name="in-vm" server-id="0"/>
</connectors>
<acceptors>
    <http-acceptor name="http-acceptor" http-
    listener="default"/>
    <http-acceptor name="http-acceptor-throughput"
    http-listener="default">
        <param key="batch-delay" value="50"/>
        <param key="direct-deliver" value="false"/>
    </http-acceptor>
    <in-vm-acceptor name="in-vm" server-id="0"/>
</acceptors>
<broadcast-groups>
    <broadcast-group name="bg-group1">
        <socket-binding>messaging-group</socket-
        binding>
        <connector-ref>http-connector</connector-
        ref>
    </broadcast-group>
</broadcast-groups>
<discovery-groups>
    <discovery-group name="dg-group1">
        <socket-binding>messaging-group</socket-
        binding>
    </discovery-group>
</discovery-groups>
<cluster-connections>
    <cluster-connection name="my-cluster">
        <address>jms</address>
        <connector-ref>http-connector</connector-
        ref>
        <discovery-group-ref discovery-group-
        name="dg-group1"/>
    </cluster-connection>
</cluster-connections>
<security-settings>
    <security-setting match="#">
        <permission type="send" roles="guest"/>
        <permission type="consume" roles="guest"/>
```

```
            <permission type="createNonDurableQueue"
            roles="guest"/>
            <permission type="deleteNonDurableQueue"
            roles="guest"/>
        </security-setting>
    </security-settings>
    <address-settings>
        <!--default for catch all-->
        <address-setting match="#">
            <dead-letter-address>jms.queue.DLQ</dead-
            letter-address>
            <expiry-
            address>jms.queue.ExpiryQueue</expiry-
            address>
            <redistribution-delay>1000</redistribution-
            delay>
            <max-size-bytes>10485760</max-size-bytes>
            <page-size-bytes>2097152</page-size-bytes>
            <message-counter-history-day-
            limit>10</message-counter-history-day-
            limit>
        </address-setting>
    </address-settings>
    <jms-connection-factories>
        <connection-factory
        name="InVmConnectionFactory">
            <connectors>
                <connector-ref connector-name="in-vm"/>
            </connectors>
            <entries>
                <entry name="java:/ConnectionFactory"/>
            </entries>
        </connection-factory>
        <connection-factory
        name="RemoteConnectionFactory">
            <connectors>
                <connector-ref connector-name="http-
                connector"/>
            </connectors>
            <entries>
                <entry
                name="java:jboss/exported/jms
                /RemoteConnectionFactory"/>
            </entries>
            <ha>true</ha>
```

```
            <block-on-acknowledge>true</block-on-
            acknowledge>
            <retry-interval>500</retry-interval>
            <retry-interval-multiplier>1.5</retry-
            interval-multiplier>
            <max-retry-interval>60000</max-retry-
            interval>
            <reconnect-attempts>-1</reconnect-attempts>
        </connection-factory>
        <pooled-connection-factory name="hornetq-ra">
            <transaction mode="xa"/>
            <connectors>
                <connector-ref connector-name="in-vm"/>
            </connectors>
            <entries>
                <entry name="java:/JmsXA"/>
                <!-- Global JNDI entry used to provide
                a default JMS Connection factory to EE
                application -->
                <entry
                name="java:jboss
                /DefaultJMSConnectionFactory"/>
            </entries>
            <ha>true</ha>
            <block-on-acknowledge>true</block-on-
            acknowledge>
            <retry-interval>500</retry-interval>
            <retry-interval-multiplier>1.5</retry-
            interval-multiplier>
            <max-retry-interval>60000</max-retry-
            interval>
            <reconnect-attempts>1000</reconnect-
            attempts>
        </pooled-connection-factory>
    </jms-connection-factories>
    <jms-destinations>
        <jms-queue name="ExpiryQueue">
            <entry name="java:/jms/queue/ExpiryQueue"/>
        </jms-queue>
        <jms-queue name="DLQ">
            <entry name="java:/jms/queue/DLQ"/>
        </jms-queue>
        <jms-queue name="WildFlyCookbookQueue">
            <entry name="queue/test"/>
            <entry
            name="java:jboss/exported/jms/queue/test"/>
```

```
            <durable>true</durable>
        </jms-queue>
    </jms-destinations>
  </hornetq-server>
</subsystem>
```

3. Now it's time to run our WildFly `live` instance as follows:

```
$ cd $WILDFLY_HOME
$ ./bin/standalone.sh -Djboss.server.base.dir=hq-live --server-config=standalone-full-ha.xml -Djboss.socket.binding.port-offset=100
```

4. While starting the `live` server, edit the file `standalone-full-ha.xml` of the `hq-backup` server, and replace the `messaging` subsystem with the following:

```
<subsystem xmlns="urn:jboss:domain:messaging:3.0">
    <hornetq-server>
        <clustered>true</clustered>
        <persistence-enabled>true</persistence-enabled>
        <cluster-user>us3r</cluster-user>
        <cluster-password>p@ssw0rd</cluster-password>
        <backup>true</backup>
        <allow-failback>true</allow-failback>
        <failover-on-shutdown>true</failover-on-shutdown>
        <check-for-live-server>true</check-for-live-server>
        <backup-group-name>backup-group-2</backup-group-name>
        <shared-store>true</shared-store>
        <journal-type>NIO</journal-type>
        <journal-min-files>2</journal-min-files>
        <journal-file-size>102400</journal-file-size>
        <paging-directory path="hq-data/paging" relative-to="user.home"/>
        <bindings-directory path="hq-data/bindings" relative-to="user.home"/>
        <journal-directory path="hq-data/journal" relative-to="user.home"/>
        <large-messages-directory path="hq-data/large-messages" relative-to="user.home"/>
        <connectors>
            <http-connector name="http-connector" socket-binding="http">
                <param key="http-upgrade-endpoint" value="http-acceptor"/>
            </http-connector>
```

```
    <http-connector name="http-connector-
    throughput" socket-binding="http">
        <param key="http-upgrade-endpoint"
        value="http-acceptor-throughput"/>
        <param key="batch-delay" value="50"/>
    </http-connector>
    <in-vm-connector name="in-vm" server-id="0"/>
</connectors>
<acceptors>
    <http-acceptor name="http-acceptor" http-
    listener="default"/>
    <http-acceptor name="http-acceptor-throughput"
    http-listener="default">
        <param key="batch-delay" value="50"/>
        <param key="direct-deliver" value="false"/>
    </http-acceptor>
    <in-vm-acceptor name="in-vm" server-id="0"/>
</acceptors>
<broadcast-groups>
    <broadcast-group name="bg-group1">
        <socket-binding>messaging-group</socket-
        binding>
        <connector-ref>http-connector</connector-
        ref>
    </broadcast-group>
</broadcast-groups>
<discovery-groups>
    <discovery-group name="dg-group1">
        <socket-binding>messaging-group</socket-
        binding>
    </discovery-group>
</discovery-groups>
<cluster-connections>
    <cluster-connection name="my-cluster">
        <address>jms</address>
        <connector-ref>http-connector</connector-
        ref>
        <discovery-group-ref discovery-group-
        name="dg-group1"/>
    </cluster-connection>
</cluster-connections>
<security-settings>
    <security-setting match="#">
        <permission type="send" roles="guest"/>
        <permission type="consume" roles="guest"/>
```

```
                <permission type="createNonDurableQueue"
                roles="guest"/>
                <permission type="deleteNonDurableQueue"
                roles="guest"/>
            </security-setting>
        </security-settings>
        <address-settings>
            <!--default for catch all-->
            <address-setting match="#">
                <dead-letter-address>jms.queue.DLQ</dead-
                letter-address>
                <expiry-
                address>jms.queue.ExpiryQueue</expiry-
                address>
                <redistribution-delay>1000</redistribution-
                delay>
                <max-size-bytes>10485760</max-size-bytes>
                <page-size-bytes>2097152</page-size-bytes>
                <message-counter-history-day-
                limit>10</message-counter-history-day-
                limit>
            </address-setting>
        </address-settings>
        <jms-connection-factories>
            <connection-factory
                name="InVmConnectionFactory">
                <connectors>
                    <connector-ref connector-name="in-vm"/>
                </connectors>
                <entries>
                    <entry name="java:/ConnectionFactory"/>
                </entries>
            </connection-factory>
            <connection-factory
            name="RemoteConnectionFactory">
                <connectors>
                    <connector-ref connector-name="http-
                    connector"/>
                </connectors>
                <entries>
                    <entry
                    name="java:jboss/exported/jms/
                    RemoteConnectionFactory"/>
                </entries>
                <ha>true</ha>
```

```
                <block-on-acknowledge>true</block-on-
                acknowledge>
                <retry-interval>500</retry-interval>
                <retry-interval-multiplier>1.5</retry-
                interval-multiplier>
                <max-retry-interval>60000</max-retry-
                interval>
                <reconnect-attempts>1000</reconnect-
                attempts>
            </connection-factory>
            <pooled-connection-factory name="hornetq-ra">
                <transaction mode="xa"/>
                <connectors>
                    <connector-ref connector-name="in-vm"/>
                </connectors>
                <entries>
                    <entry name="java:/JmsXA"/>
                    <!-- Global JNDI entry used to provide
                    a default JMS Connection factory to EE
                    application -->
                    <entry
                    name="java:jboss
                    /DefaultJMSConnectionFactory"/>
                </entries>
                <ha>true</ha>
            </pooled-connection-factory>
        </jms-connection-factories>
        <jms-destinations>
            <jms-queue name="ExpiryQueue">
                <entry name="java:/jms/queue/ExpiryQueue"/>
            </jms-queue>
            <jms-queue name="DLQ">
                <entry name="java:/jms/queue/DLQ"/>
            </jms-queue>
            <jms-queue name="WildFlyCookbookQueue">
                <entry name="queue/test"/>
                <entry
                name="java:jboss/exported/jms/queue/test"/>
                <durable>true</durable>
            </jms-queue>
        </jms-destinations>
    </hornetq-server>
</subsystem>
```

5. You can now start the WildFly `backup` instance as follows:

```
/bin/standalone.sh -Djboss.server.base.dir=hq-backup -c
standalone-full-ha.xml -Djboss.socket.binding.port-offset=200
```

6. Within the live server's log you should find the following entries:

```
...
16:48:42,918 INFO  [org.hornetq.core.server] (ServerService Thread
Pool -- 68) HQ221034: Waiting to obtain live lock
16:48:42,918 INFO  [org.hornetq.core.server] (ServerService Thread
Pool -- 68) HQ221035: Live Server Obtained live lock
16:48:43,073 INFO  [org.hornetq.core.server] (ServerService Thread
Pool -- 68) HQ221007: Server is now live
16:48:43,073 INFO  [org.hornetq.core.server] (ServerService Thread
Pool -- 68) HQ221001: HornetQ Server version 2.4.5.FINAL (Wild
Hornet, 124) [adcd3a5c-1e60-11e5-877d-c36458d7eaba]
...
16:48:43,326 INFO  [org.jboss.as] (Controller Boot Thread)
WFLYSRV0060: Http management interface listening on
http://127.0.0.1:10090/management
16:48:43,327 INFO  [org.jboss.as] (Controller Boot Thread)
WFLYSRV0051: Admin console listening on http://127.0.0.1:10090
16:48:43,327 INFO  [org.jboss.as] (Controller Boot Thread)
WFLYSRV0025: WildFly Full 9.0.0.Beta2 (WildFly Core 1.0.0.Beta2)
started in 3298ms - Started 249 of 481 services (282 services are
lazy, passive or on-demand)
```

7. Whilst within the backup server's log, you should find the following entries:

```
16:51:21,298 INFO  [org.hornetq.core.server] (HQ119000: Activation
for server HornetQServerImpl::serverUUID=adcd3a5c-1e60-11e5-877d-
c36458d7eaba) HQ221032: Waiting to become backup node
16:51:21,301 INFO  [org.hornetq.core.server] (HQ119000: Activation
for server HornetQServerImpl::serverUUID=adcd3a5c-1e60-11e5-877d-
c36458d7eaba) HQ221033: ** got backup lock
16:51:21,329 INFO  [org.hornetq.core.server] (HQ119000: Activation
for server HornetQServerImpl::serverUUID=adcd3a5c-1e60-11e5-877d-
c36458d7eaba) HQ221013: Using NIO Journal
16:51:21,636 INFO  [org.hornetq.core.server] (HQ119000: Activation
for server HornetQServerImpl::serverUUID=adcd3a5c-1e60-11e5-877d-
c36458d7eaba) HQ221043: Adding protocol support CORE
16:51:21,641 INFO  [org.hornetq.core.server] (HQ119000: Activation
for server HornetQServerImpl::serverUUID=adcd3a5c-1e60-11e5-877d-
c36458d7eaba) HQ221043: Adding protocol support AMQP
```

```
16:51:21,645 INFO  [org.hornetq.core.server] (HQ119000: Activation
for server HornetQServerImpl::serverUUID=adcd3a5c-1e60-11e5-877d-
c36458d7eaba) HQ221043: Adding protocol support STOMP

16:51:21,667 INFO  [org.hornetq.core.server] (HQ119000: Activation
for server HornetQServerImpl::serverUUID=adcd3a5c-1e60-11e5-877d-
c36458d7eaba) HQ221109: HornetQ Backup Server version 2.4.5.FINAL
(Wild Hornet, 124) [adcd3a5c-1e60-11e5-877d-c36458d7eaba] started,
waiting live to fail before it gets active

16:51:21,742 INFO  [org.jboss.as] (Controller Boot Thread)
WFLYSRV0060: Http management interface listening on
http://127.0.0.1:10190/management

16:51:21,742 INFO  [org.jboss.as] (Controller Boot Thread)
WFLYSRV0051: Admin console listening on http://127.0.0.1:10190

16:51:21,742 INFO  [org.jboss.as] (Controller Boot Thread)
WFLYSRV0025: WildFly Full 9.0.0.Beta2 (WildFly Core 1.0.0.Beta2)
started in 3001ms - Started 235 of 475 services (281 services are
lazy, passive or on-demand)

16:51:23,288 INFO  [org.hornetq.core.server] (Thread-0 (HornetQ-
server-HornetQServerImpl::serverUUID=adcd3a5c-1e60-11e5-877d-
c36458d7eaba-640469128)) HQ221031: backup announced
```

Both the live and backup servers' log entries confirm our configuration: the live server had gained the lock of the data directory, while the backup is waiting to acquire the lock and it has announced itself as the backup.

Now it's time to do some tests.

## Testing

To test our configurations, we need to first produce some messages, then check if the messages have been stored, and then consume them. In this case, compile the `jms-producer` project as follows:

1. Let's produce some messages with the `jms-producer` project as follows:

```
$ cd $WILDFLY_HOME/github/wildfly-cookbook
$ cd jms-producer
$ mvn clean package
$ mvn exec:java
...
Attempting to acquire connection factory "jms/
RemoteConnectionFactory"
Found connection factory "jms/RemoteConnectionFactory" in JNDI
Attempting to acquire destination "jms/queue/test"
Found destination "jms/queue/test" in JNDI
```

```
Sending messages with content: A message by WildFly Cookbook
    Sending messages with content [0]: A message by WildFly
    Cookbook
    Sending messages with content [1]: A message by WildFly
    Cookbook
    Sending messages with content [2]: A message by WildFly
    Cookbook
    Sending messages with content [3]: A message by WildFly
    Cookbook
    Sending messages with content [4]: A message by WildFly
    Cookbook
    Sending messages with content [5]: A message by WildFly
    Cookbook
    Sending messages with content [6]: A message by WildFly
    Cookbook
    Sending messages with content [7]: A message by WildFly
    Cookbook
    Sending messages with content [8]: A message by WildFly
    Cookbook
    Sending messages with content [9]: A message by WildFly
    Cookbook
[INFO] ------------------------------------------------------------
-------------
[INFO] BUILD SUCCESS
[INFO] ------------------------------------------------------------
-------------
[INFO] Total time: 11.234 s
[INFO] Finished at: 2015-06-29T16:03:33+02:00
[INFO] Final Memory: 15M/298M
[INFO] ------------------------------------------------------------
-------------
```

2. Now, if you check the message count, you will find ten messages on the live server. To check, execute the following:

```
[standalone@127.0.0.1:10090 /] jms-queue count-messages --queue-address=WildFlyCookbookQueue
10L
[standalone@127.0.0.1:10090 /]
```

3. If you invoke the preceding command on the backup server, you will get the following error:

```
[standalone@127.0.0.1:10190 /] jms-queue count-messages --queue-address=WildFlyCookbookQueue
WFLYMSG0066: Resource at the address [
    ("subsystem" => "messaging"),
    ("hornetq-server" => "default"),
    ("jms-queue" => "WildFlyCookbookQueue")
] can not be managed, the hornetq-server is in backup mode
[standalone@127.0.0.1:10190 /]
```

4. If you stop the live server, the backup server should become the new live server. You should find the following log entries on the backup server:

```
17:58:09,698 WARN  [org.hornetq.core.client] (Thread-1 (HornetQ-client-global-threads-1744891225)) HQ212037: Connection failure has been detected: HQ119015: The connection was disconnected because of server shutdown [code=DISCONNECTED]
17:58:09,898 INFO  [org.jboss.messaging] (MSC service thread 1-10) WFLYMSG0016: Registered HTTP upgrade for hornetq-remoting protocol handled by http-acceptor acceptor
17:58:09,898 INFO  [org.jboss.messaging] (MSC service thread 1-16) WFLYMSG0016: Registered HTTP upgrade for hornetq-remoting protocol handled by http-acceptor-throughput acceptor
17:58:09,900 INFO  [org.hornetq.core.server] (ServerService Thread Pool -- 72) HQ221003: trying to deploy queue jms.queue.ExpiryQueue
17:58:09,905 INFO  [org.hornetq.core.server] (ServerService Thread Pool -- 76) HQ221003: trying to deploy queue jms.queue.WildFlyCookbookQueue
17:58:09,916 INFO  [org.jboss.as.messaging] (ServerService Thread Pool -- 75) WFLYMSG0002: Bound messaging object to jndi name java:jboss/exported/jms/RemoteConnectionFactory
17:58:09,916 INFO  [org.hornetq.core.server] (ServerService Thread Pool -- 74) HQ221003: trying to deploy queue jms.queue.DLQ
17:58:09,918 INFO  [org.jboss.as.messaging] (ServerService Thread Pool -- 73) WFLYMSG0002: Bound messaging object to jndi name java:/ConnectionFactory
17:58:09,918 INFO  [org.hornetq.core.server] (HQ119000: Activation for server HornetQServerImpl::serverUUID=adcd3a5c-1e60-11e5-877d-c36458d7eaba) HQ221010: Backup Server is now live
17:58:09,956 INFO  [org.jboss.as.connector.deployment] (MSC service thread 1-2) WFLYJCA0007: Registered connection factory java:/JmsXA
```

```
17:58:09,971 INFO  [org.hornetq.ra] (MSC service thread 1-2)
HornetQ resource adaptor started
17:58:09,971 INFO  [org.jboss.as.connector.services.
resourceadapters.ResourceAdapterActivatorService$ResourceAdapter
Activator] (MSC service thread 1-2) IJ020002: Deployed: file://
RaActivatorhornetq-ra
17:58:09,973 INFO  [org.jboss.as.connector.deployment] (MSC
service thread 1-4) WFLYJCA0002: Bound JCA ConnectionFactory
[java:/JmsXA]
17:58:09,973 INFO  [org.jboss.as.messaging] (MSC service thread
1-11) WFLYMSG0002: Bound messaging object to jndi name java:jboss/
DefaultJMSConnectionFactory
```

5. If you invoke the count message command on the old backup server again, you will see it has all the messages that were produced earlier:

```
[standalone@127.0.0.1:10190 /] jms-queue count-messages --queue-
address=WildFlyCookbookQueue
10L
[standalone@127.0.0.1:10190 /]
```

## How it works...

The mechanism behind the failover is pretty simple; because HornetQ bases its persistence on filesystem, it makes a lock on the data storage folder. Basically, for the same folder, the first server to arrive owns the lock and hence, wins. The second server then keeps on trying to gain the lock on the same data directory until it gets it, which means the live server has shutdown or crashed.

When the backup server gains the lock, it reads all the messages stored in the data directory; it is available to store more messages and clients consume them.

What happens if the live server crashes while a client is producing or consuming messages?

Because of the failover and high-availability configuration (`<ha>true</ha>` in both, `<connection-factory name="RemoteConnectionFactory">` and `<pooled-connection-factory name="hornetq-ra">`), the client automatically reconnects to the first available live server. The client has the topology on the live and backup servers.

While producing the messages, try stopping the live server. You should get an output similar to what is depicted in the following image:

```
Attempting to acquire connection factory "jms/RemoteConnectionFactory"
Found connection factory "jms/RemoteConnectionFactory" in JNDI
Attempting to acquire destination "jms/queue/test"
Found destination "jms/queue/test" in JNDI
Sending messages with content: A message by WildFly Cookbook
                Sending messages with content [0]: A message by WildFly Cookbook
                Sending messages with content [1]: A message by WildFly Cookbook
                Sending messages with content [2]: A message by WildFly Cookbook
                Sending messages with content [3]: A message by WildFly Cookbook
                Sending messages with content [4]: A message by WildFly Cookbook
                Sending messages with content [5]: A message by WildFly Cookbook
Jun 29, 2015 3:59:02 PM org.hornetq.core.protocol.core.impl.RemotingConnectionImpl fail
WARN: HQ212037: Connection failure has been detected: HQ119015: The connection was disconnected
because of server shutdown [code=DISCONNECTED]
                Sending messages with content [6]: A message by WildFly Cookbook
                Sending messages with content [7]: A message by WildFly Cookbook
                Sending messages with content [8]: A message by WildFly Cookbook
                Sending messages with content [9]: A message by WildFly Cookbook
[INFO] ------------------------------------------------------------------------
[INFO] BUILD SUCCESS
[INFO] ------------------------------------------------------------------------
[INFO] Total time: 11.245 s
[INFO] Finished at: 2015-06-29T15:59:06+02:00
[INFO] Final Memory: 15M/296M
[INFO] ------------------------------------------------------------------------
```

Client reconnects to the first available live server while producing messages

The same applies when consuming messages. Following is an image showing what you should get:

```
Attempting to acquire connection factory "jms/RemoteConnectionFactory"
Found connection factory "jms/RemoteConnectionFactory" in JNDI
Attempting to acquire destination "jms/queue/test"
Found destination "jms/queue/test" in JNDI
Receiving messages with content: 0A message by WildFly Cookbook
Receiving messages with content: 1A message by WildFly Cookbook
Receiving messages with content: 2A message by WildFly Cookbook
Jun 29, 2015 6:19:46 PM org.hornetq.core.protocol.core.impl.RemotingConnectionImpl fail
WARN: HQ212037: Connection failure has been detected: HQ119015: The connection was disconnected
 because of server shutdown [code=DISCONNECTED]
Receiving messages with content: 3A message by WildFly Cookbook
Receiving messages with content: 4A message by WildFly Cookbook
Receiving messages with content: 5A message by WildFly Cookbook
Receiving messages with content: 6A message by WildFly Cookbook
Receiving messages with content: 7A message by WildFly Cookbook
Receiving messages with content: 8A message by WildFly Cookbook
Receiving messages with content: 9A message by WildFly Cookbook
```

Client reconnects to the first available live server while consuming messages

## See also

- As mentioned in the introduction, there is a lot to talk about HornetQ, JMS, and MOM in general, but it's out of the scope of this book. For this reason, I suggest you read the book *HornetQ Messaging Developer's Guide, Piero Giacomelli, Packt Publishing*, which goes deep into the development aspects of the framework and the JMS specification.

- Also, the jboss.org community has done a great job in providing us all with information about HornetQ, which is freely available at `http://hornetq.jboss.org`.
- Last, but not least, the JMS specification is available at `https://jcp.org/aboutJava/communityprocess/final/jsr343/index.html`.

# Clustering HornetQ using message replication

In this recipe, we will learn how to configure a cluster with a live and a backup HornetQ server.

HornetQ cluster environment can be achieved by using a shared store (live and backup servers share the same and the entire data directory) as per the previous recipe, or via message replication which happens at the network layer—message replication mode can be achieved using the following setting:

```
<shared-store>false</shared-store>
```

Our final configuration should provide the following architecture:

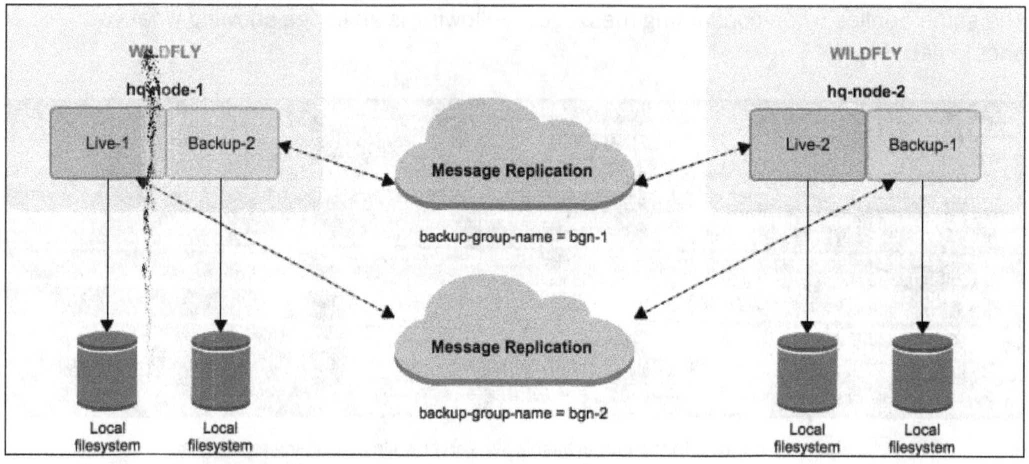


Message replication configuration

## Getting ready

To get started, let's first create an `adhoc` folder to run our WildFly.

1. In a terminal window, enter the following commands:

```
$ cd $WILDFLY_HOME
$ cp -a standalone hq-node-1
$ cp -a standalone hq-node-2
```

2. Provide the application user for both the servers to send and receive messages, as follows:

```
$ cd $WILDFLY_HOME
$ ./bin/add-user.sh --silent -a -u jmsuser -p jmsuser.2015 -g guest -sc hq-node-1/configuration
$ ./bin/add-user.sh --silent -a -u jmsuser -p jmsuser.2015 -g guest -sc hq-node-1/configuration
```

3. For this recipe, we will need an application named `cluster-jms-replication`, which you can find in my GitHub repository. If you skipped the *Managing applications using the deployments folder* recipe of *Chapter 2, Running WildFly in Standalone Mode*, please refer to it to download all the source code and projects that you will need.
4. To build the application, run the following commands:

```
$ cd $WILDFLY_HOME/github/wildfly-cookbook
$ cd cluster-jms-replication
$ mvn clean package
```

Now it's time to configure our HornetQ servers in WildFly!!!

## How to do it...

To configure our servers, we will rely on the configuration present in my GitHub repository, named `wildfly-cookbook`. There you can find a project named `cluster-jms-replication`, which has been provided by the reviewer Kylin Soong.

1. In the folder where you download the repository (`~/WFC/github/wildfly-cookbook`), there is a project called `cluster-jms-replication`. From within the folder of the project, execute the following:

```
$ mvn clean install
$ cp standalone-full-ha-1.xml $WILDFLY_HOME/node1/configuration/
$ cp standalone-full-ha-2.xml $WILDFLY_HOME/node2/configuration/
$ cp queue-jms.xml $WILDFLY_HOME/node1/deployments/
$ cp queue-jms.xml $WILDFLY_HOME/node2/deployments/
$ cp target/cluster-demo-jms.jar $WILDFLY_HOME/node1/deployments/
$ cp target/cluster-demo-jms.jar $WILDFLY_HOME/node2/deployments/
```

2. Now we are ready to start our servers as follows:

```
$ ./bin/standalone.sh -c standalone-full-ha-1.xml -Djboss.server.base.dir=node1
$ ./bin/standalone.sh -c standalone-full-ha-2.xml -Djboss.server.base.dir=node2 -Djboss.socket.binding.port-offset=100
```

3. Once the servers are started, go to the `cluster-jms-replication` project folder and invoke the following command:

```
$ mvn exec:java
```

4. This will send ten messages to the HornetQ cluster. In the `node1` server log entries, you should find the following:

```
12:07:02,323 INFO  [stdout] (Thread-7 (HornetQ-client-global-threads-1050658442)) 3: WildFly 9 HornetQ Messaging High Available
12:07:12,334 INFO  [stdout] (Thread-7 (HornetQ-client-global-threads-1050658442)) 5: WildFly 9 HornetQ Messaging High Available
12:07:22,344 INFO  [stdout] (Thread-7 (HornetQ-client-global-threads-1050658442)) 7: WildFly 9 HornetQ Messaging High Available
12:07:32,355 INFO  [stdout] (Thread-7 (HornetQ-client-global-threads-1050658442)) 9: WildFly 9 HornetQ Messaging High Available
```

Within the `node2` server log entries, you should find the following:

```
12:06:52,350 INFO  [stdout] (Thread-7 (HornetQ-client-global-threads-589728564)) 2: WildFly 9 HornetQ Messaging High Available
12:07:02,358 INFO  [stdout] (Thread-7 (HornetQ-client-global-threads-589728564)) 4: WildFly 9 HornetQ Messaging High Available
12:07:12,363 INFO  [stdout] (Thread-7 (HornetQ-client-global-threads-589728564)) 6: WildFly 9 HornetQ Messaging High Available
12:07:22,370 INFO  [stdout] (Thread-7 (HornetQ-client-global-threads-589728564)) 8: WildFly 9 HornetQ Messaging High Available
12:07:32,379 INFO  [stdout] (Thread-7 (HornetQ-client-global-threads-589728564)) 10: WildFly 9 HornetQ Messaging High Available
```

5. Now we will try a failover test by sending the first couple of messages to `node1`, and then stop it (regular shutdown or kill is the same). Again go to the `cluster-jms-replication` project folder, and invoke the following command:

```
$ mvn exec:java
```

6. Now, as soon as you get the first two messages on server `node1`, stop it. At the end of the process, you should get the following log entries:

   - `node1`

```
12:15:44,592 INFO  [stdout] (Thread-13 (HornetQ-client-global-threads-1050658442)) 1: WildFly 9 HornetQ Messaging High Available
12:15:54,602 INFO  [stdout] (Thread-13 (HornetQ-client-global-threads-1050658442)) 3: WildFly 9 HornetQ Messaging High Available
```

- node2

```
12:15:44,599 INFO  [stdout] (Thread-12 (HornetQ-client-
global-threads-589728564)) 2: WildFly 9 HornetQ Messaging
High Available

12:15:54,606 INFO  [stdout] (Thread-12 (HornetQ-client-
global-threads-589728564)) 4: WildFly 9 HornetQ Messaging
High Available

12:16:04,613 INFO  [stdout] (Thread-12 (HornetQ-client-
global-threads-589728564)) 6: WildFly 9 HornetQ Messaging
High Available

... Errors and Warnings ...

12:16:14,622 INFO  [stdout] (Thread-12 (HornetQ-client-
global-threads-589728564)) 8: WildFly 9 HornetQ Messaging
High Available

12:16:24,629 INFO  [stdout] (Thread-12 (HornetQ-client-
global-threads-589728564)) 10: WildFly 9 HornetQ Messaging
High Available

12:16:34,642 INFO  [stdout] (Thread-12 (HornetQ-client-
global-threads-589728564)) 5: WildFly 9 HornetQ Messaging
High Available

12:16:44,653 INFO  [stdout] (Thread-12 (HornetQ-client-
global-threads-589728564)) 7: WildFly 9 HornetQ Messaging
High Available

12:16:54,663 INFO  [stdout] (Thread-12 (HornetQ-client-
global-threads-589728564)) 9: WildFly 9 HornetQ Messaging
High Available
```

## How it works...

There are quite a few things that need to be explained. Beware that only the persistent messages are replicated to the backup server. Thus, non-persistent messages will not fail over. In the live configuration, we added the following directives:

```
<backup>false</backup>
<failover-on-shutdown>true</failover-on-shutdown>
<check-for-live-server>true</check-for-live-server>
```

The first one is quite obvious; it defines that the server will be the live one. The `failover-on-shutdown` means that the server will fail over to the backup servers, even in case of normal server shutdown, as we did in our test.

The `check-for-live-server` directive is used along with the `allow-failback`, present in the backup server configuration:

```
<backup>true</backup>
<failover-on-shutdown>true</failover-on-shutdown>
<allow-failback>true</allow-failback>
```

Basically, when the live server comes back up, it checks if there was a failover by contacting the other backup servers, and issuing a shutdown on the current live one for it to take over.

## See also

- As mentioned in the introduction, there is a lot to talk about HornetQ, JMS, and MOM in general, but it's out of the scope of this book. For this reason, I suggest you read the book *HornetQ Messaging Developer's Guide, Piero Giacomelli, Packt Publishing*, which goes deep into the development aspects of the framework and the JMS specification.
- Also, the jboss.org community has done a great job in providing us all with information about HornetQ, which is freely available at `http://hornetq.jboss.org`.
- Last, but not least, the JMS specification is available at `https://jcp.org/aboutJava/communityprocess/final/jsr343/index.html`.

# 14

# WildFly into the Cloud with OpenShift

In this chapter, you will learn the following recipes:

- Registering to OpenShift Online
- Installing the WildFly cartridge for our first deployment
- Taking control of your WildFly server via SSH
- Deploying your code to OpenShift Online

## Introduction

In this chapter, you will learn what OpenShift is, and how you can take advantage of it by deploying your application directly to the Internet on the cloud.

First of all, OpenShift is a **Platform as a Service**, which stands for the famous acronym **PaaS**. OpenShift is Red Hat's PaaS, and you can find it in three different versions:

- **OpenShift Origin**: This one is the free and open source version of OpenShift. You can find its code stream on GitHub at `https://github.com/openshift/origin`.
- **OpenShift Online**: OpenShift Online (OSO) is the version that we will use in this chapter. For the moment you just need to know that it's a free PaaS, where you can deploy your application based on your favorite environment. We will discuss it later in the chapter. OpenShift Online is available for free at `https://www.openshift.com`.
- **OpenShift Enterprise**: OpenShift Enterprise (OSE) is the version for which Red Hat provides support at the enterprise level.

As mentioned in the book *Getting Started with OpenShift, O'Reilly*:

> *OSE is intended for customers who want stability and a production-ready install out of the box. Since stability is paramount, some of the features found in Origin or Online may not be in Enterprise for a release or two.*

Anyway, what is OpenShift all about? OpenShift is a lot of things, but from my experience, I think that the word self-provisioning is the one that fits it better. Developers and/or sysadmins can access the system and provision themselves their own environment, on the fly. Resources, runtime, network: all you need is there for you at one click.

Another thing OpenShift can do for you is autoscaling. If you deploy your application on OpenShift and flag the option for "autoscaling", whenever your site gets more traffic, your infrastructure scales; more "nodes" are added in order to handle more and more requests. Still, "automagically", whenever your application traffic decreases, OpenShift gets back the extra resources.

In OpenShift you need to understand three main concepts:

- **Gear**: Think about it as a server that provides you the resources that you need, such as RAM, CPU, and disk space. In OpenShift Online you can find three types of gear: small, medium, and large. They all have 1 GB of disk space. The small gear has 512 MB of RAM, medium gear has 1 GB of RAM, and the large gear has 2 GB of RAM.

> OpenShift Online gives you three small gears for free. If you want more or want to get different types, you need to purchase them.

- **Cartridge**: Think of it as a plugin. A cartridge is the host of your services or applications. For example, if you have a Java web application, your cartridge might be WildFly, JBoss AS, or Tomcat. Cartridges can be of two types:
    - **Standalone**: This is like WildFly, JBoss AS, and Vert.x; basically the application server that your application runs on
    - **Embedded**: This is a functionality cartridge such as a database cartridge
- **Application**: Without turning around too much, it's your application that runs on OpenShift. OpenShift exposes three ports for incoming traffic: SSH on port 22, HTTP on port 80, and HTTPS on port 443.

This is essentially the basics you need to know in order to work with OpenShift Online. A plus would be an understanding of the basis of Git (a distributed version control software), but we will see it when needed.

Let's begin!

# Registering to OpenShift Online

In this recipe, you will learn how to register for a free OpenShift Online account. This is a warm-up recipe, which will enable us to get acquainted with the overall infrastructure.

## Getting ready

As we will operate just online, all you need to have is an Internet connection for the next 10 minutes.

## How to do it...

1. Open a browser of your choice and point it to `http://www.openshift.com`.
2. Once there, click on the **Online** box (to the extreme left), as depicted in the following image:

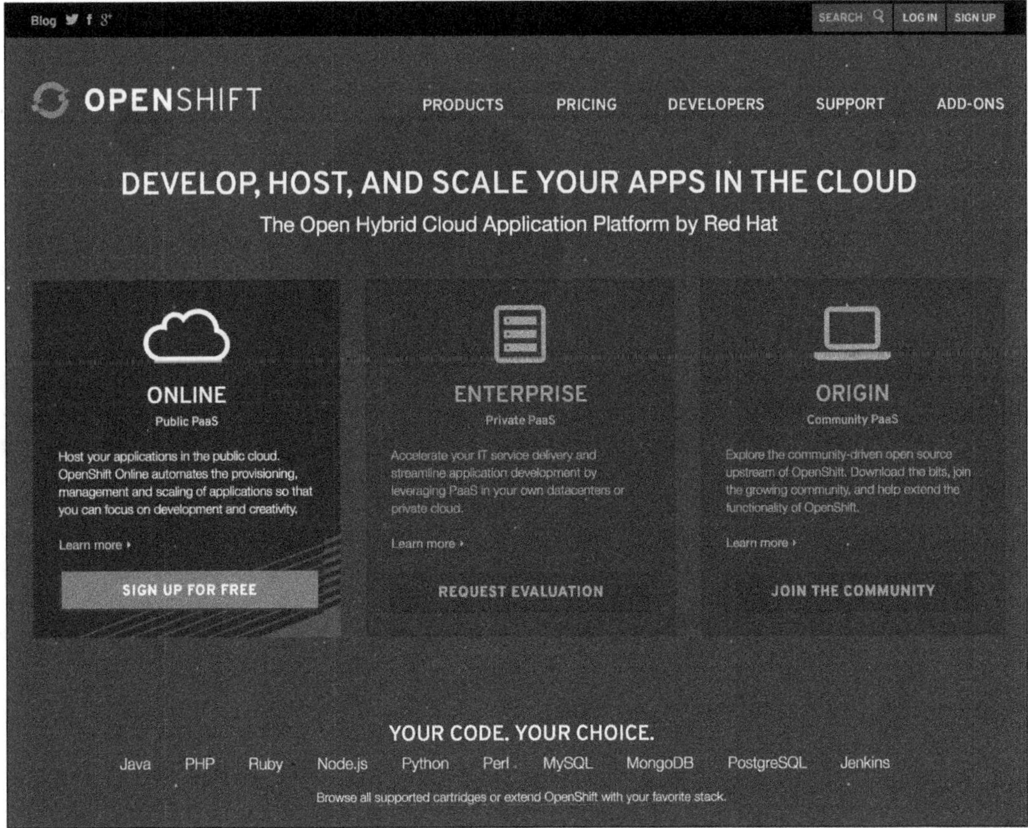


OpenShift home page

3. The next step is to fill in the registration form by providing a valid, working e-mail ID and choosing a password, as shown in the following screenshot:

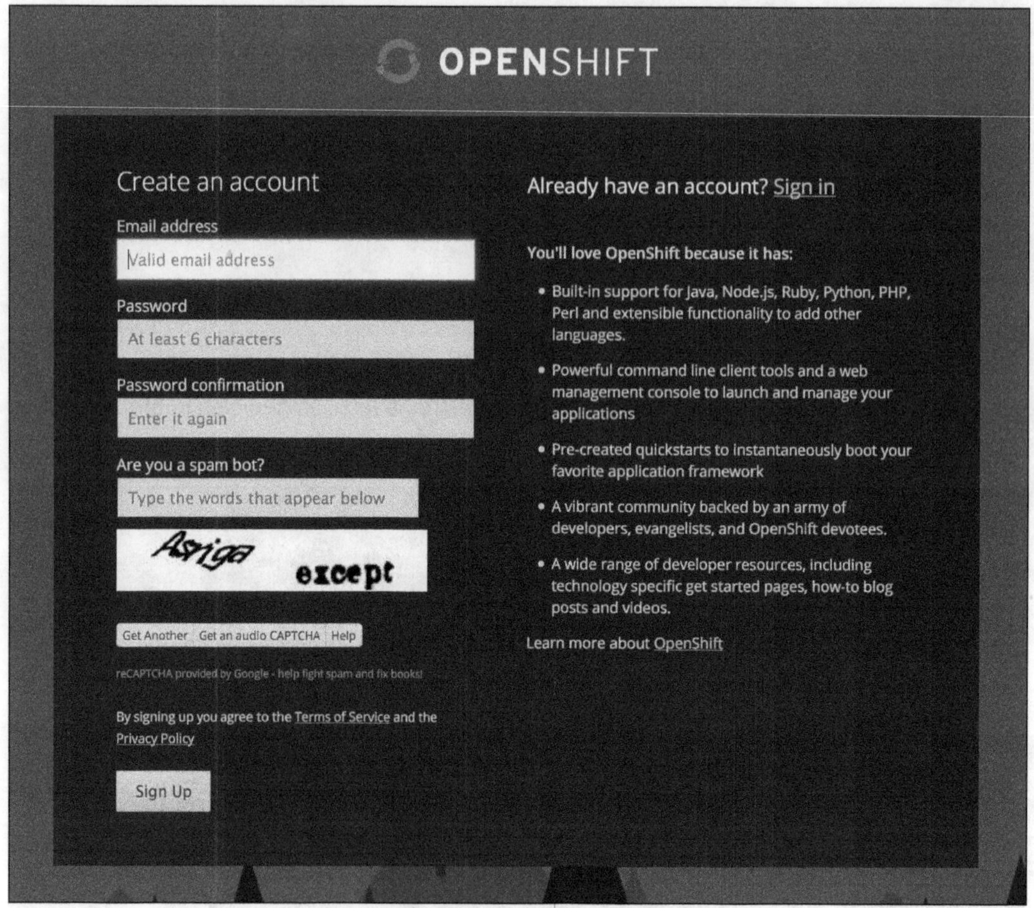


OpenShift Online registration form

4. Once done, hit the **Sign Up** button and wait for a confirmation mail, as warned in the following message:

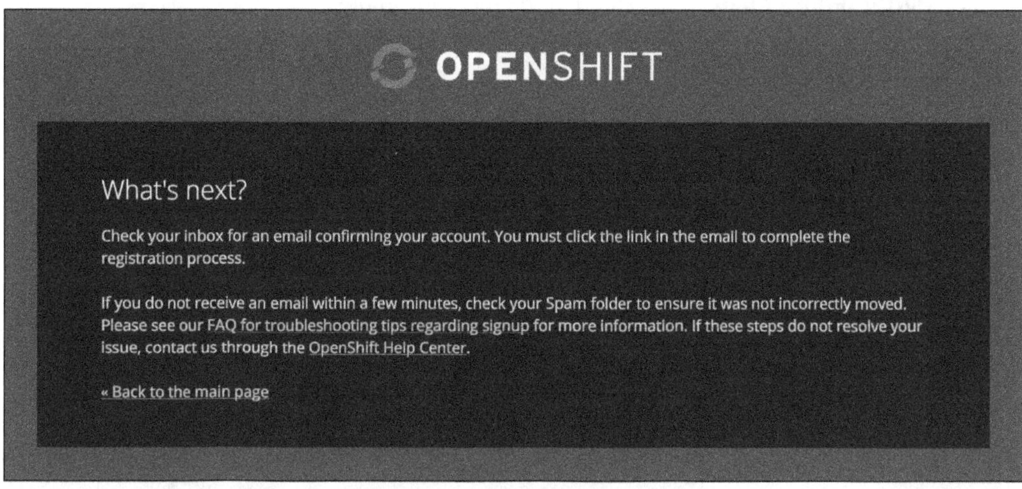


Message warning for a confirmation mail

5. You may need to wait a few minutes and even check for it in the **Spam** folder. The mail should look like the following screenshot:

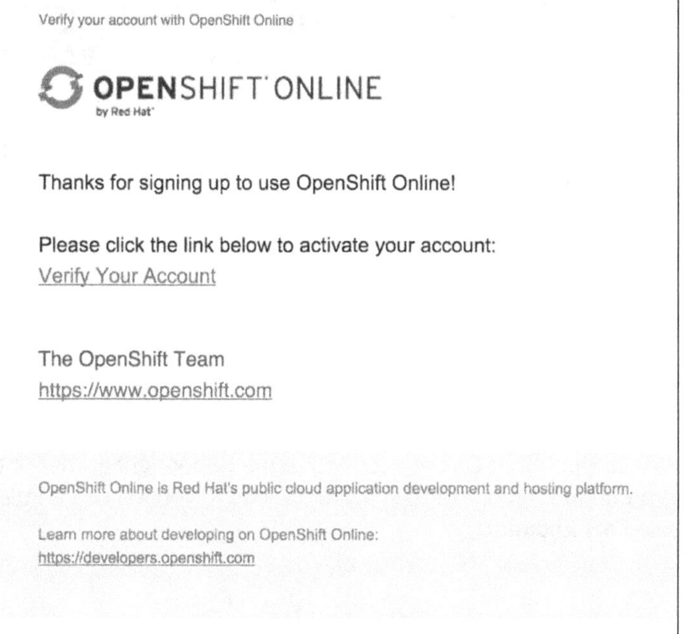


The e-mail sent by OpenShift Online

6. Click on the link labeled **Verify Your Account** to activate your account.
7. You will be prompted to accept the **OpenShift Service Agreement** and **Red Hat Portal Terms of Use**, as depicted in the following image:

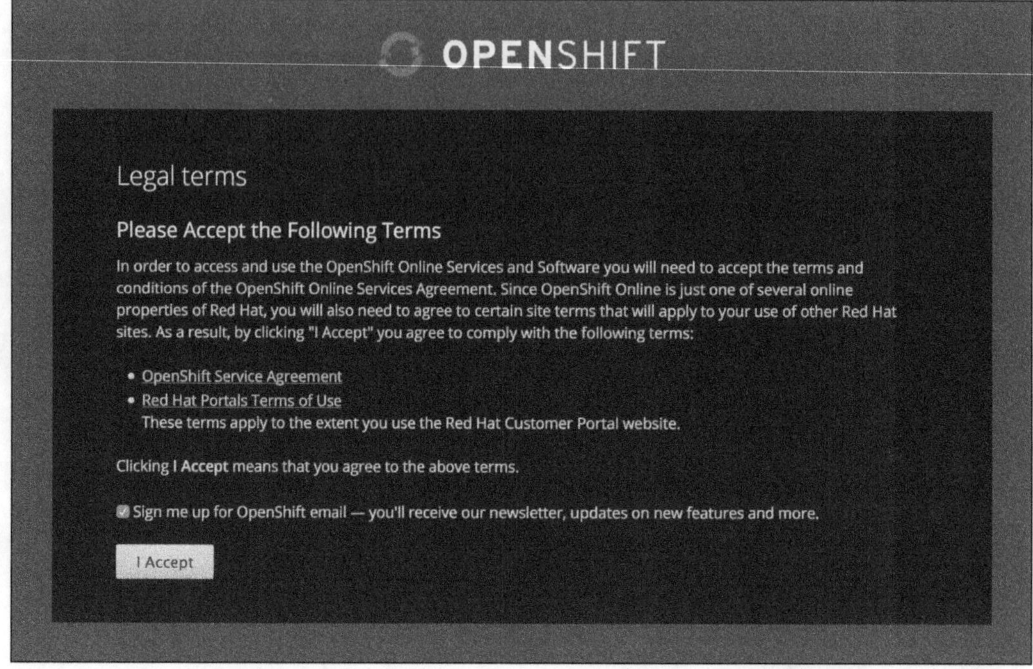


OpenShift service agreement and Red Hat portal terms of use acceptance form

8. If you want, you can also flag the **Sign me up for OpenShift email** and click the **I Accept** button.

Great, you are now ready to deploy into the cloud and provide your applications to the world!

## How it works...

The process is pretty straightforward and quick. What is worth mentioning again, is the type of account you get.

Once you log in to your OpenShift Online account, at the upper-right corner of the screen, you can find your username with a down arrow. If you click on it, you will see a little menu; click on the first item labeled **My Account**.

It should provide you with a page like the following:

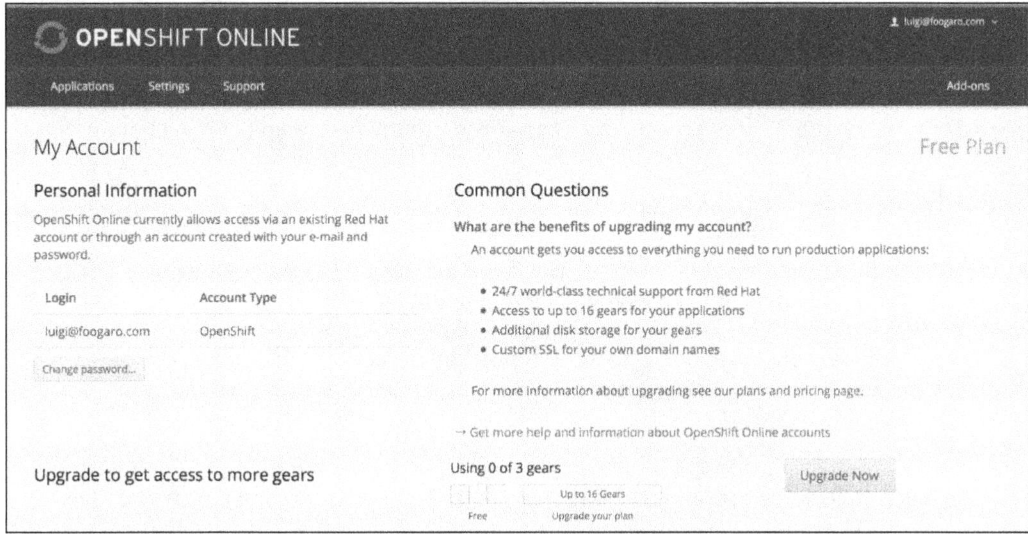


OpenShift Online "My Account" page

In that page there are four things that need to be noticed:

- On the left is your login e-mail and your account type; it's always better to check.
- On the upper-right side of the screen is a grayed bold label specifying the **Free Plan**.
- Towards the bottom-center is the information that at the moment you are using zero (**0**) gears out of three (**3**), and that they are free. Also, at the same location, there is a hint that you can have a maximum of **16 Gears**, not more! This is something you should consider when choosing between OpenShift Online and OpenShift Enterprise, which is totally customizable.
- Last, but not least, is the **Upgrade Now** button, which provides you with all the information that you need to upgrade to the **Bronze** or **Silver** Plans.

## See also

- For all the services that OpenShift Online provides and how it works, please refer to the documentation at `https://www.openshift.com/walkthrough/how-it-works`
- If you are looking for documentation from a developer's point of view, you can go to `https://developers.openshift.com`

# Installing the WildFly cartridge for our first deployment

In this recipe, you will learn how to configure the WildFly cartridge using your OpenShift Online account. If you still don't have an account, please refer to the first recipe of this chapter.

## Getting ready

As we will operate online most of the time, you need to have an Internet connection. On the other hand, all we need locally is a web application to deploy.

1. For this reason, download the entire repository named `wildfly-cookbook-oso`, from my GitHub account at `https://github.com/foogaro/wildfly-cookbook-oso.git`.
2. You can `git-clone` the project or just download it as a ZIP archive. Either way, place the source in our `~/WFC/github` path. There you can find a project called `openshift-welcome`. To compile the project, execute the following commands:

   ```
   $ cd ~/WFC/github/wildfly-cookbook-oso
   $ cd openshift-welcome
   $ mvn clean package
   ```

3. In the `target` folder, generated by maven, you should find the `openshift-welcome.war` artifact ready to be deployed.

Let's start for real now!

## How to do it...

1. First things first; log in to your OSO account at `https://openshift.redhat.com/app/console`.

2. Use the e-mail and password chosen at the time of registration, as depicted in the following image:

OpenShift Online login form

3. Once there, the first thing to do is to create an application, as depicted in the following screenshot:

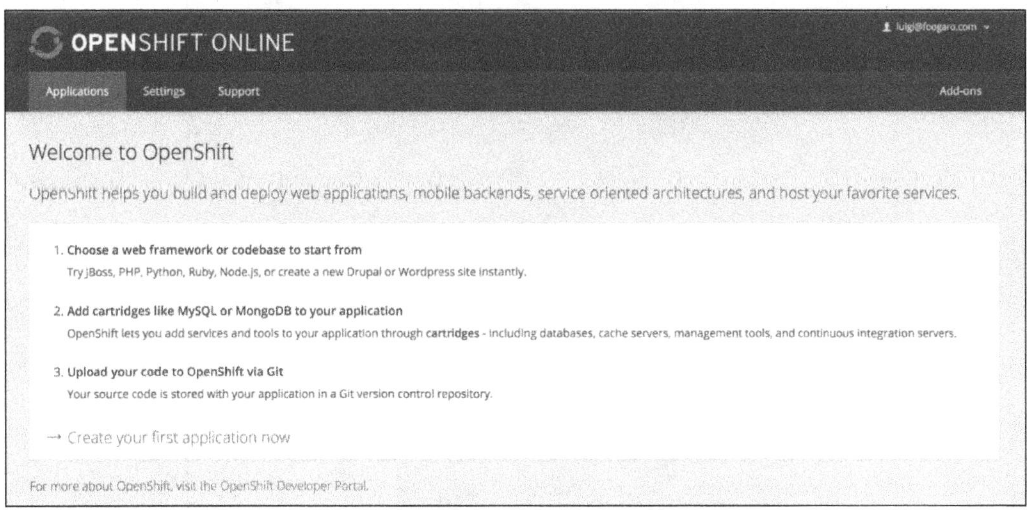


OpenShift Online welcome page

4. Follow the **Create your first application now** link. In the next page, select the WildFly cartridge, as shown in the following image:

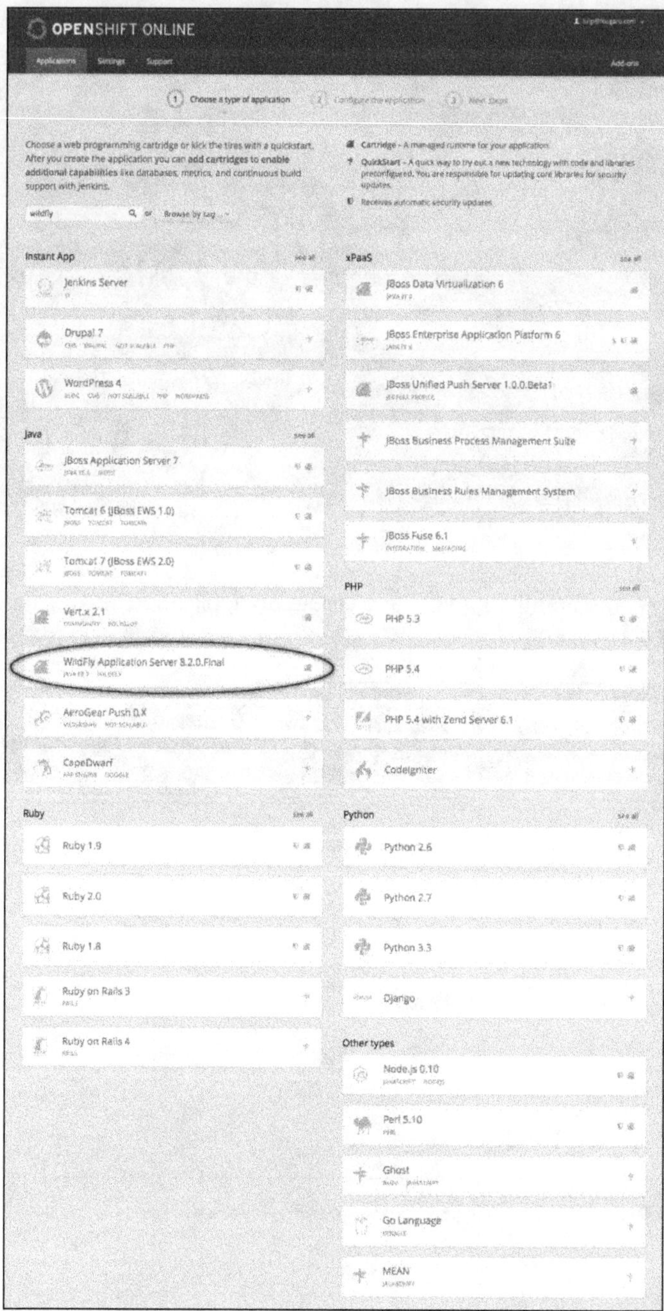

OpenShift Online list of most used cartridges

While writing the book, the latest available stable cartridge for WildFly is version 8.2.0.Final. Obviously, this is the application server which we will be using to provide our application.

5. Next, we need to configure our namespace, where all our applications will belong, and configure the application name; both of these together become the **Public URL**, as shown in the following image:

OPENSHIFT ONLINE
Applications Settings Support Add-ons
1 Choose a type of application 2 Configure the application 3 Next steps

Based On: WildFly Application Server 8.2.0.Final Cartridge

Public URL: http:// openshiftwelcome - wildflycookbook .rhcloud.com

Source Code: Optional URL to a Git repository Branch/tag

Gears: small

Cartridges: WildFly Application Server 8.2.0.Final

Scaling: No scaling

Region: No preference / aws-us-east-1 / aws-eu-west-1 / aws-ap-southeast-2

Back Create Application

redhat

OpenShift Online—applications settings form

6. What you need to change in the preceding form is the domain name, which is on the right side of the hyphen symbol (-); I chose `wildflycookbook`. The domain name must be unique within OpenShift Online at **rhcloud.com**. So choose your own domain name to which all your application names will belong.
7. For this very first try, leave all defaults as such and click the **Create Application** button. It will take a few minutes to do all that's necessary—it took me 4 minutes.
8. Then you will be asked if you will be changing the code:

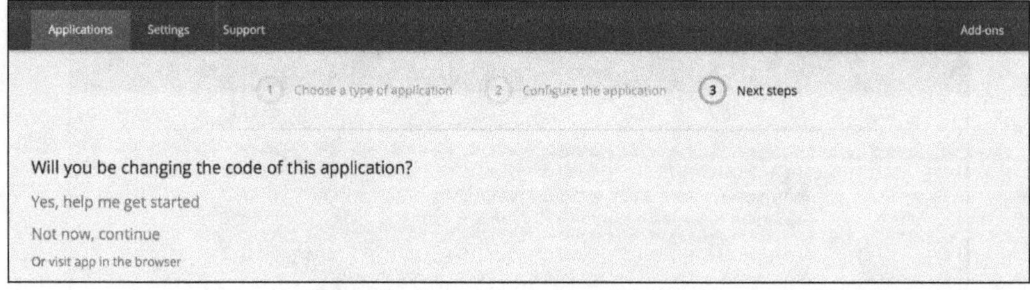


9. For the moment, we just skip this step and click on the link labeled **Not now, continue**—we will see the other option with a specific recipe, later in this chapter.
10. The next page will be our recap page, which will give us all the information to manage our WildFly instance, such as deploying our applications.

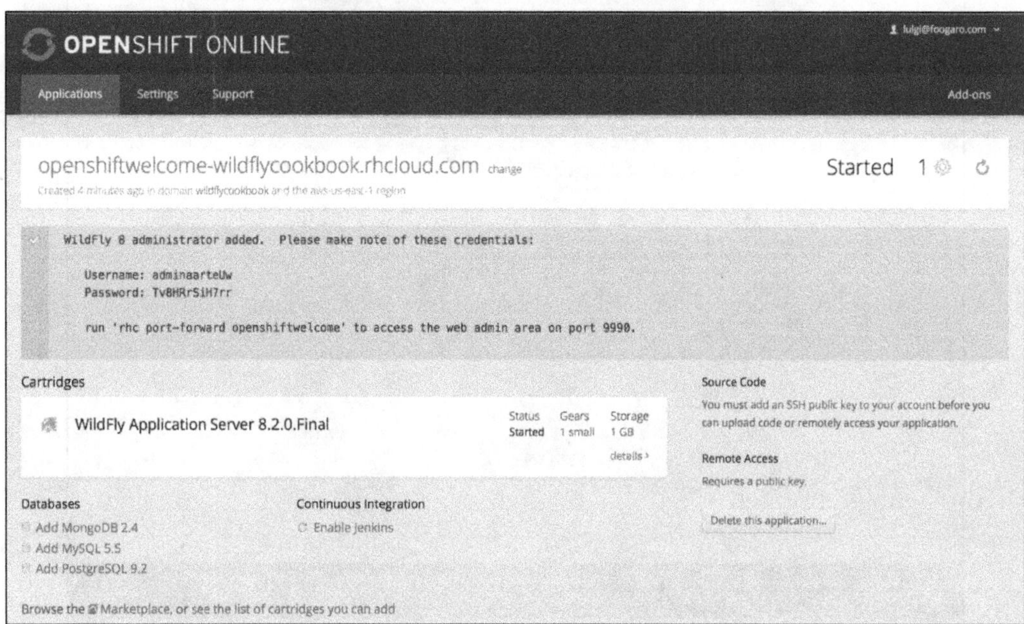

11. The green box in the preceding screenshot, depicts the **Username** and **Password** of an administrator user—basically, a user bound to `ManagementRealm` with administrator privileges. By the way, in order to access the Web Console, we need to use a tool called RHC which can forward for us all requests to port 9990 of the Admin console present in our new OpenShift Online environment.

    There is one more thing to do which is to install the client tool named RHC, which will provide us with a command-line interface to manage the OSO locally from our PC.

12. Open a terminal window and run the following commands:

    ```
    $ sudo yum -y install rubygems git
    $ sudo gem install rhc
    ```

13. Now that whole software has been installed, we need to setup the RHC tool, as follows:

    ```
    $ rhc setup
    OpenShift Client Tools (RHC) Setup Wizard


    This wizard will help you upload your SSH keys, set your
    application namespace, and check that other programs like Git are
    properly installed.


    If you have your own OpenShift server, you can specify it now.
    Just hit enter to use the server for OpenShift Online: openshift.
    redhat.com.
    Enter the server hostname: |openshift.redhat.com|


    You can add more servers later using 'rhc server'.


    Login to openshift.redhat.com: luigi@foogaro.com
    Password: ********


    OpenShift can create and store a token on disk which allows to
    you to access the server without using your password. The key is
    stored in your home directory and should be kept secret.  You can
    delete the key at
    any time by running 'rhc logout'.
    Generate a token now? (yes|no) yes
    ```

```
Generating an authorization token for this client ... lasts about
1 month

Saving configuration to /home/luigi/.openshift/express.conf ...
done

No SSH keys were found. We will generate a pair of keys for you.

    Created: /home/luigi/.ssh/id_rsa.pub

Your public SSH key must be uploaded to the OpenShift server to
access code.  Upload now? (yes|no) yes

Since you do not have any keys associated with your OpenShift
account, your new key will be uploaded as the 'default' key.

Uploading key 'default' ... done

Checking for git ... found git version 2.1.0

Checking common problems .. done

Checking for a domain ... wildflycookbook

Checking for applications ... found 1

  openshiftwelcome http://openshiftwelcome-wildflycookbook.
rhcloud.com/

  You are using 1 of 3 total gears
  The following gear sizes are available to you: small

Your client tools are now configured.
```

As you can see, the output fits my configuration. Yours should be similar, too.

Okay, let's go back to where we were. We were ready to deploy our application, but we needed to access the management console.

14. Now we can do it by first providing the following RHC command:

```
$ rhc port-forward openshiftwelcome
Checking available ports ... done
Forwarding ports ...

To connect to a service running on OpenShift, use the Local
address

Service Local               OpenShift
------- -------------- ---- ---------------
java    127.0.0.1:3528  =>  127.7.222.1:3528
java    127.0.0.1:8080  =>  127.7.222.1:8080
java    127.0.0.1:9990  =>  127.7.222.1:9990

Press CTRL-C to terminate port forwarding
```

    As described in the last line, keep this process running.

15. Now let's open a browser and point it to the OpenShift Online Admin Console, at `http://127.0.0.1:9990`.
16. When requested, insert the credentials provided to you when we created our first application, in the green box.

You should now see the following page:

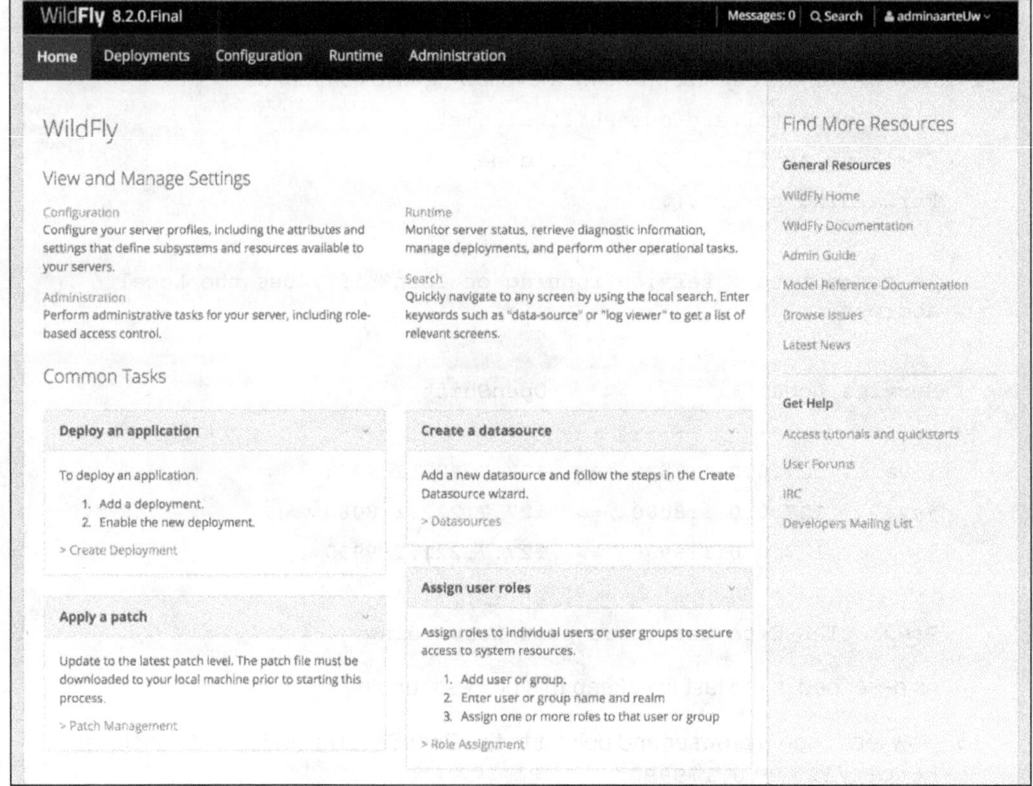


WildFly management console on OpenShift Online

17. We can deploy our application by clicking on the **Deployments** tag:

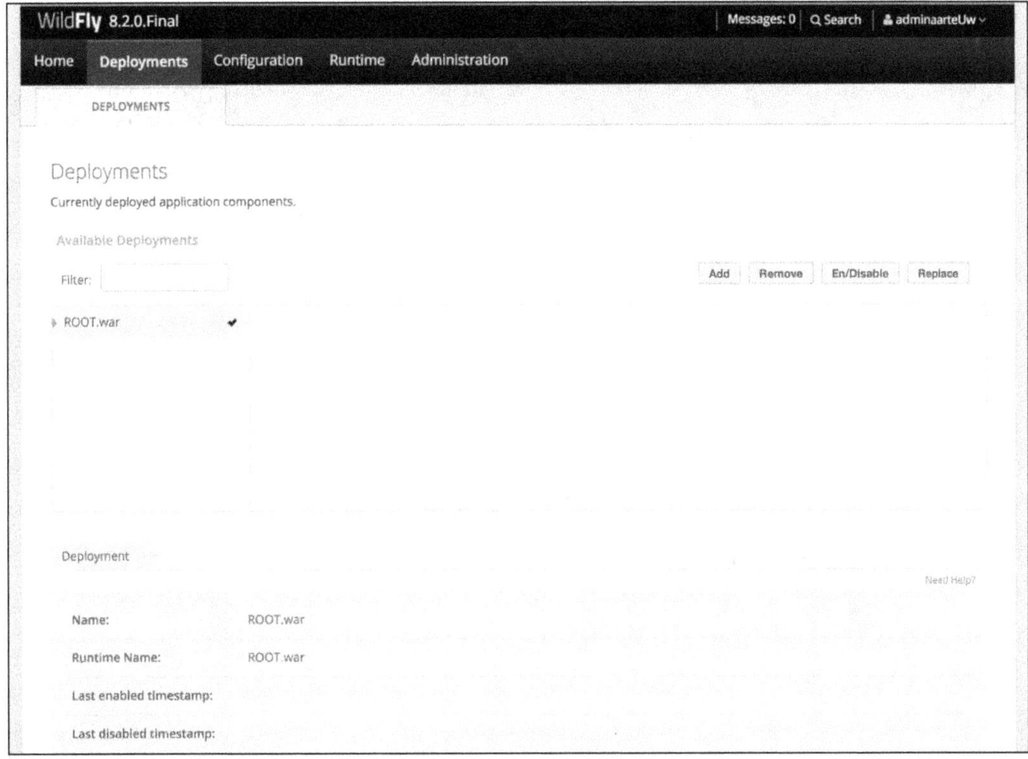


Deployments management

18. Click on the **Add** button, and choose the `openshift-welcome.war` artifact that we previously compiled with the maven command. Once we have chosen it, enable and confirm it as follows:

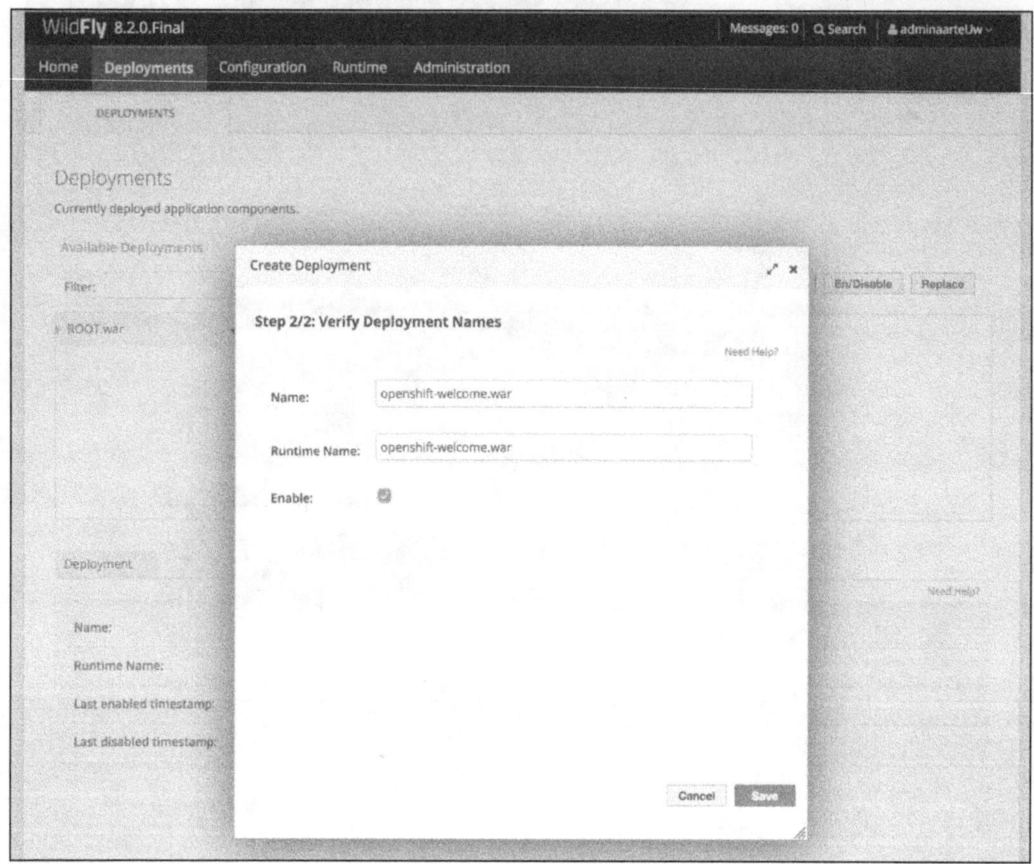


Deploying the openshift-welcome.war application

19. Once we have successfully deployed the application, let's try it by opening it at `http://openshiftwelcome-wildflycookbook.rhcloud.com`.

    That's our first application running on WildFly on OpenShift Online:

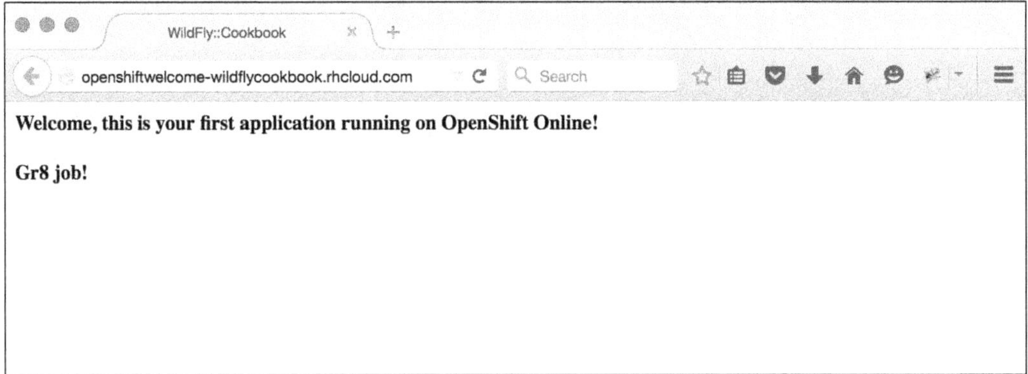


OpenShift-welcome application up and running

The page is designed to be as comprehensive as possible; I've also used the bold font style!

## How it works...

Well, here the tough job is done by OpenShift Online. The only thing we have done essentially is install the Ruby programming language environment to be able to install and run the RHC tool, which is the client tool used to mange the OpenShift Online environment.

Let's recap what we have done during the deployment of our first application in the cloud.

First we have chosen the cartridge. As we have seen, there are many cartridges that we can use for our gear: WildFly, JBoss AS, Tomcat, Drupal, WordPress, Node.js, and **MongoDB Express Angular Node** (**MEAN**). There are many of them, and you can find them all at the OpenShift Online site at `https://openshift.redhat.com/app/console/application_types`.

Once we have selected the WildFly cartridge, the platform asked us the **Public URL** to be used to publish our application, as shown in the following image:

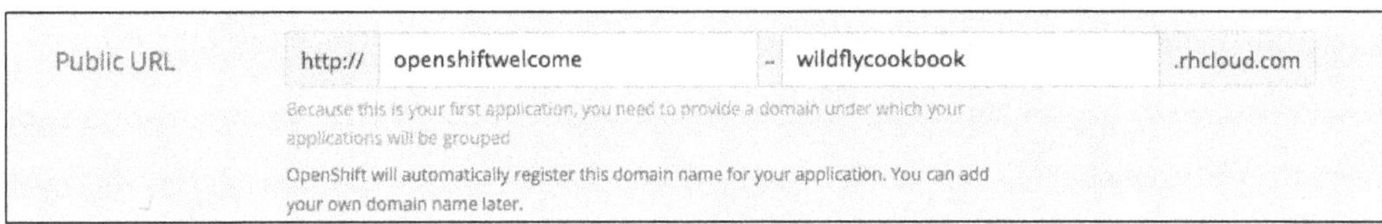


The Public URL to publish the application

The URL, besides the suffix **.rhcloud.com**, is composed using the application name and a namespace. The last one is essentially your domain, the one where all your applications reside. Remember, it has to be unique! In my case, I've chosen the namespace `wildflycookbook`.

As a matter of fact, the next time you create an application, you will be asked to give just the application name, as follows:

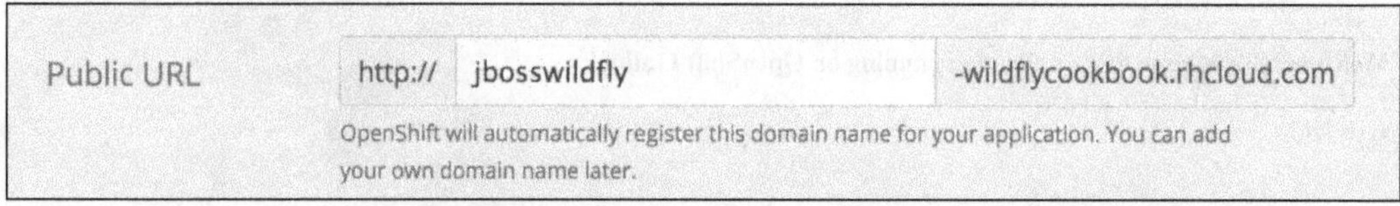
Public URL
http://
jbosswildfly
-wildflycookbook.rhcloud.com
OpenShift will automatically register this domain name for your application. You can add your own domain name later.

Defining your application name to be used into the public URL

Still remaining on the same page, there was another option we could have chosen—scaling—as shown in the following image:

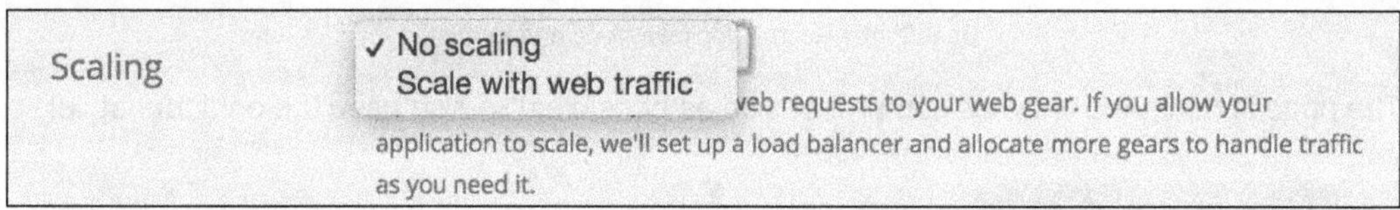
Scaling
✓ No scaling
Scale with web traffic
veb requests to your web gear. If you allow your application to scale, we'll set up a load balancer and allocate more gears to handle traffic as you need it.

Scaling option in OpenShift Online

This option would have given us the capability to automatically scale the application. In few words, as already mentioned in the introduction, OpenShift will create additional WildFly gears (as long as they are available in your plan) and a balancer gear, to scale horizontally, when the incoming traffic increases.

The next option would have been the **Region**, which is the location where the server would have run your gears: US, Europe, or Asia.

All gears of any size can be run in the **US**; only production gears can be deployed to the **EU** region (small.highcpu, medium, and large). The **Asia** region is reserved for dedicated node service.

So, with the free plan, we can only choose the **US** region, which is fine.

As you may have guessed from the name of the region (`aws-us-east-1`), OpenShift relies on the Amazon AWS, to create the servers. Because of the Amazon "pay-only-for-what-you-use" policy, whenever the incoming traffic to your site decreases, OpenShift gets back the extra resources.

Apart from the configuration settings, there was one setting I put into the application through the `WEB-INF/jboss-web.xml` JBoss specific descriptor file, which looks like this:

```
<jboss-web>
    <context-root>/</context-root>
</jboss-web>
```

The preceding configuration sets the context root of the application to `/`, so we can access it by just providing the URL `http://openshiftwelcome-wildflycookbook.rhcloud.com`, without any additional context path.

## There's more...

This recipe was a little long, and you have probably found yourself doing it in different ways. If so, you may have encountered this:

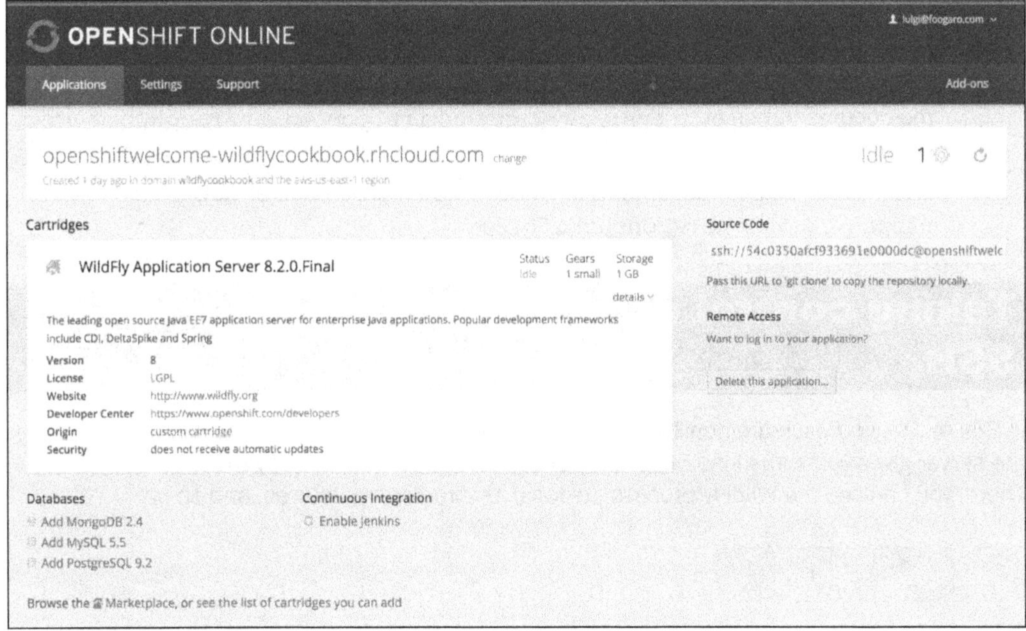


Application in the idle state

This basically means that your WildFly instance has stopped. Your application will not receive incoming traffic, and even the access to the WildFly management console will not work:

```
$ rhc port-forward openshiftwelcome

Checking available ports ... none

There are no available ports to forward for this application. Your
application may be stopped or idled.
```

The only way to move ahead is to restart the application.

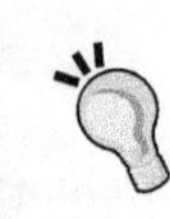

> Keep in mind that after 48 hours of inactivity, or no-traffic at all, OpenShift Online puts your application back to the idle state. To keep your application away from the idle state, you can have a kind of cron job doing a simple HTTP GET to your site, once a day.

## See also

- For all the services that OpenShift Online provides and how it works, please refer to the documentation at `https://www.openshift.com/walkthrough/how-it-works`
- If you are looking for documentation from a developer's point of view, go to `https://developers.openshift.com`

# Taking control of your WildFly server via SSH

In this recipe, you will learn how to access the server where your WildFly is running. Accessing the server gives you some kind of comfort because, I guess, it's the way we usually work. There, you can see the WildFly process, its logs, its directory structures, and so on.

## Getting ready

Before you can effectively go through this recipe, you should have an active OpenShift Online account, along with an application. In case you need to, you can follow recipe one for the registration process, and follow *Installing the WildFly cartridge for our first deployment* recipe of this chapter to create your first application.

In this recipe, I will use the environment generated while creating the application `openshiftwelcome`; yours might be different but would conceptually be the same.

## How to do it...

1. First, let's log in to your OSO account, at `https://openshift.redhat.com/app/console`.
2. Then enter the username and password that you chose during the registration process.
3. Once logged in, select the application that you have created, or create a new one as described in the second recipe. I'll select my `openshiftwelcome` application.

   The following are my application details:

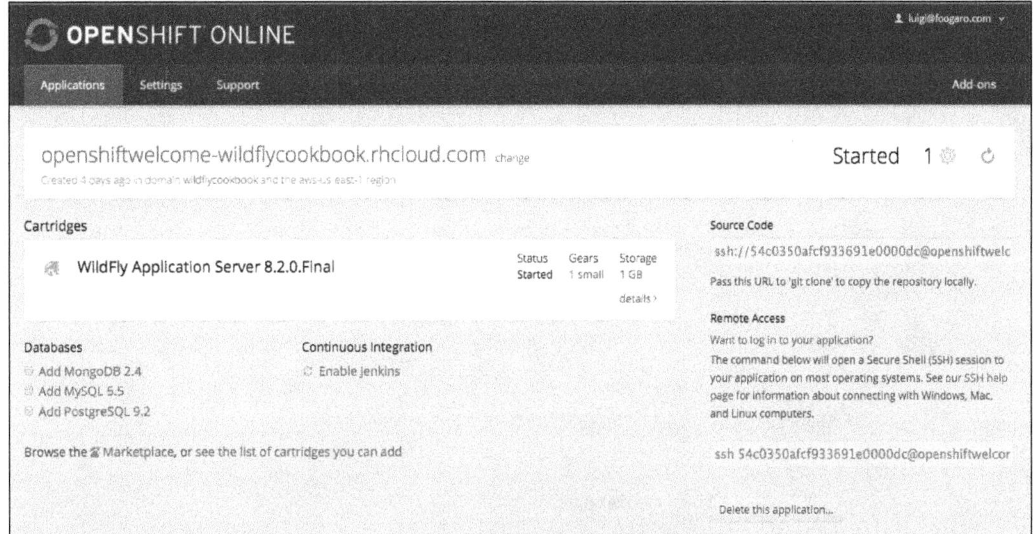


Application details

   In the preceding screenshot, there are two sections on the right named **Source Code** and **Remote Access**.

4. In the **Remote Access** section, click on the **Want to log in to your application?** label. It describes how to log in to the server which is hosting your application, obviously along with its cartridge.
5. Open a terminal window and copy-paste the `ssh` command that the page is providing you. Mine is as follows:

```
$ ssh 54c0350afcf933691e0000dc@openshiftwelcome-wildflycookbook.
rhcloud.com

    *************************************************************
*******

    You are accessing a service that is for use only by authorized
users.
```

```
    If you do not have authorization, discontinue use at once.
    Any use of the services is subject to the applicable terms of
the
    agreement which can be found at:
    https://www.openshift.com/legal

    *************************************************************
*******

    Welcome to OpenShift shell

    This shell will assist you in managing OpenShift applications.

    !!! IMPORTANT !!! IMPORTANT !!! IMPORTANT !!!
    Shell access is quite powerful and it is possible for you to
    accidentally damage your application.  Proceed with care!
    If worse comes to worst, destroy your application with "rhc
app delete"
    and recreate it
    !!! IMPORTANT !!! IMPORTANT !!! IMPORTANT !!!

    Type "help" for more info.


[openshiftwelcome-wildflycookbook.rhcloud.com
54c0350afcf933691e0000dc]\>
```

Once there, you can view the WildFly logs and see everything else that you want to.

Be careful, if you delete something that you shouldn't, you will need to create your application again.

Let's take a look at the WildFly logs.

1. Execute the following:

```
[openshiftwelcome-wildflycookbook.rhcloud.com
54c0350afcf933691e0000dc]\> tail -f wildfly/standalone/log/server.
log

2015-01-23 11:17:20,864 INFO  [org.jboss.as.server] (XNIO-1 task-
4) JBAS018559: Deployed "openshift-welcome.war" (runtime-name :
"openshift-welcome.war")

2015-01-23 11:20:21,227 INFO  [org.wildfly.extension.undertow]
(MSC service thread 1-2) JBAS017535: Unregistered web context: /
openshift-welcome

2015-01-23 11:20:21,379 INFO  [org.hibernate.validator.internal.
util.Version] (MSC service thread 1-1) HV000001: Hibernate
Validator 5.1.3.Final

2015-01-23 11:20:21,590 INFO  [org.jboss.as.server.deployment]
(MSC service thread 1-2) JBAS015877: Stopped deployment openshift-
welcome.war (runtime-name: openshift-welcome.war) in 386ms

2015-01-23 11:20:21,676 INFO  [org.jboss.as.server] (XNIO-1 task-
9) JBAS018558: Undeployed "openshift-welcome.war" (runtime-name:
"openshift-welcome.war")

2015-01-23 11:20:21,677 INFO  [org.jboss.as.repository] (XNIO-1
task-9) JBAS014901: Content removed from location /var/lib/openshi
ft/54c0350afcf933691e0000dc/wildfly/standalone/data/content/6a/248
1425c24beff9c840891145f6ea0ae5d1058/content

2015-01-23 11:20:34,820 INFO  [org.jboss.as.repository] (XNIO-1
task-4) JBAS014900: Content added at location /var/lib/openshift/5
4c0350afcf933691e0000dc/wildfly/standalone/data/content/1b/65c52cb
d69dc9f2fd0dbab59f1fb82c3c05038/content

2015-01-23 11:20:35,195 INFO  [org.jboss.as.server.deployment]
(MSC service thread 1-2) JBAS015876: Starting deployment of
"openshift-welcome.war" (runtime-name: "openshift-welcome.war")

2015-01-23 11:20:35,305 INFO  [org.wildfly.extension.undertow]
(MSC service thread 1-2) JBAS017534: Registered web context: /

2015-01-23 11:20:35,418 INFO  [org.jboss.as.server] (XNIO-1 task-
8) JBAS018559: Deployed "openshift-welcome.war" (runtime-name :
"openshift-welcome.war")
```

2. Obviously, you are not limited to the logs; you can see the process, as follows:

```
[openshiftwelcome-wildflycookbook.rhcloud.com
54c0350afcf933691e0000dc]\> ps -efa | grep java | grep -v grep
```

```
4028      94579  94303  0 Jan23 ?        00:08:07 /var/lib/open
shift/54c0350afcf933691e0000dc/wildfly/usr/lib/jvm/jdk1.8.0_05/
bin/java -D[Standalone] -server -Xmx256m -XX:MaxPermSize=102m
-XX:+AggressiveOpts -Dorg.apache.tomcat.util.LOW_MEMORY=true
-DOPENSHIFT_APP_UUID=54c0350afcf933691e0000dc -Dorg.jboss.
resolver.warning=true -Djava.net.preferIPv4Stack=true -Dfile.
encoding=UTF-8 -Djboss.node.name=openshiftwelcome-wildflycookbook.
rhcloud.com -Djgroups.bind_addr= -Dorg.apache.coyote.http11.
Http11Protocol.COMPRESSION=on -Dorg.jboss.boot.log.file=/var/
lib/openshift/54c0350afcf933691e0000dc/wildfly//standalone/log/
server.log -Dlogging.configuration=file:/var/lib/openshift/54c0
350afcf933691e0000dc/wildfly//standalone/configuration/logging.
properties -jar /var/lib/openshift/54c0350afcf933691e0000dc/
wildfly//jboss-modules.jar -mp /var/lib/openshift/54c0350afcf9
33691e0000dc/app-root/runtime/repo//.openshift/config/modules:/
var/lib/openshift/54c0350afcf933691e0000dc/wildfly//modules org.
jboss.as.standalone -Djboss.home.dir=/var/lib/openshift/54c0350a
fcf933691e0000dc/wildfly/ -Djboss.server.base.dir=/var/lib/opens
hift/54c0350afcf933691e0000dc/wildfly//standalone -b 127.7.222.1
-bmanagement=127.7.222.1
```

3. Or you can see the server resources by executing the `htop` command:

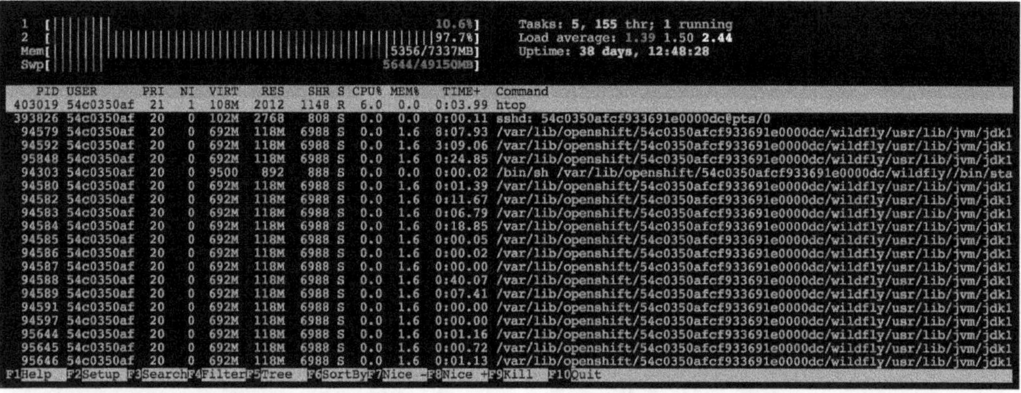


Keep in mind that you can see and control everything as long as your user (the hash that identifies your application; mine is `54c0350afcf933691e0000dc`) has permissions.

## How it works...

Whenever you create an application, you are actually creating an environment along with a cartridge that enables your application. OpenShift Online creates everything for you, assigning the whole process a hash. That hash will be your username to log in to your server, and it also identifies your application. The rest of the process of how OpenShift creates things is out of the scope of this book.

If you want to learn more about how things work under the hood, I suggest you start with this book: *Learning OpenShift, Grant Shipley, Packt Publishing*.

## See also

- Make it a point to always refer to the official documentation, which, in this case, can be found at `https://docs.openshift.org/`

# Deploying your code to OpenShift Online

In this recipe, you will learn how to re-deploy an application whenever the source code updates happen. This is done automatically for you by OpenShift Online, which triggers compilation and deployment every time a commit is applied to your code.

## Getting ready

1. First of all, we need a project on GitHub that we can use for our test. For this reason, I've created a project called `openshiftcoding-wildflycookbook` on my GitHub repository, available at `https://github.com/foogaro/openshiftcoding-wildflycookbook`.
2. If you do not have an account on GitHub, this might be a good reason to have one. Sooner or later you will need one. To get started quickly, go to the GitHub site at `https://github.com` and sign up. Once the registration process is complete, you will be ready to create a repository, which will host the source code of your application. If you don't have an application, you can borrow mine.
3. Anyway, this time you don't have to download or `git-clone` my GitHub repository locally, as it will be used to feed the next OpenShift application. But we do need to install the `git` client tool. If you are using an OS similar to Red Hat, run the following command:

   ```
   $ sudo yum -y install git
   ```

4. Once done, you can check that everything is installed successfully, by issuing the following command:

```
$ git version
git version 2.1.0
```

Okay, now we are ready to begin!

## How to do it...

1. First of all, you need to access your OpenShift Online account at the following address `https://openshift.redhat.com/app/console`.
2. Use the e-mail and the password chosen at the time of registration, as depicted in the following screenshot:

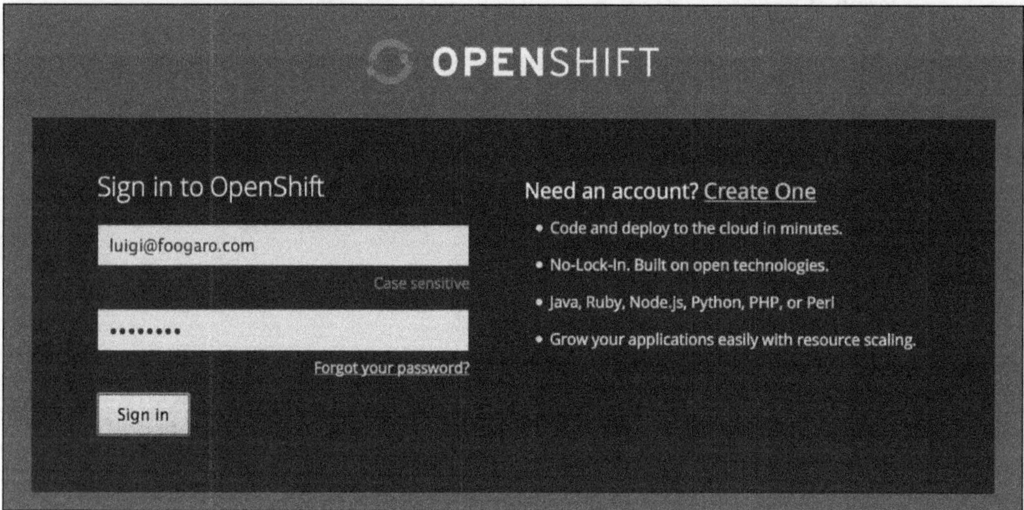


OpenShift Online login form

If you don't have an OpenShift Online account yet, follow the registration process described in the first recipe of this chapter.

3. Once you log in, on the main page, click the **Add Application...** button to create a new application:

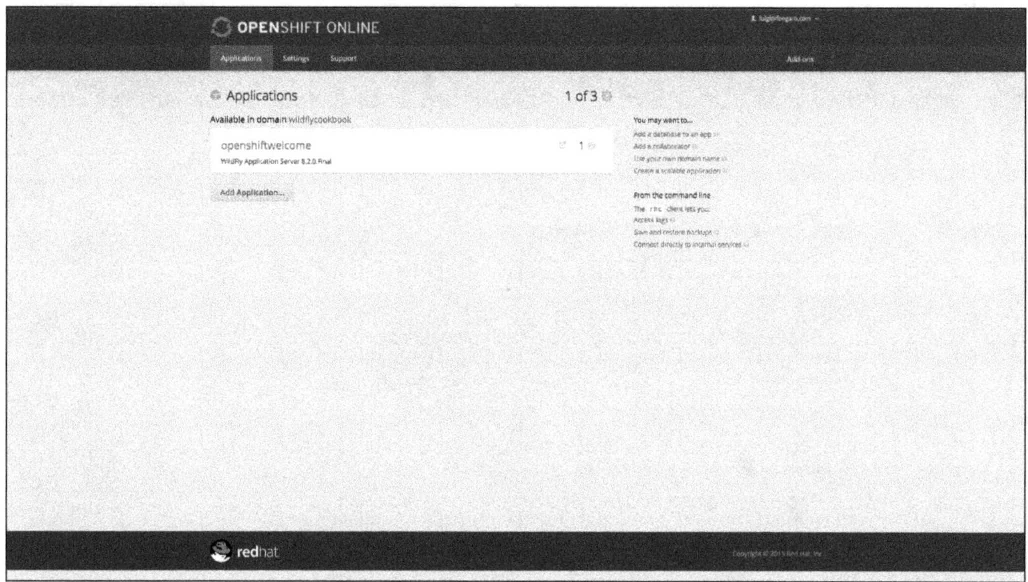


OpenShift Online initial console for adding a new application

4. Next we need to select the WildFly cartridge. As there are tens of cartridges, we can search for it by providing a criteria filter, as depicted in the following screenshot:

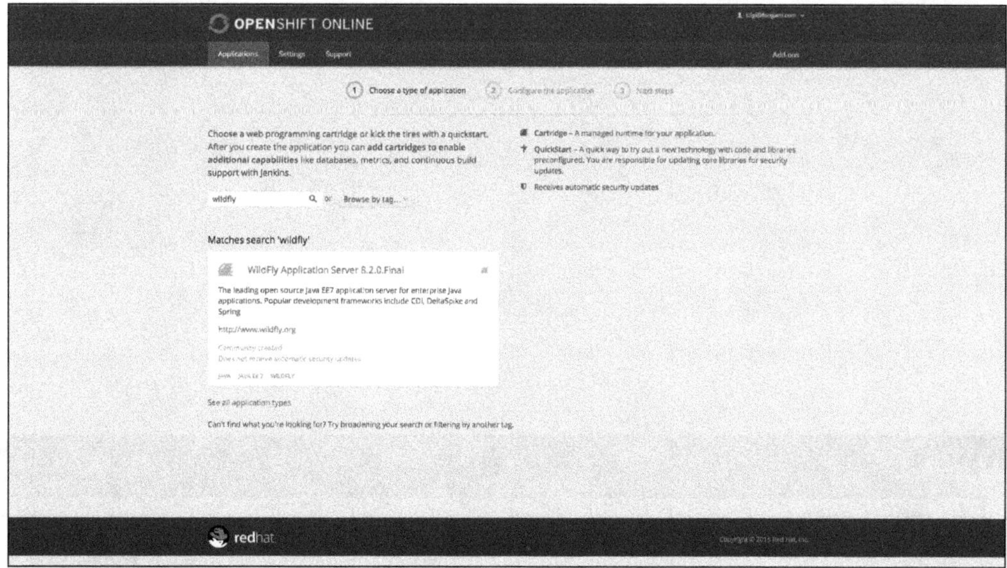


Selecting the WildFly cartridge by filtering it

5. Afterwards, select the cartridge and fill in the form with the details of our application, as follows:

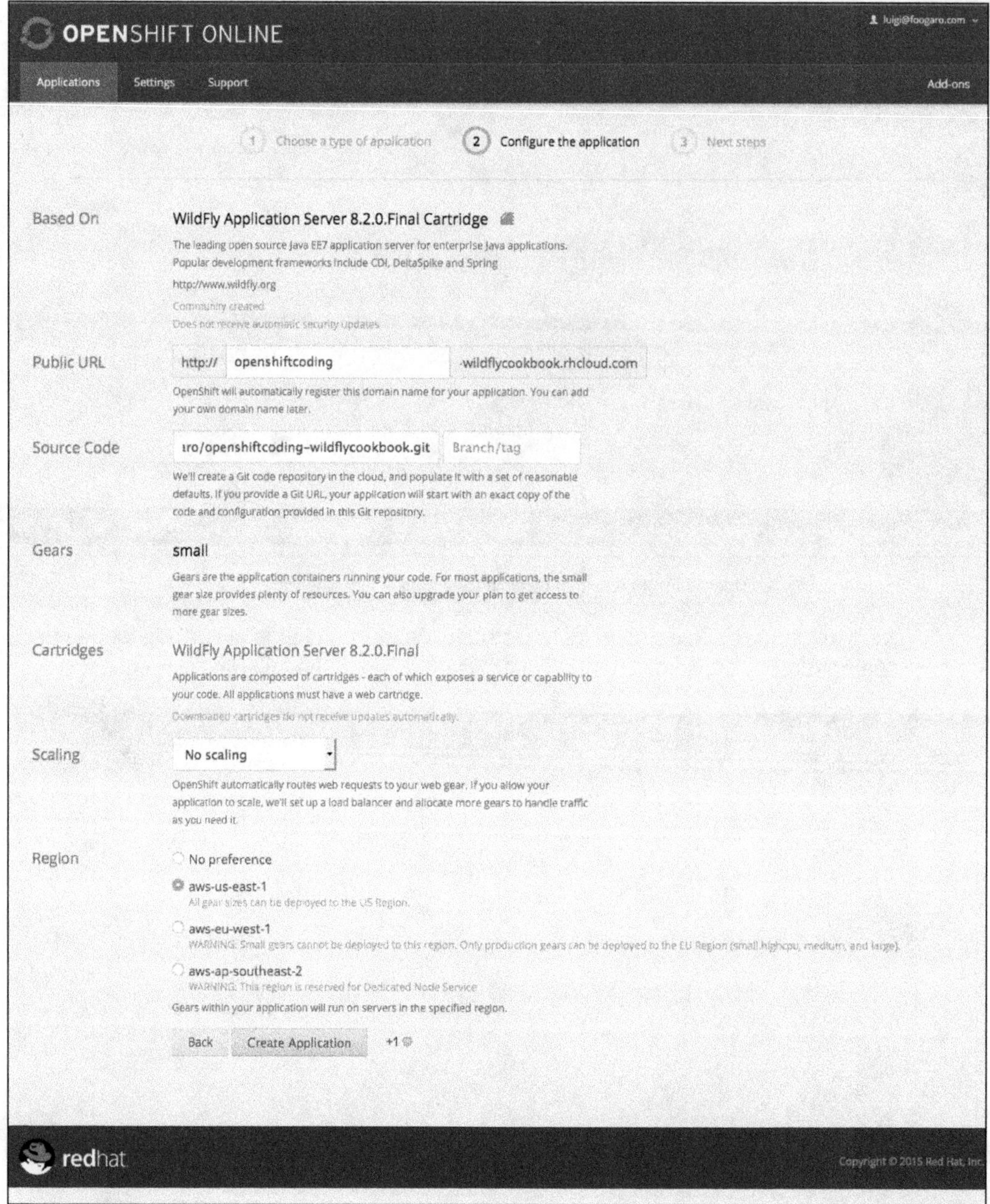


Setting application details

In my case, I've called my application `openshiftcoding`. This time I've specified my GitHub repository, where my application is available, that is, at `https://github.com/foogaro/openshiftcoding-wildflycookbook.git`. You will need to specify yours.

6. Complete the form by leaving the other default values as such and by clicking the **Create Application** button. It may take few minutes to complete.
7. Once the process is complete, you should see a page like the following:

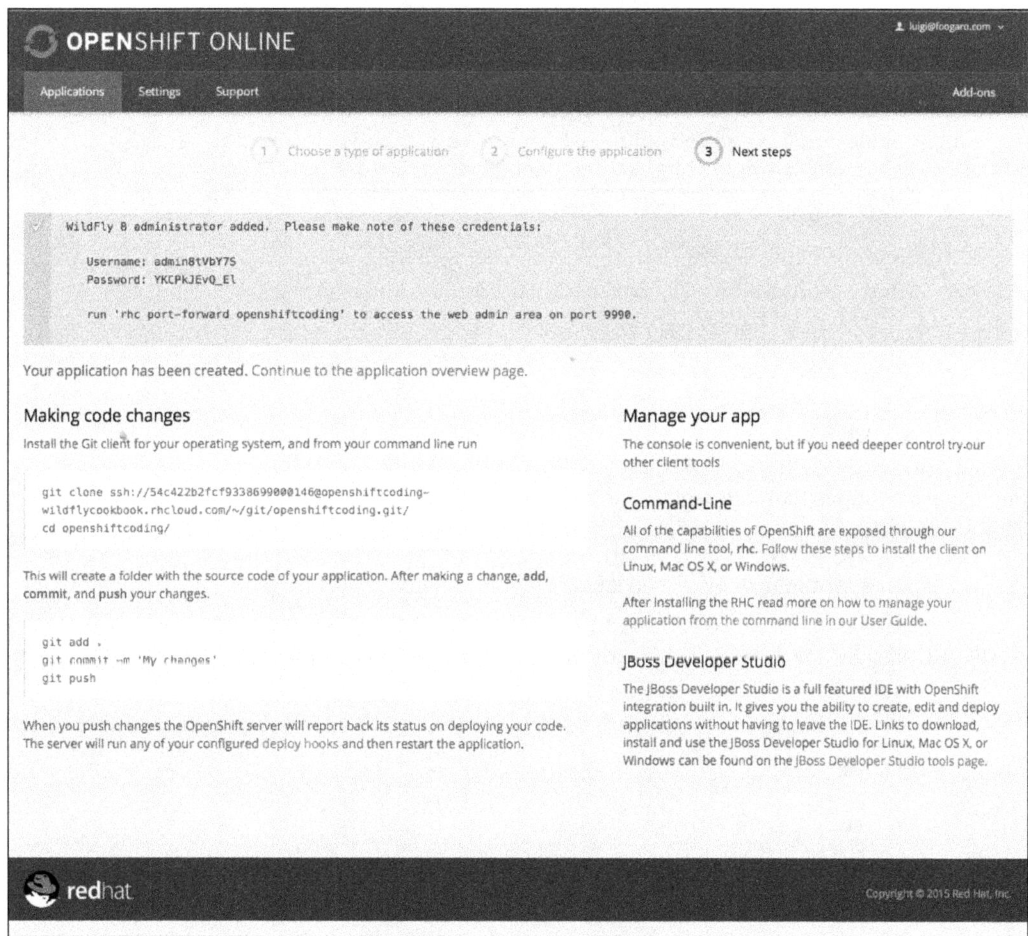


Recap of the newly created application

As you can see from the preceding image, there is a section labeled **Making code changes**, that describes what we need to do in order to modify the source of our application, and have it automatically updated whenever we modify the code.

Therefore, open a terminal window and issue the `git clone` command identifying your application repository in OpenShift Online—it is not the one on GitHub, but will be cloned locally into the server that OpenShift will create for you.

These are the commands that I enter now:

```
$ cd ~/WFC/github
$ mkdir git-openshift
$ cd git-openshift
$ git clone ssh://54c422b2fcf9338699000146@openshiftcoding-wildflycookbook.rhcloud.com/~/git/openshiftcoding.git/
Cloning into 'openshiftcoding'...
Warning: Permanently added the RSA host key for IP address '54.234.243.133' to the list of known hosts.
remote: Counting objects: 24, done.
remote: Compressing objects: 100% (18/18), done.
remote: Total 24 (delta 4), reused 24 (delta 4)
Receiving objects: 100% (24/24), done.
Resolving deltas: 100% (4/4), done.
Checking connectivity... done.
```

We are now ready to change our source code, commit it, and see OpenShift compiling and deploying our application directly to our WildFly instance. To see all this beauty, we need to look at the logs.

1. Open a terminal window and issue the following command:

   ```
   $ ssh 54c422b2fcf9338699000146@openshiftcoding-wildflycookbook.rhcloud.com


       ***********************************************************************


       You are accessing a service that is for use only by authorized users.
       If you do not have authorization, discontinue use at once.
       Any use of the services is subject to the applicable terms of the
       agreement which can be found at:
   ```

```
    https://www.openshift.com/legal

    *****************************************************************
*******


    Welcome to OpenShift shell


    This shell will assist you in managing OpenShift applications.


    !!! IMPORTANT !!! IMPORTANT !!! IMPORTANT !!!
    Shell access is quite powerful and it is possible for you to
    accidentally damage your application.  Proceed with care!
    If worse comes to worst, destroy your application with "rhc
app delete"
    and recreate it
    !!! IMPORTANT !!! IMPORTANT !!! IMPORTANT !!!


    Type "help" for more info.



[openshiftcoding-wildflycookbook.rhcloud.com
54c422b2fcf9338699000146]\> tail -f wildfly/standalone/log/server.
log
2015-01-24 17:56:23,264 INFO  [org.jboss.as.connector.deployment]
(MSC service thread 1-5) JBAS010406: Registered connection factory
java:/JmsXA
2015-01-24 17:56:23,337 INFO  [org.hornetq.ra] (MSC service thread
1-5) HornetQ resource adaptor started
2015-01-24 17:56:23,338 INFO  [org.jboss.as.connector.services.
resourceadapters.ResourceAdapterActivatorService$ResourceAdapte
rActivator] (MSC service thread 1-5) IJ020002: Deployed: file://
RaActivatorhornetq-ra
2015-01-24 17:56:23,355 INFO  [org.jboss.as.messaging] (MSC
service thread 1-7) JBAS011601: Bound messaging object to jndi
name java:jboss/DefaultJMSConnectionFactory
2015-01-24 17:56:23,355 INFO  [org.jboss.as.connector.deployment]
(MSC service thread 1-5) JBAS010401: Bound JCA ConnectionFactory
[java:/JmsXA]
```

```
2015-01-24 17:56:23,835 INFO  [org.wildfly.extension.undertow]
(MSC service thread 1-4) JBAS017534: Registered web context: /

2015-01-24 17:56:24,069 INFO  [org.jboss.as.server] (ServerService
Thread Pool -- 32) JBAS018559: Deployed "openshift-coding.war"
(runtime-name : "openshift-coding.war")

2015-01-24 17:56:24,199 INFO  [org.jboss.as] (Controller Boot
Thread) JBAS015961: Http management interface listening on
http://127.7.132.129:9990/management

2015-01-24 17:56:24,201 INFO  [org.jboss.as] (Controller
Boot Thread) JBAS015951: Admin console listening on
http://127.7.132.129:9990

2015-01-24 17:56:24,201 INFO  [org.jboss.as] (Controller Boot
Thread) JBAS015874: WildFly 8.2.0.Final "Tweek" started in 10428ms
- Started 294 of 425 services (178 services are lazy, passive or
on-demand)
```

2. As you can see from the preceding log that has been emphasized, our application is already there; in fact, if we open the public URL that we specified while creating the application, we can see it working, as follows:

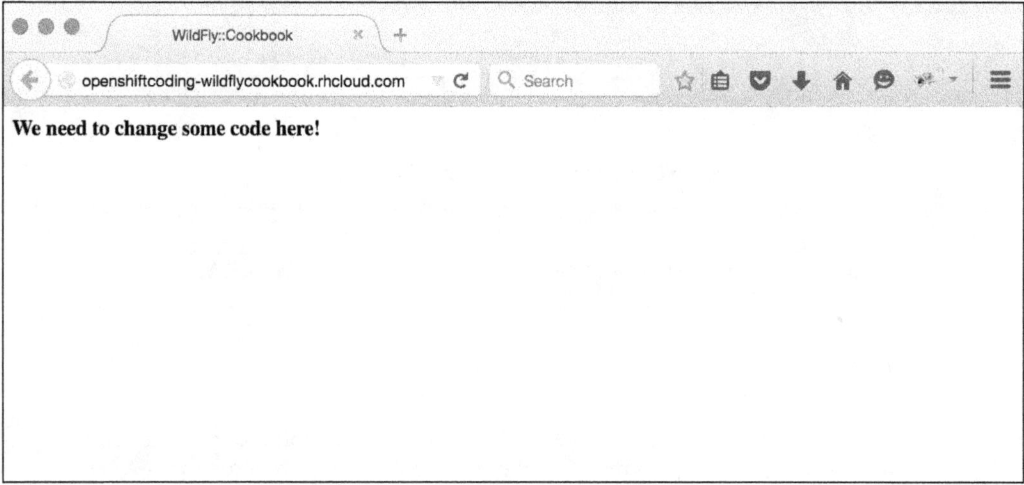


The application needs to be updated

Okay, let's update the source code. In my case, I only have a JSP, and its code is the following:

```
<!DOCTYPE html PUBLIC
"-//W3C//DTD XHTML 1.1 Transitional//EN"
"http://www.w3.org/TR/xhtml1/DTD/xhtml1-transitional.dtd">

<html xmlns="http://www.w3.org/1999/xhtml" xml:lang="en"
lang="en">
```

```
<head>
    <title>WildFly::Cookbook</title>
</head>
<body>
<b>We need to change some code here!</b>
</body>
</html>
```

3. Let's add some color to the text as follows:

```
<b style="color:red;">We need to change some code here!</b>
```

4. Now, we can update our code to the Git repository from the first terminal window (where we cloned the Git repository from OpenShift), as follows:

```
$ cd ~/WFC/github/git-openshift/openshiftcoding
$ git status
On branch master
Your branch is up-to-date with 'origin/master'.
Changes not staged for commit:
  (use "git add <file>..." to update what will be committed)
  (use "git checkout -- <file>..." to discard changes in working
directory)
  modified:   src/main/webapp/index.jsp

no changes added to commit (use "git add" and/or "git commit -a")
$ git add .
$ git commit -m "Added red color to the text"
[master c894С7c] Added red color to the text
 1 file changed, 1 insertion(+), 1 deletion(-)
```

5. Now, we need to push everything. Before doing that, let's grab the other terminal with the visible WildFly log. Now we can do the magic...

```
$ git push
warning: push.default is unset; its implicit value has changed in
Git 2.0 from 'matching' to 'simple'. To squelch this message
and maintain the traditional behavior, use:

  git config --global push.default matching

To squelch this message and adopt the new behavior now, use:
```

```
  git config --global push.default simple

When push.default is set to 'matching', git will push local
branches
to the remote branches that already exist with the same name.

Since Git 2.0, Git defaults to the more conservative 'simple'
behavior, which only pushes the current branch to the
corresponding
remote branch that 'git pull' uses to update the current branch.

See 'git help config' and search for 'push.default' for further
information.
(the 'simple' mode was introduced in Git 1.7.11. Use the similar
mode
'current' instead of 'simple' if you sometimes use older versions
of Git)

Counting objects: 6, done.
Delta compression using up to 8 threads.
Compressing objects: 100% (5/5), done.
Writing objects: 100% (6/6), 517 bytes | 0 bytes/s, done.
Total 6 (delta 2), reused 0 (delta 0)
remote: Stopping wildfly cart
remote: Sending SIGTERM to wildfly:455867 ...
remote: Building git ref 'master', commit c89467c
remote: Found pom.xml... attempting to build with 'mvn -e clean
package -Popenshift -DskipTests'
remote: Apache Maven 3.0.4 (r1232336; 2012-12-18 14:36:37-0500)
remote: Maven home: /usr/share/java/apache-maven-3.0.4
remote: Java version: 1.8.0_05, vendor: Oracle Corporation
remote: Java home: /var/lib/openshift/54c422b2fcf9338699000146/
wildfly/usr/lib/jvm/jdk1.8.0_05/jre
remote: Default locale: en_US, platform encoding: ANSI_X3.4-1968
remote: OS name: "linux", version: "2.6.32-504.3.3.el6.x86_64",
arch: "i386", family: "unix"
remote: [INFO] Scanning for projects...
remote: [INFO]
```

```
remote: [INFO] ------------------------------------------------------------------------
remote: [INFO] Building openshift-coding 1.0
remote: [INFO] ------------------------------------------------------------------------
remote: [INFO]
remote: [INFO] --- maven-clean-plugin:2.4.1:clean (default-clean) @ openshift-coding ---
remote: [INFO]
remote: [INFO] --- maven-resources-plugin:2.5:resources (default-resources) @ openshift-coding ---
remote: [debug] execute contextualize
remote: [INFO] Using 'UTF-8' encoding to copy filtered resources.
remote: [INFO] Copying 1 resource
remote: [INFO]
remote: [INFO] --- maven-compiler-plugin:2.3.2:compile (default-compile) @ openshift-coding ---
remote: [INFO] No sources to compile
remote: [INFO]
remote: [INFO] --- maven-resources-plugin:2.5:testResources (default-testResources) @ openshift-coding ---
remote: [debug] execute contextualize
remote: [INFO] Using 'UTF-8' encoding to copy filtered resources.
remote: [INFO] skip non existing resourceDirectory /var/lib/openshift/54c422b2fcf9338699000146/app-root/runtime/repo/src/test/resources
remote: [INFO]
remote: [INFO] --- maven-compiler-plugin:2.3.2:testCompile (default-testCompile) @ openshift-coding ---
remote: [INFO] No sources to compile
remote: [INFO]
remote: [INFO] --- maven-surefire-plugin:2.10:test (default-test) @ openshift-coding ---
remote: [INFO] Tests are skipped.
remote: [INFO]
remote: [INFO] --- maven-war-plugin:2.4:war (default-war) @ openshift-coding ---
remote: [INFO] Packaging webapp
```

```
remote: [INFO] Assembling webapp [openshift-coding] in [/var/lib/
openshift/54c422b2fcf9338699000146/app-root/runtime/repo/target/
openshift-coding]
remote: [INFO] Processing war project
remote: [INFO] Copying webapp resources [/var/lib/openshift/54c422
b2fcf9338699000146/app-root/runtime/repo/src/main/webapp]
remote: [INFO] Webapp assembled in [79 msecs]
remote: [INFO] Building war: /var/lib/openshift/54c422b2f
cf9338699000146/app-root/runtime/repo/deployments/openshift-
coding.war
remote: [INFO] ---------------------------------------------------
---------------------
remote: [INFO] BUILD SUCCESS
remote: [INFO] ---------------------------------------------------
---------------------
remote: [INFO] Total time: 5.855s
remote: [INFO] Finished at: Sat Jan 24 18:19:48 EST 2015
remote: [INFO] Final Memory: 7M/79M
remote: [INFO] ---------------------------------------------------
---------------------
remote: Preparing build for deployment
remote: Deployment id is 9aac8674
remote: Activating deployment
remote: Deploying WildFly
remote: Starting wildfly cart
remote: Found 127.7.132.129:8080 listening port
remote: Found 127.7.132.129:9990 listening port
remote: /var/lib/openshift/54c422b2fcf9338699000146/
wildfly/standalone/deployments /var/lib/openshift/54c422b2f
cf9338699000146/wildfly
remote: /var/lib/openshift/54c422b2fcf9338699000146/wildfly
remote: CLIENT_MESSAGE: Artifacts deployed: ./openshift-coding.war
remote: ------------------------
remote: Git Post-Receive Result: success
remote: Activation status: success
remote: Deployment completed with status: success
To ssh://54c422b2fcf9338699000146@openshiftcoding-wildflycookbook.
rhcloud.com/~/git/openshiftcoding.git/
   f2eba48..c89467c  master -> master
```

If you are familiar with `git`, you'll know that this push took a little longer than expected, but it did a lot of things:

- It stopped our WildFly
- It updated the code
- It issued a maven compilation, packaged our application as a `war`
- It copied our new application into the WildFly `deployments` folder
- It started WildFly

6. And if you have looked at the WildFly logs too, you should have noticed the following entries:

```
...
2015-01-24 18:19:36,758 INFO  [org.jboss.as] (MSC service thread 1-1) JBAS015950: WildFly 8.2.0.Final "Tweek" stopped in 1273ms
...
2015-01-24 18:20:13,374 INFO  [org.wildfly.extension.undertow] (MSC service thread 1-5) JBAS017534: Registered web context: /
2015-01-24 18:20:13,673 INFO  [org.jboss.as.server] (ServerService Thread Pool -- 32) JBAS018559: Deployed "openshift-coding.war" (runtime-name : "openshift-coding.war")
2015-01-24 18:20:13,871 INFO  [org.jboss.as] (Controller Boot Thread) JBAS015961: Http management interface listening on http://127.7.132.129:9990/management
2015-01-24 18:20:13,879 INFO  [org.jboss.as] (Controller Boot Thread) JBAS015951: Admin console listening on http://127.7.132.129:9990
2015-01-24 18:20:13,879 INFO  [org.jboss.as] (Controller Boot Thread) JBAS015874: WildFly 8.2.0.Final "Tweek" started in 23656ms - Started 294 of 425 services (178 services are lazy, passive or on-demand)
```

7. Let's see if everything worked correctly. Open the browser and go to `http://openshiftcoding-wildflycookbook.rhcloud.com`.

You should see something like the following page:

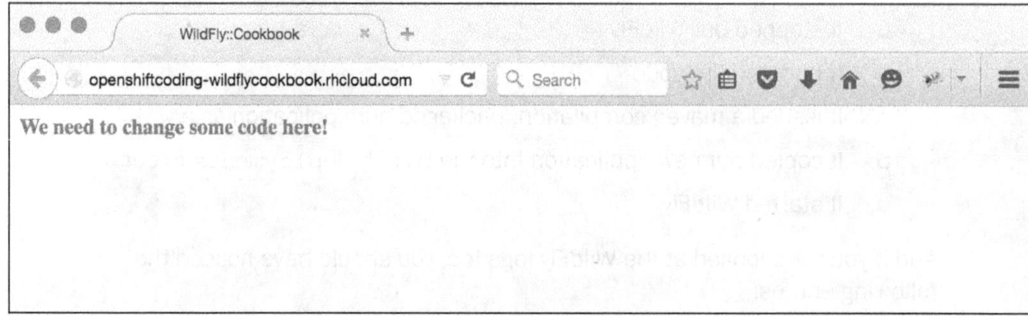


Application updated through a git push

Great, it worked!

## How it works...

OpenShift Online hides and does a lot of things under the hood, making our lives easier, much easier. The only thing that we actually did was on the development side.

To let OpenShift Online easily compile, package, and deploy our application, we need to instruct it about how to compile the source, how to package it, and where to deploy it. We can give these directives through the maven project file, the `pom.xml`.

The following is the complete `pom.xml` file of the `openshiftcoding-wildflycookbook` project (also available at `https://github.com/foogaro/openshiftcoding-wildflycookbook/blob/master/pom.xml`):

```
<project xmlns="http://maven.apache.org/POM/4.0.0" xmlns:xsi="http://
www.w3.org/2001/XMLSchema-instance"
        xsi:schemaLocation="http://maven.apache.org/POM/4.0.0
        http://maven.apache.org/maven-v4_0_0.xsd">
    <modelVersion>4.0.0</modelVersion>
    <groupId>com.packtpub.wildfly-cookbook</groupId>
    <artifactId>openshift-coding</artifactId>
    <packaging>war</packaging>
    <version>1.0</version>
    <name>openshift-coding</name>

    <properties>
        <project.build.sourceEncoding>UTF-
        8</project.build.sourceEncoding>
    </properties>

    <profiles>
```

```
        <profile>
            <id>openshift</id>
            <build>
                <finalName>${project.name}</finalName>
                <plugins>
                    <plugin>
                        <groupId>org.apache.maven.
                        plugins</groupId>
                        <artifactId>maven-war-plugin</artifactId>
                        <version>2.4</version>
                        <configuration>
                            <failOnMissingWebXml>false
                            </failOnMissingWebXml>
                            <outputDirectory>deployments
                            </outputDirectory>
                            <warName>${project.name}</warName>
                        </configuration>
                    </plugin>
                </plugins>
            </build>
        </profile>
    </profiles>

</project>
```

The key point here is the profile named `openshift`. By default, OSO uses Maven to compile the source code, asking to use the `openshift` profile. The profile that it finds will be used along with its settings; otherwise, the code will be just compiled and packaged, but OSO will not know where to deploy it.

The `openshift` profile that I've provided, defines (with the `build` tag ) the settings to be used during Maven's build phase. Particularly, I've used the standard `maven-war-plugin` and set the `outputDirectory` to `deployments`, which is the one that WildFly uses.

## See also

From a developer's point of view, I recommend that you refer to the official documentation at the following sites:

- `http://www.openshift.org/documentation/index.html`
- `https://developers.openshift.com/en/managing-modifying-applications.html`

# 15

# Using WildFly with Docker

In this chapter, you will learn the following recipes:

- Setting up the Docker environment
- Running WildFly in Docker
- Logging WildFly outside Docker
- Running WildFly in domain mode in Docker using different Docker containers

## Introduction

In this chapter, we will start learning the basics of Docker, and how you can take advantage of it by deploying your applications along with the environment.

Docker is an open source platform to develop, ship, and run applications. The basic idea of Docker is to get rid of the problems that occur when you promote your applications (actually the whole thing, such as the runtime environment) from environment to environment; that is, from development, to test, to pre-production, to quality, till production. There are so many variables involved that even if you do your best, something can go wrong in the traditional software life cycle.

With Docker, you can replicate your entire environment at every stage. The word "replicate" probably doesn't explain the concept well enough; "resubmit" would be better.

Docker is composed of the following:

- **Images**: A Docker image is just like a template. Suppose you have an image with Fedora, Java 8, WildFly, and your installed application. Images can be downloaded or built with a descriptor file called `Dockerfile`. From images you can run your containers.
- **Registries**: These are the places where images are stored. There can be private and public registries, such as Docker Hub (`http://hub.docker.com`).
- **Containers**: They are, essentially, the running component of Docker. Basically, it's a running instance of a Docker image. A container can be started, stopped, deleted, and so on. Each container is isolated from the host that is running it and from other containers as well.

By the way, how can we achieve a no bad surprises result when promoting our application at various stages with Docker? Think of Docker as a tool for creating a stack of pluggable layers. The first layer is the OS layer, then comes your environment layer (it might be your specific Java runtime version), then your application layer—you can have as many layers as you want/need.

Once your stack is all filled in, what you get is your Docker image, which is ready to be committed into the registry. After that, you grab your image and install that exact image on the production hardware. You then get what you had before, when everything was working smoothly—hope you get the idea.

For a better understanding of what Docker is, I strongly suggest you read the default documentation and user guide at the following URLs:

- `http://docs.docker.com/introduction/understanding-docker`
- `http://docs.docker.com/userguide`

Within this chapter, we will mainly use the Docker client, available for different operating systems, which is the tool that interfaces with the Docker daemon. There are so many settings and features to talk about that it would require another book. For this reason, I will focus on installing the client tool, and will explain the commands and parameters that we will use in our recipes, that is, in some basic WildFly scenarios.

# Setting up the Docker environment

In this recipe, you will learn how to install Docker and get acquainted with the basic commands. You will see how to create and build an image based on Fedora, and how you can run it.

## Getting ready

We will need to have access to the Internet in order to download and install Docker and its dependencies.

## How to do it...

1. To install Docker on Fedora, issue the following commands:

   ```
   $ sudo yum -y remove docker
   $ sudo yum -y install docker-io
   ```

   The installation should look like the following screenshot:

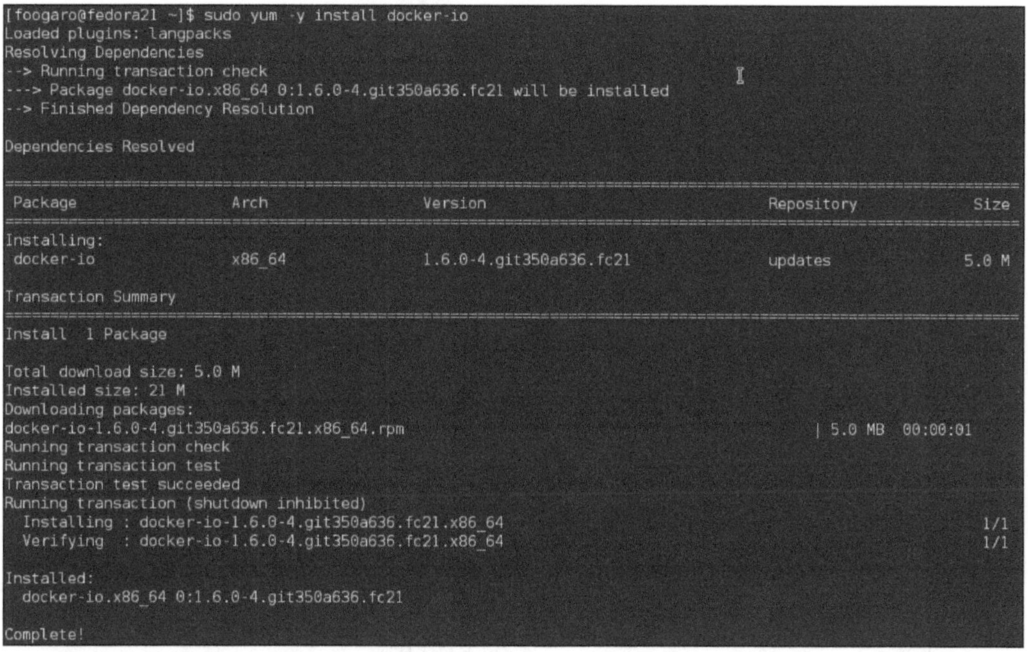

```
[foogaro@fedora21 ~]$ sudo yum -y install docker-io
Loaded plugins: langpacks
Resolving Dependencies
--> Running transaction check
---> Package docker-io.x86_64 0:1.6.0-4.git350a636.fc21 will be installed
--> Finished Dependency Resolution

Dependencies Resolved

================================================================================
 Package          Arch          Version                      Repository    Size
================================================================================
Installing:
 docker-io        x86_64        1.6.0-4.git350a636.fc21      updates      5.0 M

Transaction Summary
================================================================================
Install  1 Package

Total download size: 5.0 M
Installed size: 21 M
Downloading packages:
docker-io-1.6.0-4.git350a636.fc21.x86_64.rpm                | 5.0 MB  00:00:01
Running transaction check
Running transaction test
Transaction test succeeded
Running transaction (shutdown inhibited)
  Installing : docker-io-1.6.0-4.git350a636.fc21.x86_64                     1/1
  Verifying  : docker-io-1.6.0-4.git350a636.fc21.x86_64                     1/1

Installed:
  docker-io.x86_64 0:1.6.0-4.git350a636.fc21

Complete!
```

2. Okay, now that Docker is installed, let's run it:

   ```
   $ sudo systemctl start docker
   ```

3. If you want to start Docker at boot time, use the following command:

   ```
   $ sudo systemctl enable docker
   Created symlink from /etc/systemd/system/multi-user.target.wants/
   docker.service to /usr/lib/systemd/system/docker.service.
   ```

4. Also, ensure that your user is in the `docker` group, by executing the following:

   ```
   $ groups
   luigi wheel docker
   ```

5. In case the `docker` group is not listed, add it with the following command:

```
$ sudo usermod -a -G docker luigi
```

   Obviously, replace the user `luigi` with yours.

6. Check Docker's version by issuing the following command:

```
$ docker version
Client version: 1.6.0
Client API version: 1.18
Go version (client): go1.4.2
Git commit (client): 350a636/1.6.0
OS/Arch (client): linux/amd64
Server version: 1.6.0
Server API version: 1.18
Go version (server): go1.4.2
Git commit (server): 350a636/1.6.0
```

   Great, we are now ready to dockerize whatever we want!

7. To do this, first we need to check if there are any images available, as follows:

```
$ docker images
REPOSITORY          TAG                 IMAGE ID
CREATED             VIRTUAL SIZE
```

8. As there is no image available, we need to look for it by issuing the following command:

```
$ docker search fedora
NAME                             DESCRIPTION
STARS      OFFICIAL   AUTOMATED
fedora                           Official Fedora 21 base image and
semi-off...   128        [OK]
fedora/apache
28         [OK]
fedora/couchdb
25         [OK]
fedora/mariadb
22         [OK]
fedora/memcached
19         [OK]
fedora/earthquake
17         [OK]
```

```
fedora/ssh
16         [OK]

...
```

9. The Docker image we want is the official Fedora 21. We can download it as follows:

```
$ docker pull fedora:21
fedora:latest: The image you are pulling has been verified

511136ea3c5a: Pull complete
00a0c78eeb6d: Pull complete
834629358fe2: Downloading [>                    ] 2.681 MB/250 MB
3m20s
```

10. When all the pulls are complete, we get the following output:

```
$ docker pull fedora:21
fedora:latest: The image you are pulling has been verified

511136ea3c5a: Pull complete
00a0c78eeb6d: Pull complete
834629358fe2: Pull complete
Status: Downloaded newer image for fedora:latest
```

11. We can now use our first Fedora Docker image by executing the following command:

```
$ docker run -it --rm fedora /bin/bash
bash-4.3# ls -la
total 60
drwxr-xr-x.  18 root root 4096 Jan 29 09:52 .
drwxr-xr-x.  18 root root 4096 Jan 29 09:52 ..
-rwxr-xr-x.   1 root root    0 Jan 29 09:52 .dockerenv
-rwxr-xr-x.   1 root root    0 Jan 29 09:52 .dockerinit
lrwxrwxrwx.   1 root root    7 Aug 16 09:24 bin -> usr/bin
dr-xr-xr-x.   3 root root 4096 Dec  3 00:56 boot
drwxr-xr-x.   5 root root  380 Jan 29 09:52 dev
drwxr-xr-x.  47 root root 4096 Jan 29 09:52 etc
drwxr-xr-x.   2 root root 4096 Aug 16 09:24 home
lrwxrwxrwx.   1 root root    7 Aug 16 09:24 lib -> usr/lib
lrwxrwxrwx.   1 root root    9 Aug 16 09:24 lib64 -> usr/lib64
drwx------.   2 root root 4096 Dec  3 00:56 lost+found
```

```
drwxr-xr-x.   2 root root 4096 Aug 16 09:24 media
drwxr-xr-x.   2 root root 4096 Aug 16 09:24 mnt
drwxr-xr-x.   2 root root 4096 Aug 16 09:24 opt
dr-xr-xr-x. 233 root root    0 Jan 29 09:52 proc
dr-xr-x---.   2 root root 4096 Dec  3 00:58 root
drwxr-xr-x.   2 root root 4096 Dec  3 00:56 run
lrwxrwxrwx.   1 root root    8 Aug 16 09:24 sbin -> usr/sbin
drwxr-xr-x.   2 root root 4096 Aug 16 09:24 srv
dr-xr-xr-x.  13 root root    0 Jan 19 06:57 sys
drwxrwxrwt.   7 root root 4096 Dec  3 00:58 tmp
drwxr-xr-x.  12 root root 4096 Dec  3 00:56 usr
drwxr-xr-x.  18 root root 4096 Dec  3 00:56 var
bash-4.3# env
HOSTNAME=141b250d4361
TERM=xterm
PATH=/usr/local/sbin:/usr/local/bin:/usr/sbin:/usr/bin:/sbin:/bin
PWD=/
SHLVL=1
HOME=/root
_=/usr/bin/env
bash-4.3#
```

## How it works...

How long did it take to start the container with Fedora? Milliseconds? How long would it take to start a Fedora VM in a traditional virtualization environment? Tens of seconds? What about the overall installation? With Docker, everything gets extremely fast.

We have finally installed the Docker tool and downloaded the latest Fedora image (which is version 21 while writing this book). We can use this as a base for our next recipe, *Running WildFly into Docker*.

When you first install Docker, there are no images available, and you need to get them from the Docker registry. The default registry is the online Docker Hub, where you can also sign up for free and have your own space to share your Docker images.

Before you can pull (that is, download) a Docker image, you need to know at least its name. By issuing the command `docker search IMAGE_NAME`, you are essentially filtering all the images stored in the DockerHub that have the specified filter in the name or in the description.

Once you have pulled the image of your choice, you can use it to run a container, as per the following command:

```
$ docker run -i -t fedora /bin/bash
bash-4.3#
```

In the preceding command, we are using the Docker client tool to communicate with the Docker daemon, which is active and listening in our system.

Specifically, we instruct Docker to `run` a container based on the `fedora` image, and finally execute the `/bin/bash` command in it.

We also specified the following flags:

- `-i`: Which enables the STDIN
- `-t`: Which allocates a pseudo-tty, the terminal

# Running WildFly in Docker

In this recipe, you will learn how to run WildFly in a Docker container by creating a `Dockerfile`, which describes how the image should be composed. To go through this recipe, you need to have a working Docker installation, along with a Fedora 21 image; if you don't have these installed, please follow the first recipe in this chapter.

## Getting ready

In this recipe, you will need an internet connection to download WildFly directly from the container. Also, we will need a Java web application to test our WildFly installation. If you want, you can use one of my projects from my GitHub account, at `https://github.com/foogaro/wildfly-cookbook.git`.

You can `git-clone` the repository or just download it as a ZIP archive:

1. Place the source at `~/WFC/github`.
2. There you will find a project called `docker-example`. To compile the project, run the following commands:

   ```
   $ cd ~/WFC/github
   $ cd wildfly-cookbook
   $ cd docker-example
   $ mvn clean package
   ```

In the `target` folder generated by Maven, you should find the `docker-example.war` artifact, ready to be deployed.

3. Next, create a folder in which we will place all our Docker files that we will create along the way, as follows:

   ```
   $ cd ~/WFC && mkdir -p docker/wildfly
   ```

Let's Docker now!

## How to do it...

The first thing we need to do is create the `Dockerfile` file in the `~/WFC/docker/wildfly` folder.

1. Open a text editor and create a file named `Dockerfile`. Now copy and paste the following code:

   ```
   FROM fedora:latest

   MAINTAINER Luigi Fugaro l.fugaro@gmail.com

   RUN yum -y install java-1.8.0-openjdk

   RUN yum -y install tar net-tools

   RUN cd /opt && curl http://download.jboss.org/wildfly/9.0.0.Beta2/
   wildfly-9.0.0.Beta2.tar.gz | tar zx

   RUN ln -s /opt/wildfly-9.0.0.Beta2 /opt/wildfly

   RUN groupadd -r cookbook -g 12345 && useradd -u 54321 -r -g
   cookbook -d /opt/wildfly -s /sbin/nologin -c "WildFly user"
   wildfly

   RUN /opt/wildfly/bin/add-user.sh wildfly cookbook.2015 --silent

   RUN chown -R wildfly:cookbook /opt/wildfly/*

   EXPOSE 8080 9990

   USER wildfly

   CMD ["/opt/wildfly/bin/standalone.sh", "-b", "0.0.0.0",
   "-bmanagement", "0.0.0.0"]
   ```

   Save it in the previously mentioned folder.

2. Now, with `Dockerfile`, we can build our image, specific for WildFly, and call it `foogaro/wildfly`, as follows:

```
$ cd ~/WFC/docker/wildfly
$ docker build -t foogaro/wildfly .
Sending build context to Docker daemon 5.12 kB
Sending build context to Docker daemon
Step 0 : FROM fedora:latest
 ---> 834629358fe2
Step 1 : MAINTAINER Luigi Fugaro l.fugaro@gmail.com
 ---> Running in 29c6d2ecbe12
 ---> 54af5e1a15b6
Removing intermediate container 29c6d2ecbe12
Step 2 : RUN yum -y install java-1.8.0-openjdk
 ---> Running in 7d73ef1137ea
Resolving Dependencies
--> Running transaction check
---> Package java-1.8.0-openjdk.x86_64 1:1.8.0.31-3.b13.fc21 will
be installed
...
Complete!
Step 3 : RUN yum -y install tar net-tools
 ---> Running in 6a147261f3a7
Resolving Dependencies
--> Running transaction check
---> Package net-tools.x86_64 0:2.0-0.31.20141124git.fc21 will be
installed
---> Package tar.x86_64 2:1.27.1-7.fc21 will be installed
...
Complete!
Step 4 : RUN cd /opt && curl http://download.jboss.org/
wildfly/9.0.0.Beta2/wildfly-9.0.0.Beta2.tar.gz | tar zx
 ---> Running in 90738a7cb6c0
  % Total    % Received % Xferd  Average Speed   Time    Time
Time  Current
                                 Dload  Upload   Total   Spent
Left  Speed
100  112M  100  112M    0     0   771k      0  0:02:29  0:02:29
--:--:--  778k
```

```
 ---> 5e1138497058
Removing intermediate container 90738a7cb6c0
Step 5 : RUN ln -s /opt/wildfly-9.0.0.Beta2 /opt/wildfly
 ---> Running in 34d760c4ba59
 ---> 5c9b207bd2aa
Removing intermediate container 34d760c4ba59
Step 6 : RUN /opt/wildfly/bin/add-user.sh wildfly cookbook.2015
--silent
 ---> Using cache
 ---> 4cf96ff92355
Step 7 : EXPOSE 8080 9990
 ---> Running in 51703bccf71e
 ---> 7fbb535ab85a
Removing intermediate container 51703bccf71e
Step 8 : CMD /opt/wildfly/bin/standalone.sh -b 0.0.0.0
-bmanagement 0.0.0.0
 ---> Running in e8537f97615a
 ---> 56d5fea9c4ff
Removing intermediate container e8537f97615a
Successfully built 56d5fea9c4ff
```

3. Great! We have successfully created our first Docker image named `foogaro/wildfly`. Try issuing the following command now:

```
$ docker images
REPOSITORY       TAG     IMAGE ID      CREATED        VIRTUAL
SIZE
foogaro/wildfly latest  56d5fea9c4ff  3 minutes ago  745.8 MB
fedora           latest  834629358fe2  4 weeks ago    250.2 MB
```

As you can see, in addition to the other images, we have ours that has just been created.

4. Now, let's run WildFly as follows:

```
$ docker run -it -p 8080:8080 -p 9990:9990 --rm foogaro/wildfly
```

You should get the following output:

```
==============================================================

  JBoss Bootstrap Environment

  JBOSS_HOME: /opt/wildfly

  JAVA: java

  JAVA_OPTS:  -server -Xms64m -Xmx512m -XX:MaxPermSize=256m
-Djava.net.preferIPv4Stack=true -Djboss.modules.system.pkgs=org.
jboss.byteman -Djava.awt.headless=true

==============================================================

OpenJDK 64-Bit Server VM warning: ignoring option
MaxPermSize=256m; support was removed in 8.0
19:24:17,226 INFO  [org.jboss.modules] (main) JBoss Modules
version 1.3.3.Final
19:24:17,448 INFO  [org.jboss.msc] (main) JBoss MSC version
1.2.2.Final
19:24:17,514 INFO  [org.jboss.as] (MSC service thread 1-5)
JBAS015899: WildFly 8.2.0.Final "Tweek" starting
19:24:18,673 INFO  [org.jboss.as.server] (Controller Boot Thread)
JBAS015888: Creating http management service using socket-binding
(management-http)
19:24:18,694 INFO  [org.xnio] (MSC service thread 1-5) XNIO
version 3.3.0.Final
19:24:18,726 INFO  [org.xnio.nio] (MSC service thread 1-5) XNIO
NIO Implementation Version 3.3.0.Final
19:24:18,752 INFO  [org.jboss.as.clustering.infinispan]
(ServerService Thread Pool -- 32) JBAS010280: Activating
Infinispan subsystem.
```

```
19:24:18,768 INFO  [org.wildfly.extension.io] (ServerService
Thread Pool -- 31) WFLYIO001: Worker 'default' has auto-configured
to 8 core threads with 64 task threads based on your 4 available
processors

19:24:18,788 INFO  [org.jboss.as.naming] (ServerService Thread
Pool -- 40) JBAS011800: Activating Naming Subsystem

19:24:18,818 INFO  [org.jboss.as.connector.subsystems.datasources]
(ServerService Thread Pool -- 27) JBAS010403: Deploying JDBC-
compliant driver class org.h2.Driver (version 1.3)

19:24:18,840 INFO  [org.jboss.as.jsf] (ServerService Thread Pool
-- 38) JBAS012615: Activated the following JSF Implementations:
[main]

19:24:18,848 WARN  [org.jboss.as.txn] (ServerService Thread Pool
-- 46) JBAS010153: Node identifier property is set to the default
value. Please make sure it is unique.

19:24:18,865 INFO  [org.jboss.as.security] (ServerService Thread
Pool -- 45) JBAS013171: Activating Security Subsystem

19:24:18,871 INFO  [org.jboss.as.connector.logging] (MSC service
thread 1-8) JBAS010408: Starting JCA Subsystem (IronJacamar
1.1.9.Final)

19:24:18,914 INFO  [org.jboss.as.connector.deployers.jdbc] (MSC
service thread 1-8) JBAS010417: Started Driver service with
driver-name = h2

19:24:18,916 INFO  [org.jboss.as.security] (MSC service thread
1-3) JBAS013170: Current PicketBox version=4.0.21.Final

19:24:18,927 INFO  [org.jboss.as.webservices] (ServerService
Thread Pool -- 48) JBAS015537: Activating WebServices Extension

19:24:19,017 INFO  [org.wildfly.extension.undertow] (MSC service
thread 1-7) JBAS017502: Undertow 1.1.0.Final starting

19:24:19,023 INFO  [org.jboss.as.mail.extension] (MSC service
thread 1-2) JBAS015400: Bound mail session [java:jboss/mail/
Default]

19:24:19,027 INFO  [org.wildfly.extension.undertow] (ServerService
Thread Pool -- 47) JBAS017502: Undertow 1.1.0.Final starting

19:24:19,034 INFO  [org.jboss.remoting] (MSC service thread 1-5)
JBoss Remoting version 4.0.6.Final

19:24:19,050 INFO  [org.jboss.as.naming] (MSC service thread 1-4)
JBAS011802: Starting Naming Service

19:24:19,155 INFO  [org.wildfly.extension.undertow] (ServerService
Thread Pool -- 47) JBAS017527: Creating file handler for path /
opt/wildfly/welcome-content

19:24:19,183 INFO  [org.wildfly.extension.undertow] (MSC service
thread 1-7) JBAS017525: Started server default-server.
```

```
19:24:19,217 INFO  [org.wildfly.extension.undertow] (MSC service
thread 1-1) JBAS017531: Host default-host starting

19:24:19,473 INFO  [org.wildfly.extension.undertow] (MSC service
thread 1-3) JBAS017519: Undertow HTTP listener default listening
on /0.0.0.0:8080

19:24:19,622 INFO  [org.jboss.as.server.deployment.
scanner] (MSC service thread 1-3) JBAS015012: Started
FileSystemDeploymentService for directory /opt/wildfly/standalone/
deployments

19:24:19,730 INFO  [org.jboss.as.connector.subsystems.datasources]
(MSC service thread 1-6) JBAS010400: Bound data source
[java:jboss/datasources/ExampleDS]

19:24:19,887 INFO  [org.jboss.ws.common.management] (MSC service
thread 1-1) JBWS022052: Starting JBoss Web Services - Stack CXF
Server 4.3.2.Final

19:24:20,033 INFO  [org.jboss.as] (Controller Boot
Thread) JBAS015961: Http management interface listening on
http://0.0.0.0:9990/management

19:24:20,033 INFO  [org.jboss.as] (Controller Boot Thread)
JBAS015951: Admin console listening on http://0.0.0.0:9990

19:24:20,034 INFO  [org.jboss.as] (Controller Boot Thread)
JBAS015874: WildFly 8.2.0.Final "Tweek" started in 3113ms -
Started 184 of 234 services (82 services are lazy, passive or on-
demand)
```

5. Now try opening your browser, and point it to `http://127.0.0.1:9990/`.
6. The browser should prompt you for the username and password for the WildFly `ManagementRealm`; just enter the following credentials:
   - **Username**: `wildfly`
   - **Password**: `cookbook.2015`

   The preceding credentials are those specified in the `Dockerfile` file used to build the image.

There you go; you are in your dockerized WildFly instance!

Now we have quite a few options to deploy our `docker-example` application. We can go to the `Deployments` page of the WildFly Admin Console, add our artifact, upload it, and enable it. Or we could ship our application along with Docker itself, which is much better, as you will soon find out:

1. From the *Getting ready* section, you should have my GitHub `wildfly-cookbook` repository installed in a path, which I named `CODE_PATH`. From there, you should create another `Dockerfile` in the `docker-example` folder. Fill in the `Dockerfile` with the following code:

```
FROM foogaro/wildfly:latest

MAINTAINER Luigi Fugaro l.fugaro@gmail.com

COPY target/docker-example.war /opt/wildfly/standalone/
deployments/

EXPOSE 8080 9990

CMD ["/opt/wildfly/bin/standalone.sh", "-b", "0.0.0.0",
"-bmanagement", "0.0.0.0"]
```

2. Once again, create a Docker image from it by executing the following command:

```
$ docker build -t foogaro/wildfly-docker-example .
Sending build context to Docker daemon 33.28 kB
Sending build context to Docker daemon
Step 0 : FROM foogaro/wildfly:latest
 ---> 56d5fea9c4ff
Step 1 : MAINTAINER Luigi Fugaro l.fugaro@gmail.com
 ---> Using cache
 ---> ab0e63c8c1a9
Step 2 : COPY target/docker-example.war /opt/wildfly/standalone/
deployments/
 ---> 3b46d10fde74
Removing intermediate container 919ef5d6bc45
Step 3 : EXPOSE 8080 9990
 ---> Running in 7a33da460750
 ---> b741119c54bb
Removing intermediate container 7a33da460750
Step 4 : CMD /opt/wildfly/bin/standalone.sh -b 0.0.0.0
-bmanagement 0.0.0.0
 ---> Running in 71e0fff696e4
```

```
 ---> 0668770878ab
Removing intermediate container 71e0fff696e4
Successfully built 0668770878ab
```

3. Great! We have successfully created the preceding Docker image, which contains WildFly, along with our `docker-example` application. We can also see it listed as a Docker image, as follows:

```
$ docker images
REPOSITORY                     TAG     IMAGE ID      CREATED
VIRTUAL SIZE
foogaro/wildfly-docker-example latest  0668770878ab  7 seconds ago
745.8 MB
foogaro/wildfly                latest  56d5fea9c4ff  34 minutes
ago       745.8 MB
fedora                         latest  834629358fe2  4 weeks ago
250.2 MB
```

4. Now we just need to run this image in a container and test our application, as follows:

```
$ docker run -i -t -p 8080:8080 -p 9990:9990 --rm foogaro/wildfly-
docker-example
```

You should get the following output:

```
==============================================================

  JBoss Bootstrap Environment

  JBOSS_HOME: /opt/wildfly

  JAVA: java

  JAVA_OPTS:  -server -Xms64m -Xmx512m -XX:MaxPermSize=256m
-Djava.net.preferIPv4Stack=true -Djboss.modules.system.pkgs=org.
jboss.byteman -Djava.awt.headless=true

==============================================================

OpenJDK 64-Bit Server VM warning: ignoring option
MaxPermSize=256m; support was removed in 8.0
19:52:10,808 INFO  [org.jboss.modules] (main) JBoss Modules
version 1.3.3.Final
```

```
19:52:11,037 INFO  [org.jboss.msc] (main) JBoss MSC version
1.2.2.Final

19:52:11,109 INFO  [org.jboss.as] (MSC service thread 1-6)
JBAS015899: WildFly 8.2.0.Final "Tweek" starting

19:52:12,288 INFO  [org.jboss.as.server] (Controller Boot Thread)
JBAS015888: Creating http management service using socket-binding
(management-http)

19:52:12,308 INFO  [org.xnio] (MSC service thread 1-1) XNIO
version 3.3.0.Final

19:52:12,320 INFO  [org.xnio.nio] (MSC service thread 1-1) XNIO
NIO Implementation Version 3.3.0.Final

19:52:12,379 INFO  [org.jboss.remoting] (MSC service thread 1-1)
JBoss Remoting version 4.0.6.Final

19:52:12,388 INFO  [org.wildfly.extension.io] (ServerService
Thread Pool -- 31) WFLYIO001: Worker 'default' has auto-configured
to 8 core threads with 64 task threads based on your 4 available
processors

19:52:12,424 INFO  [org.jboss.as.clustering.infinispan]
(ServerService Thread Pool -- 32) JBAS010280: Activating
Infinispan subsystem.

19:52:12,453 INFO  [org.jboss.as.jsf] (ServerService Thread Pool
-- 38) JBAS012615: Activated the following JSF Implementations:
[main]

19:52:12,465 INFO  [org.jboss.as.naming] (ServerService Thread
Pool -- 40) JBAS011800: Activating Naming Subsystem

19:52:12,467 INFO  [org.jboss.as.security] (ServerService Thread
Pool -- 45) JBAS013171: Activating Security Subsystem

19:52:12,478 WARN  [org.jboss.as.txn] (ServerService Thread Pool
-- 46) JBAS010153: Node identifier property is set to the default
value. Please make sure it is unique.

19:52:12,494 INFO  [org.jboss.as.security] (MSC service thread
1-1) JBAS013170: Current PicketBox version=4.0.21.Final

19:52:12,518 INFO  [org.jboss.as.connector.logging] (MSC service
thread 1-4) JBAS010408: Starting JCA Subsystem (IronJacamar
1.1.9.Final)

19:52:12,537 INFO  [org.jboss.as.webservices] (ServerService
Thread Pool -- 48) JBAS015537: Activating WebServices Extension

19:52:12,552 INFO  [org.jboss.as.connector.subsystems.datasources]
(ServerService Thread Pool -- 27) JBAS010403: Deploying JDBC-
compliant driver class org.h2.Driver (version 1.3)
```

```
19:52:12,573 INFO  [org.jboss.as.connector.deployers.jdbc] (MSC
service thread 1-4) JBAS010417: Started Driver service with
driver-name = h2

19:52:12,617 INFO  [org.wildfly.extension.undertow] (MSC service
thread 1-7) JBAS017502: Undertow 1.1.0.Final starting

19:52:12,618 INFO  [org.wildfly.extension.undertow] (ServerService
Thread Pool -- 47) JBAS017502: Undertow 1.1.0.Final starting

19:52:12,687 INFO  [org.jboss.as.naming] (MSC service thread 1-1)
JBAS011802: Starting Naming Service

19:52:12,689 INFO  [org.jboss.as.mail.extension] (MSC service
thread 1-2) JBAS015400: Bound mail session [java:jboss/mail/
Default]

19:52:12,814 INFO  [org.wildfly.extension.undertow] (ServerService
Thread Pool -- 47) JBAS017527: Creating file handler for path /
opt/wildfly/welcome-content

19:52:12,835 INFO  [org.wildfly.extension.undertow] (MSC service
thread 1-5) JBAS017525: Started server default-server.

19:52:12,997 INFO  [org.wildfly.extension.undertow] (MSC service
thread 1-4) JBAS017531: Host default-host starting

19:52:13,060 INFO  [org.wildfly.extension.undertow] (MSC service
thread 1-5) JBAS017519: Undertow HTTP listener default listening
on /0.0.0.0:8080

19:52:13,348 INFO  [org.jboss.as.server.deployment.
scanner] (MSC service thread 1-8) JBAS015012: Started
FileSystemDeploymentService for directory /opt/wildfly/standalone/
deployments

19:52:13,356 INFO  [org.jboss.as.server.deployment] (MSC service
thread 1-1) JBAS015876: Starting deployment of "docker-example.
war" (runtime-name: "docker-example.war")

19:52:13,413 INFO  [org.jboss.as.connector.subsystems.datasources]
(MSC service thread 1-8) JBAS010400: Bound data source
[java:jboss/datasources/ExampleDS]

19:52:13,616 INFO  [org.jboss.ws.common.management] (MSC service
thread 1-2) JBWS022052: Starting JBoss Web Services - Stack CXF
Server 4.3.2.Final

19:52:14,008 INFO  [org.wildfly.extension.undertow] (MSC service
thread 1-4) JBAS017534: Registered web context: /docker-example

19:52:14,082 INFO  [org.jboss.as.server] (ServerService Thread
Pool -- 28) JBAS018559: Deployed "docker-example.war" (runtime-
name : "docker-example.war")

19:52:14,157 INFO  [org.jboss.as] (Controller Boot
Thread) JBAS015961: Http management interface listening on
http://0.0.0.0:9990/management
```

```
19:52:14,157 INFO  [org.jboss.as] (Controller Boot Thread)
JBAS015951: Admin console listening on http://0.0.0.0:9990

19:52:14,158 INFO  [org.jboss.as] (Controller Boot Thread)
JBAS015874: WildFly 8.2.0.Final "Tweek" started in 3640ms -
Started 249 of 304 services (92 services are lazy, passive or on-
demand)
```

5. Reading the last log entries, we can see that our `docker-example` application has been deployed. To see the application in action, open the browser and point it to `http://127.0.0.1:8080/docker-example`.
6. You should see the following page:

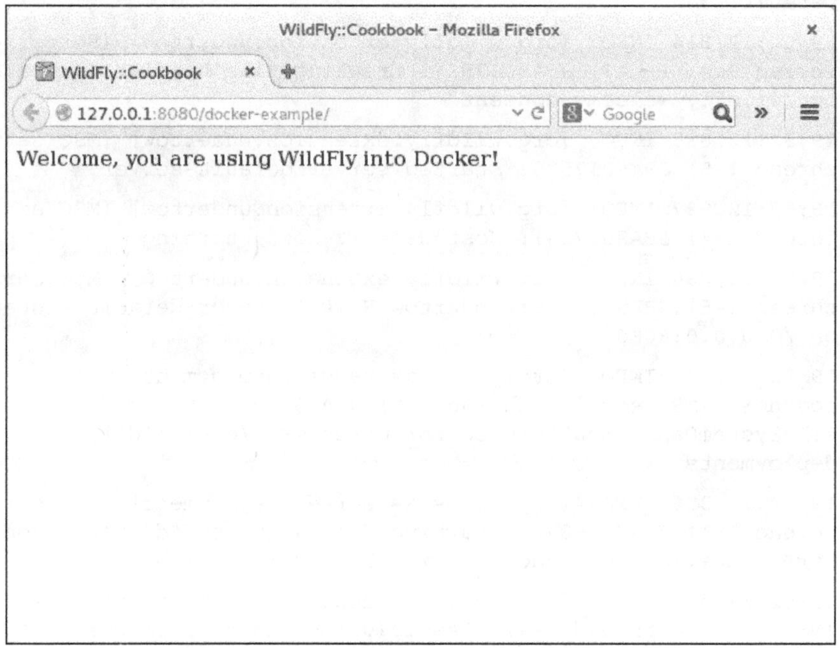


docker-example application running from a Docker container

Excellent, we have just deployed and run our first application in a Docker container running WildFly!

## How it works...

Besides the Docker tool itself, and all that it comes with, there are some relevant things to talk about.

When running the WildFly container in the `docker run` command, we used a new flag `-p`, followed by some suspicious numbers. The flag `-p` is used to map the ports exposed by the container with the local ports; that is, the host's ports:

```
$ docker run -i -t -p 8080:8080 -p 9990:9990 --rm foogaro/wildfly
```

In this case, we mapped the ports `8080` and `9990` with the same ones as in our host. That's why we could access the WildFly Admin Console with a local address. The same thing happened while accessing the `docker-example` application.

There is also another flag used in the preceding command: `--rm`.

The `--rm` flag instructs the Docker daemon to eliminate the container from the list of the container's history when the container gets stopped. To view all containers, even the non-running ones, you can give the following command:

```
$ docker ps -a
CONTAINER ID        IMAGE           COMMAND                    CREATED
STATUS                    PORTS                      NAMES
2f8fd2fbd0a0        ab0e63c8c1a9    "/bin/sh -c '#(nop)   38 hours ago
hungry_brown
794901deea3c        1816b615e0ce    "/bin/sh -c 'cd /opt 39 hours ago
Exited (2) 39 hours ago                                  drunk_pike
3fdc9d5c1680        1816b615e0ce    "/bin/sh -c 'cd /opt 39 hours ago
Exited (2) 39 hours ago                                  adoring_mcclintock
5035b7e0a76c        5200fb462c18    "/bin/sh -c 'cd /opt 39 hours ago
Exited (127) 39 hours ago                                prickly_hawking
981dd5f92e24        5200fb462c18    "/bin/sh -c 'cd /opt 39 hours ago
Exited (127) 39 hours ago                                elegant_hawking
```

As you can see, after a while, the list can get very long. Eventually, you can manually remove old containers that you don't need anymore, by issuing the following command:

```
$ docker rm 981dd5f92e24
981dd5f92e24
```

List all the containers again, and the container with ID `981dd5f92e24` should be gone, as follows:

```
$ docker ps -a
CONTAINER ID        IMAGE           COMMAND                    CREATED
STATUS                    PORTS                      NAMES
2f8fd2fbd0a0        ab0e63c8c1a9    "/bin/sh -c '#(nop)   38 hours ago
hungry_brown
794901deea3c        1816b615e0ce    "/bin/sh -c 'cd /opt 39 hours ago
Exited (2) 39 hours ago                                  drunk_pike
```

```
3fdc9d5c1680        1816b615e0ce  "/bin/sh -c 'cd /opt 39 hours ago
Exited (2) 39 hours ago                                   adoring_mcclintock

5035b7e0a76c        5200fb462c18  "/bin/sh -c 'cd /opt 39 hours ago
Exited (127) 39 hours ago                                 prickly_hawking
```

So, if we try to run our `foogaro/wildfly` container without the `--rm` flag, when we stop the container it should appear in the container's history list.

There is still one more thing to talk about, and that's the second Dockerfile that we created, the one used to create the `foogaro/wildfly-docker-example` image.

The structure and the commands used in the file are pretty straightforward:

- **FROM**: It's used to declare the base or starting image.
- **MAINTAINER**: It's used to declare the owner of the Dockerfile; that is, the image.
- **RUN**: It's used to run commands in the container itself.
- **EXPOSE**: It's used to expose a set of ports from the container.
- **CMD**: It's typically used as the final instruction to run a service/command in the container when we start it. This instruction is basically an array of parameters, where even the command to execute is a parameter itself.

There are many more instructions you can use, and they are all available and explained in detail at the Docker site at `https://docs.docker.com/reference/builder`.

Keep in mind that every instruction in the Dockerfile is run sequentially and is atomic. Each instruction starts its own temporary container, executes the task it has to do, when done it commits its work, and it destroys its temporary container. The next instruction will do the same, and so on.

This is a great feature because if something goes wrong while building an image, you don't need to restart once the bug has been fixed; the instructions previous to the error are cached, so you can quickly test and run your build again.

## See also

Keep in mind that, nowadays, there are plenty of official images in the DockerHub registries, such as the official WildFly docker image. To obtain and work on that image, you can simply search and pull it from the repository, as depicted in the following image:

```
$ docker search wildfly
NAME                       DESCRIPTION                                     STARS     OFFICIAL   AUTOMATED
jboss/wildfly              WildFly application server image                97                   [OK]
piegsaj/wildfly            WildFly 9.0.0.CR2 and 8.2 on Java 8             1                    [OK]
sewatech/wildfly           Debian + WildFly, in HA mode                    1                    [OK]
andreptb/wildfly           Debian Wheezy based image with JBoss Wildf...   1                    [OK]
jamesnetherton/wildfly     A minimalistic Docker image for WildFly ru...   0                    [OK]
caltha/wildfly             Self contained WildFly application server       0                    [OK]
tandrup/wildfly            WildFly application server image with JRE7...   0                    [OK]
sledsoft/wildfly                                                           0                    [OK]
cnry/wildfly               WildFly Application Server                      0                    [OK]
mihahribar/wildfly         Dockerfile for Wildfly running on Ubuntu 1...   0                    [OK]
$ docker pull jboss/wildfly
Pulling repository jboss/wildfly
2ac466861ca1: Download complete
511136ea3c5a: Download complete
782cf93a8f16: Download complete
7d3f07f8de5f: Download complete
1ef0a50fe8b1: Download complete
20a1abe1d9bf: Download complete
cd5bb934bb67: Download complete
379edb00ab07: Download complete
4d37cbbfc67d: Download complete
2ea8562cac7c: Download complete
7759146eab1a: Download complete
b17a20d6f5f8: Download complete
e02bdb6c4ed5: Download complete
72d585299bb5: Download complete
90832e1f0bb9: Download complete
b2b7d0c353b9: Download complete
3759d5cffae6: Download complete
5c98b1e90cdc: Download complete
8ac46a315e1e: Download complete
Status: Downloaded newer image for jboss/wildfly:latest
```

# Logging WildFly outside Docker

When dealing with an application server, and thus web applications, often we really need to look at the logs. As we have seen in the previous recipe, we have run WildFly in a container and we have looked at the logs automatically because of the terminal flag being enabled (`-t` when executing the `docker run` command).

Without the terminal flag enabled, we would have needed to access the container (`docker attach CONTAINER_ID` or `docker logs CONTAINER_ID` command). That's not the most comfortable way to look at logs, and we would like to store our logs locally, on our host, and group them.

In this recipe, you will learn how to store your application logs outside the container, and store them on the host.

## Getting ready

To be able to follow this recipe, you need to have followed the previous one, which is about running WildFly in Docker.

## How to do it...

First of all, we need to create a directory on the host to store our logs, and enable the container-writable permissions to access the directory:

1. Open a terminal window and execute the following commands:

   ```
   $ mkdir -p /opt/docker/wildfly/logs
   $ groupadd -r cookbook -g 12345
   $ useradd -u 54321 -r -g cookbook -s /sbin/nologin -c "WildFly
   user" wildfly
   $ chcon -t svirt_sandbox_file_t /opt/docker/wildfly/logs
   ```

2. Now, in a different terminal window, run a container using our `foogaro/wildfly` Docker image, as follows:

   ```
   $ docker run -d -v /opt/docker/wildfly/logs:/opt/wildfly/
   standalone/log -p 8080:8080 -p 9990:9990 --rm foogaro/wildfly
   ```

3. In the terminal where we created the `/opt/docker/wildfly/logs` folder, list the contents of the folder as follows:

   ```
   $ cd /opt/docker/wildfly/logs
   $ ls -la
   total 32
   drwxr-xr-x. 2 wildfly cookbook  4096 Feb  5 17:32 .
   drwxr-xr-x. 4 wildfly cookbook  4096 Feb  5 12:43 ..
   -rw-r--r--. 1 wildfly cookbook 10261 Feb  5 17:36 server.log
   ```

Great, our `server.log` file is there!!!

Obviously, this is not the best way to handle logs in general; you should look at integrating with `syslog`, `rsyslog`, `logstash`, and other tools with more powerful and higher performance features.

Take this recipe as an example to deal with folders that are outside the container. Nonetheless, in a development environment, people might want to have the logs stored on their PCs.

### How it works...

First of all, we needed to create a directory to store the WildFly logs, and then add the same user and group that we used in the `Dockerfile` to build the `foogaro/wildfly` Docker image. As a matter of fact, in the `Dockerfile` there was the following instruction:

```
RUN groupadd -r cookbook -g 12345 && useradd -u 54321 -r -g cookbook
-d /opt/wildfly -s /sbin/nologin -c "WildFly user" wildfly
```

The preceding code adds a group and a user in the container environment, and it creates them using a fixed group ID and user ID. Thus, to allow the container to have read-write permissions on the host, we need to use the same user and group for the directory.

Once everything was configured, we launched the `docker run` command using the `-v` flag, which is about mounting volumes with the `from:to` pattern. That is, everything from the host `from` (at the specified path) will be present in the container environment in the specified path, `:to`. Furthermore, every update made in the specified folder would have persisted in the host folder.

## Running WildFly in domain mode in Docker using different Docker containers

In this recipe, you will learn how to run WildFly in the domain mode using containers. We will use one container to act as the domain-controller and two other containers, each to act as the servers of a server-group.

### Getting ready

To properly follow and understand the topics treated in this recipe, we need to know what the WildFly domain mode is, along with its principles. You can also refer to *Chapter 3, Working with XAML*, which is about running WildFly in the domain mode.

Furthermore, you need to have followed the first two recipes of this chapter, of having a working Docker installation and a WildFly image available for use.

Nevertheless, to simplify our recipe, we will rely on the WildFly default configuration files: `domain.xml`, `host-master.xml` and `host-slave.xml`.

## How to do it...

1. First of all, we need to create a new `Dockerfile` based on the `foogaro/wildfly` image, which will contain the entire configuration needed to run WildFly in the domain mode. Following is the whole file:

```
FROM foogaro/wildfly

MAINTAINER Luigi Fugaro l.fugaro@gmail.com

RUN sed -i '/secret value/d' /opt/wildfly/domain/configuration/
host-slave.xml
RUN sed -i '/<server-identities>/a <secret
value="Y29va2Jvb2suMjAxNQ==" \/>' /opt/wildfly/domain/
configuration/host-slave.xml
RUN sed -i 's/remote host/remote username="wildfly" host/' /opt/
wildfly/domain/configuration/host-slave.xml
RUN sed -i 's/jboss.domain.master.address/env.DOMAIN_CONTROLLER_
PORT_9999_TCP_ADDR/' /opt/wildfly/domain/configuration/host-slave.
xml
RUN sed -i 's/jboss.domain.master.port/env.DOMAIN_CONTROLLER_
PORT_9999_TCP_PORT/' /opt/wildfly/domain/configuration/host-slave.
xml

EXPOSE 8080 9990 9999

USER wildfly

ENTRYPOINT ["/opt/wildfly/bin/domain.sh"]

CMD ["--host-config", "host-master.xml", "-b", "0.0.0.0",
"-bmanagement", "0.0.0.0"]
```

2. To build the image, use the following command:

```
$ docker build -t foogaro/wildfly-domain .
```

3. Once the build process is done, we can run the `foogaro/wildfly-domain` image in a container. The first thing we are going to run is the domain controller without any operative servers, as follows:

```
$ docker run -i -t -p 9990:9990 -p 9999:9999 --name=DC --rm
foogaro/wildfly-domain
...
[Host Controller] 10:05:17,590 INFO  [org.jboss.as] (Controller
Boot Thread) WFLYSRV0025: WildFly Full 9.0.0.Beta2 (WildFly Core
1.0.0.Beta2) (Host Controller) started in 2830ms - Started 50 of
50 services (13 services are lazy, passive or on-demand)
```

4. Now you can access the Admin Console from the host at `http://localhost:9990/`.
5. As we can see from the following image, in the **Domain** | **Topology** section, there is no running server:

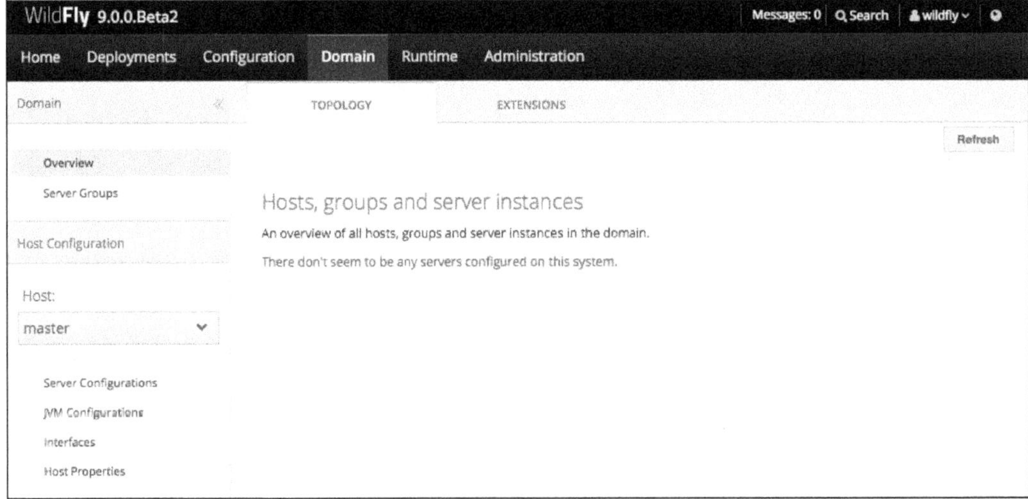


WildFly in domain mode running into a Docker container

Let's run another container with the WildFly default configuration provided by the `host-slave.xml` file.

6. Open a new terminal window and execute the following:

```
$ docker run -i -t -p 8080:8080 --link=DC:DOMAIN_CONTROLLER
--name=HC-1 --rm foogaro/wildfly-domain --host-config host-slave.
xml -b 0.0.0.0 -bmanagement 0.0.0.0
```

7. Once the container has successfully launched WildFly, refresh the topology overview section of the Admin Console that we loaded earlier, and you should now see two running servers, as depicted in the following image:

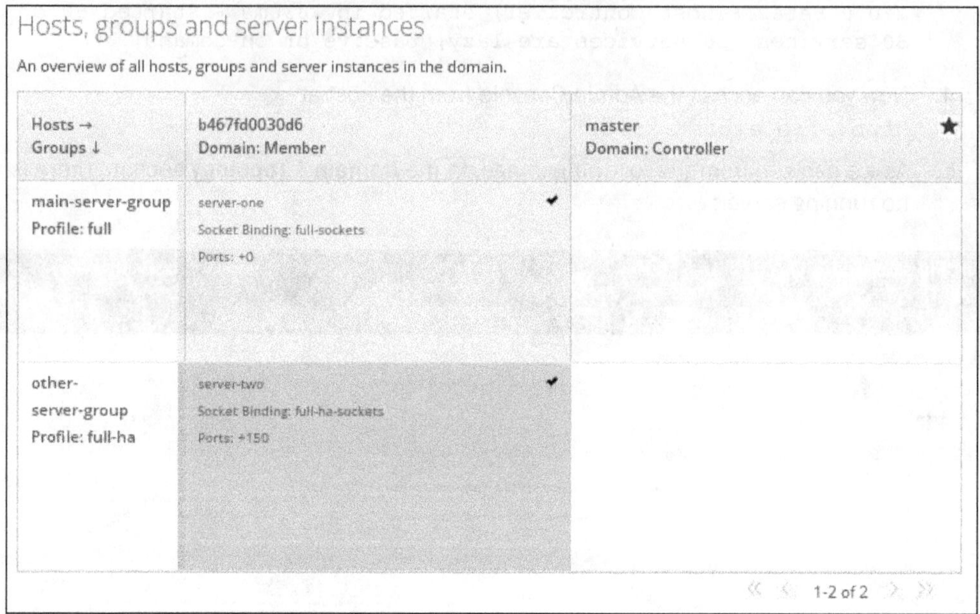


WildFly's domain mode topology showing two servers running on a different Docker container

## How it works...

In this recipe, we saw some new `Dockerfile` instructions, such as `ENTRYPOINT`. This instruction is almost like the `CMD` one; it is used to run a service. The `ENTRYPOINT` instruction uses the `CMD` instruction to hold the command parameters. As a matter of fact, you can specify both the instructions with the option to override the `CMD` instruction from the command line, which is exactly what we have done when running the host-controller.

We used the `sed` command to modify the `host-slave.xml` file; further information on this command is out of the scope of this book.

As you should already know, communication between the domain controller and the host controller needs to be verified. Thus, I inserted the hashed password of the `wildfly` user of `ManagementRealm`—the first and second `sed`. The third `sed` basically instructs the host controller to authenticate the domain controller with the `wildfly` user.

[ Remember that if you do not specify the `username` attribute in the `remote` XML element, the name of the host, `<host name="slave">`, will be used instead. ]

The last two `sed` commands instruct which address and port to use to connect to the domain controller. As we don't know which IP the container would have, we can rely on Docker's environment variables, which it automatically sets when it starts. This particular mapping is due to the `--link` flag used when launching the second container.

```
$ docker run -i -t -p 8080:8080 --link=DC:DOMAIN_CONTROLLER --name=HC-1
--rm foogaro/wildfly-domain --host-config host-slave.xml -b 0.0.0.0
-bmanagement 0.0.0.0
```

In the first container, we used the `--name` flag to give it a significant name, like `DC`. Then we used that same name with the `--link` flag to bind that container with the second one and map it to the `DOMAIN_CONTROLLER` alias.

## There is more...

When running a container, you can specify the hostname that it will have. In our example, we could have run the slaves, as follows:

```
$ docker run -i -t -p 8080:8080 -h host-1 --link=DC:DOMAIN_CONTROLLER
--name=HC-1 --rm foogaro/wildfly-domain --host-config host-slave.xml -b
0.0.0.0 -bmanagement 0.0.0.0
```

And in the topology overview, we would have seen the following page:

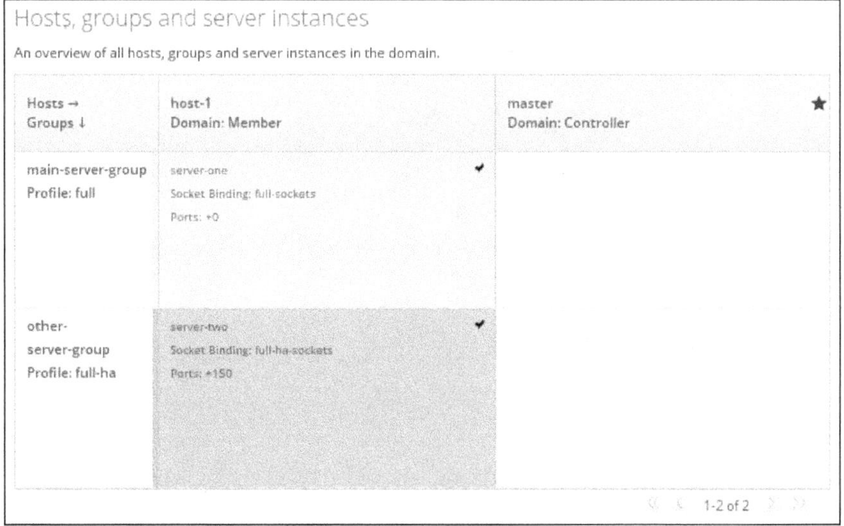


The slave running in a Docker container with a significant name host-1

This is a nice feature that can be handy, instead of trying to remember which hash a host belongs to.

In conclusion, the same kind of mechanism used in this recipe to configure and run the domain mode could be used to run a WildFly cluster.

## See also

- More information about linking Docker containers can be found at `https://docs.docker.com/userguide/dockerlinks/`

# Index

## D



## E



## F



## G

## H



## I



## J



## K



## L



## M

# X

**Thank you for buying**

# WildFly Cookbook

## About Packt Publishing

Packt, pronounced 'packed', published its first book, *Mastering phpMyAdmin for Effective MySQL Management*, in April 2004, and subsequently continued to specialize in publishing highly focused books on specific technologies and solutions.

Our books and publications share the experiences of your fellow IT professionals in adapting and customizing today's systems, applications, and frameworks. Our solution-based books give you the knowledge and power to customize the software and technologies you're using to get the job done. Packt books are more specific and less general than the IT books you have seen in the past. Our unique business model allows us to bring you more focused information, giving you more of what you need to know, and less of what you don't.

Packt is a modern yet unique publishing company that focuses on producing quality, cutting-edge books for communities of developers, administrators, and newbies alike. For more information, please visit our website at `www.packtpub.com`.

## About Packt Open Source

In 2010, Packt launched two new brands, Packt Open Source and Packt Enterprise, in order to continue its focus on specialization. This book is part of the Packt open source brand, home to books published on software built around open source licenses, and offering information to anybody from advanced developers to budding web designers. The Open Source brand also runs Packt's open source Royalty Scheme, by which Packt gives a royalty to each open source project about whose software a book is sold.

## Writing for Packt

We welcome all inquiries from people who are interested in authoring. Book proposals should be sent to `author@packtpub.com`. If your book idea is still at an early stage and you would like to discuss it first before writing a formal book proposal, then please contact us; one of our commissioning editors will get in touch with you.

We're not just looking for published authors; if you have strong technical skills but no writing experience, our experienced editors can help you develop a writing career, or simply get some additional reward for your expertise.

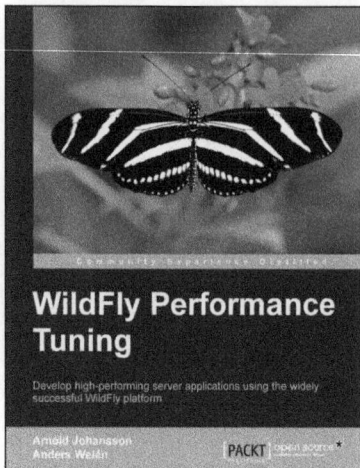

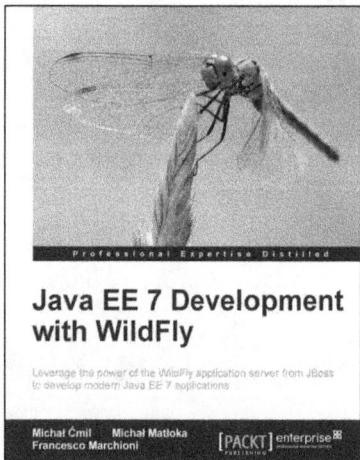

## WildFly Configuration, Deployment, and Administration

### *Second Edition*

ISBN: 978-1-78328-623-2 Paperback: 402 pages

Build a functional and efficient WildFly server with this step-by-step, practical guide

1. Install WildFly, deploy applications, and administer servers with clear and concise examples.
2. Understand the superiority of WildFly over other parallel application servers and explore its new features.
3. Step-by-step guide packed with examples and screenshots on advanced WildFly topics.

---

## Advanced Java® EE Development with WildFly®

ISBN: 978-1-78328-890-8 Paperback: 416 pages

Your one-stop guide to developing Java® EE applications with the Eclipse IDE, Maven, and WildFly® 8.1

1. Develop Java EE 7 applications using the WildFly platform.
2. Discover how to use EJB 3.x, JSF 2.x, Ajax, JAX-RS, JAX-WS, and Spring with WildFly 8.1.
3. A practical guide filled with easy-to-understand programming examples to help you gain hands-on experience with Java EE development using WildFly.

Please check **www.PacktPub.com** for information on our titles

www.ingramcontent.com/pod-product-compliance
Lightning Source LLC
Chambersburg PA
CBHW060942210326
41598CB00031B/4698
* 9 7 8 1 7 8 4 3 9 2 4 1 3 *